THE BLUE GUIDES

Countries **Austria**
Belgium and Luxembourg
Channel Islands
Corsica
Crete
Cyprus
Egypt
England
France
Germany
Greece
Holland
Hungary
Ireland
Northern Italy
Southern Italy
Malta and Gozo
Morocco
Portugal
Scotland
Sicily
Spain
Switzerland
Turkey: Bursa to Antakya
Wales
Yugoslavia

Cities **Boston and Cambridge**
Florence
Istanbul
Jerusalem
London
Moscow and Leningrad
New York
Oxford and Cambridge
Paris and Versailles
Rome and Environs
Venice

Themes **Churches and Chapels of Northern England**
Churches and Chapels of Southern England
Literary Britain and Ireland
Museums and Galleries of London
Victorian Architecture in Britain

D1287418

János Pasztor's 'The Fisherman', Balatonfüred

BLUE GUIDE

HUNGARY

Bob Dent

Maps and plans by András Bereznay

A & C Black
London

W W Norton
New York

First edition 1990
Reprinted with corrections 1991

Published by A & C Black (Publishers) Limited
35 Bedford Row, London, WC1R 4JH

ISBN   0–7136–3030–2

A CIP catalogue record for this book
is available from the British Library.

Published in the United States of America by
WW Norton & Company, Incorporated
500 Fifth Avenue, New York, NY 10110

Published simultaneously in Canada by
Penguin Books Canada Limited
2801 John Street, Markham, Ontario LR3 1B4

ISBN   0–393–30687–9   USA

Bob Dent lives in Budapest. He works as a journalist, researcher,
language editor and broadcaster. Apart from feature articles for the
Western press, he also writes a regular column in the 'Daily News',
an English-language newspaper published in Hungary.

Typeset by CRB Typesetting Services, Ely, Cambs.
Printed and bound in Great Britain by
BPCC Hazell Books
Aylesbury, Bucks, England
Member of BPCC Ltd.

PREFACE

This is the first book on Hungary in the Blue Guide series. In keeping with the tradition of the series the aim has been to produce the most comprehensive guidebook on Hungary in English for the independent traveller. The author hopes that readers will find that this aim has been achieved.

Up to the time of writing the number of English speaking visitors to Hungary has been relatively low. This is not to say that the country is not geared to tourism. On the contrary, the annual number of foreign visitors to Hungary well exceeds the total population and facilities provided for them are in general very good. Hungary is not a difficult country to enter, nor are there obstacles to travelling around.

In terms of food, drink and general relaxation Hungary has plenty to offer. Although having no coastline of its own, the shores of Lake Balaton, the 'Hungarian Sea', are full of resorts with ample bathing facilities. The country has a rich and varied architecture. Every town is different with its particular development closely tied to historical processes. Indeed history is all important in Hungarian culture generally and for this reason much attention has been paid to historical aspects both in the introductory notes and in the main texts of the routes.

The overwhelming majority of visitors to Hungary rarely get beyond Budapest, the Danube Bend and Lake Balaton. Concentrated attention has been duly given to these areas, in particular the capital which is naturally and overwhelmingly the centre of Hungary, but it is hoped that the information about other places will tempt visitors to venture further afield. The provincial towns, partly because of their relative quietness, are well worth visiting.

Hungary is a small country with a unique language, culture and history. For more than twenty years it has been at the forefront of change in Eastern Europe, although outside specialist circles this fact is often unknown. The best way of finding out about the country is to visit it. It is hoped that this book will both encourage and help those who wish to do that.

A work of this nature could not have been possible without the help of many people and organisations. Special thanks are due to the Hungarian Tourist Board, and in particular Vera Vadas and Rita Szekeres, for much help with introductions, information and accommodation. Thanks are also due to Hungar Hotels, Szeged Tourist, Balatontourist and the Helikon Hotel, Keszthely, for help with accommodation.

Tourinform, the central tourist information office in Budapest, has been particularly helpful with practical information of all kinds. Special thanks are due to Ágnes Padányi, Mariann Tóth and Katalin Koronczi.

The author would furthermore like to gratefully acknowledge the help received from the following individuals: the late Gábor Bándi of the Ministry of Culture, Marianne Rozsondai of the Academy of Sciences Library, Ádám Horváth and Éva Pröhle of the Parliamentary Library, Edit Pataki of the Tourism Specialist Library, Gyöngyi Török, Katalin Szabó and Zsuzsa Jobbágyi of the Hungarian National Gallery, Zsuzsa Urbach of the Museum of Fine Arts, István Román of the National Inspectorate for Historical Monuments, László Kozma of Útinform, Gabriella Steklács of IBUSZ, Ágnes Szabó of the

Pannonia Hotel in Pécs, András Bereznay, László Cseh, Charlie Coutts, Ildikó Deák, Hilda Faragó, Katalin Gellér, Jeremy Hawthorne, Gyula Honyek, Tünde Kecskés, Éva Kisfaludi Strobl, John Macsai, Mária Murai, Attila Pénzes, Zsuzsa Rác, György Rajna, the late Louis Scully, Mónika Szabó, Erzsébet Visy, and Richard Aczel who contributed the chapter on literature.

Gemma Davies of A & C Black had the difficult job of checking and preparing the manuscript for the printers. Her editorial precision and searching questions greatly helped to improve the text.

A very special thanks is due to Katalin Rácz for much help with research and translations, and for writing the section on food.

Needless to say any errors are the sole responsibility of the author who would be grateful to receive any suggestions for corrections, improvements or additions.

Bob Dent

For permission to reproduce the illustrations in the guide the publishers would like to thank Bob Dent, Csaba Gabler, David King, the Hungarian National Museum and the National Inspectorate for Historical Monuments in Hungary.

Note. Since the first printing of this book, a number of street names have changed in Budapest and other towns. A list of changes is given after the index on page 367.

A NOTE ON BLUE GUIDES

The Blue Guide series began in 1918 when Muirhead Guide-Books Limited published 'Blue Guide London and its Environs'. Finlay and James Muirhead already had extensive experience of guide-book publishing: before the First World War they had been the editors of the English editions of the German Baedekers, and by 1915 they had acquired the copyright of most of the famous 'Red' Handbooks from John Murray.

An agreement made with the French publishing house Hachette et Cie in 1917 led to the translation of Muirhead's London Guide, which became the first 'Guide Bleu'—Hachette had previously published the blue-covered 'Guides Joanne'. Subsequently, Hachette's 'Guide Bleu Paris et ses Environs' was adapted and published in London by Muirhead. The collaboration between the two publishing houses continued until 1933.

In 1931 Ernest Benn Limited took over the Blue Guides, appointing Russell Muirhead, Finlay Muirhead's son, editor in 1934. The Muirheads' connection with Blue Guides ended in 1963 when Stuart Rossiter, who had been working on the Guides since 1954, became house editor, revising and compiling several of the books himself.

The Blue Guides are now published by A & C Black, who acquired Ernest Benn in 1984, so continuing the tradition of guide-book publishing which began in 1826 with 'Black's Economical Tourist of Scotland'. The Blue Guide series continues to grow: there are now more than 40 titles in print with revised editions appearing regularly and many new Blue Guides in preparation.

'Blue Guides' is a registered trade mark.

CONTENTS

	Page
Preface	5
Note on Blue Guides	7
Explanatory Notes	10

BACKGROUND INFORMATION

Historical Summary	13
Hungary Today	29
Art and Architecture in Hungary	34
Hungarian Literature, by *Richard Aczel*	43
Music in Hungary	52

PRACTICAL INFORMATION

Getting to Hungary	55
Visas, Customs and Currency	56
Where to Stay	59
Getting Around	60
Useful Addresses	65
General Information	67
Hungarian Language	74
Hungarian Food, by *Katalin Rácz*	78

Route	1	HEGYESHALOM TO BUDAPEST	87
	2	GYŐR	91
	3	SOPRON	100
	4	SOPRON TO GYŐR	110
	5	BUDAPEST	114
		A. The Castle District	119
		B. The Royal Palace	135
		C. Gellért Hill and the Tabán	143
		D. Water Town (Víziváros)	148
		E. The Inner City	153
		F. The Little Boulevard (Kiskörút)	164
		G. The Northern Inner City	173
		H. From March 15th Square to the Eastern Railway Station	185
		I. Népköztársaság útja and the City Park	195
		J. The Great Boulevard (Nagykörút)	205
		K. Margaret Island and Óbuda	215
		L. The Buda Hills	221
		M. Other Places of Interest in Budapest	223
		N. Additional Specialist Museums	225
	6	THE DANUBE BEND	228
		A. Szentendre	230
		B. Szentendre to Esztergom via Visegrád	235
		C. Esztergom	238
		D. The Left Bank	248
	7	LAKE BALATON	254
		A. The Northern Shore	258
		B. The Southern Shore	268
	8	SZÉKESFEHÉRVÁR	271
	9	VESZPRÉM	279
	10	BUDAPEST TO PÉCS	287

Route   11   PÉCS   289
          12   BUDAPEST TO SZEGED VIA KECSKEMÉT   301
          13   SZEGED   310
          14   BUDAPEST TO EGER   318
          15   EGER   321
          16   BUDAPEST TO DEBRECEN   331
               A. Via Szolnok   331
               B. Via the Hortobágy   334
          17   DEBRECEN   337
          18   NORTH EAST HUNGARY   347
          19   OTHER PLACES OF INTEREST:
                   Hollókő   352
                   Ják   352
                   Zsámbék   354
                   Ráckeve   355

Index   357

Changed names of streets   367

Maps and Plans

Map of Hungary   84–5
The Danube Bend   228
Lake Balaton and Environs   256–7

Budapest, Castle District   123   Kecskemét   303
        Central   120–1   Pécs   290–1
        Inner City   154–5   Sopron   101
        Northern Inner City 174   Szeged   311
Debrecen   338   Székesfehérvár   272
Eger   322   Szentendre   231
Esztergom   239   Veszprém   280
Győr   92

Budapest, Inner City Parish Church   186
        Matthias Church   127
        National Gallery   138

EXPLANATORY NOTES

Hungarian Names. In Hungarian family names come first, followed by Christian names, e.g. Kossuth Lajos, Kovács Anna etc. In the Blue Guide they are written in English style (Lajos Kossuth, etc.), except when people's names are used as names of streets or squares. This is very common and in these cases the text follows the order which appears on the street sign (Kossuth Lajos utca etc.). Usually the Hungarian form of names has been retained and not anglicised (e.g. János and not John). Exceptions include some names well-known abroad (e.g. George Lukács) and names of kings of Hungary, many of whom came from non-Hungarian dynasties (e.g. Charles Robert of Anjou).

Abbreviations

c = circa
C = century
km = Kilometre
m = metre
Rte = route

Hungarian Terms

u./utca = street
út/útja = road
tér/tere = square
körút = ring boulevard
köz = alley or mews
sétány = walkway
fasor = boulevard
hegy = hill
lépcső = steps
sor = row
tó = lake
udvar = courtyard

Architectural Glossary

COPF (or Zopf), a Hungarian and Central European term for Louis XVI style.
ECLECTIC, a mixture of various historical styles which was common in the design of buildings in the late 19C.
HUNGARIAN NATIONAL ROMANTICISM, a combination of Art Nouveau and traditional Hungarian folk styles, often influenced by the English Arts and Crafts movement.
ICONOSTASIS, a partition, usually covered with icons which separates the main body of the church from the sanctuary in Orthodox churches.
LOGGIA, an arcade or gallery, usually with columns, open on one side.
ORIEL WINDOW, a bay window on an upper storey.
PILASTER, a rectangular column which projects a little from a wall.
PORTICO, covered colonnade forming the main entrance of a building.

SECESSIONIST, a Hungarian term for Art Nouveau.
SEDILIA, Gothic seating recess in a wall.
TYMPANUM, triangular upper part of a building, often above a portico.

József Róna's statue of Prince Eugene of Savoy, which stands outside the National Gallery, Budapest.

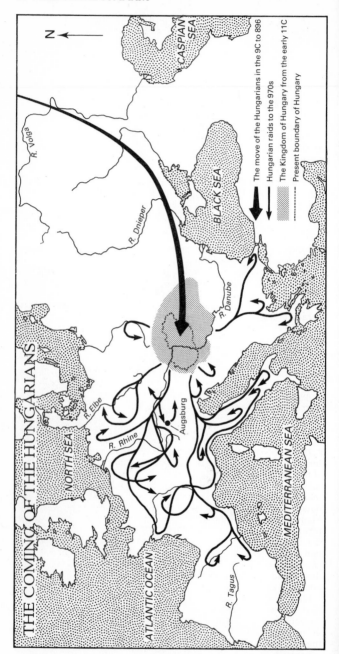

THE COMING OF THE HUNGARIANS

The move of the Hungarians in the 9C to 896
Hungarian raids to the 970s
The Kingdom of Hungary from the early 11C
Present boundary of Hungary

N

CASPIAN SEA
R. Volga
R. Dnieper
BLACK SEA
R. Danube
R. Elbe
R. Rhine
Augsburg
NORTH SEA
ATLANTIC OCEAN
MEDITERRANEAN SEA
R. Tagus

BACKGROUND INFORMATION

Historical Summary

Hungarians have been occupying the Carpathian Basin for about 1100 years. Little is known about their history before that time, but current knowledge indicates that they became an independent people around 1000–500 BC in the northern steppes of western Siberia, to the east of the Urals. When they separated from the Ob-Ugors, a closely related tribe, they also adopted a new way of living—nomadism.

Warfare and raiding took the Hungarians, or Magyars, further and further afield. By the middle of the 1C AD they were living between the Volga river and the Ural mountains in what is now Bashkiria. Around AD 700 the majority moved south-west and settled in Kazar Kaganate and neighbouring areas around the Don, Donets and Sea of Azov. In their way of life and dress the Magyars were similar to the Turkish and Iranian peoples who surrounded them, except that they maintained their own language of Finno-Ugric origin.

When they eventually arrived in the Carpathian Basin in the last decade of the 9C, the Magyars found Avars, Slavs, and Franks, who themselves had been preceded by many different peoples. Celts had settled along the Danube early in the first millennium BC; Scythians grazed their horses on the Great Plain around 500 BC; Goths, Gepids and Huns followed, while Dacians of Thracian origin moved into Transylvania. The Romans founded towns in their province of Pannonia, west of the Danube, and in the early centuries AD maintained a moderately prosperous economy and defended it against the attacks of various 'barbarian' clans from the east and north. In the 5C the Romans retreated in the face of the Huns, who were followed by the Avars. Charlemagne sent missionaries into the area and Christianity was adopted by many of the Slavs living here.

Thus the Magyars were following in a long line of settlers. Initially they were keen to expand their territories and wealth. In the first half of the 10C they launched campaigns into the west and south-east of Europe. They even reached the Pyrenees. The invaders terrified the inhabitants of western Europe who believed that their attackers must have been related to the feared Huns. Hence the legend of Hun-Magyar kinship, strengthened by the names given to the Magyars in other languages—'ungar', 'hongrois', 'Hungarian', etc.

A serious defeat at Augsburg in 955 ended the conquering ambitions of the Magyars. The descendants of Árpád, who had led the conquest of the Carpathian Basin, realised that in order to survive they would have to adapt to European ways, which essentially meant adopting Christianity.

Missionary work and conversion began under Prince Géza (972–997) but it was his son, Stephen (István), who accomplished the conversion of the Hungarians to Christianity. In recognition of this achievement, Pope Sylvester sent a royal crown to Hungary, granting the title of Apostolic King to its ruler. Stephen, who was later canonised, was crowned on Christmas day 1000.

King Stephen I, the founder of the Hungarian state, and his wife, Gizella. This statue, by József Ispánky, stands in Veszprém.

Stephen's memory has been cherished by Hungarians over the centuries. He is regarded as the real founder of the Hungarian state. During the four decades of his rule he organised the formerly tribal territories into royal counties and appointed administrators for them. He invited scholars, priests, and skilled craftsmen to Hungary. Stephen used force to defend himself against internal uprisings aimed to restore the heathen ways and the former clan system. Rebellious relatives were dealt with, sometimes brutally.

King Stephen's only son, Imre, died at an early age, and so when Stephen himself died in 1038 the country was left without a direct heir to the throne. Struggles for the throne broke out and the conflicts, which lasted for years, seriously weakened the newly founded state. Nevertheless, feudal Hungary continued to develop from the second half of the 11C to middle of the 13C. During this period one parish church was built for every ten villages. Chapels were constructed at the royal seats. Initially, monks from abroad supervised the building operations. The art of the ancient Magyars was fused with the French Romanesque style. Hungarian words began to appear more and more frequently in Latin documents.

The descendants of the former chieftains, however, were not always ready to accept central rule. In the absence of strong kings such as László I (1077–95), Kálmán (1095–1116) and Béla III (1172–96) struggles for the throne and 'pagan revolts' bred instability. The Byzantine and Holy Roman Empires both tried to take advantage of the situation.

Great numbers of foreigners, such as Germans of various descent or Cumans from central Asia, were settled in the country. In the 13C Hungary was a country of many different ethnic groups: there were Czechs, Poles, Greeks, Armenians, Saxons, Thuringians, people from the Rhineland, Slavs and some Latins. The mixed, though mainly Hungarian, feudal nobility relied on the king for protection against despotic lords or barons. Lesser nobles owned medium-sized estates and had their own arms. They were powerful enough to insist on a type of 'Magna Charta', the Golden Bull granted by King András (Andrew) II in 1222, which granted certain privileges such as exemption from taxation.

Hungarian history could be viewed as a series of national disasters prompted by foreign invasion. The first such disaster began in the spring of 1241 when Mongol fighters appeared on the eastern border of the country. Internal dissention and lack of external support allowed the invading troops to ravage the country. The king, Béla IV, was forced to flee to an island in the Adriatic. Austrian troops taking advantage of the situation pillaged the western borderlands.

It was only the death of the Great Khan, in 1242, which led to the withdrawal of the Mongol forces. They retreated, leaving behind them a devastated country and carrying off thousands of prisoners. Only a few places had been able to withstand the Mongol onslaught, and after his return King Béla was determined to rebuild the country such that it could not happen again. Towns with strong fortifications were built all over the country. Béla invited foreign architects to restore the churches and build new ones. Alongside the traditional coronation town of Székesfehérvár, Buda also began to develop.

Further settlements of various national groups took place as a means of restoring the level of the population. Medieval Hungary continued to be a country of several languages although for many centuries Latin remained the language of the educated. Despite this, the importance of the Hungarian language increased at the same time. The first piece of Hungarian poetry, the 'Lament of the Virgin', a free translation of a Latin hymn, dates from around 1300.

The death of András III in 1301 meant that the male branch of the Árpád dynasty became extinct. Conflict over the throne inevitably flared up between members of the royal family descended through the female line and their supporters. Victory was finally achieved by Charles Robert of the Anjou dynasty who reigned as king of Hungary from 1308 to 1342. His reign and that of his son, Louis the Great (1342–82), are characterised as the Hungarian age of chivalry, though it was also an important time economically, during which the Hungarian gold florin became one of the strongest currencies in

HUNGARY IN THE MIDDLE AGES

- Hungary in the early 12C
- Brought under Hungarian rule by the Árpádians (to 1301)
- Brought under Hungarian control by the Árpádians at times
- —— Boundary of Hungarian rule at the death of Louis the Great, 1382
- ········· Boundary of the kingdom of Matthias Corvinus at his death, 1490
- ------ Present boundary of Hungary

Europe. One of the first European universities was established in Hungary in 1367, although it was short-lived. Castles and churches were built and illuminated chronicles and prayer books designed.

Sigismund of Luxemburg ascended the Hungarian throne in 1387 and ruled the country for fifty years. In 1411 he was proclaimed Holy Roman Emperor, and because of his imperial position and the wars in Bohemia he was no longer able to pay much attention to matters in Hungary. Nevertheless the towns continued to develop and integrate into the commercial life of Europe. Tranquillity was disturbed towards the end of his reign by a revolt of Hungarian and Romanian peasants in Transylvania who had been inspired by the revolutionary Hussite doctrines.

In the mid-1440s there was an interregnum when the nobles once again could not agree on a king. Between 1446 and 1453 János Hunyadi was appointed Governor of Hungary. Hunyadi was a powerful lord who had shown great military talent under King Sigismund. This was fortunate, as military matters were beginning to assume priority and urgency because the Turks, in a series of victories, were beginning to penetrate into Europe.

In 1456 Hunyadi, with a motley collection of enthusiastic troops recruited by an Italian friar, Giovanni Capistrano, found himself encircled by the Turks at Nándorfehérvár (today Belgrade, Yugoslavia). Despite the apparent overwhelming odds in favour of the besiegers, he managed to break out, overwhelm the Turkish artillery and destroy their fleet. His victory, which held up the Turkish advance into Hungary for several decades, was celebrated throughout Europe, the Pope ordering that church bells chime every day at noon in commemoration.

Hunyadi's younger son, Mátyás (Matthias), was elected king by the Hungarian nobles in 1458. Until his death, in 1490, Hungary enjoyed a period of prosperity and flourished on a cultural level of European significance.

King Matthias, who was also called Matthias Corvinus after the raven (corvus) in his coat of arms, was a Renaissance ruler who broke the power of the barons and created a strong central system of government. He was a patron of the arts and not afraid of introducing foreign influences. He looked to Italy and aimed at creating a similar Renaissance environment in Hungary. His palace at Buda became one of the Renaissance centres of Europe, famous for its library of codices and illuminated manuscripts. His opposition to the powerful barons and his 'democratic' spirit find echoes even today in the myths of 'Matthias the just king'.

Decline set in after Matthias's death. The throne was offered to the king of Bohemia and the reign of Wladislas II was characterised by weakness and laxity, symbolised by the selling of parts of Matthias's library to pay for royal household expenses. Battles against the Turks continued and in 1514 a new crusade against them was proclaimed. The appointed commander, György Dózsa, was a military leader of Transylvanian Székely origin. Peasant dissatisfaction was rife and Dózsa eventually turned his army against the nobles instead of the Turks. The peasant army fought victoriously throughout the summer of 1514 until the nobles united and suppressed the movement. Dózsa was captured and put to death with great cruelty, and laws and restrictions on the peasantry were tightened. However, internal politics now took a back seat in face of the second great disaster of Hungarian history, the invasion and 150-year occupation by the Turks.

By 1526 the Turkish army had conquered the Balkans and was ready to invade Hungary. At the battle of Mohács on 29 August of that year King Louis II of Hungary was defeated by the forces of Süleyman I, the king and most of the Hungarian army losing their lives in the battle. Although the Turks retreated for a while after their victory, by 1541 they were in control of Buda.

Hungary was now divided into three parts. The central and southern area of the country became part of the Ottoman Empire. Northern Hungary and the western borderlands were under the rule of the Habsburgs, while Transylvania, to the east and south-east, became a principality mainly under Turkish tutelage. The Turks have understandably had a 'bad press' over the years in Hungarian historical writing, being held responsible for much destruction and little creation apart from a few baths and mosques. However, some towns prospered under Turkish rule and even enjoyed a degree of

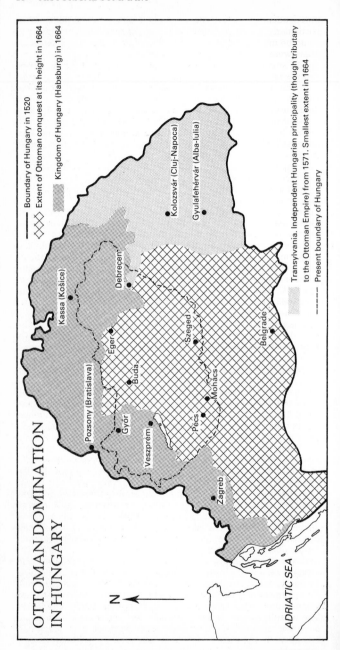

OTTOMAN DOMINATION IN HUNGARY

Boundary of Hungary in 1520

Extent of Ottoman conquest at its height in 1664

Kingdom of Hungary (Habsburg) in 1664

Transylvania. Independent Hungarian principality (though tributary to the Ottoman Empire) from 1571. Smallest extent in 1664

Present boundary of Hungary

Kassa (Košice)
Debrecen
Kolozsvár (Cluj-Napoca)
Gyulafehérvár (Alba-Iulia)
Eger
Szeged
Belgrade
Buda
Pozsony (Bratislava)
Győr
Veszprém
Mohács
Pécs
Zagreb

N

ADRIATIC SEA

independence. What is true is that the constant state of warfare, particularly in the border regions, hampered whatever progress could be made. The border fortresses, as the castles in the disputed areas were called, became the scene of bloody battles and heroic deeds, such as István Dobó's defence of Eger in 1552 and Miklós Zrínyi's battle at Szigetvár four years later.

At the same time two contested questions split the Hungarian nobility. Should a king of Hungarian nationality be elected or should the Habsburgs be acknowledged as the rulers of Hungary? The other question concerned religion—remain faithful to Catholicism or adopt one of the fast-spreading new Protestant doctrines? For the nobility the answers to both questions could have material consequences of some significance. Loyalty to the Habsburgs could lead to the granting of estates and, similarly, joining the Reformation might lead to the acquisition of expropriated church lands.

During the Turkish period Transylvania under its princes developed more or less independently and preserved its culture, giving rise to the notion of Transylvania as the seat of 'Hungarian authenticity', which has emotional echoes even today in the concern for the Hungarian minority in Romania. Calvinist influence and educational practices brought international contacts to eastern Hungary and the military exploits of the princes István Bocskai (1604–06) and Gábor Bethlen (1613–29) managed to preserve a precarious independence for Transylvania, wedged between Vienna and Istanbul.

In 1683 the Turks advanced on Vienna and almost occupied the city. The siege prompted the Habsburgs to counter resolutely and with an international army, supported and partly financed as a crusade by Pope Leo XI, they captured Buda from the Turks in September 1686 and eventually expelled them from most of Hungary's territory in 1699. Liberation from the Turks, however, brought immense suffering in its wake. The 'liberating' soldiers, as often happens in history, ransacked, looted and plundered, terrifying those Hungarians who stood in their way. Estates were confiscated and given to imperial supporters. In short, Hungary had exchanged one set of foreign rulers for another.

The colonising policy and attitude of the Habsburgs prompted the peasantry and nobles to unite in the War of Independence of 1703–11. Their leader was the landowner and elected Prince of Transylvania, Ferenc Rákóczi II. The Rákóczi War of Independence, as it is known, has gone down in Hungarian history as one of the heroic periods in the country's past, and its leader is extolled as one of the great national figures. In the end, however, Rákóczi and his *kuruc* fighters were no match for the might of the Habsburgs, particularly in view of the fact that international assistance was minimal.

The 18C was one of 'Germanization' in Hungary, symbolised artistically by the rise of Baroque and ecclesiastically by the Counter-Reformation. Maria Theresa (1740–80) and Joseph II (1780–90) introduced some reforms but only within the framework of an agricultural Hungary tied to an industrially developing Austria. Hungary, which in pre-Turkish times had been an independent European country of some importance, was now reduced to being a colonial province with backward, impoverished villages and towns. The wealthy spoke German or French, though the language of the Diet was still Latin. Hungarian was spoken in parts of eastern Hungary, by peasants generally throughout the land and by adherents of the Enlightenment among the intelligentsia.

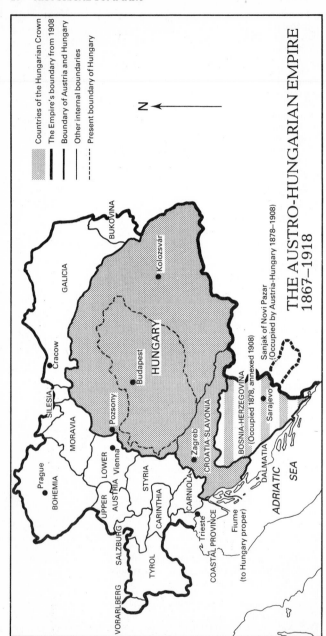

THE AUSTRO-HUNGARIAN EMPIRE
1867–1918

Countries of the Hungarian Crown
The Empire's boundary from 1908
Boundary of Austria and Hungary
Other internal boundaries
Present boundary of Hungary

N ←

BUKOVINA

GALICIA

Kolozsvár

Cracow

HUNGARY

Budapest

SILESIA

Pozsony

MORAVIA

Prague
BOHEMIA

LOWER
AUSTRIA
Vienna

UPPER
AUSTRIA

STYRIA

Zagreb

CROATIA-SLAVONIA

BOSNIA-HERZEGOVINA
(Occupied 1878, annexed 1908)

Sanjak of Novi Pazar
(Occupied by Austria-Hungary 1878–1908)

Sarajevo

SALZBURG

CARINTHIA

CARNIOLA

Trieste

COASTAL PROVINCE

Fiume
(to Hungary proper)

DALMATIA

ADRIATIC
SEA

TYROL

VORARLBERG

French revolutionary ideas, with their notions of sovereignty and national freedom, spread into Hungary at the end of the 18C, but the movement of the so-called Hungarian Jacobins was decisively nipped in the bud when their leader, Ignác Martinovics (ironically a former spy for Vienna), and six of his colleagues were executed in 1795.

One of the 'Jacobins' was Ferenc Kazinczy, a writer, translator, critic and language reformer. At the turn of the century the issue of the revival of Hungarian as a literary and national language took on political aspects in lieu of concrete political reforms. An audience developed for literary works treating national subjects in Hungarian; poets increasingly turned their attention to Hungarian heroes of the Middle Ages and through language national consciousness grew. The movement affected the non-Hungarian ethnic groups as well, though lack of sympathy among the Hungarians for them assisted Habsburg rule and caused serious difficulties during the nationalist, anti-Habsburg movements of the 19C.

The second quarter of the 19C in Hungary is known as the Reform Period. It was the age when Hungarian politicians and statesmen sought greater development and progress for their country, though the degree to which this could be done without political independence from Vienna was a matter hotly debated. An outstanding statesman of the time was Count István Széchenyi (1791–1860), who advocated economic and scientific progess very much based on the model of England, which country he visited several times, and from where he 'imported' many ideas ranging from the use of flush toilets to steam shipping on the Danube. He could write on credit in the economy or on horse-breeding and always find an eager readership. Innumerable projects are associated with his name, the most famous of which are the foundation of the Hungarian Academy of Sciences and the construction of the Chain Bridge in Budapest (designed by an Englishman and supervised by a Scotsman). It was the first permanent river crossing in the capital and a great symbol of economic and commercial progress.

His rival was Lajos Kossuth (1802–94) who eventually became the leader of the 'no progress without independence' school. Kossuth, born into a landless gentry family, became a lawyer. He was a representative in the Diet in the 1830s and sprang into prominence by publishing the proceedings of that body in a journal. His journalistic activities earned him a prison sentence after which he started a paper, 'Pesti Hirlap', in which he advocated a radical transformation of society.

The Reform Period and the agitations of politicians like Kossuth culminated in the revolution which broke out in Pest on 15 March 1848 in response to revolutionary events unfolding in Vienna. The young radicals of the city, whose leading representative was the poet Sándor Petőfi, stormed through the town distributing uncensored leaflets and making speeches demanding radical changes. They were too radical for most members of the Diet, which, in the initial stages, merely demanded faster modernisation within the framework of the Habsburg Empire.

The achilles heel of the Hungarian movement concerned the non-Hungarian ethnic minorities living within the country. Serbs, Croats and Romanians feared domination by the Hungarians should the empire be overthrown and many of them preferred, therefore, to side with Vienna. It was the governor of Croatia, Josip Jelačić, who led the first invasion of Hungary in the autumn of 1848, thus unleashing the armed struggle of the War of Independence.

Events forced the Hungarian politicians to take a more radical stand. The government moved to Debrecen and Kossuth proclaimed the overthrow of the House of Habsburg and the establishment of an independent Hungarian government. Despite his and others' valiant efforts at rallying the people, in the end the Hungarians were defeated by the combined might of the Habsburg emperor and the Russian Tsar, who had intervened on behalf of Vienna. It was all over by August 1849 and was followed by a period of military occupation and bloody reprisals carried out as a deliberate policy of punishment. On 6 October Lajos Batthyány, the former Hungarian Prime Minister, was executed in Pest, and at Arad (Oradea, Romania) 13 Hungarian generals also faced the firing squad. Many others were imprisoned, executed or forced into exile. The latter group included Lajos Kossuth who continued his agitations on behalf of Hungarian independence in England, America and other countries for many years.

The seeds of change had been sown, however, and although the movement for Hungarian independence had been suppressed the issue had not been wiped off the agenda. Hungarian politicians around Ferenc Deák sought some way in which a settlement could be reached with Austria. Their opportunity came during the Austro-Prussian war with the defeat of Austria at Sadowa (Königgrätz) in July 1866. The defeat severely shook the Habsburg Empire and to help restore equilibrium an agreement with Hungary was sought. Hence was born the 1867 Compromise (*Kiegyezés* in Hungarian, *Ausgleich* in German) by which the Empire was to be transformed into a Dual Monarchy with two separate governments and parliaments, though with common foreign, defence and finance ministries. It was a partial independence which pleased some and displeased others, in particular Lajos Kossuth who warned from exile that Hungary would remain tied to alien interests.

Nevertheless, in the period between the Compromise and the First World War Hungary experienced an unprecedented growth of agricultural, industrial and commercial development. Banks, factories, railways and town planning became the order of the day. The population rose from 15.4 to 21 million. The rivers Danube and Tisza were regulated. Wheat, potato and sugar beet yields all rose. In the 1870s Budapest's milling industry was the largest of any city in the world and was based on an enormous grain production.

Industrialisation made great strides, especially in Budapest. After the Compromise there were 170 industrial joint-stock companies and a few hundred private firms in Hungary. Their employees numbered less than 100,000. By the end of the century there were 2700 industrial plants with 300,000 workers. Improved communications and credit facilities provided the infrastructure for this growth. Between 1867 and 1913 the length of railway track increased tenfold from 2200 to 22,000km. At the beginning of the period there were about 60 small credit institutions functioning with 700 million crowns, by 1914 there were 5000 institutions with over 13,000 million crowns at their disposal.

In 1873 Buda, Pest and Óbuda were administratively united to form the city of Budapest. This was followed by an upsurge of urban development. Sewage pipes, water mains and tram lines were laid. Whole areas were pulled down and massive road-building projects undertaken (cf. today's Népköztársaság or the Great Boulevard). Café life took off and Budapest became a rival to Vienna as a Central European metropolis. Architecturally, present-day Budapest is still very much a 'turn-of-the-century' city with its mixture of Eclecticism and Hungarian Art Nouveau.

The successes achieved since the Compromise were crowned, so to speak, by the enormous celebrations organised in 1896 to mark the 1000th anniversary of the Magyar Conquest of the Danube Basin. Huge construction projects were planned and the City Park was designed and laid out especially to accommodate the Millenary Exhibition, which with much pomp and great splendour and in the presence of the chief dignitaries of the Austro-Hungarian Empire was ceremoniously opened by Emperor Francis Joseph on 2 May.

The pride and complacency of the celebrations was only partially justified. Beneath the surface of prosperity there was overcrowding in the workers' districts and outside the capital extensive rural unemployment. Massive emigration of Hungarians to America and other countries started at this time. Industrial development was inevitably accompanied by the growth of a labour movement. The first workers' party was founded in 1880 and the Hungarian Social Democratic Party in 1890. The strength and influence of trade unionism, socialism and Marxism ebbed and flowed in line with the industrial and political situation. Several bloody clashes with the police occurred throughout the period.

Because of its relation with Austria, Hungary was dragged into the First World War in alliance with the German empire. Although only a small part of the country was actually involved in the fighting, the four years' war brought immense suffering and hunger which lead to protest movements, strikes and mutinies. Towards the end of the war demonstrations demanding peace, universal suffrage, a secret ballot and democratisation were almost daily occurrences. There was a three-day general strike in January 1918, a naval mutiny in the Adriatic in February and a major mutiny of troops in May. As desertion rates increased, political opposition rallied around Count Mihály Károlyi whose party opposed the war in Parliament.

The end of the war brought the collapse of the Austro-Hungarian Empire. On 16 November 1918 Hungary's independence was proclaimed and a Republic adopted, although revolutionary events in the preceding weeks had in practice already established the first independent Hungarian government since 1848. On 11 January Mihály Károlyi became Hungary's first president. Universal suffrage with the secret ballot and freedom of the press, assembly and association were proclaimed.

The Károlyi government was faced with many problems. Hunger and shortages were still rife, land reform was a pressing problem, and relations with non-Hungarian ethnic groups were left unresolved. The Western powers disliked Károlyi's democratic politics and his sympathy for, and support from, radical circles. Furthermore they were determined to treat Hungary as a vanquished nation and dismember its territory in line with secret treaties and promises made during the war. Revolutionary disturbances in Soviet Russia also made the Western powers determined to establish more compliant states which could act as a *cordon sanitaire* against the infection of revolution from the East.

Western pressure on the Hungarian government to pull back its troops and create a neutral zone on the Romanian border led to the resignation of Károlyi and the subsequent formation of a new government composed of Social Democrats and Communist Party leaders. On 21 March 1919 this Revolutionary Governing Council took office and proclaimed Hungary a Republic of Councils on the

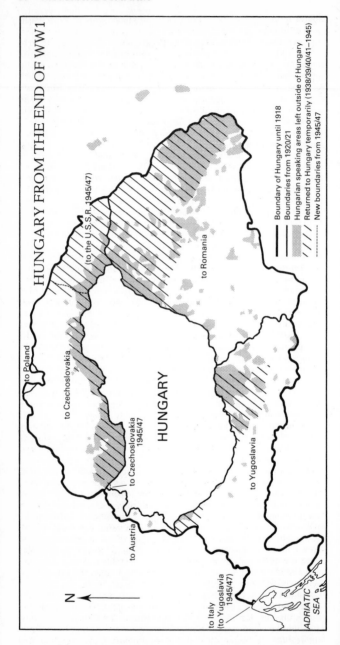

HUNGARY FROM THE END OF WW1

HUNGARY

to Poland

to Czechoslovakia

(to the U.S.S.R. 1945/47)

to Romania

to Czechoslovakia 1945/47

to Austria

to Yugoslavia

to Italy (to Yugoslavia 1945/47)

ADRIATIC SEA

N

Boundary of Hungary until 1918
Boundaries from 1920/21
Hungarian speaking areas left outside of Hungary
Returned to Hungary temporarily (1938/39/40/41–1945)
New boundaries from 1945/47

Soviet model. Apart from the workers' movements and circles of radical intellectuals support also came from all those who opposed the pressure and intervention of the Western powers.

The 133 days of the Republic of Councils were a hectic time of attempts at radical transformation. Many enterprises were nationalised, food and housing shortages were tackled and an attempt was made to make culture more accessible. However, opposition among the large numbers of peasants was generated by the refusal of the government to distribute land and its attempts at enforced collectivisation. Disturbances, including strikes, were dealt with in a heavy-handed manner by the security detachments known as the 'Lenin Boys'.

The overwhelming problem, however, was that posed by the military intervention in April of Romanian and Czechoslovak forces, backed by the French. Although the Hungarian Red Army won some victories, the approaching foreign troops and insistent diplomatic demands from the West forced the resignation of the Revolutionary Governing Council on 1 August 1919, just a few days before Romanian troops entered Budapest.

The ruler of Hungary for the next 25 years was to be Miklós Horthy, a naval officer, aide-de-camp to Francis Joseph and the last naval commander of the monarchy with the rank of rear admiral. He was Minister of Defence of the government that had been formed in Szeged to overthrow the Soviet Republic and entered the capital at the head of his counter-revolutionary army on 16 November 1919. A reign of 'white terror' now ensued against communists, their sympathisers or those suspected of being such, and Jews.

The key international event for the Horthy period took place on 4 June 1920 with the signing of the Peace Treaty in the Trianon Palace at Versailles. Under the Trianon Treaty about 70 per cent of the territory, which included around 60 per cent of the population, of the former Kingdom of Hungary was surrendered to the neighbouring countries of Romania, Czechoslovakia, Yugoslavia and Austria. (Sopron and its surroundings were given back by Austria following a referendum in 1921.) Revision of the Treaty became the key item of Hungarian foreign policy. This eventually led to the alignment with Nazi Germany in the 1930s and during the Second World War.

Domestically the Horthy period was one of ultra-conservatism with fascist leanings. The Communist Party was banned, the Social Democrats were restricted to mainly trade union representation (i.e. they were not allowed to organise among the peasantry), the entry of Jews to university was restricted in the late 1930s and leading strata preferred to dwell on the loss of Hungarian territories rather than tackle the problems of poverty and rural destitution which led to the designation of Hungary in the 1930s as 'a land of three million beggars'. In 1937–38 per capital national income was only half the European average and less than a third of western European countries. Political and economic considerations led many Hungarians to emigrate in the inter-war period.

In 1939 Hungary signed the Anti-Comintern pact, directed against the Soviet Union and which had been concluded by Germany and Japan in 1936. In November 1940 Hungary joined the formal alliance of Germany, Italy and Japan. Hungary participated in the German attack on Yugoslavia in April 1941, just a few months after it had concluded a 'Treaty of Eternal Friendship' with that country, and on the 27 June of that year Hungarian troops crossed the Soviet border, five days after the initial German assault.

During the Second World War Hungary was mainly a source of war supplies for Germany. It provided bauxite, cheap agricultural produce and labour. In military terms the war was a human disaster. The entire Second Hungarian Army was lost near the River Don in the first two months of 1943. After this defeat the government refused to send major new Hungarian forces to the front and later peace initiatives in the form of secret negotiations with the Allies were begun.

In other matters, too, Hungary was reluctant to fall in line with the Germans. In 1939 the borders had been opened to about 100,000 Polish refugees and, despite German pressure, Jews initially were neither confined to ghettos nor deported. Hungary, the unreliable ally, was occupied by German troops on 19 March 1944. The realities of war now began to hit the population at home. Thousands of opponents of Nazism were arrested, the rounding up and deportation of Jews began and Anglo-American aircraft started to bomb the country.

Soviet troops reached Hungarian territory in September 1944 and proceeded towards Budapest. The following month, after failed attempts to get out of the war, the Horthy regime finally fell and the Hungarian Nazis, the Arrow-Cross Party, took over and instituted a reign of terror against their opponents. By Christmas the Red Army was blockading Budapest and fighting continued until the capital was liberated the following February. The German army was finally driven out of the country on 4 April 1945.

The early post-war years in Hungary were times of reconstruction in which a popular creative spirit played a large role. As elsewhere in Europe central administration had collapsed and local committees were spontaneously formed to assume local political and administrative power. These were gradually displaced, however, as central authority reasserted itself.

For the first three years after the war Hungary was governed by a coalition of four parties—the Smallholders' Party, National Peasant Party, Social Democrats and Communists. In the elections of November 1945 the Smallholders' Party had gained an overall majority of 57 per cent. The Social Democrats and the Communists had approximately 17 per cent each.

The new government was faced with enormous problems. The war had left the country in ruins. Over half a million people had died (out of a total population of under ten million), war damage was estimated at five times the pre-war national income, 40 per cent of the country's national assets had been destroyed. Budapest was devastated. All the bridges linking Buda and Pest had been blown up by the Germans. One of the world's severest ever hyper-inflations took off in Hungary in 1946, but miraculously stabilised quite quickly with the introduction of the new currency, the forint. Popular support from the still largely agricultural population was assured by the Land Reform Decree of 1945 in which 35 per cent of the country's land was distributed. Most of this went to peasant families who had had no land previously.

A turning point was reached in 1948. In line with similar movements elsewhere in the Moscow-dominated international communist movement, the Hungarian communists adopted a new, more aggressive approach to the manipulation of power. A merger was arranged with the Social Democrats and a new Communist-controlled government took over. The following few years saw the consolidation of a Stalinist, one-party, state system which in its use of both legal and illegal terror was one of the worst in Europe.

Hungary's Stalinist leader was Mátyás Rákosi. Around him a cult of the personality developed to ridiculous proportions. Fear ruled as denunciations, trials, deportations and executions engulfed both opponents and supporters of the regime. The most notable trial and execution was that of László Rajk in 1949 on trumped up charges of 'Titoism'. (Tito, Yugoslavia's leader, had broken with Stalin.) Rajk had been a long-standing member of the Communist Party, had fought in the Spanish Civil War and had been part of the internal underground movement during World War II (all suspicious to the more Moscow-oriented Rákosi clique). A staunch communist, he was Minister of Interior from 1946 to 1948, in which post he helped pave the way for the later Stalinist consolidation. Nevertheless, he fell victim to the very system he supported.

1950 saw the beginning of the first Five Year Plan on Soviet lines. The emphasis was on heavy industry to the neglect of other sectors— it was called 'building a country of iron and steel' in the classical Stalinist jargon. Compulsory plan targets were centrally determined, allowing little room for independent initiatives. Although the economic indicators showed a sharp rise in industrial production, real wages actually fell. Compulsory agricultural deliveries to the State were enforced, causing resentment and disruption of supplies.

A relaxation began in 1953 following the death of Stalin. Imre Nagy replaced Rákosi as Prime Minister and announced the 'New Course', a programme of economic and social reforms including political amnesties and loosening of political rigidity. Over the next two years the internal struggle between the reformers and the hard-line old guard spilled over into non-party circles, particularly writers and journalists. Eventually the old-guard regained power, denounced the 'New Course' and removed Nagy from all official posts. However, demands for reforms continued outside the party.

Krushchev's 'secret speech' denouncing Stalin at the 20th Congress of the Soviet Communist Party early in 1956 caused major political ripples throughout Eastern Europe and the communist world. Agitation for reforms and the return of Imre Nagy continued in Hungary, particularly among the newly-formed circles of writers and other intellectuals. The rehabilitation of László Rajk became a *cause célèbre* and his ceremonial reburial on 6 October brought 200,000 people on to the streets, prefiguring the events which began 17 days later.

A mass student demonstration on 23 October 1956 spilled over into a generalised revolt with attacks on official buildings, the radio, party and police headquarters. Soviet troops intervened and there followed several days of bitter street fighting and strikes with the revolt finally ending after a second Soviet military intervention on 4 November. Some of the workers' councils and factory committees which had sprung up during the events continued rearguard strike actions until the end of the year.

The Hungarian uprising of 1956 essentially only lasted two weeks, but its impact was enormous, both internationally and internally. On a world scale the Soviet intervention damaged the traditional communist movement irreparably. In Britain, for example, one third of the entire party membership resigned in protest. The break, in Britain and elsewhere, facilitated the eventual emergence of new forms of Marxism, the so-called New Left, and the re-emergence of other libertarian approaches to radical politics, all of which played a part in the social upheavals of 1968 and the varied radical movements of the 1970s.

The most symbolic act of 1956. Stalin's statue is pulled down on 23 October, the first day of the uprising.

Inside Hungary the impact of the events was also huge, although this is usually only alluded to since for over thirty years 'a counter-revolution' was the standard designation of the 1956 events. What was generally agreed, however, was that Stalinism had generated tension and disaffection and that a return could not be made to the old ways. In one way or another, almost everything in Hungary changed or began to change after 1956. János Kádár, the new political leader, was no hard-liner. He himself had been imprisoned during the Rákosi period. Despite the executions and imprisonments of the 1956–63 period, a consensus between leadership and people was sought. A catch-phrase of Kádár's came to represent the new policy—'those who are not against us are with us'.

Along with the end of dogmatism in cultural and social life, important changes were initiated in the economy. These culminated in 1968 with the introduction of the so-called 'New Economic Mechanism' which started a process of decentralisation of decision-making in favour of enterprises at local level, encouraging them to operate on a profit basis, and allowing greater play for market forces. This economic reform process has continued, with fits and starts, to this day. The 1980s, and particularly the second half of the decade, saw an acceleration of the process such that today Hungarian economic life, albeit still operating under public or cooperative ownership, is very much market oriented.

Hungary Today—Everyday Life

Hungary today does not conform to the traditional Eastern European stereotype of political repression and serious basic economic shortages. More importantly, it has not conformed to that stereotype for many years, since long before the Gorbachev era of *perestroika* and *glasnost* in the Soviet Union. True, the stereotype had a basis in Hungarian reality. The years between 1949 and 1953 were the years of Stalinist terror in Hungary, but over the decades following 1956, one could almost say because of 1956, the country changed and was one of the leading models of reform in Eastern Europe, although officially the notion of being any kind of 'model' was always denied.

Great changes have been taking place in Hungarian economic life in recent years. The second half of the 1980s witnessed an acceleration of the economic reform process which started in 1968 as the awkwardly-named New Economic Mechanism. Market mechanisms have been more widely introduced and a great emphasis placed on profit-oriented initiatives. For the citizen this has meant various things. For some it has meant the possibility of relative enrichment by the setting up of private businesses or by exploiting the market opportunities of selling their specialised labour. For others, probably the majority, it has had a dual impact, both positive and negative. Greater choice in consumer products and services there has been, but it has been accompanied by relatively steep price rises. The introduction of a personal income tax system has also made people more wary about adding to their incomes at every opportunity.

Sign of the times? A discarded placard of Lenin in the back yard of a factory in Budapest's Kőbánya district.

Work in Hungary has a peculiar nature. Most adults (both men and women) are still employed in some basic activity by a state cooperative or other large enterprise. Many, however, are also engaged in second, third or even fourth jobs, either regularly or on an ad hoc basis, to supplement their incomes. It is not the equivalent of the 'black economy' of Western countries, as this 'second economy' as it is known in Hungary, is perfectly legal and above-board. People may work in the second economy using the same skills as in their normal job (for example teachers taking private lessons) or at entirely different activities (professors driving taxis). They may even hire the equipment or premises of their permanent employers to engage in 'private' work after hours. The intensity of labour in the official, first economy is relatively low and hence people can often work at a second job during their official working hours. The interesting and varied practices that this can lead to in working habits are countered by the fact that in total people work extremely long hours in order to make ends meet.

Until recent years full employment was guaranteed in Hungary. This is changing in line with a shift towards 'efficient' employment, meaning that if a firm does not make a profit it will not be subsidised from the state budget and will have to close, making the employees redundant. Fears of unemployment and other changes in the labour market, which include an increasing tendency on the part of the economic authorities to regard labour 'simply' as a factor of production, are having an effect on the trade union movement, for many years considered more or less as an arm of the state. The unions are beginning to take on a more autonomous role, particularly in view of the establishment of several independent trade union formations. Unlike in Poland, however, the emergence of such bodies has not as yet led to any kind of crisis situation.

Hungary, despite its increasing integration into the world's financial networks, still has a domestic cash economy. Cheques are virtually unknown. Wages and salaries are received in cash and most purchases are paid for in cash, even when quite large amounts are involved. Savings accounts exist, but for the general population they are pretty inflexible in terms of cash withdrawal facilities. The cash system has its peculiar features. These include chasing around from one office to another to collect payments for various pieces of work in the second economy. An awful lot of hours are spent running around by people trying to get paid. Cash payments can be sent in the post and this produces another phenomenon unusual to the western eye. Postmen and postwomen regularly carry around with them huge amounts of cash, usually without any threat of attack. By Western standards Hungary is a safe country. Crime, however, is on the increase.

Helping to deal with the social problems generated by youth alienation has meant a return to public life for organised religion. Today the state welcomes the involvement of the churches in this field. But it is not that the churches have suddenly emerged from a state of repression. Cardinal Lékai, the Catholic Primate of Hungary from 1976 to 1987, gradually guided the church in its relations with the state from a situation of mutual tolerance to friendly cooperation. For many years now, Catholic churches have operated freely and practising Catholics have not suffered on account of their religion. Many would argue that Lékai's success was achieved by controlling the internal church dissidents who wanted change at a faster pace. Nevertheless, the churches are full in Hungary today and attract increasing numbers of young people.

While the Catholic church is the largest in Hungary, having the formal allegiance of about two thirds of the population, there are also active Protestant communities, particularly in the Calvinist strongholds of eastern Hungary. The country can also boast of the only Jewish seminary in the whole of Eastern Europe.

Increasing press and television freedom is a significant recent phenomenom in Hungary. Today there are numerous publications dealing with all aspects of society, and outspoken criticism of official policy is not unusual. There are two television channels, but their monopoly has been eased in recent years by the introduction of satellite TV. In terms of the availability of Western and Eastern radio, TV, and newspapers Hungary has, in a sense, one of the most free media in the world.

More mundane matters, of course, are generally on the mind of the average Hungarian. Housing, for example, is one of the central problems. Most people live in flats and have only one or two rooms, apart from kitchen and bathroom. Many families feel under constant pressure to move, to find a bigger place in which to live. But decreasing public investment (recently only ten per cent of new flats have been built from public resources), rising prices and the difficulties of obtaining large loans or mortgages makes moving impossible for most people. The result is that most urban dwellers live either in old, run-down (though often large) inner-city flats or in relatively cramped, modern high-rise blocks, although given the difficulties of moving these often contain a remarkably varied mixture of professional and manual workers, which perhaps explains the somewhat less delipidated nature of tower-blocks than would normally be found in Britain.

Of course, for those who can afford it—and their numbers seem to be on the increase—there are the more 'exclusive' areas in every town, as any visitor passing through certain districts of the Buda Hills can observe. In rural areas the housing problem is not so acute in the sense that families live in houses, usually detached, on one floor and with a largish garden.

The transformation of Hungarian agriculture and its associated social life can be counted among the major successes of post-World War II Hungary. After various experiments in centralised, command systems for agricultural production, Hungary has settled down to a mixture of mainly cooperative and state farm production methods. Private plots belonging to individual farmers or employees of large farms are common, as is the interchange of goods and services between the private, family economy and the cooperative and state sector. All this, with its accompanying incentives for all involved, has led to a thriving agricultural sector in which exports play a large role. Today about 20 per cent of the population is engaged in agriculture.

Becoming ill presents problems anywhere, but sickness in Hungary can be a complicated and expensive business, despite the formally free and universal health service. The established practice is that nurses and doctors receive tips or gratuities from their patients. Although illegal, the custom is widespread enough to be regarded as a social habit. There are a variety of causes but it is generally agreed that what sustains the practice is the relatively low—some would say appallingly low—pay of doctors and medical staff. The official pay of a doctor who has spent years studying and undertaking special training can be well below the national average.

Men and women are formally, constitutionally equal in Hungary, and in many ways Hungarian women are more independent than their Western counterparts. The notion of women going out to work and not being tied to the home is primarily the reason for this. But beneath the surface equality there are deep differences. In most social, economic and political positions, it is men rather than women who have the power. In schools, for example, teachers are mainly women, but head teachers are invariably men. Although there is equal pay for equal work, women generally occupy the lowest-paid jobs. Sexist attitudes are most clear in the many jokes and cartoons about stupid women, interfering mothers-in-law, and so on. In the home it is traditionally the woman who does most of the work, meaning that as she goes out to work as well, hers is a double burden. However, things are changing and among younger people there is generally a greater sharing of household tasks.

In some senses children are highly regarded in Hungary. You will often see adults standing on the underground, for example, while they allow their child to sit when there is a limited number of seats free. Child-care leave is generous in Hungary; you can have a child and then go on child-care leave for up to three years while your job is held for you. A second child entitles you to a further three years. Nor does it have to be the mother who takes the leave. It can be the father, or even a grandparent. By international standards this is a remarkably long period of time. In practice it is usually the woman who takes the leave and she will often return to work for financial reasons before the three years have expired. There is relatively good nursery provison in Hungary for all children from the age of three, though even younger children can usually be found places in crèches.

Concern for children is not entirely divorced from wider social policy concerns. In Hungary the birth rate dropped dramatically from around 18 per thousand in the mid-1970s to about 12 per thousand at the end of the eighties, and since 1980 there has been a natural decrease in the population. Attempts have been made, therefore, to encourage people to have more children, but shortage of living space and economic difficulties are working against this.

Despite the general desire to encourage more births, Hungary is not uniformly a child-centred society. This can be experienced by anyone searching for children's clothes. Shortages in particular sizes are common. In addition, the withdrawal of state subsidies on children's clothes has meant that they have changed from being very cheap to being relatively expensive.

Schooling in Hungary is undergoing many changes but the basic pattern is that of the Prussian system, with eight years of primary followed by four years of secondary school. Schools start at 8.00 and continue through until 13.00 or 14.00, with every lesson lasting 45 minutes. The secondary level is not comprehensive, but has three types of school—grammar, technical and vocational. Entry into the generally preferred grammar schools is by grades and sometimes entrance exams. School leaving certificates at the age of 18 are based on mainly oral examinations in three compulsory subjects (mathematics, Hungarian language and history) plus other optional ones.

Music education has played a major role in Hungarian schools since World War II and has generally followed the internationally acclaimed approach of the composer and musicologist Zoltán Kodály. In the field of special education Hungary has also been hitting the international headlines in recent years. Budapest's Pető Institute for Conductive Education of the Motor Disabled, with its holistic approach and its high success rate in teaching children with severe disabilities to walk, has gained world renown not least since the children of hundreds of English families passed through its walls in the late 1980s.

Relatively few pupils manage to get into university or further education because of limited places and strict entrance requirements. University education is mostly for five years and is generally based on continuous assessment and oral examinations.

In their everyday social interactions Hungarians are very polite, at least in a formal, verbal sense. Strangers will often say good-day, for example, if they meet in a lift or on a staircase. A polite word of greeting and parting is also uttered when entering and leaving shops or taxis. Shaking hands is common when meeting and close friends, both men and women, greet each other with a kiss on each cheek.

For foreigners the forms of address are fairly straightforward (see the section on language). But among Hungarians there is a whole range of words and phrases which are deemed appropriate depending on the age and sex of the person concerned and on the relative formality or informality between the people in the given situation. Saying 'hello' in Hungarian is no simple matter. A child is addressed differently from an adult, a friend differently from a stranger, and so on. Once the introductions are over there are further complications as there are three words for 'you', both in singular and plural, and the form of accompanying verb also changes depending on the relative formality of the situation, which itself can change as people move from a formal to a friendly relationship.

Visitors need not be too concerned about all this but some knowledge of other formal social practices could be useful if visiting or being invited to a Hungarian home. It is customary, for example, to take flowers as a gift for the hostess. In fact the giving of flowers on all sorts of occasions is very common in Hungary. Flower shops and stalls abound and the practice is usually not to take a huge bunch, but rather just one or a few flowers bought individually and carefully wrapped in cellophane.

Social drinking usually takes place in the home or sometimes at restaurants, although rising prices have caused this once popular practice to change. When bought in shops, alcohol is relatively cheap, even by Hungarian standards. A bottle of Soviet vodka, for example, costs less than in Moscow. It is customary when drinking to wait until everyone's glass has been filled and until the host has raised his or her glass in a toast. Then, and throughout the drinking session, countless cries of *egészségedre* (cheers!) can be heared.

Politically, the last three decades have seen many changes in Hungary. There has been a steady opening up and the jettisoning of dogmatism and restrictions greatly accelerated in the second half of the 1980s.

One of the most dramatic developments has involved an official reassessment of and public debate about the events of 1956. This was symbolized by the public reburial of Imre Nagy and his associates on 16 June 1989. (Nagy, a reform Communist, became Prime Minister during the 1956 uprising and was executed after a secret trial two years later.)

The electoral system is also livening up. For the elections to the National Assembly (Parliament) in 1985 a law was passed requiring that all seats be contested by two or more candidates. The initial two candidates (not all party members) were proposed by the Patriotic People's Front, an umbrella organisation covering the party, churches, trade unions etc. However, nominees had to be accepted as candidates at public meetings at which they could be rejected and/or further candidates nominated. In several cases 'official' candidates were rejected and in many constituencies one, two or sometimes three additional candidates were proposed.

In parallel with the electoral changes, an attempt has been made to increase the weight and role of parliament and its committees. Debates are televised and opposition is increasingly voiced there.

1989 saw the emergence of alternative political parties in opposition to the ruling Hungarian Socialist Workers' Party. The latter was thrown out of government in multi-party elections in the spring of 1990, following which a centre-right coalition government emerged dominated by the conservative and somewhat nationalistic Hungarian Democratic Forum. In addition, numerous independent associations have started up pursuing social and political goals in a way somewhat akin to the pressure groups of Western societies.

It is fair to say that the average citizen is not directly involved in these changes, though it is not through lack of information: the Hungarian media today is full of critical reports and discussions representing a variety of views. Nevertheless, administrative decisions resulting from the changed political atmosphere have had a great impact on ordinary life. As Hungary moved from the eighties into the nineties hardly a week passed without some new change of rule. One of the most important, psychologically as well as in practice, was the lifting of restrictions regarding travel abroad. Others, usually associated with economic measures, have not been so popular. The introduction of a personal income tax system, the introduction of value added tax and the reduction of subsidies on many basic goods are three major changes which have severely hit people's pockets.

At the time of writing changes are still underway and being planned in Hungary. Together these will all have a long-term impact. Perhaps, therefore, the only really definite thing that can be said about Hungary today is precisely that it is a society in transformation.

Art and Architecture in Hungary

Any discussion of the historical evolution of Hungarian art in a guidebook to modern Hungary faces the problem of the stark political fact that in 1920, at the Treaty of Trianon following World War I, Hungary lost approximately two-thirds of its territory to neighbouring countries. Large areas were ceded to Romania and Czechoslovakia, though some land was also given to Yugoslavia and Austria. Hence, many Hungarian works of art created in these regions over the centuries can now no longer be seen by the visitor to Hungary, with the important exception of those items preserved in museums. The issue is further highlighted by the fact that during the nearly 150 years of Turkish rule in Hungary, in the 16th and 17C, many medieval works of art were destroyed, carried off or simply left to decay. Those parts of the country not under Turkish rule and whose artistic creations escaped this fate were precisely those territories of which a large part were lost to Hungary in 1920. Therefore, where reference is made in this section to a place no longer part of Hungary, its present name and country is given in brackets following the old Hungarian name. By and large this practice has also been followed in the text of the routes, though sometimes simply the words 'in Transylvania' have been used to indicate that the place is currently part of Romania.

At the time of the establishment of the Hungarian state c AD 1000 the conversion of the people to Christianity became a matter of prime political importance in order to help unite the country. The development of the Church as a Hungarian institution inevitably made the building of churches and the creation of an ecclesiastical decorative art a pressing task. The many churches founded by King Stephen (1000–1038) can now only generally be traced from foundation walls and a few descriptions. The most impressive were probably those of Pécs, which was destroyed by fire in 1064, and Székesfehérvár, of which only the foundations remain. (The carved sarcophagus of King Stephen can be seen here.) Other important churches were the Episcopal Cathedral at Kalocsa and the Benedictine Monastery at Pannonhalma. However, there are some extant remains, for example the crypt in the church at Feldebrő and the crypt of the Abbey Church at Tihany, which both date from the 11C. The style of these buildings is related to German Benedictine buildings and is characteristic of early Romanesque architecture in Hungary.

The development of the Romanesque style up to the end of the 12C is often called the period of the 'Pécs workshop'. After a fire at Pécs in 1064 destroyed the early 11C church, a three-aisled basilica with four corner towers was built. The sculptural decoration of the late 11C cathedral shows the new influence of contemporary French art. Relations with France grew closer during the reign of Béla III (1172–96) who twice married a French woman, one of them a princess. Béla developed Esztergom into a royal palace: its finest ornament is the rose-windowed chapel.

Churches founded by rich landowning families generally followed the style of the predominantly Benedictine monasteries and churches of the time. The earliest surviving example of this is the church at Lébénymiklós not far from the road between Mosonmogyaróvár and Győr on the main Vienna–Budapest highway. It dates from the first decade of the 13C and is considered one of the earliest examples of Hungarian Romanesque architecture. The richest relic in this category is, however, the Benedictine Abbey Church at Ják, near Szombathely in western Hungary, begun c 1220.

Building activity by the Cistercian and Premonstratensian orders began in the 13C. The small church at Bélapátfalva (1232) to the north of Eger is a rare survival of Cistercian architecture, while the Premonstratensians' work can be seen in the ruins of the church at Zsámbék, some 20km west of Budapest. (The church at Élmunkás tér in Budapest is a 1930s copy of the Zsámbék church.)

Few Romanesque paintings have survived. One of the earliest is the series of frescoes in the church at Feldebrő from the second half of the 11C. An example of 12C painting can be seen in the church at Hidegség near Sopron. Some of the most important murals from the mid-13C are the Byzantine-style apostles in the Gizella Chapel at Veszprém.

Romanesque art was finally terminated by the Mongol invasion of 1241–42. Many works of art were destroyed and their creators were forced to flee. After the invaders had retreated from Hungary King Béla IV (1235–70) was determined to organise the building of a series of fortifications in various parts of the country. New settlers to replace the population that had been killed or had fled were invited in. The wave of immigration included many German craftsmen and the new mendicant orders which had an influence on the development of the arts. The occupation of the throne by Charles Robert (1307–42) of the House of Anjou also brought wider European influences to bear, and in the 14C Gothic finally superseded Romanesque.

It was in the new capital, Buda, that construction work was carried out on the largest scale. The Matthias Church on Castle Hill was begun at the end of the 13C, but building continued with various reconstructions over the next 200 years. The development of the Royal Palace gained momentum in the 14C. Sigismund of Luxemburg, King of Hungary (1387–1437) and Holy Roman Emperor, took an active part in the development of the palace, inviting many Italian and French craftsmen to Hungary. Another large-scale undertaking was the construction of the Summer Palace at Visegrád on the Danube Bend. As with the Royal Palace at Buda it was completed and enriched by King Matthias (1458–90), the great patron of Renaissance arts in Hungary, and hence Renaissance elements were incorporated into the Gothic structure.

Gothic castles and churches were erected throughout the country. The Castle at Diósgyőr, near Miskolc, is a good example of the architecture of this period, as are St. Michael's church at Sopron, the Franciscan church at Pozsony (Bratislava, Czechoslovakia), the church at Eperjes (Prešov, Czechoslovakia), St. Jacob's at Lőcse (Levoča, Czechoslovakia) and the cathedral at Kassa (Košice, Czechoslovakia). Mention can also be made of the Transylvanian churches such as St. Michael's in Kolozsvár (Cluj, Romania), the Black Church at Brassó (Braşov, Romania) and the cathedral at Nagyvárad (Oradea, Romania).

Several houses, or parts of houses, in Gothic style have survived notably in Sopron, near the Austrian border, and in the Castle District of Buda. Much of the sculptural material has been destroyed, however, although during the excavations of the Gothic palace of Buda after World War II some late 14C sculptures were unearthed.

Márton and György Kolozsvári created a sculptural art in the second half of the 14C which is considered to be the finest of its period. Much of their work has been destroyed but their statue of St. George and the Dragon (1373) survives in Prague. (There are copies below the Fishermen's Bastion in Budapest and near Dóm tér in Szeged.)

The mural paintings in the Royal Palace at Esztergom which show Italian influence are among the most magnificent artistic relics of the 14C. The 15C is best represented by the paintings on winged altarpieces, examples of which are exhibited in a unique collection at the Hungarian National Gallery in Budapest. The most prominent master of Hungarian Gothic painting was active in the mining towns around Selmecbánya (Banská Stiavnica, Czechoslovakia). He is known as Master MS, these being the initials with which he marked his pictures. Some of his works can be seen in the Christian Museum at Esztergom and in the Hungarian National Gallery.

The ornamented gilded silver reliquary bust of King (St.) Ladislas (1077–95) is one of the finer surviving specimens of medieval applied arts. It can be seen in the St. Ladislas Chapel at Győr Cathedral.

Renaissance culture flowered in Hungary during the reign of King Matthias Corvinus (1458–90) who surrounded himself with a lively Renaissance household and developed Buda into one of the leading Renaissance centres of Europe. Many Italians were invited to Hungary, but local talents were also developed. Thus while the miniatures in the illuminated Corvina manuscripts were painted mainly by Italian artists, the bindings were the work of Hungarian masters. The library for which these were created was founded in 1470, and an illuminators' workshop was later established there. According to contemporary records the palace at Buda was sumptuously decorated with paintings, murals and statues. Almost all was lost, however, during the Ottoman period. The statues were removed or destroyed and the famous library was plundered.

Apart from Buda, Esztergom was also a centre where artistic life flourished, first under Prince Primate Ippolito d'Este and later with commissions for Archbishop Tamás Bakócz. The Bakócz Chapel in Esztergom Cathedral was begun in the first years of the 16C. Its red marble decoration is a fine and rare example of Hungarian Renaissance artwork.

Ottoman rule in the 16C and 17C called a halt to artistic and cultural development throughout most of Hungary. Treasures were carried away and buildings reduced to ruins either through constant warfare or neglect. Churches which survived were mostly turned into mosques. Some building did take place, however. Turkish-built baths are still in use in Budapest and the mosque and minaret of Yakovali Hassan in the southern town of Pécs have been restored to their original form. (The former mosque in Széchenyi tér in the centre of Pécs, which is today a Catholic church, is the largest surviving example of Turkish architecture in Hungary.)

The Turks were driven out of Hungary towards the end of the 17C. Their rule was replaced by that of the Habsburgs who brought with them the Counter-Reformation and its associated Baroque forms of ecclesiastical art. Baroque in Hungary was, therefore, initially an imported style in which Italian, and later German and Austrian artists, played a leading role. The early large Baroque buildings were ecclesiastical and include the Jesuit Church at Nagyszombat (Trnava, Czechoslovakia), the Church of St. Ignatius at Győr and the Jesuit Church in Kassa (Košice, Czechoslovakia). Here the Italian influence is clear. The Győr church (1634–41), for example, was designed by the Italian-born architect Baccio del Bianco, and the Baroque church which previously stood on the site of the Basilica at Eger (1713–17) was also the work of an Italian, Giovanni Battista Carlone. Similarly, the Baroque Esterházy Mansion at Kismarton (Eisenstadt, Austria, 1760s) was designed by Carlo Martino Carlone in the 1760s.

The Baroque style gained ground in Hungary throughout the 18C, with Italian influence being superseded by Austrian. The earliest large works of that period were the reconstruction of Buda Castle and the huge building designed in 1726–37 by Anton Erhard Martinelli which today houses the Budapest City Council offices on Városház u. After the explusion of the Turks from Hungary, one of the first mansions to be built in the Baroque style was at Ráckeve to the south of Budapest. It was designed by Johann Lucas Hildebrandt and built during the first twenty years of the 18C for Prince Eugene of Savoy, the Commander of the anti-Turkish armies. A good example of ecclesiastical Baroque architecture from the first half of the century is the University Church tucked away at the side of Egyetem tér in Pest. Outside Budapest, notable Baroque churches include the cathedral at Vác, designed by the French architect I.M. Amadé Canevale between 1763 and 1777 and the Minorite church at Eger, which dates from 1758–73.

In secular building mention has to be made of the Esterházy Palace at Fertőd (1764–66), between Sopron and Győr in western Hungary, which shows some French Baroque influences. It was the largest such undertaking of the period and due to the lavish lifestyle which centred around it in the late 18C it was spoken of as the 'Hungarian Versailles'. Also significant was András Mayerhoffer's Grassalkovich Mansion at Gödöllő, which was built in the 1740s and which virtually created a 'school' of mansion design, reflecting the impact of late Viennese Baroque.

The leading master of late Hungarian Baroque architecture was Jakab Fellner (1722–80). One of his most important works is the Episcopal Palace at Veszprém. He lived at Tata and designed many buildings in and around the town which can still be seen.

In painting and sculpture, as with architecture, the Baroque style was transmitted through first Italian and then Austrian examples. One of the most gifted sculptors was the Austrian Georg Rahael Donner (1693–1741) who was active in Pozsony (Bratislava, Czechoslovakia) in the 1720s and 1730s. Italian fresco painters came to Hungary, and in the 18C some of the best Viennese painters worked on commissions from Hungarian aristocrats and Church leaders. Good examples are Paul Troger's ceiling frescoes in the Church of St. Ignatius at Győr, Caspar Franz Sambach's work in Székesfehérvár and Johann Lucas Kracker's masterpiece, the ceiling fresco depicting the Council of Trent in the library of the Lyceum at Eger. Franz Anton Maulbertsch (1724–96) painted frescoes in many Hungarian churches. His series of frescoes in the parish church of Sümeg (1757–58) is the most renowned. However, the artist receiving the largest number of commissions was István Dorfmeister (1729–97).

Hungarian applied arts also flourished at this time. The wrought-iron work of Henrik Fazola is especially beautiful as can be seen on the gates at the County Hall in Eger (1761) and on several other buildings in that town.

The painter Ádám Mányoki (1673–1756) is an exception to the dominating Austrian Baroque style of the first half of the 18C. After working as a portrait painter in Hamburg and Berlin he later became the court painter to Prince Ferenc Rákóczi II. After the defeat of the latter's fight for independence in 1711, Mányoki went to Poland and later to Dresden. His work was strongly influenced by late-Renaissance portrait painting. His depiction of Ferenc Rákóczi II (hanging in the Hungarian National Gallery and reproduced on 50 forint notes) has become a classic among Hungarian historical portraits.

At the beginning of the 19C, in the years that led up to the Reform Period, Hungary experienced a growth of national consciousness which sought a new programmatic style in the arts. Baroque was rejected in favour of neo-classicism. Although neo-classical elements can be detected in some late-17C projects, for example I.M.A. Canevale's cathedral at Vác (1762–72) and his triumphal arch in the same town (the only one in Hungary), classicism became influential really only in the 19C. The process was assisted by changes in the system of patronage. Where earlier works had been generally commissioned by the aristocracy and ecclesiastical authorities, now an emerging middle class and landed gentry committed to national tasks appeared on the scene ready to support new ideas.

The first major example of neo-classical architecture is the Great Calvinist Church in Debrecen, which was built between 1803 and 1819 to the designs of the military engineer, Mihály Péchy. Its stark but imposing simplicity fitted well with the Protestant culture predominant in eastern Hungary.

While Protestant Debrecen was a fitting place to begin the neo-classical rebuttal of Austrian Baroque, it was Pest, on the left bank of the Danube, that grew into the centre of neo-classical architecture. The so-called 'Embellishment Committee' or 'Committee for Beautifying Pest' was set up in 1808 to organise the city's town planning and building activities. In doing so it promoted a uniform neo-classical style. The leading architect of this period was Mihály Pollack (1773–1855). His chief achievement was also a political project—the Hungarian National Museum, which he built in the 1840s. József Hild's (1784–1867) classical designs for town houses determined to a large extent the urban face of Pest in the first half of the 19C.

The outstanding figure in sculpture at this time was István Ferenczy (1792–1856), for the simple fact that almost single-handedly he tried to lay the foundations of a Hungarian sculpture without any traditions to build on. His sense of vocation and his self-proclaimed role as a pioneer of Hungarian artistic life had an impact probably of greater importance than his actual works. His main piece, a crouching, half-naked female figure (1820–22; National Gallery, Budapest), was curiously and rather pompously entitled 'The Beginnings of Fine Arts' (A Szép Mesterségek Kezdete), often more simply known as 'The Shepherdess'. In many ways, however, Ferenczy's project was a false start to be taken up only by a later generation.

The Reform Period saw the consolidation of the middle classes and the development of Hungarian industry. As a spin-off several branches of the applied arts began to flourish at the time. Furniture making, for example, became an important trade and Hungarian china achieved international fame through the products of the Herend Porcelain Factory near Veszprém.

The failure of the War of Independence of 1848–49 had an impact on the arts, just as the development of the arts in the first half of the century had been part of the nationalistic tendencies which led up to 1848. The defeat engendered a pathos in much of the arts though many artists still felt that they were performing social tasks. The tranquillity of neo-classicism began to give way to romanticism and a new search for what could be considered 'Hungarian'. The roots were sought in eastern Moorish and Byzantine styles. The outstanding example of this was the building of the Vigadó concert hall in Pest (1859–65), which was designed by Frigyes Feszl (1821–84). The building was severely damaged in World War II but restoration has managed to retain the façade. Feszl also had a hand in the design of the Central Synagogue on Budapest's Dohány u., a building where the romantic eastern elements are clear. A similar approach was employed on the parish church at Fót, to the north-east of Budapest. The designer, Miklós Ybl, (1839–1902) was one of the great figures in Hungarian architecture in the second half of the 19C. His works include the Budapest Opera House (1884).

In the last quarter of the 19C building activity increased tremendously in the Hungarian capital, assisted by the unification of Buda, Pest and Óbuda in 1873 and boosted by the preparations for the celebrations of the 1000th anniversary of the Magyar conquest in 1896. The style adopted was the international Eclectic or Historical style, in essence a mixture of various architectural forms. In the course of demolition and clearing for the huge projects, including today's Népköztársaság útja and the Great Boulevard, along with other individual buildings, much of the earlier neo-classical Pest was destroyed. What was created in its place determined the face of Pest, even up to this day.

In the southern town of Szeged, a huge flood in 1879 destroyed virtually the entire stock of buildings in the town centre. Szeged was rebuilt almost entirely in Eclectic style thus becoming a 'perfect' example of late-19C town planning in this architectural style.

Towards the end of the century Hungarian sculpture was under the influence of the international academic style. One sculptor, however, Miklós Izsó (1831–75), attempted to carry on the work begun by István Ferenczy in creating a national Hungarian sculptural art. Some of his monuments are highly acclaimed (for example his statues of Petőfi in Budapest, Csokonai in Debrecen, and Dugovics in Szeged) but greater significance is usually accorded to his small terracotta figures of dancing peasants. However, like Ferenczy before him, Izsó was unable to create a vigorous school or following.

As with the rest of Europe, Hungarian painting was searching for new forms in the second half of the 19C. One of the representatives of romanticism, Mihály Zichy (1827–1906), achieved success in Paris and later became a court painter to the Russian Tsar. Historical painting developed in the 1860s with the works of Viktor Madarász (1830–1917) and Bertalan Székely (1835–1910). Madarász had his first success in Paris with his 'Lamentation over László Hunyadi', which won him a gold medal from the Paris Salon in 1859. Returning to Hungary he produced historical paintings and was faithful to the memory of the ideals of 1848–49. Székely was close to the Munich school of historical painting and was also a noted fresco painter. One of the most prolific and successful fresco painters of the period, however, was Károly Lotz (1833–1904) who employed Baroque and Rococo elements in his work. His paintings survive on the ceilings of countless buildings in Budapest and elsewhere. Gyula Benczúr (1844–1920) also had Munich connections as he taught at the Academy there. His principle work, the 'Recapture of Buda Castle from the Turks' (1896), is acknowledged as one of the best creations of academic historical painting.

The best-known Hungarian painter of the 19C, Mihály Munkácsy (1844–1900), combined romanticism with dramatic realism. In the 1870s Munkácsy settled in Paris and painted a series of realistic genre pictures followed by a number of more spectacular subjects. Although living abroad, he had a direct influence on Hungarian painting and his international fame encouraged a host of young painters. There are special rooms devoted to his paintings in the Hungarian National Gallery in Budapest and in the Déry Museum in Debrecen.

The 'Hungarian impressionist' Pál Szinyei Merse (1845–1920) came to *plein air* painting almost simultaneously with Manet and Monet, although he was Munich-based and had never lived in Paris. His most noted masterpiece, 'Picnic in May' (1872–73) hangs in the Hungarian National Gallery.

Towards the turn of the century architects expressed their growing dissatisfaction with the officially-sponsored Eclectic style. Again it was felt that something more Hungarian should be developed. Prominent in this trend was the architect Ödön Lechner (1845–1914). He, too, with his colleague Gyula Pártos, turned to eastern elements in his search for Hungarian roots (Budapest Museum of Applied Arts, 1896), but he also made use of Hungarian folk art motifs as dramatic decoration on his Art Nouveau buildings—the Geological Institute (1898–99) and the Postal Savings Bank (1900) in Budapest, and the Town Hall in Kecskemét (1896). Lechner's views failed to find favour with the authorities and eventually commissions from official sources dried up. Yet he had started something which others were able to take up.

Detail of Ödön Lechner's Postal Savings Bank (1900) in Budapest.

Two trends emerged from Lechner's work via Art Nouveau, or Secessionist style as it is known in Hungary. One is represented by Béla Lajta (1875–1920) who began with an Art Nouveau style but soon turned to a functionalism which enables him to be described as the first Hungarian architect of modernism. The 'Rózsavölgyi' building in Budapest's Martinelli tér (1910–11) designed for separate retail, office and living functions, has become the classic example of early Hungarian modernism. However, the folkish decoration on this and on some of his other buildings (for example the Vas u. Commercial School in Budapest, built in 1912) betrays the earlier influences of Lechner.

The other trend, although critical of Lechner, was perhaps more faithful to his concepts. A Hungarian style of architecture, the argument went, could not be developed simply by using folk decoration as ornamentation, as Lechner tended to do. What was required was an adaptation of traditional, mainly peasant styles of design. Hence was born Hungarian National Romanticism which had similarities with other national trends in architecture appearing throughout Europe at the time. In so far as traditional folk architecture was being applied, one could say that at last here was a genuine Hungarian architecture. The fact that Transylvanian styles of building were often employed adds weight to the argument in the sense that this was the area where Hungarian culture had suffered some of the least disruptions.

While there are some examples of National Romantic style in the capital, such as The Palace Hotel on Rákóczi út. (Marcell Koor and Dezső Jakab, 1910), much of the production in this style was done outside of Budapest. A good example is the so-called New College at Kecskemét, designed by Valér Mende and Lajos Dombi and built in

1911–13. Its traditional 'rural' elements can be compared with Lechner's decorated Town Hall of 1893–96 which stands nearby, and with Géza Márkus's colourful 1902 'Ciffra' Mansion in typical Art Nouveau style across the road. Also nearby is the Romantic synagogue of János Zitterbarth (1862–71). Together these buildings make the centre of Kecskemét a veritable treasure of architectural styles.

One of the adherents of the National Romantic tendency, and a major figure in 20C Hungarian architecture was Károly Kós (1883–1977). In keeping with his attachment to the roots of Hungarian traditions he lived and worked for the most part in Transylvania, but some of his early works can be seen in the territory of Hungary today. There is, for example, the church house next to the Óbuda Reformed Church (1908) and the church at Zebegény (1908) on the left bank of the Danube Bend not far from the Czechoslovak border.

The Zebegény church is decorated inside with paintings by Aladár Körösfői Kriesch (1863–1920), a leading member of the Gödöllő school which flourished in the first two decades of the 20C. The painters and craftsmen at Gödöllő, a small town some 30km northeast of Budapest, were strongly influenced by the English Pre-Raphaelites, the English Arts and Crafts movement, and the works and ideas of John Ruskin and William Morris. The circle included a variety of artists such as weavers, glass-makers and painters, but these ideas had a wide circulation in Hungary and also influenced architects such as Kós.

The school which had a great impact on painting was that of the colony of artists established at Nagybánya (Baia Mare, Romania) in 1896 by the painter Simon Hollósy (1857–1918). Initially representing various styles and individual painters it eventually grew into a movement. Several other artists' colonies were formed, amongst them the colony of realistic painters at Szolnok whose leading personality was Adolf Fényes (1867–1945).

József Rippl-Rónai (1861–1927), who lived for a long time in Paris, was a Hungarian representative of Post-Impressionism and Art Nouveau and often worked as an industrial designer. The paintings of Tivadar Csontváry Kosztka (1853–1919) are also related to Post-Impressionist art, though really they belong to no special trend.

The work of the Nagybánya painters reflected the influence of French art, which had gained ground steadily in Hungary in the years before World War I. Cubist along with German Expressionist trends blend in the art of the first Hungarian avant-garde artists' association, the Group of Eight, which included Károly Kernstok (1873–1940), Dezső Czigány (1883–1939) and Lajos Tihanyi (1855–1939). They introduced the new artistic movements of the 20C into Hungary, and so became the originators of avant-garde in Hungarian fine arts.

The Group of Eight influenced many young artists who became known as the 'Activists' whose organising force was the journal 'Tett' (Action) and later 'MA' (Today) which was edited by the writer and painter Lajos Kassák (1887–1967). Kassák was drawn towards the international Constructivist trend which included the Hungarian painter László Moholy-Nagy (1895–1946) at the Bauhaus. An important time for these experimentalists and all modern tendencies was during the short-lived Republic of Councils in 1919. Under the wing of George Lukács, who was appointed 'commissar' for culture, artistic trends were given a free rein, though Kassák and others did fall foul of the Communist authorities for their 'extremist' positions.

The excitement, however, ended with the crushing of the revolutionary government and the emergence of the Horthy regime.

Official trends in the inter-war period opposed modern movements in all artistic fields, preferring the eclecticism of various historical styles and, from the 1930s, the Italian neo-classicism of the so-called School of Rome. Progressive artists, either because of political persecution or simply to find some cultural air to breathe, emigrated in great numbers. Developments after World War II were hindered for a number of years by the rigidities and formalities of a Stalinist approach to artistic creation which demanded the priority of a political content acceptable to the authorities. As in other fields, all that began to change and open up after 1956, since when the arts in Hungary have developed along the many and various lines as are found elsewhere in Europe.

Footnote. Certain recurring images and themes in Hungarian iconography are perhaps unfamiliar to English-speaking readers.

Statues of St. John of Nepomuk, for example, can be found throughout Hungary. This 14C priest was born in southern Bohemia and became the confessor of the wife of Wencel IV. Because he refused to reveal the confessional secrets of the queen, the king had him thrown into the river Moldva in 1383. He was canonised in 1729 and because of the way in which he was martyred he is regarded as the patron saint of bridges. His statue can often, therefore, be found near bridges and water crossings.

Three Hungarian saints, SS. Stephen, Imre and Ladislas, are often portrayed together, particularly in statues on the façade of churches. Stephen (István) I was the first king of Hungary and the founder of the Hungarian state. He reigned from 1000 to 1038 and was instrumental in the conversion of the country to Christianity. Imre was his son. He was brought up in Christian ways by Bishop Gellért who came from Italy. He died in his early twenties following a hunting accident. Ladislas, as László I, was king of Hungary from 1077–95. Although he clashed with the Pope over his attempts to gain Croatia and Dalmatia, he was regarded as one of the main figures in the consolidation of Christianity in Hungary, founding many dioceses and monasteries, and keeping the threat of a pagan revival at bay.

When Imre died in 1031 Stephen was left without a direct heir. To avoid dependency on either the Papacy or the Holy Roman Empire, he is said to have offered the Hungarian crown directly to Our Lady for her protection. From this come two very common themes of Hungarian ecclesiastical art—*Stephen offering the crown to the Virgin* and the depiction of Mary as Our Lady of Hungary, *Patrona Hungariae*.

Many of the items and places mentioned in this chapter are covered in greater detail in the various routes—see index.

Hungarian Literature

By *Richard Aczel*

'It might be more reassuring,' writes Péter Esterházy, one of Hungary's most exciting and challenging younger novelists, 'if the writer thought less in terms of the people and the nation, and more in terms of subject and predicate.' History is not on Esterházy's side. At least for the past 400 years, the history of Hungarian literature has been a highly polemical affair, with the writer occupying a privileged place in society as spokesperson of the nation.

Before the Reformation it is perhaps misleading to speak of 'Hungarian literature' as such. For the first five centuries after the beginnings of recorded literature in Hungary—which can be dated back to the adoption of Christianity by the first Hungarian king, St.

Stephen, in the year 1000—the literary language was almost exclusively Latin, and the most important texts were historical chronicles, hymns and sacred legends. Latin literature in Hungary reached the peak of its achievement in the Renaissance, during the reign of the highly cultivated King Matthias Corvinus (1458–90), whose court became one of the major centres of humanist culture and scholarship in Europe. The most celebrated literary representative of Hungarian humanism was Janus Pannonius (1434–72) who studied at the University of Padua at the height of the Italian Renaissance and went on to become the first Hungarian poet to achieve widespread European acclaim. Pannonius's poetry ranges from bitterly satirical epigrams on his enemies and extremely candid poems on themes of love and desire to the first poetic depictions of the Hungarian landscape and profound philosophical elegies on the antinomies of the Renaissance soul.

While the earliest known continuous text in Hungarian is the *Halotti Beszéd* (Funeral Oration, c 1200) and the first surviving poem in Hungarian is the *Ómagyar Mária-siralom* (Old Hungarian Lament of Mary) dating from around 1270, literature in the Hungarian tongue received its first major impetus from the Reformation. The Reformation, by definition, required the creation of a vernacular literature capable of circumventing the 'intercession' of the priesthood. Thus one of its most important achievements was the first full Hungarian translation of the Bible (by Gáspár Károli, published in 1590), which, as the most widely read Hungarian text for several centuries, had a considerable effect on the development of the literary language. The Reformation also provided Hungarian literature with what has remained one of its key characteristics ever since: a firm commitment to non-literary (religious, political, social and national) ideals and causes.

Hungarian prose in the Reformation—the purpose of which was above all to argue and persuade—is lively and dramatic. Perhaps the most outstanding example is the work of Péter Bornemisza (1535–84). In addition to publishing five volumes of sermons which present a fascinatingly vivid picture of 16C Hungarian life, and include a volume of partly confessional stories about his dramatic encounters with temptation—*Ördögi kísértetekről* (The Temptation of the Devil, 1578)—Bornemisza also wrote the earliest known tragedy in Hungarian: an adaptation of Sophocles' *Electra*. In keeping with the general character of the Hungarian Reformation, Bornemisza emphasised the political implications of the play, asking the question 'Is it right to oppose a tyrant when the nation lies in cruel bondage?' and answering—in a major departure from Sophocles—by having the tyrant murdered on stage.

The second half of the 16C also produced the first great lyric poet to write in Hungarian, Bálint Balassi (1554–94). Among Balassi's finest achievements are his two cycles of love poetry, the first of which suggests the influence of Petrarch. Balassi's love poetry, however, goes well beyond the conventions of its Petrarchan model in its richly sensual representation of the beloved not merely as a poetic ideal, but as a flesh-and-blood character with changing, unpredictable moods. Balassi's childhood tutor was Péter Bornemisza, and the attitudes and aspirations of the Reformation can be clearly identified in Balassi's religious poetry which forms the most impressive part of his *oeuvre*. Balassi's religious lyrics are intensely personal, addressing God through prayers and confessions in a remarkably direct and immediate manner. His poetry remained entirely without parallel until the national revival at the end of the 18C.

The Counter-Reformation—the effects of which began to be felt in Hungary at the beginning of the 17C—made an equally important contribution to the development of the national literature. The most significant religious author of the period was Péter Pázmány (1570–1637) who became Archbishop of Esztergom in 1616 and founded the University of Nagyszombat in 1635, which, after its transfer to Buda, then to Pest, in the 18C became (and remains) the most important university in Hungary. Pázmány, whose greatest work is a masterpiece of Baroque prose, *Isteni igazságra vezérlő kalauz* (Guide to Divine Truth, 1613), is still regarded as among the greatest of Hungarian stylists and two of the finest prose writers of the 20C, Dezső Kosztolányi and Zsigmond Móricz, both acknowledged his influence on their work.

Like Bornemisza before him, Pázmány too served as personal tutor to the most outstanding Hungarian poet of his century. This poet was Miklós Zrínyi (1620–64), whose greatest work was a major national epic which sets out to retrieve for the public memory his great-grandfather's heroic, if finally unsuccessful, defence of the fortress of Sziget against the Turkish army of Süleyman the Magnificent in 1556. *Szigeti veszedelem* (The Peril of Sziget, 1651) can be interpreted as an appeal to the Hungarians of Zrínyi's own day to live up to the glorious and patriotic example of their forefathers—an example the poet would himself emulate as a military commander leading raids against the occupying Turks. While in the 17C and 18C Zrínyi never enjoyed the popularity of his less demanding contemporary, István Gyöngyösi (1629–1704)—the author of a number of highly polished and entertaining narrative poems on themes of love and marriage—Zrínyi's identification of the role of the poet with the political and historical cause of the nation made him the poetic ideal of the more politically committed poets of the 19C.

With the peace of Karlowitz in the last year of the 17C, nearly 150 years of Turkish occupation came to an end. It was to be followed, however, by a period of Habsburg domination in which Hungary was treated as little more than a dependent province, and, during the first two-thirds of the 18C, Hungarian literature developed at a more moderate pace. Only one major Hungarian poet emerged during this period, Ferenc Faludi (1704–79), who never lived to see the publication of his poetry. In addition to his refined, often witty and exquisitely crafted Rococo verse, Faludi also introduced a form of pastoral idyll in which conventional classical allusions give way to the language of 'humble and rustic life' and the idiom of the Hungarian folk-song.

The finest literary prose of the period was produced by a succession of major Transylvanian writers of memoirs, confessions and literary letters. Among the most accomplished of these was Kelemen Mikes (1690–1761) who had served Prince Ferenc Rákóczi II in the unsuccessful war of independence against the Habsburgs (1703–11) and followed his master into exile in Turkey where he would remain until his death. It was from here that Mikes wrote most of his fascinating and often deeply moving *Törökországi levelek* (Letters from Turkey), completing the last, No. 207, in 1758. These letters, addressed to a ficticious aunt, provide a compelling and insightful study of exile as both a political and psychological condition, and represent one of the finest examples of Hungarian prose style in the history of the national literature.

The beginnings of modern Hungarian literature are conventionally dated from 1772. It was in this year that György Bessenyei (1747–1811), a member of Maria Theresa's Royal Hungarian Guard in Vienna, published four important literary works. Of these, Bessenyei's free adaptation of Alexander Pope's poetic compendium of the central ideas of the English Enlightenment, the *Essay on Man* (1733), is the most revealing as a characterisation of the early modern period in Hungarian literature. Bessenyei is unable to reproduce Pope's 'enlightened' optimism and confidence in the essential rationality and virtue of the world ('Whatever is, is right'), and his text emphasises the stifling limits, rather than the omnipotence, of human reason. Often referred to somewhat misleadingly as a *belated* 'Age of Englightenment', the Hungarian literary revival which took place during the last third of the 18C is actually far more modern and more closely in touch with contemporary European developments than is generally recognised. Most of the key elements of the European Age of Sensibility—from graveyard poetry and the cult of Ossian, through Rousseau's new individualism and celebration of solitude, to the fashionable sentimentalism of Goethe's *Werther*—find significant counterparts in late-18C Hungarian literature. Nowhere more so than in the work of Ferenc Kazinczy (1759–1831) who, as a prodigious translator (of, among others, Shakespeare, Ossian, Gessner and Laurence Sterne), literary organiser, and reformer of the national language, dominated Hungarian literary life for a period of nearly 40 years.

It was above all the radical reforms of the 'enlightened despot' Joseph II—and in particular his Language Decree of 1784 proposing German as the standard language of his empire—which began to arouse Hungarian fears concerning their national integrity and identity. With the threat of Germanization from the West and the development of Slav consciousness in the East, Hungarian writers became increasingly aware of the need to cultivate a strong, coherent and distinctively *national* literature. The two most important elements of this literature had already begun to emerge in the 1780s and 90s: the literary representation (and thus preservation) of the glories of the national past, and an identification with the values and idiom of the national folk culture. Thus the most popular Hungarian novel of the 18C, András Dugonics' *Etelka* (1788), tells the story of a young maiden in the 10C court of Prince Árpád, who—for all her characteristically 18C sensibility—is made to speak the dialect and idiom of a peasant from the southern plains. At the same time, various attempts were being made to write a great national epic on the origins of the Hungarians and on their occupation of the Carpathian Basin at the end of the 9C. Success only came in this genre with the publication of Mihály Vörösmarty's *Zalán futása* (The Flight of Zalan) in 1825.

1825 also marks the beginning of the Age of Reform, the key aspiration of which was the transformation of feudal Hungary into a modern nation state. Sharing this aspiration, the literature of this period is characterised primarily by a growing interest in folk poetry and the common past as the cornerstones of a national culture capable of addressing and representing all layers of Hungarian society. A good illustration of the national literature's development from 18C 'sensibility' to 19C 'literary populism' is provided by the career of perhaps the most representative writer of the Age of Reform, Ferenc Kölcsey (1790–1838). Kölcsey's early poetry of the 1810s continues to show the sentimental influence of Matthisson and the German *Sturm und Drang* while his literary criticism reflects the individualism, cosmopolitanism and emphasis on style over content of his first important mentor, Kazinczy. By the mid-1820s, however, Kölcsey has rejected his earlier 'Europeanness' and now objects vehemently to the imitation of foreign literary models. In a seminal essay of 1826, *Nemzeti hagyományok* (National Traditions), he makes the following statement which was to have enormous influence on the development of Hungarian literature throughout the 19C: 'the original spark of our authentic national poetry must be sought in the songs of the common people.'

In the 1840s the identification with both the culture and the plight of the 'common people' dominated all forms of literary writing. On the stage it became fashionable to perform plays which incorporated folk-songs and scenes from peasant life. Peasant figures were afforded not only sympathetic treatment, but also—and for the first time—central roles in Hungarian novels. Thus, in the most celebrated novel of the decade, *A falu jegyzője* (The Village Notary)—a full-scale satire on the hypocrisy of provincial county politics by József Eötvös (1813–71)—of the novel's two positive moral heroes, one is a peasant forced by penury and persecution to live the life of an outlaw, while the other is his conscientious benefactor, a liberal reformer from the lesser nobility.

The literary populism of the 1840s found its most accomplished (and politically radical) expression, however, in the poetry of Sándor Petőfi (1823–49). Petőfi's poetry has all the immediacy of the Hungarian folk-song, but is far more wide-ranging in theme and content. For Petőfi, all experience seems to be inherently poetic, and it is almost impossible to distinguish in his work between poetry and biography, art and life. Whether he goes into the kitchen to look at a pretty girl, or addresses a revolutionary mob, the result is poetry in the same straightforward idiom. Thus, in any account of the outbreak of the Hungarian revolution against Habsburg rule on 15 March 1848, Petőfi's *Nemzeti dal* (National Song), written to inspire the people into action, will figure not so much as a description of the events, but as one of key events itself.

It was largely the imitation of the established and communal idiom of folk poetry which prevented the emergence of a coherent Romantic Movement in Hungarian literature in the first half of the 19C. There is only one major poet in this period whose verse consistently shows the visionary approach to nature, the celebration of the unfettered imagination, and the highly individual symbolism so characteristic of European Romanticism. This is Mihály Vörösmarty (1800–55) to whom we have already referred as the author of the first successful epic on the Hungarian Conquest. While several of his early epics show the influence of the German *Märchen*, his richly symbolic drama *Csongor és Tünde* (Csongor and Tünde, 1831) is a profoundly original and beautifully crafted study of the ultimate futility of man's search for happiness. His great lyrics of the 1840s and 50s develop a remarkably rich and intense metaphorical language through which the poet projects his vision of personal, national, human and even cosmic tragedy.

The high hopes of the Age of Reform were dashed by the defeat of the revolution and War of Independence in 1849. Petőfi, already hailed by many as the nation's greatest lyric poet, had died on the battlefield. The 1850s and 60s saw a period of profound reflection and introspection, producing some of the most broadly philosophical works in the history of the national literature. The leading poet of the period was undoubtedly János Arany (1817–82), who had been Petőfi's close friend and literary ally in the 1840s and whose first successful work was a major narrative poem entitled *Toldi*, a masterpiece in the popular genre on a legendary Hungarian hero. His later epic poetry is characterised by a type of Romantic irony where the poet repeatedly intervenes to undermine his own narrative and turns the narration of a story into the story of a narration. The same kind of irony characterises Arany's lyric poetry—which has much of the cynicism, but avoids the elevated diction, of Vörösmarty's work—and also his ballads, which are among the most polished of Arany's works.

An equally ironic attitude is represented in the great pyschological and historical novels of Zsigmond Kemény (1817–74). Kemény's irony is based above all on the often entirely arbitrary relationship between the motives and weaknesses of character (portrayed with a degree of detail, depth and insight unprecendented in the history of the Hungarian novel) and the blind forces of history or fate. A lighter approach to fiction was taken by the most popular novelist of the second half of the 19C, Mór Jókai (1825–1904). Jókai was a master story-teller who subordinated everything in his novels (including the depiction of character) to the requirements of an intriguing plot. Jókai was attacked by contemporary critics for 'saying nothing to the nation', but the nation itself was, and still is, only too delighted to listen.

The greatest dramatist of the age was Imre Madách (1823–64), whose masterpiece, *Az ember tragédiája* (The Tragedy of Man) is still widely held to be the finest drama in the language. In fifteen scenes Lucifer leads Adam and Eve through the various stages of human 'progress' from Creation to a futuristic phalanstery and an age of space travel. In each historical episode fallen man appears to have discovered his ideal existence only to have his illusions shattered by visions of exploitation, persecution and bloody revolution. The closing command of the Lord at the end of the play offers only dubious comfort: 'Struggle, and have faith in faith'.

The historic compromise (*Ausgleich*) with Vienna in 1867 took much of the sting out of the tail of Hungarian literature as a *littérature engagée*, and was not celebrated by any literary work. The period which followed, lasting until the end of the 19C, saw few major developments in the national literature. Although Jókai's novels continued to be popular—transporting their readers from a barren present to a colourful, melodramatic, and often exotically Oriental past—the subtly ironic and anecdotic prose of Kálmán Mikszáth (1847–1910) was far more in touch with contemporary Hungarian realities. Mikszáth's novels and stories are concerned above all with the attempt of the declining gentry—Mikszáth's own class, which he treats with a curious mixture of sympathy, irony and outright scorn—to keep up appearances of grandeur and tradition in a rapidly changing society. One of Mikszáth's best-loved novellas, for example, *Gavallérok* (The Gentry), describes a respendent country wedding at which all the fine clothes, coaches, gifts and other trappings finally turn out to be on loan.

The period produced little major poetry, although the language of the three most interesting poets (János Vajda, Gyula Reviczky and Jenő Komjáthy) does to some degree anticipate the impressionism, symbolism and decadence of the great literary renewal which was soon to follow at the beginning of the 20C. Mihály Babits, one of the leading representatives of this renewal, would sum up his immediate predecessors as follows: 'We critical youths took a very dismissive view of the whole of contemporary verse. In our eyes it was nothing but empty rhetoric or vulgar sentimentality. Platitudes on the one hand and popular songs on the other.'

The turn of the century produced a major cultural revival throughout the Austro-Hungarian monarchy—precisely during the years of the monarchy's most rapid decay and decline. The age of Wittgenstein, Freud and Hofmannsthal in Vienna, and of Kafka and Rilke in Prague also produced a golden age in all the arts in Hungary. Hungary's greatest literary contribution to the culture of the monarchy—a contribution which, largely because of the unfamiliarity of the Hungarian language, has never been fully recognised internationally—is represented by the achievements of the journal *Nyugat* (Occident), founded in 1908. As its title suggests, *Nyugat* took a great interest in literary developments in the West and sought to stir the national literature from its provincial slumbers. It did not, however, wish to reject Hungarian literary traditions, but merely to rejuvenate them. *Nyugat's* key contributors were well aware of their mission as literary innovators and reformers; and none more so than the most controversial Hungarian poet of the first two decades of the 20C, Endre Ady (1877–1919). Ady burst onto the Hungarian literary scene in 1906 with his third volume of poetry entitled simply, but most accurately, *Új versek* (New Poems). As he would claim in the opening poem of the volume, Ady brought 'new songs for new times'. He was uncompromising in his criticism of contemporary society, took unprecedented liberties with the (sacred) national language, and created a system of poetic symbols evoking a mythological vision at once strikingly personal and profoundly Hungarian.

The great hopes of the early *Nyugat* movement were temporarily shattered by the disastrous consequences of the First World War: a brief and finally bloody attempt to establish a communist republic, and the loss of two-thirds of the former kingdom of Hungary to Romania and the new successor states. *Nyugat* continued, however, to enjoy considerable influence until its demise in 1941, and three of its most eminent early contributors (Babits, Kosztolányi and Móricz) produced much of their best work in the period between the two World Wars. The poetry of Mihály Babits (1883–1941), while constituting less of a direct affront to conservative taste than that of Ady, was no less innovative and probably exerted more influence over subsequent generations of Hungarian poets. By the 1930s Babits had become the nation's most respected poet and saw himself as a kind of prophet and defender of timeless moral and aesthetic values. The impressive fusion of broadly European and specifically Hungarian elements in Babits' poetry represents the finest realisation of the aspirations of *Nyugat*, which Babits edited from 1929 until his death in 1941.

Dezső Kosztolányi (1885–1936) is one of the few Hungarian writers to have secured a fully deserved reputation in both poetry and prose. In one of his most impressive volumes of poetry *A szegény kisgyermek panaszai* (Complaints of a Poor Child), Kosztolányi offers a perceptive and often touching vision of the world through the eyes of a child, while his last poems represent a mature and philosophical, if often bleak and painful, search for faith and meaning. His novels are penetrating studies of the unconscious and the nature of human motivation, and remain largely unsurpassed as masterpieces of Hungarian prose style.

Zsigmond Móricz (1879–1942) was the master of a very different type of prose. His novels and short stories are concerned primarily with the life and conditions of the Hungarian peasantry, represented naturalistically in all its harsh reality without any of the idealism of the 19C. Móricz grew apart from the 'aestheticism' of *Nyugat* in the 1930s and joined the new Hungarian populists whose sociographical and novelistic studies of contemporary peasant realities constitute one of the most fascinating aspects of Hungarian literature between the two wars. Among the classics of 20C Hungarian populism is Gyula Illyés' semi-autobiographical depiction of life on the Great Hungarian Plain, *Puszták népe* (People of the Puszta) published in 1936.

The finest new poet to emerge in this period, and the greatest representative of the Hungarian literary avant-garde, was Attila József (1905–37) who demonstrated that images of urban, working-class life and the sights and sounds of the factory could also provide fitting subjects for poetry. Among József's most memorable poems are his great urban, industrial landscapes which evoke not only an outer world of poverty, toil and hardship, but also an inner state of spiritual turmoil which errupts in a demand for radical social change. A committed socialist, József was none the less expelled from the underground communist movement in the 1930s, largely because of his attempts to fuse the ideas of Marx and Freud—a fusion which can also be observed in his poetry. Not long after his expulsion from the party, he threw himself under a freight train near Balatonszárszó, where a small museum now stands to commemorate his life and work.

The Second World War was soon followed by a period of ideological dogmatism in which the new Stalinist regime insisted on Socialist Realism in all the arts. Few works of great literary merit appeared in the 1950s; 'production-novels' celebrating exemplary workers, and poetic paeans to the communist leadership written in the idiom of folk-songs survive as bizarre documents of literary distortion and manipulation. By the mid-1960s, however, the party began to loosen its grip on literature, and literary life in Hungary today is as lively, varied and controversial as ever.

By far the most interesting poet to emerge in the post-war period was János Pilinszky (1921–81). While his stark and unembroidered imagery owes much to the idiom of Attila József, the tone of Pilinszky's poetry is quite different. His is a world of timeless spiritual suffering and existential anguish, often set against the background of the labour camp, in which the poetic voice achieves a kind of epiphany in the very intensity of its own self-awareness. An excellent selection of Pilinszky's poems exists in English, translated admirably by Ted Hughes.

The last ten years have witnessed a remarkable period of renewal in Hungarian prose fiction, with the novel and short story representing all that is best in contemporary Hungarian literature. The master of the contemporary Hungarian short story is Ádám Bodor (born 1936), who left his native Transylvania to settle in Budapest in 1982 after the conditions of Romania's Hungarian minority had become intolerable. Bordor's stories bear eloquent testimony to these conditions; bleak and bizarre, combining the mundane with the menacing, they portray a world of almost Kafkaesque ambiguity, suspicion and surveillance.

The two most outstanding representatives of a highly talented generation of younger Hungarian novelists are Péter Nádas (born 1942) and Péter Esterházy (born 1950). Nádas has developed a highly distinctive and sensitive prose style which places great emphasis on descriptive and emotional detail. He writes in long periodic sentences which uncover layer by layer the hidden mysteries of the complex emotional relationships he portrays. His most successful novel to date is *Emlékiratok könyve* (A Book of memoirs, 1986), a powerful study of memory, historical continuity and confession employing several narrators whose relationship is only revealed at the end of the work. Péter Esterházy's prose is characterised above all by its inexhaustable linguistic virtuosity and capacity for undermining the cliches and historical preconceptions of the national culture. In 1986, five of his recent novels, together with a number of shorter prose pieces, were brought together under the provocative title *Bevezetés a szépirodalomba* (An Introduction to Literature). The collection constitutes a remarkably resourceful challenge to the various social and national roles imposed upon the Hungarian writer not only by the ideological dictates of the Stalinist 1950s, but also—as we have seen—by four centuries of didacticism in the native prose tradition.

Hungarian Literature in English Translation
A Short Bibliography

Old Hungarian Reader, ed. Tibor Klaniczay, Corvina, Budapest, 1985. An excellent introduction to Hungarian literature from 1100 to the middle of the 18C.

Ocean at the Window, ed. Albert Tezla, University of Minnesota Press, Minneapolis, 1986. An anthology of Hungarian poetry and prose since 1945.

Hungarian Short Stories, ed. A. Alvarez, London O.U.P., 1967. An interesting selection from the work of 19C and 20C authors.

Modern Hungarian Poetry, ed. Miklós Vajda, Corvina, Budapest and Columbia University Press, New York, 1977.

Present Continuous Contemporary Hungarian Writing, ed. István Bart, Corvina, Budapest, 1985.

Today: An Anthology of Contemporary Hungarian Literature, ed. Éva Tóth, Corvina, Budapest, 1987.

Nothing's Lost, ed. Lajos Illés, Corvina, Budapest, 1988. An anthology of contemporary short stories including texts by Ádám Bodor, Péter Nádas and Péter Esterházy.

Sándor Petőfi, *Petőfi: Rebel or Revolutionary?*, Corvina, Budapest, 1974. A good selection of Petőfi's poetry and prose.

Imre Madách, *The Tragedy of Man*, trans. George Szirtes, Corvina, Budapest and Püski Publishing, New York, 1987.

Mór Jókai, *The Man with the Golden Touch*, Corvina, Budapest, 1975 (3rd ed.); *The Dark Diamonds*, Corvina, Budapest, 1978 (2nd ed.).

Kálmán Mikszáth, *The Siege of Beszterce*, Three Short Novels, Corvina, Budapest, 1982.

Endre Ady, *Poems of Endre Ady*, trans. Anton N. Nyerges, New York, 1969. *The Explosive Country* A Selection of Articles and Studies, 1898–1916, Corvina, Budapest, 1977.

Mihály Babits, *The Nightmare*, Corvina, Budapest, 1966. A short novel. *Mihály Babits: 21 Poems*, trans. István Totfalusi, Maecenas, Budapest, 1988.

Dezső Kosztolányi, see *The New Hungarian Quarterly*, Vol. XXVI, No. 98, Budapest, 1985, for three poems and two short stories in English. (Corvina plan to publish a revised translation of the novel *Nero* in 1990.)

Zsigmond Móricz, *Seven Pennies*, Short Stories, Corvina, Budapest, 1988.

Gyula Illyés, *People of the Puszta*, Corvina, Budapest, 1967.

Attila József, *Selected Poems and Texts*, trans. John Bátki, Carcanet, Cheadle, 1973.

János Pilinszky, *Selected Poems*, trans. Ted Hughes and János Csokits, Carcanet New Press, Manchester, 1976.

Sándor Weöres, *Eternal Moment* Selected Poems, Corvina, Budapest, 1988.

Péter Nádas, *Episode from a Memoir* (excerpt from *A Book of Memoirs*) in *The New Hungarian Quarterly*, Vol. XXV, No. 95, Budapest, 1984.

Péter Esterházy, *Auxiliary Verbs of the Heart* (excerpts), *Edinburgh Review*, 80–1, Edinburgh, 1988.
Ádám Bodor, *The Euphrates at Babylon* (Bodor's latest collection of short stories) will be published by Polygon (Edinburgh) in 1990.
George Konrád: *The Case Worker*, Penguin Books, Harmondsworth, 1987. *The City Builder*, Penguin Books, Harmondsworth, 1987. *The Loser*, Penguin Books, Harmondsworth, 1984.

Music in Hungary

Medieval Hungary experienced the birth of a flourishing musical culture closely connected with European trends. Music was an integral element of court life and ceremonies, though wandering musicians appeared both at royal gatherings and among the general population. The royal chapels were the scenes of musical performances of a high standard, and organs were constructed for these and also in other churches and monasteries.

Court music attained its highest level during the reign of King Matthias Corvinus (1458–90). His Italian wife, Beatrice of Aragon, helped continue the international influences on musical life. Their wedding in 1476 was accompanied by singing and instrumental music. Matthias increased the number of court musicians and provided them with a large collection of instruments which were often commented upon in contemporary descriptions.

In the 16C a Hungarian musician of European importance emerged. This was Valentin Bakfark (1507–76), composer and lute-player. He worked at the court of Henry II in Paris, at the Polish court, and at the Imperial Court in Vienna. His compositions have survived in numerous collections.

At first poetry in the Hungarian language was usually sung, the words were inseparable from the music. One of the masters of this type of sung poetry was Sebestyén Tinódi Lantos (died 1556) who accompanied his own songs on the lute (*lantos* means lute-player).

Hungarian compositions of the 17C are characterised by dances written for the virginal, which was the favourite musical instrument of the well-to-do as well as of the aristocracy. As with the music of previous centuries European influences are clear.

During the following century musical life was mostly connected with colleges and the choirs belonging to them. The Protestant colleges of eastern Hungary were pioneers in this, as in other fields of education. The Debrecen music teacher, György Maróthi (1715–44), had studied abroad, and after his return reorganised the choir of the Calvinist College and published a book on musical theory as well as psalms in Hungarian.

The aristocracy increasingly looked abroad to satisfy their musical tastes. They engaged foreign composers to direct the musical life of their households. The most noted of these was Joseph Haydn who from 1761 worked for many years for the Esterházy family. His concerts at the Esterháza (today Fertőd) mansion were the venues for several of his premières.

The 18C also saw the rise of a new Hungarian instrumental genre the *verbunkos*, a word derived from German meaning recruiting. Many factors contributed to its development, including the music written in support of the fight for independence under the leadership of Rákóczi in the first decade of the century. The verbunkos soon became separated from the act of recruiting but maintained its lively style and possibilities for improvisation. The influence of the verbunkos can be felt in several works of Haydn, Mozart, Beethoven, Schubert and Brahms. The style of its most celebrated masters, János Bihari, János Lavotta and Antal Csermák, who all lived into the first two decades of the 19C, became that of Hungarian Romantic music and the music of the Reform Age.

During the first half of the 19C culture and politics were closely intertwined. Music was no exception and the creation of an operatic culture in particular was seen as a national project. The efforts resulted in the establishment of the Pest National Theatre in 1837, where operas were also performed. A year after its opening Ferenc Erkel (1810–93) became its conductor and musical director. He was a composer, conductor, pianist and enthusiastic organiser of musical life. It was he who composed the National Anthem in 1844, using the words of the poet Kölcsey. Two of his operas, *László Hunyadi* and *Bánk Bán* are regarded as among the most important Hungarian operas. He was instrumental in organising the first professional Hungarian symphony orchestra and the first network of amateur choirs, and when the Hungarian Academy of Music was founded in 1875 he was its first director. Eight years later, in 1883, the Hungarian national opera found a permanent home of its own with the building of the State Opera House in Budapest (on Népköztársaság útja; see p 196).

The first President of the Academy of Music was Ferenc (Franz) Liszt (1811–86). Although he lived many years of his life abroad, Liszt always kept in touch with musical developments in Hungary, and during the last years of his life he spent much time in Budapest. Through his Presidency of the Academy he did much to ensure the future of Hungarian musical culture and as a teacher, training pianists, created a school of performing arts.

The second half of the 19C also witnessed, for the first time in about 300 years, Hungarian-born performers gaining a degree of fame outside the country. Ede Reményi gave violin concerts around Europe and also in the United States. The soloist and music teacher Joseph Joachim established a violinists' school in Berlin as did Leopold Auer at the Music College in St. Petersburg. The conductors Hans Richter and Arthur Nikisch were also both of Hungarian origin.

Twentieth century Hungarian music is dominated by two names: Béla Bartók (1881–1945) and Zoltán Kodály (1882–1967). Both were public figures, active as composers, teachers and musicologists. Bartók was essentially oriented towards instrumental music and teaching from the piano. Kodály's music was for the voice and the starting point of his pedagogy, the so-called Kodály method which is widely used in Hungarian schools, was singing, and in particular choral singing. 'An instrument is the privilege of the few,' he wrote in 1941. 'The human voice, an instrument accessible to all, free and still the most beautiful, can be the only soil where a general music culture may grow.'

Both Bartók and Kodály put the study of Hungarian folk-songs and folk music on a systematic basis. They travelled around the country recording songs in villages, their analysis of which provided the first real basis of Hungarian ethnomusicology. Kodály was particularly interested in Hungarian folk music and folklore and his works have a strong historical orientation.

Over the centuries Hungarian folk music had survived in the villages, passed down orally from generation to generation. Bartók and Kodály preserved a great many folk-songs by recording them.

The characteristic element of ancient Hungarian folk-songs is the use of the pentatonic (five-note) scale as opposed to the general European heptantonic (seven-note major or minor) scale. The wind instruments which accompanied the songs or were played on their own were typically the shepherd's flute or pipe, often made of elderberry, and the bagpipe, the use of which played a significant role in Hungarian life up to the end of the 19C. Stringed instruments widely employed included the zither, the rotary lute and the trapeze-shaped cymbalom played with two specially carved wooden sticks with the striking ends bent up. A larger, metal-framed variant of the cymbalom is often seen in the present-day gypsy bands of Hungarian restaurants.

There has been much confusion and dispute over what actually constitutes, differentiates or unites 'real' Hungarian folk music, traditional popular songs and 'gypsy' music. At the end of the day, perhaps it is like the controversy over 'real' ale in Britain—the best is surely what you most enjoy.

PRACTICAL INFORMATION

Getting to Hungary

By Air. There are regular daily flights to Hungary from all capitals and other major cities in Europe operated by both Malév, the Hungarian airline, and other national airlines. There is at least one flight per day between London and Budapest (flying time 2 hours 10 minutes) operated on alternate days by Malév and British Airways. Usual concessions apply, APEX tickets, etc. By shopping around it is possible to find bargain flights.

Budapest Ferihegy airport is situated approximately 20km to the SE of the city centre and has two terminals, Ferihegy 1 and 2. (There are plans to reopen some disused airfields for internal and international traffic.) Malév flights land at the more modern terminal, Ferihegy 2. Foreign airlines and flights operated jointly by Malév and Air France land at Ferihegy 1. Passport control takes about two minutes per person and a standard red/green channel system operates for customs control. Hence delays depend entirely on the numbers of people arriving, but passengers can expect to be held up no longer than is common in most Western airports. The usual airport services (currency exchange, hotel service, car rental, duty-free shop etc.) are all available.

A regular airport bus service operates from both terminals to Engels tér in the city centre (about 40 minutes). Tickets are issued on the bus. Alternatively bus No. 93 runs from the airport to the Kőbánya–Kispest terminus of the No. 3 metro line. Tickets for this bus and the metro have to be obtained before boarding.

Taxis are usually at hand outside the airport. Taxi drivers are not permitted to demand hard currency in payment. The starting rates and rates per kilometre are usually pasted on the dashboard. Check that the meter is turned to the starting rate before setting off.

By Rail. Thirty international trainlines link Budapest with the main European cities. There is a daily connection from London Victoria (approx. 28 hours). The Hungarian State Railways (MÁV) has reciprocal agreements allowing for various concessions for people travelling to Hungary. In summer the Saxonia Express road-rail service runs daily between Dresden and Budapest carrying private cars and trailers. *Note*—rail passengers cannot get a visa at the border. Visas have to be obtained in advance (see below).

By Bus. From Austria regular bus services run to many places in Hungary, including Budapest and Lake Balaton. From West Germany there is a regular service on the Munich–Vienna–Budapest line.

By Boat. A hydrofoil service on the Danube operates from April to October between Vienna and Budapest, arriving at the International Boat Station on Belgrád rakpart in the city centre. Visitors can also enter by private boat with a valid passport and visa.

By Car or other private vehicle. Hungary is a landlocked country with five neighbours—Austria, Czechoslovakia, Yugoslavia, Romania and the Soviet Union. Entry can be made by car from all five countries at more than 30 crossing points. From Czechoslovakia there are 11 crossing points, most of which are open 24 hours per day. From Austria there are six crossings, all of which are open round the clock. The main Vienna–Budapest road crosses at Hegyeshalom (see Rte 1). Third party insurance is compulsory, but an international driving licence is not necessary.

Some road distances to Budapest

Amsterdam	1404km	Paris	1511km
Berlin	911km	Prague	560km
Copenhagen	1302km	Rome	1294km
Frankfurt/Main	952km	Vienna	248km
London	1732km	Zürich	1007km

Visas, Customs and Currency

To enter Hungary you need a valid travel document showing your nationality and identity. In most cases this means a passport. Visas are no longer required for British citizens, nor for citizens of the following countries: Austria, the Benelux countries, Bulgaria, the People's Republic of China, Cuba, Czechoslovakia, Finland, France, Germany, Italy, Malta, Mongolia, Nicaragua, Poland, Romania, Sweden, the Soviet Union and Yugoslavia.

Visas, when necessary, can be obtained before departure, personally or by post, at Hungarian consulates and foreign diplomatic missions. Two photographs are required with the application form. Visas are normally issued within 24 hours but extra time has to be allowed for postal delivery.

Visas can also be obtained on arrival at road border-crossing points, at Budapest Ferihegy Airport and at the International Boat Station. However, it is advisable to obtain a visa in advance as getting one on arrival can cause delays and is more expensive. Visas are not available at the border for people arriving by train.

Visas can be for single, double or multiple entry. The period of stay is for 30 days. This can be extended for a further 30 days twice by application at the police station nearest to the place of residence in Hungary 48 hours before the visa expires. People wishing to extend their stay may be asked to provide evidence they have the financial means to support themselves. Transit visas are valid for 48 hours. With a transit visa you cannot enter and leave the country at the same border section. Visas are not required for children and young people under 14 included in their parent's passport and travelling with them.

A 72-hour sightseeing pass can be obtained by foreigners staying in Austria who wish to take part in a group tour to Hungary organised by an Austrian travel office. Transit passengers can also obtain a sightseeing permit at the airport or at the International Boat Station.

Addresses for visa applications:
Australia—Hungarian Consulate, Unit 6, 351/a Edgecliff Road, N.S.W. 2027 Sydney (328-7859, 328-7860).
Canada—Hungarian Embassy, 7 Delaware Avenue, Ottowa K2 P OZ 2, Ontario (232-1549, 232-1711).
Great Britain—Hungarian Consulate, 35/b Eaton Place, London SW1 (235-2664).
USA—Main Consulate, 8 East 75th Street, New York NY 10021 (879-4127).

Registration. Visitors staying longer than one month must register their address at the local police station. All subsequent changes of address must similarly be registered. This is done automatically for you if you are staying at a hotel, camping site, boarding house or in a private room rented through a travel agency. If you are staying with relatives, friends, acquaintances, or in rented rooms found privately, the registration can be done by either you or the person providing the accommodation. Registration forms *(Lakcímbejelentő lap)* are available from post offices and some tobacconist's. Take this to the police station with your passport and exit slip. The process usually only takes a few minutes.
   Visitors should keep their travel documents with them during their stay and produce them on request to the authorities (although this rarely happens). If a passport is lost the matter should be reported to the local police station where an exit permit can be obtained. The police also issue a certificate which should be taken to your local embassy.

Customs. For bona-fide visitors the customs formalities at the Hungarian border are minimal. At the airport and the International Boat Landing Stage there are 'green channels' for people with nothing to declare. Delays may occur at road crossings due to the volume of traffic. The annual number of visitors to Hungary is consistently greater than the total population and as there are no visa requirements for citizens of Austria, Hungary's nearest western neighbour, the procedures for dealing with incoming tourists are well worked out and by and large smooth and efficient.
   All personal items connected with the purpose and length of stay can be brought in duty free. This includes cameras, cine cameras, binoculars, a portable radio cassette player, portable tape-recorder, typewriter or TV set, prams, tents, bicycles, skis, surfboards, etc. A special permit is required for a CB radio and for sporting guns and ammunition. Duty has to be paid on large items brought as gifts. (At the time of publication the Hungarian customs regulations are undergoing considerable changes. For the latest situation regarding duties payable contact the Hungarian Consulate before departure.)
   In addition to the above, people over 16 may bring in 2 litres of wine, 1 litre of spirits, 250 cigarettes or 50 cigars or 250 grammes of tobacco.
   Dogs, cats and other pets can be brought into Hungary only with a valid veterinary certificate. There is a compulsory veterinary check at the border.

Currency Regulations. There is no compulsory money exchange in Hungary. Currency should be exchanged only at official places which include the National Bank, branch offices of the National Savings Bank, travel agencies, tourist offices, hotels, camping sites etc. There is no difficulty in finding places to exchange money. Rates of exchange are set by the National Bank and are quoted daily in the *Daily News*. No identification is required to exchange banknotes but it is advisable to have your passport number shown on the receipt as you may need proof of exchanging currency for taking goods out of the country, re-exchanging currency or reclaiming VAT.

The unit of currency in Hungary is the *Forint* (Ft) which is divided into 100 Fillers. Although they are still widely used, the value of fillers is so small that they can be ignored when making calculations.

Cheques and cards. Apart from banknotes exchange offices also accept travellers' cheques and Eurocheques for a guaranteed maximum of 10,000Ft per cheque. These, as well as several credit cards (including American Express, Bank of America, Carte Blanche, Diners' Club, Eurocard, Universal Air Travel Plan and Visa Card) are accepted in larger hotels and restaurants and some department stores for payment of goods and services. Loss of travellers' cheques should be reported to the Hungarian National Bank Central Foreign Currency Department which will organise the cancellation of the cheques. Address: 8–9 Szabadság tér, Budapest V. Tel: 1532-600, 1123-223. (Open Mon–Fri 9.00–13.00.)

Re-exchanging money. A maximum of 100Ft can be taken out of the country by foreign citizens. You can change back up to 50 per cent of the officially exchanged sum (up to a maximum of 100 dollars) at any authorised travel office or branch of the National Savings Bank. Any amount in excess of this should be handed over to the Customs Office for which an official receipt will be given. Upon request and according to the details on the back of the receipt, this amount can be transferred to your home address in hard currency. To avoid delays and complications it is advisable to organise one's spending to avoid having to re-exchange forints on departure.

Reclaiming VAT. Hungary introduced a VAT-type system in 1988. Foreign citizens can claim a refund of the VAT on goods costing at least 25,000Ft. The refund, however, will only be paid in forints in Hungary. At the time of writing the procedures are still not very clearly worked out, but are as follows: the item and receipt have to be declared at the border on departure where a certificate of export will be issued. (Proof of exchange of currency will be required.) This together with the receipt should be sent with any other documents issued at the border to the Municipal Tax Authority (Fővárosi Adófelügyelőség, 1096 Budapest, Hámán Kató út 3–5) which will respond by post. Alternatively, arrangements can be made before departure at the OTP-IKKA office at No. 3 Csarnok tér, Budapest IX (tel: 1188-544).

Leaving Hungary. Certain items (e.g. coffee, medicines, tools) need a special permit to be taken out of the country. Information regarding these can be obained from the Customs Office, 11/b Szent István tér, Budapest V. Tel: 1326-943. (Open Mon–Thurs 8.00–17.00, Fri 8.00–16.00.) Non-protected works of art and antiques may need a permit from the relevant museum, for the address of which ring Tourinform 1179-800. Goods purchased in convertible currency shops can be taken out duty free and without a permit on presentation of the official receipt.

Where to Stay

The Hungarian Tourist Board publishes a booklet every year, 'Hotel-Camping', which gives a brief description of the major places of accommodation in Hungary. It is available at travel offices. In the summer months it can be very difficult to find accommodation. It may be wise, therefore, to book in advance where possible. The range of accommodation for visitors in Hungary is quite varied.

Hotels in Hungary follow the international practice of categorisation by stars ranging from one to five. Due to the construction of several hotels in the 1980s, mainly with Austrian finance, Budapest is well provided with top-ranking hotels, which in terms of service and facilities are on a par with such hotels in the West. Middle-ranking hotels are not so easy to find, though there are plans to construct more hotels in this category.

Pensions offer accommodation for individuals or small groups with catering facilities.

The so-called *Tourist Hotel* (*Turista szálló*) is like the youth hostel in the West. There may be five or more beds in a room and the shared facilities will be minimal. They are inexpensive and suitable for people who are wanting to mix with Hungarians on their travels.

Camping Sites are plentiful in Hungary, particularly around Lake Balaton. There are eight sites in Budapest. Camping sites are categorised according to a star system, from one to four. The minimum facilities for all sites in Hungary include running water, at least cold water washstands and showers, toilets, a stove for cooking, First Aid facilities, fencing around the camp, proper lighting and a 24-hour reception service. A map is available showing the situation of camping sites and listing their facilities. There are reduced rates for children and young people, and at some sites there may be a reduction for holders of an FICC-AIT-FIA international camping carnet.

Holiday Homes are separate buildings made of stone or wood, suitable for families or small groups. The range of domestic facilites provided depends on the categorisation. Public utilities are nearby as most holiday homes are in or near camping sites.

Private rooms may be rented through a travel agency, tourist office or directly. Around Lake Balaton and the Danube Bend there are many signs by the roadside indicating rooms to let. (The signs are usually in German—*Zimmer*.) Rooms rented through agencies are often in part of a flat in which the owners are living.

Flats can also be rented either through an agency or directly. In Budapest the prices of large, well-furnished and well-situated flats can reach Western levels. The prices of flats, as with private rooms, fall into the free price category and can vary enormously.

In Hungary there is no problem regarding staying with relatives, friends or acquaintances. No special invitation or permit is required. The only requirement is that you or your host register your address with the local police. (See 'Registration' in the Visa, Customs and Currency section.)

Useful addresses

Accommodation can be booked in advance at the following places:
Great Britain
Danube Travel (agents for IBUSZ), 6 Conduit Street, London W1R 9TG (493-0263)

Hungarian Air Tours (representative of Pannonia Hotels), 3 Heddon
Street, London W1R 7LE (437-1622)
USA
IBUSZ Travel Bureau, 630 Fifth Avenue, Rockefeller Center, Suite
24-55, New York, NY 10111 (582-7412)
HungarHotels-Pentatours, Norwalk, Connecticut 06856, PO box 305
(655-6700)
Hungarian Hotels Sales Office, 1888 Century Park East, Suite 827,
Century City, Los Angeles, CA 90067 (448-4321)

Information about camping sites can be obtained from:
The Hungarian Camping and Caravanning Club—Travel Office, 6
Üllői út, Budapest VIII (1336-536)
The IBUSZ office at No. 3 Petőfi tér, Budapest V (1185-707) runs a 24-
hour non-stop service for booking accommodation and private
rooms. (It is situated near the Petőfi statue and the Intercontinental
Hotel a short distance to the north of the Pest end of Elizabeth Bridge.
The nearest metro station is Felszabadulás tér.)

Getting Around

By Rail. The railway network in Hungary is extensive and a considerable amount of domestic traffic is handled by the railways. Express
train services operate between Budapest and the main provincial
towns. Smaller towns and villages can be reached via connections.
On domestic railways tickets can be purchased and seats reserved 60
days in advance. Concessions are available in the form of group
travel, season tickets and senior citizens' reduced rates.
   Information and tickets both national and international can be
obtained from the office of MÁV (Hungarian Railways), 35
Népköztársaság útja, Budapest VI or from travel agencies. There is
an English speaking rail information service on 1228-056 and
1228-049 (Mon–Fri 9.00–18.00, Sat 9.00–13.00).
   The three main railway stations in Budapest are the Western
Railway Station (Nyugati pályaudvar) and the Eastern Railway
Station (Keleti pályaudvar) in Pest, and the Southern Railway Station
(Déli pályaudvar) in Buda. All three are situated on metro lines. (The
Nyugati pályaudvar metro station is also called Marx tér. 'Pályaud-
var' is often shortened to *pu.*)

Vocabulary and useful phrases
ticket,   *jegy*
train,   *vonat*
station,   *pályaudvar*
platform,   *peron*
arrival,   *érkezés*
departure,   *indulás*

Can you tell me where the station is, please?   *Megmondaná hol a
pályaudvar?*
I'd like to buy a ticket (two tickets) for Siófok,   *Egy (két) jegyet kérek
Siófokra.*
What time does the train leave for Esztergom?,   *Mikor indul a vonat
Esztergomba?*
From which platform?,   *Melyik vágányról?*

Note—Foreigners can purchase tickets for domestic routes in forints. For international journeys, tickets have to be paid for, either wholly or partly, in hard currency.

By Bus. All villages with at least 200 inhabitants can be reached by bus. Bus services also run to excursion spots and resort centres. It is advisable to book tickets in advance. The three main long-distance bus stations in Budapest are:

Engels tér Bus Station, Engels tér, Budapest V (Deák tér metro station). Buses for Vienna depart from here.

Népstadion Bus Station, 46–48 Hungária körút, Budapest XIV (by the Népstadion metro station).

Árpád híd Bus Station (by the Pest end of Árpád Bridge, next to the Árpád híd metro station).

By Boat. Depending on the weather there are regular boat services on the Danube and Lake Balaton from spring to late autumn. Boat services run from Budapest to Szentendre, Visegrád, Esztergom and other places on the Danube Bend and there are several places to the north of the capital where the Danube can be crossed by ferry, including car ferries (see Rte 6).

For information about boat services, including pleasure trips, contact:

In Budapest. MAHART Passenger Traffic Office, Belgrád rakpart, Budapest V (on the Pest side between the Elizabeth and Liberty bridges) tel. 1181-704. MAHART Vigadó tér Boat Station (on the Pest side between Elizabeth Bridge and the Chain Bridge) tel. 1181-223 BKV (Budapest Transport Authority) Boat Station, Jászai Mari tér (near the Pest side of Margaret Bridge) tel. 1295-844

At Lake Balaton. MAHART Balaton Shipping Company, Siófok Boat Station, tel. 184/10-050, or any tourist information office.

Motoring in Hungary. The through roads in Hungary are generally good, although the motorway network is not very extensive. Only part of the main Vienna–Budapest highway, for example, is motorway, though there are plans to extend it. A new orbital motorway, the M0, is being constructed around Budapest. The condition of the roads in towns varies from very good to very poor.

Road signs are generally good and follow the standard continental system. A flashing amber traffic light means proceed with caution. At junctions the yellow diamond gives priority, a black cross through the diamond ends priority, and the inverted triangle means stop. At unmarked junctions, traffic from the right has priority. Public transport should always be given priority. On urban roads with more than one lane Hungarian drivers have a habit of not keeping to the nearside lane, hence overtaking on the inside is common. Care should always be taken, therefore, when changing lanes. Extreme caution is also required at open level crossings. Certain sections of the Vienna–Budapest highway are particularly dangerous (see Rte 1). The average car in Hungary is relatively old and the 'driving culture' is relatively young, which tends to mean that the standard of driving is not particularly good.

Road distances in the Blue Guide are given in kilometres. The figures have been derived from officially published maps giving distances, written information supplied by the relevant authorities, road signs and personal experience. In hardly any case did the figures derived from these sources tally exactly. Those in the text, therefore, should be taken as a close approximation.

Some traffic regulations. There is a speed limit of 60km/hr in built-up areas (50km/hr for motorcycles). This includes villages and is operative from the village or town sign. (Caution—there is usually no change of speed limit sign when entering towns and villages.)
The speed limit on motorways is 120km/hr and on main roads 80km/ hr.
Safety belts must be used in the front seats.
Children under six may not sit in the front seat.
Horns should not be used in built-up areas except in emergencies.
Headlights must be used from dusk to dawn and in conditions of poor visibility.
There is a total ban on alcohol while driving.
Motor cyclists and their passengers must wear crash helmets. The use of dipped headlight is compulsory day and night.

Accidents. Accidents should be reported to the police immediately (tel. 07). Insurance claims must be made as soon as possible, preferably by the following working day. In Budapest contact Hungaria International Vehicle Insurance Office, 69 Gvadányi u., Budapest XIV (1633-079, 1836-527). In the provinces contact vehicle insurance branch offices—information from the police or tourist information office.
Fuel. Petrol stations are situated in all parts of the country, although they are sometimes in rather obscure corners. There are not as many as are normally found in Western countries, and on motorways and major roads are not as frequent. It is advisable to fill up well in advance as queues at filling stations are common and it may be easier to drive on to the next petrol station. Most pumps are not self-service and a tip of five or ten forints is common.
86, 92 and 98 octane petrol is available, although 98 octane cannot be found at every filling station. Lead-free petrol is available at selected places. A map showing their location should be available at the border. Diesel can be purchased only for coupons available at IBUSZ offices, border crossings and in hotels. The coupons are not refundable.
Breakdown. The Hungarian Automobile Club (Magyar Autó Klub) runs an emergency service which can be called in case of breakdown (tel. Budapest 1691-831, 1693-714, 24 hours). There are emergency telephones on the motorways and technical stations in major towns. The service is free for members of foreign affiliated motoring organisations. In Britain the AA is affiliated to the Hungarian Club.
Spare parts, particularly for western cars, are not easy to come by in Hungary and there is no well-established network of official servicing centres for Western makes of car. (Budapest is an exception in respect of certain makes.) It is strongly recommended, therefore, that drivers bring with them their own set of spares.
Car Rental. Several international car-rental agencies operate in Hungary and cars can be ordered in advance before departure. Western citizens can rent cars only for hard currency, with travellers' cheques or with credit cards. Drivers must be at least 21 and have had a licence for more than one year.
Parking. Parking in central Budapest is not easy. Much of the inner city area is prohibited to traffic other than that belonging to residents and service operators. It can be much easier to use the excellent

public transport system (see below). Some areas have parking metres or attendants. Parking is allowed on the curb in many places, and the vehicles of people with disabilites may also be parked in places not normally allowed. In the Castle District parking is only allowed in Dísz tér and only cars with a special permit may be driven into the inner streets of the area. In the inner city area of Pest there are multi-storey car parks at Martinelli tér and Aranykéz utca.

Cycling. Cycling is not common in Hungary and is illegal not only on motorways but also on most major trunk roads. There are few segregated cycle lanes, although plans are being made to extend cyclists' facilities, particularly around Lake Balaton. Bicycles can be taken on the train and certain stations rent bikes throughout the year. By arrangement these can be returned to any station. In Budapest bicyles can be hired at the Southern and Western railway stations. (Further information from MÁV, tel. 1228-049.) Help with routes, maps and other practical matters can be obtained from the Hungarian Cycling Federation, 1146 Budapest, Millenáris Sporttelep, Szabó János u. 3, (1836-965).

Hitch-hiking. Hitchhiking is common in Hungary and legal except on motorways.

Transport in Budapest. Public transport in Budapest is one of the best in the world in terms of both price (tickets are only a few forints) and efficiency (number of routes, short waiting times, etc.) The network consists of buses, trams, trolleybuses, three metro lines and four suburban railway lines. Tickets have to be purchased in advance and are available at metro stations, bus terminals, tobacconist's (*trafik*) or dispensing machines (yellow tickets for trams, trolleybuses, metro and HÉV within the city limits, blue tickets for buses). Maps showing the transport network (*BKV térkép*) are available from the same places. There are no conductors, but there are inspectors. Day passes are available either for all forms of transport, or all forms excluding buses. Monthly season tickets, valid from the first of the month to the fifth of the following month, can also be purchased. The 'rush hour' is between 6.30 and 8.30 and again between 14.30 and 16.30. During these times all forms of public transport can be very crowded. There are night bus services but the basic transport system closes down after 23.00. Smoking is forbidden on all forms of public transport.

The Metro has three lines. The first and last trains on all three begin at 4.30 and 23.10 respectively. Waiting time is a maximum of five minutes, usually much less. Routes are clearly marked inside all trains and most stations have a large city map showing the underground routes near the entrance to the platform. Trains stop at all stations and the driver usually announces the name of the following station in advance. All three lines intersect at Deák tér in the city centre. In fact this is the only place where metro lines meet. When changing lines a new ticket is required.

'Yellow' Line No. 1 (*földalatti* = underground) is the oldest (it was originally constructed in 1896) and runs from Vörösmarty tér to Mexikói út beyond the City Park. Tickets have to be punched on the train. 'Red' Line No. 2 crosses under the river and runs between Déli pu. (Southern Railway Station) in Buda to Örs vezér tere in Pest, roughly in a W–E direction. 'Blue' Line No. 3 runs in a N–S direction through the centre of Pest from Árpád híd to the Kőbánya-Kispest terminal. An extension of this line north of Árpád Bridge to Újpest is under construction. On Lines No. 2 and 3 tickets have to punched before boarding the train.

Buses run between 4.30 and 23.00. Buses with red numbers are faster but stop only at a limited number of places (usually major junctions). Buses marked 'E' run from one terminus to the other non-stop. In the city centre bus stops usually have a plate showing a map of the route and listing the stops. There is no organised queueing system and you can board and alight through any door. Blue tickets have to be punched after boarding the bus. Drivers usually announce the name of the following stop. To ensure the bus stops when you want to get off press the button above the door. This ensures that that particular door will open.

Trams usually run between 5.00 and 23.00. They stop, and all doors open, at every stop. Tickets have to be punched on the tram.

The HÉV suburban railway has four lines. Yellow tickets can be used for travelling within the city boundary. For longer journeys tickets can be purchased at the termini. The HÉV is a convenient way of reaching three places near Budapest as lines run from Batthyány tér to Szentendre, from Örs vezér tere to Gödöllő and from the Soroksári út/Kvassay Jenő út junction to Ráckeve.

Other public transport facilities in the capital include the Cog-wheel Railway, Pioneers' Railway (see Rte 5L) and the Furnicular Railway which ascends from Clark Ádám tér at the Buda end of the Chain Bridge to the top of Castle Hill by the former Royal Palace.

Useful phrases
I'd like 10 bus tickets and 10 metro tickets please,   *Kérek tíz buszjegyet és tíz metrójegyet.*
Excuse me, can you tell me where the nearest metro station is?   *Megmondaná hol a legközelebbi metróállomás?*
Where can I get a No. 5 bus?   *Hol van az ötös busz megállója?*
Does this go to Deák tér?   *Ez megy a Deák térre?*
Which bus do I need for Moszkva tér?   *Melyik busz megy a Moszkva térre?*
How many stops is it to Marx tér?   *Hány megálló a Marx térig?*
I'm going to the camp site/the Hilton, can you tell me when to get off?   *A campingbe/Hiltonba megyek, megmondaná mikor kell leszállnom?*

Taxis. There are many taxis in Budapest and by Western standards are still cheap. Some are run by large cooperatives, others by private operators. Most have meters and it is advisable only to use those that do. Check that the meter is turned to the starting price when setting off. Starting prices and basic rates are usually pasted on the dashboard. A tip of 10–15 per cent is common. Taxis can be picked up at taxi ranks, hailed in the street, or ordered by phone, in which case a small charge may be added. Ordering by phone is efficient. Except at busy periods it usually takes 10–15 minutes for a taxi to arrive. To order by phone give the number of the district and the address of your location (the same street name can appear in different districts), your name and the telephone number from where you are ringing. Taxis can also be booked in advance.

Useful phrases
Good evening, I'd like a taxi please,   *Jó estét, egy taxit szeretnék.*
Twelfth district,   *Tizenkettedik kerület.*

32 Zsolna street ... *Zsolna utca harminckettő*
My name is ..., *A nevem ...*
Telephone number 1333-451, *Telefon szám ezerháromszáz-
harminchárom* (or simply *egy, három, három, három)—négyszáz-
ötvenegy (négy, öt, egy).*
I'm going to the centre, *A belvárosba megyek.*

Some phone numbers
Főtaxi: 1222-222 (advanced booking: 1188-888)
Volántaxi: 1666-666
Citytaxi: 1228-855
Budataxi: 1294-000
Rádiótaxi: 1271-271

Useful Addresses

Tourist Information Offices. Hungary has a good network of tourist
information offices. In Budapest the central tourist information
bureau is *Tourinform* which deals with tourist enquiries of all kinds.
Foreign languages are spoken here, including English. Tourinform is
situated near the Deák tér metro station at No. 2 Sütő utca, which is
the short pedestrian precinct leading off from the SW corner of Deák
tér. The bureau is open for personal enquiries every day from 8.00 to
20.00 (tel. 1179-800).

Outside the capital the tourist information bureaux (*idegen-
forgalmi hivatal*) are the county tourist offices. There is usually
someone who speaks English in each office, but opening times vary.
Below is a list of county tourist offices in various towns. Where towns
have their own special route in the guidebook they are also listed
before the route and mentioned in the body of the text if they appear
on the route.

(The four-figure number indicates the post code. The telephone
numbers in brackets are preceded by the local code where one exists.
From Budapest first dial 06. If there is no code dial 01 for the
operator.)

Badacsony Balatontourist, 8261 Park u. 10 (87/31-249). Summer only.
Balatonföldvár Siótour, 8623 Hősök útja 9-11 (84/40-099).
Balatonfüred Balatontourist, 8230 Blaha Lujza u. 5 (86/42-822,
43-435, 43-471).
Balatonkeresztúr Siótour, 8648 Ady Endre u. 26 (84/76180). Summer
only.
Balatonszárszó Siótour, 8624, next to the railway station (84/40-456).
Summer only.
Balatonszemes Siótour, 8636, by the railway station (84/45-057).
Summer only.
Boglárlelle Siótour, 8630 Dózsa György u. 1 (84/50-665). Summer
only.
Debrecen Hajdútourist, 4026 Kálvin tér 2/a (52/15-588).
Dunaújváros Dunaújváros Tourist Office, 2400 Korányi Sándor u. 1
(25/16-607).
Eger Eger Tourist, 3300 Bajcsy-Zsilinszky u. 9 (36/11-724) and 3300
Szarvas tér 1 (36/11-724).

Esztergom Komturist, 2500 Széchenyi tér 13 (484).
Fót Dunatours, 2151 Kossuth Lajos u. 3 (27/58-146).
Gödöllő Dunatours, 2100 Szabadság u. 6 (28/20-977).
Gyöngyös Eger Tourist, 3200 Szabadság tér 2 (37/11-565).
Győr Ciklámen Tourist, 9021 Aradi vértanúk útja 22 (96/11-557).
Hajdúszoboszló Hajdútourist, 4200 József Attila u. 2 (52/60-114).
Hévíz Zalatour, 8380 Rákóczi u. 8 (11-048).
Hollókő Nógrád Tourist, 3176 Petőfi u. 7 (4).
Hortobágy Hajdútourist, 4071 Pastoral Museum (52/69-039).
Kecskemét Pusztatourist, 6000 Szabadság tér 2 (76/29-499).
Keszthely Zalatour, 8360 Fő tér 1 (12-560).
Kőszeg Savaria Tourist, 9730 Várkör 57 (195).
Lillafüred Borsod Tourist, 3517 Losonci út 21.
Mezőkövesd Borsod Tourist, 3400 Tanácsköztársaság u. 114 (339).
Miskolc Borsod Tourist, 3525 Széchenyi u. 35 (46/88-036).
Miskolctapolca Borsod Tourist, 3519 Martos Ferenc u. 7 (46/68-917).
Mosonmagyaróvár Ciklámen Tourist, 9200 Lenin u. 88 (98/11-078).
Nagyvázsony Balatontourist, 8291 Kinizsi Castle (80/31-015).
Nyírbátor Nyírtourist, 4300 Szabadság tér 14 (271).
Nyíregyháza Nyírtourist, 4400 Dózsa György u. 3 (42/11-544).
Pannonhalma Ciklámen Tourist 9090 Vár 1 (96/70-191).
Pécs Mecsek Tourist, 7621 Széchenyi tér 1 (72/14-866).
Ráckeve Dunatours, 2300 Hídfő u. 1 (26/85-372).
Sárospatak Borsod Tourist, 3950 Kossuth Lajos u. 46 (11-073).
Siklós Mecsek Tourist, 7800 Castle (6).
Siófok Siótour, 8600 Szabadság tér 6 (84/10-900) and 8601 Batthyány u. 2/b (84/13-111). Siótour also has offices in Siófok by the railway station, at the Aranypart camp site, at the Ifjúság camp site and at the Hungaria Hotel.
Sopron Ciklámen Tourist, 9400 Ógabona tér 8 (99/12-040, 14-434, 12-694).
Sümeg Balatontourist, 8330 Kossuth u. 29 (114).
Szeged Szeged Tourist, 6720 Victor Hugo u. 1 (62/11-711), 6720 Dorozsmai út 2 (62/24-450) and 6720 Klauzál tér 7 (62/21-800).
Szentendre Dunatours, 2000 Bogdányi u. 1 (26/11-311).
Székesfehérvár Albatours, 8000 Szabadság tér 6 (22/12-818).
Szigetvár Mecsek Tourist, 7901 Zrínyi tér 2 (284).
Szolnok Tiszatour, 5000 Ságvári körút 32 (56/11-383).
Szombathely Savaria Tourist, 9700 Mártírok tere 1 (94/12-348).
Tapolca Balatontourist, 8300 Kisfaludi u. 1 (87/11-179).
Tata Komturist, 2890 Ady Endre u. 9 (34/80-694).
Tatabánya Komturist, 2800 Győri út 12 (34/11-936).
Tihany Balatontourist, 8237 Kossuth u. 20 (86/48-519). Summer only.
Vác Dunatours, 2600 Széchenyi u. 14 (27/10-940).
Várpalota Balatontourist, 8100 Felszabadulás u. 27 (80/50-579).
Veszprém Balatontourist, 8200 Münnich Ferenc tér 3 (80/29-630).
Visegrád Dunatours, 2025 Fő u. 3/a (26/28-330).
Zalaegerszeg Zalatour, 8900 Kovács Károly tér 1 (92/11-443).

Foreign Embassies and Diplomatic Representations

All the following are in Budapest. The second and third numbers of the four-figure postal code indicate the number of the district.
Australia 1062 Délibáb u. 30 (1534-233).
Austria 1068 Benczúr u. 16 (1229-467, 1229-266, 1229-691).
Belgium 1015 Donáti u. 34 (1153-099).
Canada 1021 Budakeszi út 32 (1767-711).

Czechoslovakia 1143 Népstadion út 22 (1636-600, 1636-608, 1636-609).
Denmark 1023 Vérhalom u. 12–16, Building B, ground floor 1 (1152-066, 1355-952).
Finland 1023 Vérhalom u. 12–16, Building B, ground floor 3 (1150-600).
France 1062 Lendvay u. 27 (1324-980).
Federal Republic of Germany 1125 Nógrádi u. 8 (1559-366).
Great Britain and Northern Ireland 1051 Harmincad u. 6 (1182-888).
Holland 1146 Abonyi u. 31 (1228-432, 1228-446).
India 1025 Búzavirág u. 14 (1153-243).
Italy 1143 Népstadion út 95 (1428-722, 1225-219, 1225-077).
Japan 1024 Rómer Flóris u. 56-58 (1150-044).
Norway 1122 Határőr út 35 (1551-729, 1551-811).
Sweden 1146 Ajtósi Dürer sor 27/a (1229-880, 1229-888, 1413-507).
Switzerland 1143 Népstadion út 107 (1229-491, 1426-721).
United States of America 1054 Szabadság tér 12 (1126-450/51-52-53-54-55-56-57-58-59).
USSR 1062 Bajza u. 35 (1320-911, 1324-748, 1327-729) Consulate: 1062 Népköztársaság útja 104 (next door) (1318-985).
Yugoslavia 1068 Dózsa György út 92/b (1420-566, 1229-838, 1428-512).

Offices of Foreign Airlines in Budapest

Aeroflot 1052 Váci u. 4 (1185-955, 1185-892. Airport: 1572-780).
Air Canada 1012 Sziklai Sándor u. 1 (1754-618).
Air France 1052 Kristóf tér 6 (1180-411, 1180-469. Airport: 1571-163).
Air India 1051 Vörösmarty tér 6 (1184-804, 1184-961).
Alitalia 1053 Felszabadulás tér 1 (1186-882, 1186-898).
Austrian Airlines 1052 Régiposta u. 5 (1171-550, 1171-676. Airport: 1674-374).
British Airways 1052 Apáczai Csere János u. 5 (1183-229, 1183-041. Airport: 1579-123 ex. 8380).
Finnair 1052 Váci u. 19–21 (1174-022/026/296).
KLM 1051 Vörösmarty tér 2 (1174-522/742. Airport: 1572-425).
Lufthansa 1052 Váci u. 19 (1184-511. Airport: 1570-290).
Pan American 1052 Apáczai Csere János u. 4 (1187-922. Airport 1471-972).
Sabena 1052 Váci u. 1–3 (1184-111).
SAS 1052 Váci u. 1–3 (1185-582, 1185-675).
Swissair 1052 Kristóf tér 7–8 (1172-500/900/806. Airport: 1574-374).

MALÉV (Hungarian Airlines) Offices Abroad
Great Britain: 10 Vigo Street, London W1X 1AJ (439-0577/8); USA: Room 1900, Rockefeller Center, 630 Fifth Avenue, New York, NY 10111 (757-6480).

General Information

Churches. Access to churches is unpredictable. It used to be that Catholic churches, which predominate in Hungary, were always open. Today the practice is that apart from mass times access is restricted to the porch by the main entrance. This does not apply, however, to large churches which are major monuments. These are usually open throughout the day.

Church Services. The following church services in English are held in Budapest:
British Embassy, No. 6 Harmincad u., Budapest V. Morning Service or Holy Communion on the third Sunday of the month at 11.00.
Scottish Mission Church, No. 51 Vörösmarty u., Budapest VI. First Sunday of the month at 11.15.
Catholic Church of Christ the King, No. 9 Reviczky u., Budapest VIII. Mass in English on the last Sunday of the month at 11.15.
Catholic Church of St. Elizabeth, Rózsák tere, Budapest VII. Mass in English on the second Sunday of the month at 17.00.

Climate. Hungary has a continental climate which varies greatly through the seasons. The hottest months are June, July and August, when the daytime temperature can reach into the 30s (centigrade). The coldest month is January with a mean monthly temperature of -1.7°C, though it can often drop well below that. Warm clothing is obviously needed, but all buildings and public transport are adequately, often more than adequately, centrally heated. The most comfortable times of year for sight-seeing are usually April–May and September–October.

Electric Current. The voltage in Hungary is 220 volts. British appliances made for 240 volts function normally in Hungary. Sockets are for 2-round-pin plugs and many are not earthed. A standard continental adaptor allows the use of 13 amp, square-pin plugs. Shavers can be used in either standard shaving sockets or ordinary wall sockets. It may be necessary to file down the inside edge of the shaving plug's pins. This can be done without detriment to the use of the appliance on return home.
   Television in Hungary operates on the Secam system. TVs and video recorders brought from Britain will only operate if they are dual-system or are adjusted. Video TV recordings made from a Pal (British) TV, however, can be used in Hungary.

Emergencies
Ambulance—04
Fire Brigade—05
Police—07

Theft. Hungary is generally still a safer place than most Western countries. However, in recent years the number of thefts has been rising dramatically, particularly in the crowded tourist areas of central Budapest. Visitors should take especial care of their personal possessions when on the street, shopping, etc. Cases of theft and attack can be reported to the Budapest Central Police Station—Reports Office (Budapest Rendőrfőkapitányság—Panaszfelvétel) at No. 16–18 Deák Ferenc u., Budapest V (by Deák tér metro station). Open 24 hours a day. Tel. 1123-456. This is also probably a better number for general police emergencies than the 07 number in terms of finding someone who speaks English. It should be possible to find someone who speaks English on the 04 ambulance number, but for the fire service the call will probably have to be made by a Hungarian speaker.

Lost Property. For property lost:
—on public transport in Budapest: BKV (Budapest Transport Authority) No. 18 Akácfa u., Budapest VII (1344-787)
—on a long-distance or pleasure boat: MAHART (Hungarian

Shipping Company, Belgrád Rakpart Boat Station, Budapest V
(1181-704)
—in a taxi: FŐTAXI, No. 20 Akácfa u., Budapest VII (1344-787);
VOLÁNTAXI, No. 56 Jerney u., Budapest XIV (1633-228); CITY,
BUDA, RÁDIÓ taxi, TAXIUNIÓ, No. 5 Engels tér, Budapest V
(1174-961)
—on a train: Southern Railway Station: information office by platform 12; Western Railway Station (1490-115); Eastern Railway Station (1225-615); on a flight: Ferihegy 1 (1427-784), Ferihegy 2
(1578-108).

English Language Publications and Broadcasts. The 'Daily News' is
a newspaper published in English and German every day except
Sunday and Monday. Apart from national and international news of
interest to visitors it also carries a regular listing of English-language
films in Budapest and other cultural events. It is available at newsagents and hotels. A more comprehensive list of cultural events is
contained in the monthly 'Programmes in Hungary', which is available at travel offices and hotels. The quarterly 'Hungarian Travel
Magazine' has feature articles about tourist services and places of
interest. It is distributed on Malév flights and at some travel offices.
The 'Hungarian Observer' is a monthly news and feature magazine
mainly distributed abroad but available at some newsagents. Foreign
newspapers, including the 'Times', 'Financial Times' and 'International Herald Tribune' are available at large newsagents and at
hotels.
    Hungarian Radio broadcasts the news in English, German and
Russian every day on the Petőfi Channel after the midday news in
Hungarian. Broadcasts of news and features about Hungary in
English are transmitted on shortwave at regular times throughout the
day.
    News in Esperanto is broadcast on Sundays at 13.05 on the Bartók
Channel.
    Danubius Radio is a German-language broadcast of travel
information, light music and news aimed at tourists. It is broadcast
daily from May to September between 6.30 and 21.00 on 100.5 MHz
for Lake Balaton and western Hungary and on 103.3 MHz for
Budapest and central Hungary.
    Satellite TV (Super, Sky, and the German SAT 1) is available in
Hungary as is Soviet, Czech and, in western Hungary, Austrian TV.
Several large hotels are equipped to receive the satellite broadcasts.

Further Reading. 'The New Hungarian Quarterly' is consistently one
of the best sources of information about Hungarian history, literature,
arts, and contemporary society. The standard is invariably high,
albeit a little over-academic. The journal is available in several
public libraries in Britain and the United States and can also be
obtained from the foreign agents of Kultúra, the main distributor of
Hungarian books and newspapers abroad.
    Books about Hungary in English and in print are not easy to come
by. Two that have been published in Britain recently are Hans-Georg
Heinrich, 'Hungary: Politics, Economy and Society' (Frances Pinter,
1986) and Jörg K. Hoensch, 'A History of Modern Hungary 1867–
1986' (Longman, 1988). The huge 'Information Hungary' was
pubished by Pergamon Press in 1968 in association with the Hungarian Academy of Sciences. A new edition is in preparation and it

promises to be a weighty tome of basic facts and background information.

Corvina is the main foreign language publisher in Hungary. They have an extensive range of titles in English about Hungary available at their own bookshop at No. 4 Kossuth Lajos u. Budapest V. They are represented abroad by Kultúra. Corvina's 'One Thousand Years: A Concise History of Hungary' (ed. Péter Hanák, 1988) is a very readable and clear account of the country's complex history.

Health and Medicine. Foreigners in Hungary can receive first aid treatment and transport to hospital free of charge. Generally all other treatment will be charged. There is an agreement, however, between the UK and Hungary that allows for UK residents to receive, in addition to transport and first aid, free emergency health care and emergency dental treatment.

For the ambulance service ring 04. Round-the-clock emergency dental services—Dental Surgery Clinic, Institute of Stomatology, No. 52 Mária u., Budapest VIII (1330-189).

Pharmacies (Gyógyszertár or Patika) can be found in all parts of the country. The system is to queue to place your order, then queue at the cash till to pay, then queue again to collect your items. Hence it can take some time. Some basic medicines are 'Quarelin' for headaches, 'Faringoszept' for sore throats, 'Amidazophenum' for high temperature, and 'Demalgon' for toothache. There are several pharmacies providing an emergency, all-night service in Budapest, including those at Lenin körút 95, Rákóczi út 86 and Boráros tér 3.

Herbs and more natural health products can be obtained in the 'Herbaria' chain of shops.

It is advisable for people with contact lenses to bring with them whatever they might require. Supplies can usually be obtained, however, at the Ofotért shop towards the end of Bajcsy-Zsilinszky út (No. 16), near Engels tér in Budapest.

Museums. There are over 700 museums in Hungary covering a wide variety of themes. Entrance charges are low and there is often free entrance on one day a week, the particular day varying from one museum to another. The standard opening times are 10.00–18.00 every day except Monday, when museums are usually closed. However there are many exceptions to this general rule. The opening times given in the text are based on personal visits and the latest published information at the time of writing, but it may be wise, particularly for out-of-the-way museums, to check the opening times beforehand with the local tourist information office. Smaller museums are often closed or open for shorter hours in the winter, and where possible this has been indicated. Entrance is often not permitted during the last half hour of opening time. Items in museums are usually accompanied by a text in Hungarian, occasionally in German and sometimes in English. However, brochures and booklets in English are often available. It is worth asking even if nothing is on display. (*Van valami a múzeumról angolul?*—Is there something about the museum in English?)

The major national museums are situated in Budapest. They include the Hungarian National Museum (Hungarian history), the Hungarian National Gallery (Hungarian painting and sculpture), the Museum of Fine Arts (non-Hungarian painting and sculpture), the Museum of Applied Arts and the Ethnograhical Museum. This does not mean that there are no important museums in the provinces. The

Déri Museum in Debrecen, for example, has a good fine arts collection and the town of Pécs in southern Hungary has several major art collections. Many specialist museums and ethnograpical collections are also to be found outside the capital.

Orientation in Budapest. Finding your way around Budapest is relatively easy. The city is divided into 22 districts. The inner city on the Pest side is district V. This is surrounded by districts VI, VII and VIII, running from N–S roughly along the line of the Great Boulevard. District I is the Castle and Watertown areas of Buda. The middle figures of the four-figure post code of addresses indicates the district (e.g. 1107 is district X, 1056 is district V etc).

Even street numbers invariably ascend on the left-hand side, odd numbers on the right. The lower numbers usually begin either from the Danube end, or, in Pest, from the end nearest the Kossuth Lajos u./Rákóczi út axis. Street name plates usually indicate the street numbers in the adjoining block. The numbers generally refer to a whole building and do not differentiate between shops which might occupy the ground floor and have separate entrances.

There is a map of the city in most metro stations. Maps of Budapest and other places can be found in many bookshops and at specialist map shops at 1065 Bajcsy-Zsilinszky út 37 and 1072 Nyár u. 1 (entrance to the latter in Dohány u.). The Cartographia company publishes a 'Budapest Guide' city map-book which has places marked in English as well as other information.

Photography. Western brands of 35mm colour films are readily available, but those of black and white films are not. Long-life batteries are available. Photographic items can be found in Ofotért, Főfotó and Fotex shops which also offer a developing and printing service comparable to that found in the West.

Post Office Services. Post offices are normally open on weekdays from 8.00 to 18.00 and on Saturdays from 8.00 to 14.00. Two post offices in Budapest are open 24 hours a day including Sunday—at 105 Lenin körút (near the Western Railway Station) and at Baross tér, on the left-hand side of the Eastern Railway Station. Postcards, envelopes, stationery and stamps can also be purchased at tobacconist's shops. Letters to Britain normally take under a week, but it can take three times as long for mail sent from Britain to arrive in Hungary. Mail sent 'poste restante' Budapest will arrive at the Main Post Office (entrance No. 18 Városház u. tel. 1184-811). Mail can be directed to other towns and will be kept at the main post office in that town (addresses are given before the routes of the major towns).

The number to dial for sending a telegram is 02. An English speaking operator can occasionally be found on this number. Telegrams are commonly used in Hungary for sending quick messages, though they cannot be sent from public phone boxes.

There are four public telex stations in Hungary: in Budapest at the office of the Telephone Directorate, 17–19 Petőfi Sándor u. (there is also a public telefax service here); in Debrecen at the post office on Hajdú u. (No. 18); in Keszthely at No. 1–3 Kossuth Lajos u.; and in Miskolc at the post office on Széchenyi István u. (No. 3–9). Most hotels also have telex (and sometimes telefax) machines which guests can use.

Local telphone calls, at the time of writing, are 2Ft for 3 minutes between 7.00 and 18.00, and 2Ft for 6 minutes after 18.00. (In a call box lift the receiver, put the money in, wait for the uninterrupted dialling tone, then dial.) For long-distance calls in Hungary dial 06, wait for the tone, then dial the district code and subscriber's number. For districts not on the long-distance network, dial 01. Red push-button public telephones can be used for international calls. They operate with 2, 10 and 20Ft coins. To make an international call first dial 00 and wait for the purring tone, then dial the country code (44 for Britain, 1 for the USA), the area code and the subscriber's number. (For dialling Britain the initial zero of the area code is not required, thus that of Liverpool would be 51, Birmingham 21, etc.) The country code for Hungary when dialling from abroad is 36. The Budapest code is 1. Hence to reach a Budapest number from Britain dial 010 361 and then the subscriber's number.

Warning. The Hungarian telephone system is acknowledged to be one of the worst and most underdeveloped in Europe. It can take a long time to get through! Telephone directories are not published every year and are therefore usually a little out of date. There is an English language enquiry service in Budapest (1172-200, 7.00 to 20.00).

bélyeg = stamp
levelezőlap = postcard
távirat = telegram
telefonszám = telephone number
légiposta = airmail
posta = post office

Public Toilets. Public toilets in Hungary are not easily found but when they are they are not often in a clean condition. It is better to use the toilet facilites in a café, bar or, best of all, in a hotel. A payment of 2 or 3Ft is usually expected and there is often a saucer or plate by the entrance for this.

Public Holidays
1 January—New Year's Day
15 March—Anniversary of the outbreak of the 1848 Revolution in Hungary
1 May—International Labour Day
20 August—Feast of St. Stephen, first King of Hungary, and traditional celebration of 'new bread'
23 October—Anniversary of the outbreak of the 1956 Uprising and of the 1989 declaration of Hungary as a Republic (ie. no longer a 'People's Republic')
25–26 December—Christmas (the holiday period begins on the afternoon of Christmas Eve)

Shopping. In general food shops open early, around 6.00 or 7.00 in the morning and stay open until 19.00 or 20.00 in the evening. Other shops tend to open only at 10.00 in the morning and close around 18.00, except on Thursdays when many shops stay open until 20.00. Most shops are closed on Sundays *and* on Saturday afternoon after 13.00 or 14.00. Some food shops, tobacconists and sweet shops are open on Saturday afternoon and Sunday, but not many. In Budapest food can be obtained day and night, every day at the Skála Csarnok store in Klauzál tér. In the larger, non-food shops the procedure is to select the items, receive a bill, pay at a separate till and then return to the counter to collect the goods. Alcohol can be obtained in supermarkets and some sweet shops.

Two major markets in Budapest are the large covered market on

Tolbuhin körút, at the Pest end of Liberty Bridge, and the 'Lehel' open-air market in the XIIIth district just north of the centre in Pest (Élmunkás tér metro). The latter is open on Sunday mornings. There is a flea market in the XIXth district to the SE of the centre on Nagykőrösi út, near the start of the M5 motorway (bus No. 54 from Boráros tér by Petőfi Bridge).

There are folk art shops in Budapest at the following addresses: 14 Váci u. (open Saturday and Sunday), 6 Vörösmarty tér, 12 Régiposta u., 13 Kecskeméti u., 26 Szent István körút and 16 Országház u. (the last-mentioned is in Buda, the others are in Pest).

Duty-free goods are available for hard currency in Intertourist, Utastourist and Konsumtourist shops and at hotels.

Shops are often situated in premises which were originally built as residential blocks and hence, from the outside, often do not look like shops in the Western sense. The following short vocabulary may help with identification:

trafik/dohánybolt = tobacconist's
csemege = delicatessen
áruház = department store
élelmiszer = food shop
édességbolt = sweetshop
illatszer = toiletries and cosmetics
kincsesbolt = jewellery
zöldség = vegetables
gyümölcs = fruit
hentesáru/hús bolt = butcher's
könyvesbolt = bookshop
lemezbolt = record shop
közért = supermarket

Useful phrases:
How much is this please?   *Mennyibe kerül?*
Can you show me that one?   *Megmutatná azt?*
I'll take this,   *Megveszem*
Is there anything similar?   *Van valami hasonló?*
Have you got any...?   *Van...?*
It's too big/small,   *Túl nagy/túl kicsi.*

Special Interests. Information about the following special interests can be obtained by contacting the agencies listed below:
Angling. Magyar Országos Horgász Szövetség (Hungarian Anglers' Association) 1051 Budapest, Október 6 u. 20 (1325-315, 1315-332). There are waters suitable for fishing in all parts of the country, but a permit is required. Special rules apply to fishing at Lake Balaton.
Camping. Hungarian Camping and Caravaning Club Travel Office, 1085 Budapest, Üllői út 6 (1336-536, 1141-880).
Horse Riding. Pegazus Tours, 1053 Budapest, Károlyi Mihály u. 5 (1171-644). National and international equestrian events take place in different parts of the country from early May until late August.
Hunting. MAVAD, 1014 Budapest, Úri u. 39 (1556-715). HUN-TOURS, 1024 Budapest, Retek u. 34 (1352-313). VADCOOP, 1052 Budapest, Apáczay Csere János u. 4 (Duna Intercontinental Hotel) (1175-122).
Motoring and caravanning. Autó Tours, travel agency of the Hungarian Automobile Club. 1024 Budapest, Rómer Flóris u. 4/a (1152-040).

Naturist beaches. Naturisták Szövetsége (Naturists' Federation) 1133 Budapest, Kárpát u. 8.

Open-air pursuits. Walking, bird-watching, skiing, water sports etc. Magyar Természetbarát Szövetség (Hungarian Nature-lovers' Federation) 1065 Budapest, Bajcsy-Zsilinszky út 31, 2nd floor, (1112-467, 1117-498, 1319-705).

Spas and water treatment. Danubius Travel, 1052 Budapest, Martinelli tér 8 (1173-652, 1173-115). Based on the many warm-water natural springs found throughout the country, thermal tourism, as it is called, is one of the growth areas of the Hungarian tourist industry.

Vintage Trains. Máv Tours, 1051 Budapest, Guszev u. 1 (1173-723). Travel agency of the Hungarian Railways.

Youth activities. Express, 1054 Budapest, Szabadság tér 16 (1317-777) and 1052 Budapest, Semmelweis u. 4 (1176-634).

Theatre and Concert Tickets. In Budapest theatre tickets can be obtained in advance from the Central Theatre Ticket Office (Színházak Központi Jegyirodája) at No. 18 Népköztársaság útja (nearest metro—November 7 tér). Open Monday to Friday 10.00–14.00 and 14.30–19.00. Tel. 1120-000. Concert tickets are available at the National Philharmonia Central Ticket Office (Országos Filharmónia Központi Jegyirodája) at No. 1 Vörösmarty tér (through the glass doors and to the right on the ground floor of the modern building facing the Vörösmarty statue). Open Monday to Friday 11.00–14.00 and 14.30–18.00. Tel. 1176-222.

Tickets are also available at the appropriate theatre or concert hall. Last minute tickets may be available at the venue half an hour before the performance starts. Occasionally, for large productions, tickets are available for hard currency from the IBUSZ office at No. 1 Felszabadulás tér (1186-666).

Time. Hungary is on Central European Time which means that it is six hours ahead of the USA and Canada, one hour ahead of Great Britain, and at the same time as the rest of Western Europe. The clocks are adjusted one hour for summer time at the end of March and the end of September.

Tipping. Conventions regarding tipping are similar to other countries in terms of who is tipped (taxi drivers, porters, waiters and waitresses, etc.). The standard amount is 10–15 per cent.

Wheelchair Access. Hungary is not at the forefront of countries making provision for people with disabilities. Although ramps do exist at certain places where there are steps, by and large public buildings and facilities are poor as regards wheelchair access.

Hungarian Language

In Hungary English is spoken in hotels, tourist information offices and at some other places frequented by tourists. The first language of tourism, however, is German and visitors may often find themselves being addressed in this language rather than either Hungarian or English. Knowledge of a few phrases in Hungarian, therefore, is not only useful but also necessary in some basic situations, for example when shopping. Teaching materials for English speakers are few and far between. 'Colloquial Hungarian' by Jerry Payne (Routledge, 1987) is one of the more recent books.

Hungarian belongs to the Finno-Ugric group of languages, which includes Finnish, Estonian and some languages spoken in northern areas of the Soviet Union. It is unrelated to the Indo-European languages and therefore there are relatively few words with which visitors will feel familiar. Grammatically the language is also quite different from English. Suffixes abound. With 'to our house', for example, the possessive and directional suffixes are added to the word for house (*ház*) making one word—*házunkba*. This can make some words confusingly long. Verbs are also difficult. They have different endings depending on whether there is a definite or indefinite object.

On the positive side the Roman script is familiar and pronunciation, once learned, is simplified by the fact that letters and combinations of letters are always pronounced in the same way. There is also a regular stress pattern, with a slight emphasis on the first syllable of a word and each following syllable being clearly and evenly pronounced.

Hungarian is a 'non-sexist' language in that words have no grammatical gender, and in that there is no distinction in the terms for 'he' and 'she'. This can lead to some confusion, however, and Hungarians who speak English are apt to say 'he' when they mean 'she' and vice-versa.

Pronunciation

Vowels

a   confusing for English speakers as it is pronounced like the *o* in 'hot'
á   like the *a* in 'car'
e   as in 'ten'
é   like the *a* in 'day'
i   as in 'hit'
í   lengthens the above, as the double *e* in 'feet'
o   as in 'open'
ó   lengthens the above
ö   like the *e* in 'bitter'
ő   lengthens the above, like the *u* in 'fur'
u   short as in 'put'
ú   long as in 'rule'
ü   short as in the French 'tu'
ű   lengthens the above

Consonants

Consonants are pronounced much as they are in English except for the following:
c   like the *ts* in 'cats'
cs   like the *ch* in 'chapel'
g   is always hard, like in 'gun'
gy   like the soft *d* of 'during'
j   like the y in 'yes'
ly   also like the y in 'yes'
ny   like the *gn* in 'cognac'
s   like the *sh* in 'ship'
sz   like the *s* in 'sit'
ty   like the soft *t* of 'tube'
zs   like the *s* in 'pleasure'

A Glossary of Words and Phrases

Good day/hello, *Jó napot kivánok*
Good morning (early), *Jó reggelt (kivánok)*
Good evening, *Jó estét*
Good night, *Jó éjszakát*
Goodbye, *Viszontlátásra*

The above phrases are used continuously in Hungary on meeting and parting, even in situations where you would not necessarily use them in English (for example in shops or before buying a ticket, or with strangers in a lift).

Szia and *Szervusz* (in plural *sziasztok* and *szervusztok*) are familiar forms which are used among friends and among young people in general on meeting and parting. Both can mean either 'hello' or 'goodbye' depending on the situation. It is not as confusing as it sounds and is easily picked up. It explains why Hungarians, when leaving you, will often wave and say 'hello'!

Yes, *Igen*
No, *Nem*
Thank you, *Köszönöm*
Good/OK!, *Jó*
Very good, *Nagyon jó*
Thank you very much, *Köszönöm szépen*
Thank you very much indeed, *Nagyon szépen köszönöm*
Please, *Kérem*
Excuse me, *Bocsánat*
Do you speak English/German?, *Beszél angolul/németül?*
Sorry, I don't understand, *Elnézést, nem értem*
I'm English/American, *Angol/amerikai vagyok*
Monday/on Monday, *Hétfő/hétfőn*
Tuesday/on Tuesday, *Kedd/kedden*
Wednesday/etc., *Szerda/szerdán*
Thursday, *Csütörtök/csütörtökön*
Friday, *Péntek/pénteken*
Saturday, *Szombat/szombaton*
Sunday, *Vasárnap/vasárnap*

Fortunately the months of the year in Hungarian are similar to the English: *Január, Február, Március, Április, Május, Június, Július, Augusztus, Szeptember, Október, November, December.*

Numbers are quite different, but fairly straightforward:

One, *Egy*
Two, *Két/kettő*
Three, *Három*
Four, *Négy*
Five, *Öt*
Six, *Hat*

Seven, *Hét*
   (hét also means 'week')
Eight, *Nyolc*
Nine, *Kilenc*
Ten, *Tíz*
Eleven, *Tizenegy*

Twelve, *Tizenkettő*
Thirteen, *Tizenhárom*
...etc.
Twenty,*Húsz*
Twenty one, *Huszonegy*
Twenty-two, *Huszonkettő*
Twenty three,
Huszonhárom
...etc.
Thirty, *Harminc*
Thirty one, *Harmincegy*
Forty, *Negyven*
Fifty, *Ötven*
Sixty, *Hatvan*
Seventy, *Hetven*

Eighty, *Nyolcvan*
Ninety, *Kilencven*
One hundred, *Száz*
Two hundred, *Kétszáz*
...etc.
One hundred and twenty,
Százhúsz
One hundred and twenty one,
Százhuszonegy
Two hundred and twenty one,
Kétszázhuszonegy
One thousand, *Ezer*
One thousand two hundred,
Ezerkétszáz
...etc.

Years are derived simply from the relevant numbers. In writing the figures are normally used but if the year is written as spoken it is written as one word and hence appears extremely long, but on inspection its derivation is obvious, for example 1956 is *ezerkilencszázötvenhat*.

One Hundred Basic Words (see also other sections, especially 'Food and Drink')

ajándék, gift
állomás, station
amerikai, American
angol, English
angolul, in English
ár, price
asztal, table
balra, to the left
bejárat, entrance
benzinkút, petrol station
bocsánat, excuse me!, sorry
bolt/üzlet, shop
busz, bus
cigaretta, cigarette
cím, address
délben, at noon
délelőtt, (in the) morning
délután, (in the) afternoon
drága, expensive
éjszaka, night
emelet, floor
emlékmű, monument
eső, rain
este, (in the) evening
fagylalt, ice cream
falu, village
fehér, white
fekete, black
feleség(em), (my) wife
férj(em), (my) husband
filmszínház, cinema
fürdő, bath

fürdőszoba, bathroom
gyufa, matches
hajó, boat, ship
ház, house
híd, bridge
hideg, cold
hol van a...?, where is the...?
holnap, tomorrow
hónap, month
időjárás, weather
itt, here
jobbra, to the right
kastély, mansion
kerékpár, bicycle
kép, picture
kevés, little, few
kijárat, exit
kicsi, small, little
kirándulás, excursion
kórház, hospital
könyv, book
kulcs, key
ma, today
magyar, Hungarian
magyarul, in Hungarian
Magyarország, Hungary
megálló, (bus, tram, etc.) stop
meleg, warm
messze, far
mosdó/WC, toilets
mozi, cinema
nagy, big

nagykövetség, embassy
nagyon, very
nap, day: sun
népművészet, folk art
név, name
nincs..., there is no...
nyár, summer
olcsó, cheap
orvos, doctor
ott, there
pénz, money
pénztár, booking, cash office
pénzváltás, exchange
rendőrség, police (station)
repülőtér, airport
ruhatár, cloakroom
segítség, help
sok, many, much

szálló(da), hotel
szám, number
szép, lovely, beautiful
szivar, cigar
szoba, room
tánc, dance
tegnap, yesterday
templom, church
új, new
újság, newspaper
útlevél, passport
vám, customs
végállomás, terminus
villamos, tram
virág, flower
víz, water
vonat, train
zene, music

Hungarian Food

By *Katalin Rácz*

Hungarians like eating and drinking. It takes up much of their time using any occasion like name-days or birthdays and festivities like Christmas or Easter for elaborate meals and social drinking. These celebrations may take place in somebody's home, a café or a restaurant, where large tables for ten or more people are reserved.

The main meal of the day is likely to be lunch taken at the office or factory canteens and schools on weekdays, and at home or in a restaurant on Sundays. What you find on the table largely depends on the season, partly because the hot summers and very cold winters used to determine people's eating patterns and this is still reflected in today's habits, and partly because of the strictly seasonal availablity of fresh foodstuff which the country largely produces for itself.

There are a few dishes whose names are familiar to most foreigners. They may be suprised to see, however, that what they have known as Hungarian goulash is not a stew in its home country but a rather thick soup exclusively made of beef and three or four types of vegetables or that the best strudels are made from the thinnest possible pastry.

Among the spices of most savory dishes paprika prevails. It is believed to have been introduced into Hungarian cuisine by the Turks and it has remained here ever since in many varieties. Paprika is generally understood as ground red paprika, though Hungarians call the fresh yellow or green peppers of various shapes and flavours by the same name. The yellow paprikas can be found in all the markets from May to October and they are used in many dishes. One of these is called *lecsó* and is made of onions, tomatoes and fresh yellow paprika cooked together. Another is stuffed paprika *(töltött paprika)* when very large yellow paprikas are stuffed with minced pork and rice boiled in water and served in freshly made tomato sauce. Ground red paprika is naturally used in a different way. It adds flavour and colour to dishes.

Paprika is grown in most gardens in Hungary but the main paprika growing regions are around Szeged and Kalocsa, which produce many varieties like *különleges* (special) paprika with a full red colour, finely ground and with a mild taste, *édesnemes* (sweet-noble) paprika, darker and mildly sharp, *rózsapaprika* (rose paprika), medium ground and quite sharp, *erős paprika* (sharp), the strongest in flavour with a brownish red to yellow colour. It is not only the different kinds of paprika that make Hungarian dishes very special but also the way it is used. Dishes that contain paprika are begun by frying chopped onion in oil or fat and when lightly brown paprika powder is added and stirred in. Another important ingredient is sour cream, which is either cooked with the food or added at serving.

Hungarians eat a lot of meat, mainly pork and beef, but many restaurants also serve veal and game. Poultry is plentiful and so is fish. Hungary has many rivers and lakes, so river fish like carp, pike, catfish and trout, are widely eaten. A meat dish is most often served with potatoes or rice and hardly any vegetables, unless a side salad is served. A favourite dish on restaurant menus and for Sunday dinners is pork or veal slices coated in breadcrumbs and deep-fried in oil. Its origin is not Hungarian but Austrian hence the name *Bécsi szelet* (wiener schnitzel), though commonly it is known as *rántott hús*. Side salads differ according to season. In the summer months there are fresh green salads and tomatoes. The standard dressing is made from vinegar, sugar and water. In the winter months there will be pickles on the table. They might include gherkins, pickled peppers (normally very sharp), beetroot and mixed pickles.

Boiled vegetables are called *angolos zöldségek* (English vegetables) showing that boiling is really not a Hungarian way of cooking them. An important part of Hungarian meals, especially at home, in small restaurants and in school meals, is *főzelék*: vegetables chopped and fried in a small amount of oil, then boiled in a little water until completely cooked. Either sour cream sprinkled with flour or roux is stirred in before serving.

For most Hungarians a meal starts with soup, followed by the main course with some side salad, and finishes with a sweet. Desserts are very varied and include pastries, pies and cakes. Hungarians go to a *cukrászda* (pastry-shop) for *torta* (gateaux), very often taking home big trays of these richly layered cakes. Ice cream is popular throughout the year, and in the summer most cafés open up their windows and sell cones.

A meal usually finishes with coffee. Tea is normally only drunk at home for breakfast, though some cafés in the centres of towns serve tea, which is drunk with lemon and sugar. Coffee is drunk not only after meals but on any occasion between meals. The beverage was introduced by the Turks, but later the style of making it was influenced by the Italians. It is made in coffee-makers, where boiling water is forced through ground coffee and a very strong drink is produced, similar to the Italian espresso. It may be served with whipped cream.

Hungary, with its meat-eating culture, is not the best country for vegetarians, though in the summer months the markets have a plentiful supply of fruit and vegetables. There are no vegetarian restaurants at the time of writing, though as healthy ways of eating are slowly gaining in popularity so may vegetarian dishes. Nevertheless, vegetarians can find lots of suitable items among traditional Hungarian dishes, such as *főzelékek* (braised vegetables), mushrooms made in different ways, like *rántott gomba* (mushrooms coated with breadcrumbs, deep fried and served with tartar sauce) or *gombapörkölt* (mushroom stew), and *rántott sajt* (cheese coated with breadcrumbs and deep fried). *Lángos*, a deep-fried yeast dough, which can be found anywhere near stations, markets and in the summer by swimming pools and Lake Balaton, is eaten at any time.

Restaurants. Eating out is popular in Hungary. Visitors to the country often want something that is typically Hungarian with gipsy music in the background. For this one can either go to one of the big hotels which serve meals of a generally international flavour or to the restaurants in the Castle District and in the centre of Budapest which have gipsy bands specially to entertain tourists. Budapest and all the other towns have plenty of small restaurants where sometimes excellent cuisine can be discovered at very reasonable prices. Restaurants are usually open from 11.00 to 22.00 or 24.00.

Cafés are open from 9.00 (some earlier) till 23.00. They serve alcoholic drinks together with coffee, soft drinks, cakes and sandwiches throughout the day.

Always ask for the bill in good time as it invariably takes a while to be produced. There is nothing sinister in this, it is just the general custom, but it is advisable to check the bill when it comes. Tipping is normally between 10 and 20 per cent. The tip is never left on the table. It is included when paying the bill: either say how much change you want, to allow for the tip, or say how much you want to pay including the tip.

Some Hungarian specialties

Soups
Gulyás leves (Goulash soup) is a thick soup made from beef cubes, vegetables such as carrots, parsnips, celeriac, onions, potatoes, and small dumplings. It often replaces the main course and is followed by a more substantial dessert.
Halászlé (fish soup) can also be a main course. The best fish soup is made from several types of fresh river fish, carp being the main ingredient. Both fish soup and goulash are red in colour due to the red paprika used sparingly.
Újházi tyúkhúsleves (hen soup Ujházi style) is a golden colour soup, made from hen and various vegetables. It is served with thin noodles.
Meggyleves (Morello cherry soup) is a summer speciality. It is made of morello cherries with sour cream or single cream. It is eaten cold and is a light, refreshing soup in the hot summer months.

Starters
Hortobágyi palacsinta (pancakes Hortobágy style) is eaten as a hot starter. The pancakes are filled with pork stew and covered with a sauce made from the stew and sour cream.
Gombafejek rántva (mushrooms coated with breadcrumbs) is also a hot starter but it is substantial enough to be a vegetarian dish. The mushroom heads are put in flour, eggs and breadcrumbs, which makes the Hungarian batter for not only mushrooms but cheese, meat and poultry or fish. Then they are deep-fried and served with rice and Tartar sauce.

Rántott sajt (cheese slices coated with breadcrumbs) is made and served in the same way as the above.

Main courses

Pörkölt (stew) is made of one type of meat, thus it can be *disznópörkölt* (pork stew), *marhapörkölt* (beef stew) or *borjúpörkölt* (veal stew). The meat cubes are cooked with chopped onions and red paprika. It can be served with boiled potatoes or *nokedli* (gnocchi).

Paprikáscsirke (chicken paprika) is similar to pörkölt, the basic ingredient being chicken joints. It is served with sour cream and gnocchi.

Töltött paprika (stuffed peppers). The peppers are stuffed with minced pork and spices and served with freshly-made tomato sauce and boiled potatoes.

Töltöttkáposzta (stuffed cabbage) is a filling winter dish. The basic ingredient is soured cabbage, with meat balls, smoked ham and sausage. Sour cream is added at serving. It is often made in large pots and warmed up several times whenever eaten. This popular dish has gone into a frequently used Hungarian saying: 'Love is not like stuffed cabbage, it cannot be heated up several times.'

Bélszín Budapest módra (beefsteak Budapest style) has a ragout made of paprika, mushroom, green peas and chicken liver pieces poured on top of the steak.

Rácponty (carp Rác style) is like a pörkölt but instead of using meat it is made with carp. It is served with gnocchi and sour cream.

Savoury dishes made with onion, meat and red paprika are prepared by frying the onion in oil then sprinkling it with red paprika and only after that the meat is added and braised.

Desserts

Gundel palacsinta (pancakes Gundel style). This delicious pudding bears the name of a famous chef and restaurateur. The pancakes have a walnut filling and chocolate sauce on top. Brandy is poured on and lit when served at the table.

Somlói galuska (chocolate cream pudding) is a cold pudding. Sponge with walnuts and raisins is served with a thick chocolate sauce and whipped cream.

Rétes (strudel), which might be *almás rétes* (apple strudel), *cseresznyés rétes* (cherry strudel), *mákos rétes* (poppy seed) or *túró rétes* (curd cheese and raisins).

Vargabéles is a hot dessert. Very thin noodles are baked with sweetened curd cheese and raisins.

Menu

Levesek (Soups)
Gulyásleves, Goulash soup
Csontleves, Clear soup
Újházi tyúkhúsleves, Hen soup
Gombaleves, Mushroom soup
Zöldségleves, Vegetable soup
Hideg almaleves, Cold apple soup

Főzelékek (Braised Vegetables)
Finomfőzelék, Carrots, parsnip and green peas
Karalábéfőzelék, Kholrabi
Parajfőzelék, Spinach
Lencsefőzelék, Lentils
    Braised vegetables may be served with *tükörtojás* (fried egg), *vagdalthús* (slice of mince pork) or *füstölt tarja* (smoked ham).

Köretek (Side dishes)
Főttburgonya, Boiled potatoes
Sültburgonya, Roast potatoes
Hasábburgonya, Chips
Petrezselymes burgonya, New potatoes with parsley
Rizs, Boiled rice
Rizibizi, Boiled rice with green peas

Meleg előételek (Hot starters)
Hortobágyi palacsinta, Pancake Hortobágy style
Rántott sajt, Cheese slices in breadcrumbs
Rántott gomba, Mushrooms in breadcrumbs

Halak (Fish)
Halászlé, Fish soup
Rántott ponty, Fillet of carp in breadcrumbs
Ponty roston, Grilled fillet of carp
Süllő roston, Young pike-perch grilled
Fogas, Pike-perch

Szárnyasok (Poultry)
Paprikáscsirke, Chicken paprika
Rántott csirke, Chicken pieces in breadcrumbs
Kacsasült, Roast duck
Pulykamell ananásszal, Turkey breast with pineapple

Készételek (Ready-made dishes)
Marhapörkölt, Beef stew
Bácskai rizseshús, Pork risotto
Töltött káposzta, Stuffed cabbage

Frissensültek (Freshly-made meat dishes)
Rántott borjúszelet, Veal in breadcrumbs
Rántott sertésszelet, Pork in breadcrumbs
Brassói aprópecsenye, Braised pork Brassó style (thinly chopped with
    spices)
Bélszin Budapest módra, Beefsteak Budapest style
Csülök Pékné módra, Roast pork loin

Saláták (Salads)
Csemegeuborka, Gherkins
Ecetes paprika, Pickled hot paprika
Céklasaláta, Beetroot salad
Babsaláta, Pickled beans with onions

Édességek (Desserts)
Gundel palacsinta, Pancake Gundel style
Vaniliás palacsinta, Pancakes filled with curd cheese and served
    with vanilla sauce
Izes palacsinta, Pancakes filled with jam
Somlói galuska, Chocolate cream pudding
Rétesek, Strudels

A Note on Drinks. The Hungarian spirit is *pálinka*, a clear brandy made from apricots (*barackpálinka*), cherries (*cseresznyepálinka*) or other fruits. Wines are plentiful with different tastes from different regions. The main vine-growing areas are around Balaton, Bada-csony, Sopron, Pécs and Eger. *Minőségi bor* on the label is the equivalent of 'appellation contrôlée'. Classic grapes—Riesling, Syl-vaner, Pinot, Cabernet, etc.—have been brought to Hungary and wines made from these are available. (In an interesting reversal of this practice Ágoston Haraszthy planted Hungarian vines in Califor-nia in the 19C. He later became known as the 'Father of Californian wine'!) A special Hungarian dessert wine is Tokaj, of which *Tokaji Aszú* is generally considered the best. It comes both sweet (*édes*) and dry (*száraz*) (see p 350).

Beers are generally in half litre bottles though draught beer (*csapolt sör*) can be obtained in some restaurants and 'pubs' (*söröző*). Prices vary, usually according to quality. Good Czechoslovak beers at reasonable prices are available. Austrian and German beers, and beer in cans are always more expensive. By and large the beers are of the lager type, though occasionally a beer similar to English brown ale can be found (*bak sör*). Good quality Soviet vodka and Soviet champagne are particularly cheap by Western standards.

Drinks are always much more expensive in cafés and restaurants than in the shops. It is advisable always to ask for the drinks menu (*az itallap*) to check the prices before ordering.

wine = *bor* (red = *vörös*, white = *fehér*, sweet = *édes*, dry = *száraz*, medium-dry = *félszáraz*)
beer = *sör* (bottled = *üveges*, canned = *dobozos*)

MAIN ROADS AND PLACES OF HUNG

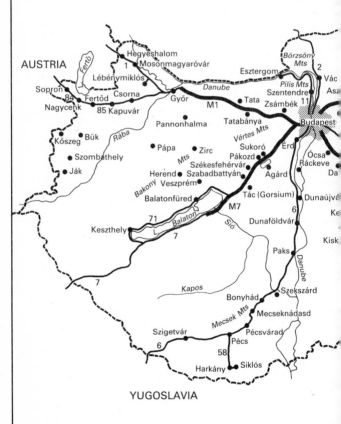

0   km   50

CZECHOSL

AUSTRIA

Fertő

Hegyeshalom
Mosónmagyaróvár
Lébénymiklós   1

Sopron
84   Fertőd   Csorna
Nagycenk   85 Kapuvár

Győr   M1   Tata
Danube

Esztergom
Szentendre
Zsámbék   11

Börzsöny Mts   2
Pilis Mts   Vác
Asz

Budapest

Kőszeg   Bük   Rába
Szombathely
Ják

Pápa   Zirc
Mts
Herend   Szabadbattyán
Bakony   Veszprém

Pannonhalma
Tatabánya
Vértes Mts
Sukoró
Pákozd
Székesfehérvár
Agárd

Érd
Ócsa
Ráckeve
Da

Balatonfüred
71   Balaton
Keszthely   L.   7

Tác (Gorsium)
M7
Sió
Dunaföldvár

Dunaújvá
6   Ke

Paks
Danube   Kisk

Kapos
Bonyhád
Mecsek Mts
Szigetvár   Pécsvárad
6   Pécs
58
Harkány   Siklós

Szekszárd

Mecseknádasd

YUGOSLAVIA

—— Main roads (with official Hungarian road n
▬▬ Motorways (N.B. Some lengths of motorw

RY

ΚΙΑ

llókő

Aggtelek

3

Sárospatak

Miskolc

Bükk Mts

Eger

Feldebrő

25

Mezőkövesd

Gyöngyös

Hatvan

ászberény

Abony

Cegléd Szolnok

Nagykőrös

Lajosmizse

ét

yháza

Ópusztaszer

5

Tápé

undorozsma

Szeged

Mátra Mts

3

Mts

Zemplén

Karcsa

37

Tokaj

37

Nyíregyháza

Nyírbátor

4

4

Hortobágy

Tiszafüred Hortobágy

Tisza

Hajdúszoboszló

Debrecen

Karcag

Kisújszállás

Törökszentmiklós

Zagyva

Körös

ROMANIA

Szarvas

Gyula

Tisza

U.S.S.R.

N

ing)

tably the entire stretch of the M1 between Győr and Tatabánya are incomplete)

1   Hegyeshalom to Budapest

Roads 1 and M1. Total distance 175km. **Hegyeshalom**—Road 1
14km **Mosonmagyaróvár** —15km turning for (5km) **Lébénymiklós**
—23km **Győr**—M1 54km turning for **Tata** —6km turning for
Tatabánya—63km **Budapest**.

The Nickelsdorf-Hegyeshalom border crossing is the main Austro–
Hungarian border crossing for motorists and the 175km route from
here to Budapest is the most popular way for Western drivers to
approach the Hungarian capital.

Despite the volume of traffic, only the last 56km, between Tatabánya and
Budapest, is a fully-constructed motorway, although there are plans to extend
this to cover the full distance between the capital and the border. The 70km
stretch between Vienna and Hegyeshalom is similarly non-motorway, and the
volume and speed of traffic, together with the narrowness of the road have led
to many accidents. Hence, although the shortest distance between Vienna and
Budapest, the route via Hegyeshalom is not an easy drive. The nearest
alternative crossing is at Klingenbach-Sopron. This adds just 33km to the
Vienna–Budapest route but joins the main highway just before Győr and so fails
to cut out another dangerous and difficult section after that city (see below).
The border crossing at Hegyeshalom is open 24 hours a day. Entry visas can
be obtained here, but this can take a long time and costs slightly more than in
the country of departure. The passport, visa and customs check takes only a few
minutes but the volume of traffic means that crossing times can vary from ten
minutes to one and a half hours or more. Lack of visa requirements for citizens
of Austria and Hungary, together with the loosening of travel restrictions for
Hungarians in the late 1980s, has resulted in a dramatic increase in the numbers
of short-term visitors travelling between Vienna and Budapest. It is advisable,
therefore, to avoid crossing into Hungary at the end of the day and at weekends.
If the proposed joint Budapest-Vienna World Expo goes ahead in 1995 it is
likely that the motorway between the two cities will be completed and that
crossing times will be speeded up. In the meantime, however, it is best to be
prepared for some delay.
The border station has parking, toilet, refreshment, telephone and money
exchange facilities. There is no requirement to change money at the border and
places to change money are easily found elsewhere, including at several points
on the road to Budapest. Petrol, which is substantially cheaper in Hungary than
in Austria, is not available at the border, but can be obtained in the village of
Hegyeshalom, 4km from the border just off the main highway (unleaded petrol
is available here), or in Mosonmagyaróvár, 14km after the border on the main
road.

MOSONMAGYARÓVÁR (pop. 30,000) is the first major town after
the border on Road 1. Although today mainly an important junction
for through traffic, there are a number of historic sights.

For centuries Mosonmagyaróvár has been a commercial centre and an important point on the east–west mail routes. During the various wars it was
frequently occupied and plundered. Magyarórvár received its royal charter in
1354 from Queen Elizabeth, the widow of King Charles Robert. Further
prosperity followed a decree of King Sigismund (1387–1487) which stated that
Magyaróvár should be the only place through which goods could pass between
Hungary and Austria. In addition, for a long time shipping was only safe along
the Moson branch of the Danube. The two settlements of Moson and
Magyaróvár were united in 1939. Industrial development after the war brought
a number of large factories to the town.

The *Castle*, is in old Magyaróvár just off Road 15, which enters the
town from the NW. (From Road 1 take the turning signposted
Bratislava.) Although originally built in the second half of the 13C,
the castle has been constructed several times over the centuries.
Today it accommodates a section of the Keszthely University of
Agricultural Science.

In Building B of the university there is a small exhibition of the 'Fauna of the Hanság'. The Hanság is a nature conservation area lying to the south of Mosonmagyaróvár. In the last century this low-lying basin was an impassable moorland covered with reeds, groves of alder trees and marshy meadows. At the end of the century a significant portion of the Hanság was drained by means of large-scale water-control projects. (Open 10.00–17.00 except weekends and holidays.)

The *Salt House* (Sóház) stands nearby, to the W of the Castle. The Capuchins had a church and monastery built here in 1689. When the order was dispersed in 1787 the monastery became a salt warehouse. Also nearby, E of the castle in Lucsony u., there are a number of peasant Baroque houses.

The *Hanság Museum* at No. 135 Lenin út (on the right of Road 1 just after the Bratislava turning) is one of the oldest established provincial museums in Hungary, although its present neo-classical building dates from 1912. The collections of the museum cover the history of Mosonmagyaróvár and its region from the Roman times to 1848. (Opening times are normally 10.00–18.00; Nov–March 10.00–17.00; closed Mondays. At the time of writing the museum is closed for long-term restoration work.)

At No. 103 Lenin út, in the so-called Cselley House, built in Baroque style around 1730, there is a *Fine and Applied Arts Exhibition*. Items on display date from the 17C to the 19C and there is also a collection of Hungarian paintings from the 19C and 20C. (Open 10.00–18.00; Nov–March 10.00–17.00; closed Mondays.)

One of the most tragic and bloody incidents of the Hungarian events of 1956 occurred in Mosonmagyaróvár. Here, on the morning of Friday 26 October, the ÁVH (secret police) without warning fired two machine guns on an unarmed crowd of demonstrators, killing about 80 and wounding over a hundred. The incensed crowd, having obtained weapons from the local soldiery, then attacked the ÁVH headquarters and eventually killed or lynched several officers.

One of the earliest surviving monuments of Romanesque architecture in Hungary is situated at **Lébénymiklós**, 5km off Road 1 and c 15km to the S of Mosonmagyaróvár. The *Benedictine Church* here was originally built between 1208 and 1213 and came under the jurisdiction of the Benedictine Abbot at Pannonhalma. Although untouched by the Mongol invasion it suffered serious fire damage, first in 1478 and twice later during Turkish times. The church was renovated in Baroque style by the Jesuits in the mid-17C, but in 1858–79 the structure was restored in its original Romanesque style. At *No. 5 Iskola u.* there is an exhibition of the economy and agriculture of the Hanság in the 19C and 20C. (Open Wed, Thurs, Sat and Sun 10.00–16.00.)

Road 1 can be rejoined at Öttevény, 8km to the SE via Mosonszentmiklós.

Road 85 from Sopron joins Road 1 3km after the village of Abda. Approximately 5km after this junction on the right there is a statue of Miklós Radnóti (1909–44), the poet who was killed by the Nazis near here whilst on an enforced march westwards (Miklós Melocco, 1980).

This flat region is known as the *Little Plain* (Kisalföld). A sunken basin, which was filled up and flattened by waters from the Alps, it includes some of the country's most valuable agricultural land. Its excellent soil and fair climate facilitate highly productive plant-cultivation and livestock breeding.

Hungarians settled on the Little Plain at the time of the Magyar conquest. National minorities have also lived in the region in considerable numbers.

There were Germanic settlers from as early as the 13C, and Croatians began to arrive from the 16C. The grander houses of the Little Plain's villages represent the highest level reached by the traditional peasantry in Hungary. A selection of peasant houses, characteristic of the local vernacular architecture, have been moved and set up in the open-air Ethnographical Museum near Szentendre (see p 235).

In the centre of this rich farm region, the town of **Győr** (see Rte 2 was founded at the intersection of four rivers. Road 1 runs through the town, along Tanácsköztársaság útja and past the late 19C neo-Baroque Town Hall in Szabadság tér. Győr is treated as a separate route (starting from the Town Hall) which can be found on p 91.

The 60km stretch of Road 1 between Győr and Tatabánya is one of the most dangerous in Hungary. The road is actually a half-completed motorway (M1) and although there is only one lane in each direction the eastbound lane towards Budapest has a hard shoulder with a good tarmac surface. Drivers heading towards the capital often move wholly or partially onto the hard shoulder to allow faster cars to overtake. Although common, this is both illegal and dangerous as the hard shoulder should be left free for vehicles with problems. What is worse is that drivers heading in the opposite direction, towards Győr, are aware of the habit and often begin to overtake even when the road is not clear, flashing their lights at oncoming vehicles to try and force them off the carriageway and onto the hard shoulder. Foreign drivers visiting Hungary should take especial care on this section.

TATA (pop. 26,000) lies 54km beyond Győr just to the N of Road 1. The town is situated between the Vértes and Gerecse mountains and the area is full of springs, lakes and canals. There is a large lake, the **Old Lake** (Öreg-tó), in the centre of Tata itself.

Much of the rebuilding of Tata, after centuries of wars, took place in the 18C under the direction of the architect Jakab Fellner. He was born in Moravia in 1722 and moved to Tata when he was 22 years old. He designed many of the Baroque buildings in Tata and the surrounding area, and also worked in Veszprém and Eger. He died in Tata in 1780. A *statue of Fellner* (Lajos Ungvári, 1940) stands beside the twin-spired *Nagytemplom* (Large Church) in Kossuth tér. The late-Baroque church itself was designed by Fellner and József Grossman, and was constructed between 1751 and 1787. In front of the church, on top of a 17m-high obelisk, is a Baroque *Immaculata* statue (Antal Schweiger, 1785). It stands on the site of the sanctuary of a 15C Church of St. Blaise which used to be here.

The former *Esterházy Mansion* nearby in November 7 tér was also designed by Fellner and built in 1765–69. The Habsburg king, Francis (Ferenc I of Hungary), fled from Napoleon and lived here for three months. On 14 October 1809 he signed the Schönbrunn Peace Treaty here. Today the building serves as a hospital. In the former synagogue in November 7 tér there is now a *Collection of Replicas of Greek and Roman Statues*. (Open May–Oct 10.00–18.00 except Monday.)

The **Old Castle** (Öreg-vár) stands surrounded by a moat in the middle of Tata by the NW end of the lake. A palace was built here in the early years of the 15C. King Sigismund lived here for a while in the 1420s. Of the original four towers, only one is still surviving. The building was badly damaged during the Turkish wars and the Habsburgs had it burned down in 1707. In 1755 Jakab Fellner redesigned the bridge over the moat and in 1897 the castle was rebuilt for a visit of Ferenc József.

The castle today houses the *Domokos Kuny Museum*. Kuny (1754–1822) was a ceramist and master of faience who learnt his skills in Tata. The exhibitions include archaeological finds from the earliest times, a medieval stonework collection, and a selection of old Tata pottery and ceramic art. (Open 10.00–18.00 except Monday; Nov–April Tues–Sat 10.00–14.00, Sun 10.00–16.00.)

In Bartók Béla u., stands the former *Capuchin Church*, built in Baroque style in the 1740s to the design of József Kuttner from Komárom. The attached monastery was added in the following years. Országgyűlés tér, at the end of Bartók Béla u., is so-called because a 'parliamentary' session took place here under Ulászló II in 1510. (The name means 'national assembly square'.) The wooden *Clock Tower*, with four clock faces, which stands in the square was designed by Fellner and made entirely from wood in 1763 by József Éder.

A large number of water-mills used to exist in Tata and several can still be seen today. The former Nepomucenus Mill, at No. 1 Alkotmány u., was designed by Jakab Fellner and built in 1758. Today it is the *German Ethnic Minority Museum* which covers the history of the German ethnic group in Hungary. (Open 10.00–18.00 except Monday; Nov–April Tues–Sat 13.00–16.00, Sun 10.00–16.00.) Nearer the castle, at No. 3 Bartók Béla út.,is the *Cifra Mill* (Ornate Mill), with red marble window frames. It was originally built in the 16C and reconstructed in 1753.

By the northern side of the lake, along Tópart, there is a former small abbatoir. The thatched Baroque building was designed by Fellner and built around 1780. Today it is the *Butchers Museum* exhibiting items relating to the local trade in the 18C and to the history of the butchers' guilds in Tata. (Open May–Sept 10.00–18.00 except Monday.)

Vértesszőlős is 5km to the SE of Tata on Road 100. The archaeologist László Vértes made some sensational finds here in the 1960s when the remains of a prehistoric human settlement thought to be almost half a million years old were discovered in a cave. It is one of the oldest such finds in Europe. Some relics are displayed at the National Museum in Budapest but other remains can be seen in situ in the former cave. (Open in the summer months Tues–Fri 10.00–15.00, Sat and Sun 10.00–18.00.)

Road 1 becomes a completed two-lane motorway (the M1) at **Tatabánya**, 56km from Budapest. Tatabánya (pop. 76,000) is an industrial town noted for its coal-mining industry. It is also the capital of Komárom county. At No. 38 Felszabadulás tér there is an *Industrial and Labour History Museum* covering the period between the two world wars. (Open 10.00–20.00 except Monday.)

One of the largest bird statues in Europe can be seen at the top of the hill to the left as the motorway begins to climb on the northern side of Tatabánya. The *Turul Statue* standing here, representing the mythical, eagle-like bird and symbol of the ancient Magyars, was sculpted by Gyula Donáth and erected in 1896 as part of the Millenary celebrations marking the 1000th anniversary of the Hungarian conquest. The bird's wing-spread is 14m and the sword of Prince Árpád in its claws is 12.5m long.

Just before the outskirts of the capital, at Budaörs, the M1 motorway joins the M7 from Lake Balaton, and enters Budapest from the SW. The two major signposted routes are for Petőfi-híd (Petőfi Bridge) and Erzsébet-híd (Elizabeth Bridge). The former crosses the Danube to Boráros tér at the southern end of the Great Boulevard in Pest. The latter crosses the river to Felszabadulás tér in the centre of Pest.

2   Győr

GYŐR (pop. 131,000) is the major industrial town of western Hungary. Its engineering works with its associated football team are known throughout Europe. The manager of the Rába engineering company, Ede Horváth, was a noted pioneer of new styles of management in Hungary in the 1980s. Notwithstanding its industrial connections and despite the fact that most visitors simply pass through the town, situated as it is on the major through-route from Vienna to Budapest, Győr has a significant history and many valuable monuments and places of interest, almost all of which are in a relatively confined area which can be visited quite easily.

Tourist Information: Ciklámen Tourist, 22 Aradi Vértanúk útja (96/11-557).

Rail Station: Révai Miklós u. 2 hours by express from the Western and the Eastern Railway Station, Budapest.

Bus Station: Hunyadi u. 2¼ hours from Engels tér, Budapest.

Post Office: 46 Bajcsy-Zsilinszky u.

Police: 54 Zrínyi u.

History. Győr is situated in the centre of the Kisalföld (Little Plain) at the junction of three rivers, the Danube, Rába and Rábca. In the Roman period it was called *Arrabona*, a name which originates from the Celts who inhabited the area in the last centuries BC. King Stephen established an episcopal see at Győr in the 11C and during the Middle Ages the town was an important economic centre due to its riverside position.
   A fortress was built in the mid-16C to protect the town against the approaching Turks, who only managed to occupy Győr for four years in the 1590s. For most of the period when the Turks were in Hungary Győr belonged to that part of the country under the rule of the Habsburgs. Thus Baroque art appeared in Győr much earlier than in other places, where its development was delayed until after the Turks had been driven out.
   In 1809 the town was occupied by Napoleon's armies who were pressing into Hungary from Italy. Napoleon himself stayed in Győr on one occasion. The occupation was considered to be important by the French who inscribed Győr's German name, Raab, on the Arc de Triomphe in Paris.

The itinerary begins in SZABADSÁG TÉR on Tanácsköztársaság útja, which is the Győr stretch of the main Vienna–Budapest road. The neo-Baroque *Town Hall* with its 58m-high tower on the S side of the square was designed by Jenő Hüber and built in 1896–98. A musical clock made in the Pécs workshop of Lajos Gulácsi was added in 1985. It occasionally plays a short piece by the local composer, Attila Reményi.
   In front of the Town Hall to the W stands the *1919 Republic of Councils Monument* (Ferenc Kovács) and to the E is the *Liberation Monument* (János Konyorcsik). Farther to the E, on the other side of the road leading up to the Lenin bridge, in the corner of the small park, there is a large bronze memorial erected on the *30th anniversary of the liberation* in 1975. The sculptor was Pál Pátzay (1896–1979) who was born at Kapuvár not far from Győr.
   The modern building (József Cserhalmy and Tamás Fátay, 1971) opposite the Town Hall on the N side of the square is occupied by offices including those of the County Council and the local water authority. The *bronze relief* in front by Sándor Mikus commemorates the 700th anniversary of the town and depicts the following scenes from the history of Győr (from left to right): Stephen V (1270–72) endows the town with privileges; recapture of the castle from the Turks in 1598; the March events of 1848; armed workers in 1919; 1945 liberation; the new coat of arms of the town.

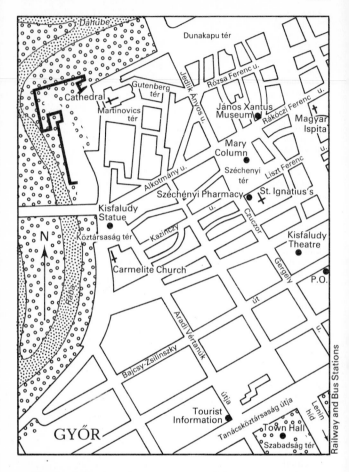

The county *Tourist Information Office* (Ciklámen Tourist) is on the W side of the square at No. 22 Aradi Vértanúk útja, on the corner with Tanácsköztársaság útja (tel. 11-557).

Aradi Vértanúk útja leads northwards to KÖZTÁRSASÁG TÉR passing the former Carmelite monastery in Egység tér which is today a modern hotel. Next to the monastery, facing northwards onto Köztársaság tér, there stands the **Carmelite Church**.

The Carmelites settled in Hungary in the Middle Ages. They were especially supported by the Angevin King, Louis the Great who ruled Hungary from 1342 to 1382 and who founded a monastery for the order on Castle Hill in Buda. The monastery at Győr was founded in 1697. Four years later in April 1701 the Austrian Carmelite province separated from the German order and became independent which gave an impetus to construction work.

The church was built extremely quickly between 1721 and 1725 to the plans of Martin Wittwer a lay brother of the order. Two other lay brothers were also central in the construction and decoration of the church. One of them, Martino Altomonte, painted the altarpieces. Born in Naples in 1657, he became an important figure of Austrian and Central European Baroque painting. The wooden carvings of the high altar, side altars, pulpit and pews are the work of the other lay brother, Franz Richter, originally a joiner's mate from Münster.

The main façade of the church is divided into three parts by four piers with Doric capitals. A strongly emphasised cornice also divides it horizontally into two. Above the stone-framed double gate, which bears the date 1724, the Carmelite coat of arms can be seen. Above it is a hand holding the fiery sword of Elijah and a ribbon with a Latin inscription reading 'I worked zealously for the Lord of hosts'. The statues in the niches represent 16C reformers of the Carmelite Order—on the left, St. Teresa of Avila showing a book with her heart pierced by an arrow, and on the right St. John of the Cross. In the centre, above the cornice, there is a statue of the Virgin Mary.

To the right of the façade there is an open chapel built in 1891. Inside there is a statue of *Mary of the Foam* brought here from an island on the river Rába. The name derives from the belief that the statue's powers once held back a flood on the Rába. The sculptor is unknown but written sources indicate that it dates from the first half of the 18C.

The *high altar* was the last to be completed among the furnishings of the interior. It is vertically divided into three parts. The lower part, about 2m high, is decorated with reliefs illustrating events in the life of Mary, such as the Nativity, Annunciation and Flight into Egypt. The four gilded wooden statues standing in front of the columns are the work of Franz Richter and represent Albert, Patriarch of Jerusalem, Elijah, Elisha and Cyril, Patriarch of Jerusalem. The main altarpiece shows King Stephen and his son Imre paying homage to the Holy Virgin. The upper, smaller painting shows Moses in front of the burning bush. The ornate *pulpit* was designed by Wittwer and carved by Richter. It was finished in 1726. Seated figures of the four evangelists can be seen on the lower protruding part of the rail. The central part has a relief of the Madonna and two smaller reliefs depict the Carmelites St. John of the Cross and St. Teresa of Avila. Beside the sanctuary Wittwer designed a chapel known as the 'dark chapel' because it has no windows. It is known also as the *Loreto Chapel* because it was built after the Santa Casa occupying the centre of the basilica of Loreto in Italy. A Black Madonna, made in 1717, crowned and with the infant Jesus on her arm, stands in the chapel. It is a copy of a statue also found in Loreto. The chapel has been built of brick and its interior is mostly unplastered.

An earthquake in 1763 did much damage to the church but it was repaired in the following years. In the 1780s Joseph II ordered that the properties be turned into a county or district office. In fact this never happened but because the order had to move from Buda Győr became the largest Carmelite centre in Hungary in the 19C. During the French occupation of the town in 1809 many people took refuge in the monastery as happened later following the 1848–49 War of Independence. Dénes Pázmándy, for example, a former President of the National Assembly, sought refuge here. The church suffered badly during World War II but restoration was undertaken in the following years.

The statue in front of the Carmelite church in the middle of Köztársaság tér is of *Károly Kisfaludy* (1788–1830) a poet and playwright (Lajos Mátrai, 1890). At the NE corner of Köztársaság tér by the river there is a statue of *King Stephen I*, the work of Ferenc

Medgyessy. The house with the Copf façade and balcony at *No. 13* to the E of the church was built in 1778–82 for Ferenc Zichy, Bishop of Győr. Above is the coat of arms of the Ott family, who owned the house at a later date. *No. 12* dates from the 16C. The two corner oriel windows are characteristic of Győr.

Alkotmány u. starts on the N side of the last-mentioned house. No. 4, just into the street on the right, is the so-called *Napoleon House*, where Napoleon stayed on 31 August 1809 while on a fleeting visit to Győr. Originally 17C, it was rebuilt c 1767 in Baroque style and then again in the 1890s. Since 1963 it has housed the *Picture Gallery* of the János Xantus Museum. (Open 10.00–18.00; Oct–March 10.00–17.00; closed Mondays.)

The northern corner building at the end of Alkotmány u. is actually numbered *No. 11* Köztársaság tér. Dating from the beginning of the 18C it is probably the first three-storey building of the town. At the end of the 19C the Győr branch of the Austro-Hungarian Bank rebuilt both the interior and the exterior giving it an Eclectic façade, though the windows retain some Baroque elements.

The route now begins the short climb northwards up Káptalan-domb (Chapter Hill). Immediately on the left, at the bottom of the incline, in the building numbered No. 5 Köztársaság tér, there is the entrance to the *Collection of Stonework* from Roman and later times, which is housed in the part 16C, part 17C underground fortifications. Access to a section of the old bastions and town walls can also be had from inside. (Open April–Oct 10.00–18.00 except Monday.)

KÁPTALANDOMB is dominated by the **Cathedral**. (Open 9.15–12.00, 14.00–18.00.) The foundations are thought to date back to the time of St. Stephen though much rebuilding has taken place ever since. The chancel with three apses, however, is 12C Romanesque. The Mongol invasion resulted in serious damage and afterwards, in the 1480s, the church was enlarged in Gothic style. The cathedral was further damaged during the Turkish wars. It was reconstructed in the 17C when the Baroque elements appeared. Further work in the 1820s resulted in the present basic form of the cathedral, though some items are even later, such as the bronze gate which was made by a local craftsman in 1938.

The interior is decorated with frescoes by the Austrian painter, Franz Anton Maulbertsch. The *Transfiguration* (1781) is depicted on the ceiling above the nave, the *Assumption of the Blessed Virgin* on the main altarpiece, and the *Hungarian Saints before God* above the chancel. The late-Baroque main altar and the other interior furnishings follow the designs of Menyhért Hefele.

The *bishop's throne* was a gift from Maria Theresa. Above it is a painting depicting the foundation of the Győr episcopacy. The richly decorated Baroque *organ* was begun in the early 1760s and the middle part survives from that time. In the middle of the ornamentation King David is shown with a harp. Around him six angels are playing instruments. Above is a ceiling fresco with the words of the Magnificat.

The Gothic *St. Ladislas Chapel* by the S aisle just beyond the main entrance was built in 1404. On the altar is the **reliquary bust of St. Ladislas** which is considered one of the most valuable surviving examples of medieval Hungarian goldsmith's work. It dates from around 1400, though some parts are later additions. It was originally made for the cathedral at Nagyvárad (today Oradea in Romania) where Ladislas I (1077–95) was buried. In the 16C it was moved to various places and was finally brought to Győr in 1606.

The reliquary bust of St. Ladislas in Győr Cathedral is an outstanding piece of medieval applied art.

Opposite the main façade of the cathedral is the *Bishop's Palace*. The oldest parts are 13C but much rebuilding has taken place over the years particularly in the last century. Medieval Gothic sedilia can be seen in the gateway under the tower to the NW of the Cathedral.

The large building with three protruding façades that can be seen from here to the NE of the cathedral is the former *Priests' Seminary* (Papnevelő Intézet). One of the largest buildings on the hill, it was constructed between 1686 and 1688, though the third floor was added in 1732. The earthquake in 1763 necessitated rebuilding over the next four years which was when it achieved its present form.

MARTINOVICS TÉR is on the S side of the cathedral. It is named after Ignác Martinovics (1755–95) the leader of the Hungarian Jacobins who was executed in Buda. In the middle of the small square is a Rococo statue of *St. Michael the Archangel* (*Szent Mihály-szobor*) which dates from 1764. The Latin inscription associated with St. Michael, 'Quis sicut Deus' (who is like unto God) can be seen on the statue. In front of the statue there are the foundation stones of an 11C Romanesque chapel.

On the wall of the cathedral, facing the square there is a *memorial relief* to the 19th Győr Infantry of World War I (Adorján Horváth, 1926). The inscription reads: 'Was all that blood shed in vain?'—a reference to the loss of Hungarian territory after the war. The relief and the sentiment are a typical product of the inter-war period.

The modern building on the S side of the square was constructed in the 1980s and is the guest house of the Rába engineering firm. On the E side, at No. 2, is a building originally dating from the 17C–18C built from the stones of a former bishop's palace, though the present façade is from c 1800. Today it houses the *Miklós Borsos Collection* where a selection of the artist's sculptures, paintings and graphics are permanently exhibited. (Open 10.00–18.00; Oct–March 9.30–16.30; closed Mondays.)

Miklós Borsos, a self-taught artist, was born in 1906 and has had a somewhat chequered career, which included being expelled from the Győr grammar school, being refused admittance to the Budapest Academy of Fine Arts and being dismissed from a teaching post at the Academy of Applied Arts. Today, however, he is widely acknowledged for his sculptures: he is the creator of the most commonly referred to monument in Hungary—the 'Zero Kilometre' stone in Budapest's Clark Ádám tér from which all distances to and from the capital are measured.

From the NE corner of the square at the back of the cathedral the route continues down KÁPTALANDOMB UTCA. The building at *No. 15* with a Copf façade and two entrance gates framed in red marble was constructed in 1655 from four previous buildings. It later became the Győr Provost's house. *No. 13*, a two-storey house with a Baroque façade, at one time belonged to István Telekessy, the Canon of Győr, who later became Bishop of Eger in which post he was the only Hungarian Catholic prelate to support Ferenc Rákóczi's War of Independence against the Habsburgs in the first decade of the 18C. From here Telekessy directed the rebuilding of the cathedral after the Turkish period. The statue of the Madonna in the niche in the courtyard was brought here by him in 1695.

GUTENBERG TÉR is at the bottom of the short Káptalandomb u. The **Ark of the Covenant** standing here is one of Győr's finest Baroque monuments. It was constructed in 1731 probably to the design of Joseph Emanuel Fischer.

Tradition has it that here in 1729 soldiers knocked the monstrance out of the priest's hands during the Corpus Christi procession as they were trying to capture a fugitive soldier. To assuage the ensuing general anger over the incident King Charles III had the monument erected two years later.
Duna-Kapu tér is 30m to the N along Jedlik Ányos u. In the middle of this open area which is used for markets there is one of Győr's symbols on top of the well, an *iron weather-cock*. The Turks placed such a weather-cock above one of the gates of the town and vowed they would never leave Győr until the cock crowed.

Rózsa Ferenc u. runs E from Gutenberg tér. No. 1, on the corner with Jedlik Ányos u., is a classical building dating from c 1820. Inside is the *Margit Kovács Collection*. Kovács (1902–77) was born in Győr. The exhibition is a selection of her ceramics. (Open 10.00–18.00; Oct–March 10.00–17.00; closed Mondays.)

The route now continues S to SZÉCHENYI TÉR, Győr's main square and formerly a market place. The Baroque building at the NW corner, *No. 17 Alkotmány u.*, has fine wrought-iron work dating from c 1770 showing the coat of arms of Gábor Esterházy. To the left of the oriel window is a niche with a statue of the crowned Mary.

Moving from W to E along the N side of the square, the simple

Baroque building at *No. 1* dates from the 18C. The two niches contain an Immaculata and St. John of Nepomuk. *No. 2* dates from the 17C, while *No. 3*, with four pilasters and a tympanum, got its present form in the 19C. *No. 4* is the so-called 'Iron Beam House' (Vastuskós-ház). It was built in early-Baroque style in the 17C though the third floor was added later. The name comes from the wooden beam studded with iron nails at the corner of the building. It was placed here in the early 19C by a tradesman, Mátyás Zittritsch, who owned the house at the time. It was an old Viennese custom for travelling journeymen to knock nails into such a beam as a sign that they had stayed there.

No. 5, to the E across Stelczer Lajos u., is today the *János Xantus Museum*. The exhibitions cover the history of Győr and its region from ancient times to the present day and include a collection of tiled stoves. Inside the museum there is also a specialist stamp collection of all the series of stamps printed in Hungary. (Open 10.00–18.00; Oct–March 10.00–17.00; closed Mondays.)

The main collection of the museum was originally started by Ferenc Rómer Flóris (1815–89), a priest, teacher, and one of the founders of Hungarian archaeology. It is named after another archaeologist and ethnographical researcher, János Xantus (1825–94) who finished school in Győr. Imprisoned for his participation in the events of 1848–49, he later travelled to England and then the United States where he worked as a labourer but subsequently joined a scientific expedition to Texas. He travelled to China and elsewhere on research projects commissioned by the US government.

The building was constructed in Baroque style for the Abbot of Pannonhalma in 1741–42. It belonged to the Benedictines until 1786 when it was taken over by the military, but it was returned to the order in 1802. From 1857 it was a theological academy and from 1910 a teachers' hostel. It has been a museum since 1948. The Baroque statues in the niches on either side of the oriel window are of St. Stephen and St. Benedict. The frescoes inside the main hall (the former refectory) are the work of a local artist, István Schaller, and date from 1756.

The building to the right of the museum at *No. 1* Rákóczi Ferenc u. was constructed between 1753 and 1774. It functioned as the Town Hall until 1898 when the new building was opened on today's Szabadság tér. A short way along Rákóczi Ferenc u., at *No. 6* on the right just beyond Gorkij u., is the *Magyar Ispita* (Hungarian Hospice) and its chapel. The hospice was founded as a home for the poor and aged in 1666 and rebuilt in 1724. Two arcaded Renaissance court-yards with Tuscan columns are notable features of the building. The Italian influence came from Italian craftsmen who worked on Győr Castle in the 16C and 17C. The fountain adorned with birds in the rear courtyard is the work of Miklós Borsos. The *chapel* dates from c 1730. It may have been designed by Martin Wittwer, the architect of the Carmelite church which also has its spire by the sanctuary.

The *Column of the Virgin Mary* standing in Széchenyi tér was erected by the Bishop of Győr, Lipót Kollonits, to commemorate the recapture of Buda Castle from the Turks in 1686. This type of column was very common in Austria. The base is decorated with reliefs above which are four statues—St. Stephen, St. John the Baptist, St. Anthony of Padua and St. Leopold. Behind them are more reliefs depicting events of church history. At the top of the marble column is a sculpture of Mary with the Child Jesus. Their Baroque crowns were removed in the 1870s during restoration work but replaced during further work 100 years later. The balustrade around the base of the statue is 20C.

LISZT FERENC U. runs eastwards from the SE corner of the square and has a number of historic buildings. *No. 1* was originally built in 1565 for László Alsoky. The Latin inscription 'Curia Nobilitaris' asserts that the owner had the nobleman's privilege of being exempt from taxation and from having to billet soldiers. This privilege was granted by the Habsburg Emperor, Maximilian I. *No. 6* used to be a college for the nobility but from 1777 to 1869 belonged to the National Academy of Drawing. The Copf façade is late 18C. Today it is a music school. The large, neo-classical building at *No. 13* used to be the County Hall, though a church and house belonging to the Franciscans originally stood on the site. The building has been redesigned several times and gained its present form in 1826 when the County purchased the property. Today it houses the County Archives.

The **Church of St. Ignatius**, on the S side of the square, was originally built between 1634 and 1641 for the Jesuits who had been in Győr since 1627, but it later passed into the hands of the Benedictines. The architect of this Baroque church was the Italian-born Baccio del Bianco. The domes on top of the two towers were added in 1726. Much of the interior is 18C. Of particular interest is the painting in the sanctuary of the Apotheosis of St. Ignatius, by the Viennese artist Paul Troger (1744), and an altarpiece (1642, oil on canvas) in one of the side chapels depicting the Patron of Hungary with her Saints.

The former Jesuit monastery stands to the right of the church. It was started in 1651 and completed under the direction of Bishop György Széchényi in 1667. The room to the right of the gateway, at the corner of the square, was made especially for a pharmacy. It has a beautiful interior design. Today the *Széchényi Pharmacy* is unique in that it is both a museum and a working pharmacy. The vaulted ceiling is richly coated with stuccoes in Rococo style and Baroque frescoes made between 1660 and 1670. The frescoes on the ceiling, depicting the Assumption in the middle and the four drug plant symbols on the vaults, have religious iconographic interpretations. The Latin names given to the medicinal plants do not correspond with either their contemporary or their later denominations: they are references which glorify the Virgin Mary. Behind the counter is an oil painting of the founder, Bishop György Széchényi, painted at the end of the 18C. (Open 8.00–17.00; Wed 13.00–17.00; Sun 9.00–13.00; closed Saturdays.)

Czuczor Gergely u. leads S from the side of the pharmacy. On the left across Schweidel u. stands one of Hungary's most modern theatres, the *Kisfaludy Theatre*. The 700-seat theatre was opened on 7 November 1978. The ceramic design on the exterior is the work of the Hungarian-born Victor Vasarely. The theatre is the home of the Győr Ballet Company which, under the direction of Iván Markó, has won international acclaim.

The class graduating from the Budapest State Ballet Institute in 1979 stayed together to set up the then newest ballet company in Hungary. They requested as their leader Iván Markó who had been for seven years the leading dancer of Maurice Béjart's 20th Century Ballet. He gave up his international career to start another promising but risky venture in this provincial town of Hungary. The aim of the new company was to be an ensemble different from the traditional. 'Since my childhood I have had a permanent conflict with classical ballet,' Markó once stated. 'I could not express myself and I sense the reason for it. Contemporary man is missing from classical ballet.'

Czuczor Gergely u. ends at Tanácsköztársaság útja which, to the right, leads to Szabadság tér.

Excursions from Győr

Pannonhalma is 20km to the SE of Győr on Road 82. The **Benedictine Monastery** and **Church** here have a history dating back to the early years of the Hungarian state. The monastery was founded by Prince Géza in 996 and, according to the deed of foundation dating from 1001, the building was completed by his son, King (St.) Stephen I. Destroyed by fire, the church was rebuilt in 1137. During the first quarter of the 13C it was completely remodelled. Work began in 1217 under the direction of Abbot Oros who had brought masons and other craftsmen from Italy. It was around this time that the regulations governing the Hungarian Benedictine order were redrafted along stricter Cistercian lines and this may explain why this church was built with certain characteristic features of Cistercian architecture, such as the eastern rose window. The church was finally consecrated in November 1225 in the presence of Andrew II (1205–35).

No serious damage occurred during the Mongol invasion and the structure remained more or less intact up to the time of King Matthias. In 1486 the side aisles were enlarged and a Gothic chapel added on the N side. During the Turkish period the hill on which the monastery stood was turned into a fortified complex, nevertheless serious damage was sustained by the building. In the early 18C repairs included the construction of the two neo-Romanesque gates by the side of the steps leading up to the raised chancel and the installation of Baroque furniture.

In the late 1820s neo-classical elements, such as the 55m-high tower were added. (The mosaic above the door at the base of the tower was added later in 1907 and is the work of Miksa Róth.) New wings were added to the monastery and for a number of years from 1867 Ferenc Storno of Sopron was engaged on restoration, recarving the walls and sculptures, and providing the church with a new, neo-Romanesque interior. The marble and cedar-wood altar is his work, as is the red marble, neo-Romanesque gate on the S side by the cloisters. Above the five double columns on either side of the gate there are rich limestone carvings, and above the door St. Martin is depicted cutting his cloak.

In the early 1940s a secondary school and dormitory were added to the buildings which are divided by a number of courtyards. There is still a Benedictine monastery and school at Pannonhalma today. It was one of the few ecclesiastical institutions belonging to a religious order which did not fall victim to the anti-religious measures of the early 1950s.

The **Pannonhalma Abbey Collections** contain items of great value including rare documents from the Middle Ages. Among the archives, which lead from the cloisters, is the Latin deed of foundation of the Benedictine Abbey at Tihany dating from 1055, which contains a considerable number of words in Hungarian and represents the earliest surviving record of written Hungarian. The library on the N side was founded by King (St.) Ladislas (1077–95) and is the oldest in the country. The classical library building dates from

1824–27. The furnishings are in Empire style. The finely carved, cherry-wood book-cases contain some illuminated codices and other material from later periods. The art gallery has mainly 16C–18C works, including Italian, German and Dutch paintings.

(Open 8.30–17.00; Sundays and Church Holy days 10.30–17.00; closed Mondays.) Guided tours of the Abbey in English can be arranged, they are organised by the Benedictines (tel. 96/70191, 70022, 70024).

3   Sopron

SOPRON (pop. 57,000) is situated near Hungary's NW border with Austria, 6.5km along Road 84 from the Kligenbach–Sopron border crossing, which is SE of Eisenstadt. The town lies at the foot of the 300–400m-high Lövér Hills. Proximity to Austria means that the town is full of Western cars and that German is widely spoken in public places. Entry into Hungary is so easy for Austrians (no visa being required of them) that they readily cross the border for shopping, hairdressing or dental treatment at prices much lower than at home. There are plans to make a tariff-free commercial zone in the neighbourhood of Sopron.

Sopron has no large monuments, its attraction rather lies in its compact town centre which has retained a medieval atmosphere, with a remarkably high number of listed buildings. Being the centre of a vine-growing region (the local wine is 'kéfrankos') Sopron also has many wine cellars.

Tourist Information: Ciklámen Tourist, 8 Ógabona tér (99/12-040).

Rail Station: Baross u. 3 hours by express from the Southern or the Eastern Railway Station, Budapest.

Bus Station: Lackner Kristóf u. 4¼ hours from Engels tér, Budapest.

Post Office: 7–10 Széchenyi tér.

Police: 7 Lackner Kristóf u.

History. The area has been inhabited continuously since neolithic times. In the late Iron Age several settlements surrounded by earthworks developed on the neighbouring hills. The Romans founded the town of *Scarbantia* here, which flourished for four centuries. During the following age of migrations various Germanic, Avar and Slav tribes settled in the area in quick succession. The Magyars arrived in the 10C.

The medieval walls of the town followed the previous line of the Roman walls. Sections can still be seen in Színház u. and Lenin körút which surround the inner city in the form of a horse-shoe. Neither the Mongols nor the Turks reached Sopron hence the town managed to escape the destruction that plagued most other Hungarian settlements. As a consequence Sopron is the most 'medieval' of any Hungarian town in that numerous Gothic architectural elements have survived although most of them are incorporated into later Baroque structures.

The town suffered serious damage in World War II but careful restoration of medieval and Baroque buildings took place in the 1960s and 1970s and in 1975 the Hamburg-based FvS Foundation awarded Sopron the gold medal of its Europe Prize for its success in protecting its historic monuments. Sopron has more buildings (mainly former dwelling houses) listed as historic monuments than any other provincial Hungarian town.

Most of Sopron's sights are within and around the compact historic town surrounded by the town walls. The route begins at the *Fire Tower* (Tűztorony) at the N end of the historic town. The 61m-high tower stands on the site of a former Roman gate. The lower, square part, dates from the 10C–12C, the cylindrical part is 16C and the Baroque upper section, with arcaded balcony and spire, dates from the early 1680s. It was used as a look-out tower to warn of fire. Trumpeters used to play when dignitaries arrived or to signal the time of day. This tradition has been revived today in that a recorded fanfare is played from the tower at selected times. Visitors can ascend the tower for a fine view of Sopron. Inside there is a small historical display. (Open 10.00–18.00; Nov–March 10.00–16.00; closed Mondays.)

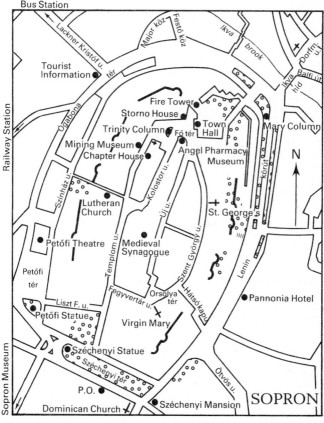

The neo-Baroque *Fidelity Gate* (Hűség-kapu) at the bottom of the tower on its S side was added in 1922 (Zsigmond Kisfaludi Strobl and Rezső Hikisch). A sitting Hungaria is shown surrounded by kneeling citizens. There is the Sopron coat of arms and the inscription 'Civitas Fidelissima' (The most faithful town).

Sopron and its surroundings had been given to Austria as part of the Trianon Peace Treaty in 1920. In the only such referendum to be held the population voted by 72 per cent in December 1921 to return to Hungary, hence the 'most faithful' epithet.

The famous *bronze key* on the wall on the left by the N side of the Tower was placed here in 1977 to mark the 700th anniversary of Sopron's designation as a city.

The itinerary begins in the direction of FŐ TÉR, a few metres to the S of the Fire Tower. The large Eclectic building on the left, adjoining the Tower, is the *Town Hall* (Városház). When it was being built in 1895 three large Roman marble statues of Jupiter, Juno and Minerva were unearthed. They can be viewed in the Fabricius House nearby.

The decorated Baroque *Trinity Column* (Szentháromság-szobor) which stands in the middle of Fő tér dates from 1695–1701. The sculptor is unknown but it was commissioned by Jakab Löwenburg and his wife Katalin Thököly. There are two kneeling statues of them on the E side and their patron saints are shown on the base.

All the houses in the square are listed buildings. No. 2 on the S side is the *Angel Pharmacy Museum* (Angyal Patika Múzeum) based in the oldest pharmacy in the town. The first apothecary's shop in Sopron was founded by Tóbiás Marb in c 1601. It moved here in the mid-17C and functioned for over 300 years. The museum-pharmacy displays documents and materials relating to the history of pharmacy in Sopron. (Open 9.00–18.00; Nov–March 9.00–17.00; closed Mondays.)

The original Gothic building was transformed into a two-storeyed house in 1656–58. It was reconstructed in 1850 to the plans of Franz Wasitzky. During renovations in 1966–67, prior to the opening of the museum, the building regained its 18C look. The interior walnut fittings in Biedermeier neo-classical style date from the first half of the 19C.

The *Gambrinus House* is round the corner to the right of the museum at No. 3 Fő tér. The two-storey building was originally Gothic. The façade with its cast-iron balcony is 18C Baroque. In the 15C the building served as the town hall.

The *Storno House* stands on the corner at No. 8 on the N side of the square. Built originally in the 15C it was transformed into a Renaissance corner house in 1560 and then rebuilt in Baroque style in the 18C. The Renaissance courtyard has been retained. Above the Baroque gate is the coat of arms of the Festetich family who owned the building at one time. The plaques on the wall record that both King Matthias, in 1482–83, and Ferenc Liszt, in 1840 and 1881, stayed here. Inside is a small museum of modern Sopron (16C to today) and the private collection of the Storno family who lived here from 1872. Ferenc Storno (1821–1907) was a painter, restorer and architect who restored several medieval churches in Hungary. His son, also called Ferenc (1851–1938), was likewise a painter and restorer. The family amassed a large collection of household items, furniture, paintings, jugs, decorated boxes, clocks etc. The private collection can only be viewed in guided groups. (Open 10.00–18.00; winter months 10.00–16.30; closed Mondays.)

No. 7 next door is the 'Lackner' or 'Tábornok' House, also originally medieval. In 1631 Kristóf Lackner, the mayor of Sopron, left the house to the town in his will. Later, members of the military command had their headquarters here (*tárbornok* means general). Lackner's coat of arms can be seen with his saying 'Fiat Voluntas tua' (Let your will be). The building has an interesting courtyard. The

Fabricius House (No. 6 Fő tér) was built on Roman foundations in Gothic style but received its present form in the 17C and 18C. In the Gothic cellar there is a collection of Roman stonework. On the upper floors there are exhibitions of archaeological finds in the Sopron area and a section showing furniture from the 17C–18C. (Open 10.00–18.00; Nov–March 10.00–17.00; closed Mondays.)

No. 5 on the W side of the square is the former County Hall designed by Vincel Hild in neo-classical style and built in 1828–34. In the tympanum is the old Sopron shire arms, designed by Zsigmond Kisfaludi Strobl. The building today houses the county archives and has an exhibition about the town's history from the 12C. The building on its left at *No. 4* dates in part from the Middle Ages as can be seen from the Gothic windows. Ferdinand II of Habsburg stayed here in the 17C as did Leopold I, King and Emperor, later.

The triple-aisled *Goat Church* (Kecske templom) was originally built from 1280 to 1300 for the Franciscans but later came into the possession of the Benedictines, so it is also known as the Benedictine Church. The 48m-high tower dates from the first quarter of the 14C. The small tabernacle dates from 1491 and the Gothic pulpit is also 15C. Otherwise the interior is mainly Baroque and Rococo. The altarpiece was painted in the 1770s partly by István Dorfmeister (1729–97) an Austrian artist who came to live in Sopron and who was one of the leading masters of Baroque painting in Hungary.

The name of the church is taken from the coat of arms of Henrik Gaisel, who donated considerable sums towards its construction. In the 17C five sessions of the Diet and three coronations were held here.

The Chapter House, Sopron. A fine relic of medieval architecture.

TEMPLOM UTCA leads S from Fő tér. *No. 1* on the left, next to the church, was once a medieval monastery that was later ruined. Its present shape dates from 1745 but the original 14C *Chapter House* inside is a fine example of medieval architecture. It was originally a hall with a flat ceiling which was converted around 1330 into a hall with two side aisles and cross vaulting. The vaulting is supported by octagonal pillars. The capitals, consoles and bosses are decorated with images said to represent the deadly sins. Tracery windows and fragments of frescoes have also survived. (Open 10.00–12.00, 14.00–16.00 except Mondays.)

The former Esterházy Mansion at *No. 2* opposite has the arms of the Esterházy family above the gate and above that a statue of Mary of Mariazell. The Baroque building today houses the *Central Mining Museum* (Központi Bányászati Múzeum) of the Ministry of Industry. The oldest coal mines in Hungary were opened in the 18C at Brennberg near Sopron. The museum deals with all aspects of the history of mining in Hungary. (Open 10.00–18.00; Nov–March 10.00–16.00; closed Wednesdays.) *No. 4* was where the Entente Committee counted the votes in the historic referendum of 1921. *No. 6* was built on medieval foundations. It received its present form c 1710. During the Reform Period of 1825–48 the house was a frequent meeting place for progressive intellectuals.

The late-Baroque *Lutheran Church* on the right was built in 1782–83 though the 52m neo-Romanesque tower, designed by Lajos Förster, was added 80 years later.

In 1674 all Evangelical churches were confiscated and the Lutherans in Sopron had to conduct their services in various houses. In 1676 permission was granted for a wooden church to be built on this site but it burnt down two years later and was rebuilt in the form of a prayer house. In the early 1720s a small stone church was built, which was replaced by the present building in the 1780s. The tower came later because of a decree of Joseph II forbidding towers on Lutheran churches at the time.

The *Sopron Collection of the National Lutheran Museum* (Evangélikus Országos Múzeum Soproni Gyűteménye) is at No. 12 Templom u. on the right after the church. The original two-storey medieval building had an additional floor added c 1770. It was bought by the Lutherans in 1866. (Open April to mid-Sept: Mon, Thurs, Sat and Sun 10.00–13.00).

No. 15 on the left has a neo-Renaissance loggia in the courtyard. The building was originally Gothic, but it was rebuilt in the 18C. The richly ornamented façade and gateway of the so-called *Töpler House* at No. 22 on the right dates from the second half of the 19C although the three-storey house was originally Baroque.

Dr Károly Töpler bought the house in 1828 and lived here for over 20 years. He devoted his life to the fight against contagious diseases and was active in the cholera epidemic of 1830–31. Struck down by disease himself, he died in 1850.

FEGYVERTÁR UTCA branches off Templom u. to the left. *No. 3* on the right is a two-storey Baroque house built c 1680. Ferenc Greiner bought it in 1695 and his family ran a coach service and Sopron's first mail service from here for three generations. *No. 2–2/a* was originally built in 1619 to serve as an armoury (*fegyvertár*), from which the street derives its name. In 1778 the arms were auctioned off and the building then functioned as a school until 1857 when it was sold to a private owner.

Fegyvertár u. leads into ORSOLYA TÉR, the site of a former market known as Salt-market. *No. 3* on the right is today a school. Formerly two residential houses, the Ursuline order bought it in 1848. The Romantic neo-Gothic façade is the work of Ferdinand Handler who also designed the neo-Gothic *Church of the Virgin Mary* next door, which was built in 1861–64. An Ursuline convent stood here in the 18C. The *Catholic Collection of Sopron* (Soproni Katolikus Egyházművészeti Gyűtemény) is based at No. 2 on the left of the church in the former Ursuline school building. (Open in summer months Mon and Thurs 10.00–16.00; Sun 11.00–16.00.)

The *Mary Fountain* in the middle of the square dates from the second half of the 18C but has only been standing here since the 1930s. Seriously damaged in the Second World War it was restored by Ernő Szakál. No. 5, to the N of the fountain, is the *Lábas-ház* (Arcaded House). Bombing in World War II revealed the arcade which dates from c 1570. It was probably walled-in during the 19C. There used to be slaughter houses under the arches. Today the building houses an information office and is also used for temporary exhibitions.

ÚJ UTCA leads off from the NW corner of Orsolya tér. In the Middle Ages it was known as Zsidó u. (Jewish Street) and was the centre of the Jewish community in Sopron. Documents indicate that Jews inhabited Sopron from the 9C–10C. They were expelled in 1526 and from then until the mid-19C there were no Jews in Sopron. At No. 22–24, about half-way along the street on the left, is a *Medieval Synagogue* which was probably built c 1300–20. The building was converted into a Renaissance dwelling house following the expulsion of the Jews. It came to light in 1967 and has been carefully restored. There are two rooms and a ritual bath in the courtyard. The synagogue, one of the smallest in Europe, is set back from the street because of rules regarding the necessity of a fenced courtyard for dealings with Christians. A text in English is available. (Open 10.00–17.00; Nov–March 10.00–16.00; closed Tuesdays.)

The attractive two-storey building at *No. 16* on the left, with a red façade, was originally a medieval residential house and dates from c 1480. It was later converted into Baroque style but during World War II the Gothic parts were revealed and these were carefully restored in the 1950s. Today it is the local office of the National Inspectorate for Historical Monuments.

No. 8, today a tourist hostel, has a half-storey above the first floor which was used for grain storage and is characteristic of buildings in Sopron. The house itself was originally medieval but has been rebuilt several times.

At the N end of Új utca SZENT GYÖRGY UTCA swings to the right and leads southwards. In 1677 Leopold I gave the building at *No. 3* Szent György u. to the Jesuits who remained here until their order was dissolved in 1773. The Festetics family bought it in 1786 and later rebuilt it, together with the adjoining No. l, to the designs of Lőrinc Nenmayer. When the building was restored in the 1950s Gothic elements were revealed. The medieval windows are clearly visible on the exterior, as are the vaults in the café on the ground floor. The building is a good example of the results of restoration work in Sopron.

The Baroque *Káptalan-ház* (Chapter House) at No. 7 was built c 1650 by István Vitnyédi, an official of the town.

The building materials were provided free by Vitnyédi but many citizens objected to his grandiose plans. Above the gate are sculpted two men's heads, one with his tongue sticking out. Legend has it that this refers to the owner's quarrel with the town. The house was confiscated from Vitnyédi following his participation in the so-called Wesselényi plot against the Habsburgs and given to the Jesuits in 1674. From 1779 and for the following 200 years it was owned by the Society of St. George.

The adjoining *St. George's Church* (Szt. György templom) was built in Gothic style at the turn of the 14C and 15C. Serious damage caused by a fire in 1676 was followed by reconstruction in Baroque style though several medieval elements remain. Above the gate, for example, there is original Gothic work with reliefs of St. Margaret of Antioch and St. George and the Dragon. Above these are statues of Mary and Joseph. The baptistery, near the front of the church on the left, has a fragment of a 15C fresco of St. George. The tower behind the chancel, however, is late 19C.

No. 12 opposite the church has the Brandenburg coat of arms above the exterior gate. Protestant services were held in the courtyard in the 1670s, the ornamental ballustrade on the first floor serving as a pulpit. *No. 14* is the temporary home of the *Forestry Museum*. (Open 9.30–13.30 except Wednesday.) *No. 11* on the left was designed by György Unger in 1852 for the Lenk family. Under the window above the gate on the Romantic façade is a relief entitled 'Marvellous fishing'. On either side is a Moorish head, the symbol of the Lenk family. *No. 16*, on the right, is the former Erdődy mansion, rebuilt by the Széchény family in early-Rococo style in 1740. The ground floor is decorated with shells and Rococo patterns; there is fine floral ornamentation on the Corinthian pilasters.

No. 13 across the street was built at the end of the 17C though the façade was altered in the mid-19C. The three-storey building at *No. 15* was originally medieval and received its Baroque form in the late 17C. Two small Gothic windows can be seen on the first floor and one on the ground floor. The courtyard gives access to a view of a *rondella* of the medieval town walls. The so-called *Sax House* stands at No. 22 on the right of Szent György u. The late-Renaissance façade dates from the end of the 17C. The plaque on the wall indicates that the linguist, writer and university teacher Miklós Révai (1750–1807) once lived here.

Turning left into the short HÁTSÓKAPU, *No. 2* on the right-hand corner is the so-called 'Caesar House'. Originally medieval, it was rebuilt following fire damage. Medieval stone windows can still be seen on each side of the balcony and on the façade which overlooks Szent György u. The gateway and garden give access to a view of the medieval town walls.

No. 1 on the left was the first residential tenement house in Sopron. It was built in neo-classical style in 1821–25. *No. 3* was built in 1773 for János Herbst, a chemist. The Golden Crown pharmacy operated here until 1866.

The route now continues to the left along LENIN KÖRÚT, and in an anti-clockwise direction along Színház u. and through Széchényi tér encircles the town on the outside of the line of the old medieval walls. The walls and some bastions are clearly visible on the left from parts of the first stretch of Lenin körút.

The *Pannonia Hotel* on the right at No. 75 is the former Arany Szarvas (Golden Stag) Inn. Johann Strauss the Younger is believed to have composed some of his works here. The building has suffered fire damage on several occasions. The present structure was designed by Móricz Hinträger and built in 1893. *No. 74*, further along on the left, with a rich Romantic exterior, was designed by Nándor Handler c 1860.

At the point where Lenin körút begins to turn to the left there stands the *Column of the Virgin Mary* (Mária-oszlop). In the Middle Ages the Church of Our Lady used to stand here. Later it was a site for regular markets. The column was designed by Andreas Altomonte and built in 1745 by Jakob Schletterer, a Viennese sculptor, and local craftsmen. At the top of the four corners of the base are angels with torches. The four reliefs depict Mary and Elizabeth; the Adoration of the Shepherds, Jesus in the Temple and the Angels' Welcome.

The two-storey house across the road at *No. 39* on the right just before the short Ikva híd is Baroque with original Gothic parts incorporated. IKVA HÍD (Ikva Bridge) crosses the hidden Ikva Brook and leads to Szentlélek u. on the left and Balfi út on the right. The *Church of the Holy Ghost* (Szentlélek-templom) here is 15C, rebuilt in 1782 with a Baroque interior. Inside are frescoes by István Dorfmeister (1729–97). No. 9–11 Balfi út houses the private *Zettl-Langer Collection* of weaponry, porcelain, paintings and other items accumulated by the manufacturer Gusztáv Zettl (1852–1917) and his grandson Herbert Langer. (Open 10.00–12.00.)

Dorfmeister u. at the side of the church leads N to Pozsonyi u., where at No. 9 on the left is the so-called *House of Two Moors* (Két mór-ház) which gets its name from the statues on either side of the gateway. The building is an example of rustic Baroque and was fashioned in the early 18C from two former gabled peasant houses. It was once in the possession of a stonemason who decorated the façade with carvings designed from trade sample books.

St. Michael's Church (Szent Mihály-templom) stands further up Pozsonyi út on the right. Construction was begun in the 13C but only finally completed in the early 16C. The lower part of the tower is medieval but the spire was added in the late 19C by Ferenc Storno. The sacristy to the right of the chancel dates from 1482 but most of the interior is Baroque. The altarpiece, 'Patrona Hungariae', is the work of Bartolomeo Altomonte (1739). In the cemetery to the right of the church is Sopron's oldest architectural monument, *St. James's Chapel* (Szent Jakab-kápolna), built in the mid-13C in a Romanesque-Gothic style. The chapel was renovated in 1960.

Returning to Ikva híd the route continues westwards along Lenin körút. *No. 37*, just after Ikva híd on the right' was designed by János Schármár and built in Eclectic style at the end of the 19C. The statue of St. Barbara on the façade dates from c 1750 and has survived from a previous building on this site. Across the road on the corner at *No. 42* Lenin körút is the smallest shop in Sopron. This watch repairer's, just 4 sq m, is probably also the smallest shop in the whole of Hungary.

No. 35 and *No. 33* are both examples of 19C neo-classical architecture, the latter being the earlier of the two. *No. 31* is a Baroque residential house from the 17C, though the present façade was added during the following century. The *Golden Lion Pharmacy* (Arany Oroszlán gyógyszertár) is at No. 29 Lenin körút. It was founded c 1600 by Márton Becher under the name 'Golden Eagle' at the neighbouring No. 31 and moved here in 1724. The portal is early 20C and was made at the Zsolnay factory in Pécs. To the right the tiles show a lion under a palm tree. The neo-Rococo interior fittings date from 1873. The building was renovated in 1988.

The building at *No. 25* received its present form in the 1730s and is a former Catholic convent. The courtyard has balconies and an arcaded first floor. Here there is a fresco of Mary Immaculate dating from 1752, though repainted by Kálmán Storno in 1925. *No. 19* with a Rococo façade was a public baths until 1830. Just past the mid-18C house, at No. 9, is the narrow *Festő köz* (Artist's Alley) and beyond that, at No. 7, a late-16C Renaissance house preserving medieval elements, the so-called *Rejpál House*. Just beyond this lies Májor köz on the right. The large yellow building (No. 3) set back from the main road is a former dwelling house of the employees of the Festetics family. It was built in 1760 though redesigned by Vencel Hild in 1820 and restored in 1985.

Lenin körút now curves round to the left to Ógabona tér. Lackner Kristóf u. joins from the right. On its corner, at No. 8 Ógabona tér, is the office of *Ciklamen Tourist*, the local county tourist information office for Győr-Sopron county. On the exterior wall overlooking Lackner Kristóf u. there is a large relief by Ernő Szakál in memory of Kistóf Lackner (1571–1631) a former mayor of Sopron.

SZÍNHÁZ UTCA begins on the other side of the small square and, running southwards, forms the western arc of the outer circle of the town walls. The Kraffka House is at *No. 10* on the right. This late-Baroque residential house, with six copf-style Corinthian pilasters and a wrought-iron balcony, was built in 1779. *No. 21* on the left was built in the early 19C in classical style as a residential house. Its richly ornamented façade has reliefs above the first floor windows depicting the four seasons (c 1815). An octagonal pavilion stands in the courtyard. The two-storey, neo-classical building at *No. 31* was designed by Ferdinand Hild and built in 1846. Towards the end of the century it was redesigned in Eclectic style. The courtyard has a well with a sculpture entitled *Fishergirl* which dates from the first half of the 19C. A bastion from the old walls can also be seen from here.

Színház u. ends in PETŐFI TÉR at the N end of which stands the *Petőfi Theatre* (Petőfi színház) designed by István Medgyasszay in 1909 in National Romantic style with folk motifs, a rare example of this style in Sopron.

Hungary's second stone theatre was built in Sopron in 1769 (the first was in Pozsony). It stood nearby on today's Liszt Ferenc u. A theatre was built on the present site in the early 1840s and functioned until 1909 when it was pulled down for fire safety reasons. Only the Doric columns remain from that building. Across from the theatre in the southern part of the square stands a statue of Sándor Petőfi (1823–49), the poet and revolutionary leader of the 1848–49 period.

From the SE corner of Petőfi tér the route leads into SZÉCHENYI TÉR, which marks the southern end of the inner city. Immediately on the left, at No. 15, is the large grey Eclectic building of the *Ferenc Liszt Cultural Centre* (Liszt Ferenc Kultúrház) which was built in 1872 to the designs of the Viennese architect Lajos Wächtler. The building houses the city library and is also the venue of concerts and other performances. To its right, occupying the W side of the square at No. 14, is the three-storey so-called *Újhelyi House*, designed by József Handler c 1850.

A bronze statue of *István Széchenyi* (1791–1860), the leading social and economic reformer of the 19C, stands in the W part of the square (1896; by Lajos Mátrai from a model by Miklós Izsó). There used to be a lake here in the early 19C. In 1829 it was drained and converted into a park for which Széchenyi donated 50 trees. At the other end of the square there are memorials to the heroes of the 1919 Republic of Councils and to those who gave their lives in 1944–45.

The four-storey Secessionist decorated building of the *Post Office* is at No. 7–10 in the middle of the S side of Széchenyi tér (Ambrus Orth and Emil Somló, 1911–13). It is worth entering to see the red marble staircase on the left, the woodwork of the doors and telephone boxes, and the interior with its 40m-wide iron and concrete structure.

No. 11, to the right of the Post Office, is the *Berzsenyi Dániel gimnázium* (secondary school). There was a building here standing in the 1650s. It was reconstructed in neo-classical style in 1825 and then in Eclectic style in 1894. In 1666 the rich library of the former Evangelical Lyceum was founded here. The wall plaques recall noted former pupils of the school including the poet Dániel Berzsenyi (1776–1836) after whom it is currently named.

The two-storey building with a classical façade at *No. 5* to the left of the Post Office dates from the mid-19C. The neighbouring *No. 3–4* dates from 1745–50 and is a former Dominican monastery. In the niche to the left of the first floor stone-framed windows is a statue of St. Dominic. The former *Dominican Church* stands at the SE corner of Széchenyi tér.

The Dominicans settled in Sopron in 1674 and bought this plot of land in 1700. The Baroque church was built between 1719 and 1725 under the direction of Lórinc Eisenkölbe. The two towers were added in 1775 and in 1777 the bells were commissioned from a Sopron master, György Köchel. The interior carvings are the work of Dominican monks from the mid-18C.

No. 1–2 on the E side of the square is the former *Széchenyi mansion*. The present three-storey neo-classical building dates from 1851 when Henrik Koch was commissioned to redesign the three separate houses which stood here. To the right of this building facing its southern wall at No. 2 Móricz Zsigmond u. is the so-called 'Somogyi' *House*. This three-storey Baroque building dates from 1766 though the façade was rebuilt in the first half of the 19C. The wooden gate with carved Rococo ornamentation is particularly attractive.

The three-storey Romantic building at the NE corner of Széchenyi tér was built in 1856 and today functions as a students' hostel. *No. 20* to its left was originally two-storeys and was designed by József Handler in 1855.

Other places of interest. The *Sopron Museum Ethnographical Collections* is housed in an Eclectic villa designed by Ottó Hofer in 1890, and is situated at No. 1 Május 1 tér on the corner of Múzeum u. to the SW of the town centre. The garden contains several medieval and Baroque stone monuments. Inside is a rich collection of varied materials relating to the history of Sopron and its region from the 17C to modern times, a collection of old stoves and a special Ferenc Liszt memorial room. (Open 10.00–18.00; Nov–March 10.00–17.00; closed Mondays.)

The *Bakery Museum* (Pékmúzeum) is situated in a former bakery at No. 5 Bécsi u. to the N of the centre. The building was originally a 17C dwelling house which was reconstructed in 1749. The display inside covers confectionary, bread and cake-making in Sopron. (Open 10.00–18.00; Nov–March 10.00–17.00; closed Mondays.)

Excursions from Sopron

The **Lövér Hills** to the S of the town provide an attractive setting for walking and recreation. They can be approached from several roads which ascend from Szabadság körút, which runs through the Lövérek suburbs south of the centre. A road near the Lövér swimming baths on the körút leads up towards the 23m-high *Károly Look-out Tower* (Károly-kilátó) from which a magnificent view of the surroundings can be had. (Open 9.00–18.00, winter months 9.00–16.00.)

Sopronbánfalva was once a separate village but is now a garden suburb of Sopron to the SW (c 8km) of the centre. (Take either Ady Endre út or Bánfalvi u.) The *Church of St. Mary Magdalene* (Mária-Magdolona-templom) has a 12C nave. The tower is early 14C and the chancel 15C. There are fragments of 12–13C frescoes. A series of 18C Baroque steps, with statues and balustrades, leads up to the *Church on the Hill* (Hegyi-templom) which originally belonged to the Pauline order and which from the end of the 19C was a Carmelite church. The Gothic 15C building was damaged by fire in the 18C and restored in Baroque style.

Brennbergbánya is 5km beyond Sopronbánfalva near the Austrian border in the middle of the Sopron Hills. Hungary's first coal mine was opened here in the mid-18C. Today one of the old engine houses at 14 Óbrennbergi u. contains a *Mining Museum* displaying items about the history of the mine and the local labour movement. (Open 9.00–13.00 except Monday.)

Fertőrákos is 8km NE of Sopron near *Lake Fertő*. (Leave the town via Pozsonyi u. past St. Michael's Church.) The road passes through Sopronkőhida where, on Christmas Eve 1944, the anti-fascist, liberal politician, Endre Bajcsy-Zsilinszky, was executed. *Fertőrákos Quarry* dates back to Roman times. Huge chambers cut into the rock have remained and in the summer concerts and performances are given here in the cave theatre fashioned out of the rocks. The *Castle Museum* at 153 Fő u. is situated in the former bishop's palace and has an exhibition of furniture. (Open May–Sept 9.00–15.00; Sat and Sun 9.00–17.00; closed Mondays.)

Most of Lake Fertő belongs to Austria. The shallow water is surrounded by a wide belt of reeds in which many varieties of waterfowl live. The lake itself is rich in fish. Plans are afoot to develop the recreational facilities around the lake.

4   Sopron to Győr

Roads 84, 85 and 1 connect Sopron and Győr, a distance of some 87km. The road is flat and passes through the so-called Small Plain (Kisalföld) region of NW Hungary.

Sopron—Road 84 6km turning for (2km) **Balf**—6km turning for Road 85—1km **Nagycenk**—12km turning at *Fertőszentmiklós* for (3km) **Fertőd**—12km **Kapuvár**—17km **Csorna**—15km turning at Enese for (14km) **Lébénymiklós**—12km junction with Road 1—6km **Győr**.

Road No. 84 leaves Sopron from the SE of the centre via Ötvös u. and Győri út. At the village of Kópháza, 6km from Sopron, there is a turning to **Balf**, which is 2km to the N. Bathing facilities were built here centuries ago following the discovery of sulphuric springs by the Romans. Today it is a spa and offers treatment for rheumatic disorders. The *Catholic Church*, which was restored at the end of the 1980s, dates from the 14C but was rebuilt later in Baroque style.

The junction of Roads 84 and 85 is 12km from Sopron. The route follows the left fork, Road 85, which is signposted for Győr. 1km along this road, on the right, stands the **Nagycenk Mansion** of the Széchényi family. It is one of the most famous country seats in Hungary. Although seriously damaged in the Second World War it has since been carefully restored.

For the past two centuries the village of Nagycenk has been closely associated with the Széchényi family. The place played an important part in Hungarian history and has often been referred to in Hungarian literature. Count Ferenc Széchényi (1754–1820) the founder of the Hungarian National Museum, and his son, Count István Széchenyi (1791–1860), the outstanding politician of the Reform Period, both lived here and are buried nearby.

The Baroque mansion was built at the end of the 18C though it was reconstructed between 1834 and 1840 under the direction of Ferdinand Hild, a Sopron architect. An avenue of lime trees planted in the mid-18C stretches for 3km in front of the mansion, across the main road.

István Széchenyi (he spelt his name differently from his father, omitting one of the accents) took over the management of Nagycenk in 1820 with the intention of establishing a model farm. Eight years later he divided the fields of Cenk between the estate and the bondmen living there, commenting in a letter at the time 'Let us set an example . . . [and] work for the public good, not only for our own profit'.

The mansion was lit by gas—the first time such a method had been used in Hungary. Széchenyi had smuggled the gas-generating equipment out of England in 1815 following his first visit there. A great anglophile, he introduced several technical novelties from England such as bathrooms and flush lavatories. He established the first stud in Hungary importing stallions and mares from England for the purpose. With a view to developing breeds he promoted horse-racing and encouraged English trainers and jockeys to come to Hungary.

Since 1973 the mansion has been the home of the *Széchenyi Memorial Museum* (Széchenyi Emlékmúzeum) which has a permanent exhibition about Széchenyi's household, his work and his achievements (a good guided tour on cassette is available in English and other languages) and an exhibition covering Hungarian industry from Széchenyi's time to the present century. (Open 10.00–18.00; Nov–March 10.00–17.00; closed Mondays.) A hotel and restaurant were opened in one of the restored outbuildings of the mansion in 1988.

Across the road from the mansion is a small *open-air transport museum* with old steam engines and railway equipment. From April to October at weekends a steam engine runs on a narrow-gauge railway to Fertőboz, a distance of approximately 4km.

Nagycenk village is 1.5km along the road on the W side of the mansion. In the centre of the village stands the neo-Romanesque *St. Stephen's Parish Church*, designed by Miklós Ybl and consecrated on St. Stephen's Day, August 20, 1864. Above the portal the coat of arms of the Széchényi family, held by two eagles, can be seen surrounded by the family motto: 'Si Deus pro nobis, quis contra nos' (If God is with us, who can be against us). The interior furnishings are in Romantic style. The altarpiece, 'St. Stephen offering the crown to the Virgin', is by a local painter, Károly Blaas (1863).

In front of the church stands a bronze statue of *István Széchenyi* (Alajos Stróbl, 1897). The inscription below the coat of arms on the base is Széchenyi's famous saying 'Magyarország nem volt, hanem lesz' (Hungary was not—but will be).

To the left of the parish church, in the cemetery across the road, stands the *Széchenyi Mausoleum*. The oval-shaped inner chapel was built in 1778 and the outer, neo-classical entrance hall was designed by József Ringer and constructed in 1806–10. The ceiling of the domed chapel has a fresco by István Dorfmeister. The crypt includes the graves of István Széchenyi and his wife Crescentia Seilern.

Following the events of 1848 Széchenyi was an inmate of a private asylum at Döbling near Vienna. Towards the end of the 1850s his health improved and he was able to resume some of his political activities, which included writing articles published anonymously in the London 'Times'. A relapse followed the confiscation of his papers by the police and on 8 April 1860 he put a bullet through his head.

His funeral deeply moved the whole country. His body was brought by train to Sopron and from there his coffin was carried on people's shoulders to Nagycenk. The Viennese police ordered the funeral to be held on 11 April, a day earlier than planned. Nevertheless about 6000 people attended the ceremony, and on the following day thousands more mourners arrived including a delegation from the Academy of Sciences which Széchenyi had founded. In three days as many as 50,000 people paid their respects.

1.5km to the E of Nagycenk along Road 85 is a turning for **Hidegség** situated 3km to the N. The apse of the *Roman Catholic Church* has one of the earliest frescoes of its kind in Hungary, dating from the 12C.

The **Esterházy Palace**, known as the 'Hungarian Versailles' stands 15km E of Nagycenk in the village of **Fertőd**, which lies 3km N of Road 85. (Take the left turning in the middle of Fertőszentmiklós.) It was built in the 1760s in Baroque style with Rococo and Louis XVI stylistic elements for the Hungarian nobleman, Prince Miklós Esterházy (1714–90). Restoration following decades of neglect and serious damage during World War II have made the building presentable, though somewhat bare and lifeless. The building is open to the public but individuals are only allowed to look round in the company of a guide. (Open 8.00–12.00, 13.00–17.00; mid-Sept to mid-April 8.00–12.00, 13.00–16.00; closed Mondays.)

A tripartite, richly ornamented, wrought-iron Rococo gate opens into the ceremonial courtyard. On both sides single-storey wings arch from the gates and continue in three-storey side-wings. A two-flight ceremonial staircase lined with Rococo iron railings leads to a balcony supported by double columns on the façade of the central section. To the rear of the building is a former French garden which is being re-planned.

The palace's 126 rooms were decorated with rich Rococo furniture and ornamentation, some of which has been restored. On the ceiling of the Banquet Hall there is Johann Basilius Grundemann's large fresco, 'Apollo on the Chariots of the Sun'. The two fireplaces are original. The Sala Terrena on the ground floor has been almost completely restored. The ceiling frescoes here are by Josef Ignaz Milldorfer; the floor is of white marble.

Most of the furnishings in the many rooms of the palace have been brought from elsewhere, but the fashion for chinoiserie at the time of its construction is clearly visible in several salons. The stoves collected and exhibited in one of the rooms on the ground floor are all original pieces from the palace.

The foundations of the Esterházy family's wealth were laid down in the period of the Counter-Reformation when Catholic and re-Catholicised nobles who had been loyal to the Habsburgs received enormous estates following the defeat of the 1703–11 Rákóczi War of Independence.

In the 1770s the palace was the scene of one dazzling, large-scale festival after the other. Games, feasts, garden festivities, ballets, concerts, hunting expeditions, balls, fireworks—all added to the French-style court atmosphere. A highlight was the visit of Empress Maria Theresa in early September 1773.

In 1761 the prince engaged Joseph Haydn, and from then on the composer spent much time here not only composing and conducting the orchestra but also handling administrative matters involving the musicians and the concert performances. Under Haydn's direction the opera and musical life at Esterháza (as it was then known) reached a very high level. During its golden age of 1770–90 at least one new opera performance was given each month. Today there is a *Haydn Memorial Room* inside the building.

Following the death of Miklós Esterházy in 1790 the palace started to decline. Within a quarter of a century it was in a state of virtual ruin and the park had fallen into decay. The former picture gallery, puppet theatre, Chinese house, pavilion-temples, hermitage and music house disappeared leaving only the main building in a ramshackle state. Some of the rooms were used for agricultural purposes. Sheep, for example, were kept in the Sala Terrena.

The building was neglected for nearly a century after which some restoration was undertaken by the Esterházy family, but war damage, neglect and theft in the 1940s all took their toll. The process began to be reversed only when a Botanical Experimental Station and a section of the Agricultural Technical School were located in the palace. Serious reconstruction started in the 1950s but due to the enormous costs is still unfinished today. There are plans to open an international hotel in the grounds and revive some of the former atmosphere by transforming Fertőd into a modern tourist centre.

Kapuvár lies 12km E of Fertőd on Road 85. A late-12C fortress used to stand here. Its castle was destroyed by the *Kuruc* forces during the Rákóczi War of Independence lest it would again become an imperial base. The *Rábaközi Múzeum* at No. 1 Fő tér is situated in a 1750 Baroque mansion formerly belonging to the Esterházy family. The museum exhibits items relating to the history of the region from prehistoric times to the present day and also has a display of local costumes. (Open 10.00–18.00 except Monday.)

The sculptor Pál Pátzay (1896–1979) was born in Kapuvár and a permanent exhibition of his work is displayed in the *Pál Pátzay Collection* at No. 1 Rába sor. (Open April–Oct 10.00–18.00 except Monday.)

Csorna, a further 17km to the E, has a *local history collection* (Helytörténeti Gyűjtemény) at No. 16 Szabadság tér, next to the late-18C Baroque church. The opening hours are unavailable at the time of writing due to repairs being undertaken.

At Enese, c 15km W of Csorna, there is a turning for **Lébénymiklós** which is about 14km to the N via Bezi and Győrsövényház. Here there is a former Benedictine Abbey Church which is one of the most important historic monuments of Romanesque architecture in Hungary (for further details see p 88). Those undertaking this short excursion can rejoin the main road to Győr at Öttevény, 8km to the E.

12km beyond Enese Road 85 joins Road 1 approximately 6km N of Győr.

5   Budapest

Beautiful Budapest—it is not an exaggeration. The Hungarian capital (pop. 2.1 million) straddles the River Danube in an almost perfect setting. On the right bank, the Buda Hills reach almost to the river side. Gellért Hill and Castle Hill provide splendid panoramas in all directions. Pest, on the left bank and connected to Buda by a series of attractive bridges, each with its own history, is the administrative and commercial centre of the capital.

From the turn of the century up to the Second World War Budapest was one of the outstanding cultural capitals of Central Europe, on a par with Vienna and Prague. Much of that old atmosphere has returned, partly as a result of a policy of liberalisation and opening up to the West, but more concretely because the city to a large extent looks very much as it used to before 1939. You will not find any towering office blocks in the centre of Budapest. New buildings have to conform in their proportions to the old ones, which, where possible, have been carefully restored.

Modern Budapest, with its predominant mixture of Eclectic and Art Nouveau architecture, is still very much a turn-of-the-century city. With its marvellous views, rich history, long hours of summer sunshine, street cafés and (for Westerners) cheap prices, it is an ideal place to visit.

Tourist Information: Tourinform, No. 2 Sütő u., Budapest V (tel. 1179-800).

Rail Stations: Western Railway Station, Lenin körút (by Marx tér); Eastern Railway Station, Baross tér; Southern Railway Station, Krisztina körút. (All three are on metro lines.)

Bus Stations: the Central Bus Station at Engels tér, Budapest V, is the main terminus for long-distance routes, though others also depart from the bus stations by Árpád Bridge metro and Népstadion metro.

Central Post Office: 13–19 Petőfi Sándor u., Budapest V. (There is a 24-hour post office at No. 105 Lenin körút, near the Western Railway Station and at the side of the Eastern Station in Baross tér.)

Central Police Station: No. 2 Deák tér, Budapest V.

History. Strictly speaking one can only refer to the history of Budapest after 1873, the year when the two parts, Buda on the right bank of the Danube and Pest on the left, were administratively united along with Óbuda. There had been plans to unify the capital prior to that, notably during the upheavals of 1848. The construction of the Chain Bridge in the 1840s, the first permanent link across the river, was both a symbolic and a practical step in uniting the divided capital. But it was not until the autumn of 1872 following the years of repression after 1848–49 and the Compromise with Austria in 1867 that the appropriate legislation to create Budapest was enacted.

The history of the area, however, can naturally be traced back much farther. Excavations show that people lived on both sides of the Danube here in the second millennium BC, though archaeological relics from even earlier times have also been discovered. Ornamented items from between the Copper and the Bronze Age have been discovered on Csepel island and cemeteries with hundreds of graves dating from the Bronze Age have been found at several places.

Among the various waves of immigrants the Scythians are known to have arrived in the 6C BC from the area of what is today the Soviet Union. In the 4C and 3C BC the Celts arrived from the territory which is now France. The most important of these were the Eravisci who settled around Gellért Hill. They introduced the potter's wheel and were the first to coin money in the region. The Eravisci stayed when the Romans arrived and assimilated into their culture. A wide range of archaeological relics have survived from the Eravisci period. They are preserved in the Hungarian National Museum and the Aquincum Museum.

In the 2C AD the Romans divided their province of Pannonia (today's Transdanubia, or western Hungary) into two parts. *Aquincum* was made the capital of Pannonia Inferior. (The name 'Aquincum' is probably of Celtic origin. 'Ak-Ink' is believed to mean 'good water' or 'abundant waters'.) The military camp was based in Óbuda in the area which is today at the Buda end of Árpád Bridge. The civilian town was further north, where the Aquincum Museum is today. In the 2C and 3C some 10,000 soldiers were garrisoned here. They built a series of fortifications along the right bank of the Danube to protect what was then the border of the Roman Empire.

With the decline of the Empire the attacks of nomadic peoples from the east could no longer be resisted. In the early 5C Aquincum was evacuated and the Huns moved in. Few Hun graves have been found in the area, but some medieval records suggest that the right bank was named after the Hun king Attila's brother, Buda. After Attila's death in 453, various Germanic peoples, Eastern Goths and Lombards occupied the area. Then from the 7C the Avars controlled the region.

The Hungarians arrived c 896 and besides Avars also found Slavs here. According to Anonymus, the mysterious chronicler of the 12C and 13C, the Hungarian leader, Prince Árpád settled his tribe on Csepel Island while the six other tribes spread out over the Carpathian basin. Following Árpád's death, princes from his family ruled the country. Prince Géza began the process of Christianising the Hungarians, realising that a spiritual and cultural adaptation to the West would help the Hungarians to survive. His son, Stephen, was crowned King of Hungary at Christmas 1000 with a crown sent by Pope Sylvester II. Stephen began to create a strong, centralised, Christian state but during his reign and that of his successors it was first Esztergom and then Székesfehérvár that was the administrative centre. It was only in the 12C that Buda and Pest started to develop, partly because of the French, German and Walloon settlers who were involved in commerce and crafts.

In 1241 the Mongols invading from Asia burnt Pest to the ground. People fled across to Buda. But in the winter the Danube froze over and the invaders were able to cross and plunder Buda, after which they proceeded to devastate the territory of Transdanubia. The Mongols retreated in 1242 after which King Béla IV, fearing another invasion, ordered that a series of castles be built around the country. One of them was at Buda. He also invited German settlers to repopulate the town which had been decimated by the invaders. The German name for Buda was Ofen which means 'oven', as does the word 'pest' which is of Slav origin. The names probably derive from the lime-kilns that could be found here. The older settlement to the north now became Óbuda (Old Buda).

With the death of Andrew III in 1301 the House of Árpád came to an end and several years of struggle for the throne ensued. It resulted in the victory of the Anjous of Naples. The first Angevin king, Charles Robert (1308–42) had his seat at Visegrád on the Danube Bend, but later moved it to Buda. His son, Louis I (1342–82) had a royal palace built on Castle Hill and granted rights to Buda whereby all passing merchants were obliged to stop there. Thus the importance of Buda rose considerably in relation to Pest.

During the reign of Sigismund of Luxembourg (1387–1487) a vast royal palace was built at Buda, the remains of which were only unearthed following World War II. Many mansions for aristocrats were built on Castle Hill at the same time.

The Turks were advancing on Hungary during the 15C but their advance was considerably delayed by the victory of János Hunyadi at Nándorfehérvár (Belgrade) in 1456. Two years later Hunyadi's younger son, Mátyás (Matthias), was elected king. Matthias Corvinus (his emblem was a raven—'corvus' in Latin) reigned from 1458 to 1490. He transformed Buda into one of the liveliest Renaissance cultural and artistic centres of Europe. Italian influence gained ground, helped by Matthias's second marriage to Beatrice of Aragon. One of the largest libraries in Europe was assembled and it was then that the celebrated 'Corvinae' manuscripts were created. Scholars and writers of all sorts flocked to the court as the King became a great patron of classical learning. The palace itself was enlarged in Renaissance style. The historian Antonio Bonfini spent several years at Buda and in his 'Rerum Hungaricarum Decades' recorded his observations of 'marble baptismal fonts ... spacious banqueting halls and superbly furnished bedchambers ... gilded ceilings ... lawns, gravel paths, fishponds and fountains'.

Following the death of Matthias a decline set in which resulted in a weakening of central power. The defeat of the Hungarian army by the Turks at Mohács in 1526 spelt disaster for the country and in 1541 the Ottomans were able to capture Buda Castle almost without a fight. For the next 145 years Turkish rule prevailed over both Pest and Buda, though the latter underwent 11 sieges during this period as the Habsburgs, who controlled the territories in the west and north-west of the country, tried to capture the castle.

Under the Turks the population declined, most churches were turned into mosques and little building took place apart from strengthening the defensive walls and, importantly, the building of several splendid baths which still survive today both as architectural monuments and as bathing establishments. To Evliya Çelebi, a Turkish scholar who travelled in Hungary in the 1660s, however, Buda was an impressive sight. According to his account, which may be slightly exaggerated, there were 34 mosques, four djamis, three dervish monasteries, six elementary schools, five high schools, a hundred leather workshops and four thermal baths in and around the Castle district.

In 1686, on the initiative and with the financial help of Pope Innocent XI, a pan-European Christian army was organised to recapture Buda (one of the volunteers was James FitzJames, the 16-year-old son of James II of England). The siege lasted for six weeks before the castle was finally retaken on 2 September. After the siege the Castle Hill was in ruins. In addition, as often happens with 'armies of liberation', looting, plunder and destruction followed. Pest, destroyed and looted, had less than 4000 inhabitants as late as 1700.

The new Habsburg rulers brought in settlers from Austria and Germany to replace the diminished population. Hungary had had one set of foreign rulers replaced with another. The Habsburgs, however, stayed much longer than the Turks. Their rule lasted well over 200 years and was only finally brought to an end with the First World War.

Hungary was now governed from Vienna. The Diet, when it did meet, convened in Pozsony (Bratislava). The armed struggle for Hungarian independence under Ferenc Rákóczi II, between 1703 and 1711, although heroic, ended in defeat. The reforms of Maria Theresa (1740–80) and her son, Joseph II (1780–90) were enacted with Austria's interest in mind and were coupled with Germanisation.

In the second half of the 18C development of both Buda and Pest took on a more intensive nature. The population, including the Hungarian proportion, grew, and cultural and political movements of a national character became stronger. The university was moved from Nagyszombat (Trnava in Czechoslovakia) first to Buda in 1777 and then to Pest in 1784. The political aspirations of the 'Hungarian Jacobins', however, were nipped in the bud with the execution in Buda in 1795 of Ignác Martinovics and his associates.

The 19C witnessed a great number of building projects in Pest. In 1808 the so-called Embellishment Committee was set up to direct the construction of the city according to modern town-planning principles. Its work was supported by the King's representative, the Archduke Joseph, who was Palatine of Hungary from 1796 to 1847. The great flood of 1838 caused very serious damage but gave an opportunity to rebuild Pest. It was at this time that Pest adopted the neo-classical style for its architecture, the most significant example being the National Museum (Mihály Pollack, 1848). Many classical town houses, however, also survive in the area between today's József Attila u. and Szent István körút.

It was also the time, particularly in the second quarter of the 19C, when Pest became the centre of the Reform Movement, which aimed at greater economic progress and cultural and political independence for the country. The Academy of Sciences was initiated in 1830, the National Theatre constructed in 1837 and the Chain Bridge commenced in 1839. The economic and cultural progress of the 19C finally shifted the balance of importance in the direction of Pest and away from Buda.

Pest was the centre of the 1848 revolution which broke out on March 15 in support of the Austrian uprising. Demonstrations were organised, the censorship was ignored and proclamations for independence were delivered from the steps of the newly completed National Museum. By 1849, however, the ensuing War of Independence had been lost and the short-lived Hungarian government dispersed. Hungary fell under even more repressive Austrian control. The citadel was built by the Austrians on Gellért hill as a symbol of their power.

The Compromise of 1867 which established the Austro-Hungarian Dual Monarchy and gave a limited amount of independence to Hungary paved the way for an upsurge of capitalist development which was centred, initially almost exclusively, in the capital. In 1870, as a successor to the Embellishment Committee, the Council of Public works was founded based on the example of the London Metropolitan Board of Works. This, together with the establishment of a unified Budapest in 1873, led to an architectural reorganisation of the city which included the construction of the great avenue now called Népköztársaság útja, the Great Boulevard and later the rebuilding of the inner city around today's Felszabadulás tér, all of which has given Budapest its characteristic late-19C Eclectic and turn-of-the-century Secessionist appearance.

The capital started to develop very fast. The population grew from under 300,000 in 1873 to 733,000 by 1900. Municipal public services were set up including gas, water, sewage and transport services. Budapest was the scene of the main Millenary celebrations of 1896 marking the occasion of the 1000th anniversary of the Magyar conquest. Bridges and public buildings were constructed, the European continent's first underground railway opened, Heroes' Square developed and the whole city decked out with the trappings of national pomp to mark the occasion. In 1902 the neo-Gothic parliament building by the Danube was completed. It is still one of Budapest's most impressive structures. Café society took off in the early years of this century and Budapest began to rival Vienna as a place to see and in which to be seen.

Hungary entered World War I as part of the Austro-Hungarian monarchy. Initial enthusiasm, as in other countries, soon wore off in the face of casualities, inflation, food shortages and increasing economic difficulties. Opposition movements with roots in the early workers' and trade union movement of the late 19C together with liberal political circles eventually forced the proclamation of a Hungarian Republic in November 1918. This was soon followed in 1919 by the short-lived Republic of Councils which based itself on the model of Soviet Russia. Primarily strong in Budapest (it failed to win the support of peasants by not decreeing the distribution of land) the Council Republic was overthrown after 133 days by a combination of external military intervention on the part of Romania and Czechoslovakia with the support of France, and internal conservative forces.

The years of the Horthy regime in the inter-war period saw an increasing number of nationalistic statues and monuments erected in the capital lamenting the loss of Hungarian territories at the Treaty of Trianon after World War I (most were removed after 1945). The rulers of the country were also occasionally disturbed by manifestations of opposition. One of these in Budapest, a hunger-march along the avenue to Heroes' Square, on 1 September 1930, was particularly large.

It was in the 1930s that Budapest became a spa centre on the map of European tourism. International celebrities including members of the British royal family flocked to the city. In 1938 Budapest was once again decked out with pomp for the occasions of the 34th World Eucharistic Congress, the 900th anniversary of the death of King (Saint) Stephen and the World Scout Jamboree.

The political drift to the right inevitably led to alliance with Nazi Germany and Hungary's entry into the war in 1941. On 19 March 1944 German troops occupied Hungary which was followed by one of the most tragic and difficult years for the Hungarian capital. Not only communists, but also all anti-fascist and democratic activists were rounded up. A Jewish ghetto was created and the deportation of the Jews began. When the Hungarian fascist Arrow Cross took over in the autumn of 1944 terror was unleashed on a wide scale. Many people were taken to be shot by the banks of the Danube.

The Soviet Red Army reached Budapest in December 1944. For nearly two months a bitter siege took place of the remaining Germans who were holding out on Castle Hill (they had previously blown up all the bridges). In the course of the fighting many buildings were damaged or destroyed. The Castle District and the Royal Palace were in ruins before the Soviets finally took the whole city on 13 February 1945.

Reconstruction of the city's basic services was the priority immediately after the war. Under the direction of the Communist mayor, Zoltán Vas, the population participated with an enthusiasm that is often shown at such times of emergency and rebuilding: buildings were repaired, the food supply restored and the bridges rebuilt all relatively quickly.

In 1950 Greater Budapest was created by merging the suburbs and neighbouring townships. By that time, though, the capital, like the rest of the country, was in the grip of the worst period of Stalinist rule under the Communist leader Mátyás Rákosi. Achievements tended to be recorded in terms of grandiose constructions such as the opening of the massive People's Stadium near the Eastern Railway Station in 1952.

The major events of the 1956 uprising all took place in Budapest— the demonstrations of 23 October, the shooting outside the radio building, the pulling down of Stalin's statue near the City Park, the attack on the party headquarters, and so on. The general strike continued in Budapest and factory councils continued to operate even for some time after the second Soviet intervention on 4 November.

Since 1956 Budapest, like the rest of the country, has undergone many changes. On the outskirts, tower-block estates have replaced the old slum areas. In the centre the Elizabeth Bridge, the last bridge to be rebuilt after the war, was opened in 1964, a modern metro network was constructed and the reconstruction of the Royal Palace was finally completed in the 1970s. A noteworthy architectural feature of the modern city centre is the lack of skyscrapers. The intention has been to restore what could be restored and only allow new buildings to be erected if they blended with the former environment. The best example of this is the Hilton Hotel on Castle Hill next to the Matthias Church. The achievements in this regard were recognised in 1988 when the panorama of the Danube embankment in Budapest was added to UNESCO's World Heritage List.

Today Budapest is a modern European capital city and increasingly the host of major international events of all descriptions.

A. The Castle District

The **Castle District** (Várnegyed) is the name give to the area of predominantly former dwelling houses in the northern part of Castle Hill (Várhegy). It stretches from Dísz tér in the S to Bécsi kapu tér and Kapistrán tér in the N, a distance of approximately 1km. This route, however, which includes the Coronation or Matthias Church, one of the symbols of Budapest, weaves around the various streets of the Castle District covering some 3km.

Castle Hill rises up to 60m above the Danube and is topped by an 11m-thick layer of limestone. A system of caves and passages running through the limestone was developed in the Middle Ages for defensive purposes. Archaeological investigations reveal that the hill was inhabited in prehistoric times but it was not until the mid-13C that there was any major settlement. It was then that, after the Mongol invasion of 1241–42, King Béla IV had a fortress built on the hill and a civilian population gathered around the royal quarters. Buda only became the permanent royal seat, however, in the 14C and 15C after the so-called New Palace was built during the reign of Sigismund of Luxemburg (1387–1487).

During the 15C King Matthias Corvinus (1458–90) had the Gothic palace enlarged and enriched with Renaissance elements. A humanist court developed

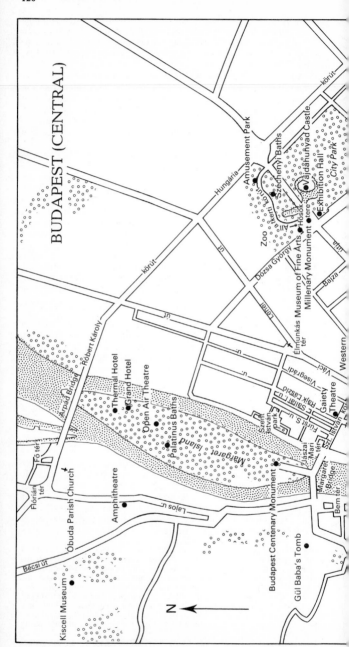

BUDAPEST (CENTRAL)

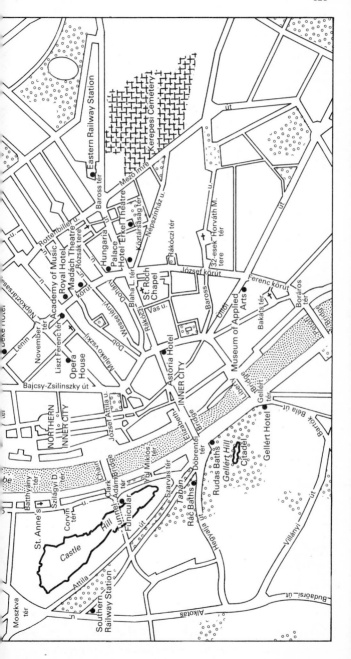

around Matthias representing one of the major centres of Renaissance culture in Europe and a golden era in Hungarian history. Decline set in following Matthias's death and the Turkish occupation of Buda in 1541 initiated a period of plunder and destruction. The churches were turned into mosques, most of the wealthy population fled and the houses were left to ruin.

Buda Castle was recaptured in 1686 by a united Christian army set up with the support of Pope Innocent XI. The victory over the Turks was proclaimed and celebrated all over the Christian world. But the long years of Ottoman rule, the destruction of the siege and the ravaging of the victorious armies had left the castle district with only just over 600 inhabitants as against 8000 in the time of Matthias. Reconstruction began slowly and continued into the following century. Former Gothic dwelling houses were rebuilt in Baroque style. This can clearly be seen today in the many houses which have Gothic sedilia in their gateways but Baroque upper floors.

Buda became a royal free borough in 1703 but the former splendour did not return as the Habsburgs maintained their rule from Vienna and the important government offices were situated in Pozsony (today Bratislava in Czechoslovakia).

During the 1848–49 War of Independence Buda Castle was occupied by the Hungarians and later recaptured by Austrian troops. Many dwellings again suffered serious damage and the Royal Palace which had been partially reconstructed in the previous century was burnt down. Following the unification of Buda, Pest and Óbuda in 1873 the Castle District started to develop once again. New government and official offices were built, the Matthias Church was reconstructed and the Palace enlarged.

World War II brought a further wave of destruction when, in the winter of 1944–45, German troops entrenched on Castle Hill attempted to hold out in face of the encroaching Red Army. By the time Budapest was finally liberated on 13 February not a single habitable house remained in the Castle District. Reconstruction of the area took place over the following 40 years.

The itinerary begins in DÍSZ TÉR at the southern end of the Castle District. It can be reached on bus No. 16 from the SE corner of Engels tér and on bus No. 116 from the University Library on Károlyi Mihály u. Private cars are only allowed into the Castle District with special permission but there is some parking space in and near Dísz tér.

The square was originally the site of St. George's Church which was built in the 14C, and after which it was called St. George's Square. The present name means 'Parade Square' and recalls that military parades were held here in the 19C. The *statue of a hussar* in the uniform of the time of Maria Theresa stands in the SW corner of the square (Zsigmond Kisfaludi Strobl, 1932).

The first hussars were South Slav light cavalry organised by King Matthias into a regiment in 1480. The name comes from the Latin *cursor* meaning runner. The hussars' fighting ability was based on speed as they carried no heavy armour. They excelled in close combat, surprise attacks and unexpected manoeuvres. Their arms were the curved sabre (later a broadsword); the pike, and the pointed dagger. They were noted throughout Europe for their heroic deeds and striking uniform. The word *hussar* is one of the few words which have passed from Hungarian into English.

To the SE of the square, across the cobbled area designated as Szent György tér, stands the **Castle Theatre** (Várszínház) the oldest extant theatre building in Budapest.

The Carmelite Church of St. John the Evangelist, founded by Béla IV in 1269, used to stand here. András III, the last of the Árpád kings, was buried here in 1301. During the Turkish period it was transformed into a mosque but in the siege of 1686 was destroyed. The Carmelites rebuilt a church here in 1736. Then in 1784 Joseph II dissolved the order and the church was vacated. The altar went to Sárospatak in eastern Hungary and the organ to St. Anne's in Watertown. Three years later Farkas Kempelen redesigned the interior as a theatre with an auditorium seating 1200. The German Theatre Company gave performances here from 1787. In October 1790 the first professional group of Hungarian actors, the Hungarian Theatre Company of László Kelemen, gave

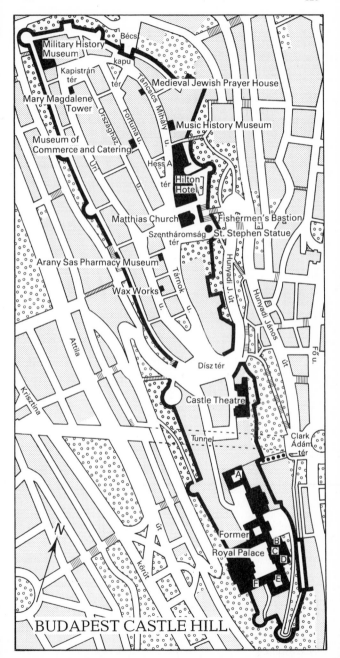

BUDAPEST CASTLE HILL

Military History Museum

Bécs kapu

Kapistrán tér

Tárnics Mihály

Medieval Jewish Prayer House

Mary Magdalene Tower

Országház

Fortuna u.

Music History Museum

Museum of Commerce and Catering

Úri

Hess A tér

Hilton Hotel

Matthias Church

Szentháromság tér

Fishermen's Bastion

St. Stephen Statue

Arany Sas Pharmacy Museum

Tárnok u.

Hunyadi J. út

Hunyadi János út

Fő u.

Wax Works

Attila

Kristina

Dísz tér

Castle Theatre

Tunnel

Clark Ádám tér

körút

Úri

Former Royal Palace

A

B
C
D

E

F

their first presentation here. Throughout most of the 19C German and Hungarian companies alternated. The theatre functioned until 1924 when parts of the gallery collapsed and then in 1943 the wooden furnishings were demolished for fire safety reasons. Serious damage in World War II necessitated structural reinforcements in 1948–50 and excavations preceded slow reconstruction. The original Baroque façade of Kempelen was restored and the theatre finally reopened in 1978.

The recently reconstructed building to the N of the theatre is the former *Alexander Palace*, the official residence of Hungarian Prime Ministers from 1867 to 1944.

In the northern part of Dísz tér is György Zala's 1893 *Honvéd Memorial* commemorating the 'honvéds' (soldiers) who broke into the castle during the 1848–49 War of Independence.

The former Batthyány Mansion stands at *No. 3* on the S side. It was designed in Baroque style by Márton Sigl and built in 1745–48. The neo-classical building opposite, at *No. 13*, dates from 1815. Reliefs above the first floor windows depict Diana, Rhea Sylvia and Pallas Athene. The neighbouring *No. 15* is an 18C building constructed on the remains of two medieval houses. *No. 6* on the S side is today the Algerian Embassy. The intricate wrought-iron work above the door is actually 20C, the work of Sándor Sima.

TÁRNOK UTCA. runs northwards from the NE corner of Dísz tér and derives its name from the 'tárnokmester' (treasurer), a court dignitary who dealt with the royal revenues. The street was a centre of commerce in the Middle Ages.

The house at *No. 1* on the right dates from the 15C but was rebuilt around 1700. The stone door frame was added in 1795. *No. 5* was built in Baroque style c 1725 using the walls of three former medieval houses. *No. 14* on the left was constructed in stages during the 14C and 15C. On the protruding first floor there used to be a 'palatinum', a hall characteristic of buildings in the Castle District. The paintwork on the façade was originally 16C though it was restored after the war in the early 1950s. *No. 16* dates from the 14C and 15C and has been rebuilt several times. Today it is the *Arany Hordó* (Golden Barrel) restaurant and beer-hall.

The *Arany Sas* (Golden Eagle) *Pharmacy Museum* occupies the building at No. 18 Tárnok u. (Open 10.30–17.30 except Monday.) The pharmacy was established in 1688 by Ferenc Ignác Bősinger, a former mayor. It was the first pharmacy in Buda Castle after the expulsion of the Turks. Originally in Dísz tér, it moved here in the mid-18C. The building was formerly a merchant's house and dates from the first half of the 15C. The present neo-classical façade is from 1820. Pál Pátzay's 1973 statue of a nude female stands just beyond the museum at the end of Balta köz.

Tárnok u. ends in SZENTHÁROMSÁG TÉR (Holy Trinity Square) in the middle of which stands the 16m limestone *Holy Trinity Column* (Szenháromság-szobor) which was originally commissioned by the Buda Council following a plague and made between 1710 and 1713 by Anton Hörger and Philip Ungleich. Seriously damaged in the Second World War it was resculpted in the 1960s. A relief on the plinth depicts the plague, another the construction of the column.

The Baroque building at the SW corner of the square and running the length of Szentháromság u. is the **former Buda Town Hall** (Buda Városháza) which was built at the beginning of the 18C by the Italian architect Venerio Ceresola. Today it houses the Academy of Sciences' Institute of Linguistic Research. On the corner of the building overlooking the square is a copy of a statue of Pallas Athene made in

1784 by Carlo Adami which used to stand nearby. The coat of arms of Buda is on the shield in the goddess's right hand. (The original statue can be seen inside the southern gateway of the Budapest City Council on Városház u. in Pest.)

The statue has become the symbol of the numerous architecture protection associations throughout Budapest. Twenty years ago a young cameraman, Mihály Ráday, used the statue as the centrepiece of a programme about the decay of architectural heritage (the spear in the goddess' left hand was often vandalised). Subsequently Ráday had a popular monthly TV series—'Unokáink se fogják látni' (Our grandchildren won't see it)—and the movement for the protection of the city's built environment became widespread.

The *Ruszwurm pastry-shop* has been at No. 7 Szentháromság u. since 1827. There used to be a gingerbread shop here in the Middle Ages.

The white building on the W side of Szentháromság tér at No. 7–8 belongs to *Pressinform*, the office which assists foreign journalists. The bronze statue of *Mercury* by the entrance is the work of Greek sculptor Agamemnon Makrisz (1981). The building to the right of Pressinform, actually *No. 2* Országház u., has been reconstructed since the war to reveal several medieval details. Traceried niches can be seen in the gateway as well as some arches of the 15C arcade in the courtyard. The wine cellar of the restaurant here has been fashioned out of a cave cut into the rock.

The *former Ministry of Finance* stands on the N side of Szentháromság tér. It was designed by Sándor Fellner in late-Eclectic style with Hungarian Secessionist ornamentation. Today it appears simpler than when it was first built in 1906. Some spires, for example, were destroyed in the war. In the 1960s the building functioned as a student hostel. It now houses the New Hungarian Central Archives, a management training school and other offices.

The Church of Our Lady (Nagyboldogasszony-templom), commonly known as the **Matthias Church** (Mátyás-templom) stands on the E side of the square. It has become a symbol of Buda and a popular tourist attraction, though it is still a working church with masses every morning and on Sundays.

Tradition has it that King Stephen built a small church dedicated to the Virgin Mary here in 1015 which was destroyed during the Mongol invasion of 1241–42. The present church was originally founded by Béla IV following that invasion. A 1255 charter mentions it being under construction. It was a basilica constructed in a style comparable with the northern French Gothic architecture of the period. It became the parish church of the Germans who had recently settled in Buda and whose numbers were growing due to the expanding trade of the town. The poorer Hungarians, who were mostly farmers, vinegrowers and craftsmen, had to make do with the less grandiose Church of Mary Magdalene at the northern end of the Castle District.
In 1302, after the death of András III, the last of the Árpád kings, the church was the scene of an extraordinary event in Hungarian history. The citizens and clergy of Buda 'excommunicated' Pope Boniface VIII for supporting Charles Robert of Anjou's claim to the throne in opposition to their favoured candidate, King Wenceslas of Bohemia. However, resistance crumbled after a few years and Charles Robert was crowned in the church in 1309. Apart from this occasion the church was not used as a coronation church in the Middle Ages. Hungarian kings were usually crowned in Székesfehérvár.
At the turn of the 14C the church was remodelled into a hall church in high Gothic style by Louis the Great and Sigismund of Luxemburg. A royal oratory was built during the reign of King Matthias Corvinus and the tower which had collapsed in 1384 was rebuilt. The church became the scene of ceremonies and political events. Matthias's two marriage ceremonies (with Catherine Podebrad and Beatrice of Aragon) both took place here amidst great splendour.

Following the Turkish victory over the Hungarians at the battle of Mohács in 1526 the ecclesiastical treasures of the church were transferred to Pozsony (today Bratislava). The Turks occupied Buda in 1541 and converted the church into the city's main mosque. It was called 'Eski' or 'Büyük' Djami ('Old' or 'Great' mosque). The medieval furnishings were destroyed as were the wall decorations. The two ornamental chandeliers above the high altar were taken to Constantinople where they still hang in St. Sophia's. Buda was finally recaptured from the Turks in 1686, following which the church was given first to the Franciscans and then later to the Jesuits who restored the building, decorating its interior with a rich Baroque style.

The church regained some of its former importance in the second half of the 19C. In 1867 the splendid coronation of Emperor Francis Joseph as king of Hungary (Ferenc József I) took place here to the music of Liszt's Coronation Mass, which had been specially composed for the occasion. Deterioration, however, necessitated reconstruction of the church and this took place under the direction of the architect Frigyes Schulek between 1873 and 1896. Where possible original structural and decorative elements were preserved but Schulek designed new elements of his own with the result that only parts of the main walls, the square bottom part of the southern tower, the interior pillars and some parts of the Mary Portal on the S façade are genuinely medieval.

The last king of Hungary, Charles IV, was crowned here in 1916 during World War I. During the siege of Budapest in the winter of 1944–45 the church was badly damaged and post-war restoration work was not completed until 1970.

The acoustics of the church have always been excellent. As early as the 15C, in the reign of King Matthias, a choir of 70 was singing chorales here. Today 50 to 60 concerts are held every year, particularly during the Budapest Spring Festival and the summer season.

On the tympanum of the main portal of the W façade overlooking Szentháromság tér there is a relief of the Madonna enthroned with angels. The work of Lajos Lantai (c 1890), it is made from coloured pyrogranite from the Zsolnay factory in Pécs. To the left is a large rose window and to its left is the N tower, named *Béla tower* after Béla IV, the founder of the church. The *S tower*, the most decorative part of the church, has two lower square storeys, which are medieval, below three octagonal upper storeys which are more or less a faithful copy of the tower built in Matthias's time. On the second of the upper storeys there is a copy of the Hungarian coat of arms together with the Corvinus coat of arms showing Matthias's symbol, the raven. The open-work structure and the stone spire decorated with crockets and gargoyles above is Schulek's design from the late 19C.

The *Mary Portal* stands on the S façade near the tower and dates from the reign of King Louis the Great (1342–82). On the exterior of the porch, in niches on either side of the gate, are statues of the 11C Hungarian kings St. Stephen and St. Ladislas. Inside, above the entrance, there is a multifigural scene of the Death of the Virgin. In the lower part Mary is seen kneeling with the 12 disciples and in the upper part Christ, surrounded by the four seated Evangelists, is receiving his mother's soul. The work is largely 14C. The parts that have been added later are painted brown.

Through the portal, on the inside wall of the S tower to the left, the original coat of arms of King Matthias can be seen. To its left, above the Mary Portal, are five circular paintings by Károly Lotz showing the birth and childhood of Christ. The walls and pillars of the interior of the church are covered by decorative painting made up of coloured floral and geometrical elements partly of medieval, partly of Art Nouveau character, designed by Bertalan Székely at the end of the 19C.

The *Loreto Chapel* is on the ground floor below the S tower. Above its wrought-iron gate is a wall-painting of the Virgin and inside is a Baroque Madonna of Italian style from c 1700.

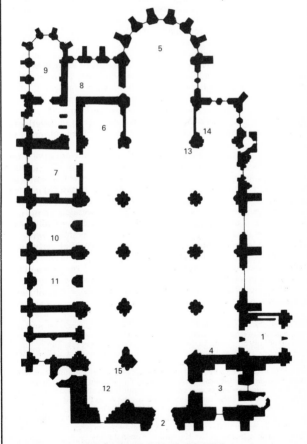

1 Mary portal
2 Main portal
3 Loreto Chapel below the South Tower
4 Coat of arms of King Matthias
5 High altar
6 St. Ladislas Chapel
7 Oratory of the Knights of Malta (above)
8 Royal oratory (above)
9 St. Stephen Chapel
10 Tomb of Béla III
11 St. Imre Chapel
12 Baptismal font below the Béla Tower
13 Pulpit
14 Entrance to the crypt
15 Medieval figural capitals

THE MATTHIAS CHURCH

There are two figural capitals from the Middle Ages in the bay
beneath the Béla tower. One represents a monster fighting with
dragons, the other a hooded and a bearded man with an open book.
The W wall of the tower has a recessed round window with the figure
of a lamb symbolising the Good Shepherd. The N wall is decorated
with a painting by Károly Lotz showing Pope Calixtus III ordering the
church bells to be tolled at noon every day in memory of János
Hunyadi's victory over the Turks at Nándorfehérvár (Belgrade) in
1456, which halted the Ottoman advance for nearly a century. In the
centre of the bay is a neo-Romanesque baptismal font.

The *St. Imre Chapel* is the first chapel on the N side of the church.
It has a wall-painting by Bertalan Székely depicting scenes from the
life of St. Francis of Assisi. The cabinets of the neo-Gothic triptych
contain wooden sculptures of St. Stephen, the first king of Hungary,
St. Imre, Stephen's son who died at the age of 24 in 1031, and St.
Gellért, Imre's tutor. The pictures on the wings by Mihály Zichy
represent four scenes from Imre's life: the prince's birth; visiting the
Benedictine Abbey at Pannonhalma in western Hungary; being
taught by Bishop Gellért; and on his death bed.

In the next chapel is the double sarcophagus of King Béla III and
his wife Anne of Châtillon. They were originally buried in the
cathedral at Székesfehérvár. Their graves were discovered during
excavations in 1848 and they were then brought here. The richly
carved sepulchral ornament above the sarcophagus (the work of
Ference Mikula and István Hausen) is an imitation of a portal of a
12C French cathedral and dates from the time of Schulek's
restoration.

The side chapel to the left of the chancel is covered with wall-
paintings by Károly Lotz depicting the life and funeral of St. Ladislas,
king of Hungary 1077–95. The chancel has a fine wrought-iron gate
and around the apse is a series of *sedilia* which had figural wall-
paintings in the Middle Ages. The *stained glass windows* in medieval
style are by Ede Kratzmann to the designs of Bertalan Székely and
Károly Lotz. On the left and above, the stone balcony with lions on
either side indicates the position of the royal oratory which was
added in Matthias's time. The high altar composed of early-Gothic
elements is the work of Schulek and replaced the former Baroque
altar. The neo-Gothic stone pulpit shows the four Evangelists and the
four Fathers of the Church. The stained glass windows on the
southern wall of the church represent the Virgin, St. Elizabeth and St.
Margaret.

Access to the *Museum of Ecclesiastical Art* is via the *crypt*, the entrance to
which is on the right of the chancel. (Open 8.30–20.00; Oct–March 9.00–19.00.)
Fragments of the original church are displayed in the crypt. The red marble
sarcophagus contains the bones found in the royal tombs of Székesfehérvár.
Stairs lead to the *St. Stephen Chapel* which Schulek designed. On the walls are
scenes from Stephen's life (Bertalan Székely) and on the columns are statues of
King Stephen and his wife Queen Gizella. The stained glass windows depict
various Hungarian saints and holy people and below the windows are sedilia
with rich tracery. Ecclesiastical items are displayed in the glass cabinet.
A neo-Gothic staircase leads up to the *Royal Oratory* (on the left) which
overlooks the chancel. Here is a small display of vestments including priests'
coronation robes and the coronation thrones of Francis Joseph and Charles IV.
There is also a replica of the Hungarian Crown Jewels.
Along the passage to the W is the *Oratory of the Knights of Malta* (Schulek's
design). The W wall is decorated with coats of arms of the Knights of Malta.
There is a copy here of the first Hungarian bible of 1626. The stairs lead to a
gallery stretching along the N wall of the church where monstrances, chalices
and various other ecclesiastical items are exhibited.

The large equestrian statue of *St. Stephen* by the exterior SE corner of the Matthias Church was designed by Alajos Stróbl in 1906. The neo-Romanesque limestone plinth was designed by Frigyes Schulek. The relief at the rear shows Schulek as a bearded figure kneeling before the king holding a model of the church.

The neo-Romanesque **Fishermen's Bastion** (Halászbástya) was also designed by Frigyes Schulek and built at the turn of the century as part of the reconstruction of the Matthias Church and its surroundings. Tradition has it that this stretch of the medieval ramparts used to be defended by the fishermen's guild, though the name might also derive from a nearby former fish market. The function of the present bastion was both decorative and to serve as a look-out terrace over the Danube. One of the best panoramas of the city can be viewed from here with Margaret Island, Margaret Bridge and the Parliament to the left, and the Chain Bridge, Forum and Intercontinental Hotels, Inner City Parish Church, Elizabeth Bridge and Gellért Hill to the right. Below the Fishermen's Bastion in Hunyadi János út which weaves up the hill stands a bronze statue of *János Hunyadi*, the 15C commander of battles against the Turks. There is also a replica of *St. George and the Dragon* by the noted 14C Hungarian sculptors, the Kolozsvári brothers. (The original is in Prague Castle.)

On the pillars of the NE tower of the Bastion are limestone statues of *Álmos* and *Előd*, two leaders of the ancient Magyar tribes (Ferenc Mikula, 1902). At the far N end of the Fishermen's Bastion, up the steps and through the gate, in the ruins of a former 13C Dominican church stands Károly Antal's 1937 statue of *Julianus and Gellért*, two Dominican friars who travelled to the East in 1235 in order to find the Hungarians who had remained there when the majority moved westwards in the mid-9C. Only Julianus, seen here pointing, was able to reach his goal, and on returning home he brought Béla IV news of the approaching Mongol invasion.

The Budapest *Hilton Hotel* was built in 1976 to the N of the Matthias Church. A Dominican church and monastery stood on this site in the Middle Ages, the ruins of which have been incorporated into the design of the modern hotel. The W façade of the hotel, by the main entrance in Hess András Tér, integrates the remains of an 18C Jesuit college, and on the outer wall of the so-called *St. Nicholas Tower*, to the left of the entrance, is a copy of the 1486 *Matthias relief*, which is held in the East German city of Bautzen and which was the only authentic representation of King Matthias made in his lifetime.

HESS ANDRÁS TÉR was named after the first Hungarian printer who had a workshop here and who printed in Latin the first book in Hungary in 1473, the so-called Buda Chronicle. In the middle of the square is a statue of *Pope Innocent XI* who supported and helped finance the Christian armies who came to drive the Turks out of Hungary In the 1680s. The statue, by József Damkó, was erected in 1936 on the 250th anniversary of the recapture of Buda Castle. The reliefs on the plinth commemorate the Polish king, Jan Sobieski, the Doge of Venice, and Leopold of Habsburg who also supported the anti-Turkish struggle.

No. 3 Hess András tér behind the statue is the former *Red Hedgehog* (Vörös Sün) *Inn*, mentioned in a census as early as 1686. In the 18C theatrical performances were also held here. The building was formed around 1700 by joining three medieval houses and in the early 19C it was rebuilt in neo-classical style. The first floor window frame on the Fortuna u. façade to the left and the 15C door in the gateway are Gothic, while the main façade, with the hedgehog relief above the door, is neo-classical.

The neo-classical building at *No. 4* on the W side of the square was also formed from three originally medieval houses. In the gateway of the building, which now houses the Fortuna restaurant, sedilia characteristic of the Castle District's medieval houses can still be seen.

The route now continues northwards from Hess András tér along TÁNCSICS MIHÁLY UTCA. Mihály Táncsics (1799–1884) was a champion of the peasants and of national independence. He was set free from prison in Buda by young revolutionaries on 15 March 1848. His radical demand the following year that any land over 2000 hold (2133 acres) in the possession of landlords be distributed amongst the needy was rejected by the leaders of the independent Hungarian government.

Until the age of twenty Táncsics worked as a serf; then he became a weaver. He was self-taught and travelled all over Europe. In 1846 he was the first to demand the emancipation of the serfs without compensation. After the defeat of the War of Independence he went underground for eight years under a death sentence, but reappeared in political life for a short time after the Compromise of 1867.

The *National Inspectorate for Historical Monuments* (Országos Műemléki Felügyelőség) has its headquarters at No. 1 Táncsics Mihály u. on the right, in an originally Baroque house built c 1775. The specialist *Museum of Hungarian Architecture* (Magyar Építészeti Múzeum) based here has a collection of documents, manuscripts and photographs relating to the history of architecture in Hungary over the centuries. Occasional temporary exhibitions are also staged in the building. (Open 10.00–18.00; Sun 10.00–16.00.)

No. 5 houses the 'Art Galerie' of the Creative Circle of Etchers where drawings, water-colours, medallions, plaques, statuettes, prints and other items can be purchased and exported duty free. The gateway is adorned with a copy of a relief from St. Stephen's Chapel in the Vatican of the Ellipse of History by the Hungarian-born sculptor Amerigo Tot (1909–84).

The *Music History Museum* occupies the former Erdődy Mansion at No. 7 Táncsics Mihály u. (Open Mon 16.00–21.00; Wed–Sun 10.00–18.00; closed Tuesdays.) The building was designed in Baroque style by Máté Nepauer and constructed between 1750 and 1769. The museum follows the development of Hungarian musical instruments from private production to the rise of an instrument-making industry. Inside there is also a reproduction of Béla Bartók's workshop and a collection of musical medals. Upstairs musicologists conduct their research and the Bartók archives are available to scholars. Concerts are often held in the building.

No. 9 is the site of the former Royal Mint which stood here in the Middle Ages. The present three-storey building, the former Joseph Barracks, was built c 1810 for military purposes and later served as a prison. Memorial plaques recall that it was here that Mihály Táncsics was imprisoned in 1847–48 and again from 1860 to 1867, and that Lajos Kossuth was also imprisoned here for three years in the late 1830s. Many other Hungarian patriots also spent time within these walls during the 19C.

No. 16 on the left was built c 1700 on medieval foundations and received its present Baroque façade in the second half of the 18C.

The fresco on the first floor shows Christ and the Virgin Mary surrounded by saints. The plaque at *No. 13* records that the poet and translator Árpád Tóth (1886–1928) spent the last ten years of his life here.

The *Medieval Jewish Prayer House* (Középkori Zsidó Imaház) at No. 26 Táncsics Mihály u. dates from the late 14C though the present building is 18C Baroque. Religious inscriptions and frescoes have been found here. In the doorway are some Jewish tombstones unearthed nearby and in the ground floor rooms religious objects and documents relating to the history of the Castle District's Jewish population are exhibited. (Open May–Oct 10.00–14.00; Sat and Sun 10.00–18.00; closed Mondays.) The remains of a 15C synagogue have been found in the garden of the house at No. 23 opposite but at the time of writing excavations have not been completed and nothing can be viewed.

Táncsics Mihály u. ends in BÉCSI KAPU TÉR (Vienna Gate Square), which gets its name from that of a medieval town-gate. The small single-steepled *Lutheran Church* on the left was designed by Mór Kollina and built in 1895–96. Concerts are occasionally held here in the summer. The present *gate* to the right was built in 1936 on the 250th anniversary of the recapture of Buda Castle from the Turks. The statue of the angel holding a cross in front of the gate, which is a *Monument to the recapture of Buda*, also dates from the same year and is the work of Béla Ohmann. Across the road is a memorial plaque in Latin commemorating the Swabian, Hessian, Würtembergian, Bavarian, Austrian, Flemish, Walloon, Spanish, Italian and Hungarian soldiers who formed the united Christian army which liberated Buda in 1686. Through the gate and to the right is the so-called *Europe Grove*, which has a collection of various types of trees planted by different European mayors in 1872 in commemoration of the unification of Buda, Óbuda and Pest.

In the middle of Bécsi kapu tér is a statue of *Ferenc Kazinczy* (1759–1831), a leading figure in the development of Hungarian literature and of language reform (János Pásztor, 1936). The huge neo-Romanesque building of the *National Archives* (Országos Levéltár; by Samu Pecz, 1913–20) stands to the right of the statue on the N side of the square and houses charters and other historic documents. The Archives themselves date back to 1756 when they were founded in Pozsony. The coloured patterned roof of the building was restored as original in 1988.

The houses in a row on the W side of the square are of medieval origin but they were reconstructed in the 18C following damage which occurred during the siege of 1686. *No. 5* on the right, with the balustrades and stucco ornaments, was built c 1780 in Rococo style. It shares a roof with *No. 6*, which has a statue of St. John of Nepomuk in the niche on the façade. The reliefs on the façade of *No. 7* were added in the early 19C. At the top Pallas Athene is surrounded by symbolic figures of the arts and sciences. Between the first floor windows are portraits of Virgil, Cicero, Socrates and Livy, with Quintilian and Seneca in the middle. Baron Lajos Hatvany (1880–1961) a writer, literary historian and one of the founders of the 'Nyugat' journal, lived here in the mid-1930s, during which time Thomas Mann stayed here on his three visits to Hungary. *No. 8* has been rebuilt several times. The corner bay window dates from 1929–30.

The route now continues S along FORTUNA UTCA, which in the Middle Ages was called French Street (Francia u.) after the French craftsmen who lived here. The present name dates from the late 18C and refers to the Fortuna Inn which used to be situated here. The street numbers are in descending order in the direction of the route.

Like many buildings in the Castle District the houses in this street had to be rebuilt after the sieges of 1686, 1849 and 1945. Nevertheless many original parts of buildings remain such as the Gothic doorframes and window-frames at *No. 14* on the right. The house at *No. 10*, two doors away, dates back to the 13C. It has been rebuilt several times and now stands in its late 18C Louis XVI style, but medieval details can be seen on the façade. The building belonged to the Order of Malta before World War II, hence the Maltese Cross over the door. The door-frame with its keystone decorated with a mask at *No. 13* on the other side of the road is Baroque (c 1730).

No. 6 on the right was built on medieval foundations in the early 18C though the façade is early 19C. Above the double door is a relief of Cupid. *No. 4* next door was built in Louis XVI style from the remains of three medieval houses. The Fortuna Inn was situated here from 1784 to 1868. Today it houses the *Museum of Hungarian Commerce and Catering* (Magyar Kereskedelmi és Vendéglátóipari Múzeum) which, when it opened in 1966, was the world's first catering museum. The museum has permanent exhibitions on the history of confectionery and pastry-shops, and on Hungarian commerce in the first half of the 20C. A recorded message about the content and background of the museum is available in English in the coin-operated box. (Open 10.00–18.00 except Monday.) The house opposite the museum at *No. 9* has a relief of the goddess Fortuna on the first floor (Ferenc Medgyessy, 1921).

The route now continues westwards along the short Fortuna köz at the side of the museum to ORSZÁGHÁZ UTCA, the main thoroughfare of the Castle District in the Middle Ages. *No. 18*, which faces Fortuna köz, was rebuilt in its original 15C form after World War II. *No. 20* on its right is 14C and has survived fairly well. Above the ground floor is a trefoil-arched cornice. The initials J.N. and the date 1771 on the keystone of the Baroque gate refer to Johann Nickl, a butcher and former owner of the house. *No. 22* was originally 15C but was rebuilt in the 16C and again in the 18C. There is Renaissance graffiti on the bottom of the bay window and mid-18C Baroque stucco ornamentation on the balcony.

Proceeding northwards, the house at *No. 9* on the right has 14C traceried sedilia in the gateway. The large building at *No. 28* on the left is the former Cloister of the Poor Clares and was built in the late 18C to the design of Franz Anton Hillebrandt. The wing facing Országház u. was for a time in the 1790s used by the Diet (Parliament) which is the origin of the present name of the street ('Országház' means Parliament). Both the Lower and the Upper House used to meet here. Today the building belongs to the Hungarian Academy of Sciences.

The Baroque house at *No. 17* on the other side of the street (today a restaurant) was built c 1700 from two medieval houses. The gate's keystone has a relief showing a croissant, indicating the trade of a former owner. In front of No. 21, across Hatvany Lajos u., there is a zinc statue of *Márton Lendvay* (1807–58) an actor and prominent member of the National Theatre (László Dunaisky, 1860).

Országház u. ends in KAPISZTRÁN TÉR at the N end of the Castle District. Here stands the *Mary Magdelene Tower*. The church to which it belonged was badly damaged in the last war and had to be pulled down though the outline of the foundations can still be seen.

Sedilia are characteristic of gateways in the Castle District.

The church was built in the 13C and was used by the Hungarian population of the district. A parish school was added in the 15C. For a while under the Turkish occupation it was the only Christian church in Buda. Catholics used the chancel, Protestants the nave. Then it 1605 it was turned into a mosque. Following the expulsion of the Turks in 1686 it was given to the Franciscans. The Habsburg Francis was crowned here as Ferenc I in 1792, and from 1817 it served as a garrison church for troops stationed nearby. The tower was reconstructed after World War II copying the original 18C Baroque spire.

In the NW corner of Kapisztrán tér is József Damkó's 1922 statue of *St. John Capistranus*, (1386–1456) an Italian Franciscan friar who accompanied János Hunyadi in his campaign against the Turks. The complex of buildings behind the statue stands on the site of a former municipal barracks which were redesigned by Márton Dankó in 1847. After various names it assumed the title of Nándor Barracks. The N wing was transformed in 1892 by Guido Hoepfner then after 1926 the wing accommodating troops was converted into a military museum which opened in 1937. Restored after World War II the building today houses the **Museum of Military History** (Hadtörténeti Múzeum). The museum exhibits items of military history connected with the 1848 Revolution and the following War of Independence, the Austro-Hungarian Monarchy and the First World War, the revolutionary army in the 1919 Republic of Councils, and military history from that time up to the present. (Open 9.00–17.00; Sundays and holidays 10.00–18.00; closed Mondays. Entrance on the W side of the building from Tóth Árpád sétány.)

TÓTH ÁRPÁD SÉTÁNY runs along the western ramparts of Castle Hill and affords an excellent view of the Buda Hills and the area to the west of the Castle. In front of the entrance to the Military History Museum cannons from different ages are exhibited. At the NW corner of Castle Hill is the so-called *Esztergom Round Bastion*, 48m in diameter. Nearby along the northern rampart in the direction of the Vienna Gate is a memorial stone to *Abdurrahman*, the last Pasha of Buda. The inscription, in two languages, reads 'Vezir Abdurrahman Abdi Arnaut Pasha, the last governor of Buda during 143 years of Turkish occupation, fell close to this spot in his 70th year on the afternoon of 2 September 1686. A valiant foe, may he rest in peace.'

The route now continues from Kapisztrán tér S along ÚRI UTCA which runs the length of the Castle District to Dísz tér. The street numbers are in descending order.

No. 51, on the left, is a former Franciscan monastery built between 1701 and 1753. Here the Hungarian Jacobins and their leader, Ignác Martinovics, were imprisoned and sentenced to death in 1795. The well in the front of the building has a 19C cast-iron copy of the classical Greek sculptor Praxiteles' statue of Artemis, the goddess of hunting. *No. 49* is the Úri u. façade of the former Cloister of the Poor Clares (see p 132). The Baroque-style statues in the first floor niches of the building at *No. 54–56* on the right represent the four seasons. The house itself was completely rebuilt in 1902. *No. 48–50* was built in the 18C from two medieval houses. There are Gothic sedilia in the gateway. *No. 40* was also formed from two medieval dwelling houses. The neo-classical façade dates from c 1830. The cross-vaulted gateway has Gothic sedilia.

The striking façade of *No. 31*, on the left, is almost entirely Gothic. Despite the various wars and sieges enough has survived to be able to reconstruct the mansion in detail. In the 14C a two-storey house was built here, to which another floor was added in 1440. Several remodellings followed until 1686 when the building was severely damaged. It was rebuilt at the beginning of the 18C and the original façade was kept. Then in 1862 the façade was redesigned in Romantic style. During the siege of 1944–45 the Romantic decorations fell off revealing the original walls. Extensive archaeological research enabled the medieval façade to be restored.—This type of restoration to reveal and maintain original Gothic elements can be clearly seen in the gateways of the buildings opposite at *Nos 38, 36, 34 and 32*.

At the junction of Úri u. and Szentháromság u. there is an equestrian statue of *András Hadik* (György Vastagh Jr, 1937).

Hadik (1711–90) rose from being a rank-and-file hussar to become a field-marshal under Maria Theresa, in whose service he commanded a Hungarian unit alongside the Austrians in the Seven Years War, holding Berlin to ransom for a time. From 1764 to 1768 he was governor of Transylvania, and from 1773, with the title of count, he was head of the Vienna military council—the first and last Hungarian to hold this post. He was also an early advocate of the abolition of serfdom in Hungary.

The entrance to the *Buda Castle Wax Works* (Budavári Panoptikum) is situated a short way along Úri u. at No. 9 on the left. (Open 10.00–18.00 except Tuesday.)

The exhibition is actually underground in one of the caves constituting a system of galleries running under the Castle District. The network extends for more than 10km and was formed artificially by connecting cavities fashioned by thermal springs. The system was developed mainly in the Middle Ages and Ottoman period primarily for defensive purposes. About 80 wells were also dug to ensure the water supply. Later the caves were partitioned and used as cellars by occupants of the houses above. In World War II they served as an air-raid shelter and an army hospital was also established underground.

Úri u. leads southwards into Dísz tér which was the start of the route.

B.   The Royal Palace

The first royal residence was established on Castle Hill in the second half of the 13C by Béla IV following the Mongol invasion. No remains of either the residence or the accompanying fortress have been found and their existence is only known from documents.

In the following century, during the reign of the Angevin kings Charles Robert (1307–42) and Louis the Great (1342–82), a new castle was built. Then a large Gothic palace arose under Holy Roman Emperor Sigismund of Luxemburg who was king of Hungary from 1387 to 1437. According to records its large hall was 70m long and 20m wide. A system of fortifications was also built to defend the palace.

The reign of King Matthias (1458–90), is regarded as the golden age of the palace and of Buda generally. He had most of the Gothic buildings rebuilt in Italian Renaissance style and had new buildings added. The Royal Palace became an important centre of politics, culture and art in Europe.

During the period of Turkish rule the palace suffered little damage but the structure was destroyed during the three-month siege of 1686 when the united Christian armies finally expelled the Turks from Buda.

In the early decades of the 18C under Charles III the ruins of the medieval palace were pulled down and a new smaller palace was built. During the reign of Maria Theresa, in the second half of the 18C, a large palace comprising 203 rooms was constructed according to the plans of the chief imperial architect Jean Nicolas Jadot, Franz Anton Hillebrandt and Ignác Oracsek. The university was based here between 1777 and 1784 after it had been moved from Nagyszombat (Trnava, Czechoslovakia). Later the Viennese court assigned the palace to the Palatine.

Reconstruction of the buildings which had been damaged during the 1848–49 War of Independence were completed in 1856. Then following the Compromise and the establishment of the Austro-Hungarian Dual Monarchy in 1867 large-scale extensions were planned under the direction of the architect Miklós Ybl. He added a new building looking westwards (today Building F, the National Széchényi Library). After Ybl's death work was resumed by Alajos Hauszmann in 1893. He more than doubled the length of the buildings overlooking the Danube by adding a replica of the Maria Theresa wing to the N and connecting the two wings by a central block topped by a dome. This symmetrical neo-Baroque palace was completed in 1905.

The palace was completely burnt out in 1945. Reconstruction under the direction of István Janáky started in 1950, during the course of which excavations revealed remains of the former medieval palace. Hauszmann's large block was rebuilt though with a simpler roof and a neo-classical dome. The interior was reconstructed to serve the purpose of a complex of museums. Work was only finally completed in the 1980s.

Today the former Royal Palace comprises five wings given over to the following purposes: the *Modern History Museum* (Building A) containing material relating to the history of the Hungarian labour movement in the 19C and 20C (though it is due to move; see below); the *Hungarian National Gallery* (Buildings B, C and D) exhibiting collections of Hungarian works of art; the *Budapest History Museum* (Building E) containing exhibitions of the history of the Hungarian capital and of the excavated medieval royal palace; and the *National Széchényi Library* (Building F).

The reliefs and statues which can be seen on and around the building all date from the turn of the century. By the NE corner at the top of the funicular railway is a pillar supporting Gyula Donáth's bronze representation of the Hungarian mythical *Turul eagle*, erected in 1905. (According to legend a 'Turul', a mythical bird resembling an eagle begat Álmos, the son of Emese. It was Álmos' son, Árpád, who led the Magyars in the conquest of 896 AD.) The neo-Baroque wrought-iron gateway and fence behind the bird is the work of Jungfer Gyula, a noted 19C iron work craftsman.

In front of the Danube façade of Building A is Károly Senyei's fountain statue *Children Angling* (1912). Nearby, in front of Building C by the entrance to the National Gallery, stands József Róna's equestrian statue of *Prince Eugene of Savoy* (1663–1736).

The architect József Róna (1861–1939) was a self-made man from a poor background. Although he only had three years of schooling, he managed to obtain a scholarship to study at the academy in Vienna and later received many commissions for public statues erected in the last quarter of the 19C, a period of growing civic and national pride. His neo-Baroque Eugene of Savoy is considered his finest work.

The town authorities of Zenta (today in Yugoslavia) wanted to commemorate the 200th anniversary of the battle of Zenta in 1697 where Eugene of Savoy's victory sealed the fate of Ottoman rule in Hungary. They commissioned the statue from Róna at short notice and set about raising the money in the town with a lottery. The sculpture was completed within a year but not enough money had been raised. The architect wrote to Emperor Francis Joseph who bought the statue and ordered that it be placed in the Castle. Róna is reported as saying that it 'was placed in one of the most beautiful spots in the world'. Two reliefs on the base show scenes from the 1697 battle.

On either side are Miklós Ligeti's 1903 bronze statues of *Csongor* and *Tünde*, the two lovers in Mihály Vörösmarty's 19C drama which bears their name.

The statue in the middle of the courtyard on the W side of the palace bounded by Buildings A, B and C is entitled *Horseman* and is by György Vastagh the Younger (1901). On the wall N of the statue is the so-called *Matthias Fountain* (Alajos Stróbl, 1904) which recalls one of the romantic tales associated with the popular King Matthias.

On the right below the King is the legendary Szép Ilonka (Ilonka the Beautiful) who is said to have fallen in love with the king after she met him by chance when he was hunting in the forest and who later, on discovering who he was, died of a broken heart believing her love to be hopeless. On the right is Galeotto Marzio, the Italian humanist who was a chronicler at the court of King Matthias.

The *Lion Court*, which is to the S through the archway, derives its name from the statues there by János Fadrusz (1901–02). The two statues flanking the entrance to the Budapest History Museum on the S side of the courtyard represent *War* and *Peace* and are the work of Károly Senyei (1900).

The **Modern History Museum** (formerly the Museum of Labour History) at present occupies Building A, at the N end of the former Royal Palace. Exhibitions cover Hungarian social and political developments over the past century and a half. (Some time in the mid 1990s the museum is due to move to the building of the Hungarian National Museum in Pest and merge with the present display there to make a new exhibition of the History of the Hungarian People. The Natural History Museum, at present on the top floor of the Hungarian National Museum, will in turn move here, to Building A of the former Royal Palace.

The **Hungarian National Gallery** occupies Buildings B, C and D of the former Royal Palace. The main entrance is on the E façade of Building C by the statue of Eugene of Savoy. (Open 10.00–18.00 except Monday.)

That a public collection covering the entire development of Hungarian fine arts could be established was largely due to the middle-class reform movements of the first half of the 19C. The Founding Society of the National Picture Gallery was set up in 1845 with the express aim of embracing the cause of Hungarian and Hungarian-born artists. Its first exhibition showing items from the collection of the archbishop of Eger, László Pyrker, opened at the National Museum in March 1846. The National Picture Gallery was opened five years later in 1851 and this can be regarded as the precursor of today's Hungarian National Gallery. The acquisition in 1870 of the Esterházy collection containing 637 paintings, over 3000 drawings and 50,000 prints signified a great boost to the national art collection. It was opened to the public in the Academy of Sciences' building in 1871. Just over a year later 60 masterpieces from the 13C–15C were added from the collection of Arnold Ipolyi, Bishop of Besztercebánya and a noted scholar of old Hungarian art.

An Act of 1896 at the time of the Millenary celebrations stipulated that a Museum of Fine Arts should be established. Elek Petrokics, the director of the museum which opened in 1906, increased the collection and separated the works of Hungarian artists under the label New Hungarian Picture Gallery, which in 1928 was housed in the building which is today the Academy of Fine Arts on Népköztársaság útja. Meanwhile, the municipality of Budapest had been actively patronising and purchasing works since the 1880s and in 1933 the Municipal Picture Gallery was opened in the Károlyi mansion in the centre of Pest. In 1953 this merged with the Museum of Fine Arts and the resulting collection of Hungarian works constituted the core of the collections of the National Gallery.

The Hungarian National Gallery was established as an independent national museum in 1957 in the building of the former Supreme Court in Kossuth tér (today the Ethnographic Museum). It moved to its present location in 1975. There are over 70,000 paintings, sculptures, medals, prints and drawings preserved in the National Gallery. Over 60,000 documents about Hungarian artists are held by the Documentation Department and the Registration Department handles information about works of art held in private collections. A special library of some 80,000 volumes is at the disposal of researchers.

The permanent exhibition of *14C wood sculpture and 15C panel painting and wood carvings*, the exhibition of *11C–15C stonework* and the collection of *Renaissance stone carvings* can all be found on the ground floor of Building D. The medieval stone carvings on display are rare survivals of Hungarian Romanesque and Gothic architecture and sculpture which almost entirely disappeared during the centuries of wars and occupations. The earliest remains include 11C cornice fragments from Pilisszentkereszt and Veszprém. 12C Romanesque is represented by fragments from, among others, the cathedral at Pécs in southern Hungary. Architectural fragments from the royal palace at Esztergom make up part of the early Gothic remains from the late 12C and early 13C. The most outstanding late-Romanesque carvings are from the Abbey of Ják in western Hungary. Red marble carvings from King Matthias's Buda palace are among the Renaissance stonework collection as are pieces from the following Jagello period. The most noted examples of 14C wooden sculpture are two Madonnas from the Szepes region.

The permanent exhibition of *late 15C and 16C winged altarpieces* is in the former grand throne room of the palace on the first floor of Building D and represents a unique collection of such items in Central Europe. The majority of altarpieces and panel pictures on display come from churches in Upper Northern Hungary (now part of Czechoslovakia). Hungarian late Gothic painting reached its climax at the beginning of the 16C in the art of Master MS. His work, The Visitation, on display here used to belong to an altarpiece in Selmecbánya (Banská Stiavnica, Czechoslovakia).

Also on the first floor of Building D is the exhibition of *Late Renaissance and Baroque Art (1550–1800)*. Apart from works created in Hungary this section also reflects the wider horizon of patronage and collecting activities of the aristocrats of the age and hence includes German, Bohemian and Silesian works. Hungarian painters whose major creations fell outside Hungary are also included (Jakab Bogdány, Ádám Mányoki). 18C commissions for Baroque ecclesiastic art generally went to Austrian artists and the exhibition includes

NATIONAL GALLERY

1 Lapidarium. Medieval and Renaissance Stone Carvings
2 Gothic Wood Sculpture and Panel Paintings
3 Late Gothic Winged Altars, Wood Carvings and Panel Paintings
4 Late Renaissance and Baroque Art
5 19th Century Paintings, Sculpture and Medals
6 20th Century Paintings, Sculpture and Medals (up to 1945)
7 Contemporary Art
8 Temporary Exhibitions

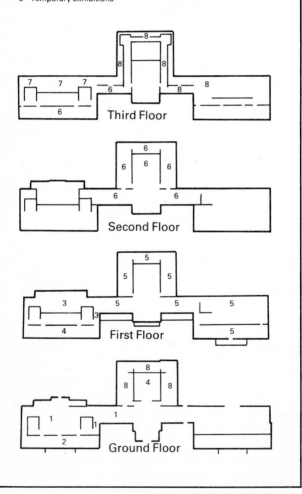

Third Floor

Second Floor

First Floor

Ground Floor

paintings by one of the most prominent creators in this field, F.A. Maulbertsch, who made several of his major works in Hungary.

The collection of *19C painting* covers the period from about 1790 to 1900 and is situated on the first floor of Buildings B and C. The works are displayed in chronological order and grouped by stylistic trends. The transition from Baroque to classicism is represented by the portraits of János Donát while the emergence of Romanticism is most clearly seen in the landscapes of Károly Kisfaludy. Romanticism blossomed in Hungary in the mid-19C, with portraiture, genre-painting, landscape and mythological painting represented here by Miklós Barabás (The Arrival of the Bride, 1856), József Borsos (Girls After the Ball, 1850), Károly Markó the Elder (Visegrád, 1826–30) and Károly Brocky.

Historical painting emerged originally in classical style, with examples here by Bálint Kiss, Soma Orlai Petrich and Mihály Kovács. In the 1860s and 1870s romantic styles took over historical themes— Victor Madarász (The Bewailing of László Hunyadi, 1859), Bertalan Székely (The Women of Eger, 1867), Mór Than (The Capture of Nyári and Pekry, 1853) and in the work of Mihály Zichy. New trends of the second half of the 19C are represented by the plein-air work of Géza Mészöly (Fishermen's Camp at Lake Balaton, 1877) and the near Impressionism of Pál Szinyei Merse (Picnic in May, 1873). A romantically tinted realism dominated the works of Mihály Munkácsy (The Condemned Cell, 1870) and László Paál (Pond of Frogs, c 1875). Both of these artists' work is displayed in a special room.

In addition this section displays some late realistic landscapes of Bertalan Székely, graceful portraits of Károly Lotz, and some late historical paintings by Sándor Wágner (Titusz Dugovics, 1859) and Gyula Benczúr (The Recapture of Buda Castle, 1896).

The permanent exhibition of *19C sculpture* is displayed together with the 19C paintings (B and C first floor). István Ferenczy's 'Shepherdess' (1820–22) was intended to lay the foundations of a Hungarian sculpture at a time when national consciousness and the development of national culture were primary aims. Ferenczy's notions, however, were drowned in a sea of classicism which dominated the Reform Period in Hungary to the middle of the century and beyond (Lőrinc and László Dunaiszky, András Schossel, Jakab Guttmann, Ferenc Kugler and others).

In the second half of the 19C the national theme proposed by István Ferenczy was taken up in a way by Miklós Izsó who formulated a popular national ideal with his authentic chronicles of peasant life (Grieving Shepherd, 1862; Woman Reaping, 1863). He is considered by many to be the founder of Hungarian sculpture proper.

Rapid urbanisation and improving economic conditions led to a growth in the number of sculptors in the last three decades of the 19C. There were a wide variety of genres, based on different schools (Vienna, Munich, Paris) and a multiplicity of styles which eventually merged with the universal trend of Eclecticism. In post-Compromise Hungary and the years leading up to and around the Millenary celebrations of 1896 there was a boom in commemorative sculpture represented by the works of Alajos Stróbl, Barnabás Hollós, György Zala, Károly Senyei, Adolf Huszár, János Fadrusz and others. The innumerable competitions of the period demanding designs for public statues produced a plethora of models by these artists which are on display in the collection. But despite all this, portrait sculpture did not lag behind as is shown by the work of György Zala and the busts of Alajos Stróbl.

The small sculpture of the time involved diverse subjects often deriving from literature and folk themes, e.g. Barnabás Holló (Highwayman on Horseback, 1896) and János Fadrusz (Toldi's fight with the wolves, 1901).

The permanent exhibition of *20C Hungarian painting, sculpture and medals* covers the period up to 1945 and can be found on the second floor of the central section of the museum (Building C) and on the third floor of the southern wing (Building D). All the major schools and currents of the period are represented in the collection. It begins with the plein-air works of the leading artists of the Nagybánya colony, in particular Károly Ferenczy (Sermon on the Mount, 1896; Sunny Morning, 1905; Archers, 1911), Simon Hollósy, János Thorma, Béla Iványi Grünwald and Oszkár Glatz. The artists' colony at Szolnok is represented by Adolf Fényes (Poppy-seed cake, 1910) and the so-called Great Plain school by József Koszta, János Tornyai and Béla Endre.

László Mednyánszky's work, which fits no category neatly, is represented by some landscapes and dramatic portraits (Farmstead, c 1905; Head of a Tramp, 1905–10). The colourful work of Tivadar Csontváry Kosztka, fusing expressionism and symbolism is shown here in 'Ruins of the Greek Theatre at Taormina' (1905).

One trend of Art Nouveau in Hungary was greatly influenced by the English pre-Raphaelites John Ruskin, William Morris and Walter Crane. The Hungarian pre-Raphaelites established a colony at Gödöllő represented here by works of two of their leading members, Aladár Körösfői Kriesch and Sándor Nagy. József Rippl-Rónai, trained in France and a leading Hungarian post-Impressionist, is given a prominent place in the exhibition (Woman with Bird Cage, 1892; The Manor House at Körtvélyes, 1907).

French Cubism and German Expressionism influenced the so-called Group of Eight (Róbert Berény, Dezső Czigány, Béla Czóbel, Károly Kernstok, Ödön Márffy, Dezső Orbán, Bertalan Pór and Lajos Tihanyi). Their efforts were taken further towards Expressionism and Constructivism by the so-called Activists who included József Nemes Lampérth (The Bier, 1912), János Kmetty and Lajos Kassák. The suppression of the Hungarian Republic of Councils in 1919 and the subsequent white terror forced many of the Hungarian avant-garde into exile. A sample of the works of Béla Kádár, Armand Schönberger, Hugo Scheiber and others give some idea of the fate of these trends.

Official cultural policy in the 1930s supported the neo-classicist tendency of the Rome School as shown in the work of Vilmos Aba Novák, Pál C. Molnár and Jenő Medveczky. The influential post-Nagybánya school of the inter-war period is represented by Aurél Bernáth (Riviera, 1926–27; Morning, 1927) and István Szőnyi (Evening, 1934). A group of Socialist Artists active in the 1930s evolved around the painter Gyula Derkovits whose works epitomised the left-wing creations of the time (For Bread, 1930; Generations, 1932; Along the Railway, 1932). The varied trends of the artists' colony at Szentendre are shown here in works by Jenő Barcsay (Hilly Landscape, 1934), Lajos Vajda (Self-Portrait with Lily, 1936; Icon with Mask, 1936), Dezső Korniss (Motif from Szentendre, 1935) and Imre Ámos (Self-Portrait on the Bier, 1934).

Although the museum's collection of 20C sculpture is wideranging the exhibition (displayed with the paintings of the same period) gives priority to progressive tendencies which attempted to break away from academic stereotypes and the formalities of Viennese neo-Baroque. The neo-classicists are represented by János Pásztor (The Waters of Lethe, 1918), István Szentgyörgyi (Complaint, 1908), Zsigmond Kisfaludi Strobl (Finale, 1912) and others. The influences of Art Nouveau are shown here in works of Alajos Stróbl and Miklós Ligeti. The experiments of the Activist circle connected with Lajos Kassák's journal 'MA' (Today)—Pál Pátzay (Standing Boy, 1919), Sándor Gergely (Dancing Woman, 1918)—were cut short in the early 1920s and only developed abroad. Sculptors belonging to the group of Socialist Artists are represented by László Mészáros (Liberty, 1936), György Goldmann (Sitting Worker, 1934), István Gádor, Tibor Vilt et al.

The permanent exhibition of *Contemporary Art* covers the major trends from 1945 up to the end of the 1960s and can be found on the third floor of Building D. Shown here are representatives of the European School (Dezső Kornis, Ferenc Martyn, et al.) and survivors of the inter-war Gresham Group. As in other fields artistic creation was restricted and stylised in the late 1940s and early 1950s, but after 1956 aritists were able to experiment more freely with different styles. Jenő Barcsay, Endre Bálint, Lajos Kassák and others are represented here. The final section shows a sample of more modern works exhibiting features of international Constructivist, Surrealist, Pop Art and other tendencies.

The largest collection of the Gallery, with over 40,000 drawings, water-colours, miniatures and prints, belongs to the Department of Drawings and Prints. However, these works of art are only available to the public in occasional temporary exhibitions. Such exhibitions, as well as temporary exhibitions of Hungarian and foreign works are displayed on the ground floor of Building C, near the main entrance, and on the third floor of the same wing.

The **Budapest History Museum** is situated in Building E, the southernmost wing of the former Royal Palace. (Entrance via the Lion Courtyard.) Inside are two permanent exhibitions: *The 2000 Years of Budapest* and *The Royal Palace and Gothic Statues of Medieval Buda.* (Open 10.00–18.00 except Monday.)

The first exhibition, on the ground floor, covers the history of the capital from Roman times to the present century. Carvings, documents, prints, ceramics, glass objects, tapestries, photographs and various items and works of art illustrate the history of Pest, Buda and Óbuda up to their unification in 1873 and the development of the modern metropolis since their union.

The exhibition of the *Medieval Royal Palace* was made possible by archaeological excavations which took place over a considerable period of time following World War II when the entire Royal Palace had to be reconstructed. The exhibition is in the basement of the building and weaves around a series of underground galleries and reconstructed halls.

The three vaulted halls of the Treasurer House (Rooms 5, 6 and 7) were found almost intact. Matthias Hunyadi (later King Matthias Corvinus) spent time here as a prisoner of the Habsburg King László V in 1457. Two of the halls exhibit ceramics, including samples of valuable glazed oven tiles from the 14C palace. A reconstructed oven is on display. Hall No. 6 has some 15C kitchen utensils—pots, pans, storage vessels, etc. Hall No. 7 has some arms finds and prison memorabilia. The building was used as a prison over the centuries including during the Turkish times. An inscription in Latin from the 16C reads: 'You who are reading this writing here now may know that three captains are paying the penalty for the surrender of the Visegrád fortress'.

Quarries near Esztergom supplied the Palace with soft and malleable red marble suitable for use by the Italian masters brought to Buda by King Matthias, especially after his marriage in 1476 to his second wife, Beatrice of Aragon. The richly decorated fireplaces were a constant attraction at the palace and two friezes from these red marble fireplaces can be seen in the Renaissance Hall (9).

The ruins of the cross-vaulted late-Gothic Hall (11) date from the turn of the 14C and 15C. They remained hidden until 1950 and full reconstruction was only achieved in the 1960s. On display here are a number of Gothic statues of court personnel, squires, society ladies and servants. They are displayed as they were found in 1974, without additions. The 14C Tower Chapel (16) was found relatively intact. A 14C triptych has been placed here.

From the Southern Palace Yard (25) there is a good view of the southern fortifications (15C–16C). The Great Round Bastion (28) was built against expected Turkish attacks. It was heavily damaged in 1686 during the siege by the Christian armies. Bavarian troops led the assault on Bastion which at the time was surrounded by a moat. The Turks held out for two months but were finally defeated on 2 September 1686.

The **National Széchényi Library** occupies Building F, the far western wing of the former Royal Palace complex. The central collection of books consists mostly of 'Hungarica', i.e. of publications printed in Hungary or abroad if written in Hungarian, or by a Hungarian, or relating to Hungary. In addition there are collections of newspapers and journals, ancient books, manuscripts, graphics and small prints, a map collection, a music collection and a theatre history collection. The Hungarian ISBN and ISSN offices are based here, having been introduced in Hungary in 1974 and 1977 respectively. The library also operates an international exchange service. The holdings are at the disposal of all users, be they researchers or the general public, though it was not until 1989 that all restrictions on 'politically sensitive material' were finally lifted. (The central reading rooms of the library are open Mon 13.00–21.00 and Tues–Sat 9.00–21.00.)

The National Széchényi Library was founded in 1802 on the initiative of Count Ferenc Széchényi (1754–1820) the father of István the noted 19C Hungarian reformer. Széchényi searched the entire country and at his own expense amassed a collection of books which he donated to the nation. The Library opened its doors to the public in Pest on 20 August 1803. In 1804 the King granted the Library the right to deposit copies which it has maintained ever since, thus enabling the Library to acquire copies of all material printed in the country. The National Museum, which opened in 1846, was the home of the library for many years and by 1848 the Library had accumulated approximately 100,000 volmes.

A period of stagnation ensued following the defeat of the 1848–49 War of Independence when the Habsburg rulers were reluctant to support Hungarian national endeavours. With the relaxation of political tension the reading room was opened to the public in 1866 after having been closed for 28 years. József Eötvös, the Minister of Education from 1867 to 1871 began to transform the library into a general collection of international scholarly achievements. Recognition of the national importance of the Library was further signified in 1879 when the entire National Museum including the Library was included in the state budget. The period up to 1914 was one of great expansion and progress for the Library but in the inter-war period lack of funds and space hindered growth and narrowed perspectives. In 1949 the Széchényi Library was separated from the Hungarian National Museum and was officially declared the National Library, becoming an independent state institution.

C. Gellért Hill and the Tabán

Gellért Hill (Gellérthegy) stands over 230m above sea level and, with the Liberation Monument on top, is one of the dominating elements of the Danube panorama in Budapest. It takes its name from Bishop Gellért, the first ecclesiastical writer in Hungary, who came from Italy to participate in the conversion of the Hungarians to Christianity during the reign of King Stephen (1000–38).

This route begins in GELLÉRT TÉR at the Buda end of Liberty Bridge (see p 164) climbs to the top of the hill and down the other side to the Elizabeth Bridge, and then explores some of the sights of the Tabán, the low-lying area between Gellért Hill and Castle Hill.

The Art Nouveau building of the **Gellért Hotel and Baths** was built between 1912 and 1918 to the designs of Artúr Sebestyén, Ármin Hegedüs and Izidor Sterk. The entrance to the baths is on the right side of the hotel in Kelen-hegyi út. The ornate Secessionist interior can be viewed from just inside the entrance here. On opening the baths were one of the most up-to-date spas in Europe. Apart from medicinal steam, mud and salt baths where treatment is available, there are also public indoor and outdoor thermal and swimming pools. There was a hospital on this site as early as the 13C and the Turks also operated medicinal baths here.

On the S side of Gellért tér stands a 12m-high limestone obelisk. This *memorial to Soviet heroes*, erected in 1945, is one of the earliest post-war monuments in Budapest. It is the work of Károly Antal who also designed the larger Soviet memorial in Szabadság tér.

The complex of buildings S of Gellért tér, between Liberty Bridge and Petőfi bridge, belongs to the *University of Technology* (Műszaki Egyetem). It was from the Technical University that many students set off to demonstrate on 23 October 1956, marking the beginning of the uprising of that year.

Tucked away in the side of Gellért Hill on Szent Gellért rakpart just N of Gellért tér is an unusual building designed by Károly Weichinger and built in 1932. A former monastery, today it belongs to the State Ballet Institute and functions as a students' hostel.

The top of GELLÉRT HILL can be reached on foot via any of the paths which lead up from Kelen-hegyi út. Alternatively, bus No. 27 goes to the summit from its terminus at the beginning of Villányi út, by Móricz Zsigmond körtér, 500m S of Gellért tér along Bartók Béla út (two stops on tram No. 47 or 49). Cars can ascend via any of the roads that weave around to Szirtes út on the W side of the summit.

In the Middle Ages vines were cultivated on the slopes of the hill. They were destroyed, however, by an epidemic of phylloxera in the middle of the last century. A variety of hot-water medicinal springs are found at the foot of the hill which are used in all three baths (Gellért, Rudas, and Rác) nearby. In the 19C Gellért Hill was a popular recreational area and the annual Easter Monday fair used to be held on the hill's gentler sloping western side.

The **Liberation Monument** (Felszabadulási Emlékmű) stands at the top of Gellért Hill facing SE in the line of the hill (Zsigmond Kisfaludi Strobl, 1947). It was erected in honour of the Soviet soldiers who liberated the capital from the Germans in 1945. Below the 14m-high female figure holding the palm of victory is a Soviet soldier with a flag. To the sides are figures symbolising progress and destruction. On the back of the pedestal are the names of Soviet soldiers who died during the siege of Budapest.

Soviet troops crossed the Hungarian border in the autumn of 1944 and soon captured Debrecen on the Great Plain. By Christmas Budapest was already blockaded and following two unsuccessful attempts to persuade the Germans to surrender the two-month 'Battle of Budapest' began, which was when most of the war damage to the capital occurred. Official history has it that two officers who approached the Germans under a flag of truce to parley were shot by the Germans. Monuments to the memory of Captain Ostapenko and Nicolai Steinmetz (the latter a Hungarian-born Soviet captain), stand on the outskirts of Budapest by the beginning of the M1/M7 Motorway and near the Ferihegy 2 airport terminal respectively.

The Pest side of the capital was liberated on 18 January 1945 but due to the last desperate resistance of the Germans on Castle Hill Buda had to wait until 13 February. The last German units were finally driven from Hungarian territory on 4 April, which date, until 1990, was always a public holiday.

Behind the Liberation Monument stands the **Citadel** (Citadella). The fortress (220m by 60m) was built by the Austrians in 1851 as a symbol of their power following the defeat of the Hungarians in the War of Independence although the architects, Ferenc Kasselik and Mátyás Zitterbarth, were Hungarian. In 1897 the thick walls were breached at a few places, signifying that the fortress no longer served military purposes. Today it is a tourist attraction with restaurant, café and splendid look-out platforms giving a marvellous view of the city.

Some of the earliest inhabitants of the region, the Celts and Eravisci, used to have settlements on the hill. Their story and a potted history of Budapest's 2000 years is displayed in a series of glass wall cases through the entrance and on the left inside the Citadel. To the right, up the incline, is a memorial stone to the astronomer *Imre Dániel Bogdanich* (1762–1802). An astronomical observatory stood here from 1813 until its destruction during the 1848–49 war.

The ramparts on the W side of the citadel look out on to the *Jubilee Park* (Jubileumi park) below. The park was laid out on the 50th anniversary of the 1917 Russian Revolution. It is decorated with statues, fountains and flower beds.

Two thirds of the way down the E side of Gellért Hill, above the Buda end of Elizabeth Bridge, stands the **Gellért Monument** (Gyula Jankovits, 1904). According to legend Bishop Gellért (c 980–1046), who had come from Italy to help King Stephen's crusade to convert the Hungarians to Christianity, was thrown down this hill to his death during a pagan rebellion eight years after the death of Stephen. The bronze figure of Gellért (11m) is holding a cross above a heathen Magyar accepting conversion.

The monument was one of ten statues commissioned and paid for by Emperor Francis Joseph at the turn of the century. 470,000 crowns were spent on the work which involved cutting into the hill and constructing the artificial waterfall. The structure below the statue was aimed at strengthening the base of the hill and was completed by the engineer János Bakó in 1902. A competition for the design was won by architects Mór Kallina and Aladár Árkay.

The **Rudas Baths** lie at the bottom of the hill to the S of the Buda end of Elizabeth Bridge. There were baths here as early as the time of King Sigismund (1387–1437). In the mid-16C Ali, the Pasha of Buda, and later Pasha Sokoli Mustapha, had new baths constructed. The octagonal pool (for men only), vaulted corridor and dome have all remained from that time. To the left, built into the end of the bridge, is the well room where waters from the Juventus, Hungária and Attila springs can be sampled. As a drinking cure they are recommended for kidney stones, gastric ailments and catarrh.

The thermal waters gushing from the Buda Hills on the right bank of the

Danube have always played a part in history. There is archaeological evidence that neolithic people were drawn to the warm springs along the Danube. The Romans brought their bathing habits and built conduits, aqueducts and bathing establishments. The Magyars who conquered the Carpathian basin around 896 continued the tradition of utilising the natural spring waters. The Turks, in what is often regarded as their only positive contribution to Hungary, created a golden age of bathing such that their architectural and bathing customs are still apparent. It was not until the 19C, however, that medical science and balneology made great headway.

Nevertheless, bathing in the thermal waters has been a popular pastime in Budapest for centuries. A British traveller, Robert Townson, visited one of the former Turkish baths in 1793 and recorded the following amusing observation: 'In a common bath I saw young men and maidens, old men and children, some in a state of nature, others with a fig-leaf covering, flouncing about like fish in spawning-time. But the observer must be just. I saw none of the ladies without their shifts. Some of the gentlemen were with drawers, some without; according, no doubt, to the degree of their delicacy, and as they thought themselves favoured by nature or not. But no very voluptuous ideas arise in these suffocating humid steams...'

The route now continues through the underpass at the end of ELIZABETH BRIDGE (Erzsébet híd). The present 380m cable bridge was designed by Pál Sávoly and opened in 1964. It was built on the site of a former chain bridge of the same name, built between 1897 and 1903, which, until 1926, was the largest single-span bridge in Europe. That bridge, the construction of which was accompanied by considerable urban redevelopment on the Pest side, was destroyed by the Germans in January 1945. All the bridges in Budapest were similarly destroyed but the Elizabeth Bridge was the only one not to be reconstructed according to its original design.

In the small park on the N side of the underpass (part of Döbrentei tér) is a seated statue of *Empress Elizabeth* (1837–98), wife of Francis Joseph and Queen of Hungary. Elizabeth learnt Hungarian and spent much time in the country. She was friendly with artists, aristocrats and politicians and helped pave the way for the Compromise of 1867. She was a very popular figure and so much money was collected to set up a statue after her death that it prevented the closure of recurring competitions for the design. A design submitted by György Zala finally won in the fifth version of the competition in 1919, but it was not until 1932 that the statue was eventually erected. It originally stood in today's March 15th Square by the bridge on the other side of the river but in 1953 it was removed. Restored by Walter Madarassy the Younger, it was placed here in 1986.

The tablet on the ground nearby records that on 6 October 1944 Hungarian anti-fascists blew up a statue of Gyula Gömbös which stood here. Gömbös (1886–1936) was a conservative politician with fascist sympathies who was Prime Minister of Hungary from 1932 until his death. He was the first foreign statesman to visit Hitler after the latter had come to power in Germany. (6 October is a historic date in Hungary. It was on that date in 1849 that Austria took revenge on Hungary following the War of Independence by executing 13 Hungarian generals at Arad in Transylvania.)

The **Rác Baths**, which takes its name from the Serbians or Rác people who used to inhabit this area, stands at the foot of Gellért Hill to the W of Döbrenti tér, across both Attila út and Krisztina körút. The 19C exterior, designed by Miklós Ybl, belies the fact that the baths date from Turkish times. Inside, the original octagonal pool and dome still remain. The 40°C water comes from springs under the building. Due to its sulphurous content it is considered beneficial to the skin and in treating neuralgia and diseases of the joints. (Mon, Wed and Fri women only; Tues, Thurs and Sat men only.)

In front of the baths, in the corner of the park area, is a small memorial stone in the form of a cube. This commemorates the *51st Esperanto Congress* which took place in Budapest in 1966.

Hungarians were among the first to join the Esperanto movement. At the turn of the century the world's then only Esperanto journal was published in Hungary. In the early 1950s Esperanto was suppressed as it conflicted with Stalin's theory of linguistics which deemed that the time was not ripe for an international language. Like many associations the Esperanto Society was refounded after 1956 and today there are around 50,000 Esperanto speakers in Hungary. The language is an optional subject in some schools.

The area which lies just to the N of the Rác Baths and which today is covered with grass and trees is known as **The Tabán**. The name probably comes from the many tanning workshops which existed in this area during the Turkish period. Towards the end of the 17C many Serbians fled here from the Turks and around 1700 of the nearly 3000 inhabitants 95 per cent were Serbian. The Tabán became a densely populated, poor area, unhealthy because of a sewer that ran along the line of today's main road, though with a certain romantic charm for some observers. In 1908 the Budapest Council of Public Works decided to demolish the area, but the work was not finally completed until the 1930s.

A few buildings remain from the old Tabán including the **Tabán Parish Church** (Church of St. Catherine of Alexandria). The church was planned by Keresztély Obergruber and built between 1728 and 1736 on the site of a previous medieval church which the Turks had used as a mosque. On the façade are statues of St. Gellért and St. Carlo Borromeo. Inside, on the right in the little window, is a copy of a 12C carving known as the Tabán Christ. (The original is in the Budapest History Museum.) Further along the same wall in a window recess there is a picture of 'St. Florian and the 1810 fire' which swept through the Tabán destroying 600 houses and in which more than 50 people perished.

The statue of the *woman with plate* standing behind the church and in front of the house at No. 10 Apród u. is a memorial to the poet Benedek Virág (1754–1830). Virág, a representative of Hungarian classicism, lived in a former house here. He was a member of the Pauline order and often gave masses in the parish church.

The route now continues down the E side of Apród u. to YBL MIKLÓS TÉR, named after the celebrated architect of the Opera House and many other public buildings. There is a *statue of Ybl* (1814–91) in the middle of the square (Ede Mayer, 1896). The building behind the statue, the *Várkert* (Castle Garden) *Kiosk*, was designed by Ybl and built in 1874–79 to house the then pump room of the Castle waterworks. A popular restaurant functioned on the terrace and in the garden up to the 1960s. In a dilapidated state since then, some original *sgraffito* by Róbert Scholtz can still be seen on the building. (There are plans to renovate the building.)

The neo-Renaissance ornamental arcade and stairs on the NW side of the square at the bottom of the hill is the so-called *Várkert Bazár*, also designed by Ybl and constructed in 1875–82. The originally open archway was intended for a display of statues. It later became a row of shops and today houses several sculptors' studios.

Returning towards Apród u. the route passes *No. 6 Ybl tér* on the W side. The plaque on the wall records that Adam Clark died here on 23 June 1866. Clark, who was born in Edinburgh in 1811, came to Hungary to supervise the building of the Chain Bridge (see p 148), after which he decided to settle in Budapest. He is buried in the Kerepesi Cemetery. The present building dates from 1875–80 and was designed by Miklós Ybl.

The **Semmelweis Museum of Medical History** is at No. 1–3 Apród u. on the right. (Open 10.30–17.30 except Monday.) The building dates from the 17C but received its present Louis XVI façade following the Tabán fire of 1810. The physician Ignác Semmelweis, who discovered the cause of puerpal fever (see p 192), was born here in 1818, and is buried here. The museum named after him exhibits items connected with the history of medicine from ancient, Oriental, Greek and Roman times, as well as that of Christian Europe and Hungary up to 1914. The furnishings of one of the oldest pharmacies in Pest, the Szentlélek Patika (Holy Ghost Pharmacy), founded in 1786, can be seen inside. In the inner courtyard is a statue, *Anyaság* (Motherhood) by Miklós Borsos (1965).

Apród u. ends at SZARVAS TÉR from where there is access via steps to the southern side of the Royal Palace. No. 1 Szarvas tér, on the right, is the so-called *Stag House*, a triangular building in Louis XVI style which takes its name from the inn-sign with the relief of a stag which has survived on the façade. The triangular courtyard with gallery and iron railings recalls the atmosphere of the old Tabán. Today the building houses the 'Arany Szarvas' (Golden Stag) restaurant.

Opposite the Stag House on the other side of Attila út is a bust of *Vuk Karadzic* (1787–1864) one of the pioneers of Serbian literary language. It is the work of Mitric Nebojsza and was placed here in 1987.

ATTILA ÚT runs for approximately 2km NW from Szarvas tér. Bus No. 5 runs the full length. 500m from Szarvas tér in Dózsa György tér, below the western wing of the Royal Palace, is a group of statues commemorating *György Dózsa* the leader of the Hungarian peasant rising of 1514 (István Kiss, 1961). Steps lead up from the square to a lift which gives access to the Royal Palace above.

Further along Attlia út, before Alagút u., is the small Haydn Park with a *monument to Haydn* erected on the 150th anniversary of the composer's death (András Kocsis, 1959). To the right Alagút u. leads to the Tunnel, while to the left stands the *Christina Town Parish Church* (Krisztinavárosi plébániatemplom). Originally built in Louis XVI style in 1795–97 it was rebuilt in Eclectic style in the 1880s. In 1939 the chancel was moved back and a transept was added. On the façade are sculptures of 11C Hungarian kings: St. Stephen and St. Ladislas. The first two side altars are Baroque, the next two in Empire style. The ornamental pulpit is early 19C. On the right of the church stands a statue of Mary Immaculate on a column. The work of Matthias Janish in 1702, it is one of the oldest statues in Budapest still standing in a public place.

The *Vérmező* (Blood Meadow) lies 500m beyond Alagút u. on the left of Attila út. In 1795 Ignác Martinovics and the other leaders of the Hungarian Jacobin movement were beheaded here. 'An example had to be set to make the country live in fear', wrote Ferenc Kazinczy, one of a number of writers who were imprisoned at the time. A monument to the martyrs· can be found at the northern end of the park. The present-day park was laid out at the end of the 1940s when the Blood Meadow was filled over with debris from the many buildings in the Castle District which had been damaged in the war.

The **Southern Railway Station** (Déli pályaudvar) stands to the W of the Vérmező. It is Budapest's most modern major railway station and was built in 1970–77 to the design of György Kővári. The sunken area in front of the station has patterned enamel work by Victor Vasarely. Most of the trains for Lake Balaton depart from here, and underneath is a metro station which is the Buda terminus of the the No. 3 metro line.

In the northernmost corner of the Vérmező, at the junction of Attila út and Krisztina körút is a statue of *Béla Kun* (1886–1939) one of the early leaders of the Hungarian Communist Party and of the 1919 Republic of Councils. The work, which depicts Kun urging on a revolutionary crowd, is by Imre Varga and was erected for the centenary of Kun's birth.

A short distance to the N lies Moskva tér, a major junction of Buda from where buses, trams and underground run to all parts of the city.

D.   Víziváros (Water Town)

The narrow part of Buda between Castle Hill and the Danube has been called **Water Town** (Víziváros) since the Middle Ages. At that time it was surrounded by walls and was inhabited by sections of society poorer than their neighbours up the hill. In the main, people here were craftsmen, tradesmen and, very importantly at that time, fishermen. The Turks transformed the local churches into mosques but they also built baths and one of these, the Király Baths, is still functioning in the area. Intensive building at the turn of the century brought an end to the small-town atmosphere of Water Town, but enough sights have remained to make it an interesting area (not much visited by tourists) in the heart of the city.

This route (c 2km) begins at CLARK ÁDÁM TÉR, at the Buda end of the Chain Bridge, continues along Fő u. (the main street of Water Town) and after crossing Bem tér ends at the Buda side of Margaret Bridge. Clark Ádám tér can be reached on the No. 16 bus which departs from the SE corner of Engels tér in the centre of Pest every few minutes.

The **Chain Bridge** (Lánc híd) was Budapest's first permanent stone bridge across the Danube. Prior to its construction between 1839 and 1849 the only structural link between Buda and Pest was a pontoon bridge which had to be dismantled when vessels passed by.

The idea of a permanent bridge was developed by Count István Széchenyi. Its construction was a necessary and integral part of the social and economic reforms that he promoted. William Tierney Clark, an Englishman, was commissioned to design the bridge and the Scottish engineer Adam Clark (no relation) was brought to Hungary to supervise the construction work. The building of the bridge aroused much public interest. A large painting by Miklós Barabás depicting the ceremonial laying of the foundation stone can be seen in the National Museum.

In May 1849 during the War of Independence, before the bridge was finally completed, the Austrians planned to blow it up. Adam Clark thwarted their plans by having the chain-lockers flooded with water. When it finally opened on 21 November 1849 the bridge, at nearly 380m and with its 2000 tons of ironwork, was one of the largest suspension bridges of the time. It is a similar, though larger, design to that of Tierney Clark's earlier Hammersmith Bridge in London.

A toll was levied on all who used the bridge thus breaching the privileges of those nobility who had previously been exempt from taxes. In practice tolls ceased in 1918 though they were not legally abolished until May 1920. The bridge was reconstructed during World War I since when it has been officially called the Széchenyi Chain Bridge. Destroyed by the Germans in the last war it was reconstructed and reopened on 21 November 1949, the centenary of its original inauguration. The statues of lions at either end of the bridge are the work of János Marschalkó (1850).

On the W side of Clark Ádám tér is the neo-classical entrance to the
350m **Tunnel** (Alagút) which leads under Castle Hill to the Christina
Town (Krisztinaváros) area of Buda. Adam Clark was also involved in
the planning of the tunnel, which was built in 1853–57 and modernised in the 1970s. As with the bridge a toll was levied on the use of the
tunnel until 1918.

On the left of the tunnel entrance is the **Buda Castle Funicular**
(Sikló) which connects Clark Ádám tér with the Royal Palace above.
The carriages run every few minutes and the journey takes under
one minute. It is closed on alternate Mondays for maintenance. There
is wheelchair access.

The world's second funicular railway was constructed here on the initiative of
Ödön, the younger son of Count István Széchenyi, and opened on 2 March
1870. It functioned continuously until the end of World War II when a direct hit
put it out of action. It was not until 1986 that it was reconstructed and reopened.
The design of the carriages is as original, but in place of the earlier steam
engine they are now pulled by electric operation.

In the small park in front of the funicular stands the white *'Zero
Kilometre' Stone* (Miklós Borsos, 1975). It is from this spot that all
distances from Budapest are measured.

FŐ UTCA begins at the N side of Clark Ádám tér. *No. 1* on the right
is the headquarters of the Buda High Court. *No. 3* next door was built
in neo-classical style by Hugó Máltás in 1862 and at one time served
as a town hall. Jégverem u. is the first street to cross Fő u. The three-
sided Romantic building at *No. 2* on the right was also designed by
Hugo Máltás (1860–61). It was built for the widow of Dutch ship-
builder J.A. Majson who came to Hungary on the invitation of István
Széchenyi. The leading 19C sculptor István Ferenczy had a studio at
No. 1 opposite until 1834.

In front of the modern building at *No. 14–18* Fő u. on the left are
some remains of a medieval house which was reconstructed in the
17C. *No. 20* at the corner of Pala u. also originally dates from the
Middle Ages but its present form with cylindrical corner oriel
window and reliefs above and below the windows dates from 1811
when András Dankó rebuilt it for a Greek trader called Kapistory.

The *Former Capuchin Church and Monastery* stands at No. 30–32.
The original medieval church was used as a mosque by the Turks.
On the southern wall of the church, visible from both outside and
inside, there are Turkish door-frames and window-frames. The
Matthias Corvinus coat of arms is on the outer N wall (a crown with a
raven holding a ring in its beak).

CORVIN TÉR follows immediately after the church. In the square is
a bronze statue of a *Hungarian warrior* from the time of the conquest,
drinking from an ox-horn (Barnabás Holló, 1904). On the limestone
base is a relief of Lajos Millacher, a wealthy citizen who had the
statue/fountain erected 'out of gratitude'. The Baroque house at *No.
3 Corvin tér* was built in the 18C. A statue of St. John of Nepomuk
stands in the niche on the façade. Behind the large doors a cellar-like
passage leads to an interesting courtyard. The 18C neo-classical
house next door, at *No. 4*, has reliefs above the windows depicting
King Matthias as a farmer, scholar and commander. The relief above
the door, with a satyr on either side, shows the interior of an
alchemist's workshop. The *Buda Vigadó*, which stands on the N side
of the square, is the home of the Hungarian State Folk Ensemble. It
was built at the turn of the century to the designs of Mór Kallina and
Aladár Árkay.

The neo-Gothic *Calvinist Church* in Szilágyi Dezső tér was designed by Sámuel Pecz and built in 1893–96. There is a statue of the architect at the SW corner of the square (Béla Berán, 1919).

The stretch of the Danube embankment by Szilágyi Dezső tér is where many Hungarian Jews, anti-fascists, and others were brought and shot during the last war. Erzsébet Róna, the daughter of the sculptor József Róna who made the equestrian statue of Eugene of Savoy in front of the Royal Palace, has recorded how she was arrested in January 1945 by the Hungarian Arrow Cross and taken in a group to Szilágyi Dezső tér and told to line up by the river. 'The Arrow Cross were right behind us with their guns ... We stood in line obediently, with our faces to the Danube. Nobody said a word because it happened so suddenly, then a command, and they shot. Those who were hit fell down at once ... I was not hit ... [but] instinctively I dropped to my side on one arm and remained motionless. They believed that I was dead ... if I had breathed that would have been the end of me. Anyone they saw moving was given a second shot.' Believed to be dead she was dumped in the Danube. Luckily the water was shallow and she later managed to crawl to safety.

Vám u. crosses Fő u. a short way after Szilágyi Dezső tér. To the left is the modern building of MVMT (Hungarian Electrical Trust), which shows an ingenious use of the narrow space. The building on the right at *No. 1/b Vám u.*, with an unusual curved façade, was designed by Loránd Sebestyén and Dezső Beregszászy and built in 1937. *No. 37/a–37/c* Fő u. has some sculpted reliefs above the first floor level of Danaides-type figures. To the bottom right is the symbol of the sculptress, Alice Lux. The new building opposite belongs to the National Water Authority (Országos Vízügyi Hivatal) and was built in 1972 to the design of Dezső Dul.

Fő u. now enters BATTHYÁNYI TÉR, the historic centre of the Water Town district.

Like many streets and squares in Budapest it has had a variety of names. It was once called Bomba (bomb) tér because a cannon and ammunition depot was situated here for the defence of the Danube waterway. In the 18C it was the site of a market and hence called Upper Market Square. The present name refers to Lajos Batthyányi, the Prime Minister of the 1848 Hungarian government.

The terminus of the HÉV suburban railway, which goes northwards to Szentendre, is situated here. It shares an entrance with the Batthyányi tér metro station, which is on the No. 2 line.

The twin-towered **Church of St. Anne** in the square is considered to be one of Hungary's outstanding Baroque monuments. It was built by Kristóf Hamon, Mátyás Nepauer and Milály Hamm between 1740 and 1762. The façade of the church was seriously damaged during World War II but it has been meticulously restored. The Buda coat of arms can be seen in the tympanum and above it the triangular 'God's eye' motif between two kneeling angels. A statue of St. Anne with the child Mary stands in a niche in the middle of the façade and above the entrance are allegorical figures of Faith, Hope and Charity.

The high altar has a group of statues representing the young Mary being presented by her mother, St. Anne, in the Temple in Jerusalem. It is the work of Károly Bebó and was completed in 1773. Bebó also built the pulpit although the reliefs on it were added later. The painting of the Holy Trinity in the cupola of the chancel is by Gergely Vogl (1771) while the ceiling frescoes depicting the life of St. Anne and the triumph of the Eucharist were only added in 1928 by Pál C. Molnár and Béla Kontuly.

The building to the left of the church, *No. 7 Batthyányi tér*, was adapted from a former tavern in 1724 by Henrik Ferenc Fiedler. Today it houses the presbytery and a café. The relief to the left is in memory of Ferenc Faludi (1704–79) a poet, prose-writer, translator and Jesuit priest.

The *Market Hall* on the W side of the square has been standing here since 1902. On its right is a Louis XVI-style house which was built in the 1790s. The two-storey sunken building at No. 4 is the *former White Cross Inn*, a rare surviving example of Rococo architecture in Budapest. It acquired its present shape around 1770. The asymmetrical character indicates that it was formed from two buildings. In the late 18C the inn was a popular and elegant place of entertainment where theatrical performances were given. Tradition has it that Casanova once stayed here, hence the name of the present-day night club on the ground floor. The Louis XVI-style dwelling house at *No. 3* next door was built in the 1790s. The reliefs above the ground floor symbolise the four seasons.

The large building on the N side of Batthyányi tér is the *former Franciscan monastery* and later hospital of the nuns of St. Elizabeth. In front of the building, facing the square, is a seated statue of the poet *Ferenc Kölcsey* (Ede Kallós, 1939).

Kölcsey (1790–1838) is the author of the Hungarian national anthem 'Himnusz', which was written in 1823. The words on the statue, however, are from another of his works written in 1838 and entitled 'Huszt', the name of a town then in Hungary but today across the border in the Soviet Union. They read:

Look to the distant future and
confront the present wisely;
Produce, create, enrich—from this our
homeland will flourish and be brighter.

The route continues N along Fő u., which leaves Batthyányi tér at the NW corner. On the right is the *Church of St. Elizabeth*, built between 1731 and 1757. It originally belonged to Franciscan friars hence the statues of St. Francis of Assisi and St. Anthony of Padua on the façade between the image of the Immaculate Conception. The interior is Baroque though the frescoes are late 19C. The pulpit and the carvings on the benches were the work of the friars. A fresco on a side altar to the right depicts the fire of 1810 with St. Florian protecting the Christians.

The three-storey, neo-classical building next to the church on the corner of Csalogány u. is the *former Marczibányi-menház* (almshouse). It was built by philanthropist István Marczibányi (1752–1810) for charitable purposes. The inscription above the door reads 'A shelter for the defenceless ill, 1805'.

BOLGÁR ELEK TÉR is a few metres further along Fő u. The large building on the immediate left facing the square was designed by István Janáky and Jenő Szendrői and constructed at great speed during the harsh winter of 1941–42 for the Ministry of Light Industry. The relief on the wall with an industrial theme is the work of Zoltán Borbereki Kováts. Today it is the home of the Federation of Technical and Natural Scientific Associations. The statue of a bear in the park is the work of sculptor Ferenc Medgyessy (1937). Behind the bear, at No. 70–78 Fő u. is the imposing *Military Court of Justice*. The building was a police headquarters and prison for many years and was used by both the Gestapo and the secret police in Hungary's Stalinist period. It was here, in 1958, that the former Prime Minister Imre Nagy and his associates were tried in secret and condemned to death.

The **Király Baths** at No. 82–86 Fő u. on the left is one of Budapest's most significant monuments of the Turkish period. Construction started under Pasha Arshlan in 1566 and was finished by Pasha Sokoli Mustapha around 1570. From considerations of defence the baths were built inside the then walls of Water Town and water had to be piped in from springs to the N where the Lukács Baths now stands. The surviving Turkish parts are in the wing which faces Ganz u. The neo-classical wing with Ionic pilasters and tympanum facing Fő u. was built in 1826. The present name of the baths, which means 'King' baths recalls the 19C owners, the König family, who later adopted the Hungarian equivalent of their name—'Király'. The original 16C Turkish pool is still in use and relics of Turkish times are on display inside. (Open alternate days for men/women only.) Various facilities and services are offered here by the Institute for Balneotherapy particularly for the treatment of rheumatism and arthritis.

Across Ganz u. is the Baroque *Chapel of St. Florian* which was built in 1760 and designed by Mátyás Nepauer. On the façade are statues of St. Blaise, St. Florian and St. Nicholas. The church, which originally stood lower, was raised in 1936–37 to the present level of the street. It is today a Greek Catholic parish church.

Fő u. ends in BEM JÓZSEF TÉR. Joseph Bem (1794–1850) was a Polish general who fought in the Polish uprising of 1830–31, then against the Habsburgs in the 1848 Vienna uprising and later with the Hungarians during the 1848–49 War of Independence. A *statue of Bem* stands in the middle of the square (János Istók, 1934) showing the wounded general with his arm in a sling. Under his command the revolutionary army managed to liberate almost the entire territory of Transylvania in a period of three months. During that campaign Sándor Petőfi was his aide-de-camp and his poem about Bem is engraved at the back of the pedestal. After the defeat of the 1848–49 war Bem went into exile, eventually becoming a Muslim and a Turkish citizen. He fought as a colonel in the Turkish province of Syria and is buried in that country at Aleppo.

A huge rally took place in front of the statue on the first day of the 1956 uprising, which had partly been sparked off by sympathy for events unfolding in Poland.

The building on the W side of Ben tér at *No. 3* is today the HQ of the Hungarian Democratic Forum. It was built in 1897 and is the former Radetzky Barracks, the home of the Budapest sappers.

The *Foundry Museum* (Öntödei Múzeum) stands 200m away at No. 20 Bem József u., which runs westwards from Bem József tér. In 1844 the Swiss cast-iron worker Ábrahám Ganz established a foundry here which became the core of the internationally known Ganz Machine Works. The foundry functioned until 1964 after which it was turned into a museum. The original wooden structure can be seen inside as well as jib cranes and ladles in their original setting. The museum exhibits the history of metal work in Hungary and has a collection of stoves made in different regions. (Open 10.00–17.00 except Monday.)

The *row of busts* outside is of noted Hungarian metallurgists and the *seated figure of a worker* in front of the entrance is a side statue from an original memorial to András Mechwart (Alajos Stróbl, 1913) which was destroyed in the last war. Mechwart (1834–1907) was an engineer who started working at the Ganz works in 1859 and who rose to become the general manager. He developed and perfected the milling machine such that before World War I Budapest had become the milling capital of Europe.

The route continues from the NE corner of Bem József tér along Bemrakpart in the direction of Margaret Bridge (for details of the bridge see p 215). In the small park just by the Buda end of the bridge is a *statue of a lion* (Szilárd Sződy, 1932) raised to the memory of those who fell in World War I at Przemyśl Castle in Poland which at the time stood in a part of the Austro-Hungarian Empire. The inscription on the plinth reads 'They fought like lions'.

The large yellow building standing 100m N of the bridge end today belongs to the *National Rheumatological and Balneological Institute*. It was built in 1901 for the Sisters of Charity who had run a hospital on this site during the 19C. The statue of a *young man on horseback* standing in the park area between the Institute and the river is by Pál Pátzay (1957).

The next building, across Üstökös u., is the **Lukács Baths** which has two open air swimming pools. The original neo-classical building has been rebuilt several times. The adjoining **Császár Baths** date from Turkish times and the 16C bath-hall is still in use. The entrances to both the Lukács and Császár Baths are on the E side of the buildings in Frankel Leó út at Nos 25–29 and 31 respectively. (The Hungarian Leó Frankel was a colleague of Karl Marx and Commissioner of Labour during the Paris Commune. He was later one of the first to introduce Marxism into Hungary.)

The **Tomb of Gül Baba** (Gül Baba Síremléke) is situated not far from the end of Margaret Bridge (follow Mártírok útja W from the bridge, then, as it swings to the left, straight on up Margit u., immediate right into Mechet u. and up the steps on the left). Gül Baba, which means 'Father of Roses', was a Muslim Dervish of the Bektashi order who took part in the capture of Buda in 1541 but died soon after in September of the same year. Yahjapashazade Mehmed, the third Pasha of Buda, had an octagonal sepulchral chapel with hemispherical dome built here between 1543 and 1548. Although it has been rebuilt several times and for a while was used as a Christian chapel it was reconstructed in its original form by architect Egon Pfanni in 1962. Inside is the tomb of Gül Baba and objects recalling his life and religious order. For centuries it has been a place of pilgrimage for Muslims, in fact the only such place in Hungary. (Open May–Oct 10.00–18.00 except Monday.)

E.   The Inner City

This route, some 2km in length, describes a circular walk around the heart of the historic inner city (Belváros) which originally was bounded by the ancient town walls which ran in a semicircle on the inner side of today's Tolbuhin körút, Múzeum körút, Tanács körút and Deák Ferenc u. (The first three are described in Rte 5F.)

Much of the inner city was pulled down at the beginning of the 20C as part of the redevelopments associated with the building of the first Elizabeth Bridge. World War II also took its toll as the Red Army fought it out from here with the retreating Germans who were making a last desperate attempt at resistance from their remaining positions on Castle Hill on the other side of the Danube.

Today's Inner City is the commercial and shopping centre of Budapest. Here also can be found most of the travel bureaux, tourist offices and foreign airline companies.

The route starts at the Szabad Sajtó út end of VÁCI UTCA, Budapest's most fashionable shopping street and, for the most part, a pedestrian precinct. The large building on the left is the **Eötvös Loránd University Arts Faculty**. Built by Dezső Hütl during World War I it

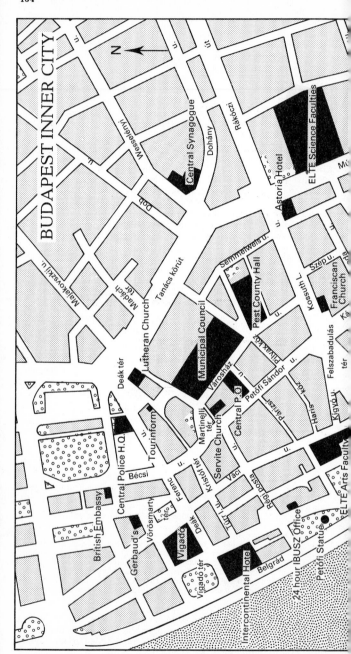

BUDAPEST INNER CITY

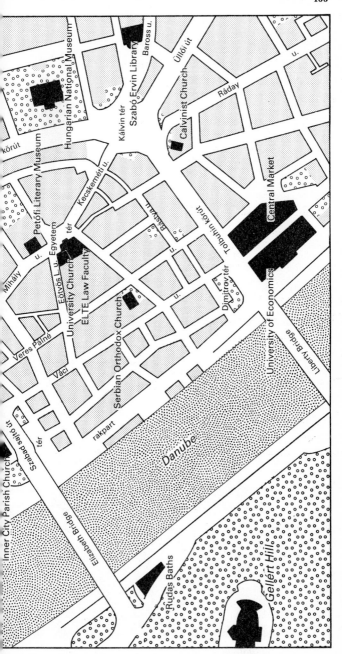

has been occupied by the university since 1950. On the ground floor at the end of the street is the *Gorky Bookshop*, a specialist shop for Soviet books and records. Since 1987 the short road which runs through the archway in the middle of the building has been called *Piarista köz* as a reminder that the building used to be a Piarist secondary school.

According to documents there was a parish church school on this site in the 13C. In 1717 the Pest authorities invited the Piarist Order to establish a secondary school here, and this became one of Pest's first such secondary educational establishments. The school became an important place for teaching and developing the Hungarian language and for the teaching of sciences. The physicist Loránd Eötvös, who invented the torsion pendulum and after whom the present university is named, studied at the Piarist school from 1857–65. The old school building was demolished in the early years of the 20C as part of the redevelopment linked with the construction of the first Elizabeth bridge. The present building was begun in December 1913 and completed in February 1917. In 1948 the Piarist school was nationalised, though the Order was given another school in Budapest. Above the arch facing Váci u. there is a statue of *St. Joseph Calasanctius*, the founder of the Piarist Order, and some pupils (Béla Radnai).

The chemists at *No. 34* on the corner of Kígyó u. traces its origins back to the Szentháromság (Holy Trinity) Pharmacy, the oldest pharmacy in Pest. The *bronze fountain* at the junction here is the work of Béni Ferenczy (1977). In the middle of the next block on the right is the *Foreign Language Bookshop* which sells imported titles and books published in Hungary in foreign languages. The *Second Hand Bookshop* in the next block also has some titles in English.

The building at *No. 28* on the corner of Párizsi u. was designed by Imre Steindl and built in 1877. An 1889 guidebook carried an advertisement for Mátyás Hezella's general shop which was situated

Váci utca in the 1840s.

here saying that all manner of English gentlemen's tennis, riding, cricket and croquet sports equipment was available here and that the gunpowder for shooting came directly from the English Curtis & Harvey Co. *No. 26* on the far corner of Párizsi u. was built in 1890 to the plans of Alajos Hauszmann though reconstruction has taken place due to severe damage during the war.

It took some time after World War II before Váci u. returned to its former status as the most fashionable street in Pest, which it had enjoyed for many years. In the record of his travels in 1834, the Austrian painter F.S. Chrismar, commented on the animated life he found in central Pest: 'It is especially pleasant to walk along Váci street in fine weather, in the noonday hours, when everyone belonging to the elegant world of Pest is about. Here, dressed in all their finery, the beauties of the country stroll past the elegant shop-windows to look at the articles of luxury and fashion. The tastefully arranged windows provide a brilliant frame to the two sides of the street.' If the artist returned today, he might think that very little had changed!

No. 24, which has the Adidas shop on the ground floor, was built in 1927–28 and designed by the then 60-year-old Emil Vidor, an ardent follower of the Hungarian Secessionist school. By the late 1920s this style was no longer fashionable so he confined the Secessionist part to the upper floors only and designed the lower part in the more popular Modern style. The ground floor was rebuilt in 1964. The *Akadémia Bookshop* at No. 22 stands on the site of a former watchmakers. In 1857 the first public clock in Pest was erected here. It was lit by gas at night until midnight.

Next to the bookshop is the modern building of the *Taverna Hotel* designed by József Finta and opened in 1987. The same architect planned the modern building of the *International Trade Centre* (1985) opposite at No. 19–21. It has a plaque on the right of the façade which records that two 19C poets, Károly Kisfaludy (1788–1830) and Mihály Vörösmarty (1800–55) both died in the building which used to stand here.

No. 18 next to the hotel, which is decorated with blue ceramic tiles, was designed by Gál Bertalan and built in 1907. The *Fontana Department Store* stands next to it at No. 16 (György Vedres, 1984). On the other side of Váci u. at *No. 15* is a building with a knight in an upper niche and much wood carving, including carved gateways with Hungarian motifs. *No. 13* next to it is the oldest building in Váci u. It was built c 1805 in early classical style by Ferenc Schorndorfer although its appearance has changed a lot over the years. Round the corner on the Régi posta u. side are four remaining inset reliefs above the windows. These used to stretch all around the building. On the building a little further along at *No. 13* Régi posta u. there is a coloured ceramic of the old post coach above the door. It is the work of Margit Kovács and was placed here when the building was completed in 1937.

The Rondella, a tower which legend says was erected by King Sigismund (1387–1437) for the protection of the town used to stand at the far, Danube end of Régi posta u. Here the National Hungarian Stage Company was born and the first Hungarian theatre performance in Pest took place here on 27 October 1790. The Rondella was pulled down in 1815.

Next to the Fontana Department Store is the bronze *Hermes Fountain*, which was previously an emblem of the Merkur bank which used to stand nearby. The *Folkart Centrum* is on the ground floor of No. 14, the corner building to the left of the fountain. This is one of the largest shops in Budapest for folk and craft goods. The

Hungarian coat of arms with a crown can be seen on the corner near the top of the building. It is a reminder that the 'Hungarian Crown' café used to occupy a former building on this site.

No. 12 was designed by Ignác Alpár and originally dates from 1919–21 though it was reconstructed in 1946. Opposite, at No. 11a on the left, is the so-called **Thonet House**, which was built in 1888–90 to the designs of Ödön Lechner and Gyula Pártos. The building, panelled in coloured majolica, was constructed for the furniture-making company of Jakab Thonet. Miraculously it escaped damage in the war and it stands today as original.

The *Gondolat Bookshop* at No. 10 on the right is on a site which has been occupied by a bookshop for many decades. In the 1930s the Librairie Française bookshop was situated here. The plaque in the window says that the writers Attila József, Lajos Kassák and Miklós Radnóti often used to frequent the premises. *No. 8* next door was designed by Ferenc Fazekas and Gyula Katona Mihály and was built in 1906–09.

No. 9 opposite, which today houses the **Pest Theatre** (Pesti Színház), has had a varied and interesting history. Formerly here stood the *Inn of the Seven Electors*, a gathering place noted for its magnificent balls. An 11-year-old Ferenc Liszt gave a concert here in 1823. The present building is the work of József Hild and was constructed in 1840. In the last four decades of the 19C it was the National Hotel (Nemzeti Szálló). A cinema was added in 1913 which was rebuilt for the theatre in the 1960s. The *Philantia* florists on the ground floor at the left opened in 1905 and is the oldest flower shop in Budapest. The interior is original turn-of-the-century Art Nouveau.

No. 6 on the right of Váci u. at the corner of Kristóf tér dates from 1911 and is the site of the former pharmacy belonging to Kristóf Nagy. In the middle of the small square is László Dunaisky's 1862 *Fisher-girl Well* (Halász-lány kút). For many years it stood in the Népliget (People's Park) several kilometres SE of the city centre. Restored by Sándor Lovas it was placed here in 1985.

The office of the Soviet airline *Aeroflot* occupies the ground floor of No. 4. The building, designed by József Hild, dates from 1839. Türr István u. leads off Váci u. opposite.

István Türr (1825–1908) fought in the 1848–49 War of Independence after which he went into exile. He served the British during the Crimean War and British intervention saved his life in 1856 after he had been captured by the Austrians in Romania. Having fought alongside Garibaldi in Italy in 1860 he returned to Hungary following the Compromise of 1867. He was involved in developing the canal system in Hungary and even participated in the preparatory plans for the construction of the Panama Canal.

The *Váci kapu* (Vác Gate), one of the major gates in the old Pest walls, stood at the end of Váci u. It was pulled down in 1870 but an outline of the gate can be seen on the ground here. On the left is the large building known as the **Bank Palace**. It was designed in 1913–15 for the First Pest Savings Bank Association by Ignác Alpár who won an international tender from among ten architects.

Alpár, who also designed the former Stock Exchange and the National Bank in Szabadság tér, wrote at the time that it was his biggest project and that after the First World War such expensive building would probably no longer be undertaken. A whole series of master craftsmen were employed on the project. The bronze gate of the main entrance (round the corner in Deák Ferenc u.) is the work of Gyula Jungfer. The reliefs above the first floor level are by Géza Maróty. The rich interior is by Ödön Faragó and the windows are by stained glass-maker Miksa Róth. Although partly burnt at the end of World War II the building has been carefully restored. Today it is occupied by the Budapest Bank and the State Development Bank.

The corner building on the other side of Váci u. was built in 1877 to the design of Mór Kallina. Critics thought the building too simple and not ornate enough having just one balcony on the N side overlooking the large square. Ironically that balcony played a larger role in history than the critics might have guessed, for during World War I the supporters of the radical liberal politician Mihály Károlyi, who became Prime Minister in 1918, had an office in the building and Károlyi himself often used to address the crowds in the square from the balcony above.

Váci u. ends in VÖRÖSMARTY TÉR, a large, pleasant square popular with street musicians and artists in the summer. In the middle of the square is Ede Telcs' 1908 Carrara marble statue of **Mihály Vörösmarty** (1800–55) one of the leading literary figures of the Reform Period. Carved on the front of the monument are the words 'Rendületlenül légy híve hazádnak, óh Magyar' (Be always faithful to your country, oh Magyar), the opening lines of Vörösmarty's 'Szózat' (Appeal) which is regarded almost as a second national anthem.

The modern building facing the statue on the W side of the square (Elemér Tallós and Tibor Hübner, 1971) contains offices of the Hungarian PEN Club, the Corvina foreign language publishing house, the Hungarian Recording Company (Hungaroton), Artisjus (the copyright protection office) and, on the ground floor, an art showroom, concert ticket agency (through the swing doors in middle) and a large record shop. The German Theatre of Pest used to stand on this site. Beethoven composed an overture for its opening in 1812.

On the N side of the square stands the **Gerbeaud pastry-shop and café**. It was founded in 1858 by Henrik Kugler, a pioneer of the Hungarian confectionary industry, and moved here from its original site in nearby József Nádor tér in 1870. It was bought by the Swiss Emil Gerbeaud in 1884 and from the turn of the century Gerbeaud's became well-known both as a meeting place and for the quality of its cakes. For many years after the war it was called the 'Vörösmarty' but in the 1980s reverted to its more popular, present name. The Secessionist style interior furnishings date from the turn of the century.

Vörösmarty tér has had many names over the years and its appearance has also changed with time. Some of the different names together with old pictures of the square can be seen on the round pillar-like structure standing by the edge of the trees towards the NE corner. The Vörösmarty metro station is the city centre terminus of the Small Underground Line. The entrance is down the steps in front of the Gerbeaud café.

The **British Embassy** is situated in a former bank building at No. 6 Harmincad u., which runs eastwards from the NE corner of Vörösmarty tér. (The street name means 'one thirtieth' and comes from an ancient form of toll.) The *British Council Library* is situated in the building (access via the door to the left of the main entrance) and has a selection of British newspapers and magazines. (Open Mon–Fri 10.00–12.45 and 14.30–17.00.) The Visa Department and Consulate are reached via the same entrance and are normally open 8.30–11.30 but British passport holders may be allowed access in the afternoons.

Basil Davidson in his autobiographical wartime memoir, 'Special Operations Europe—Scenes from the anti-Nazi war', recalls an ironic incident about the British Legation which was then based here. He had been sent to Budapest to

assist the underground resistance while officially running a news service for
Britain. Early in 1941 he was called to the Legation and told that the plastic for
explosives intended for the resistance, which had been stored at the Legation,
had been dumped in the Danube and that if he did not cease his clandestine
activities he would be denounced to the Hungarian police. The Minister (not
named) sincerely believed that Britain would soon lose the war, a not uncom-
mon attitude in Central Europe at that particular time.

The route continues along Deák Ferenc u. at the SE corner of
Vörösmarty tér. On the left, its main façade overlooking the square, is
the *Luxus Department Store* built in 1911 to the designs of Flóris
Korb and Kálmán Giergl. The building was renovated in 1988. On
the right is the *Chemolimpex Building*. It was designed by Zoltán
Gulyás and built in 1964. Its modern style became, in the words of
one commentator, 'a repository of architectural cliché' copied on
countless occasions over the following 20 years.

The building stands on the corner of Bécsi u. and it is along here, to
the right (S), that the itinerary continues, arriving after 100m at
MARTINELLI TÉR. In the centre of the small square, on a column, is a
statue of the Virgin Mary which originally dates from 1729 though
the present structure is a copy made in 1943 by Dezső Erdey. At the
base of the column are figures of Joseph, Anne and Joachim.

*This striking Secessionist gable can be seen in Martinelli
tér.*

The **Servite Church** behind the statue was built between 1725 and
1732 to the designs of János Hölbling and György Pauer. The façade
was rebuilt in the early 1870s but the interior has retained its
Baroque character. The large relief on the right of the entrance is a
memorial to the members of the VIIth Wilhelm Hussar Regiment who
fell in World War I (János Istók, 1930). Above the level of the door to
the right and the left are statues of St. Anne and St. Peregrin. At the
top stand St. Augustine and St. Philip.
On the right of the church is the modern building (1975) of the

Inner City Telephone Exchange. Adjoining it, at No. 13–19 Petőfi
Sándor u. is the building of the *Central Post Office* (Antal Skalniczky,
1875). 'Poste restante' mail can be collected here, while in the
modern building next door international telephone, telex and telefax
directories can be found. There is also a public telex and telefax
service here.

No. 5 Martinelli tér is the so-called **Rózsavölgyi House** designed
by Béla Lajta in 1910–11. With its stylistic distinction between the
retail, office and residential parts of the building, it is considered a
precursor of modern Hungarian architecture. Although Lajta is often
regarded as the father of modernism, the ceramic decorations on the
upper floors betray his earlier connections with the National Romantic school. On the ground floor is a chemist's and a record shop which
also stocks a large range of music books and music scores.

To the right at *No. 3* is the former 'Turkish Banking House' built in
1906 and designed by Henrik Böhm and Ármin Hegedüs. At the top
on the gable is a striking Secessionist coloured mosaic showing a
glorified Hungaria surrounded by angels and shepherds. *No. 1* to the
right was originally built with just two storeys. It was rebuilt in 1922
by two fashionable architects, Töry and Pogány, which was when the
Renaissance-style embellishments were added.

VÁROSHÁZ UTCA leaves Martinelli tér from the left side of the
Servite church. The building which stretches for nearly 200m on the
left of the street is the **Municipal Council**. Designed in the early 18C
by Anton Erhard Martinelli as a hospital for veterans of the anti-
Turkish war it is the largest Baroque building in Budapest, though
much of the original ornamentation was destroyed in World War II.
Just inside the third, southernmost gateway, on the right, is a 1785
statue of *Pallas Athene* by Italian-born sculptor, Carlo Adami. It
originally stood by the old Buda Town Hall near the Matthias
Church, hence the Buda coat of arms on the goddess' shield.

In the small square (Kamermayer Károlyi tér) on the left at the far
end of the Council building is an aluminium statue of *Károlyi
Kamermayer* (1829–97), the first mayor of the united city when Buda
and Pest were administratively joined in 1873 (the statue is by Béla
Szabados, 1942).

Pilvax köz on the right is the site of the former *Pilvax Kávéház*, a popular 19C
meeting place for political radicals. 'If you write,' Sándor Petőfi once advised
János Arany in a letter of 1847, 'then address the letter to the Pilvax Coffee
House. It is more likely to reach me, as I am more often here than at home.'

It was from here that Petőfi and the revolutionary youth set out on 15 March
1848. The original coffee house was pulled down in 1911 though one of the tables
and various memorabilia can be seen in the Petőfi Literary Museum on Károly
Mihály u. Inside today's Pilvax café, which stands almost on the same spot,
there are photographs and items around the walls appertaining to the political
atmosphere of its 19C predecessor.

The **Pest County Hall** stands at No. 7 Városház u., beyond Kamermayer Károly tér. It was built in several stages in the first half of the
19C. The neo-classical façade with its six Corinthian columns and
tympanum is the work of Mátyás Zitterbarth Jr. The building has an
interesting triple courtyard which it is possible to inspect during
working hours. The first of these has arcades around three sides and
a cast-iron neo-Gothic well dating from the early 19C.

The route now passes through the gateway of *No. 6* Városház u. on
the right, and through the buiding's two inner courtyards to emerge
through the far gateway at *No. 3* Petőfi Sándor u. This is the largest

neo-classical building in the Inner City and was built in the 1830s to the plans of József Hild.

For more than 30 years until 1865 it was the home of the Academy of Sciences. The Trattner Printing House, also based here, was associated with the magazine 'Tudományos Gyűjtemény' (Scientific Collection) an important critical, literary and historical journal of the 19C and a forum for young Pest writers. The building was damaged by cannon fire in 1849 but restored later by Hild.

No. 6 on the far side of Petőfi Sándor u. is the home of the *József Katona Theatre* (Katona József színház), noted for its contemporary productions. To the left is Felszabadulás tér which the route now crosses via the underpass emerging at the beginning of KÁROLYI MIHÁLY UTCA. (For the Fransciscan church here see p 189.) Just beyond the *Catholic Repository* on the left is the *Kárpáthia restaurant* which has a striking neo-Gothic interior. Beyond it, at No. 10 Károlyi Mihály u., stands the **University Library**, which was originally founded in 1635. The present building was designed by Antal Skalnitzky and Henrik Koch and constructed in 1873–76.

Diagonally across the junction, on the corner of Irányi u., is the university students' *Eötvös Club*, which stands on the site of the fomer Centrál kávéház, a popular literary meeting place from the 1890s to the 1930s. The club here is a venue for all kinds of youth events and foreigners are welcome.

The **Petőfi Literary Museum** (Petőfi Iródalmi Múzeum) is at No. 16 Károlyi Mihály u. on the left, in the former Károlyi Mansion. The building was originally Baroque, the work of András Mayerhoffer in 1759–68, though Anton Riegl of Vienna rebuilt it in neo-classical style in 1832. The museum is devoted to the lives and works of the great names of Hungarian literature including Sándor Petőfi, Mór Jókai, Zsigmond Móricz, Miklós Radnóti, Attila József and Tibor Déri. (Open 10.00–18.00 except Monday.)

Count Mihály Károlyi, the liberal progressive politician and President of the 1918–19 Hungarian Republic, was born here in 1875. In exile during the Horthy era, Károly spent much time in England trying to rally democratic forces to have an influence on Hungary. He returned to Hungary after World War II and served as Hungarian ambassador to Paris. Disagreements over the Rajk trial in 1949 (see p 214) led to a second exile and he died in France in 1955. Originally buried on the Isle of Wight, his body was moved to Budapest and reburied in the Kerepesi Cemetery in 1962. Inside the museum is a *memorial room* to Károlyi which includes an amusing 1925 letter to him from Bertrand Russell as well as material from his anti-fascist campaigns in Britain and America. The Károlyi memorial plaque on the N wall of the building is by Viktor Kalló (1964).

The Austrian general Julius Haynau who was sent to counter the Hungarians in the 1848–49 War of Independence had his headquarters in this building. The relief on the S side, by Henszlmann u., shows the arrest which took place here of Count Lajos Batthyány, the Prime Minister of the first independent Hungarian government in 1848. Batthyányi was later executed on 6 October 1849.

Behind the building in the small garden (Károlyi kert) is a bust of *Dániel Irányi* (1822–92) a lawyer and one of the leading politicians of the 1848–49 period (Ede Kallós, 1904). In exile after the events, Irányi wrote prolifically in support of Hungary's independence. He returned in 1867 and later formed the Independence Party, of which he was the chairman until his death.

Károlyi Mihály u. ends at EGYETEM TÉR. The large neo-Baroque building at No. 1–3 on the right is the central building and Law Faculty of the **Loránd Eötvös University** (Eötvös Loránd Tudomány Egyetem—ELTE). It was built in 1898–99 and inaugurated in May

1900. The University was founded in 1635 in Nagyszombat (today Trnava in Czechoslovakia) by Péter Pázmány, the Archbishop of Esztergom. In 1777 it moved to Buda, and in 1784 to Pest where it occupied the former Pauline Monastery near the present building. (Loránd Eötvös, 1848–1919, was a physicist noted for his invention of the torsion pendulum used in geological research and his theories concerning the measurement of gravity and magnetism.)

The *University Pharmacy* at No. 5 Egyetem tér was opened in 1928 and originally carried the name of Péter Pázmány. Inside there is a bust of him by György Zala, the sculptor of the Millennial Monument.

On the right-hand corner of the university building is a typically inter-war patriotic bronze relief dedicated to the students who died fighting in World War I (György Zala, 1930).

To the right stands the **University Church** (Egyetemi Templom) one of the most impressive pieces of Baroque architecture in Budapest. Consecrated in 1748 it was built for the Pauline order, the only religious order founded in Hungary (by Canon Eusebius in 1263). The design is believed to be the work of András Mayerhoffer. Above the tympanum at the top of the façade are statues of St. Paul and St. Anthony. Between them is the Pauline arms, a palm tree with a raven between two lions. The door is particularly beautiful with its carved wooden interior porch. The now somewhat dilapidated frescoes on the ceiling show scenes from the life of Mary (Johann Bergl, 1776). The statues on the high altar are the work of József Hebenstreit who also carved the stalls in the chancel. Above the altar is a copy of the Black Madonna of Czestochowa painted on copper (c 1720). The richly decorated pulpit on the right and the carvings on the pews are the work of the Pauline monks who also made the balustrade in the organ loft, the Louis XVI confessionals on each side and all the other interior carvings of the church.

The Pauline monks also worked on the library of the *Central Seminary* (Központi Papnevelő Intézet) at No. 7 Eötvös Loránd u. to the right of the church. Unfortunately, however, the library is not open to the public.

No. 2 at the far end of Eötvös Loránd u., on the corner with VERES PÁLNÉ UTCA, used to be the *Golden Lion* (Arany Oroszlán) *Pharmacy*. Founded nearby in 1794, it moved here in 1810. The original furnishings have been removed and reconstructed in the Kiscell Museum in Óbuda. The Baroque parts of the house were rebuilt in classical style in 1841 by József Hild.

The **Serbian Orthodox Church** is 150m to the left along Veres Pálné u., at the junction with Szerb u. Large numbers of Serbs fleeing from the Turks arrived in Pest in the late 17C. Many were tradesmen and merchants. The church was completed in the mid-18C on the site of a former church. It is probably the work of András Mayerhoffer. The iconostasis inside has carvings dating from 1845, the paintings, which show Italian Renaissance influence, are by Károly Sterio, a painter of Greek origins (1856–57).

The route now continues northwards along Veres Pálné u. A few metres after Eötvös Loránd u. on the right is *Szivárvány köz* (Rainbow Alley) one of the narrowest streets in Budapest. The *Ady Memorial Room* (open 10.00–18.00 except Monday) is on the first floor of No. 4–6 Veres Pálné u. (on the right after Irányi u.). The poet Endre Ady (1877–1919) lived the last two years of his life here. Ady was one of the outstanding Hungarian poets of the 20C whose appearance on the scene coincided with the emergence of a radical democratic intelligentsia. The innovative and creative spirits which gathered around him resulted, among other things, in the establishment of 'Nyugat' (Occident), the progressive literary journal. The bronze memorial tablet outside is the work of sculptor Imre Varga and was placed here in 1977 when the memorial room was first opened.

Veres Pálné u. ends at Felszabadulás tér.

F. The Little Boulevard (Kiskörút)

This route, some 1.5km in length, runs from Liberty Bridge (Szabadság híd) just S of the inner city along Tolbuhin körút, Múzeum körút and Tanács körút, ending in Deák tér in the city centre. It follows the line of the former town walls of Pest. The ancient walls can still be seen in certain places and these have been indicated in the text. Trams No. 47 and 49 run along the length of the route.

Liberty Bridge, 331m in length, was originally opened on 4 October 1896 to the design of János Feketeházy. Destroyed in World War II it was the first Budapest bridge to be rebuilt in 1946 whence it takes its present name. However, the two original customs houses on the Pest side survived and are still standing today. At the top of the iron structure are two 'Turul' birds, the legendary birds of the ancient Hungarians.

Just N of the Pest end of the bridge, at No. 2 BELGRÁD RAKPART by the riverside, is the former home of the Hungarian Marxist philosopher George Lukács (1885–1971). His fifth floor flat today houses a library and research archive belonging to the philosophy department of the Hungarian Academy of Sciences.

Perhaps the most surprising thing about George Lukács is that this maverick Marxist managed to survive all the twists and turns of the international Communist movement and die a natural death in his own country at the age of 86.

The son of a bank manager he had a conventional upbringing attending grammar school and university. The period 1906–11 found him in Berlin pursuing his studies of literature and philosophy. During the First World War, back in Hungary, he began to mix in radical intellectual circles and turned towards Marxism, a shift which was encouraged by the outbreak of the Russian Revolution in 1917. He joined the Communist Party in December 1918 and a few months later found himself working as a People's Commissar for Education and Culture during the short-lived Republic of Councils of 1919.

While in exile in Vienna in the 1920s he continued writing, producing 'History and Class Consciousness' in 1923—a work which was to inspire many Western New Left radicals over four decades later. His unorthodox Marxist approach, not limited to purely economic concepts, has often been compared to the work of other critical Marxists of the time, notably the Italian Antonio Gramsci and the German Karl Korsch, though there are differences between all three.

A dispute over strategy in 1929 in the Comintern led Lukács to withdraw into purely theoretical work. He moved to Moscow in 1933 and stayed in the Soviet Union until the end of the Second World War. Devoting himself primarily to Marxist aesthetics he managed to escape the purges to which many of his Hungarian colleagues in Moscow fell victim, including Béla Kun the leader of the Hungarian Party.

Returning to Budapest in 1945 he took up a post at the university and actively encouraged intellectuals to work for a new Hungary. In 1949–50 he was strongly criticised in a campaign of the emerging cultural dogmatism and he once again withdrew into theoretical work. He reappeared on the political scene in 1956 becoming Minister of Culture in Imre Nagy's short-lived government. Although he spent time with Nagy in exile in Romania he was allowed to return to Hungary unharmed in April 1957. He spent the rest of his life studying and writing about aesthetics, philosophy and questions of socialism and democracy.

Lukács is one of the few Eastern European Marxists to have gained a degree of respect in the West, both in academic and political circles. Yet he always retained an orthodox attachment to the Party and often displayed elements of dogmatic simplicity: 'Even the worst socialism is better than the best capitalism', he said in 1967.

DIMITROV TÉR is the name of the square at the Pest end of Liberty Bridge. The plaque on the wall at *No. 2 Dimitrov tér* (on the N side) indicates that the writer Zsigmond Móricz (1879–1942) lived and worked here for eight years. The quotation reads 'I am not a man of dreams, but of life—my dream is life'.

On the W side of the square stands a bronze statue of *Georgi Dimitrov* (1882–1949) the Bulgarian Communist leader who played a major role in the Comintern in the 1930s. The statue, by J. Kratchmarov, was presented as a gift from Bulgaria in 1954. The limestone memorial in the middle of the square, somewhat hidden by trees and bushes, is to the *First Honvéd Infantry Regiment* of World War I (Árpád Domján, 1949).

The large building at No. 8 on the S side of the square is the **Karl Marx University of Economics**. It was designed by Miklós Ybl in early Eclectic, neo-Renaissance style and built between 1871 and 1874 as the Main Customs Office. A series of tunnels connected the building to the Danube embankment. The 170m façade overlooking the river has ten allegorical statues by the Viennese sculptor, August Sommer. The building was reconstructed after the war and opened as a university in 1951.

TOLBUHIN KÖRÚT leaves the square on the E side and is the first section of the Little Boulevard. Next to the university at No. 1–3 Tolbuhin körút stands the **Central Market Hall** (Samu Pecz, 1893–96) the most impressive of the five Budapest market halls built in the 1890s.

The huge iron framework covering more than 10,000 sq m was originally built to serve as the city's main wholesale market. The wholesale market has since moved to Csepel island and the building is now used entirely for retail purposes. Always a popular attraction with visitors (Margaret Thatcher was filmed and photographed buying paprika here in 1984) at the time of writing it was due to close for three years while renovations take place.

The neo-classical building opposite at *No. 2*, on the corner of Váci u., is the former Nádor Hotel built in 1840 to the design of Ferenc Kasselik. In the butchers on the ground floor some original coloured picture tiles can still be seen. The building is a characteristic example of mid-19C Pest construction as is the classical building nearby at *No. 6* (Antal Diescher, 1854).

Veres Pálné u., the first street to the left off Tolbuhin körút, is named after Hermin Beniczky (1815–95) one of the pioneers of education for girls in Hungary. (Ironically perhaps in this context, she is usually referred to through her husband's name, Pál Veres.) The wall tablet at the end of the street records that at No. 36 she founded the National Association for Female Education (Országos Nőképző Egyesület) and at No. 38 the first high school for girls.

From the corner of Bástya u., the first street on the right along Veres Pálné u., the original 15C town wall of Pest can be clearly seen at the back of the block which faces Tolbuhin körút. A free-standing section of the wall can also be seen clearly in the courtyard of the classical building at No. 16 on the körút.

Tolbuhin körút (named after the Soviet Marshal Fyodor Tolbuhin who was a participating commander during the liberation of Hungary) ends at KÁLVIN TÉR, one of the main junctions of Pest. The Kecskemét Gate, part of the old city walls, used to stand here until it was pulled down in 1794. A modern hotel has been built on the site where the gate used to stand, at the end of Kecskeméti u. An 80 sq m red limestone memorial of the gate stretches along one of the walls of the central area in the Kálvin tér pedestrian subway (Gyula Illés, 1983). The subway and the metro station below were opened in 1976.

The square received its present name in 1874 after the single-nave **Calvinist Church** which stands here. Designed by József Hofrichter it was built between 1816 and 1830 although the entrance and tympanum were added by József Hild in 1848 and the spire dates from 1859. Hild also added the upper part of the pulpit (1831) and the organ loft (1854). The neo-Gothic sepulchre of the Countess Zichy can be found in the wall of the church on the left. The statue is by the Frenchman Raymond Gayard and the framework by Frigyes Feszl (1854). The church is normally closed, but access can sometimes be gained by application at the church house to the rear.

The two stone lions above the entrance to the two-storey neoclassical building at *No. 9* Kálvin tér are a reminder that the building, until 1881, used to be the 'Two Lions' inn (Mátyás Zitterbarth, 1816–18). Hector Berlioz is believed to have first heard the 'Rákóczi Song' here after which he composed his 'Rákóczi March'. In the courtyard through the gateway is a row of single-storey 19C houses and a single seated female figure from the *Danubius fountain* which originally stood in Kálvin tér. Damaged, like much of the area, in World War II, the fountain was eventually restored and today stands in Engels tér.

Ráday u. runs off Kálvin tér by the side of No. 9. About 200m along here, at No. 28 on the left, in the building of the Ráday Calvinist College, there is one of Budapest's newest museums, the small *Bible Museum* (Biblia Múzeum) which opened in late 1988. (Open 10.00–17.00 except Monday.)

The college and the street are named after Pál Ráday (1677–1733) a Protestant nobleman who was Ferenc Rákóczi II's secretary during the early 18C War of Independence. After that war he played an important political role as a spokesperson of Protestant interests. He supported various cultural activities and at his mansion in Pécel near Budapest he established the first significant collection of books published in Hungarian.

The strange white limestone figure in Kálvin tér near the beginning of Ráday u. is called *Music* (Zene) and is by Róbert Csíkszentmihályi (1983). Üllői út, the next street, which leads away from the square to the SE, has a plaque at No. 4 to the memory of the Dutch Consul General, Jan Fledderus who did much to help Budapest children in the years after the 1914–18 war.

The next street, Baross u., leads immediately to Szabó Ervin tér and the neo-Baroque **Municipal Szabó Ervin Library** (Artur Meining, 1887). (Open Mon, Tues, Thurs and Fri 9.00–21.00; Sat and Sun 9.00–13.00; closed Wednesdays.) The library is a public lending social sciences library with over 100 branches throughout the city. It has a specialist collection of material on Budapest.

Ervin Szabó (1877–1918) was a social scientist, an internationally recognised authority on statistics and librarianship, a left-wing political activist with both Marxist and syndicalist sympathies and the first director of the library. There is a marble relief of him on the wall of the library (Gyula Kiss Kovács, 1954).

The bronze and limestone *Fountain of Justice* (Justitia-kút) in front of the library is by István Szentgyörgyi (1929) and depicts Justitia, the goddess of justice, with sword and scale in hand. Originally there was also on the fountain a side relief of the British Lord Rothermere who befriended post-Trianon Hungary in the 1920s. This was removed in 1949.

The large wrought-iron gates (1897) of the library are a good example of the fine work of Gyula Jungfer.

The route continues northwards from Kálvin tér along MÚZEUM KÖRÚT. The first street off to the right is Múzeum u. No. 7 is the headquarters of TIT, the Society for the Promotion of Scientific Knowledge (Tudományos Ismeretterjesztő Társulat). Called this since 1958 the society actually traces its roots back to 19C movements for public enlightenment. TIT organises a wide range of voluntary educational activities such as foreign language teaching, lectures, discussions and (in Hungarian) guided walks round Budapest. The building also houses the Kossuth Klub, a literary, artistic, political and social club. 1956 saw the formation here of the Petőfi Circle, one of the main groupings of opposition intellectuals whose discussions prefigured the uprising of that year.

Some 100m along Múzeum körút, at No. 17, is the neo-Baroque building of the *National Technical Library*, (Országos Műszaki Információs Központ és Könyvtár). Built for the Károly family in 1881 by the Viennese architects Fellner and Helmer, the building was used as the French Embassy in the 1920s and then in the 1930s by the Baross Federation, a commercial organisation with right-wing political leanings. After the war it was the home of the Teachers Free Trade Union and since 1955 that of the Technical Library. The beautiful carved large wooden stairway inside was made in the workshop of Endre Thék, one of the most noted furniture makers of the day. The neo-Renaissance courtyard is also worth seeing.

Immediately beyond Múzeum u., on the körút, stands the large neo-classical building of the **Hungarian National Museum** (Magyar Nemzeti Múzeum). (Open 10.00–18.00 except Monday.)

The museum dates from 1802 when Count Ferenc Széchényi (1754–1820), the father of István Széchenyi and himself a promoter of Hungarian national identity, donated his own collection of over 11,000 prints, 1150 manuscripts, hundreds of maps, coats of arms and coins to the nation for the founding of a national museum and library. The news was greeted with enthusiasm by intellectuals and progressive aristocrats not only in Hungary but throughout Europe.

Construction began in 1837 to the designs of Mihály Pollack (1773–1855) who although born in Vienna and trained in Italy adopted Hungary as his homeland. His neo-classical public buildings and town houses typified the architecture of the Reform Period in the second quarter of the 19C. When the museum was opened in 1847 it was the fourth national museum to be completed after the British Museum, the Altes Museum in Berlin and the Glyptothek in Munich.

Shortly after its opening, the Museum became the scene of one of the most celebrated events of the 1848 revolution. It was here, from the wide steps of the building, that a huge crowd was addressed by the young revolutionary leaders of Pest, including the poet Sándor Petőfi, who recited his rousing 'Nemzeti Dal' (National Song). The event, the place and the poem have all found their place in Hungarian history and today every year on March 15 the Múzeum is decked out with the national colours and an open-air rally and/or performance takes place on the steps recalling the events of 1848. The plaque on the outside of the N wall of the steps is in memory of Petőfi and his song, while that on the inside is to Pál Vasvári, one of the leaders who was present here and who was killed later in 1848.

The façade of the National Museum is dominated by a huge central portico with eight Corinthian columns supporting a large tympanum for which a group of statues was cast in zinc by Munich sculptor, Ludwig Schaller, to the design of Raffaello Monti of Milan. The central seated figure is Pannonia (the name of the Roman province occupying today's western Hungary), the Hungarian coat of arms on her shield. The three figures on each side represent the sciences and arts.

Through the main doorway is a columned entrance hall which leads to a spacious round hall in which a 3C Roman mosaic floor from Baláca near Veszprém can be seen. The frescoes are by Károly Lotz and Mór Than who also did the frescoes on the ornamental staircase leading to the first floor. The central circular hall with panelled, domed ceiling was designed after the Roman Pantheon.

The History of the Peoples of Hungary from the Paleolithic Age to the Magyar Conquest is the permanent exhibition on the ground floor. The eight rooms and one corridor display materials showing the history of settlements in the region from antiquity through the Bronze and Iron Ages, the Roman period, to the early Middle Ages.

The first floor is occupied by the permanent exhibition of *The History of the Hungarian People from the Magyar Conquest to 1849*. The exhibits illustrate the main political stages of Hungarian history to the mid-19C (the age of Árpád and the subsequent dynasties, the flowering Renaissance period under King Matthias Corvinus, the 150-year Turkish occupation, the Rákóczi War of Independence against the Habsburgs and the Revolution and War of Independence of 1848–49).

Also on the first floor are the *Hungarian Coronation Regalia*, Hungary's crown jewels. The central piece is the Hungarian crown, which is one of the oldest royal crowns in existence. It is made up of an upper, Roman crown and a lower, Byzantine portion. The upper crown was sent by Pope Sylvester II to King Stephen I for his coronation in AD 1000. It is made up of gold bands set with gems and pearls, and has cloisonné enamel images of eight apostles. It is surmounted by a gold cross leaning to one side as a result of damage sustained during Stephen's lifetime. The leaning cross can always be clearly seen on representations of the old Hungarian coat of arms.

The lower crown was sent to King Géza I in 1074 as a gift from the Byzantine emperor. It is a gold diadem set with precious stones and gold enamel images of archangels and saints. Along the upper edge are images of Christ Enthroned, the Byzantine emperor Michael Duca, Constantine the Great and Géza I. It is not known precisely when the two crowns were joined together but it was probably sometime during the reign of Béla III (1172–96) as the composite crown first appeared on coins minted in 1190.

The crown was used for centuries at the coronation of Hungarian kings. Possession of the crown and being crowned with it was always a matter of great political significance. Several times it has been removed from the country. The most recent absence lasted 34 years. At the end of the Second World War the crown jewels were taken by Hungarian Nazis to Germany from where they were later taken to the United States of America and kept in Fort Knox. They were not returned to Hungary until January 1978 after US-Hungarian relations had been normalised for some time.

Other items on display here include the coronation robe, made of crimson-coloured silk from Byzantium, the sceptre with a rock crystal head and gold setting, the 14C orb, made of gold-plated bronze, and a 16C sword made in Venice.

At the time of writing the **Natural History Museum** (Természet-tudományi Múzeum) is situated on the third floor in the Hungarian

National Museum. There are plans, however, to move the museum sometime in the 1990s to Building A at the Royal Palace in Buda, which is currently occupied by the Labour History Museum. That museum, in turn, is to move to the Hungarian National Museum and it will probably be merged with the current exhibitions here to form a new exhibition of the History of the Hungarian People.

The **Museum Garden** surrounding the National Museum (gates open 6.00–21.00) has been a popular meeting and resting place since it was laid out in 1856. A nationwide campaign was organised to create the garden and fund-raising activities included concerts by Ferenc Liszt and Ferenc Erkel. The many statues in the garden tell something about Hungarian history.

The large bronze and limestone statue in front of the museum, overlooking the körút, is of the poet *János Arany* (Alajos Stróbl, 1893). The side figures represent Miklós Toldi and Piroska Rozgonyi, characters in his epic work of Hungarian chivalry, the 'Toldi Trilogy'. János Arany (1817–82), one of the classic figures of Hungarian literature, was an epic poet and ballad writer. He translated many works of Shakespeare and was instrumental in the publication of the first complete works of Shakespeare in Hungarian. He once wrote that working on the English texts he 'laughed at the bizarre pronunciation of the written words ... the task was difficult but inspiring; a fair at Debrecen brought me cheap editions of King John and Richard II ... and before I knew it, King John spoke to me in Hungarian iambic pentameter.'

The 3m *marble column* standing just forward of the NW corner of the museum is from the Forum in Rome and was brought here in 1929. Indicative of the change in political atmosphere is the fact that pre-war guidebooks describe it as 'a gift from Mussolini' while post-war ones prefer 'from the city of Rome'.

The garden on the N side of the museum has six statues in the following order (from W to E): a bust of *Ferenc Kazinczy* (1759–1831), a leading literary figure of Hungarian Enlightenment and language reform; *Ottó Herman* (1835–1914) an ethnographer and natural scientist; *Count Ferenc Széchényi* (1753–1820) whose statue was erected here in 1902 on the 100th anniversary of his foundation of the museum; *Baron Alessandro (Sándor) Monti* (1818–54), one of the leaders of the 1848 anti-Habsburg revolt in Brescia, Italy, who came to Hungary and became a commander of the Italian legion in the Hungarian War of Independence; an eagle on a globe with a harp in its claws—a monument to the poet *Sándor Kisfaludy* (1772–1844); and, by the NE corner, a monument to three 19C archaeologists, *Flóris Rómer, Ferenc Pulsky* and *József Hampel*, whose work connected them to the museum.

In the SE corner of the garden is a marble monument to the poet and dramatist *Károly Kisfaludy* (1788–1830). By the middle of the S wall of the museum is an 1894 cast-iron copy of a 4C BC Greek sculpture, the *Apollo of Belvedere*, and in the far SW corner of the garden is a bust of the poet *Dániel Berzsenyi* (1776–1836). The bust was raised virtually in secret in the early morning of 29 May 1860 as at that time, under Austrian rule, the erection of monuments to Hungarian national figures (even poets) carried significant political connotations.

The two busts in front of the museum just S of the entrance steps date from more recent times and are both of foreign figures with Hungarian connections. On the right is *József Wysocki*, a general who fought for Polish independence and who in 1848–49 fought in Hungary in the Polish legion. The bronze bust, by Hanna Danilewicz, was presented as a gift from Warsaw in 1976. On its left is a bust of the Italian nationalist leader *Garibaldi*, erected on the 50th anniversary of his death in 1932. The relief shows him shaking hands with István Türr, a Hungarian who fought alongside Garibaldi in Italy.

BRÓDY SÁNDOR U. runs right from the körút along the N side of the Museum Garden. At the corner, on the körút, is an old Pest coffee house, the *Múzeum Kávéház*. Original ceramic wall decoration made at the Zsolnay factory in Pécs can be seen as can ceiling frescoes by Károly Lotz.

The neo-Renaissance mansion at No. 4, with a first floor loggia, was built by Antal Wéber in 1875–76 for Károly Ádám. No. 8 today houses the *Institute of Italian Culture* though it was originally built in 1865–66 for the Chamber of Deputies, the lower of the two houses of Parliament. (The Upper House met nearby in the National Museum.)

Designed by Miklós Ybl in neo-Renaissance style, construction began in September 1865. The project was regarded as a national concern. 800 people worked on the building and despite a strike for higher pay by the Hungarian carpenters, which necessitated the importing of Austrian furniture, the building was ready for use by the following March. The Parliamentary representatives met here until the new Parliament building by the Danube was opened in 1901. A stone carving of the Hungarian coat of arms and the royal crown can be seen on the ledge at the top of the façade.

Pollack Mihály tér is at the back of the Museum Gardens. The building at *No. 10*, on the corner of Bródy Sándor u., used to belong to the Festetics family and was designed by Miklós Ybl in neo-Renaissance style in 1862. For many years it housed the National Széchényi Library until this was moved to the former Royal Palace.

The yellow building further along Bródy Sándor u. at No. 7 on the right is the old entrance to *Hungarian Radio*. Shooting occurred here for the first time in 1956 as a crowd of protestors beseiged the radio on the evening of 23 October, the first day of the uprising.

The complex of buildings beyond the Múzeum Kávéház at Nos 4–8 Múzeum körút belong to the **Natural Science Faculty of the Eötvös Loránd University**. Inside the garden, which opens off the körút, is a *Memorial to Teachers who fell in World War I* (Béla Horváth, 1936). Further inside is a bronze statue of *Ágoston Trefort* (1817–88), a former Minister of Culture.

Beyond the university buildings by the newly-constructed trade centre is a white stone monument erected by the city council in 1987 to commemorate the 150th anniversary of the foundation here of the *Pesti Magyar Szinház* (Pest Hungarian Theatre). In 1840 it became the *Nemzeti Színház* (National Theatre), which was instrumental in developing Hungarian cultural life. The building was demolished in 1913.

The row of buildings on the other side of Múzeum körut, opposite the museum and the university, contains a number of book and record shops. No. 15 is the *Central Second-hand Bookshop* (Központi Antikvárium), which has a selection of books in English.

In the courtyard of the Romantic building at *No. 21* a free-standing section of the old medieval city wall can still be seen. *No. 7* was also built in Romantic style (Miklós Ybl, 1852) and has an interesting, though now somewhat dilapidated through-courtyard and a wooden floor in the gateway. The *Astoria Hotel* (see p 190) stands on the corner of Múzeum körút and Kossuth Lajos u.

Crossing this junction the route now continues along TANÁCS KÖRÚT. The corner building on the right at *No. 1* was originally built by the Academy of Sciences in 1936. It was popularly known as the 'Golden House', it being alleged that you needed a kilo of gold to buy a flat here.

The cinema at No. 3 is called the *Broadway*. It often has old and foreign films. Across the road at No. 2–8 Dohány u., on the corner of Tanács körút, stands the **Central Synagogue**, the largest synagogue in Europe. It was designed by Viennese architect Lajos Förster between 1854 and 1859 with the assistance of Frigyes Feszl, the architect of the Vigadó building by the Danube. The style is Romantic with Byzantine-Moorish elements which makes it one of the most striking buildings in Budapest. The annexe on the left was added by Ferenc Faragó and László Vágó in 1929–31. Its first floor houses the **National Jewish Museum** (Országos Zsidó Múzeum) which exhibits items from Jewish history in Hungary and has a small exhibition of photographs of the ghetto and the war years. (Open 15 May–15 October: Mon and Thurs 14.00–18.00; Tues, Wed, Fri and Sun 10.00–13.00; closed Saturdays.) The garden behind the annexe became a cemetery at the end of the war for Jews who were killed in the ghetto.

Restoration work on the synagogue started in 1988 at an estimated cost of 10 million USD. The Emmanuel Foundation, established jointly by the Hungarian government and the New York based World Association of Hungarian Jews, is helping to raise the money. Money has also been raised, partly by private donation, towards a weeping-willow shaped memorial (by Hungarian architect Imre Varga) the leaves of which bear the names of families massacred by the Nazis. It was planned to unveil the monument in 1989 on the 45th anniversary of the start of the deportation of Jews from Budapest.

The Jewish ghetto stretched from behind Tanács körút out towards the Great Boulevard. Its centre was in Klauzál tér. The area had become densely populated by Jews in the second half of the 19C, which was when it became the centre of Jewish life in Budapest. Architecturally the area has changed very little since the turn of the century and a walk along any of the streets leading off the körút (Dohány u., Wesselényi u., Dob u. and Majakovszkij u.) still gives a flavour of old Budapest.

An example of the many synagogues in the area is the *Rumbach Sebestyén u. Synagogue*, which can be reached through the entrance passageway of the modern red-brick building at No. 9 Tanács körút and then through three large connected courtyards to Rumbach Sebestyén u. where just to the left, at No. 11–13, stands the Romantic synagogue with its two huge towers and circular balconies at the top. Built in 1872 the main architect was the Viennese Otto Wagner. It was the central synagogue of the so-called 'status-quo' (middle-conservative) Jews.

A huge complex of red-brick buildings on Tanács körút opens on to and surrounds MADÁCH IMRE TÉR. Designed by Gyula Wälder in 1938, the plan was to make this the beginning of a new avenue similar to Népköztársaság útja which would sweep through the old parts of the city towards the City Park. The plans were shelved during the war and the present buildings are all that remain.

The Madách Repertory Theatre (Madách Kamaraszínház) is at No. 6 in the square. In front of the theatre is a small bronze statue entitled *Dancing Woman* (Táncosnő) by Ferenc Medgyessy (1982).

A few metres beyond Madách tér Tanács körút ends at DEÁK TÉR, named after the Hungarian politician Ferenc Deák (1803–76). It has had a variety of names including Coal Market, Cabbage Market and Lutheran Church Square but has been known as Deák tér since 1866. In 1883 the square had the dubious distinction of having the first public toilet in Budapest.

The Deák tér metro station is the main underground interchange, being the only station where all three metro lines meet. The **Underground Museum** is situated in the station's underpass. Entrance is 5 forints or one metro ticket. Opened in 1975 this small museum shows the history of underground development and outlines the plans for expansion. It has an old coach from the 'little underground' line. (Open 10.00–18.00 except Monday.)

The most significant building in Deák tér, on the left at the end of Tanács körút, is the neo-classical **Lutheran Church** designed by Mihály Pollack and János Kraus and built between 1799 and 1809. The façade with its Doric pillars and tympanum was added by József Hild in 1856. The high altar was designed by Pollack, and the altarpiece is a copy of Raphael's 'Transfiguration'. The building is normally only open for worship but occasionally concerts are given inside and these are usually advertised on the front door of the church.

The **National Lutheran Museum** (Evangélikus Országos Múzeum) is in the adjoining building. (Open 10.00–18.00 except Monday.) On display are artefacts from the history of the Lutheran church in Hungary including a facsimile of the last will and testament of Martin Luther (the original is preserved in the Lutheran archives in Budapest). The building used to be a Lutheran school and the wall plaque outside records that Sándor Petőfi attended classes here in 1833–34.

Opposite the museum, on the other side of the metro entrance, is the *NDK Centrum*, the cultural centre of the German Democratic Republic. On its right, at No. 2 Deák tér, is the *Budapest Central Police Headquarters*. Designed by Móric Pogány and Emil Tőry it was originally built in 1913 for the Adria Insurance Company. As with the New York Palace on Lenin körút, insurance companies were among the prime builders in Budapest in the years before World War I. Another such company, Anker Insurance, put up the large, columned building opposite the police headquarters on the far side of Deák tér (Ignác Alpár, 1907). On the ground floor of this building there is a good shop for postcards, posters, etc.

In the centre of the square is a small bronze statue entitled *Tavasz* (Spring) and at the northern edge of the square is a half-seated-half-standing statue of *Endre Bajcsy-Zsilinszky*, the politician and anti-fascist activist who was killed by the Nazis at Sopronkőhida in western Hungary on Christmas Eve in 1944.

The publicist and politician Bajcsy-Zsilinszky (1886–1944) had a rather varied career. In the 1920s he edited 'Szózat', a racist journal, was one of the leaders of the Racialist Party and a supporter of extreme right-wing policies. In the following decade he gradually swung to the left and joined the government's opposition forces. During the war he advocated unity with the Communists and formed a committee to direct the armed struggle against the Germans.

On the base of the statue are the words of the 19C Hungarian poet Ferenc Kölcsey, 'A Haza Minden Előtt' (The homeland before everything). The statue is the work of Sándor Győrfi and was erected in 1986.

Sütő u. leads off Deák tér to the SW (between the GDR Centre and the Lutheran Museum). Sütő means 'oven' (or 'baker') and the street used to be the site of a bakery for the nearby Károly Barracks. **Tourinform** is situated at No. 2 on the right. Tourinform is the central information office for foreign tourists and deals with all tourist enquiries. It has detailed information on cultural events, concerts, customs, exchange, passport and visa regulations, timetables, money exchange places, travel offices, restaurants and museums. English is spoken. (Open 8.00–20.00 every day. Tel. 1179-800.)

BIERMANN ISTVÁN TÉR lies at the end of Sütő u. a few metres beyond Tourinform. The *Danaides' fountain* here was erected in 1933 (Ferenc Sidló). To the rear of the fountain, overlooking the square, is the building of the former Lutheran Grammar School which has been a state school for most of the period since World War II.

The school includes among its past pupils the Hungarian political philosopher George Lukács. He once recalled that 'The Lutheran Grammar School being considered really exclusive in those days, my parents had me enrolled there ... Some of the leading personalities of Hungarian literary conservatism taught in that secondary school ... My attempts at intellectual self-liberation took on accents glorifying international modernism in opposition to a Hungarianness that I considered stupidly conservative and that I far-reachingly identified under the circumstances with the whole official world of the time. This oppositional attitude found its first expression in my homework which elicited violent professional uproar.'

G. The Northern Inner City

This route, c 3km in length, weaves around the area which started to develop in the late 18C to the north of the historic inner city which had been enclosed by the Pest walls. In 1790 it received the name Lipótváros (Leopold Town) after the Emperor Leopold II. The southern part of the area was built up in the first half of the last century in predominately neo-classical style, some of which remains. Eclecticism dominates, however, around Szabadság tér which, with the National Bank, Postal Savings Bank and Stock Exchange, became the centre of financial and commerial life. From there, northwards to Szent István körút, ministries, government and state offices were constructed and the area has retained this official character ever since.

The itinerary begins at VIGADÓ TÉR on the Danube embankment. The **Vigadó Concert Hall**, which faces the square, was designed by Frigyes Feszl and built in 1859–64 to replace a former concert hall on the same site which burnt down during the War of Independence of 1848–49. The hall opened in 1865 with Liszt's Elizabeth oratorio and over the years international artists, such as Wagner in 1875, have performed here. The building was badly damaged by fire at the end of World War II and although the Romantic exterior has been reconstructed as original the inside was completely redesigned.

The richly decorated exterior includes reliefs of dancers on the columns (Károlyi Alexy, 1863–64) and a series of busts along the freize-like ledge. In the centre is the old Hungarian coat of arms. To the left are images of King Louis the Great, János Hunyadi, István Széchenyi, Elizabeth of the House of Árpád, Béla IV and, round the corner facing Vigadó u., Maria Theresa and King Sigismund. To the right are King Matthias, Miklós Zrínyi, Palatine Joseph, Erzsébet Szilágyi, Jakab Varula (Pest's first magistrate after the Turkish era) and, round the corner facing Deák Ferenc u., Árpád and Attila.

The building to the left of the Vigadó with the maritime relief on the corner at the top and six ships hulls decorating the third floor level belongs to Mahart, the Hungarian shipping company.

The modern building on the right of the concert hall occupies the site of a former famous hotel, the Angol Királynő (English Queen).

It had been built in the early 1850s by József Hild to replace a previous hotel of the same name which had opened in 1839 at the time of the coronation of Queen Victoria and which was shelled by the Austrians in 1849. The politician Ferenc Deák lived here for 15 years and the hotel became a centre of political life which has been recorded in memoirs and on film. The hotel closed in 1916 and the building was demolished in 1940.

A 12m Swedish granite *Memorial to Soviet Airmen* stands in the middle of Vigadó tér (József Schall, 1975). It replaced an earlier one erected in 1945 which was pulled down in 1956.

The stretch of the Pest embankment to the N and S of Vigadó tér between the Elizabeth and Chain bridges is known as the **Corso** (Duna-korzó).

The embankment was built up in its present form in the second half of the 19C by the engineer Ferenc Reitter. Plans for a tramway along the embankment were made in 1884 by Siemens and Halske Co., but were realised only in 1900.

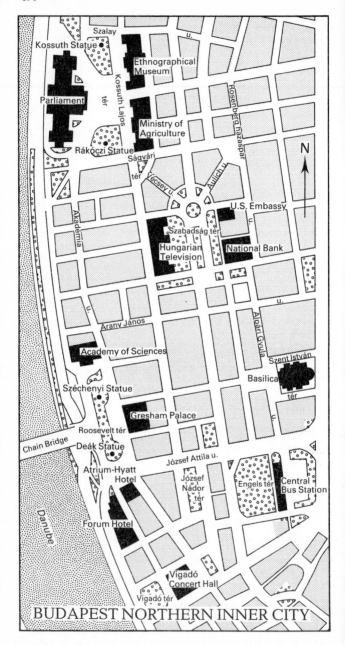

BUDAPEST NORTHERN INNER CITY

The tramway, which originally ran from today's March 15th Square to the Academy of Sciences, was constructed on a form of viaduct to allow space for storehouses underneath the river. These can still be seen today.

In the late 19C and early 20C the Corso was a favourite place for Budapest promenaders. Neighbouring hotels such as the English Queen, Europe, and Grand Duke Stephen received guests from all over the world including the Shah of Persia, Emperor Don Pedro of Brazil and the Prince of Wales. It was a place to stroll and be seen. Although some of that atmosphere has been revived in recent years the only building to have survived from the original row is the one on the N side of Vigadó tér which has the Dunakorzó café on the ground floor. One of the permanent attractions of the Corso has always been the splendid view it affords of the right bank of the Danube. In 1988 Castle Hill and this magnificent panorama across the river were added to the Unesco list of the world's cultural and natural heritage along with such places as the Acropolis in Athens and London's Westminster.

The river Danube bisects Budapest from N–S over a distance of approximately 28km. It is at its narrowest near Gellért Hill, where its width is only 285m. The depth of the river varies greatly. At medium water level it is about 9m at Liberty Bridge but only 3m in the southern part of the city. Bathing in the Danube within the boundaries of the city is not allowed (though people can often be seen fishing). Passenger transport on the river is mostly limited to excursion and pleasure boats. There is a landing stage for such boat trips on the riverside by Vigadó tér.

The *Duna Intercontinental Hotel* stands to the S of Vigadó tér where two of the old hotels, the Bristol and the Carlton, used to be before the war. Designed by József Finta and built in 1969 it was the first of a series of modern hotels to be constructed to serve Hungary's increasing tourist trade.

Two other modern hotels stand to the N of Vigadó tér. The dark-glass-fronted *Forum Hotel* (József Finta, 1981) is on the Corso, and next to it, facing Roosevelt tér, is the *Atrium-Hyatt Hotel* (Lajos Zalavári, 1981). The Forum, like several recently constructed hotels, was built with Austrian credit. On the first floor it has a reconstruction of a Viennese coffee house.

In front of the hotel is a bronze statue of *Baron József Eötvös* (1813–71) a statesman, scholar and writer, Minister of Culture in 1848 and after 1867, and from 1866 President of the Academy of Sciences (the statue is by Adolf Huszár, 1879).

Important legislation is linked with Eötvös. The 1868 Public Education Act established state-controlled compulsory elementary schooling. The Nationalities Act of the same year although liberal in some respects declared that all of Hungary's citizens belonged to the 'united Magyar nation' and did not recognise the right to autonomy of non-Magyar peoples.

The *Kossuth Museum Ship* (Kossuth Múzeumhajó) is moored at the embankment to the S of the Chain Bridge. Founded in 1986 as part of the Transport Museum, the museum (itself a steamship built in 1913) is devoted to the history of steam shipping on the Danube. (Open 15 April–31 October, 10.00–18.00 except Monday.)

ROOSEVELT TÉR is at the Pest end of the Chain Bridge (for details of the bridge see p 148). In the 19C it was a market. The present name, one of a handful of American and English place names in Budapest, dates from 1947. In 1867, for the coronation of Emperor Francis Joseph as King of Hungary, a 'coronation hill' was constructed here from earth brought from all parts of the country. The newly crowned king flourished the sword of St. Stephen in all directions as a pledge that he would protect the country. The historic soil was later dug into the earth.

In the southern part of the square amidst the trees is a large seated statue of **Ferenc Deák** who was largely responsible for the Compromise (Kiegyezés) of 1867 whereby the Austrian Empire was transformed into the Dual Monarchy and Hungary gained a degree of autonomy from Austria.

Deák (1803–76) was a well-to-do landowner who had studied law and worked in the county civil service. After 1833 he was a deputy and leader of the liberal opposition. He sided with Kossuth and in the 1848 government was Minister of Justice. Being of moderate persuasion he retired from public life during the War of Independence. During the 1860s he was the advocate of compromise with Austria, which finally came about in 1867. Afterwards he did not accept any kind of office but as a politician enjoying great prestige he was for a long time an influential figure in government circles and the enactment of a number of liberal laws is associated with his name.

The groups of side-statues show Justice (front) Patriotism (back) Popular Education and National Progress (left) and on the right Compromise (children with the Austrian and Hungarian coats of arms clasping hands). The whole ensemble is the work of Adolf Huszár, Ede Mayer and Adolf Kessler (1887).

In the northern part of the square stands a statue of **Count István Széchenyi** (1791–1860) the leading Hungarian social and economic reformer of the first half of the 19C. The four secondary figures represent Széchenyi's varied fields of activity: Minerva (trade), Neptune (navigation), Vulcan (industry) and Ceres (agriculture). The Academy of Sciences decided to raise a statue to Széchenyi two days after his death in 1860 but it was not until 20 years later that the bronze and granite statue by József Engel was finally unveiled.

The two busts across the road behind Széchenyi are of the linguist *Gábor Szarvas* (on the left) and the historian *Ferenc Salamon*. (Both by Gyula Jankovits, 1899 and 1902 respectively.)

The building at the N end of Roosevelt tér is the neo-Renaissance **Hungarian Academy of Sciences** (Magyar Tudományos Akadémia). It was completed in 1862–64 following much debate and a competition which was won by the Berlin architect Friedrich August Stüler.

On the main façade are statues representing the original six departments of the Academy: law, sciences, mathematics, philosophy, linguistics and history. At the corners, from the Danube side, are Newton, Lomonosov, Galilei, Révay (a Hungarian linguist) Descartes and Leibnitz. A detailed bronze relief on the right-hand side of the building facing Akadémia u. shows the foundation of the Academy when, on 3 November during a session of the 'Reform Diet' of 1825 Count István Széchenyi offered a year's income to help set up a 'Hungarian Scholars Society' (Barnabás Holló, 1893).

Reorganisation of the Academy took place in 1949 when it changed from being basically a private learned society into the country's supreme scientific body financed from the state budget. It performs the dual function of on the one hand giving advice and recommendations to the government in every field of science and scholarship and on the other of implementing the government's science policy by running research centres and institutes.

The Academy's library is one of the major research libraries of the country. Its origins can be traced back to 1826 when Count József Teleki, the then governor of Transylvania, offered his family collection of 30,000 volumes to serve as the basis of the library. During the siege of Budapest at the end of World War II the library suffered serious losses and its premises were badly damaged. In 1988 the library moved to new premises in the block to the rear of the Academy's main building (entrance from Arany János u.). It is only open for specialist researchers.

No. 1 Akadémia u., on the E side of the Academy, was built in neo-classical style with Corinthian pilasters in 1835 by Mátyás Zitterbarth Jr. The upper floors were added in 1927–28. One of the two wall plaques recalls that Joseph Bem, the Polish general who fought with the Hungarians in the War of Independence, stayed here for a while in 1848 when it was a hotel. The other records that general György Klapka (1820–92) spent the last few years of his life in the house.

No. 3, also neo-classical, was designed by József Hild in 1836. Hild (1789–1867) was one of the chief architects involved in the development of this part of Pest in the first half of the 19C. The house was the birthplace of *György Hevesy* (1885–1966), the discoverer of the element hafnium and the recipient of a Nobel Prize in 1943. Today the building houses the *National Council of Producer Cooperatives* (Termelő Szövetkezetek Országos Tanácsa).

Hevesy went to Berlin to continue his studies begun in Budapest. He later worked alongside Rutherford and in 1918 was appointed professor at Budapest University. With the arrival of the Horthy regime he decided to leave and went to Neils Bohr's institute in Copenhagen. He named his discovery of the 72nd element hafnium, after the Latin name of the Danish capital. From 1943 he lived in Sweden and turned more towards research into nuclear medicine.

The modern building on the E side of Roosevelt tér at *No. 7–8* was built in 1979 to the plans of Miklós Hófer and Tibor Hübner. It is the headquarters of several official economic planning offices.

To its right, across Zrínyi u., at No. 5–6 Roosevelt tér, stands the impressive Art Nouveau building known as the **Gresham Palace**. It was built in 1907 to the plans of Zsigmond Quittner and the Vágó brothers, József and László, for the London Gresham Life Assurance Company. Inside the gateway on the right a rare plaque in English testifies to this and lists the company directors. A plaque on the other side of the gateway gives details of the builders and lists the council of directors of the Hungarian branch which was founded in 1867. The entrance passageway leads to a huge T-shaped glass-roofed arcade which is today in a sad state of disrepair (although there are plans to renovate the whole building). The cast-iron gate with peacocks at the Zrínyi u. end, to the left, is original.

In the inter-war period the *Gresham Café*, which was situated on the ground floor of the building, was a well-known meeting place for progressive artists and the cultural intelligentsia. 'Such a friendly circle,' wrote Aurél Bernáth, one of the table society's regulars, 'is attractive not only because the members share an intellectual identity but also because they are lively in their judgment and humour—and there was no shortage of either of these at our table.'

The 'Gresham Circle', as they were known, were supporters of the Nagybánya school and opposed to 'official' art. They wanted to create a Hungarian national art by developing the Nagybánya tradition. The rival 'European School' embraced Hungarian members of the École de Paris, and representatives of surrealist and non-figurative trends.

The former Pest Hungarian Commercial Bank at *No. 3–4 Roosevelt tér* today belongs to the Ministry of the Interior.

The route now continues eastwards along József Attila u. 100m along on the right is JÓZSEF NÁDOR TÉR (Palatine Joseph Square). In the middle of the square is a statue of *Archduke Joseph*, grandson of Maria Theresa and son of Leopold II, who was elected Palatine (the King's deputy) of Hungary at the age of twenty in 1796. In 1804 he had plans for the development of Pest drawn up by architect János

Hild and in 1808 he was instrumental in setting up the Embellishment Commission, an early public body devoted to urban renewal and development. He died in Buda in 1847.

The statue, which shows Joseph in the ceremonial costume of the Order of St. Stephen, is the work of Munich sculptor, Johann Halbig. It was the first public statue of a layman in Pest. The sculptor offered to do the work cheaply as the Pest authorities were reluctant to pay for it entirely, arguing that Palatine Joseph was a national figure. It arrived by boat in 1860 but remained in its case for nine years. When it was finally erected it was placed, paradoxically, facing south, though much of Joseph's work had been developing the city to the north. The city council considered turning it in the 1920s but it remains today as originally erected.

No. 1 in the square, the first building on the right from József Attila u., is a characteristic example of neo-classical Pest architecture and was designed by József Hild in 1824. The arcaded side of the building by József Attila u., is post-1945. No. 2–4, next door, is the *Ministry of Finance* and was designed in 1913 by Ignác Alpár for the Hungarian General Credit Bank.

No. 5–6 at the southern end of the square is a Romantic building designed by Hugó Máltás (1859). Originally four storeys, the fifth floor was added in 1922. Medieval and Baroque motifs decorate the window-frames and the balustrades of the balconies. The *Museums Information Office* is on the ground floor of No. 7, a neo-classical building designed by Lőrinc Zofahl in 1833. (Open 10.00–18.00 Mon–Fri; Thursdays late opening till 19.30; closed Saturdays and Sundays.) The office gives information about current exhibitions throughout Budapest. The modern building at *No. 8* on the W side of the square is by Lajos Földesi (1966). At No. 12 there is a special shop for therapeutic bottled natural mineral waters from all over Hungary.

The building across the road from the N end of József Nádor tér, at No. 16 József Attila u. is a former beer-merchant's house and was constructed in 1838–39 to the plans of József Hild.

A short way along József Attila u. is the large, open ENGELS TÉR which covers c 20,000 sq m. At one time a cemetery, by the 19C it had become a market place. Today the eastern side is occupied by the *Central Bus Station* (István Nyíri, 1948). In the middle of the park section stands the *Danubius Fountain*. It was designed in 1883 by Miklós Ybl, the secondary figures being the work of Leo Feszler and Béla Brestyánszky. The fountain originally stood in Kálvin tér but was badly damaged in the war. Restored, it was placed here in 1959. The male figure at the top represents the Danube and the sitting female figures the Tisza, Dráva and Száva, at the time the three largest Hungarian rivers after the Danube.

Behind the fountain is a marble statue of *Veres Pálné*, née Hermin Beniczky (1815–95) a pioneer of girls' education in Hungary (György Kiss, 1906). On the side near József Attila u. is a bronze statue of a shepherd playing a flute entitled *Népdal* (Folksong), the work of János Horvay (1929).

The route now turns northwards along ALPÁRI GYULA UTCA which, after 200m, reaches SZENT ISTVÁN TÉR. Here stands the largest church of Budapest, St. Stephen's Church, known as the **Basilica**. 86m long and 55m wide at its maximum, the church covers an area of over 4000 sq m. The dome is 96m high.

Work began on the construction of the church in 1851 according to the neo-classical plans of József Hild. He designed the columns and tympanums of the lateral façades. Hild died in 1867 and Miklós Ybl took over contributing the neo-Renaissance aspects of the building. A misfortune occurred in January

1868 when the dome collapsed during a storm. By 1891 Ybl himself had died and a third architect, József Kauser finished the interior and finally completed the building in 1905. The church was considered to be so solidly built that during World War II the basement was used to safely store important official archives.

The exterior statues are all the work of Leó Fessler. The twelve apostles stand on the upper rim of the apse at the back of the church. The four evangelists are in the outer niches of the dome and in the niches in the front towers are statues of St. Ambrose, St. Gregory, St. Jerome and St. Augustine.

The group of statues in the tympanum above the porch, also by Fessler, represents the Virgin Mary, Patroness of Hungary surrounded by Hungarian saints. The bust above the main entrance is of King (St.) Stephen and above it is a mosaic of the Resurrection. To the left of the porch is a relief depicting the coronation of King Stephen, the work of Ernő Jálics, erected in 1938, the 900th anniversary of the death of Stephen.

To the right of the main entrance is a small *Treasury*. Inside, seven display cabinets exhibit mainly 19C Hungarian, Austrian and German chalices, ciboria and monstrances. The exhibits are accompanied by texts in English. (Open May–Sept 9.00–17.00 every day; Oct–April 10.00–16.00.)

Inside the Basilica the statues at the base of the pillars which support the dome are of King Ladislas (by János Fadrusz), St. Elizabeth of the House of Árpád (Károly Senyei) and St. Gellért, the bishop who taught Stephen's son St. Imre. This last statue is the work of Alajos Stróbl who also made the marble statue of St. Stephen on the high altar. Scenes from Stephen's life are portrayed on the bronze reliefs around the apse. On the second altar on the right is Gyula Benczúr's painting of 'Stephen offering his crown to the Virgin Mary'. Stephen, left without a successor, preferred to symbolically offer his crown to the Virgin rather than to either the Pope or the Holy Roman Emperor, and ever since Mary has been regarded as the Patroness of Hungary.

Behind the main altar is the *Szent Jobb Kápolna* (Chapel of the Holy Right Hand). Here is kept the holy relic of St. Stephen's right hand. The entrance to the chapel, which was restored in 1988 for the nation-wide celebrations in connection with the 950th anniversary of Stephen's death, is through the swing doors to the left of the chancel and across the small porch of the side exit. (Open May–Sept 9.00–17.00 every day; Oct–April 10.00–16.00.)

On 20 August 1988 the square in front of the Basilica was the scene of a remarkable event. 50,000 people attended an open-air mass to commemorate the 950th anniversary of Stephen's death. The square was decked out in the Hungarian colours and papal banners in white and yellow. The mass was the culmination of a year-long nationwide commemoration and was the biggest public religious ceremony in Hungary for many decades.

The route continues northwards from Szent István tér along Alpári Gyula u. The building with the intricate Venetian Gothic style façade at *No. 9* on the right just after the Basilica dates from the mid-1850s and was designed by Ferenc Wieser. At the next crossing on the left-hand corner of Alpári Gyula u. and Arany János u. is the head-quarters of the *National Authority for Environmental Protection and Nature Conservation* (Országos Környezet és Természetvédelmi Hivatal) which has been here since 1965. The five reliefs on the exterior wall show scenes of mining activity as the building originally

belonged to the Salgótarján Mining Company. At No. 21 Alpári
Gyula u. at the end of the street is the *Zrínyi Pharmacy*. The
furnishings are original and date from 1849 when it was known as
the 'Virgin Mary Mother of God' pharmacy.

The large late-Eclectic building at the end of Alpári Gyula u. is the
National Bank (Nemzeti Bank), the façade of which overlooks
SZABADSÁG TÉR (Liberty Square) to the left. The bank was built in
1905 to the designs of Ignác Alpár as the Austro-Hungarian Bank
and received its current name 19 years later in 1924. Nationalisation
of the bank was enacted in December 1947. The series of reliefs on
the first floor level, which stretch round three sides of the building,
show different trading and commercial activities connected with the
bank. Situated inside the building is a small *Museum of Banknotes
and Coins* (Magyar Nemzeti Bank Bankjegy és Éremgyűjteménye)
which shows the history of money circulation in Hungary. (Open
Thursdays 9.00–14.00.)

The former Ministry of Metallurgy and Machine Industry stands at
No. 5–6 Szabadság tér on the S side of the square. The eight-storey
building was designed in 1937 by István Nyíri and László Lauber. The
large relief on the right at ground floor level is by Ferenc Medgyessy
(1940) and is entitled *Szüretelők* (Grape-pickers). In the small playground in front of the building stands a memorial fountain with the
inscription 'Virulj!' (Prosper!). It commemorates the planting of trees
in Pest in 1846 (Ede Telcs, 1930). The huge Art Nouveau former Stock
Exchange building on the W side of Szabadság tér is today the
headquarters of **Hungarian Television** (Magyar Televízió-MTV).
Like the bank opposite it was designed by Ignác Alpár in 1905.

Experimental TV transmissions started in 1954 and regular programmes were
launched in 1958. Today MTV broadcasts on two channels. Two Czechoslovak
and one Soviet channel are also available and in recent years reception of
Western satellite TV transmissions has been widespread through the joint
purchase of rooftop dishes by residents in tower blocks. Austrian TV has also
been available for some time in western Hungary.

In 1989 on March 15th, the anniversary of the outbreak of the 1848 Revolution
and a public holiday for the first time in many years, tens of thousands of
demonstrators gathered in front of the steps of MTV to hear György Cserhalmi,
a well-known actor, declare the 15 points jointly agreed by several newly-
formed independent political organisations. The declaration, which included a
call for democratisation of the media, symbolically echoed the declaration of
Petőfi's 12 demands for national freedom 141 years previously.

In the small park area immediately in front of the entrance to MTV is
the *Memorial to the Martyrs of the New Building* (Az újépületi
vértanuk emléke) the work of András Dózsa Farkas (1934). The New
Building (Újépület) was a huge barracks built in 1785 on the site of
today's Szabadság tér. Representing Habsburg absolutism it was an
object of hatred to Hungarians many of whom were imprisoned and
executed within its walls. The building was demolished in 1897. The
present square was planned by Antal Palóczy and made into a park
in 1902.

In the 1930s several statues full of political symbolism used to adorn Szabadság
tér but all of them were removed in 1945 as a sign of the changed political
climate. Four of them were called North, South, East and West, and symbolised
the Hungarian regions lost at the Treaty of Trianon after World War I. There
was also a flag permanently at half-mast mounted on a pedestal inscribed with
a quotation from an article, 'Hungary's Place in the Sun', written by the British
press baron Lord Rothermere and published in his newspaper 'The Daily Mail'
in June 1927. Rothermere was an active campaigner at home and abroad for a
revision of the Treaty and the return of lost territories to Hungary. He sent his

son Esmond to Hungary in 1928 to meet Regent Horthy and Prime Minister
Bethlen. Another of the pre-war statues in the square was a gift from Rothermere entitled 'Monument of Hungarian Grief'. The British Lord's activities
aroused great interest in official, conservative, irredentist, pre-war Hungary
and much propaganda was made out of his interventions. After 1945 conservative ultra-nationalism was pushed into the background and this curious episode
in Anglo-Hungarian relations has been quietly forgotten.

Another statue which once stood here and which has been removed, though
for quite different reasons, was entitled 'Gratitude' and was erected in 1949 on
the occasion of Joseph Stalin's 75th birthday.

The obelisk towards the N end of Szabadság tér is the *Soviet Army
Memorial* (Károly Antal, 1945). The relief at the base depicts Red
Army soldiers crossing today's Felszabadulás tér during the siege of
Budapest. In the background the original Elizabeth Bridge can be
seen. The relief at the rear shows Soviet soldiers near the Parliament.

The *US Embassy* is to the right of the memorial at No. 12 in the
square. This is where Cardinal Mindszenty spent 15 years in self-
imposed confinement after 1956.

Mindszenty, head of the Catholic Church in Hungary, was a conservative, anti-
communist cleric who had been badly mistreated in prison during and after a
show-trial in 1949. Released by insurgents during 1956 his presence in the
embassy and uncompromising attitude was an obstacle to normalising church-
state relations until the Vatican persuaded him to leave for Austria in 1971.

The statue in the square just to the SW of the embassy is of Harry Hill
Bandholtz (Miklós Ligeti, 1936). Bandholtz, a US general, was
present in Budapest in 1919 after the suppression of the Hungarian
Council Republic by Allied supported troops of Romania and
Czechoslovakia. He intervened to prevent the removal to Romania of
treasures in the Hungarian National Museum. The statue was
removed after 1945, but reappeared in July 1989 when the US
President, George Bush, visited Budapest.

The colourfully decorated building behind and adjoining the
embassy at No. 4 Rosenberg házaspár u. is the **former Post Office
Savings Bank** built in 1900 to one of Ödön Lechner's classic Hungarian Art Nouveau designs. As with the Museum of Applied Arts
Lechner made use of majolica from the Zsolnay factory in Pécs.

Aulich u. at the NE corner of Szabadság tér leads to a little square
in the middle of which is a limestone plinth and ornate bronze lamp.
This is the *Batthyány Eternal Flame* erected in 1926 to the memory of
Count Lajos Batthyány, Prime Minister of the 1848 independent
Hungarian government, who was executed on this spot by the
Austrians on 6 October 1849.

Batthyány (1806–49) was a big landowner and liberal politician. Before 1848 he
was one of leading opposition aristocrats in the Hungarian Diet. As head of the
Hungarian government in 1848 he sought to avoid a conflict with Austria but
finding this way impossible he resigned on 2 October. After heading an
unsuccessful peace delegation he was arrested in Pest in January 1849.

No. 15 Szabadság tér, behind the Soviet memorial and to the left,
belonged to the Ministry of Labour for many years after the war.
Earlier it had been the headquarters of the Hungarian Fascist Arrow-
Cross (Nyilas) for a while. Since 1981 it has belonged to the
Tanimpex leather export-import company. In the tympanum at the
top of the building is a relief of Lajos Kossuth with Petőfi and
Vörösmarty. Emperor Francis Joseph once vowed that no statue of
Kossuth should be erected during his lifetime. Hence plans for the
relief only showed vague figures and the sculptor is unknown. It is
the oldest representation of Kossuth in Budapest.

Vécsey u. on the left of this building leads via the small Ságvári tér to KOSSUTH LAJOS TÉR where, on the W side, stands one of the symbols of Budapest, the neo-Gothic **Parliament Building**.

For centuries the Hungarian National Assembly had no permanent home. In 1843 a resolution was passed at the Pozsony (Bratislava) Diet to erect a permanent building in Pest though the plans were delayed by the events of 1848–49. From 1861 the Lower House met in Bródy Sándor u. and the Upper House in the nearby National Museum. In 1880 a law was passed approving the present site and work began in 1884 to the designs of Imre Steindl. The building was completed in 1902.

The building, which has 691 rooms, is 268m long, 118m wide at its maximum and is over 90m high at the top of the dome. There are 88 statues on the exterior. On the Danube side are the Hungarian rulers from the seven conquering chiefs to Ferdinand V (died 1848). On the Kossuth tér side are the princes of Transylvania and several famous commanders. Above the ground floor windows are coats of arms of kings and princes.

The main entrance from Kossuth Lajos tér leads to a ceremonial staircase with ceiling frescoes by Károly Lotz. From here there opens a 16-sided hall below the dome. It is used for official receptions and ceremonies. On the pillars are statues of Hungarian rulers. In the S wing is the meeting hall of the National Assembly. The former hall of the Upper House in the N wing is today used for congresses. Both halls are ornamented in a rich neo-Gothic style, as are the adjoining rooms. In one of these is Mihály Munkácsy's large painting 'The Magyar Conquest' (1893).

The Parliament building can only be visited in guided tours organised by travel agencies.

The National Assembly meets here several times a year. There are 386 elected members. For the 1985 general election a law was introduced making it compulsory for all seats to be contested by at least two candidates. Electors in each constituency had the right to nominate candidates in addition to the two nominated by the Patriotic People's Front. In many constituencies the seat was contested by three, four and sometimes five candidates. In recent years increasing weight has been attached to the role of the National Assembly and its parliamentary committees.

The *Library of Parliament* collects foreign and Hungarian books on political science, law and history. It is also a designated UN Library. The entrance is through door No. 25 on the Danube side, reached via the S side of the building.

In front of the Parliament building towards the southern end of Kossuth Lajos tér is a bronze statue of **Ferenc Rákóczi II** on horseback (János Pásztor, 1937). Rákóczi (1676–1735) as Prince of Transylvania led the 1703–11 struggle for independence. There are Latin inscriptions on both sides of the plinth. One reads 'For Country and Liberty', the other 'The wounds of the noble Hungarian nation burst open'—the opening lines of Rákóczi's anti-Habsburg declaration.

At the age of 12 Ferenc Rákóczi was separated from his mother, Ilona Zrínyi, when she finally surrendered the castle of Munkács (Mukachevo, Soviet Union) to Imperial troops. The Viennese court sent him to Bohemia to be educated by the Jesuits. Later he studied in Prague and in Italy, and in Vienna he led the frivolous life of a young aristocrat. He returned to his estates loyal to the Habsburgs and when rebelling peasants wanted to win him to their cause in 1697 he fled from them to Vienna.

Contact with disaffected Hungarian nobles and the expectation that he would defend the country led to a change of attitude on his part. While planning a conspiracy against the Habsburgs with French help he was arrested in 1701 and imprisoned. Escaping from prison he sought refuge in Poland from where he eventually launched the freedom struggle of 1703–11. After defeat he went into exile, first to Poland, then France and eventually to Turkey, always hoping that the struggle could be revived. He died in Rodosto in 1735.

At the northern end of the square is a group of statues whose central figure is **Lajos Kossuth** making a call to arms during the 1848–49 War of Independence. Erected in 1952 the main figure is the work of sculptor Zsigmond Kisfaludi Strobl while the others are by András Kocsis and Lajos Ungvári.

Lajos Kossuth (1802–94) is the most celebrated political leader of the struggle for Hungarian independence in the 19C. He was Minister of Finance in the first independent Hungarian government in 1848 and shortly afterwards elected Governing President of Hungary. During the war with Austria which followed he travelled the country rousing the people to arms, which activity is depicted in this group of statues. Forced to flee the country after defeat he spent many years abroad, several of them in England and the United States, defending the cause of Hungary. He first arrived in England on 16 October 1851. Landing at Southampton he surprised his audience by giving an extempore speech in English. Although a popular figure in England he refused an invitation from the Chartists to speak at a working men's dinner, an attitude which prompted Karl Marx to write that Kossuth was 'all things to all men. In Marseilles he shouts: Vive la république; and in Southampton: God Save the Queen!' He died in Turin in 1894 and his body was returned to Hungary and given a ceremonial burial in the Kerepesi Cemetery. His huge mausoleum, designed by Alajos Stróbl, is still standing today (see p 194).

Between the two statues in the middle of Kossuth Lajos tér is a *white flagpole* on which the State Flag of the Hungarian People's Republic is hoisted on festive and official occasions. The square has been the scene of many noted political demonstrations in particular during the 1918–19 period and in 1956, when Imre Nagy, returning from the political wilderness, addressed a huge crowd from the balcony of Parliament on 23 October, the first day of the uprising.

The seated bronze statue in the small park just to the S of the Parliament building is of the working-class poet **Attila József** (László Marton, 1980). The inscription by the side of the statue is taken from his poem 'A Dunánál' (By the Danube) and reads '... as if it flowed from my own heart in a spate ... wise was the Danube, turbulent and great.'

Attila József was born in the Budapest working class district of Ferencváros in 1905. Expelled from Szeged university he left for Vienna and later Paris where he mixed with left-wing and avant-garde circles. Back in Budapest in 1930 he joined the illegal Communist Party but was denounced three years later by the emigré party leadership in Moscow. Like Wilhelm Reich in Germany and George Orwell in Britain he was too much of a libertarian rebel and too interested in the wider, socio-psychological aspects of politics to fit neatly into the Communist orthodoxies of the 1930s. Political estrangement and constant difficulties with publishers led to depression and schizophrenic tendencies. He committed suicide under the wheels of a train in 1937. Since the war, however, Attila József has been revered in Hungary as one of the country's greatest 20C poets.

In front of the statue by the railings is a memorial stone marking the site of the *Kossuth Bridge* which stood here from 1946–60. Built in eight months it was the first permanent bridge erected after the war. At the time of its construction it was the only permanent bridge to span the Danube between Regensburg and the Black Sea.

The modern building behind the statue at the S end of Kossuth Lajos tér was designed by Béla Pintér in 1972 and is the headquarters of the *Hungarian Chamber of Commerce* (Magyar Gazdasági

Bronze statue of Attila József by the Danube (László Marton, 1980).

Kamara). On the ground floor is the entrance to the *Kossuth tér metro station.* In the corner of the entrance hall is a bronze statue entitled *Mother with child* (Anya gyermekkel) the work of József Somogyi (1972).

There are two large buildings facing Kossuth Lajos tér on its E side. On the right is the *Ministry of Agriculture and Food* (Mezőgazdasági és Élelmezésügyi Minisztérium) built in 1885–87 by Gyula Bukovics. On the right-hand side of the building overlooking Ságvári tér are two wall plaques. One is to *Endre Ságvári* (1913–44) one of the leaders of the illegal Communist Party who died in a skirmish with the police during the war. The other is to *Duke Mieczslaw Woronieczky*, a young Polish cavalry legion colonel who fought with the Hungarians in the War of Independence and whom the Austrians executed on this spot in October 1849.

The *row of busts* in the archways on each side of the main entrance are of people who had significant connections with agricultural science. On the far left of the façade is a small replica of *The Seed*, a vast bronze relief by Amerigo Tot which stands in the courtyard of the University of Agriculture in Gödöllő. The two statues in front of the Ministry are both by Árpád Somogyi and are, on the right, *The Reaper Lad* (1956) and, on the left, *Girl Agronomist* (1954).

The Eclectic building of the **Ethnographical Museum** (Néprajzi Múzeum) is to the left of the Ministry on the other side of Alkotmány u. It was designed by Alajos Hauszmann and built from 1893 to 1896 to house the Supreme Court. On the tympanum is a group of statues by György Zala representing a court hearing and above it on a chariot drawn by three horses is Justitia, the Goddess of Justice (by Károly Senyei) flanked by the Legislator and the Magistrate (both by János Fadrusz). The interior—through the entrance and up the steps—is particularly impressive. The large ceiling fresco depicting an enthroned Justitia surrounded by allegories of Justice, Peace, Sin and Revenge is the work of Károly Lotz.

The permanent exhibition (open 10.00–18.00 except Monday) is an ethnographic display entitled 'from ancient times to civilisation'. Temporary exhibitions are held of Hungarian folk art (costumes, ornaments, furniture and working tools) and village life.

Szalay u. runs from the NE corner of Kossuth tér at the side of the Ethnographical Museum. At No. 7 is the small *Law Museum* (Ügyvédi Múzeum) which has exhibits relating to the history of legal services. (Open 10.00–13.00; closed at weekends and throughout August.)

The statue in the small playground on the N side of the Parliament building is of **Mihály Károlyi** and is the work of the sculptor Imre Varga (1975).

Károlyi (1875–1955) was a liberal politician before the First World War and a supporter of democratic reforms. During that war he was opposed to the German alliance and in 1918 he became Chairman of the National Council, Prime Minister and from January 1919 President of the Republic. He always had some sympathy with radical and revolutionary forces and hence the Horthy regime denounced him as a traitor. In exile he was an organiser of the anti-fascist and democratic Hungarian forces abroad. From 1943 he headed the Movement for a Democratic Hungary in Britain. He returned home after World War II and from 1947–49 was Hungarian Ambassador in Paris. Disaffection over the Rajk trial (see p 214) and other violations lead to a second exile. After his death his ashes were eventually returned to Hungary and buried in the Kerepesi Cemetery.

H.   From March 15th Square to the Eastern Railway Station

This route runs in a straight line from March 15th Square (Marcius 15 tér) at the Pest end of Elizabeth Bridge along the short Szabad Sajtó út, through Fel-szabadulás tér and via Kossuth Lajos u. and Rákóczi út to the Eastern Railway Station (Keleti pályaudvar) in Baross tér. Approximately 2.5km long, it is, and has been for centuries, the main W–E axis of Pest. Buses No. 7 and 78 run the length of the route and the No. 3 (red) metro line connects one end of Rákóczi út (Astoria) with the other (Keleti pu.).

MARCH 15TH SQUARE (which name recalls the first day of the 1848 revolution) is situated underneath and on each side of the fly-over which is a continuation of Elizabeth Bridge (Erzsébet híd) on the Pest side (for details of the bridge see p 145). The most prominent building in the square is the **Inner City Parish Church** (Belvárosi plébániatemplom) which stands immediately to the N of the fly-over.

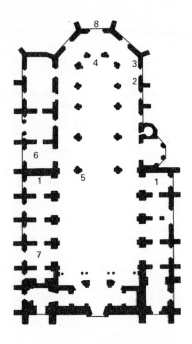

1. Renaissance tabernacle niche
2. Turkish mihrab (prayer niche)
3. 15C sedilia
4. High altar
5. Empire pulpit
6. Baptismal font
7. Tomb of István Kultsár
8. Relief of St. Florian

INNER CITY PARISH CHURCH

At the end of the 12C a triple-aisle Romanesque church was built here and Elizabeth, princess of the House of Árpád, was betrothed here to Louis, Count of Thüringia, Lord of Wartburg. It was rebuilt in Gothic style in the 14C under King Sigismund which was when it became its present size. On one occasion, following the death of King Matthias in 1490, the Diet met in the church. The Turks used the church as a mosque, but later they returned it and for a while it was the only Christian church in Pest. Following the expulsion of the Turks from Budapest in 1686 the church was damaged and in 1723 it burnt down. From 1725–39 it was rebuilt by János György Paur in Baroque style. The two spires date from 1795 and the present neo-classical organ loft from the 1830s. War damage necessitated reconstruction after World War II and the high altar dates from that time.

Outside, note the Baroque façade and front side walls, and the Gothic chancel. There is a group of statues representing the Holy Trinity above the main entrance and at the rear, on the exterior chancel wall, there is a large relief of St. Florian by Antal Hörger, erected after the 1723 fire.

Inside, you can see the Baroque barrel-vaulted nave and the Gothic chancel with its ogival vaults. The Doric columns just beyond the entrance are the work of neo-classical architect János Hild and date from 1835. On the right there are three small chapels which have Baroque interiors while in the fourth there is a red marble and white limestone Renaissance tabernacle niche commissioned by the town of Pest in 1507. It is decorated with the arms of Pest. The next chapel is Gothic. Just along the row of sedilia which stretches around the interior of the chancel wall there is a Turkish prayer-niche (mihrab) which dates from when the church was used as a mosque.

The high altar is the work of sculptor Károly Antal and painter Pál C. Molnár (1948). On its left is a reconstructed Gothic tabernacle. The Empire pulpit with Gothic motifs is the work of a Pest craftsman and dates from 1808. The two statues by the arch at the front of the chancel are of St. Joseph (on the left) and the Virgin Mary (on the right). Both are by József Damkó (1900).

On the left the first chapel beyond the entrance to the chancel has fragments of frescoes which were originally in other parts of the church and a baptismal font with small bronze sculptures (Béni Ferenczy, 1955). In the next chapel towards the entrance is another Renaissance tabernacle commissioned by the parish priest, András Nagyrévi, in 1500. This and the tabernacle on the other side are rare surviving examples of Renaissance work in Hungary. In the chapel nearest the entrance is the neo-classical tomb of newspaper editor István Kultsár (1760–1828). It was constructed in 1835 by István Ferenczy, one of the leading Hungarian sculptors of the period.

The church is usually open to visitors every day.

Not far from the church in the small park in March 15th Square is a bronze sculpture entitled *The Struggle of the Barbarians with the Romans* (István Tar, 1971). It recalls the fact that here in the 4C the Romans built a fortress called Contra-Aquincum to defend the Danube crossing and the road to the east. A small open-air *museum* has been established in the sunken area in the middle of the square showing the system of Roman fortresses in the area.

The large building on the eastern side of the square belongs to the Arts Faculty of the Eötvös Loránd University and at the far NE corner of the square (actually No. 2 Pesti Barnabás u.) is the yellow two-storey **Százéves Étterem** (100-Year-Old Restaurant). The building is one of the oldest surviving non-ecclesiastical Baroque constructions in Pest. It was designed by András Mayerhoffer in 1755 for Baron János Péterffy whose family coat of arms can be seen on the tympanum. The marble tablet on the right of the gate shows the water level during the great flood of 1838. There has been a restaurant here since 1831.

PETŐFI TÉR is at the NW corner of March 15th Square. Sándor Petőfi (1823–49) was a poet and leader of the revolutionary youth on 15 March 1848 who later died in the War of Independence. One of the most popular Hungarian poets, his poems have been translated into several foreign languages. The **statue of Petőfi** with raised arm here is by Adolf Huszár to the design of Miklós Izsó (1882). Much of the cost of the statue was raised by violinist Ede Reményi on his European concert tours.

Petőfi tér has been the scene of many political demonstrations. An illegal large-scale anti-fascist rally assembled here on 15 March 1942 to protest against Hungary's participation in World War II. In 1956 this was one of the initial rallying points on the first day of the uprising, and every year on March 15 patriotic (and often 'unofficial') celebrations take place at Petőfi's statue.

Behind the statue to the right stands the **Greek Orthodox Church**. Construction started in 1791 to the plans of József Jung though the façade was transformed in 1872–73 by Miklós Ybl when two spires were added, one of which was destroyed in the last war. The richly decorated iconostasis is the work of Serbian woodcarver Miklós Jankovich (1797–99). The pictures were added by Viennese artist Anton Kochmeister c 1801. (Open 15 April–30 September, 14.00–18.00.)

To the left of the church, at No. 2 Petőfi tér, there is a *Non-Stop IBUSZ office* which is open 24 hours a day for booking accommodation and other tourist services.

The route now proceeds from the southern part of March 15th Square on the other side of the flyover. The large yellow building at *No. 38* Váci u., across the road from the SE corner of the square (i.e. away from the river), is the former Officers Club (Tiszti Kaszinó) which was founded in 1861 and moved here in 1899 after the completion of the building. The patriotic slogan, 'A Haza Minden Előtt' (The Homeland Before Everything) can still be seen high up on the façade. There were over 8000 members in the 1930s and after the war it became the central club of the Hungarian People's Army. Today the building is occupied by the Hungarian Busexport Company.

In June 1956 the radical intellectual Petőfi Circle held an open meeting here to discuss 'Questions of Information and the Press'. Thousands of people tried to attend and the speeches which continued until late into the night had to be relayed into the surrounding streets by loudspeaker.

Diagonally across the junction of Váci u. and Irányi u. on the corner of the building at *No. 43* Váci u. is a bronze plaque recording that Charles XII of Sweden spent a night here in November 1714 during his return from exile in Turkey (Ottó Jarl, 1924). Further along this side of Váci u., at No. 47, stands the Baroque *Church of St. Michael*, which was formerly called the 'Church of the English Young Ladies' (Angolkisasszonyok temploma).

In 1609 the English woman Mary Ward founded an order of nuns in the Netherlands for the education of young girls. In 1774 Maria Theresa gave over part of the Royal Palace in Buda to the nuns, then in 1787 they resettled in the former monastery of the (disbanded) Dominicans in today's Váci u. next to the church. Until 1948 there was a school and teachers' training college here named after the founder of the order (Ward-Kollégium). The church itself dates from 1747–49. The statue above the gate, by József Hebenstreit, is of 'Patrona

Hungariae' (Our Lady, Patroness of Hungary). The carved benches inside are the work of friars and also date from the mid-18C.

Returning via Váci u., the route now continues E along the short Szabad sajtó u. (In the subway here, which links the northern and southern stretches of Váci u., there are late 19C–early 20C photographs of this part of Budapest by the noted photographer György Klösz.) The two imposing buildings on each side of Szabad Sajtó u. are known as the **Klotild Palaces**. They are best viewed from a little farther on, from the middle of FELSZABADULÁS TÉR. Named after an Austrian Archduchess they were designed in 1902 by Flóris Korb and Kálmán Giergl in Secessionist style with Spanish Rococo elements as part of the general reconstruction of this area which took place at the turn of the century. On the ground floor of the southern building is the old *Belvárosi Kávéház* (Inner City Coffee House) which, according to the wall plaque, was the first coffee house to reopen after the liberation. Today it is both a café and a night club.

The Art Nouveau building which dominates the N side of Felszabadulás tér was built by Henrik Schmahl in 1909 for the Belvárosi Takarékpénztár (Inner City Savings Bank). Today it houses one of the central offices of IBUSZ, the largest Hungarian travel agency. The ground floor entrance on the corner of Petőfi Sándor u. leads to a reception area for general tourist information, including the booking of accommodation and tours. The *Párisi udvar* is an attractive arcade which cuts through the building from the Felszabadulás side to Petőfi Sándor u. (Note the finely carved ceiling.)

Károlyi Mihályi u. leads S from the square at the beginning of which stands the *Nereids Fountain* (Ferenc Uhrl and József Fessl). It was originally placed here in 1835 but removed in 1899 to a spot outside the centre. Restored by Dezső Győri, it was replaced in 1976.

On the left of the fountain is the **Franciscan Church**. The Franciscans had a church and monastery here as early as the second half of the 13C. Under the Turkish occupation it was turned into a mosque. Nothing survives today of this original building. The present church was begun in 1727 and consecrated in 1743.

Above the entrance is a stone relief depicting Christ on the road to Calvary. The crossed wounded hands are the symbol of the Franciscan order. The statue in the central niche of the gable is of St. Peter of Alcantara. In the side niches are St. Francis and St. Anthony. The spire which stands above the chancel was constructed as early as 1758 though the decorative elements appeared in the 1860s.

The church has a nave with three chapels on either side. The statues on the high altar date from 1741 and the pulpit, with statues of the apostles, was made in 1851. The frescoes were painted partly by Károly Lotz in the 1890s and partly by Viktor Tardos Krenner in the 1920s. The stone crucifix outside the church, to the right of the entrance, dates from 1763 but the sculptor is unknown.

KOSSUTH LAJOS UTCA begins at Felszabadulás tér and runs to the E. It is the main W–E axis of the inner city and used to be a popular promenade before the days of modern traffic.

On the side wall of the Franciscan church which overlooks Kossuth Lajos u. is a high relief showing *Baron Miklós Wesselényi* rescuing people during the great flood of 1838 (Barnabás Holló, 1905).

Areas by the river bank often used to be destroyed by flood. Between 1732 and 1830 there were 12 recorded floods of which one, in 1799, devastated the whole of Francis Town. Following this, serious construction of defensive embankments began but on the night of 13–14 March 1838 the river burst its banks causing a huge flood which lasted several days. Over 400 people died and 2000 houses were destroyed.

Miklós Wesselényi (1796–1850) was a Transylvanian landowner, a reform-minded colleague of István Széchenyi, a member of the Academy of Sciences and one of the leaders of the opposition in the Hungarian and Transylvanian Diets. At the time of the great flood of 1838 he created a legend around himself due to his activities as a boatman in rescuing many people. The following year, however, he was accused of treason and imprisoned because of his political activities. In prison he lost his sight and after his release was less able to engage in political activity.

On the other side of the road under the archway at *No. 2* stands the 'Kígyó' (Serpent) chemists. It is one of the oldest working chemists in the city being originally founded in nearby premises in 1784. It moved to this building in 1899. The original interior furnishings, part neo-Rococo and part Secessionist, have been restored. *No. 3* on the right is the former Landerer and Heckenast printing works. The crowds came here on 15 March 1848 to witness an important event— the printing of Sándor Petőfi's 'National Song' and the 'Twelve Points', the radical demands of the revolutionary movement. It was the first printing without censorship for many years.

Szép u. at the side of this building runs into Reáltanoda u. which runs parallel to Kossuth Lajos u. *No. 12* is the former so-called Kincsem Palace.

The famous racehorse Kincsem (My Jewel) was kept here in stables built from the money the horse won at races all over the world. Although Kincsem was bred in Hungary she was of English ancestry. She raced for four seasons and created a world record by winning all her 54 races including the Goodwood Cup on her one venture in England. There are items relating to Kincsem in the Agricultural Museum in the City Park in the horse-breeding section.

The English influence on Hungarian horse racing was particularly strong and was encouraged by Count István Széchenyi who saw it as a way of developing good breeds. In 1844 the English jockey Thomas Benson arrived and won many important races. He stayed in Hungary and worked as a trainer for 40 years bringing several others over from England.

Reáltanoda u. was also the site of the first public hospital in Pest. Robert Townson, a visiting Englishman, was not very impressed, describing it in the 1770s as 'the worst hosital in Europe' for its bad conditions and particularly bad smell.

The *Corvina Bookshop* on the ground floor of the block at No. 4 Kossuth Lajos u. belongs to the Corvina publishing house, the main foreign language publisher in Hungary. The shop is usually well stocked with books about Hungary in English, French and German.

The *House of Soviet Culture and Sciences* (Sovjet Kultúra és Tudomány Háza) is at No. 1–3 Semmelweis u. on the corner with Kossuth Lajos u. The building was originally designed in 1896 by Győző Czigler and Béla Atzél for the National Casino (Országos Kaszinó). The luxuriously furnished rooms, libraries, billiard rooms, ballrooms and restaurant provided a central meeting place for the upper gentry, leading politicians and civil servants. The club's first president was Prime Minister Sándor Wekerle. Within the Casino the first women's club was opened in 1899. The National Casino, which was one of several English-style clubs in Budapest, operated until 1945. A glance at the staircase through the main door gives an idea of the former opulence.

On the ground floor today there is the *Melodia* Soviet book and record shop. The entrance to the Russian *Baikal* restaurant is from Semmelweis u.

At the end of Kossuth Lajos u. at No. 19 on the right is the **Astoria Hotel**, built in 1912–14 to the design of Emil Ágoston and Rezső

Hikisch. In October 1918 during the post-war republic upheavals the National Council met here and formed the first independent Hungarian government. The building suffered severe damage during the fighting in 1956 when for a time it functioned as headquarters for the Soviet forces. Today the renovated interior and the coffee lounge on the ground floor recall the atmosphere of pre-World War I Hungary.

In the Middle Ages at today's junction of Kossuth Lajos u. and the Little Boulevard stood the Hatvan Gate, one of the three major gates in the old Pest town walls. It was pulled down at the end of the 18C. The continuation of Kossuth Lajos u. on the other side of the junction is RÁKÓCZI ÚT.

It was formerly called Kerepesi út but has had this name since 1906 when it was named after Ferenc Rákóczi II (1676–1735) the Prince of Hungary who led the War of Independence in 1703–11. Taverns and inns lined both sides until redevelopment in the last quarter of the 19C when the street was broadened to become an important through road to the Eastern Railway Station.

On the side wall of the first building on the left (No. 2) is an old lamp with a tablet underneath recalling that the first electric street lights in Budapest were placed in this area in 1909.

The Romantic building at *No. 5* on the right is the former Pannónia Hotel and was built in 1876, though modified in 1892. The ground floor used to be occupied by the Pannonia Coffee House where writers and artists from the neighbouring National Theatre used to congregate. (The theatre, which stood to the right of the building on the corner of the Little Boulevard—today the site of a trade centre—was pulled down in 1908.) There is a plaque to Ferenc Rákóczi above the middle balcony. After the war the building became a female students' hostel and is today part of the Natural Sciences Faculty of the university.

Next door, *No. 7* was built in the early 1890s by Henrik Schmahl in a rich neo-Gothic style. On the third floor exterior are two frescoes by Károly Lotz. József Hild designed the classical house at *No. 13* in 1837. Originally only one storey, the rest of the building was added by József Diescher in 1852. The plaque in the gateway on the right recalls that Ödön Lechner, the architect who tried to establish a specifically Hungarian form of architecture, was born here in 1845, and that the violinist Jenő Hubay was also born here in 1858. Ferenc and Károly Doppler, both musicians, lived here for a time and their guests included Liszt, Wagner and Erkel. In the second half of the 19C the house was one of the centres of artistic and literary life in Pest. József Hild also designed *No. 15* next door in neo-classical style. As the former White Horse (Fehér Ló) Hotel it was well-known in the 19C for large dances and balls. The building was renovated in 1987–88 and today houses the Czechoslovak cultural centre.

Across the road a few metres along Síp u., on the corner with Dohány u., is the striking Art Nouveau building of the *Metroclub*. Formerly the Árkád-bazár it was designed by the Vágó brothers, László and József, in 1909. On the corner of Síp u. and Rákóczi út is one of the oldest department stores in Budapest, the *Verseny Áruház*, designed by Gyula Wälder in 1936. *No. 18* on the same side belongs to the Municipal Gas Authority (Fővárosi Gázművek). The building dates from 1911 and was designed by Béla Lajta (1873–1920) one of the founders of the modern school of architecture in Hungary.

No. 19 on the right, at the corner of Szentkirályi u., has a statue of King Matthias on the first floor (Ede Mayer). It was once the sign of a café which was situated inside the building. In this same block at

No. 21 Rákóczi út is the Eclectic building of the *Urania Cinema* (Henrik Schmahl, 1893). The Moorish style of the building is even more emphasised inside which has been renovated as original. It was once the Alhambra music hall, then a lecture theatre, a drama school and finally a cinema. It was one of the first cinemas to be reopened after the siege of Budapest in 1945. The entrance at No. 21b is for the *Theatre and Cinematic Art Highschool* (Színház-és Filmművészeti Főiskola).

The building at *No. 9–11 Vas u.*, the next street on the right, was designed by Béla Lajta in 1912 as a boys commercial school. It is still a secondary trade school today. Although regarded as a significant example of early modern Hungarian architecture, the unusual brick-work and the folkish decoration on the first floor of the façade and on the metal cladding around the entrances betray traces of National Romanticism.

The **St. Roch (Rókus) Chapel** on Rákóczi út is just beyond the next street, Gyulai Pál u. The St. Roch and St. Rosalie Chapel (to give it its full title) has its origins in a small chapel built here by the Pest council after the great plague of 17ll. The area at the time was uninhabited and an isolation barracks was also set up here. The chapel's present size dates from 1740 and the tower from 1797. The stone crucifix outside to the right of the chapel, by an unknown artist, dates from 1798. The level of the flood waters in 1838 ('vízállás') is clearly visible on the façade of the chapel which was badly damaged in World War II.

To the right, at No. 2 Gyulai Pál u., is the Pest County Council Semmelweis Hospital, usually referred to as the **St. Roch Hospital**. It stands on the site of the isolation barracks built at the time of the 1711 plague. The main building was begun by József Jung in 1781 and continued by Tamás Kardetter in 1796–98. The wing overlooking Rákóczi út behind the chapel was designed by Mihály Pollack in 1839.

Just into Gyulai Pál u. facing the hospital is a marble and limestone statue of **Ignác Semmelweis** the director of the hospital's maternity ward from 1851–57 (Alajos Stróbl, 1906).

Semmelweis (1818–65) is known as the 'saviour of mothers' due to his discovery of the cause of puerperal fever and its prevention by simple asepsis. His ideas were opposed by the leading British surgeon at the time, Sir James Young Simpson, and his contribution to protecting the health of women in childbirth was only widely recognised at the turn of the century following Lister's application of antiseptic techniques. Lister himself recalled that on his visit to Budapest in 1885 nobody even mentioned the name of Semmelweis. By 1906, however, his work was acknowledged and the cost of the statue was raised by international donations from many countries.

The arcade which starts at Nagy Diófa u. on the other side of Rákóczi út was not part of the original design. This and the other stretches farther along the street have been added to create a wider pavement. The next street is Nyár u. A few metres along, on the corner of Dohány u., there is a special *map shop* (Térképbolt).

Rákóczi út now opens on to the triangular BLAHA LUJZA TÉR. Lujza Blaha (1850–1926) known as 'the nation's nightingale' (a nemzet csalogánya) was one of the most popular actresses of her day. She frequently appeared at the National Theatre (Nemzeti Színház) which stood here from 1908 to 1964 when the building was pulled down amidst much controversy. Since then the theatre company has had temporary accommodation while awaiting the construction of a new home. Despite huge public appeals and much publicity for the plans to build a new National Theatre in the City Park lack of finance has so far left the company without its own permanent theatre.

The *Gorky Cinema*, which specialises in screening Soviet films, is a few metres into Akácfa u. on the left. Immediately beyond this street stands the building of the EMKE Hotel and Bistro. The old EMKE café which used to be here was a popular meeting place in the interwar period. The working class poet Attila József worked here as an errand boy in the summer of 1914. (The letters come from an old organisation, Erdélyrészi Magyar Közművelődési Egyesület, the Hungarian Transylvanian Association for the Promotion of Learning.)

On the other side of the square is the *Corvin department store*, one of the largest in the city. To its left, at *No. 3*, are the editorial offices of the Party's central daily, 'Népszabadság' (People's Freedom). Several other newspapers and magazines are also based in the same building.

Crossing the Great Boulevard (Lenin körút to the left, József körút to the right) the route now continues E along the second section of Rákóczi út. *No. 41* is the first building on the right. It houses a regional water authority and by the entrance there is a tablet marking the level of the flood waters of 1838. It was placed here on the 150th anniversary of the great flood of that year. The building itself was designed by István Kiss and built between 1893 and 1895.

The **Palace Hotel** at No. 43 on the right was opened at the end of 1910 to the designs of Marcell Komor and Dezső Jakab. It is a good example of Hungarian National Romantic architecture which flourished for a while before World War I and in which Art Nouveau was transformed by traditional peasant themes in an attempt to create a specifically Hungarian architecture. A noteworthy feature is the interior of the hotel's restaurant on the ground floor.

At *No. 57* is the entrance of the former Slovak Lutheran church. By the middle of the 19C there were more than 5000 Slovaks in Pest and in the following decades they continued to arrive to work on the many buildings being erected in the city. The first pastor of the church was the classic Slovak writer, Ján Kollár.

The next street on the right, Luther u., leads to KÖZTÁRSASÁG TÉR, which at 66,000 sq m is the largest square in Budapest. Formerly the site of a market it was converted into a park at the end of the last century. The present name, which means Republic Square, dates from 1946 and is in memory of a mass demonstration held here on 1 November 1918 calling for the proclamation of a republic.

At the immediate NW corner of the square is the white building of the **Erkel Theatre** (Géza Márkus, Dezső Jakab and Marcell Komor, 1911), which today belongs to the State Opera House. It has had a varied history as a cinema and theatre and has undergone modernisation several times. It has the largest seating capacity of all the theatres in Hungary and in addition to opera performances it is also used for popular concerts.

To the left of the theatre stands a 6.6m bronze figure (Viktor Kalló, 1960) erected to the memory of those who were killed during the attack on the Budapest Party Headquarters (opposite the statue at No. 26–27 Köztársaság tér) on 30 October 1956. The 45 sq m limestone wall sculpture to the left of the statue is also by Kalló (1983) and is entitled 'Memorial to the heroes of people's power'.

The attack on the headquarters of the Budapest Party Committee was one of the most brutal and tragic experiences of the 1956 uprising. Crowds of insurgents, believing that it was occupied by members of the secret police and that there were torture chambers inside, besieged the building and dragged whoever they found outside killing them on the spot. Among those thus killed was Imre Mező, a friend of János Kádár. Kádár had originally been sympathetic to the uprising and a member of the new government of Imre Nagy. Mező's death is thought to have been influential in his shifting of allegiance during the events.

Légszesz u., which runs off the NE corner of Köztársaság tér, is so named because in 1856 the Légszesz Társulat (Gas Company) built the first gasworks in Pest nearby.

The route now returns to Rákóczi út via Kenyérmező u. opposite Viktor Kalló's memorial statue. The department store at No. 74–76 on the other side of the road, the *Otthon Áruház*, was opened in 1914 by Márk Rosenberg. By 1939 it employed 1000 people. Severely damaged in 1956 it has subsequently been reconstructed.

The second street after the store, Huszár u., leads to Rózsák tere and the *Elizabeth Town Parish Church* (Erzsébetvárosi plébánia-templom). This double-spired neo-Gothic church was designed in 1893–97 by Imre Steindl, the architect of the Parliament building. To the left, immediately inside the main door, there is an intricately decorated *baptismal font* by the wrought-iron craftsman Gyula Jungfer (1900). In front of the church is a marble statue of *Árpád-házi Szent Erzsébet* (St. Elizabeth of the House of Árpád) by József Damkó (1932).

Elizabeth (1207–31) was the third child of King Andrew II. She married the Marquis of Thüringen and lived in Warburg. Following her husband's death she lived an ascetic life and gave generously to the poor, which allegedly displeased her relatives. As here, she is often depicted with roses since legend has it that once she was on her way to visit the poor with her apron full of alms when her relatives stopped her, demanding to know what was in her apron. Forced to reveal the contents, a miracle happened—the alms had turned into roses.

Rákóczi út ends at BAROSS TÉR on the far side of which stands the **Eastern Railway Station** (Keleti pályaudvar). The subway system, constructed in 1969, leads to the station and the No. 2 (red) metro line. The Eclectic neo-Renaissance station was built in 1881–84 and designed by Gyula Rochlitz and János Feketeházi. The 44m span of its steel framework was considered quite daring at the time. On the main façade are statues of the Englishmen James Watt (on the right) the inventor of the steam engine, and George Stephenson (on the left) the inventor of the steam locomotive. The (today very faded) wall-paintings in the departure hall on the left are by Károly Lotz and Mór Than. Despite its name the Eastern Railway Station is the usual arrival point for trains from the West.

To the left of the station is a statue of *Gábor Baross* (Antal Szécsi, 1898). Baross (1848–92) was a leading liberal politician and one-time Minister of Transport. He did much to create and develop a unified railway system in Hungary. The statue was moved here in 1971 from its original site in front of the station.

Beyond the statue at the side of the station is *Post Office No. 72* which is open 24 hours every day.

400m along Mező Imre út, which runs SE from Baross tér, is the **Kerepesi Cemetery** (Kerepesi temető). The entrance can be reached on tram Nos 23 and 24 (one stop) which depart from Festetics György u. on the S side of Baross tér.

In the cemetery are buried many public figures. Most of the celebrated names of 19C and 20C Hungarian political history can be found here. Several of the tombs are architectural achievements and the large cemetery, which covers 90,000 sq m, is a place of quiet and rest in the busy city. Of particular note are the mausoleums of Lajos Kossuth, Lajos Batthyány and Ferenc Deák. Many labour and communist movement leaders are also buried here. A special

Pantheon of the Working Class Movement was erected in 1958 designed by József Körner and with sculptures by Zoltán Olcsai Kiss. Here can be found the gravestones of László Rajk, the former Communist minister who was a victim of the purges and was executed after a show trial in 1949. Later exhonerated he was publicly reburied here on 6 October 1956. The most recent large-scale public burial in the cemetery took place on 14 July 1989 when over 100,000 mourners paid their last respects to János Kádár, Hungary's political leader from 1956–88.

I. Népköztársaság útja
(and the City Park)

NÉPKÖZTÁRSASÁG ÚTJA (The Avenue of the People's Republic) stretches for 2.5km from the NE corner of Engels tér to the City Park (Városliget). It was originally called Sugár út (Radial Avenue) then in 1885 was renamed after the one time Prime Minister and Foreign Minister Gyula Andrássy (1823–1890). It retained the name Andrássy út until World War II, after which for a time it was called Stalin Avenue. Today's name dates from 1957. This route runs the length of the avenue and includes at the end details of Heroes' Square and the City Park.

Construction of the avenue followed a deliberate act of law promulgated in 1870. Building started in 1872 and within 12 years most of the houses were complete. The perfectly straight avenue may be divided into three, almost equal parts. Up to November 7 tér it is 34m wide and lined with closely-built neo-Renaissance and Eclectic buildings. Then up to Kodály körönd it is still closely built but wider, at 45m, and with tree-lined side roads. Finally the stretch up to Heroes' Square is similarly wide and tree-lined, but the buildings are more in a detached villa style which today have been given over to foreign embassies and official institutions.

Metro Line No. 1 (sometimes called the 'small underground') runs under the length of Népköztársaság útja. It was inaugurated as the Millenary Underground in 1896, the thousandth anniversary of the Magyar Conquest. After London it was the second underground to be constructed in Europe. The original line ran from Vörösmarty tér to the City Park, a distance of some 3.5km. The line was extended by 1.2km in 1974 and now terminates at Mexikói út, on the far side of the City Park. Apart from the metro, buses Nos 1 and 4 also run the length of the avenue.

The neo-Renaissance building at *No. 3* on the right was built for the wealthy Saxlehner family by Győző Czigler in 1884–86. The rich interior and stairway have frescoes by Károly Lotz. The *Post Office Museum* (Postamúzeum) is today inside, occupying a former 7-room private apartment. It exhibits items connected with the Hungarian post and telegram systems and with the evolution of radio and television. (Open 10.00–18.00 except Monday.)

The five-storey, Eclectic building at *No. 7*, which today houses the Bulgarian Folk Art Centre is a listed monument and was designed by Zigmond Quittner in 1882. *No. 9* has impressive caryatids by the entrance. *No. 19* has rich reliefs and roof carvings in the gateway and *Nos 21 and 23*, which were both designed by Miklós Freund in 1885, have huge gateways. No. 23 also has impressive caryatids by the entrance.

On the northern side, the corner building at the start of the avenue, *No. 2*, is a richly decorated Eclectic house designed by Adolf Feszty for the Foncière insurance company. *No. 8*, also by Feszty (1880), has murals and frescoes in the gateway, although they are somewhat dilapidated today. The female figure holding a lamp in the staircase is by the French sculptor, A. Durenné. *No. 10*, which today belongs to the Komplex Foreign Trading Co., was cleaned and renovated in the late 1980s and gives some idea of the original splendour of the buildings. *No. 12* across Dobó u. (Zsigmond Quittner,1884) has a rich ceiling in the gateway and frescoes on the walls of the interior courtyard. The fountain there is by György Donáth (1885). The building belongs to the Interior Ministry and is the headquarters of KEOKH, the central registry of foreign citizens in Hungary. Although it is possible to enter the gateway taking photographs is prohibited.

The **State Opera House** (Állami Operaház) at No. 22 Népköztársaság útja, built in neo-Renaissance style to the designs of Miklós Ybl is the avenue's most sumptuous building.

Construction began in October 1875 on the site of the former Ócskapiac (flea-market) and took nine years mainly because of financial problems. Budgetary limitations made Ybl produce ten different sketches for the façade. During the course of construction, on 8 December 1881, there was a fire at the Ringtheatre in Vienna in which 436 people died. This was one of the most serious fire accidents which plagued theatres in those days. An Austrian engineer, Robert Gwinner, had founded a company to design new, safer theatres. The Budapest Opera House was the first to use the new design which included all-metal, hydraulic stage machinery. Technically the Opera House was the most modern in the world when it opened and the hydraulic equipment lasted for nearly 100 years. All the materials for the original building were Hungarian except the bronze chandelier, weighing 3000 kilos, which was made in Mainz.

For the opening on 27 September 1884 the conductor was Ferenc Erkel (1810–93), the first general musical director of the Opera and the creator of Hungarian national operas. Ferenc Liszt had been commissioned to write a work for the opening but because he worked in a setting of the 'Rákóczi March', the Hungarian 'rebel melody', it was not performed.

A large number of foreign conductors have worked at the Opera house including Artur Nikisch, Egisto Tango, Sergio Failoni, Otto Klemperer, Lamberto Gardelli, Giusepe Patané and Antal Doráti. Eminent singers and dancers from all over the world have appeared here and in addition there have been many guest performances by foreign opera and ballet companies. The range of music performed has included everything from pre-classics to modern works.

During the seige of Budapest towards the end of World War II thousands of people found shelter in the huge cellars of the building, which miraculously only suffered minor damage. Hence the Opera was able to open very quickly after the war, on 15 March 1945. In 1981 the building was closed for major renovations (300,000 8 sq cm pieces of 23-carat gold leaf were used). Glittering in its original brilliance it was reopened on 27 September 1984, the exact centenary of its original opening.

The façade of the building is adorned with many statues. On the balustrade above the second floor are statues of Monteverdi, Scarlatti, Gluck, Mozart, Beethoven, Rossini, Donizetti, Glinka, Wagner, Verdi, Gounod, Bizet, Mussorgsky, Tchaikovsky, Moniusko and Smetana. (These are copies of the original statues and were made by Hungarian sculptors in the 1960s.) Below them, in the corner niches of the first floor projection are Terpsichore, Erato, Thalia and Melpomene, representing dance, love-poetry, comedy and tragedy. On the ground floor, on either side of the entrance arcade are statues of Ferenc Liszt and Ferenc Erkel by Alajos Stróbl.

The interior is one of the richest in Budapest with its ornamental marble stairway, and frescoes and wall-paintings by Bertalan Székely and Mór Than. The auditorium counts among the most beautiful in Europe. The large fresco on the ceiling is the work of Károly Lotz and shows Greek gods, with the god of music, Apollo, in the centre.

The building just beyond the Opera House, at *No. 24* Népköztársaság útja, has a memorial tablet to the left of the entrance which records that here was the former Three Ravens (Három Holló) Restaurant which was a favourite meeting and working place of the poet Endre Ady. The *Opera Pharmacy* next door, at *No. 26*, was founded in 1888. It has original neo-Renaissance furnishings inside.

The Renaissance building directly opposite the Opera at No. 25 is the **State Ballet Institute** (Ödön Lechner and Gyula Pártos, 1883). The interior courtyard can be seen from the side entrance in Dalszínház u. on the right.

The *Művész Espresso*, at No. 29 on the avenue is one of Budapest's traditional coffee houses. The tablet to the right of the café records that Jenő Nagy and Vilmos Tartsay, two leaders of the anti-fascist resistance, were arrested here in November 1944 and later killed.

NAGY-MEZŐ UTCA, which crosses the avenue a short while after, is traditionally one of the centres of Budapest night life. To the left is the *Moulin Rouge* night club, the *Municipal Operetta Theatre*, and the *Microscope Theatre*. To the right is the *Miklós Radnóti Theatre*. Here also was situated the *Arizona* night club, about which director Pál Sándor made the film 'Miss Arizona', starring Hanna Schygulla and Marcello Mastroianni.

The *Ernst Museum* is at No. 8 Nagy-mező u. on the right. (Open 10.00–18.00 except Monday; Tues 12.00–20.00.) Founded in 1912 by art collector and critic Lajos Ernst (1872–1937) it is today used mainly for temporary art exhibitions. The building also dates from 1912 and is in Secessionist style. A particular feature is the colourful stained glass window in the staircase at the top of the first flight of stairs (József Rippl-Rónai, 1912).

Further along, at the corner of Nagy-mező u. and Majakovszkij u., stands the **Theresa Town Parish Church** (Terézvárosi plébániatemplom). The original design (1801–11) was by Fidél Kasselik in Louis XVI style though the exterior was changed to neo-Baroque in the late 19C. The tower has a balcony which was originally used by fire watchers. Below it is a *statue of St. Theresa* (1811) by Lőrinc Dunaiszky. The interior, which is much finer than the exterior suggests, has a high altar in neo-classic design by Mihály Pollack. The large 1832 chandelier originally hung in the Redoute, the concert hall which stood on the site of today's Vigadó hall by the Danube.

The richly decorated Romantic-Gothic corner house diagonally opposite the church at *No. 47* Majakovszkij u. was built in 1848 by Ferenc Brein for a municipal dignitary, Imre Pekáry. In the 1900s the writer Gyula Krúdy lived here and mentioned it in many of his writings. Damaged in the war it was restored in 1965.

At No. 35 Népköztársaság útja, beyond Nagy-mező u., there is a special MÁV (Hungarian Railways) office for advanced booking of railway tickets. The Art Nouveau building at No. 39 on the right is the *Divatcsarnok* department store. It was originally built in 1882 by Austrian architect Gusztáv Petschnacher for the Theresa Town Casino (one of the many gentlemen's clubs of 19C Budapest). Its present form dates from 1909 following renewals made for the Párisi Nagy Áruház (Grand Parisienne Department Store). However, the main hall from the club, with its rich frescoes by Károly Lotz, survived and this can be seen at the top of the staircase inside.

The four-storey, Eclectic building at No. 45 on the corner of Liszt Ferenc tér is the site of the former *Japan Coffee House* (Japán Kávéház) which operated on the ground floor from 1900 to 1945. In the inter-war period it was a popular daily meeting place of writers, poets and artists. Today it is a bookshop—the so-called *Writers Bookshop*. Inside, on the wall by the avenue, there are old photographs showing what the interior of the coffee house used to be like.

LISZT FERENC TÉR follows immediately on the right. The statue here is of **Endre Ady** (1867–1919) one of the greatest figures in modern Hungarian poetry (statue by Géza Csorba, 1960). Jókai tér is on the other side of the avenue. The bronze statue here is of **Mór Jókai** (1825–1904) the popular Romantic novelist (Alajos Stróbl, 1921). A branch of the *State Puppet Theatre* is at No. 10 in the square.

No. 47 on the avenue has a very impressive gateway with restored marble columns and decorated walls. Shortly afterward Népköztársaság útja reaches the large, open NOVEMBER 7 TÉR where it crosses Lenin körút.

Octagonal in shape, the square was originally called *The Octagon*. Its present name dates from 1945 and recalls the date of the 1917 Bolshevik revolution in Russia. The bronze wall plaque at No.2 (the Abbázia café on the right) recalls a huge workers' demonstration here in 1930 (András Kiss Nagy, 1973). There is a special shop for philatelists at No. 3 (closed Saturday) though the entrance is actually on the avenue at No. 51.

Beyond the junction, on the right-hand side of the avenue at No. 55, is the *Exhibition room of the Ministry of Interior* (Belügyminisztérium Kiállítóterme). Temporary exhibitions deal with police work and other activities in the Ministry's field.

The building at *No. 60* across the road, which today belongs to the Chemokomplex company, has notorious historical associations. It is the former headquarters of the secret police, the ÁVH (Államvédelmi Osztály) who inherited the building from the pre-war secret police of the Horthy period. The ÁVH were particularly active in Hungary's brutal Stalinist period in the early 1950s. Police cars with their victims inside used to drive into the courtyard via the side entrance in Csengery u.

The Eclectic building at *No. 63–65* was built c 1880 by Gusztáv Petschacher (1844–90) a Viennese architect who came to Hungary to participate in the construction of Népköztársaság útja. It was one of the oldest girls secondary schools in the capital until 1966 when it was transformed into a technical school for the clothing industry.

No. 67, was known as the centre of Hungarian musical life in the 19C, being the former Academy of Music (Adolf Láng, 1877–79). Above the windows on the second floor are reliefs of Bach, Haydn, Liszt, Erkel, Mozart and Beethoven. Ferenc Liszt (1811–86) the Academy's first president, lived here from 1881–86. The plaque on the wall to his memory is by Zoltán Farkas (1934). In 1985 Liszt's former flat was opened as the **Ferenc Liszt Memorial Room**. (Open 12.00–17.00; Sat 9.00–13.00; closed Sunday.) The entrance is in Vörösmarty u. at No. 35.

No. 69 was also designed by Adolf Láng (1875–77). This Italian Renaissance building has a full-length balcony with Corinthian pilasters. Frescoes by Károly Lotz decorate the entrance hall and first floor corridors. The **State Puppet Theatre** (Állami Bábszínház) occupies the ground floor, the rest of the building belongs to the **Academy of Fine Arts** (Képzőművészeti Főiskola). The Academy also occupies the adjoining premises at *No. 71*, a neo-Renaissance building designed by Lajos Rauscher (1875). The sgraffito on the façade is the work of Róbert Scholtz. (The first Hungarian drawing school was founded under Maria Theresa in the Fortuna Hotel on Castle Hill, Buda, in 1777. The Academy has been here since 1876.)

The *Lukács Café*, on the other side of the avenue at No. 70, has long been noted for its excellent cakes and coffee. The 1930s furnishings on the ground floor are literally museum pieces having been supplied by the Museum of Catering in Buda.

The large building at *No. 73–75* Népköztársaság útja, on the right just across Izabella u., belongs to the Hungarian Railways (MÁV) Administration. The near corner of the building has a large bronze relief to the memory of railway workers who fell in the First World War (János Zsákodi Csiszér, 1932). The relief on the far corner, by Rózsa u., was placed here in 1946 on the centenary of the first Hungarian railway (Imre Turáni Kovács). In the hand of the figure is a model of the first Hungarian railway engine which ran from Pest to Vác in 1846.

KODÁLY KÖRÖND ends the second section of the avenue. The four statues in the square, beginning on the left and moving clockwise, are of *György Szondi* (died 1552) a fighter in the anti-Turkish wars (László Marton, 1958); *Bálint Balassi* (1554–94) a lyric poet who died fighting the Turks at the siege of Esztergom (Pál Pátzay, 1959); *Miklós Zrínyi* (1508–66) Ban of Croatia who died in the defence of Szigetvár (József Róna, 1902); and *Vak (Blind) Bottyán* (died 1709) a general in Prince Rákóczi's War of Independence (Gyula Kiss Kovács, 1958).

No. 88–90 Népköztársaság útja, which is No. 3 in the square, immediately on the left, is a huge neo-Renaissance mansion built by Gusztáv Petschacher in 1880–82. The sgraffiti are by Lajos Rauscher and Bertalan Székely. The ornamental wrought-iron gate is by Gyula Jungfer. Across the square at No. 1 is a bronze relief of *Zoltán Kodály* (1882–1967) the internationally renowned composer, music teacher and researcher who lived here in the last years of his life and after whom the square is named.

The final section of the avenue is mainly occupied by embassies (Soviet at No. 102; Albanian at No. 109; Yugoslav at No. 129) and official offices (the 1903 Art Nouveau House of Journalists at No. 101; the National Women's Council at No. 124; People's Front Budapest Committee at No. 125).

The **Ferenc Hopp Museum of Eastern Asiatic Art** occupies the building at No. 103. (Open 10.00–18.00 except Monday.) It is the former home of Ferenc Hopp (1833–1919) who left the villa and the works of art he had collected on his travels in India, China and Japan to the Hungarian state. The collection has been added to over the years and today the Chinese material is exhibited at the nearby **Ráth György Múzeum** at No. 12 Gorkij fasor which runs parallel to the avenue (access via Bajza u.).

The **Yugoslav Embassy** is the last building on the right at the end of Népköztársaság útja. It was here that Imre Nagy and his colleagues found refuge after the crushing of the uprising in 1956. Tricked by false assurances given to the Yugoslav government, they emerged on 23 November only to be arrested and taken to Romania. Nagy was finally executed after a secret trial in Budapest in June 1958.

During World War I Imre Nagy (1896–1958) was a prisoner of war in Russia where he joined the revolutionary movement. He returned to Hungary in 1921 but seven years later went into exile first to Vienna, then to Moscow. After 1945 he held a number of ministerial posts but always maintained an interest in agriculture. In July 1953 he was Prime Minister during the mini thaw following the death of Stalin, but two years later was divested of his party and government offices. During the events of 1956 he was hurled back into office as Prime Minister between 24 October and 4 November (see also p 202).

Népköztársaság útja ends at HEROES' SQUARE (Hősök tere), one of the largest and most impressive squares in Budapest. On the square stands the **Millenary Monument** (Milleniumi emlékmű) the work of architect Albert Schickedanz and sculptor György Zala. Construction began in 1896, the thousandth anniversary of the Magyar Conquest but was not completed until 1929, and since then political considerations have resulted in alterations in the composition of the statues.

In the centre rises the 36m stone column with the Archangel Gabriel at the top and equestrian statues of Árpád and the other six conquering Magyar chiefs at the base. Zala's statue of the archangel won a Grand Prix at Paris in 1900 and was erected here in the following year.

The block of stone in front of the column is the Heroes' Monument, the traditional spot for wreath-laying ceremonies. The inscription reads: 'To the memory of the heroes who have sacrificed their lives for the freedom of our people and national independence.' The original memorial, placed here in 1929, was dedicated to the unknown soldiers who lost their lives in World War I, and had inscriptions on it referring to that war and the territories lost at the Treaty of Trianon.

Behind the column is a two-part colonnade. The four groups of symbolic figures on the top represent, from left to right, Work and Wealth, War, Peace, and Knowledge and Glory. These, like the statues at the base of the stone column, are the work of György Zala.

Between the columns of the colonnade are statues by various sculptors of Hungarian rulers and princes. From left to right they are: King Stephen (1000–38); King László (1077–95); King Kálmán (1095–1116); King Andrew II (1205–35); King Béla IV (1235–70); King Charles Robert (1308–42); King Louis the Great (1342–82); Regent János Hunyadi (1446–52); King Matthias Corvinus (1458–90); István Bocskay, Prince of Transylvania (1604–06); Gábor Bethlen, Prince of Transylvania (1613–29); Imre Thököly, Prince of Upper Hungary and Transylvania (1682–85 and 1690); Ferenc Rákóczi II, Prince of Transylvania (1704–11) and of Hungary (1705–11); and Lajos Kossuth, Regent of Hungary (1849).

Below each statue is a relief. All but one show some significant scene from the life of the person represented above. From left to right they are: 1. King Stephen receives the crown from the Pope in 1000; 2. László defeats the Kun knight who is abducting a girl; 3. King Kálmán abolishes witch-burning; 4. Andrew II leading a crusade to liberate Jerusalem; 5. Béla IV reconstructs the country after the Mongol invasion; 6. A battle scene from 1278 (not connected with Charles Robert); 7. Louis the Great marches on Naples 1348; 8. Hunyadi's victory at Nándorfehérvár (today Belgrade) stops the Turkish advance; 9. King Matthias among his scholars; 10. Bocskai's soldiers in battle with the Emperor's mercenaries; 11. Bethlen concludes an alliance with the Czechs in 1620; 12. Thököly's Kurucs defeat the Habsburgs at the battle of Szikszó in 1697; 13. General Tamás Esze with his serf army receives the returning Rákóczi; 14. Lajos Kossuth calls the people of the Alföld to arms in 1848–49.

The statues of the Transylvanian princes on the right-hand colonnade were all added after World War II in place of statues of Habsburg rulers. The Habsburgs had also been removed, though later replaced, during the 1919 Republic of Councils period. For May day of that year the whole square was decked out with red, and the central column covered by a huge red obelisk.

Originally the square was more like a small park with trees and bushes. The present-day ornamental paving was laid out in 1938 for the 34th International Eucharistic Congress.

The large buildings on the S and N sides of the square are the Exhibition Hall and the Museum of Fine Arts respectively. The **Exhibition Hall** (Műcsarnok) to the S is one of the country's largest.

Temporary exhibitions of the arts are held here. (Open 10.00–18.00 except Monday; Tues 12.00–20.00.) The Eclectic–neo-classical red-brick building was designed by Albert Schickedanz and Fülöp Herzog in 1895. It was used as a military hospital during World War I, after which it was renovated.

Behind the six Corinthian columns of the portico there is a fresco in three parts by Lajos Deák Ébner depicting the Beginning of Sculpture, with figures of Vulcan and Athene; the Source of Arts, with Apollo and the muses; and the Origins of Painting, with images from the mythology of antiquity. The two smaller ones in between show allegorical figures of Painting and Sculpture.

Originally the tympanum was plain. The present design, depicting St. Stephen as patron of the arts, was added by Jenő Haranghy between 1938 and 1941.

The Millenary Monument, Heroes' Square. The crowds seen here are assembling for the ceremony marking the reburial of Imre Nagy on 16 June 1989.

The steps of the Exhibition Hall were the scene of a remarkable event on the morning of 16 June 1989 which attracted world attention. The façade of the building was decorated in black and white and over 100,000 people packed Heroes' Square to witness a ceremony marking the public reburial of Imre Nagy, the Prime Minister during the 1956 uprising who was secretly executed on 16 June 1958.

The event was attended by opposition groups, members of the government, leading churchmen, foreign ambassadors and political activists prominent in 1958, some of whom had returned to Hungary from abroad for the first time in over 30 years.

Nagy's coffin was flanked by five others. Four belonged to colleagues with whom he had been executed (including Pál Maléter, the Minister of Defence) in 1956, and one was empty, representing the unknown victims of the period.

In the afternoon the coffins were taken to plot 301 in a far corner of Budapest's Új köztemető cemetery where Nagy and over 200 others had lain in unmarked graves for three decades. (The cemetery is situated on the eastern side of Kőbánya, about 10km from the city centre. Bus No. 95 runs there from Baross tér, where the Eastern Railway Station stands.)

On the left of the Exhibition Hall is a bronze copy of an original marble statue of St. Christopher (László Hüvös, 1913). On the other side of the road from this is *The Archer* by Zsigmond Kisfaludi Strobl (1929). The tablet on the right-hand side of the Exhibition Hall's façade recalls that on 1 September, 1930 the largest workers' demonstration of the inter-war, Horthy period passed through the square under slogans demanding work and bread.

The section of DÓZSA GYÖRGY ÚT which runs from the right side of the Exhibition Hall for about 1km to the S used to be used as a huge parade ground on 1 May and other festive or political occasions, in the manner of Red Square in Moscow.

No. 84/b Dózsa György út is the headquarters of the *National Federation of Hungarian Trade Unions*. Opposite, until it was removed for repairs in 1989 and never replaced, used to stand a bronze statue of Lenin in front of a pillar of Swedish granite. There is no truth in the rumour that Lenin was deliberately placed at the bottom of the pillar so that he would not be able to look into the windows of the trade union offices opposite and see how little work was being done.

Here, too, used to stand a huge statue of Joseph Stalin, erected here in 1951. The 25m statue stood on a plinth 30m high. On the evening of 23 October 1956, the first day of the Hungarian uprising, massed crowds assembled here and pulled the statue down (see p 28).

A short distance along Dózsa György út is the large bronze *monument to the 1919 Hungarian Republic of Councils* (István Kiss, 1969). The sailor is modelled on a celebrated poster of 1919 by the painter Róbert Berény.

György Dózsa (c 1470–1514) was the leader of a peasant rebellion in 1514 who was captured and brutally killed by being burnt alive on a red-hot throne.

Opposite the Exhibition Hall, on the N side of Heroes' Square, stands the **Museum of Fine Arts** (Szépművészeti Múzeum) the main collection in Hungary of non-Hungarian works of art. It is one of the major art galleries of Central Europe. Also designed by Schickedanz and Herzog, it was completed in 1906. In the tympanum above the portico is a copy of the relief on the western gable of the temple of the Olympian Zeus depicting the fight of the Centaurs and Lapiths. (Open 10.00–18.00, except Monday.)

Reconstruction of the building started in 1987 and is expected to continue well into the 1990s. At the time of writing it is impossible to give an accurate description of even the permanent exhibitions as they are constantly being rearranged and the final plans have not yet materialised. The following, therefore, should only be taken as a general guide to the contents of the museum.

The most important collection of the museum is the *Old Masters Gallery*. The core of the collection came from Miklós Esterházy's private gallery, which he sold to the state in 1871. The collection covers 13C–18C European painting including works by Titian, Rembrandt, Raphael, Brueghel, Rubens, Van Dyck, El Greco, Velázquez, Goya, Dürer, and the British masters Hogarth, Reynolds and Gainsborough. The *Modern Foreign Gallery* among others has a series of paintings by 19C French artists including Delacroix, Courbet, Millet, Manet, Monet, Gauguin, Renoir, Cézanne and Toulouse-Lautrec. Among the *20C Collection* are works by Chagall, Le Corbusier, Picasso and Vasarely. The *Collection of Prints and Drawings* is a rich collection of several thousands of drawings and engravings including three studies by Leonardo da Vinci and 15 drawings by Rembrandt.

The *Collection of European Sculpture* is mainly Italian and 17C–18C Baroque work. For the period of the museum's reconstruction most of the collection is in storage and those works that are on display are situated in various parts of the museum. The *Classical Antiquity Collection* has an Egyptian section as well as a Greek and Roman collection of 6C–1C BC ceramics.

ÁLLATKERTI KÖRÚT runs from the right side of the museum northwards encircling the City Park. Immediately behind the museum at No. 2 is *Gundel's*, one of the most famous, highly regarded and, by Hungarian standards, expensive restaurants in the capital. The popular Wampetic's restaurant was here from the late 19C. Károly Gundel (1883–1956), the son of János Gundel (1844–1915) a pioneer of the Hungarian catering industry, acquired the business in 1910. Through exhibitions he popularised and developed Hungarian specialities.

Next to the restaurant, at No. 6–12 Állatkerti körút, is the **Budapest Zoo**. The Municipal Zoological and Botanical Gardens (Fővárosi Állat-és Növénykert) opened in 1866 on the initiative of the Academy of Sciences and in particular of János Xantus (1825–94) the natural scientist who spent much of his life in the United States. Taken over by the city council in 1907 it has been modernised several times. Some of the architecture of the zoo represents significant examples of Hungarian Art Nouveau, such as Kornél Neuschloss-Knüsli's main gate (1912) and elephant house (1910). The bird house near the SW corner of the zoo, designed by Károly Kós, is also in National Romantic style. The zoo has a reputation for the high fertility rate of its hippopotamuses, attributed to the constant supply of thermal spring water.

No. 7 next to the zoo is the **Municipal Circus** (Fővárosi Nagycirkusz). The first circus in Pest, the Hetz Theatre, was opened in 1783 on the site of today's Lutheran church in Deák tér but because of fire danger it moved several times. The first permanent circus was built on the present-day site in 1891 by a German entrepreneur, Ede Wulff. It seated 2300 and operated until 1966. The present building dates from 1971.

The **Széchenyi Baths** (Széchenyi Gyógyfürdő) stands opposite the circus. Designed in 1909–13 by Győző Cziegler and Ede Dvorzsák it was extended in 1926. The baths have an open-air swimming pool (open throughout the year) and medicinal pools fed by thermal springs bored in the last century. The building is undergoing major renovation throughout the early 1990s.

The *Fun Fair* (Vidám Park) is at No. 14–16 beyond the circus. Before the war it was called the Angol (English) Park. The traditional merry-go-round in the small building through the entrance and immediately on the left, and the wooden switchback at the rear of the fairground are original and date from pre-war times. Between the circus and the Fun Fair there is a special *small children's fairground.*

The bridge immediately behind Heroes' Square leads into the CITY PARK proper (Városliget).

The City Park is the biggest in Budapest and has been a popular recreation area for many decades. Originally marshland, the area was presented to Pest in the mid-18C by Leopold I. Plans for the park were drawn up by landscape gardener Henrik Nebbien in the 1810s but the present layout mostly dates from the end of the last century when English-style gardens were popular. There were nearly 200 English gardens in Hungary in the second half of the last century.

The City Park was the site of the main exhibition during the six months of the Millenary celebrations in 1896. Over 200 halls and pavilions were erected to display the agricultural, industrial and commercial life of the country. The country's first museum village was built to represent peasant life and 'real' peasants were on hand to demonstrate authenticity. A great attraction was the balloon that rose 500m providing its passengers with a panoramic view of the city. The balloon was unfortunately ripped to pieces by a storm on 2 August of that year.

To the right of the bridge is the open-air **Skating Rink** which operates only in winter. Competitions have been held here since the 1860s when the Skating Club of Pest was founded. Membership was originally 35 but by 1897 it reached almost 8000. European championships were held here in 1895 and 1900, and in 1909 there were both European and World championships. Originally skaters used the frozen surface of the lake but an artificial rink has operated since 1926. The club house on the right was designed in 1893 by Ödön Lechner.

Beyond the skating rink on an island in the lake stands an unusual building, the **Vajdahunyad Castle**. It was originally designed by Ignác Alpár as a temporary structure for the Millenary Exhibition which opened in the park on 2 May 1896. The idea was to present in one building all the different architectural styles which could be found in Hungary. Due to its popularity the same architect was commissioned to rebuild the structure in a permanent form at the end of the exhibition. Hence the present building actually dates from 1907. There is a statue of Ignác Alpár (1855–1928) dressed as a medieval guild master by the road leading to the castle.

The section facing the lake is a copy of part of the original Vajdahunyad Castle in Transylvania (today Hunedoara, Romania) from which the whole complex of buildings takes its name. Work started on the original castle c 1450 under the direction of Erzsébet Szilágyi, the wife of János Hunyadi and the mother of King Matthias who continued the building until its completion at the end of the 15C.

To the left of the main gate across the bridge are copies of towers of former castles in Upper Hungary while to the right is a copy of the tower of Segesvár (also in Romania today).

In the courtyard on the left is the Romanesque wing and the *Chapel of Ják,* a copy of the still-standing 13C Benedictine church at Ják in western Hungary (see p 352). In fact only the gate decorated with the 12 apostles is a copy. The rest is both smaller and different from the original church. To the left of the chapel is a cloister with round arches reminiscent of the age of Árpád.

Opposite, around a small courtyard, is the façade of the so-called Palace section, containing a mixture of Romanesque and Gothic styles (on the right) and the 'Vajdahunyad' section. Further to the left is a replica of a small Renaissance house and beyond that a large sprawling Baroque building based on details of various 18C mansions. Inside this group of buildings is the **Agricultural Museum** (Mezőgazdasági Múzeum). (Open 10.00–18.00 except Monday; September–May early closing on weekdays at 17.00.)

The exhibitions inside trace the development of agriculture in Hungary including the development of tools and machines. On the ground floor is a steam engine built in 1852 by the Clayton-Shuttleworth company of Lincoln, England, which was brought to Hungary and used for nearly 50 years for driving threshing machines.

There are also sections on sheep, horse and cattle-breeding including the way of life of those who tended these animals, and on hunting and fishing.

An English speaking guide is available on three days' notice (tel. 1412 011).

Facing the entrance of the Agricultural Museum is a *Statue of Anonymus* who wrote an early chronicle of the Hungarians at the time of King Béla III in the late 12C or early 13C (Miklós Ligeti, 1903). An extremely popular statue, many bronze or ceramic copies of it ranging from mantlepiece decorations to inkpots adorned pre-war apartments.

Across the City Park, towards its SE corner, stands the **Transport Museum** (Közlekedési Múzeum). The museum was originally opened in 1896 in a specially designed building. In the Second World War, the building and its contents were almost completely destroyed and it was not until 1966 that the museum was opened in its present building. The exhibitions inside cover the history of shipping and road and rail transport. There are many models on display, both large and small scale. (Open 10.00–18.00 except Monday.)

The Transport Museum's *Exhibition of Air and Space Travel* is also in the City Park, but in a separate building, that of the Petőfi Csarnok (Petőfi Hall) some distance to the W. (Open 4 April–7 November, 10.00–18.00 except Monday.) Part of this complex also functions as a popular venue for pop concerts.

J.   The Great Boulevard (Nagykörút)

This route, some 4.1km long, follows the curve of the **Great Boulevard** from Petőfi Bridge, S of the city centre on the Pest side, round to Margaret Bridge in the N. It is divided into four parts—Ferenc körút, József körút, Lenin körút and Szent István körút. Trams No. 4 and 6 run the length of the route.

The Great Boulevard, 45m wide throughout, is the main thoroughfare circling the heart of Pest. Its construction was planned in 1871 and it was opened to traffic in 1896, on the thousandth anniversary of the Hungarian Conquest. It follows the line of a former backwater of the Danube which on old maps was called 'Magnum Fossatum' or Great Ditch. The three- and four-storey blocks of flats being constructed at approximately the same time make the Great Boulevard as a whole an outstanding example of late 19C Hungarian Eclecticism.

The route begins at BORÁROS TÉR at the Pest side of Petőfi bridge (Pál Álgyay Hubert, 1933–37). János Boráros was the chief justice and later mayor of Pest in the early 19C. There is a plaque to his memory on the wall of the building at No. 4 on the N side of this busy junction where six streets converge and where the terminus of the suburban railway (HÉV) to Csepel can be found. Soroksári út which starts here leads to the E5, the road for Kecskemét and Szeged which lie to the SE of Budapest.

The pillar standing at the S of the square just below the end of the bridge is from the old National Theatre and was placed here in 1910. Below the pillar in the underpass can be seen a bronze statue entitled *Winemaker* by Imre Varga (1983).

FERENC KÖRÚT (556m) is the main road leading away from Boráros tér to the E. The buildings at Nos 23, 22, 20 and 5 have interesting courtyards. The surrounding area, in particular to the S of this stretch of the route, is called *Ferencváros* (Francis Town) and was inhabited as early as the Middle Ages although it was named after Francis I in 1792. The great flood of 1838 devasted this area, destroying over 90 per cent of the dwellings.

The first street off to the left, Tompa u., leads to the hidden BAKÁTS TÉR in the centre of which stands the *Francis Town Parish Church* (Ferencvárosi Plébániatemplom). The original church was damaged in the great flood of 1838 and had to be pulled down in 1865. The present building was constructed over the following ten years to the plans of Miklós Ybl in late Romantic style. The interior has frescoes and painted windows by Károly Lotz and Mór Than respectively. The statue of St. Francis on the N side of the church is by Alajos Stróbl. Behind the church is the Schöpf-Merei Hospital which stands on the site of the former Erdey Sanatorium, a private hospital built in 1906 for pregnant and sick women and which the city bought in 1917.

Ferenc körút ends where it meets Üllői út, a long, straight road leading SE out of the city centre and which goes towards Ferihegy airport and beyond that to Debrecen, the major town of eastern Hungary on the Great Plain.

The huge classical block at the corner where Ferenc körút meets Üllői út is the former Maria Theresa, then György Kilián, barracks (József Hild, 1845–46). The Kilián Barracks played a major role in the events of 1956. The Hungarian troops here joined the insurgents and the building became a centre of resistance. This junction was the scene of some of the fiercest fighting. The damaged building was rebuilt in the 1960s for civilian purposes which was when the corner archways were constructed. Today it houses the Budapest City Council Repairs Office (Ingatlankezelő Műszaki Vállalat).

On the left-hand corner at the end of Ferenc körút is a curved building just beneath the top floor of which can be seen the words 'Lottó Ház'. In 1959 the flats in this newly constructed block were offered as prizes in the state lottery.

Public lotteries in Hungary originated in the second half of the 18C and continued uninterrupted until 1897, except for a short period when they were banned by the revolutionary government of 1848. In 1957 the state lottery was revived and continues to this day drawing in many millions of forints annually to the public purse.

Next to the Lottó Ház at Üllői út 33–37 is the impressive domed building of the **Museum of Applied Arts** (Iparművészeti Múzeum).

The building was planned and its construction directed by Ödön Lechner and Gyula Pártos between 1893 and 1896 and opened by Emperor Franz Joseph in 1897 as part of the Millennium celebrations. The building is a characteristic example of Lechner's individual style in which he combined elements of Hungarian folk art with Hindu and Turkish motifs with the intention of creating a unique national architecture. The building displays his typical use of coloured pyrogranite ceramics made in the Zsolnay factory in Pécs.

Critics did not like the building which they denounced as too ornamental. Even the site was unusual being in what was then a poor, unbuilt area. Lechner, who won a competition for the design, wrote later in his 'Autobiographical Sketches' that in developing his combination of folk and modern styles he had been deeply impressed by his studies in England and especially by British colonial architecture.

The principal entrance, facing Üllői út, consists of an open, projecting portal, topped by a dome, in the centre of the long building with domes at each corner. The building was damaged in World War II and again during the events of 1956. The Zsolnay ceramic factory in Pécs, which had made the original pyrogranite ornamentation, again manufactured the material required for reconstruction.

The museum was founded in 1872 and was the second of its kind in the world after the Victoria and Albert Museum in London. The permanent display has five sections: Glass, Ceramics, Porcelain; Leather, Paper, Books; Textiles; Wood, Furniture; and Metalwork, as well as old ivory. The permanent sections, however, only occupy a small part of the museum. Most of the building is devoted to temporary exhibitions of which there may be two or three at any one time. The Moorish style white interior of the museum, with its stucco ornamentation, is also worth examining. (Open 10.00–18.00 except Monday.)

The seated statue in front of the museum is of *Ödön Lechner*, the architect of the Museum (Béla Farkas, 1936).

The section of the route which continues beyond Üllői út is called JÓZSEF KÖRÚT and stretches for some 1.2km. Almost immediately on the right there is a small street, Kisfaludy köz, which leads to the *Corvina Cinema* (Emil Bauer, 1923). Like the Kilián Barracks the cinema was also a rebel stronghold in 1956.

The first part, up to Baross u., has some interesting inner court-yards worth viewing at Nos 85, 77–79, 69, 71–73 and 63 on the left and at Nos 66, 64, 62 and 60 on the right. No. 71–73 has a well-renovated double courtyard while No. 69 has an unusual, although somewhat dilapidated, triple courtyard. The passage to the courtyard at No. 62 has neo-Gothic arches. This building used to house the studio of Aladár Székely, a noted Hungarian portrait photographer of the turn of the century. Four doors along at No. 70 is the *Joseph Town Showroom and Collection of Local History* (open 10.00–18.00 every day except Monday).

The plaque on the wall at No. 83 is to the memory of the writer *Ferenc Molnár* (1878–1952). He was actually born at No. 68 nearby but moved here in 1905. His celebrated novel 'The Paul Street Boys' (A Pál utcai Fiúk), published in 1907 and later made into a film, recalls the time of his childhood spent in this area. Pál utca (Paul St) is the first street on the left along József körút.

The first major road to cross József körút is BAROSS UTCA, which on the right opens into Harminckettesek tere (Square of the 32nd). Here stands the monument of the former home regiment of Budapest, the 32nd Infantry (István Szentgyörgyi, 1933). The relief on its left shows the regiment's foundation by Maria Theresa and the one on the right marching to the First World War. At the back are listed the names of the regiment's battles.

300m along Baross u. stands the **Joseph Town Parish Church** (Józsefvárosi plébániatemplom) in HORVÁTH MIHÁLY TÉR, named after the Catholic bishop and historian who was Minister of Education in the 1849 government. The church was built in 1797–98 to the plans of József Thàllher, though it was several times rebuilt during the last century. The statue between the spires on the façade is of St. Joseph (Lőrinc Dunaisky, 1820). The high altar (1835–37) was designed by József Hild and the painting there depicting the apotheosis of St. Joseph is by the Viennese painter Leopold Kupelwieser. In front of the church, the marble statue with outstretched hand (Béla Radnai, 1914) is of *Péter Pázmány* who founded the

University of Nagyszombat (now Trnava in Czechoslovakia) the forerunner of Budapest University.

Pázmány (1570–1637) was a Jesuit who came from a Protestant family. He was Archbishop of Esztergom from 1616. With his polemical essays and political activities he won many members of the Protestant aristocracy for the Roman Catholic Church and laid the foundations for the Counter-Reformation. He was a supporter of the House of Habsburg and an enemy of the Transylvanian Principality, but at the same time a defender of the privileges of the Hungarian nobility. He founded the university in 1635.

To the left of the church at the corner of Horváth Mihály tér and Bacsó Béla u. stands the building of the *old Joseph Town telephone exchange*, one of the earliest exchanges in the city (Rezső Vilmos Ray, 1910–12). Behind the trees on the side facing the square is an unusual large relief depicting classical figures welcoming the new technology of long-distance communication.

The bronze relief on the right of the entrance (Szilárd Sződy, 1931) depicts the Puskás brothers, Tivadar (1844–93) and Ferenc (1848–84). The former, an inventor, was a colleague of Edison and both were instrumental in organising the early telephone network in Budapest.

The first exchange, built on today's József Attila u. in the city centre, was opened in 1881 and had 54 subscribers. By 1904 there were already 6300. The building here at Horváth Mihály tér still belongs to the Telephone Directorate.

Along József körút, which proceeds northwards from Baross u., the house at *No. 47*, at the junction of Krúdy u., bears a plaque which records that the writer Gyula Krúdy (1878–1933) once lived here. The small statue in front of the house (György Kiss, 1927) is entitled *Csirkefogó* (Rascal).

250m along the route brings us to RÁKÓCZI TÉR on the right, the only proper square (as opposed to large junction) on the entire length of the Great Boulevard. The large building at the far side of the square is the *Joseph Town Market Hall*, designed by the Budapest city engineering department and opened in 1897. The building suffered severe fire damage in 1988.

This area has traditionally been one of the centres of prostitution in Budapest and although brothels were officially closed down in 1948 Rákóczi tér is still the hub of a down-market red-light district. The business has a long tradition. In the spring of 1810 Vladimir Bronievsky, an officer of the Russian navy travelling through Hungary noted: 'Treacherous sirens in Pest weave dangerous nets in the dimness of the night ... they are skilled in taking advantage of men's inclinations and desires. Under the effect of their slim figures, gossamer garments and softly-calling voices the last traces of self-restraint disappear unnoticed, but at the same time your purse is emptied.'

The short Kölcsey u., opposite the NW corner of Rákóczi tér, connects the Boulevard with the small GUTENBERG TÉR, in the centre of which is a bronze bust of *József Fodor* (György Vastagh the Younger, 1909). Fodor (1843–1901) was active in public health campaigns and was the first to hold the Chair of Public Health at Budapest University. The Chair was established in 1874 and was the second in the world.

Facing the statue at No. 4 in the square is the *Book Printers' and Typesetters' Cultural Centre*. The building with its interesting curved façade was designed by József and László Vágó in 1907. The small bronze relief of *Gutenberg* by the door is by Tamás Vigh (1984). To the left of this building at Somogyi Béla u. 26 is the *Anna Frank Gimnázium*, the site of a Jewish secondary school since 1919, though only with this name since 1965.

József körút ends at BLAHA LUJZA TÉR and the junction with Rákóczi út. The last building on the left before the square (actually No. 5 József körút) belongs to *Pallas Lapkiadó Vállalat*, the main newspaper and magazine publisher, and houses the editorial offices of 'Népszabadság' (People's Freedom), the Party's central daily, and several other newspapers. The Socialist Realist relief, three storeys high on the wall facing the körút, is the work of András Beck, Jenő Kerényi and Sándor Mikus.

Diagonally across the körút from this building, at the corner of Népszínház u., is an attractive neo-Renaissance building with a façade of red bricks and terracotta ornamentation. Built to the design of Alajos Hauszmann in 1887 it today houses the Institute of Commercial Quality Control. Next door stands the *Nemzeti* (National) *Hotel*. It was built as a family hotel at the end of the 1890s in Eclectic style to the design of György Schannen and has had its present name since 1929. Its restaurant was popular at the turn of the century and the atmosphere has been maintained by restoration work which was undertaken in 1987.

Detail from the façade of the 'New York Palace' (Alajos Hausz-mann, Flóris Korb and Kálmán Giergl, 1891–95), Lenin körút.

The Nagykörút continues after Rákóczi út as LENIN KÖRÚT, which runs for approximately 1.8km towards Marx tér. The bronze relief of Lenin on the wall of No. 1 on the right is by Iván Szabó (1970).

The five-storey Art Nouveau building at No. 9–11 Lenin körút was well known before the Second World War as the **New York Palace**. It was built for an American insurance company in 1891–95 to the designs of Alajos Hauszmann working with Flóris Korb and Kálmán Giergl. The statues on the façade are the work of Károly Senyei.

The *New York Coffee House*, which occupied the ground floor, was one of the central meeting places for writers, poets, painters, sculptors, composers, singers, actors and later film directors. It played an outstanding role in the literary, artistic and cultural life of Budapest up to the Second World War. 'Here you could see everybody,' wrote Gyula Krúdy, though he once derided the building as 'an imitation of an American skyscraper'. The 'Nyugat' (Occident) circle used to meet here and its editor-in-chief for many years, Ernő Osvát (1877–1929), did much of his editorial work at a reserved table. A memorial tablet commemorates this inside the café where caricatures of the various literary figures can also be seen.

In 1945 the building became a centre of publishing and to this day it houses the editorial offices of many newspapers and magazines belonging to Pallas Lapkiadó Vállalat, the state publishing company. Hence the building is sometimes known as the *Press Palace*.

In 1954 the coffee house on the ground floor was reopened as a café and restaurant with a new name, the *Hungaria*. It still operates under this name, though the original 'New York' is slowly creeping back into use.

At the turn of the century there were 500 coffee houses in Budapest many of which, like the New York, became the meeting places of writers and artists. The coffee house culture virtually disappeared during World War II and so the Hungaria/New York, with its rich interior of marble, bronze and Venetian ground glass and its restored frescoes and paintings (the work of Gusztáv Magyar-Mannheimer, Ferenc Eisenhut and Károly Lotz) can be said to be the only surviving coffee house of the traditional type. Today it has even regained some of its former spirit by playing host to occasional literary meetings.

The fountain opposite the Hungaria on the other side of Lenin körút is entitled *Faun* and is the work of László Marton (1986). The nearby building at *No. 6* Lenin körút is the former Meteor Hotel and coffee house. In 1907 the poet Endre Ady lived here for a time and a literary circle gathered around him. Today the building houses the *VIIth District Council offices*. Further along this stretch at No. 20 is a second-hand bookshop, while the passage immediately beyond the Intertourist shop at No. 26 leads to an interesting inner courtyard.

On the other side of the körút, 100m along Barcsay u. at No. 5 is the *Madách Imre Gimnázium* which traces its origins back to 1881 when the first state secondary school was established, though it only moved to this building 11 years later in 1892. The frescoes on the exterior are the work of Károly Lotz. The courtyard opposite at *No. 6* is worth viewing.

The *Madách Theatre* at No. 29–33 Lenin körút was opened in 1961 to the plans of Oszkár Kaufmann. The five groups of three bronze statues high up on the façade are connected with theatrical art and are by József Somogyi, Jenő Kerényi and Gyula Kiss Kovács. The foyer is decorated with Eszter Mattioni's so-called decorated stone wall pictures. The theatre stands on the site of the former *Royal Orpheum*, one of the largest and most popular music hall/variety theatres. Founded by Hermann Keleti and Oszkár Fodor in 1908, many stars from all over the world performed here including Josephine Baker and Little Titch from Britain.

At No. 39 Lenin körút, on the corner of Dob u., is the *Mátra cinema* which specialises in screening cartoons for young people. 100m along Dob u. on the E side is a modern building belonging to the Postal Ministry. On the façade at the corner are statues by Gábor Boda of the seven chiefs of the Magyar conquest. The *Philatelic Museum* is situated on the mezzanine floor of this building. (Open Wed: 10.00–18.00; Sat: 10.00–15.00; Sun: 10.00–14.00.) The collection includes world stamps, private stamps, ship, balloon and airmail marks, and forgeries.

Immediately beyond Dob u. on the building at *No. 44–46* Lenin körút can be seen the words *Jókai Udvar* (Jókai Court). The outstanding representative of Hungarian romantic prose, *Mór Jókai* (1825–1904) lived here from 1899 until his death. Further along this stretch, good inner courtyards can be seen at Nos 50, 52 and 54. No. 50 has original wrought iron work on the staircase which was left undamaged by the war. The *Erzsébet Söröző* at No. 48 is an old style beer hall and eating place.

The *Royal Hotel* at No. 45 was one of the largest hotels of its day when it was opened (Rezső Lajos Ray, 1894–96). Burnt out in 1956 it was reopened in 1961 after alterations and renewals. The cast-iron statues on the façade above the main entrance represent the four seasons.

LISZT FERENC TÉR lies 100m S of the Great Boulevard along Majakovszkij u. On the corner of Majakovszkij u. and overlooking the eastern end of the square is the Art Nouveau building of the **Ferenc Liszt Academy of Music** (Liszt Ferenc Zeneakadémia), designed by Flóris Korb and Kálmán Giergl and built between 1904 and 1907. It is the most important music-teaching centre in Hungary. It has the largest music library and collection of scores in the country and its halls are the centres of concert life in Budapest.

Ferenc Liszt (1811–86) was the first president of the Academy of Music when it was originally founded in 1875. There is a seated statue of him by Alajos Stróbl above the entrance on the main façade. The six reliefs on the ledge above the base (by Ede Telcs) represent stages in the development of music. Through the main entrance and to the left is a *bust of Chopin*, which was presented by an official Polish delegation in 1958. Along the walls above the entrances to the auditorium is a fresco from 1907 entitled 'Hungarian Wedding Procession in the 14C'. The artist, Aladár Körösfói Kriesch (1863–1920), was one of the leaders of the Hungarian Pre-Raphaelites, known as the Gödöllő School. The English Pre-Raphaelite influence is clearly visible, as it is on his large wall-painting (The Fountain of Art, 1907) on the building's first floor, which is generally much richer in decoration. (If the main entrance is closed, access can usually be gained via the side door in Majakovszki u.)

The Academy of Music is noteworthy not only because of its teaching traditions (Béla Bartók and Zoltán Kodály both taught here) but also because it has been the venue for significant literary and political events. For example, it was here in 1916 at the celebrated 'Nyugat' matinée that Endre Ady, Mihály Babits, Ignótus, Frigyes Karinthy and Zsigmond Móricz gave readings from their works. And in 1956, on the eve of the uprising of that year, a packed audience gave a 15-minute ovation to Kodály after a rendering of his unaccompanied choral work based on Miklós Zrínyi's 'Szózat' (Appeal). (Zrínyi was a commander in the wars against the Turks. The clapping was accompanied by chants of his line 'Ne Bántsd a Magyart'—Let the Hungarians Alone!)

The statue 100m from the Academy in the middle of Liszt tér is of Ferenc Liszt and was erected on the 100th anniversary of the composer's death (László Marton, 1986).

The fine buildings along Lenin körút between Majakovszkij u. and November 7 tér have been cleaned and restored to their original late-19C splendour which makes this stretch of the Great Boulevard (at the time of writing) one of the most visually pleasing sights in the whole of Pest.

The shop called *ERMA* at No. 62 was founded by Erzsébet Herzman and Mariska Goldberger in 1922. The name of the shop derives from the first two letters of their names. In 1987 it was reopened in the same style as they had commissioned from Pál Rákos when it moved here in 1935. The *Octogon Pharmacy* at No. 61 Lenin körút, on the corner of Szófia u. on the right, was originally founded in 1786 in the Tabán district in Buda. It moved here in 1924 which was when the neo-Baroque furnishings were done. The wall-painting inside of *Hygieia and Asclepios* is by Kocsár Bretschneider (1936). *No. 67*, on the right, was built in 1884 to the plans of Alajos Hauszmann as a replica of the Renaissance Strozzi Palace in Florence at the behest of the owner, Count Batthyány. The intricate wrought-iron gate is by Gyula Jungfer.

Lenin körút now reaches the huge open junction of NOVEMBER 7 TÉR (see p 198). Crossing the square, and with it Népköztársaság útja, Lenin körút continues, gently curving to the NE.

The *Béke* (Peace) *Hotel* stands at No. 97 on the right. Originally built for flats in 1896 the building was redesigned by Béla Malnai to open as the Brittania Hotel in 1912. Its current name stems from the early years of the cold war. The coloured mosaic on the corner of the building is of *György Szondi* (died 1552), a legendary fortress captain at the time of the Turkish wars. The artist was Jenő Haranghy who also painted the large murals depicting scenes from Shakespeare's plays on the walls of the hotel's Shakespeare dining room. The hotel was renovated and reopened in 1985. In the Cupola Bar on the first floor some of the original stained glass from the old beer hall in the basement can be seen. Today the basement is the home of the *Orpheum*, a modern night spot which attempts to recreate the music hall/variety theatre atmosphere of old Budapest.

In the early 1920s the hotel was the meeting place of a notorious group of right-wing officers known as the 'Britannias' (a britanniások). In the 1930s the political orientation changed and the hotel was a gathering place for the progressive Friends of Nyugat group (Nyugat Barátok Köre). It was a favourite haunt of the writer Ferenc Móra and a special room was furnished for him where many of his works originated.

Further along the körút at *No. 105* is a large post office which is open 24 hours a day, every day of the year. (There is a similar one by the Eastern Railway Station.) Next to the post office is the imposing façade of the **Western Railway Station** (Nyugati pályaudvar) (August de Serres and Győző Bernardt, 1874–77). The building contractors were the Eiffel Company of Paris which built the famous tower of the same name. The large hall with its iron framework, much of which was cast in Paris, was one of the most up-to-date constructions of its time and generated much interest throughout Europe. Despite rebuilding, the original framework has been preserved.

The first railway station in Pest was built on this site and the first train left here on 15 July 1846 for Vác, 34km to the N. It covered the journey in 49 minutes and created a sensation. In the previous year a trial run of 8km had been held with the Palatine Joseph on board. After that the Town Council requested local priests to warn their parishioners 'not to walk on the rails, nor put anything on or beside the tracks'.

It had taken some persuading on the part of Count István Széchenyi to get the idea of steam trains accepted. Before that lines were being built for horse-drawn trains. Like many of his other initiatives, he had been influenced by his experiences in England. One of his diary entries reads: 'We have inspected the Manchester–Liverpool railway line. It is a staggering sight when the train passes closely by, carrying everything with diabolical force.'

In 1887 the first tram line in Budapest ran from in front of the station for 1km along the Boulevard. A small memorial plaque recalling the event was placed by the central tram stop on the centenary.

Lenin körút ends at MARX TÉR (formerly Berlin tér) an important traffic junction which was entirely replanned in 1978–81 when the pedestrian subways and the flyover were constructed. The modern dark-glass-fronted building on the left is *Skála Metro* (György Kővári, 1984), a department store belonging to the Skála chain, a huge cooperative which has done much to modernise retail trading in Hungary. (It runs the S-modell boutiques and the Vitamin Porta grocery shops.) The supermarket on the ground floor here is one of the best stocked in Budapest but, as elsewhere, lack of adequate space can make shopping seem like unarmed conflict as customers fight to get to the shelves.

350m N from the square, along Váci út, is the **Élmunkás tér church** (István Möller, 1931). It is a copy of the 13C Romanesque church at Zsámbék, 34km W of Budapest, which was built for the Premonstratensian order but ruined by an earthquake in 1763 (see p 354).

Behind the church is the **Lehel market** (Lehel piac), the largest traditional open-air market in Budapest. Both the church and the market can be reached by one stop on the metro in the direction of Árpád híd. There are photographs of old Budapest on the walls of the escalator in the Marx tér metro station.

The final section of the Great Boulevard is SZENT ISTVÁN KÖRÚT, which runs for 553m from Marx tér to Margaret Bridge. Despite some being spoilt by the appearance of private boutiques, almost all the inner courtyards on this stretch are worth viewing especially those at No. 17 on the left and, nearer the bridge, at Nos 7, 3 (a double courtyard) and 1 on the left and Nos 10, 8, 4 and 2 on the right. The street numbers are in descending order from Marx tér.

The *Memorial Room of the Foundation of the Hungarian Party of Communists* is situated at No. 15 Visegrádi u. the first street to the right off Szent István körút. (Open 10.00–18.00 every day except Sunday.)

Formerly the private flat of avant-garde artist, writer and communist sympathiser Lajos Kassák, and an exhibition room for the 'Ma' (Today) group of artists, this became the first headquarters of the Hungarian Communist Party after its foundation on 24 November 1918. A tape in English giving background information is available in the museum where there is also a special memorial room to Béla Kun, the leader of the Hungarian Communist Party in the 1920s and 1930s until his disappearance in Moscow during the Stalinist purges of 1937. (The Kádár u. which crosses Visegrád u. is, incidentally, not named after János Kádár, Hungary's political leader from 1956 to 1988, but has had this name since 1897. 'Kádár' in Hungarian means 'cooper'.)

The neo-Baroque building at No. 14 Szent István körút is the **Gaiety Theatre** (Vígszínház), which was built at the end of the 19C to the plans of two Viennese architects, Ferdinand Fellner and Herman Helmer. The first performance took place on 1 May 1896. Destroyed by fire during World War II it was restored in 1951. The inside was modernised but the exterior retains its original design. Until 1960 it was known as the Hungarian People's Army Theatre (Magyar Néphadsereg Színháza). The bronze busts in front of the theatre are of the poet-revolutionary *Sándor Petőfi* (György Baksa Soós, 1952) and *Miklós Zrínyi* (István Tar, 1952). Zrínyi (1620–64) was a politician, a poet and a military leader in the anti-Turkish wars.

The corner building beyond the theatre used to house the *Club Coffee house*. Actors, writers and members of the local intelligentsia came here. It was a meeting place for 'Nyugat's' forerunner 'Magyar Géniusz Kör'—the journal was printed nearby, behind the theatre.

Several streets beyond the Gaiety Theatre on the N side of Szent István körút bear names with political connections. At the side of the theatre is Rajk László u.

László Rajk (1909–49) was an underground communist leader in the 1930s who fought and was wounded in the Spanish Civil War. After World War II he became Hungary's Minister of the Interior, and later he was made Foreign Minister. Falsely accused of 'Titoism' he was arrested and executed in 1949, becoming the most famous victim of the Hungarian purges. Helped by the campaigning of his widow his case became a cause célèbre and in the thaw following Stalin's death he was posthumously rehabilitated and reinterned in Budapest's Kerepesi Cemetry. The reburial, on 6 October 1956, turned into a spontaneous demonstration prefiguring the uprising which broke out 17 days later. The plaque on the wall of the theatre (Imre Varga) was unveiled 20 years after his death.

The second street off Rajk László u. bears the name of *Raoul Wallenberg*, the Secretary of the Swedish Legation in Budapest who, after his arrival in July 1944, boldly and heroically saved thousands of Jews from the hands of the Nazis by issuing Swedish passports. Some of the Swedish 'safe houses' were in this area.

Wallenberg disappeared in the chaos at the end of the war and although Soviet Deputy Foreign Minister Andrei Gromyko announced in February 1957 that he had died in Moscow's Lubianka Prison ten years previously many believe that he could still be alive somewhere in the Soviet prison network.

For many years this street was the only public memorial to Wallenberg in Budapest (a statue commissioned from the sculptor Pál Pátzay mysteriously disappeared on the eve of its unveiling in the nearby Szent István Park in April 1949). Then in 1987 a prominent new bronze statue of Wallenberg (by Imre Varga) was erected on Szilágyi Erzsébet fasor, one of the main arteries of Buda.

The two streets following Rajk László u. on the N side of the Great Boulevard are named after Imre Sallai and Sándor Fürst respectively. These were two communist martyrs executed under the Horthy regime in 1932 (the first after 10 years) during a crack-down on militants following the derailment of a train.

200m along HONVÉD UTCA (which runs from the S side of the körút) at No. 26–30 stands the building of the *Ministry of Defence* (Honvédelmi Minisztérium). Built in neo-classical style with Ionic pilasters (József Hild, 1839–41) it was originally a silk factory. The large limestone memorial tablet (István Szabó) by the main entrance was erected for the centenary of 1848.

On the E side of Néphadsereg tér, which lies in front of the Ministry, stands the monument to the Hungarian members of the International Brigade who fought in Spain during the civil war of 1936–39 (Agamemnon Makris, 1970). On Markó u., to the S of the square stand the Pest District Court (No. 25), the Municipal Court (No. 27) and the Ministry of Industry (No. 16).

Szent István körút, and with it the Great Boulevard, ends at JÁSZAI MARI TÉR at the Pest end of Margaret Bridge. (Mari Jászai (1850–1926) was a renowned actress connected with the National Theatre.) The granite statue in the southern part of the square is of *Marx and Engels* (György Segesdi, 1971). To their left is the former Party Central Committee HQ, often referred to as 'The White House'. Today the building houses parliamentary offices.

The building on the N side of Jászai Mari tér which faces the river is the so-called *Palatinus House* (Emil Vidor, 1911). It is the former home of the Hungarian Geographical Institute and its publishing house. The best view of this example of National Romantic architecture is probably from some way across the bridge. In front of the building is a river landing-stage for boats to Margaret Island and beyond. (For details of Margaret Bridge see below.)

K.   Margaret Island and Óbuda

This route starts from the middle of Margaret Bridge at the S end of Margaret Island, crosses the island from S to N (approximately 2.5km) and then via Árpád Bridge explores some parts of Óbuda (Old Buda) on the right bank of the Danube around the Buda end of the bridge. Trams No. 4 and 6 which run the length of the Great Boulevard cross Margaret Bridge and stop in the middle by the island. Bus No. 26 runs from Marx tér, by the side of the Western Railway Station, to the island itself and then crosses it on the main road to the N end. Private cars are only allowed on the island at the N end from Árpád Bridge and then only as far as the car park by the Thermal Hotel.

MARGARET BRIDGE (Margit híd) links Szent István körút at the northern end of the Great Boulevard with Mártírok útja on the Buda side. Over 600m long and 25m wide, it was designed by Ernest Gouin and built in 1872–76 by the French Société des Bettignoles company following an international competition. The two arms of the bridge meet in the middle at an angle of 150° so that each is at right angles with the current of the two branches of the river. The statues on the pillars of the bridge are the work of the French sculptor Thabart.

During World War II a technical error caused the bridge to blow up early in the afternoon of Saturday 4 November 1944. Several hundred people were killed including German engineers who were planting explosives in preparation for the destruction of the bridge. (Photographs in the underpass at the Pest end of the bridge show the extent of the damage.) What remained of the bridge was destroyed by the Germans in January 1945. It was rebuilt after the end of the war.

Margaret Island (Margit-sziget) used to be known as 'The Island of Hares'. It was a royal game reserve at the time of the Árpád dynasty. From the 12C it was the home of the Premonstratensians and, from the 13C, the Franciscans. The Order of St. John had a monastery at the S end and the Archbishop of Esztergom a castle at the N end, though all traces of these last two have disappeared. Béla IV had a convent built here for Dominican nuns in the 13C and for a while under his patronage the nuns became the largest ecclesiastical landowners in the country. According to tradition Béla vowed during the Mongol invasion of 1242–44 that if Hungary were victorious his daughter Margaret would be brought up as a nun. Thus at the age of nine Margaret was brought here in 1252. She lived here until her death in 1271. The island was named after her at the end of the 19C.

After the victory of the Turks over the Hungarians at the battle of Mohács in 1526 the island became depopulated and during the Turkish occupation many of the buildings here were destroyed. After the Turks the island became the home of the nuns of St. Clare but when the order was suppressed it passed into the hands of Archduke Palatine Alexander. Palatine Joseph took over the island in 1795 and in line with his zeal for renewal had vines and rare trees planted. Many European dignitaries participated in vintage festivals here in the first half of the 19C.

An English traveller, Miss Pardoe, visited the island in the late 1840s and recorded an amusing observation indicating that vandalism has not simply been a 20C phenomenom ... '[the island] was for some time appropriated by the

Palatine as a public promenade; but the destruction among the trees and vines was so great that he was compelled to deny admission to the island from the Pest side, and to limit the permission of ingress on the other shore to such individuals as, from the respectability of their appearance, might be presumed not to indulge in wanton mischief.'

Archduke Joseph inherited the island in 1867 and further developed it into a park. It was opened to the public in 1869 but until 1900 when the connecting link with Margaret Bridge was built the only access was by boat. Baths were built on the island at the end of the last century to exploit the natural waters of the island but these were destroyed in World War II.

The city bought the island in 1908 and placed it under the management of the Council of Public Works. Visitors were charged an entrance fee which doubled on Sundays and holidays. This rather exclusive system lasted, apart from the brief period of the 1919 Republic of Councils, until 1945 when the island was declared a free public park for all citizens. Since then it has been one of the most popular recreational areas in Budapest.

To the left of the bridge-island link is the *Pioneers Stadium* used as a sports-ground and race track by school pupils. Here, according to legend, the 14C hero representing peasant aspirations, Miklós Toldi (immortalised in János Arany's 'Toldi Trilogy'), met in combat with foreign knights and champions. Here too used to be the sports field of the Hungarian Athletics Club which, when it was founded in 1875, was the first such club on the continent.

At the end of the link road stands a 10m bronze monument erected in 1973 for the centenary of the unification of Buda, Pest and Old Buda. The sculptor, István Kiss, placed inside the monument various mementoes of the city's previous 100 years.

To the left of the main road which runs the length of the island is the *Alfréd Hajós Swimming Pool*. It is named after the winner of the 100 metres and 1200 metres swimming races at the first modern Olympics held in Athens in 1896. Hajós (1878–1955) was an architect and actually designed the pool, which, when it opened in the 1930s, was the first indoor swimming pool in Hungary. Since then an open-air pool, a diving pool and childrens' pools have been added.

The *ruins of the Franciscan church* are 500m along the island to the right of the main road. These date from the late 13C–early 14C. Part of the W façade and some parts of the tower are still standing. An original window with Gothic tracery can be seen high up. The N wall of the church is also clearly visible. The statue of the *girl with pipe* on the far side of the wall is by Jenő Kerényi (1965).

On the left, farther along the main road, is the **Palatinus Baths** designed by István Janáky in 1937. The open-air pools are fed by the island's thermal springs. To the E of the baths is the *Rose Garden* at the S end of which is Tibor Vilt's 1973 bronze seated statue of the dramatist *Imre Madách* (1823–64) whose play, 'The Tragedy of Man', has frequently been translated into other languages. E of the statue, nearer the Pest side of the island, is a *Small Game Reserve* which has colourful peacocks, pheasants and other small birds and animals.

About two-thirds of the way along the island on the E side are the **ruins of the Dominican church and convent**. The convent stood for nearly 300 years and its copying workshop played an important part in Hungarian culture.

The legend of St. Margaret was first written down by Lea Ráskai, a nun who lived here in the 16C. During the Turkish occupation the nuns fled and the buildings fell into ruin. They were not discovered until the mid-19C. The convent used to stand to the S of the church and the foundations of the cloister court, well-house, chapter hall, kitchen and refectory can be seen. A marble tablet marks the original burial place of Margaret and there is a *shrine* to her in the modern brick construction nearby. Many legends and miracles are associated with Margaret's name. She was beatified after her death at the age of 29 in 1271 but was not canonised until nearly 600 years later in 1943.

The 200m stretch N of the ruins contains many busts and statues of Hungarian writers, poets, painters, sculptors, musicians and actors which were mostly erected after 1945. To the left is the **Open-Air Theatre** (Állami Operaház Szabadtéri Színpada) which belongs to the State Opera House. Open-air concerts and performances are given here during the summer months. The 57m *Water Tower* nearby was built in 1911 to the designs of Szilárd Zielinszky and Vilmos Ray Rezső.

A **Premonstratensian Chapel** stands a few metres to the NE of the tower. Built in the 12C in Romanesque style on the site of an even earlier chapel it was largely destoyed in the Turkish wars of the 16C. Excavated in the 1920s it was reconstructed in 1930–31. In the tower hangs one of the oldest bells in Hungary, the work of the 15C master Hans Strous. It was found nearby in 1914 in the roots of a walnut tree torn out during a storm.

The *Grand Ramadan Hotel* was originally a sanatorium attached to the medicinal baths built here at the end of the last century and destroyed during the war. The *Thermal Hotel* was built on the site of the former baths in 1978 (Gyula Kéry). The *rock garden* to the left of the hotel is at the same time a small botanical garden with exotic plants, streams, waterfall and ponds. Tropical water-lilies and small fish thrive in the warm-water ponds.

Towards the northern end of the island is a replica of Péter Bodor's *Musical Fountain* (Zenélő kút) built in 1820 in the centre of Marosvásárhely in Transylvania. Originally the musical mechanism played by the force of water. Today it is driven by electricity and plays for about 5 minutes on the hour. The area at the northern tip of Margaret Island under and beyond Árpád Bridge is today used for clay-pigeon shooting.

The route now continues along ÁRPÁD BRIDGE (Árpád híd) towards Buda. Árpád Bridge is the youngest site for a permanent river crossing in the city, though a new bridge is being planned for the southern end of Budapest to link with the M0 motorway which will circle the city. Work on the bridge began in 1939 but was held up by the war and so was not completed until 1950. In the first half of the 1980s the bridge was widened to twice its original width.

The bridge crosses the southern tip of **Óbuda Island** (Óbudai-sziget). On the island to the right of the bridge is the Óbuda Shipyard. The Danube Steamship Company, founded in Vienna in 1830 and later based here, employed 2000 people at the turn of the century.

Count István Széchenyi laid the foundations of steam navigation in Hungary. He entered into partnerhsip with the British ship-building company, Andrews and Richard, and as a result the steamer 'Franz I', built with money raised by Széchenyi, made its trial run between Vienna and Buda on 4 September 1830. The development of steam navigation on the Danube was a stimulus to Anglo-Hungarian connections. British engineers came to Hungary to supervise the construction of ships and the installation of engines, many of which were made by the British firm Boulton and Watt. In the early years many of the ships' captains were also British.

The **Óbuda Parish Church** (open Mon–Sat 17.00–18.30; Sun 7.00–12.00 and 17.00–19.00) stands to the S of the Buda end of Árpád Bridge (the church can be reached via the steps leading down by the tram stop). The Baroque church was designed by János György Paur and built in 1744–49. Above the door is a relief of St. Rosalie. On the façade are statues of St. Sebastian (to the left) and St. Roch and on the sides of the tower are SS. Peter and Paul after whom the church is officially named. All the statues are the work of Károly Bebó who also made the richly carved Rococo pulpit inside on the left and the frame of the picture of St. Charles of Borromeo on the other side of the triumphal arch. At the rear of the church on the external wall there is a memorial relief to the 'heroes of Óbuda' who died in World War I (István Toth, 1928).

In the area behind the church are a few renovated one-storey houses characteristic of old Óbuda. At the rear and to the right of the first modern block of flats behind the church is the small *Óbuda Calvinist Church* which was built in 1785–88. The church house next door (No. 4 Kálvin köz) was built in National Romantic style in 1908 to the design of Károly Kós and Dezső Zrumeczky.

The statues of *St. Flórián* and *St. John of Nepomuk* which stand 100m in front of Óbuda parish church are the work of Károly Bebó (1753–54). On the bases of the statues are the coats of arms of Count Miklós Zichy and his wife. The Zichy family owned much of Óbuda in the 18C.

St. John of Nepomuk, according to tradition, was a priest in 14C Bohemia who refused to reveal the confessional secrets of the queen. The king therefore had him thrown from a bridge but he miraculously survived and has since been revered as the patron saint of rivers and bridges. His image is one of the most common in Hungary and often appears on bridges and at river crossings.

The two-storey Baroque church house by the side of the statues was built in 1756 by János Schaden who used existing Roman and medieval walls. An internationally-financed thermal hotel is being constructed on the area in front of the building. A short distance to the S stands a neo-classical former synagogue designed by András Landherer and built in 1820–21. The six-columned portico supports a tympanum and at the top are the Tablets of the Commandments. The building today is used as studios by Hungarian Television.

Opposite at No. 158 Lajos u. is the *Budapest Gallery Exhibition House* (Budapest Galéria Kiállítóháza). There is a permanent exhibition of the work of sculptor Pál Pátzay and temporary exhibitions are also held here. (Open 10.00–18.00 except Monday.)

Returning to Árpád Bridge the route now passes through the subway leading to Korvin Ottó tér. There are old photographs of Óbuda on the walls of the underpass.

In the Middle Ages Óbuda was the first significant settlement in the area of today's Budapest. At that time it was called simply Buda ('ó' is an ancient form meaning 'old') and was an area of royal residences. Stones of the former Roman city were used in its construction. Mansions were built here as well as a palace, but only a few remains of these survive today. After the Mongol invasion Béla IV had the royal residence moved to Castle Hill and this area declined in importance. Following the Turkish occupation Óbuda revived as a market town and up to the end of the 19C was also well-known for its local wines. The cosy nostalgic atmosphere portrayed in some of these pictures has survived in a few small pockets up to the present day but much of old Óbuda has been demolished to make way for modern tower blocks and housing estates.

Facing the exit of the subway on the far side of Korvin Ottó tér is the two-storey white building of the **Vasarely Museum**. In 1982 the painter Victor Vasarely, who was born in the southern Hungarian town of Pécs in 1908 and who currently lives in Paris, donated 400 of his works to the Hungarian state. The museum, which was opened in May 1987, contains a selection of his paintings spanning his life's work. There is also a library, lecture hall and space for temporary exhibitions. (Open 10.00–17.00 except Monday.)

FŐ TÉR (Main Square) was the centre of Óbuda in the 18C. Today it has been renovated and often at weekends in the summer months musicians and dancers perform here. There are several restaurants in the vicinity. It is reached via the cobbled area to the left of the museum. A bronze bust of the novelist *Gyula Krúdy* (1878–1933) stands on the right at the rear of the museum's side wall (Tamás Gyenes, 1958). Krúdy once described Óbuda as an 'antique town' where the streets were 'as bent as old people, huddling like tramps in the merciless wind on the high road'.

The gateway on the right at No. 1 Fő tér leads to the former **Zichy Mansion** built in Baroque style for Miklós Zichy in 1746–57 to the design of János Henrik Jäger. War damage necessitated restoration after 1945. The building today is a cultural centre of the district and houses an *Óbuda local history collection* (Óbudai Helytörténeti Gyűjtemény) which includes a display of barrel-making instruments. (Open Tues–Fri 14.00–18.00; Sat and Sun 10.00–18.00; closed Mondays.) It also houses the **Lajos Kassák Memorial Museum** (Kassák Lajos Emlékmúzeum) which displays items connected with Kassák's work and has a small exhibition entitled 'Hungarian Collage 1920–65'. (Open 10.00–18.00 except Monday.)

Lajos Kassák (1887–1967) was an avant-garde poet, writer and artist, and editor of the 'Ma' (Today) journal. The son of a Slovak pharmacist's assistant and a Hungarian washerwoman, he failed his school exams when he was 11 and became a blacksmith's apprentice. Before World War I he wandered through Austria, Germany, Belgium and France experiencing life at the bottom, which he later wrote about after his return. He was always an internationalist and being on the margins (some would say at the forefront) of cultural trends he inevitably had clashes both with progressive cultural circles and with left-wing political leaders. He was an active supporter of the 1919 Republic of Councils, after the suppression of which he spent several years in exile.

Hajógyár u. is at the NE corner of Fő ter. The statues of three women with umbrellas here is the work of Imre Varga (born 1923), one of the most prolific of contemporary sculptors. There is a collection of his work at the **Imre Varga Gallery** situated nearby at No. 7 Laktanya u. which runs immediately to the left off Hajógyár u. The collection includes copies of his statue of St. Stephen and composition of Our Lady of Hungary which stand in the Hungarian Chapel at St. Peter's in Rome.

The Eclectic–neo-Baroque three-storey building with two large atlases at *No. 3* Fő tér was built in 1906 and today belongs to the Third District (Óbuda) Council. The two-storey Copf-style building across to the left at No. 4 was built around 1780 and today houses the **Zsigmond Kun Folk Art Collection** of pottery, textiles, carvings and furniture. Zsigmond Kun, born in Mezőtúr in 1893, was a connoisseur and collector of ceramics and folk art. His former home here has been preserved as a museum. Items inside include dishes, brandy flasks, a dowry chest, kitchen utensils and jugs collected from all over greater Hungary. (Open 14.00–18.00; weekends 10.00–18.00; closed Mondays.)

The route leaves Fő tér via Kórház u. at the NW corner. On the immediate right are the ruins of the *Acquincum Praetorian Gate* which was built at the end of the 3C. Also on the right of Kórház u., just before the last block of flats, there are some remains of a 13C *Franciscan church and monastery*.

Kórház u. finishes at Szentendrei út by the end of the flyover which connects with Árpád Bridge. To the left is the large junction of FLÓRIÁN TÉR. This area used to be the site of a Roman military camp and in the 2C and 3C AD about 6000 soldiers were garrisoned here. In the 1970s during construction work on the junction remains of the camp were found and today the whole of the underpass network beneath the square has been turned into a *Roman Settlement Museum*, with display cabinets and stone relics lining the walls (access is from the end of Kórház u. via the steps to the left). The large baths of the Roman legion were found in the late 18C and became the subject of the first excavations in Hungary made on a scientific basis. The entrance to the **Roman Baths Museum**, which constitutes a separate section of the display, is in the underpass. (Open May–Aug 10.00–18.00; Sept–Oct 10.00–15.00; closed Mondays.)

The Romans arrived in Hungary around the time of Christ but it was not until the 2C and 3C that people started to arrive from all parts of the empire to settle here in the Roman town called *Aquincum*. At its height the population was about 40,000. Military and civilian public baths were built as well as workshops, market halls, inns, gymnasiums, religious shrines and two amphitheatres. At the end of the 4C decline set in and when the Huns arrived the Romans evacuated Aquincum.

Several more sights from the Roman period are in this region of Budapest, but not all are within easy walking distance of Flórián tér. The nearest is the *Roman Camp Museum* 150m along Korvin Ottó u., which runs S from Flórián tér. (The entrance is between the first two blocks of flats on the left.) Remains of Roman buildings and graves were discovered when the foundations of No. 63 were being laid in 1950. The remains were of a 2C dwelling house which was transformed into a bathing establishment in the 3C or 4C. In addition to the architectural finds, some Roman tools and items of glass and earthenware are also on display. (Open May–Oct 10.00–14.00; weekends and public holidays 10.00–18.00; closed Mondays.)

The ruins of the **Amphitheatre of the Military Town** are situated at the corner of Korvin Ottó u. and Nagyszombat u. at a distance of about 1km from Flórián tér. (Buses No. 84 and 86 run along Korvin Ottó u.) Built in the 2C AD it could seat 13–15,000 spectators. The arena was larger than that of the Colosseum in Rome and it was used until the end of the 4C. It was probably utilised as a fortress following the Magyar conquest but was built over in subsequent centuries. Excavations of the foundations and some reconstruction took place in the late 1930s.

The **Hercules Villa** is at No. 19–21 Meggyfa u. to the N of Flórián tér (left off Szentendrei út along Raktár u. then right to the end of Vihar u.). The name refers to the 3C mosaic floors representing the Herculean myth which were unearthed here in the late 1950s. The hero of the ancient world is shown shooting an arrow into the centaur Nessos who abducted Deianeira. The mosaics probably originated abroad and were brought here 'ready-made', but the surrounding framework, which is coarser work, is in all likelihood of local origin. The mosaics are among the Roman relics of the highest artistic level found in Hungary. (Open May–Oct 10.00–14.00; Sat and Sun 10.00–18.00; closed Mondays.)

Approximately 4km N of Flórián tér, on Szentendrei út, are the ruins of the Roman civilian town and the **Aquincum Museum**. (Open May–Oct 10.00–18.00 except Monday.) (Buses Nos 42 and 134 run along Szentendrei út from their termini in Korvin Ottó tér and the HÉV suburban railway which starts out from Batthyány tér in Buda stops nearby at the Aquincum station. There is a HÉV station, Árpád híd, on the E side of Korvin Ottó tér near the Vasarely Museum.)

The neo-classical museum was built in 1894 to exhibit Roman relics found in the area of Aquincum. Apart from the statues, pottery, tools, utensils, coins, mosaics and jewellery there is a rare example of a 3C organ.

The excavated remains of part of the civilian town lie around the museum in the open-air. They include the remains of large public baths, a market place, dwelling houses and an old Christian church and a shrine of the Persian Sun-god Mithras.

By the side of the HÉV station, under the bridge and across the road from the museum, are the ruins of the *amphitheatre of the civilian town*. It was much smaller than that of the military town and was built to seat up to 8000 spectators.

L.   The Buda Hills

The wooded Buda Hills in the western part of the capital, a few kilometres from the centre, are a favourite spot for relaxation and walking. The air is much cleaner and fresher than in the city and splendid views can be had from many vantage points. A convenient and pleasant way of sampling the hills by public transport is via the Cog-wheel Railway and the Pioneers' Railway. There is also a chair-lift to one of the hills and buses to different spots run from various points in Buda.

The lower terminus of the **Cog-wheel Railway** (Fogaskerekű Vasút) is on Szilágyi Erzsébet fasor opposite the 17-storey circular *Budapest Hotel* which was designed by György Szrogh and built in 1967. (Two stops from Moszkva tér on the No. 56 or No. 18 tram.) The railway, the third of its kind in the world, was originally built in 1873 by a Swiss firm on commission from the mayor of Buda, Ferenc Házmán. The first train ran on 24 July 1874 and was driven by steam power.

The grounds of the János Hospital (János Kórház) stretch out by the side of the first stop from the bottom. It is one of the oldest established hospitals in the city. As the train climbs one can see the modern building of the Central State Hospital behind it, and beyond that the smaller modern building of the András Pető Institute which has become internationally famous in recent years due to its unique and successful methods of teaching children with motor disabilities to walk.

The railway slowly climbs up **Szabadság-hegy** (420m). The hill used to be known as Sváb-hegy as many Germans settled here after the Turks had left Hungary. Up to the 19C the hillside was covered mainly with vineyards. The construction of the Cog-wheel Railway opened up the hill and it became a popular place of recreation where many writers' and artists' villas were built. A short distance to the W of the Szabadság-hegy station in the former summer villa of the romantic novel writer Mór Jókai (1825–1904) at No. 21 Költő u. there is a *Jókai Memorial Room*. (Open 10.00–14.00 except Monday.)

The *Széchenyi Look-Out* (Széchenyi Kilátó) is to the SW of the station. A good view can be had from here. The *gloriette* standing here was designed by Miklós Ybl and used to stand in the area of today's Heroes' Square. It was moved here when the square was being planned in the 1890s. The *bust of István Széchenyi* is by Alajos

Stróbl and was made in 1891. The look-out can be reached via Evetke u. which runs off one of the roads leading up from Szabadság-hegy station.

The upper terminus of the Cog-wheel Railway is on **Széchenyi-hegy** (Széchenyi Hill, 427m). The *Vörös Csillag* (Red Star) *Hotel* on the other side of the road from the station was built in 1938 as the Golf Hotel in the style of an alpine hunting lodge. The road to the left, past the kiosks and buffet, leads to the terminus of the **Pioneers' Railway** (úttörővasút) a narrow-gauge railway constructed between 1948 and 1951. All the controllers, conductors and booking-clerks are children who are members of the 'Pioneers', a youth movement equivalent to the scouts and guides in Britain. The 11km journey takes about 45 minutes as the train slowly winds through the wooded hills.

Normafa is the first stop. It is a popular excursion centre with a beautiful view. In the winter skiing and sledging take place here on the slopes. The name comes from an occasion in 1840 when a celebrated star of the National Theatre, Rozália Klein, sang the grand aria from Bellini's 'Norma' to a company of artists gathered here. A memorial plaque today recalls the event. (Normafa can also be reached by car via Isten-hegyi út and Eötvös út, or by bus No. 21 from Moszkva tér to its terminus at the Szabadság-hegy station of the Cog-wheel Railway and then by bus No. 90.)

János-hegy (529m) is the highest point in Budapest. A path from a stop of the Pioneers' Railway with the same name leads up to the hill. It can also be reached along the road from Normafa by foot (about a 30-minute walk), though cars are not allowed. A special bus service connects the hilltop with the terminus of the No. 21 bus and occasionally one also runs to Moszkva tér. Another way to reach the hill is via the chair-lift, which is called the *Libegő* (floater) in Hungarian. Its lower station is on Zugligeti út and can be reached by bus No. 158 from Moszkva tér. The 24m-high *Erzsébet Look-out Tower* stands on the peak of the hill some way up from the top of the chair lift. The neo-Romanesque tower was built in 1908–10 to the designs of Frigyes Schulek. From the top there is a wide panorama of the surrounding hills and almost the whole of the city can be seen.

Ságvári-liget is the next stop of the Pioneers' Railway after János-hegy. Nearby are the ruins of the central Pauline monastery which was built in the early years of the 14C. The Paulines were the only monastic order founded in Hungary. The area can also be reached along Budakeszi út, one of the main arteries of Buda. Bus No. 22 from Moszkva tér runs along here.

The lower terminus of the Pioneers' Railway is at **Hűvösvölgy** (Cool Valley). A clearing called Nagyrét (large meadow) is a short way to the W. Today it is a popular excursion spot. In the inter-war period it was a meeting place for illegal political gatherings and along the path which leads to the meadow from the station several monuments have been erected as a reminder of those times.

Bus No. 56 and tram No. 56 both run from Hűvösvölgy back to Moszkva tér.

A particular attraction of the Buda Hills are the unique caves that are to be found here. The caves have been formed by thermal waters in the ground and not, as is more common, by infiltrating rain water. The high temperature and the dissolved salts brought by the thermal waters have made them particularly beautiful. Two caves that are easily accessible and which can be visited in normal clothing are the

Pálvölgy Cave and the **Szemlőhegy Cave**. (The latter has more varied rock formations and in 1986 was reopened to the public with more modern facilities for visitors.) The starting point for both is Kolosy tér, near the Buda embankment between Margit Bridge and Árpád Bridge. (Bus No. 6 goes to the square from Marx tér by the Western Railway Station.) Bus No. 65 runs from Kolosy tér up Szépvölgyi út (initially Virág Benedek u.) There is a stop outside the Pálvölgyi Cave. Bus No. 29 runs past the Szemlőhegy Cave (alight at the fourth stop).

The lower terminus of both these bus routes is, strictly speaking, not in Kolosy tér but nearby at the junction of Szépvölgyi út and Bécsi út, a few metres to the W of the square. The *Újlak Parish Church*, which stands on the corner here, was built between 1746 and 1759 to the design first of Kristóf Hamon and, after his death, Máté Nepauer. A tower which originally stood in the centre was pulled down and replaced with the present one to the left of the façade in the 1760s, though the top part was added by Miklós Ybl in 1877. The main altar is the work of Kristóf Hikisch and Frigyes Held (1799). On it is a copy of Lucas Cranach's Madonna painted by Ferenc Falkoner. The interior furnishings are mainly from the Baroque period.

M.   Other Places of Interest in Budapest

Kőbánya

Kőbánya is the name of the 10th district, which is situated to the E of the centre in Pest. The name means 'stone quarry' and refers to the fact that from the 17C to the 19C the quarries of the area provided stone for construction work in Pest. The stone was quarried in underground passages which stretched for more than 30km. These were later used by the brewery established in the district. (The output of the Kőbánya brewery today is one of the largest in Europe.)

Today Kőbánya is an industrial and working-class district, worth visiting for anyone who wants to get a glimpse of the Budapest which is not normally featured in the tourist brochures. Buses No. 9 and 17 run E from Baross u., near the junction with József körút at Harminckettesek tere. They progress along the main road of the district, Kőbányai út, to the modern centre of Zalka Máté tér.

There are, however, some special sights and places of interest in the district. In PATAKI ISTVÁN TÉR, a short distance to the N of Zalka Máté tér along Kőrösi Csoma út (one stop on the No. 13 tram) there is the beautiful little **St. Ladislas Parish Church**, built in 1906 to the design of Ödön Lechner. The style is a mixture of neo-Gothic and Hungarian Art Nouveau and bears the characteristic marks of Lechner's designs. The interior brickwork, altars and pulpit, decorated with Zsolnay ceramic ornamentation, were designed by Ottó Tándor. The church was badly damaged in World War II but was rebuilt. Restoration work undertaken throughout the 1980s has made this church a gem amidst rather dreary surroundings. The modern Pataki István Cultural Centre across the road contains a cinema and a *local history collection*. (Open Mon and Thurs 17.00–19.00.)

The *Fire Service Museum* (Tűzoltó Múzeum) is situated at No. 12 Martinovics tér, 300m E of Zalka Máté tér. There is an exhibition of fire-fighting equipment and documents relating to the great fires of the past. (Open 9.00–16.00; Sun 9.00–13.00; closed Mondays.) Nearby, at the far end of Kápolna tér, stands the oldest monument of the district, the Baroque Greek Catholic *Holy Trinity Chapel*, built in 1739–40. (At the time of writing it is fenced off for restoration work.)

100m to the S of Zalka Máté tér (under the railway bridge and to the left) there is a characteristic open-air local market, *Mázsa piac*, where produce from private and cooperative farms is sold. Saturday morning is the best time to visit.

The grounds of the *Budapest International Fair*, covering 100,000 sq m of indoor and open-air exhibition space, are situated in Kőbánya. Every year the Consumer Goods Fair takes place here in the autumn and the Investment Goods Fair in the spring. Various other exhibitions and occasionally conferences also take place here throughout the year. In the summer the grounds become a car park and site for camping trailers. The grounds can be reached by taking the No. 2 (red) Metro line to its terminus at Örs vezér tere and then bus No. 100 which runs to the grounds from a stop 100m to the right from the exit of the metro station.

The **Új köztemető cemetery**, one of the largest in Budapest, is situated in the far west of Kőbánya. Every Sunday the cemetery is crowded with visitors bringing flowers to lay on the graves. The crowds here and at other cemeteries are particularly large every year on the eve of All Souls Day (2 November).

Plot 301 in the far NE corner of the cemetery is the place where Imre Nagy and others executed after 1956 were buried in secret. For his reburial on 16 June 1989 (see p 202) the plot was transformed by the erection of 301 specially carved wooden graves posts, and public access was made easier.

Bus No. 95 runs from Zalka Máté tér to the main entrance of the cemetery on Kozma u.

Csepel

Csepel, the 21st District of the capital, is situated on the northern tip of Csepel Island (Sziget) to the S of the centre. Like Kőbánya, it is a traditional industrial and working-class area, of interest to visitors wanting to get a feel of 'ordinary' Budapest. The district is easily accessible via the HÉV suburban railway which departs from Boráros tér at the Pest end of Petőfi Bridge.

The huge Csepel Iron and Metal Works employs thousands of people in the district. Before the war it was called the Manfred Weiss Works and for a while in the 1950s was named after Hungary's Stalinist leader, Mátyás Rákosi. In recent years, like several other large enterprises, it has been broken down into smaller units, operating more or less independently with a market orientation. The statue of Lenin in front of the main gate, with the characteristic outstretched arm, was the first one to be erected in Budapest after the war. Protesting workers have on more than one occasion placed a slice of bread and dripping in its hand.

The militancy of the local labour movement in the inter-war period earned the district the epithet of 'Red Csepel'. One of the few successful acts of mass resistance to the Germans took place in Csepel towards the end of 1944 when the local population refused to be forcibly evicted from the area. In 1956 the local workers' council was one of the longest to hold out.

At No. 1 Gyepsor u., by the factory, there is a *Labour Movement Museum* which covers the history of the iron and metal works and its labour movement from 1892 to the present times. (Open 9.00–16.00 except weekends.) Not far away in the building of the local disctrict council, at No. 3 Tanácsház tér, there is a *Local History Collection* which traces the general history of Csepel from early times to the present day. The Csepel Gallery is situated in the same building. (Open 10.00–18.00 except Monday.)

Kispest

Kispest, the 19th District to the SE of the centre, was a separate village at the end of the last century. Today it is part of the industrial belt around the capital and has several large factories and tower-block housing estates. An architectural peculiarity of the area is the so-called **Wekerle Estate** at the NW corner of the district, which was built between 1908 and 1925 as a public housing estate. Of the more than 1000 houses on the geometrically-patterned streets, 70 per cent are single-storied. Many are detached or semi-detached, which makes the area somewhat akin to an English suburb. Of particular interest is the ensemble of buildings in Kós Károly tér at the centre of the estate, which were constructed between 1908 and 1913 in Hungarian National Romantic style under the direction of the architect Károly Kós, and which were designed by Kós along with Dezső Zrumeczky and Gyula Wälder. The estate can be reached by taking the No. 3 (blue) metro line to the Határ út stop, which is near the northern corner of the estate. Buses No. 154 and 99 run from here to Kós Károly tér.

N.   Additional Specialist Museums

The following is a list of some specialist museums which are not on the main routes. For a full list of museums in the capital see the items listed under Budapest-Museums in the index at the end of the book.

Buda

Béla Bartók Memorial House, No. 29 Csalán u., Budapest II. The composer and music researcher Béla Bartók (1881–1945) lived here from 1932–1940. The exhibition covers his life and work and includes a display of Bartók commemorative stamps. (Open 10.00–18.00 except Monday.)

  Gizi Bajor Theatre Museum, No. 16 Stromfeld Aurél u., Budapest XII. A villa formerly belonging to Gizi Bajor (1893–1951) a celebrated actress and member of the National Theatre. The exhibition is devoted to Hungarian actors and actresses. (Open Tues and Thurs 15.00–19.00; weekends 11.00–18.00.)

  Kiscell Museum, No. 108 Kiscelli u., Budapest III. The museum, which belongs to the Budapest History Museum, is situated in a former Trinitarian monastery and church built in Baroque style in 1744–48 to the plans of Johann Entzenhoffer. It contains an exhibition of printing machines from the 18C and 19C, a display of furniture from the central museum's collection, and prints of 19C Budapest. The furnishings of the Golden Lion Pharmacy have also been moved here. The church is used for temporary art exhibitions. (Open 10.00–18.00; Nov–March 10.00–16.00; closed Mondays.)

Nagytétény Mansion Museum, No. 9–11 Csókásy Pál u., Budapest XXII. Baroque former Rudnyánszky Mansion built in stages in the mid-18C. The collection belongs to the Museum of Applied Arts and includes European furniture from the 15C to the 17C and Hungarian furniture from the 18C and 19C. There is a display of stoves and stove tiles. The lapidarium has a collection of Roman stonework. (Open 10.00–18.00 except Monday.)

Nyugat Literary Museum, No. 48/b Városmajor u., Budapest XII. The exhibition deals with the influential, progressive 'Nyugat' (Occident) literary and critical journal which was published between 1908 and 1941. (Open 14.00–18.00 except Monday.)

Sewage Disposal Exhibition (Csatornázási Kiállítás), No. 2–4 Zsigmond tér, Budapest II. Display of techniques from Roman times to the present day. (Open 9.00–16.00; Sat 9.00–14.00; closed Sundays.)

Pest

Attila József Memorial Room, No. 3 Gát u., Budapest IX. Birthplace of the working-class poet Attila József (1905–37). (Open 10.00–16.00; Sun 10.00–15.00; closed Mondays.)

Bakery Exhibition (Sütőipari Emléktár), No. 67 Majakovszkij u., Budapest VII. (Open Wed 12.00–18.00; Thurs 9.00–15.00.)

Electricity Industry Museum (Magyar Elektrotechnikai Múzeum), No. 21 Kazinczy u., Budapest VII. (Open Tues–Sat 11.00–17.00.)

Geological Institute Collection, No. 14 Népstadion út, Budapest XIV. Collection of rocks, minerals and geological rarities. (Open Mon–Fri 8.00–15.00; advanced notification is required, tel. 1837-940) The building of the institute itself is of some architectural interest. It was built in 1898–99 and was designed by Ödön Lechner in his individual Secessionist style. It is colourfully decorated and unique in appearance.

Géza Kresz Ambulance Service Museum (Mentőmúzeum), No. 22 Markó u., Budapest V. Géza Kresz (1846–1901) was a doctor and the founder of a voluntary ambulance service in 1887. The exhibition covers the history of the service and its technical equipment. (Open Mon and Thurs 10.00–14.00; Sat and Sun 9.00–15.00.)

Lift Museum (Felvonóipari Szakgyűtemény), No. 16/c Mohács u. Budapest XIII. The history of lifts from the turn of the century to the present day. Working examples on display. (Entrance by prior arrangement, tel. 1402-932.)

Meat Processing Industry Museum (Húsipari Múzeum), No. 6/b Gubacsi út, Budapest IX. A specialist collection of the National Meat Industry Research Institute covering all aspects of the industry's history. (Open Apr–Oct Tue and Fri 10.00–15.00.)

Milling Industry Museum (Malomipari Múzeum), No. 24 Soroksári út, Budapest IX. (Open Tues and Thurs 10.00–15.00.)

Physical Education and Sport Museum (Testnevelési és Sportmúzeum), No. 3 Dózsa György út, Budapest XIV. (Open 10.00–18.00 except Monday.)

Textile and Dress-Manufacturing Industry Museum (Textil-és Ruhaipari Múzeum), No. 9–11 Gogol u., Budapest XIII. History of weaving and dress-making. (Open 10.00–18.00 except Monday.)

Veterinary Science Museum (Állatorvostörténeti Gyűtemény), No. 20–24 Bethlen Gábor u., Budapest VII. Folk and scientific remedies. History of the Veterinary Science University. Statues of animals by sculptor György Vastagh Jr. (Open Tues and Thurs 9.00–16.00.)

The **Planetarium** is not strictly a museum but temporary exhibitions dealing with physics, space research and related matters are often organised here. Built in 1977 by the Jena Zeiss works in the GDR, the mechanism inside projects the planets and their movements as seen from the earth on to a dome with a 23m diameter. The planetarium is more popularly visited for its regular lazer light shows accompanied by pop or classical music. Children's shows also take place. It is situated 5km to the SE of the centre, a few hundred metres from the Népliget metro station on the No. 3 (blue) line, in the corner of the People's Park (Népliget).

6   The Danube Bend

The Danube Bend is the name given to that part of Hungary which lies along the Danube River to the north of Budapest. The designation comes from the fact that about 40km to the north of the capital the Danube sharply alters its eastward course and starts flowing southwards. Strictly speaking the Danube Bend is that part of the river which cuts a swathe between the Börzsöny and Visegrád mountains, but the term is generally applied to the whole of the area on both sides of the river roughly encompassed by the Budapest-Esztergom-Vác triangle.

The sight of the Danube Bend around Visegrád, where the curve of the river is accompanied by mountain ranges on both sides, is quite awe-inspiring and counts among the most beautiful environments in Hungary. The hilly forests used to be favourite hunting grounds of Hungary's medieval kings. Today they offer plenty of opportunities for walks and excursions. The proximity of the river and the natural thermal springs of the region have led to the provision of ample bathing facilities, and hotels, guest houses and camping sites are dotted all over the area.

The Danube Bend is also rich in historic monuments and places of interest. Esztergom was the first royal seat of the Hungarian kings. The first stone fortification and royal palace was built here. It has been excavated and is today a museum. Esztergom is still the ecclesiastical centre of Catholicism in Hungary. The Cathedral here is a monumental work of 19C architecture. The Christian Museum in the town has an important collection of medieval art.

Szentendre (see Rte 6A), just 20km from the capital, is noted for its Serbian past. The refugees from the Balkans built Orthodox churches which still determine the look of the town. It has also been an important artistic centre in the present century and many galleries are dotted around the winding streets and narrow alleys.

At Visegrád (see Rte 6B), the most beautiful point of the Bend, a medieval royal palace was built whose riches and splendour rivalled that of Buda. 20C excavations have uncovered the remains of this palace.

The left bank of the river is visited less frequently. It has fewer monuments and relatively fewer facilities, but it does have its own points of interest. The largest town, Vác, although today small, was once an important diocesan centre as its architectural monuments indicate. The view offered by the left bank, particularly on the northern stretches towards the Czechoslovak border, is equally inspiring, and there is some fine architecture on this side of the river, too; for example, the churches at Fót and Zebegény.

Access to all points of the Danube Bend is good. Road 11 follows the river from Budapest, through Szentendre and Visegrád, to Esztergom. In the summer months many inhabitants of the capital spend the weekend at cottages on the Bend. Hence, because of overcrowded traffic conditions, the return journey along this road on a Sunday evening is best avoided.

The HÉV suburban railway runs from Budapest to Szentendre. It starts from Batthyány tér in Buda, across the river from the Parliament building. (Red metro line No. 3.) Buses run to Visegrád and Esztergom. The latter can also be reached by train from the Western Railway Station.

On the left bank Road No. 2 and, after Vác, Road No. 12 runs the

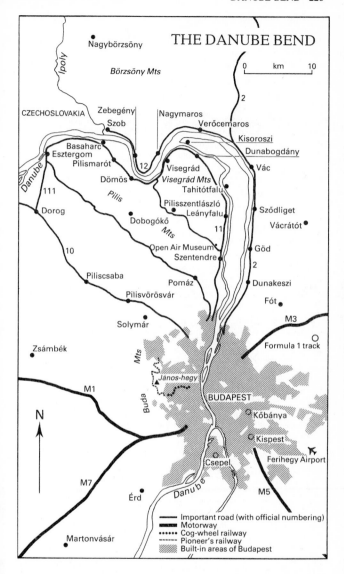

THE DANUBE BEND

length of the Bend. All places on this side can also be reached by train from the Western Railway Station.

During the summer months Szentendre, Visegrád and Esztergom can also be reached by river boat from Budapest. Drivers, hitchhikers and others can progress along one bank and return via the other by taking one of the ferries which crosses the river. There are major crossings between Tahitótfalu and Vác, Visegrád and Nagymaros, Pilismarót and Zebegény, and Basaharc and Szob.

Curiously, cycling is not permitted on the main road between the towns of the Danube Bend.

A. Szentendre

Szentendre (pop. 20,000) lies 20km to the N of Budapest on Road 11 and is the southern gateway to the right bank of the Danube Bend. Its narrow, winding streets, small squares, Serbian and Greek Orthodox churches, and art collections make it one of the most popular places to visit from Budapest, particularly in view of the fact that it is conveniently situated at the terminus of the HÉV suburban railway.

Tourist Information: Dunatours, 1 Bogdányi u. (26/11-311).

Rail Station: Állomás tér. 50 minutes on the suburban electric railway from Batthyány tér, Budapest.

Bus Station: Állomás tér.

Post Office: 4 Rákóczi Ferenc u.

Police: 11 Martinovics u.

History. The area was conquered by the Illyrian-Celtic Eravisci in 1C BC. Its name was taken over and Latinised by the Romans and thus *Ulcisia Castra* became an important stronghold of the Roman borderline fortresses built along the Danube. By the time the Magyars arrived, very little was left of the earlier Roman settlements which had been the victim of several waves of migration by different peoples.

During the 14C the Turks advanced and pushed further into the Balkan Peninsula. The Serbian inhabitants fled north to Hungary and settled in a number of towns by the Danube, including Szentendre. However, during the course of Ottoman rule in Hungary the town became deserted.

Towards the end of the 17C the Turks were driven out of Hungary by the united Christian armies. Fighting continued in the Balkans and a second wave of Serbian, Albanian, Bosnian, Dalmatian and Greek families sought refuge in Hungary. Large numbers settled in Szentendre under the leadership of Patriarch Arsen Crnojevič. At first their churches were built from timber. Later, as economic life improved, these were replaced in the second half of the 18C by stone churches built in Baroque style. The many churches built at this time are still characteristic of the townscape of Szentendre today.

It was in the 18C, too, that Szentendre became an episcopal see of the Eastern Church. The town's merchants, who possessed privileges granted by the Habsburgs, grew wealthy through their trading activities. In the following century, many of the prosperous Serbian families moved back to their own homeland, so that today although Szentendre can be regarded as a 'Serbian' town, it has relatively few inhabitants of that nationality.

The 20C saw the establishment of an artists' colony at Szentendre in the inter-war period. Modern art has thus been added as a characteristic element of the town.

Visitors arriving by the HÉV suburban railway can approach the centre of the town via KOSSUTH LAJOS UTCA which runs northwards from the underpass by the station. Some distance along here, at the junction of Római sánc u., stands the small *Flórián Chapel*, built c 1750 following a plague. It was originally dedicated to SS. Roch, Sebastian and Rosalie, but has borne the name of the patron of fire-fighters since the early 19C.

A *Collection of Roman Stonework* (Római Kőtár) can be found a short distance along Római sánc u. at No. 1 Dunakanyar körút. Here are displayed relics of the one-time Ulcisia Castra, its military camp and burial places. Approximately on this spot the Roman encampment used to stand. The eastern gate, opening on to the Danube was

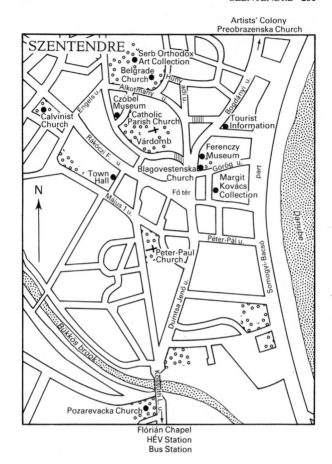

Artists' Colony
Preobrazenska Church

SZENTENDRE
Serb Orthodox
Art Collection
Belgrade
Church
Alkotmány
Czóbel
Museum
Catholic
Parish Church
Calvinist
Church
Rákóczi F. u
Engels u.
Huny
Bogdányi u.
Tourist
Information
Ferenczy
Museum
Görög u.
Várdomb
Town
Hall
Blagovestenska
Church
Fő tér
Margit
Kovács
Collection
Május 1 u.
N
Péter-Pál u.
Peter-Paul
Church
Dumtsa Jenő u.
Somogyi-Bacsó
Bükkös brook
Pozarevacka Church
Kossuth L. u.
Danube

Flórián Chapel
HÉV Station
Bus Station

guarded by two watch-towers. The western side was flanked by a
civilian settlement. (Open May–Oct 10.00–18.00 except Monday.)

The route continues northwards along Kossuth Lajos u. The early-
Eclectic building at *No. 5*, with the Baroque gates at each end, was
originally built in the late 18C, though altered during the following
century. Up to 1903 it was a courthouse and prison.

The rear of the **Požarevačka Church** touches Kossuth Lajos u. just
before the Bükkös stream. It was built between 1759 and 1763 on the
site of a former wooden church, though the Louis XVI tower dates
from the end of the century. The Byzantine-style iconostasis dates
from the mid-18C and may have been brought here having been
painted prior to the construction of the church.

DUMTSA JENŐ UTCA continues across the stream towards the
centre. *No. 7* on the left is the birthplace of the Serbian novelist Jakov
Ignjatovic (1822–89) who fought with the Hungarians in the War of
Independence of 1848–49. No. 10 across the road houses the *Barcsay
Collection*. The painter, graphic artist and teacher, Jenő Barcsay was

born in Transylvania in 1900 and worked in Szentendre from 1928. This originally 18C Baroque dwelling house, with a 19C classical façade, now contains a selection of his work. (Open 10.00–18.00; Oct–March 9.00–17.00; closed Mondays.) The plaque on the wall records that the opera singer Ferenc Stéger (1824–1911) was born and lived here.

PÉTER-PÁL U. crosses Dumtsa u. On the eastern branch, towards the Danube, the building at *No. 6* on the left is a good example of a late-18C Szentendre merchant's house. The two basement windows are fitted with wrought-iron grilles and the wings of the gate are in Louis XVI style.

The western branch of Péter-Pál u. leads to the **Peter-Paul Church**, which was built in 1753 as an Orthodox church, the Čiprovačka, dedicated to St. Nicholas. The original furnishings were taken to Yugoslavia after World War I, but the ground plan and exterior are as original. Note the red marble Louis XVI portals on both sides of the church. A history of the church in English can be found inside the porch on the N side. The statue of the Serbian writer, *Jakov Ignjatovic* (1822–89) on the S side of the church is by Frigyes Janzer (1977).

Dumtsa Jenő u. leads up to the main square of Szentendre, FŐ TÉR, a historic ensemble of Baroque, Rococo and Louis XVI-style buildings. The Orthodox *Merchant Cross* in the middle of the square was erected in 1763 in thanksgiving that the plague had not swept through the town. The three-sided pillar has a red marble pedestal and an iron cross supported by a web of iron branches. The marble pillar is ornamented with icons. Although a fine piece, at the time of writing it was badly in need of restoration. The Slavonic inscription on one side of the pedestal reads: 'This sacred cross was erected by the Serbian privileged merchants' association of Szentendre in the year of 1763.'

A number of buildings in the square are of historical interest. The row of Baroque buildings at *No. 2–5* on the E side is united by a high gable roof. It was built in the 1720s by merchant families and today houses the *Szentendre Picture Gallery* which displays works by local artists. (Open 10.00–18.00; Nov–March 9.00–17.00; closed Mondays.)

Moving round the square in a clockwise direction, the Louis XVI-style building at *No. 22* was erected c 1790. The Romantic building at *No. 21* dates from c 1850 and today is the *János Kmetty Memorial Museum*. Kmetty (1889–1975) was one of the members of the Szentendre artists' colony. (Open 10.00–18.00; Nov–March 9.00–17.00; closed Mondays.)

The group of buildings at Nos 18, 19 and 19/a closes the square on the SW side. The so-called Pálffy House at *No. 17* was built in 1781, though the present façade is a result of later rebuilding. The keystone of the Baroque gate is decorated with the sign of the Serbian Merchants' Guild. The patriarchal cross refers to the Orthodox faith, the number 4 to the commercial profit of 4 per cent recommended by the guild, and the anchor to the Danube. The two-storey building at *No 15*, the Milič House, is a merchant's house dating from the early 18C, though it has also been subject to alterations over the years.

Across the road, *No. 12/a* was originally built in the mid-18C but as the year inscribed on the keystone of the Baroque gate implies, it has undergone some changes. *No. 11* was built at the end of the 18C in provincial Louis XVI style.

The Baroque Serbian Orthodox **Blagoveštenska Church**, also called the Church of the Annunciation, is believed to have been designed by András Mayerhoffer and was built between 1752 and 1754 on the site of an earlier wooden church dating from the time of the great Serbian migration of 1690. The windows of the belfry and the oaken wings of the side gate to the right in, Görög u., are decorated with Rococo ornamentation. To the left of the side entrance is a candle niche built into the wall in 1759 below the tombstone of a Greek merchant of Macedonian origin. The paintings of the gilded iconostasis, which is carved from limewood, are by Mihailo Živkovič, a Serbian icon-painter from Buda, and were executed in the early years of the 19C.

The Baroque corner building of Görög u. and Vastagh György u., a few metres from the church down the hill, was originally built in the mid-18C as a municipal salt house. Later it became a post-house and then the residence of a Serbian merchant. Since 1973 it has housed the permanent exhibition of the **Margit Kovács Collection**. Kovács (1907–77) was first exhibited in 1926 in Budapest and then many times in France where she worked for some time as a designer of ceramic pottery. The expressive statuettes and other works of this prize-winning ceramist combine modern forms with the traditions of Hungarian folk art. (Open 9.00–19.00 every day.)

The building at No. 6 Fő tér, to the left of the church, was erected in 1793 to serve as a Serbian school. Above the carved stone doorway on the Louis-XVI style façade the emblems of science and learning can be seen and a tablet in Serbian indicating the original function. It was a teachers' training school up to 1816 and then a grammar school. Since 1951 it has been the **Ferenczy Museum**, exhibiting the works of the Ferenczy family. Károly Ferenczy (1862–1917) was a Hungarian pioneer of Impressionist painting who spent his youth in Szentendre. Noémi Ferenczy (1890–1957) was a tapestry-maker, Béni Ferenczy (1890–1967), a sculptor and medallion-maker, and Valér Ferenczy (1885–1954), a painter. Apart from works by the different members of the family, the museum also has an exhibition about local viticulture. (Open 10.00–18.00; Nov–March 9.00–17.00; closed Mondays.)

The picturesque alley and steps to the right of No. 9 Fő tér lead up to the plateau encircled by a wall and known both as Várdomb (Castle Hill) and Templom tér. The **Catholic Parish Church** here is of medieval origin and was Szentendre's first stone church. The windows suggest a late-Romanesque style but Gothic elements resulting from a 15C reconstruction are also in evidence. The church fell into disrepair during the Turkish occupation and was rebuilt in Baroque style in the 18C after it had been taken over by the Catholic Dalmatians who came to Szentendre. The early Gothic entrance on the S side came to light during restoration work in 1957. The 20C frescoes in the sanctuary are the collective work of members of the local artists' colony. There is a picturesque view of the surrounding town from the walled courtyard of the church.

The **Béla Czóbel Museum** is situated across from the main façade of the church. Czóbel (1883–1976) worked in Paris and Szentendre. Apart from his paintings, the exhibition also includes works by his wife, the painter Mária Modok (1896–1971). (Open 10.00–18.00; Nov–March 9.00–17.00; closed Mondays.)

A short street leads down from the Czóbel Museum to Alkotmány u. Here, behind the wall, stands the single-towered, Orthodox episcopal cathedral known as the **Belgrade Church**, which was built between 1756 and 1764. Notable features of the church include the Rococo carvings of the oak wings of the main gate, the pulpit decorated with wooden carvings, and paintings including a picture of St. John Chrysostom, and the richly embellished bishop's throne. The paintings on the carved Baroque iconostasis are the work of Vasilije Ostoič, a painter from Újvidék (today Novi Sad in Yugoslavia). The icons show scenes from the New Testament and various saints of the Eastern Church. The fine wrought-iron gate which leads to the church is the work of a local craftsman, Mátyás Ginesser and dates from 1772.

From the mid-18C the Serbian Orthodox bishops had their seat in a neighbouring building, thus Szentendre became the ecclesiastical and cultural centre of the Serbs in Hungary. The bishops are buried in the crypt of the cathedral here.

The **Collection of Serbian Orthodox Ecclesiastical Art** is housed in one of the former buildings of the episcopal see a few metres to the NW of the church at No. 5 Engels u. (to the right from the western end of Alkotmány u.). The collection includes icons, textiles, goldsmiths' works and other items of 16C–19C Orthodox ecclesiastical art which have been gathered from the Orthodox churches in Hungary which were vacated as the Serbians returned to the Balkans. At the time of writing the exhibition is closed but it is due to reopen in the early 1990s.

Engels u. leads S to a junction with Rákóczi Ferenc u. A short distance to the right from here stands the Baroque **Calvinist Church**. It was built as an Orthodox church in 1746 under the name Opovačka. (The names derive from the region from which the congregations who built the churches came.) It has been a Calvinist church since 1913.

To the left, Rákóczi Ferenc u. leads back towards the town centre. The *House of Folk Arts* (Népművészetek Háza) situated at No. 1, some way along on the left, has a display of folk art from the local Pest county region. (Open 10.00–18.00; Nov–March 9.00–17.00; closed Mondays.)

Across the road, on the W side of Városház tér, stands the Baroque *Town Hall*. The ground-floor rooms were fashioned in the early 18C and then enlarged in 1811. The neo-Baroque gable and protruding balcony of the main façade were added in 1924.

The route now passes through Fő tér again towards BOGDÁNYI UTCA, which runs down from the N end of the square. The local *Tourist Information Office*, Dunatours, is situated at No. 1 on the right, on the corner of Bercsényi u. Steps opposite lead up to the junction of Alkotmány u. and Hunyadi u. The corner house at the top of the steps on the right is the former home of the painter Károly Ferenczy. A short distance to the N, at No. 1 Hunyadi u., there is the *Lajos Vajda Memorial Museum*. Vajda (1908–41) was a painter who, from 1934, often worked in Szentendre. A selection of his works is exhibited here. (Open 10.00–18.00; Nov–March 9.00–17.00; closed Mondays.) From here Kígyó u. leads back down to Bogdányi u.

The *Imre Ámos—Margit Anna Collection* is some distance below the tourist information office at No. 12 Bogdányi u. on the left. Paintings of the married couple who worked in the town are on display here. (Open 10.00–18.00; Nov–March 9.00–17.00; closed Mondays.) The Baroque building which houses the exhibition dates from the mid 18C, though as the Eclectic façade indicates, later rebuilding has also taken place.

At the bottom of the incline the street opens on to a small square which is today used as a car park. The simple iron cross on top of a column standing at the NE corner of the square is known as the *Tzar Lázár Memorial Cross.*

Tzar Lázár was a Serbian ruler captured and beheaded by the Turks in revenge for the death of Sultan Murad during the battle of Kosovo in 1389 at which the victorious Turks overthrew the medieval Serbian kingdom. Lázár's coffin was brought to Hungary by refugees in 1690 and placed in a wooden church which was erected on this site.

Bogdányi u. continues from the NW corner of the square. The **Preobraženska Church**, some 400m along the street, was built by Serbian tanners between 1741 and 1746. A Serbian festival is usually held here every year on 19 August. The decorated Louis XVI gate in the surrounding wall is the work of a local craftsman, József Olhauer, and dates from the early 19C. The richly carved Rococo iconostasis divided by Corinthian columns is noteworthy, although the names of the painters of the icons are unknown.

The so-called *Vinegrowers' Cross* (Szőlősgazdák keresztje) stands at the top end of Bogdányi u., on the corner of Dézsma u. and Ady Endre u. Its column is decorated with vine tendrils, leaves and grape clusters topped by a wrought-iron patriarchal cross. It was erected in the 18C by one of the wine trade guilds. The importance of viticulture in the region of the Danube Bend has since declined.

The **Szentendre Artists' Colony** is situated opposite, at the southern end of Ady Endre u. It was founded in 1928 as the Association of Szentendre Painters. The *Gallery* here is used for temporary exhibitions. (Open 15 March–31 October 10.00–18.00, except Mondays.) Further along, at No. 5 Ady Endre u., in the park area on the left, there is the **Kerényi Memorial Museum**, which contains a permanent exhibition of the sculptures of Jenő Kerényi (1908–75). (Open 10.00–18.00; Nov–March 9.00–17.00; closed Mondays.)

B.   Szentendre to Esztergom via Visegrád

Road 11. Total distance 46km. **Szentendre**—(4km open-air Ethnographical Museum)—6km **Leányfalu**—4km *Tahitótfalu* and **Szentendre Island**—6km **Dunabogdány**—6km **Visegrád**—7km *Dömös*—4km *Pilismarót*—13km **Esztergom**.

The **Open-Air Ethnographical Museum**, (Szabadtéri Néprajzi Múzeum) which is situated a few kilometres NW of Szentendre, is the largest open-air museum of vernacular architecture in Hungary. It can be reached from Road 11, which curves around the town centre, by taking the road signposted for Pilisszentlászló. From the south it is also signed 'Skanzen', which is the original Swedish word for such open-air museums. Buses to the open-air museum depart from Stand No. 8 near the terminus of the HÉV railway from Budapest.

The science of ethnography emerged in Europe in the 19C. This was when large ethnographic museums were established, including the Ethnographic Museum in Budapest which was set up in 1872. By the end of the century a demand arose to have rural life seen on a larger scale and in a more natural setting. This led to the establishment of open-air museums. The first was built in Sweden in 1891 in the *Skansen* district of Stockholm.

Hungarian open-air museums can be traced back through international exhibitions. Hungarian buildings were included in the international village set up at the Vienna World Exhibition of 1873. At the Hungarian National Exhibition of 1885 15 peasant room interiors were shown, and within the framework of the Millennium festivities of 1896 an Ethnographic Village was set up. It consisted of 24 houses with original furnishings, plus a wooden church. The buildings were copied from samples selected in various parts of the country. Nevertheless it was the first presentation on a national scale of vernacular architecture in Hungary. The Ethnographic Village was pulled down after six months but the idea of an open-air museum was never taken off the agenda. In the inter-war period several localities took measures to protect local buildings but it was not until the 1960s that permanent open-air museums began to be planned.

The open-air museum near Szentendre was established in 1968 on an area of 46.5 hectares. The intention is to show traditional rural buildings and ways of life from different regions of the country. Houses and furniture represent farms, villages and small towns of the 18C, 19C and early 20C. Ten regional groups of buildings, brought here from their original sites, will represent Northern Hungary, the market towns of that region, Upper Tisza, Middle Tisza, North-East Hungary, the market towns of the Great Plain, South, Central and West Transdanubia, and the Small Plain in North-West Hungary.

At the time of writing two units have been completed: the Upper Tisza and the Small Plain (Kisalföld) regions. Some buildings in the West Transdanubia group, which are being completed, can also be visited. Apart from peasant houses and outbuildings, there are churches, chapels, a bell tower, trade workshops and a Calvinist cemetery. Remnants of a Roman villa are also included in the museum.

Throughout the summer months regular displays take place to show the traditional life of rural Hungary. Visitors can see traditional crafts such as pottery, basket-weaving and baking taking place. Folklore programmes are organised on traditional fair and feast days. (Open April–Oct 9.00–17.00, except Monday. For further information or advanced application for a conducted tour in English telephone Szentendre (26) 12-304.)

Leányfalu is 6km N of Szentendre on Road 11. During the past 100 years this roadside settlement between the hills and the Danube has become a popular resort near the capital. It has a warm-water open-air swimming pool set in a park area.

Towards the end of the last century Leányfalu became a favourite summer resort of actors from the Budapest National Theatre and singers from the Opera House. Villas along the hillside began to spring up. The turn-of-the-century painters, Bertelan Székely and Árpád Feszty lived here and the writer Zsigmond Móricz (1879–1942) spent much time working here.

4km to the N of Leányfalu is the small village of *Tahitótfalu*. It is actually in two parts. A bridge connects Tahi with Tótfalu on **Szentendre Island** (Szentendrei-sziget). The island stretches for 31km from just S of Visegrád at its northern tip to the border of the Hungarian capital. There are four small villages on the 56 sq km island. A car and passenger ferry service connects the E side of the island with the town of Vác on the left bank of the Danube. At *Kisoroszi* at the northern end of the island there is a golf course, a rare phenomenon in Hungary.

Dunabogdány is 6km to the N of Tahitótfalu on Road 11. This picturesque village stretches for over a kilometre along the main road. It is a characteristic example of a Hungarian village in that the former peasant houses were all built sideways on to the road. This pattern has remained and can be clearly seen today. Dunabogdány has traditionally been a German speaking village and at the small *Local History Collection* (Helytörténeti Gyűjtemény) in the former peasant house and its outbuildings at No. 93 Kossuth u., there is a display of ethnic German folk art and history. (Open 9.00–12.00; Sat 14.00–16.00; closed Sundays.)

A further 6km along Road 11 the route passes through an arch and enters **Visegrád**. This small village is the former site of one of the most sumptuous royal palaces built in Hungary.

The Romans established a fort here which was still in use in the 9C and 10C. At that time the area was inhabited by Slav peoples who gave the settlement its present name which means 'high castle'. In the middle of the 11C, as the Hungarian state was being organised and the Church was being established in the country, a monastery was built near the fortress.

A lower castle by the river and a citadel on top of the hill were built in the mid-13C following the Mongol invasion. This work was undertaken on the instructions of King Béla IV, and on its completion Visegrád became one of the strongest fortifications in the country.

King Charles Robert (1307–42) set up his royal household at Visegrád in 1316 and it was he who commenced the construction of the Royal Palace. In 1335 an important meeting took place here when Charles conferred with the Polish king, Casimir, the Bohemian king, John, Prince Rudolf of Saxony and Henrik Wittelsbach, Prince of Lower Bavaria. The guests brought knights and large retinues and envoys from other countries were also present. The congress, which lasted for two months amidst grandiose feasts and tournaments, resulted in important treaties and the opening of a commercial route by-passing Vienna.

Charles's successors, Louis the Great and Sigismund of Luxemburg, continued with the construction of the palace even though the royal court had moved back to Buda. Visegrád continued to be a place where kings and diplomats met and the Hungarian crown jewels were kept in the Visegrád citadel.

In the 15C King Matthias Corvinus (1458–90) had the palace and the stronghold completely renewed, first in Gothic style, then, after his second marriage in 1470 to Beatrice of Aragon, in Renaissance style. Matthias's palace never ceased to amaze visitors with its splendours. The Papal Legate, Cardinal Castelli, in 1483 called it 'an earthly paradise', and the Italian Bonfini wrote of 'a large number of magnificent and spacious halls, porticos with snow-white facings, and beautiful windows, as well as a terraced garden and splashing fountains with ornate red marble and bronze basins.'

Decline set in after Matthias and was completed with the occupation of the buildings by the Turkish invaders in 1543. Frequent sieges caused further destruction and after the Turks were finally displaced in 1686 German settlers were moved in and they built new houses using the stones of the former palace.

Over the centuries the rains pouring down the hillside (which had previously been channelled away before the palace was destroyed) completely buried the palace in earth and its exact whereabouts was unknown until excavations uncovered some remains in 1934.

The remains of the former **Royal Palace** can be visited from No. 29 Fő u, though much of what can be seen is a result of reconstruction work or, indeed, a copy of the original. Notable features include the reconstructed Gothic arcaded passageway; the base of the Renaissance *Hercules fountain*, with red marble side panels; and the copy of the wall fountain, known as the *Lion Fountain*, original pieces of which are in the Solomon Tower nearby. (Open 9.00–17.00; Nov–April 8.00–16.00; closed Mondays.)

The keep of the lower castle, called **Solomon's Tower** stands to the S of the ruins a little way up the hill. It was built in the 13C and 14C and today, reconstructed, is a museum displaying items found during the excavations at Visegrád. (Open 1 May–7 November 9.00–17.00 except Mondays.)

The remains of the **Citadel** at the top of the hill can be reached either by a steep footpath beside Solomon's Tower or via the winding road from the turning signposted 'Fellegvár' a short distance to the N on Road 11. The citadel contains a small pictorial exhibition of Visegrád castle and also offers a splendid view of its surroundings. (Open every day 10.00–18.00.)

Just beyond the Fellegvár turning on Road 11 there is a landing-stage for a car and passenger ferry service to Nagymaros on the other side of the Danube.

While the former splendours of the Royal Palace can now only be seen in their ruins, the natural beauty of the area, which also appealed to visitors in the Middle Ages, can still be appreciated by today's visitors. The stretch of the Danube as it curves round in a horseshoe bend in the vicinity of Visegrád is one of the most spectacular in the whole of the Danube Bend region.

The Gabčikovo-Nagymaros barrage, a joint Hungarian-Czechoslovak project to build a series of barrages and a hydro-electric power station, was suspended unilaterally in May 1989 by the Hungarian government.

The village of *Dömös* lies 7km to the N of Visegrád. In the Middle Ages this was one of the centres of the royal hunting grounds. At the beginning of the 12C an important provostry was established here. In the 15C it became a Benedictine monastery and later belonged to Esztergom. Excavations have uncovered some ruins of the building which was destroyed in Turkish times.

From *Pilismarót*, 4km along Road 11, there are ferries across the Danube to Zebegény and (from the Basaharc landing-stage some way beyond the village) to Szob. From Pilismarót, as from Dömös, several walks can be taken into the nearby hills.

Road 11 continues to **Esztergom** (see Rte 6C) which lies 13km beyond Pilismarót.

C. Esztergom

Esztergom is a small town of 33,000 inhabitants 68km from Budapest via Road 11 which follows the right bank of the Danube. It is, however, the most important ecclesiastical centre of the country, being the seat of the Archbishop of Esztergom who is also the Primate of all Hungary. The monumental Cathedral, standing on a hill overlooking the Danube and beyond that Czechoslovakia, dominates the town and is the largest church in Hungary. The town is also important historically, as it was here that the first Hungarian kings established their seat.

Tourist Information: Komturist, 13 Széchenyi tér (22/484)

Rail Station: Bem tér. 1½ hours by express from the Western Railway Station, Budapest.

Bus Station: Zalka Máté tér. 2 hours from the Árpád Bridge Bus Station, Budapest.

Post Office: 2 Arany János u.

Police: 27 Kiss János altábornagy út.

History. Celts occupied the Danube region during the 4C BC. Some relics from their times can be seen in the Castle Museum. The Romans were here, too, from the 1C AD. They built watch-towers at several points. But the great age of the Danube Bend commenced when, towards the end of the 10C, Prince Géza established his seat at Esztergom which then became the centre of the royal household for almost 300 years. Due to the efforts of Géza and his son Stephen to convert the Hungarians to Christianity, Esztergom also became the centre of the early Church in Hungary and the first cathedral of the country was built here. It was here that Stephen was crowned first King of Hungary at Christmas in 1000.

The high point in the town's history came in the late 12C during the reign of Béla III (1172–96). He had been brought up at the Byzantine court, and had been for a while heir apparent to the Byzantine throne. He wanted to evoke the splendour and image of strength of the empire to the East. Western influences were not lacking, though, particularly through the medium of the king's two French wives and from the fact that foreign knights stopped here on their way to fight in the Holy Land. It was during the reign of Béla that the unknown notary, who has been called Anonymus, wrote down one of the first chronicles of Hungarian history in Latin.

In 1241–42 the Mongols destroyed the town but were unable to capture the castle. In the years following their retreat Béla IV (1206–70) chose to move the royal residence to Buda and hence Esztergom declined in importance in royal terms. However, the Archbishop, as Head of the Church, stayed and moved into the royal palace. Some of the later archbishops developed Esztergom into a lively cultural centre. János Vitéz, for example, the humanist prelate at the time of King Matthias, turned the town into one of the Renaissance centres of Hungary. His palace was visited by scholars and artists and for some time after

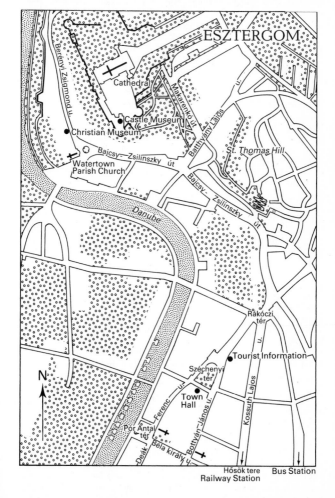

Matthias's death, under the archbishops Ippolito d'Este and Tamás Bakócz, Esztergom continued in these traditions.

The town was under Turkish rule for almost all the years of the Turkish presence in Hungary. They were driven out in 1683, three years before they were forced to leave Buda. The population had declined, however, and life returned to Esztergom only slowly. The ecclesiastical leaders had fled in the wake of the Turks and Esztergom was only re-established as the national religious centre in 1820. This explains why the huge cathedral was built on neo-classical lines, the architectural style predominant at the time, rather than in the more elaborate Baroque style which had been employed in the previous century for church buildings erected in the process of consolidating the Catholic Church after the expulsion of the Turks.

The **Cathedral**, on Castle Hill, was begun in 1822 under the direction of Archbishop Sándor Rudnay. The architects were Pál Kühneland and János Packh, though József Hild supervised the later stages of construction. The first cathedral on the hill had been ruined by the Turks. Maria Theresa (1740–80) had had a small church built here but nothing remains of it apart from the statues of King (St.) Stephen and King (St.) Ladislas in front of the present cathedral on either side some way below the statue of Our Lady of Hungary in the middle of the square.

By 1847 the 72m high dome and the roof were in place and although not fully completed it was consecrated on 31 August 1856. Ferenc Liszt conducted his Esztergom Mass here which he had composed for the occasion. (A memorial plaque recalling the event has been placed on the wall to the right in the side entrance.) The last stone was only finally put in place by Archbishop János Simor in November 1869.

The portico consists of eight 22m high Corinthian columns. On the far right there is a statue of János Hunyadi (c 1407–56) the commander of the victorious armies that defeated the Turks at Nándor-fehérvár (Belgrade) in 1456. Opposite is a statue of Dénes Széchy, the primate who crowned King Matthias in 1458. On either side of the door there are statues by György Kiss. To the right is Louis the Great, King of Hungary from 1342 to 1382. To the left, Csanád Telegdy, an archbishop of Esztergom in the early 14C. Above the door is a relief of Jesus and Zacheus by Johann Meixner. On the wall are the coats of arms of Sándor Rudnay, József Kopácsy, János Scitovszky and János Simor, the Esztergom archbishops associated with the building of the cathedral. The Latin inscriptions read, in turn, 'He Started . . . Continued . . . Consecrated . . . Finished' the building. The reliefs on the arches connecting the building to the side bell towers show the 'laying of the foundation stone' (on the right) and the 'consecration of the church'. Both are by Johann Meixner.

Inside the cathedral, on the left through the S side entrance, is the red marble **Bakócz Chapel**—a fine example of Renaissance architecture. It was built between 1506 and 15ll by a craftsman from the circle of the Italian Giuliano da Sangallo as a sepulchral chapel for Archbishop Bakócz and was originally built into the St. Adalbert Cathedral erected on the hill in the early 11C. It managed to survive the Turkish period and when the present cathedral was being built it was dismantled into 1600 numbered pieces and reassembled in its present position under the direction of János Packh. The white marble altar was carved by Andrea Ferrucci da Fiesole in 1519. The statues of Stephen and Ladislas on the altar, however, are 19C, the work of Pietro Bonani. The beauty of the chapel has never failed to receive a mention in the descriptions left by travellers to Esztergom over the centuries.

The Bakócz Chapel, Esztergom Cathedral.

The main altarpiece of the cathedral is one of the biggest oil paintings on a single canvas in the world, measuring 13m by 6.5m. The work of the Venetian painter Michelangelo Grigoletti (1801–70), it is based on Titian's 'Assumption' in the Frari Church in Venice. The main altar dates from 1856 and is by Pietro Bonani and Franz Anton Danninger. The lower marble reliefs show scenes from the Old Testament and contain a copy of Leonardo da Vinci's 'Last Supper'. On the upper part are statues of (from left to right) St. Martin, who served in the Roman province of Pannonia which is today's western Hungary; St. Gellért, depicted here with Imre, King Stephen's son; St. Adalbert, the patron of the archdiocese; and St. Mór, a former bishop of Pécs. The white marble bishop's throne is to the left of the main altar. The ceiling fresco above the chancel depicting the 'Holy Trinity among angels' is the work of Ludwig Moralt of Munich.

Around the ledge of the dome a Latin inscription reads 'Mary has been taken to Heaven and the angels are rejoicing'. The four mosaics just underneath the dome of SS. Ambrose, Gregory, Jerome and Augustine are by Ludwig Moralt. Below the dome on the left by the S transept there is a statue of the Jesuit Péter Pázmány (1570–1673) a leader of the Counter Reformation, founder of the university and Archbishop of Esztergom from 1616 until his death (statue by Pietro della Vedova, 1882).

The 'Altar of the Holy Cross' is in the middle of the S transept wall. It was carved by Pietro Bonani in 1856. The painting of the Calvary, above, is by Grigoletti and shows Adam on the left, shocked to see the consequence of his sin. To the left is the small Heart of Jesus altar. The small altars in the cathedral were commissioned by various Hungarian bishops. This one was made in 1897 and shows St. Anthony of Padua and St. Margaret Mary of Alacoque adoring the Sacred Heart. The painting of the Resurrection, above, is by Moralt. He also painted the Nativity opposite, above the small altar of St. Joseph. The statues here are the work of Johann Meixner.

The centre altar of the N transept is dedicated to the Martyrs of Kassa (Košice, Czechoslovakia), three churchmen executed for their beliefs in 1619 during the 'religious' wars of the time. Their relics are kept in a casket below the altar, and above are statues of them by György Kiss. In front of the altar there are statues of St. Elizabeth of the House of Árpád (left) and St. Margaret by Pietro Bonani. Grigoletti initiated the painting above the altar which depicts St. Stephen offering his crown to the Virgin.

This is a common theme of Hungarian iconography and refers to the fact that Stephen's son, Imre, died at an early age in a hunting accident, leaving no heir apparent to the throne. Stephen offered the Hungarian crown to the Virgin Mary for protection and thus she became the Patron of Hungary. As such she is also often portrayed in Hungarian works of art.

The small altar to the left in the N transept is dedicated to St. Adalbert. Adalbert came to Hungary from Prague and confirmed St. Stephen in Esztergom. The statues are by Meixner and the painting above by Moralt depicts the Baptism of Vajk which was King Stephen's original name. The small St. Martin altar stands against the opposite wall and apart from St. Martin there are statues of Blessed Kinga and Blessed Jolantha, two of Béla IV's daughters. Moralt's fresco above depicts the 'Conversion of the Hungarians to Christianity'. The large statue to the right is of Archbishop János Simor (1813–91) who directed the completion of the cathedral (Alajos Stróbl, 1896). He is depicted with a scroll in his hand showing a sketch of the building. Simor was also the founder of the Treasury and of the Christian Museum in Esztergom.

The *Chapel of St. Stephen the Martyr* is at the rear of the church, on the N side opposite the Bakócz Chapel. To the left there is a statue of the kneeling martyr, St. Stephen, by István Ferenczy, a pioneer of 19C Hungarian sculpture (1831). Opposite is the ornate sepulchral monument of Archbishop Ambrus Károly, the work of Giuseppe Pisani (1826). Among the various items of Church history on display here is a cabinet by the N wall containing relics of various saints including a relic of the English saint, Thomas Becket. (One of the early archbishops of Esztegom, Lukács, had studied with Thomas in Paris. This was one of several connections between Hungary and the martyr—see also St. Thomas Hill below.)

The large reliefs on the walls of the nave above the Bakócz and

Stephen chapels are by Meixner and depict 'Jesus among children' (on the N wall) and the 'entry into Jerusalem'.

The entrance to the **Cathedral Treasury** (Kincstár) is inside the church below the dome by the N transept. (Open 9.00–16.30; Nov–March 10.00–15.00. Tickets from the office in the southern bell tower.)

The original collection of the archdiocese, especially objects dating from the Middle Ages, was greatly depleted over the years by sackings, confiscations and dispersals. Items have had to be moved for safety reasons over a dozen times. The idea of presenting the religious material in the form of a museum came to fruition at the end of the 19C. The Treasury was developed and made accessible to the public by Primate János Simor in 1886.

The items on display include a Carolingian crystal cross, several Romanesque pieces of gold work, four pieces of work by 14C goldsmiths, over 20 textile pieces and nearly 30 pieces of gold work from the late Gothic or Renaissance periods. Selected items from the Treasury's large collection of Baroque and 19C works are also on display.

Of particular interest are: a pre-1408 *drinking horn* in a silver-gilt setting from the Rhineland or France with decorative statuettes, niello scenes and coats of arms; the *Calvary of Matthias Corvinus*, a 15C Gothic decorated cross made by a goldsmith who had trained in Lombardy; *Benedek Suki's Chalice*, a beautiful Hungarian late-Gothic decorated chalice; and the *Maria Theresa Chalice*, the largest and most ornate Baroque chalice in the Treasury, an embossed work decorated with many precious stones and coloured enamel pictures, a gift from the Empress to Archbishop Imre Esterházy.

Access to the Cathedral *Crypt* is from the side entrance to the church. Here are the tombs and fragments found in the old St. Adalbert Church. At the bottom of the stairs are the statues of 'Mourning' and 'Eternity', by Andreas Schrott (1823). The items in the Egyptian-style undercroft give an idea of medieval Hungarian sepulchral sculpture. The sarcophagus of Dénes Széchy (from 1465) and of János Vitéz (1472) are both richly decorated.

The side entrance also gives access to steps leading up to the external ledge of the dome. Although it is an exhausting climb a fine view of the surroundings can be had from here.

The **Castle Museum** (Vármúzeum) is to the S of the cathedral inside the reconstructed royal palace. (Open 9.00–16.30 except Monday.)

The medieval Royal Palace was the first stone fortress of Hungary. Until the 1930s it lay hidden under earth like the palace at Visegrád. This was the seat of Prince Géza and then King Stephen I. From the end of the 11C several armies on their way to the Holy Land during the Crusades passed through Hungary, including those of Louis VII of France in 1147 and Frederick Barbarossa, Holy Roman Emperor, in 1189. The reception and entertainment of visitors coupled with the normal life of the royal household led to modernisation and expansion of the palace. Eventually Esztergom became the strongest fortress of the country and apart from the fortified church at Pannonhalma was the only place able to withstand the onslaught of the Mongols in the early 1240s.

From 1249 the Archbishops of Esztergom lived in the palace after Béla IV had moved the royal seat to Buda. Primate János Vitéz (c 1408–72) turned the palace into a centre of humanist culture and a few decades later a luxurious court was furnished here for Ippolito, the nephew of King Matthias's wife, Beatrice. In the early 16C, during the period of Tamás Bakócz, the splendours of the archdiocese were on a par with the Buda court of the Hungarian kings.

Bakócz (1443–1521) was of peasant origin but rose to be King Matthias's secretary, Chancellor of Wladislas II, Bishop of Győr, then of Eger, and from 1497, Archbishop of Esztergom. In 1513 he was a contender for the Holy See but failed to be elected Pope. He was a leader of the pro-Habsburg court party and a corrupt fortune hunter but also a patron of the arts, as his Renaissance chapel in the cathedral shows.

The following gives a summary of the contents of the various rooms in the museum. ROOM 1. A room from the 15C, containing local relics from the Iron, Bronze and Copper Ages; Celtic and Roman finds. R. 2. From the 14C. Items from the period of migrations after the Romans; weapons of the Avars; relics from the time of the Magyar conquest; a 9C white limestone column from an early Christian church, probably recarved in the 12C; relics from graves from the time of the Árpád dynasty; 11C coins—the royal mint was here and was the only one in Hungary up to the 13C. R. 3. A section of the original St. Adalbert Cathedral burned down in 1130, rebuilt in 1203; a model of that cathedral's Romanesque gate, the Porta Speciosa (scale 1 to 3); opposite the model, remains of red marble decoration from above another gate of the old church; remains of an inlaid marble floor, column capitals and bases from the same church; the 12C bronze bell is from another village nearby. R. 4. Pictures showing the excavations of the royal palace in the 1930s and the 1960s. R. 5. A living room from the 12C palace. The vaulting, but not the column, is original. R. 6. Photographs showing the excavations. R. 7. A reconstructed 12C red marble throne, probably belonging to Béla III. R. 8. The wall-paintings depicting Intelligence, Moderation, Strength and Justice are probably 15C. R. 9. 15C relics; a copy of Béla IV's letter handing the palace over to the archdiocese; stove tiles, bronze and ceramic pots, candle holders, weapons. R. 10. A passage from R8 with 14C stones and fragments of frescoes. R. 11. Chapel of the royal family.

In the latter half of the 12C Hungarian architecture and related arts developed at a great pace owing to the political and cultural links established throughout Europe by King Béla III (1172–96). His two wives were both French and he settled two French monastic orders, the Cistercians and the Premonstratensians, in Hungary and gave them extensive privileges. The priests working in his chancery were educated in Paris. All this explains the appearance in Hungary, at the end of the 12C, of craftsmen familiar with French Gothic styles. They came to work on the construction of the royal palace at Esztergom. The interior of the chapel reflects the early Gothic style of building around Paris.

The chapel collapsed during the Turkish wars but was filled up with earth and converted into a defensive bastion. The layer of earth protected it and during excavations almost every rib of the vaulting was found, making an accurate reconstruction possible. Both the stone walls and the vaulting were completed with thin bricks so that the additions would be clear.

The chapel was painted twice. Of the late 12C frescoes, only the lions standing before the Tree of Life have survived. During the middle of the 14C an Italian master, probably Niccolò di Tommaso (fl. c 1343–76), painted apostles in the niches and scenes from the life of Jesus and Mary on the walls.

An exit door by Room 6 gives access to some wooden steps leading down to a small yard where there are some Turkish-head tombstones and some cannon balls. R. 12. A display of relics from Turkish times.

A path leads down from the entrance of the Castle Museum through a gate which, like the walls, was reconstructed in the 1930s. The huge bronze statue here is called *The Founder* and represents Prince Géza, who founded the first royal seat at Esztergom (Tamás Vigh, 1979).

St. Thomas Hill (Szent Tamás-hegy) can be seen across to the SE. Towards the end of the 12C a religious chapter was established on the hill dedicated to the English martyr, Thomas Becket, who had been killed in 1170 on the orders of King Henry II of England. It was set up by Margaret Capet, a French princess who had been married to Henry's son, also called Henry, who strongly disagreed with his father's action. After his death she married Béla III and came to Hungary. It was her desire to preserve the memory of Thomas. The original building was destroyed by the Turks. The present chapel was built in 1823 in memory of all the heroes killed in defence of the town. The calvary in front, however, dates from 1781 and originally stood on Castle Hill.

The path from the Castle Hill leads down to Makarenko út. The tunnel with the neo-classical entrance, which can be seen to the left, is the so-called *Dark Gate* (Sötét-Kapu). It was constructed in the 1820s to facilitate access between the various ecclesiastical buildings situated on either side. The name of the then Primate, Sándor Rudnai, and the year of construction are inscribed above in Latin. On the right is a bronze statue of *Bálint Balassi* by András Dózsa Farkas (1938). Balassi (1554–94) was an early representative of Hungarian lyrical poetry. He died in Esztergom while participating in one of the fights to recapture the town from the Turks.

The route follows the road round to the right along Batthyány Lajos u. then right again into the northern part of Bajcsy-Zsilinszky út which leads to the WATERTOWN (Víziváros) quarter, a small but pleasant district at the foot of Castle Hill on a narrow strip between the Danube and the hill.

The statue on the right, as the route enters Bajcsy-Zsilinszky út, is of *Ferenc Liszt*. It was sculpted by István Marosits and erected in 1986 on the centenary of the composer's death. The two-storey building across the road at No. 28, designed by József Hild in 1856, houses the *Cathedral Library*. It is one of the oldest established libraries in the country, mention being made of it in documents at the end of the 14C, and contains many valuable codices and incunabula.

No. 59 on the right was built during the Turkish occupation. The plaque on the wall says that here the *Bey* of Esztergom received an imperial delegation in 1602. The school at *No. 42* on the left was built in 1912, while the Theological College next door at *No. 44* occupies a former Franciscan friary. The building was erected in 1750, though the classical façade is from 1847. The Baroque *Franciscan Church* attached to it was built between 1726 and 1750, though the façade likewise dates from the last century. The two-storey Baroque building opposite at No. 63 used to be the County Hall until 1830. Today it is the *Bálint Balassi Museum* of local history. There are, however, plans to move the museum to No. 77 further along the street. (Open 9.00–17.00 except Monday.)

The street opens out into a little square where, on the left, stands a Baroque *Virgin Mary Statue* (Szűz Mária-szobor) erected in the year following the plague of 1739. The **Watertown Parish Church** (Vízivárosi plébániatemplom) was built in Italian Baroque style, 1728–38. The two frontal towers, however, date from the 1880s. The richly decorated interior was severely damaged in World War II and later replaced. The equestrian statue of *St. Stephen* in front of the church is a copy of one standing in Győr, in western Hungary. It was donated in 1978 by the widow of the sculptor, Ferenc Medgyessy.

The two-storey neo-classical building at *No. 1* Berényi Zsigmond u., which runs N from the end of Bajcsy-Zsilinszky út, was designed by József Hild c 1830. It used to be the Primate's Palace before the present one was built. The rear of the present *Archbishop's Palace* can be seen on the other side of the street. The Eclectic building, which faces the Danube, was built in the 1880s to the designs of József Lippert, who was employed by Archbishop János Simor in 1857, rising to become his chief architect in 1864. At the far end of the building is the entrance to the **Christian Museum**, the largest provincial fine arts collection in Hungary. The museum was founded by János Simor as part of the project of re-establishing Esztergom as the main Hungarian ecclesiastical centre and opened in 1875. It has the largest collection of medieval works of art outside the Hungarian National Gallery in Budapest.

Outstanding items in the collection include (in the first room to the left) eight panels from Tamás Kolozsvári's *Calvary winged altarpiece*, made in 1427 for the Benedictine church of Garamszentbenedek (Hronsky Benadik, Czechoslovakia). In the middle of the same room, and also from the same town of the former Upper Hungary region, is a unique piece of medieval Hungarian liturgical wood sculpture, the *Lord's Coffin of Garamszentbenedek*, which dates from c 1480. The upper part of the wheeled construction, which was used during Easter Week, is reminiscent of a church in form. The finely carved pillars are ornamented on all four sides with figures of the apostles. On the lower part are soldiers guarding Christ's coffin. It was brought to Esztergom in 1872 after restoration work, but was badly damaged in World War II. It was restored again in the 1970s over a period of six years and at a cost of half a million forints. For this it was broken down into 500 pieces and the gilt layers restored.

In the second room on the right-hand wall is another masterpiece of medieval Hungarian panel painting, the *Passion* of Master MS (the artist is known only by these initials). They date from 1506 and formed the upper parts of the former high altar of Selmecbánya (Banská Stiavnica, Czechoslovakia).

Other items in the museum include works by German and Dutch painters, Italian paintings of the 13C–16C, and works by the Austrian artist, Franz Anton Maulbertsch, who was a leading Baroque painter active in Hungary. There is also a collection of Flemish and German tapestries and some objects of applied art.

The route continues in SZÉCHENYI TÉR which is about 1km away, reached by returning along Bajcsy-Zsilinszky út and proceeding along its southern section to Rákóczi tér which adjoins the northern end of the funnel-shaped Széchenyi tér. Many of the buildings in and around the square are quite dilapidated, but the area gives an idea of what the town was like as it was built up in the 18C and 19C.

The *Hotel Fürdő* (Baths Hotel) is on the way at No. 14 Bajcsy-Zsilinszky út on the right. There has been a bathing establishment on the site for many centuries. The thermal waters here were used by the Romans and later the first public baths of Hungary were entrusted to the Knights of St. John of Jerusalem. 13C records show that the baths were functioning in the second half of the 12C. Destroyed by the Mongols, they were put to use again by the Turks who built a steam bath here.

The so-called *Bank House* is at the northern end of Széchenyi tér at No. 21. The three-storey Romantic building decorated with a woman's figure at the top was designed by József Hild and erected in 1860 for the National Savings Bank whose name can be seen on the ledge. *No. 24* opposite is a two-storey Louis XVI building with Ionic pilasters. It was built around 1790. There are decorative festoons above the windows and the gate.

The local county *Tourist Information Office* (Komtourist) is situated in the classical building at No. 13 Széchenyi tér on the left-hand, eastern side of the square. The two-storey Rococo house at *No. 7* on the same side was designed by Antal Hartmann and built in 1768. Interesting features include its wrought-iron work, stucco work around the windows and mansard roof. There is a statue of the Virgin Mary in a niche on the façade. The Romantic corner house at *No. 3* is today the post office.

Opposite, on the W side of the square, *No. 14* was built in 1820 in neo-classical style. *No. 6* was originally Baroque and rebuilt in early Eclectic style. Its cellar underneath dates from the Middle Ages. *No. 4* dates from 1840.

A *Holy Trinity Statue* (Szentháromság-szobor) stands in the middle towards the S end of Széchenyi tér. It was designed by György Kiss using parts of a previous Baroque statue and erected in 1900. The **Town Hall** stands behind the Holy Trinity statue stretching the length of the S side of the square. Originally just one storey, the first floor was added in 1729 though the present form dates from reconstructions undertaken from 1770 to 1773 according to the plans of Antal Hartmann. The coat of arms of the town can be seen on the tympanum. The windows of the first floor are fringed with Rococo ornamentation. To the left is an equestrian statue of *János Bottyán*, one of Prince Rákóczi's commanders in the War of Independence at the beginning of the 18C (István Martsa, 1978). Bottyán once owned the town Hall building.

BOTTYÁN JÁNOS U. runs S from the corner of the Town Hall by the statue. *No. 1* is the side of the Town Hall. Hartmann had the date of construction, 1778, inscribed on this façade, though the turret with the clock above the projection was erected in the following year. No. 3 is the *Old County Hall*. The two-storey Baroque façade has a balcony with trellised railing and decorated windows. It was designed by András Mayerhoffer in 1747 and later purchased by Esztergom County. It served as the county hall until 1952. Today the town is part of Komárom-Esztergom County. The two-storey neighbouring Baroque building at *No. 5* dates from 1755. *No. 8* across the road is a former Benedictine monastery and was built in 1724. *No. 10* is a former Franciscan monastery built in the early years of the 18C at the same time as the Franciscan church here.

Béla király u. cuts through to the right and leads to the small Pór Antal tér. Here stands the **City Parish Church**, sometimes called the Öreg-templom (Old Church). The church was built between 1757 and 1762. The main altarpiece (1896) depicting SS. Peter and Paul is by János Vaszary and the mural above the chancel by Márton Reindl. The statues of angels on the gable are by a local sculptor. The marble altar dates from the first years of the 20C, while the ornamented Baroque pulpit is thought to be the work of Károly Bebó (1763). The red marble plaque to the right of the wooden Rococo gate shows the level of the flood waters of 1832.

A medieval Franciscan church and monastery used to stand on the site of the present church and here were buried King Béla IV and his wife Mária Lascaris. This ancient church, however, was destroyed during Turkish occupation.

Deák Ferenc u. leads northwards back to Széchenyi tér.

Other places of interest in Esztergom. The *Mihály Babits Memorial House* is at No. 15 Babits Mihály út due E of Széchenyi tér. Babits (1883–1941) was a poet, translator, essayist and editor of the 'Nyugat' journal. This was his summer house. (Open May–Oct 10.00–18.00 except Monday.)

The exhibitions of the *Hydrology Museum* (Magyar Vízügyi Múzeum) situated at No. 2 Kölcsey u. to the NE of Rákóczi tér, covers the history of the Danube regulation and water management in Hungary. The Baroque building which today houses the museum is a former ecclesiastical property built in the 1830s. Items on display refer to periods as wide apart as the age of the Hungarian wandering navvie to the building of the Gabčikovo-Nagymaros barrage today. Count István Széchenyi played a central part in the regulation of the Danube in the last century and he encouraged the use of British techniques. There is a model of the 'Vidra', the first steam dredger in Hungary, which was bought from Britain as well as other pieces of English equipment. (Open 10.00–18.00 except Monday.)

The round *Church of St. Anne* stands in Hősök tere on the southern side of the town along Kossuth Lajos u. It was built between 1828 and 1835 to the plans of János Packh, one of the architects of Esztergom Cathedral, for Archbishop Rudnay whose coat of arms can be seen in the tympanum of the neo-classical portico. The statues in front were made by György Herzog, the Carrara marble altar by Ignác Számord and the main altarpiece by an Eger artist, János Mihály Hesz.

Excursions from Esztergom

St. Anne's Church in Hősök tere stands at a junction from where there are two alternative routes returning to Budapest, apart from Road 11 by the side of the Danube. (Both journeys are shorter—approximately 50km.)

The road signposted Dobogókő (c 15km) leads up through the Pilis Hills, which were one of the favourite royal hunting grounds of the Middle Ages. The hermits of the Order of St. Paul, founded by Canon Eusebius (Özséb) of Esztergom, also used to frequent the hills and later many former hunting lodges became small monasteries.

Dobogókő at 700m is one of the highest points of the hills. It is a popular resort and offers a splendid view of the surrounding area. At the end of the last century one of the earliest tourist hostels in Hungary was established here. Today the wooden building serves as a *museum of rambling and nature tourism*. (Open Thurs, Sat and Sun 10.00–16.00.) The bronze relief on the natural stone at the top of the hill commemorates a 19C pioneer of Hungarian mountain tourism, Ödön Téry.

The road to Budapest leads down through Pilisszentkereszt and Pomáz from where Road 11 can be joined just S of Szentendre, or (more quickly) the road via Budakalász can be taken.

The quickest way to return to Budapest from Esztergom is to continue due S from Kossuth Lajos u., past St. Anne's Church, in the direction of Dorog, on Road 11, from where Road 10 (the old main Vienna–Budapest highway) leads to Budapest.

Dorog (pop. 13,000) is an industrial town and an old mining centre. A small *Mining Museum* has been set up at No. 70 Sziklai u., with items relating to the 200 years of coal-mining in the region. (Open Tues and Sat 13.00–18.00; Thurs and Sun 9.00–12.00, 13.00–18.00.)

About 17km from Dorog, on Road 10 at the junction of the road leading to Solymár, there is the small *British Military Cemetery*. Apart from the British, it is also the resting place of Polish, Canadian, Australian and New Zealand airmen who were shot down over Hungary during World War II.

D.   The Left Bank of the Danube Bend

Roads 2 and 12. Total distance 85km. **Budapest**—Road 2 18km Dunakeszi and turning for (6km) **Fót**—5km **Göd**—5km Sződliget—3km turning for (8.5km) **Vácrátot**—1km **Vác**—5km junction with Road 12—5km *Verőcemaros*—8km **Nagymaros**—9km **Zebegény**—6km **Szob**—20km **Nagybörzsöny**.

The left bank of the Danube Bend is not so popular and has fewer historical monuments and tourist attractions than the right bank. Nevertheless there are a number of interesting places and sights along the route and the very quietness of the major town on this side of the Bend, Vác, has its own attraction.

Road 2 runs to Vác from the Pest side of Árpád Bridge in Budapest. A short distance beyond Vác there is a junction for Road 12 which follows the river on its northern side to Szob near the Czechoslovak border. The distance by road around the left bank from central Budapest to Szob is just under 70km. All the towns along the route can be reached by train from the Western Railway Station in Budapest.

At Dunakeszi, 18km to the N of Budapest on Road 2, there is a junction for (signposted 'Gödöllő') **Fót**, some 6km to the east. The **Catholic Church** standing on an artificially-made small hill in the centre of the village is one of the finest examples of Romantic architecture in Hungary.

The local estate owner, István Károlyi, began the church in 1845 according to the designs of Miklós Ybl who was aged 31 at the time and who later was to achieve fame with many designs including that of the Budapest Opera House. Work stopped in 1848 as Károlyi was imprisoned due to his participation in the political events of that year, which included the fitting out of a cavalry regiment at his own cost. Construction recommenced when he was freed in 1851 and continued until 1855.

Both the external and internal decorations of this unusual church show a mixture of Romanesque, Arab and Moorish motifs. The stained glass windows of the nave, the altarpiece and the paintings in the sanctuary are the work of the Austrian artist, Karl Blaas. The statues were made mainly by Viennese sculptors, though the ornamented pulpit was made in Rome. In the crypt there is a white Carrara marble statue of Christ (1858) by the Italian sculptor, Pietro Tenarari. The *church house* to the left was also designed by Ybl and built in 1850. On request visitors can look round the interior of the church. (Visiting times 10.00–12.00 and 14.00–18.00.)

The former *Károly Mansion* in the village was originally neoclassical and then rebuilt by Ybl in 1847. Since 1957 it has been the 'Children's Town', a home for children in state care.

The Fót *Local History Collection* at No. 31 Béke u. has an exhibition of works by the sculptor Kálmán Németh (1903–79). (Open 10.00–18.00 except Monday.)

Fót also has an historical claim to literary fame. It was here in the press-house of the writer and politician, András Fáy, that in 1842 the celebrated poet Mihály Vörösmarty read aloud his eulogy to wine and patriotism, the 'Fóti dal' (Fót Song), which later became famous and was set to music.

Göd is a few kilometres N of Dunakeszi on Road 2. Many holiday houses belonging to companies, trade unions and individual families stand along the riverside here. In the inter-war period the area contained one of the gathering places of underground labour movement activists. The *Göd 'Fészek'* (Arts House, though literally the word means 'nest') contains an exhibition devoted to the history of the workers' sports movement in Hungary. (Open May–Oct 10.00–18.00 except Monday.)

Sződliget, 5km further on, offers some of the best bathing facilities on the left bank.

The **Botanical Garden** at Vácrátot (No. 2–4 Alkotmány u.) can be reached via a turning to the right off Road 2 a few kilometres to the N of Sződliget. The garden was set up in the 1870s by Count Sándor Vigyázó who established a romantic landscape garden with artificial ruins, waterfalls and a large rock garden. He collected plants from all parts of the world and at the end of his life bequeathed the collection and gardens to the Academy of Sciences. The botanical garden has since been expanded and today contains thousands of different types of flowers, trees, plants and shrubs. (Open March–Oct 7.00–18.00.)

The town of **VÁC** lies on Road 2, 4km N of Sződliget and some 35km from Budapest.

The quiet, sleepy atmosphere of Vác today (pop. 36,000) belies its former importance. King Stephen I established an episcopal see here, and a Romanesque cathedral surrounded by a castle-like fortification was already standing in the early 11C. At the end of the 15C the humanist bishop, Miklós Báthori, enriched the town with Renaissance buildings, but by 1544 Vác had fallen into the hands of the Turks.

For the next 140 years the town had an eastern character. Turkish historians noted that it had 1000 houses with wooden roofs, seven mosques and a public bath. However, by the time the Turks had been driven out in 1686 Vác was in ruins. Redevelopment took place in the 18C under the direction of the various bishops of Vác, which was when the inner town received its present Baroque appearance.

The first Hungarian railway line connected Vác with Budapest in 1846, but significant industrial development had to wait until after 1945. Today there is an important photo-chemical factory and a large cement works in the vicinity.

Road 2 enters Vác across the Gombás stream. The *stone bridge* here with its Baroque statues was built in the 1750s with the financial support of Bishop Károly Althan, a patron of the arts, and is the work of Ignác Oracsek. The statues on the western side, towards the Danube are of SS. Venantius, John of Nepomuk, and Camillus. On the eastern side they represent SS. Judas Thaddeus, Peter, Paul and Barbara.

At the following open junction a road to the left leads towards the town centre via GÉZA KIRÁLY TÉR. The Baroque former *Franciscan Church* standing in the square here was finished in 1765. A member of the order carved the pulpit with allegorical figures representing the various virtues. The square was the ancient centre of medieval Vác and it was here that the fortress and original cathedral stood, where King Géza I was buried in 1077. The buildings fell victim to the Mongol invasion in the 13C.

KONSTANTIN TÉR is a short distance to the N. The **Cathedral** standing here on the E side dominates the square.

Building was begun in 1763 under the direction of Bishop Károly Esterházy according to the plans of the Austrian architect Franz Anton Pilgram. The bishop was later moved to Eger and his successor, Kristóf Migazzi, who subsequently became Prince Primate of Vienna, ordered a new design from Isidore Canevale, a French architect living in Vienna. The building was completed according to Canevale's plans in 1777. Influenced by Jacques Germain Soufflot and what was known as French 'revolutionary architecture', Canevale incorporated the latest French architectural ideas into this early neo-classical work. It was not until the beginning of the following century, however, that the neo-classical style became generally acceptable in Hungary.

The façade of the church is adorned with huge Corinthian columns. The six statues on the parapet are the work of Joseph Bechert. Inside, the *murals* on the dome and behind the main altar are the work of the Austrian painter, Franz Anton Maulbertsch. The artist's depiction of The Visitation behind the altar was not to the liking of Bishop Migazzi who had it bricked over. It only came to light during restoration work in the 1940s.

The *former Piarist monastery* and grammar school stands on the N side of the square overlooking Köztársaság útja. Building started in 1725 and the façade overlooking the square was finished in 1781. In the second half of the 18C the Piarists moved away and the building became a soldiers' quarters. The secondary school on the S side at No. 1–3 in the square was originally a seminary, built in Louis XVI style in the 1790s. The late Baroque building on the W side, opposite the main façade of the cathedral, was built in 1775 and is believed to have been designed by Joseph Meissl of Vienna.

Múzeum u. leads off Konstantin tér from the SW corner. No. 4 is the home of the *Vak Bottyán Museum*, which contains items relating to the history of Vác from the Conquest to 1900. (Open 10.00–18.00; Nov–March 9.00–17.00; closed Mondays.) Vak (Blind) Bottyán (1635–1709) was one of the military leaders in the Rákóczi War of Independence in the early 18C. For a time he was the captain of Vác.

Szentháromság tér is a short distance to the N of Konstantin tér along Köztársaság útja. The *Holy Trinity Statue* standing here dates from the 1750s. Across the road is the Baroque *Piarist Church* which was built between 1725 and 1741, though the present form of the church is a result of several rebuildings.

Today's town centre, the triangular-shaped MÁRCIUS 15 TÉR, is slightly further to the N. The *Upper City Parish Church* on the S side is a good example of local Rococo architecture. The Baroque *Town Hall* at No. 11, on the W side, was begun after a fire of 1736. Building stopped and resumed several times and was finally completed in 1764 for the visit of Maria Theresa to Vác. Notable features of the building are the wrought-iron balcony over the gate, the statue of Justitia on the gable, the female figures holding the Hungarian and Migazzi coats of arms, and the coat of arms of the town on the arch of the gable. *No. 7–9* next door used to belong to the Sisters of Charity. Note the Louis XVI-style grates on the windows. The building has been a hospital since 1785.

The building on the other side of the square at *No. 6* was erected on the town's oldest foundations. Two medieval buildings were utilised for its construction after the Turkish period. A fire of 1731, however, caused much destruction and the building has been remodelled several times. The bishops of Vác used to have their residence here but in 1802 the building was handed over to become the country's first institute for the deaf and dumb. *No. 4* next door was originally built in Louis XVI style and is the former palace of the grand provost.

Lőwy Sándor u. runs southwards from the SE corner of the square. At No. 4 there is an *exhibition room* belonging to the local museum which displays selected works of the painter Gyula Hincz (1904–86). (Open 10.00–18.00; Nov–March 9.00–18.00; closed Mondays.)

A short distance along Bartók Béla u., which leads W from Március 15 tér, there is a pleasant riverside promenade. A car ferry service operates from here to Szentendre Island. A road leads across the island to Tahitófalu where there is a bridge connecting with the right bank of the Danube.

The only **Triumphal Arch** in Hungary stands in Vác just under 1km to the N of Március 15 tér. It was erected by the Bishop of Vác, Kristóf Migazzi, for the visit of Empress Maria Theresa in 1764. The neoclassical structure was designed by Isidore Canevale, the architect of the town's cathedral. Its tripartite main cornice is decorated with festoons and eagles and has a relief of Maria Theresa and her husband, Francis of Lotharingia.

The *State Prison* which stands by the triumphal arch was originally intended for educational purposes. It was founded by Maria Theresa as an academy for noble youth and operated as such from the construction of the building in 1777 until 1784 when it was turned into a barracks. It has been a prison since 1855.

During the Horthy period, between the two world wars, many communist and labour movement activists were imprisoned here. A plaque on the wall commemorates the deaths of two such figures, Sándor Lőwry and Sándor Sztáron, who went on hunger strike in protest against maltreatment. The prison was also used to confine political opponents, or those regarded as such, during the Stalinist period of the early 1950s. The English woman Edith Bone spent some years in solitary confinement here. She came to Hungary in 1949 when in her sixties to write articles for the British Communist Party's 'Daily Worker'. Arrested at the airport when about to leave, she was charged with espionage and imprisoned, though for some time her existence in Hungary was officially denied. Later moved to Budapest, she was released during the uprising of 1956.

A specialist museum in Vác is the *József Petzval Museum of*

Photographic Techniques, which is situated at No. 9 Tragor Ignác u., near Lenin út to the SE of Konstantin tér. Petzval (1807–91) was a mathematician, engineer and pioneer of photographic technology in Hungary. The exhibition covers the history of photography and photographic techniques as well as the history of the Forte photochemical works near Vác. (Open 10.00–18.00; Nov–March 9.00–17.00; closed Mondays.)

Road 2 continues to the N of Vác. 5km from the town there is a junction where Road 12 branches off to the W and follows the Danube on its northern side. *Verőcemaros* is 5km along this road. The ceramist Géza Gorka (1894–1971) had a workshop here from 1923. His former house at No. 22 Szamos u. has been turned into a *Gorka Memorial Museum* where samples of his pottery are displayed. (Open 10.00–18.00; Nov–March 9.00–17.00; closed Mondays.)

Not far away, between the Verőce and Kismaros sections of the settlement, is the *summer residence of Bishop Kristóf Migazzi* which was built between 1766 and 1774 to the designs of Isidore Canevale (the mansion is signposted from Road 12).

Nagymaros is 8km to the W of Verőcemaros on Road 12. It lies at the foot of the Börzsöny Mountains on the bank of the Danube. The settlement dates back to the Middle Ages as is indicated by the Gothic *Catholic Church* dating from the 14C. The tower is somewhat later and acquired a new spire in the 18C, which was when the present furnishings were also installed.

From Nagymaros there is a magnificent view of the Visegrád citadel across the Danube. (A local saying proclaims that Visegrád has a castle, Nagymaros a view.) A car and passenger ferry service connects the two banks of the river here.

The road to **Zebegény**, 9km to the W, passes by the construction works of the Gabčikovo-Nagymaros barrage on the Danube (see p 238). The **Catholic Church** at Zebegény was designed by Károly Kós and Béla Jánszky and was built in 1908–10. It is the only Catholic church in Hungary designed in the National Romantic style, which combines Art Nouveau forms with traditional folk art. The interior furnishings of the church were also designed by Kós. Also noteworthy are the *interior frescoes* which depict the Vision of the Roman Emperor, Constantine, and St. Helen (his mother) finding the Holy Cross in Jerusalem. The frescoes are the work of Aladár Körösfői Kriesch, a leading member of the Gödöllő Colony, active in the first two decades of the 20C. The members of the Gödöllő circle were particularly influenced by the English Pre-Raphaelites and this is clearly discernible in the paintings inside the church.

István Szőnyi (1894–1960) was a painter and school teacher who lived in Zebegény and painted the local countryside and the life of the people. His former home and workshop at No. 7 Bartóky út has been turned into a *Szőnyi Memorial Museum* where his paintings are displayed. (Open 9.00–17.00; Dec–Feb 10.00–16.00; closed Mondays.)

Of specialist interest is the *Navigation Museum*, the private collection of Captain Vince Farkas, who accumulated the items on display during his voyages all over the world. The carved ship's figureheads are particularly noteworthy. The museum is situated at No. 9 Szőnyi u. (Open April–Oct 9.00–17.00 except Mondays.)

A car ferry service operates from Zebegény to near Pilismarót on the right bank of the Danube.

Szob is an important junction for rail traffic between Hungary and Czechoslovakia (no crossing for motorists). It is a few kilometres W of

*The church at Zebegény. A rare example of a Roman
Catholic Church built in National Romantic style.*

Zebegény along Road 12. The *Bözsöny Museum* at No. 13 Hámán
Kató u., exhibits archaeological finds from the Ipoly valley nearby
and items of regional folk art. It also has displays on local geography.
(Open 10.00–18.00; Oct–April 9.00–17.00; closed Mondays.)

There is a car ferry service operating between Szob and Basaharc
on the opposite side of the Danube.

Nagybörzsöny is 20km to the N of Szob but it has two interesting
church monuments. (It is reached by taking the road northwards
from Szob along the Ipoly valley through Ipolydamásd and
Ipolytölgyes and then via a road to the right.)

Nagybörzsöny grew prosperous in the Middle Ages because of the deposits of iron, copper and gold found here. At the end of the 14C and beginning of the 15C, Saxon miners were settled here to mine the ores. A royal decree of 1439 raised the village to the rank of a mining town and the inhabitants thus enriched were able to boast of having the first church in the region. Over the centuries, however, the minerals were exhausted and the town declined and became a small village once again.

The **Church of St. Stephen** dates from the 13C and is one of the oldest Romanesque village churches to have survived more or less intact. It did suffer some damage during the Mongol invasion but was repaired in the same style afterwards, when the tower was added. The solid church has a row of bearded heads decorating the outer wall of the sanctuary. The stone wall surrounding the church dates from the 17C. The towerless Gothic *Miners' Church* (Bányász-templom) was built in the early 15C by the miners who came to the village. Above the entrance a miner's emblem from 1417 can still be seen. Some alterations were made to the church when the Lutherans took it over in the 17C.

To preserve the memory of the mining traditions of the Börzsöny Hills, there is an *Exhibition of Ore and Mineral Mining* located in the village at No. 19 Petőfi u. Examples of folk art are also on display here. (Open Sat and Sun 10.00–17.00.)

7   Lake Balaton

At 598 sq km Lake Balaton is the largest lake in Central and Western Europe. Oblong in shape, it stretches for almost 80km with a maximum width of 14km. Where the Tihany Peninsula (12 sq km) juts into the lake, one third of the way in from the E on the northern side, the Lake narrows to about 1.5km. Although there are several ferry routes which cross the lake, the only one to take vehicles runs between Tihany and Szántód on the southern shore.

For its size Lake Balaton is extremely shallow with an average depth of only 3m. At its deepest, in the so-called Tihany 'well' by the peninsula, it reaches only 12–13m. Due to the shallowness of the water the lake warms up relatively quickly thus making it favourable for bathers. The mean temperature in summer is over 20°C and it often climbs above 25°C. The bathing season can stretch from May to September, though the high point coincides with the school holidays from early July to late August. On the northern shore the water deepens relatively quickly and apart from designated bathing places the bottom of the lake tends to be stonier and muddier. On the southern side the beaches and bed of the lake are sandy and the water is shallow for up to 500–1000m from the shore, thus making it particularly safe for children.

In recent years Lake Balaton has attracted an increasing number of foreign tourists and the facilities, services and infrastructure are generally on a high level. Overcrowding, however, particularly in the high season, is becoming more and more of a problem. In addition many Hungarians own weekend cottages near the lake and in order to avoid the weekend rush of traffic in the summer it is advisable not to travel from Budapest to Lake Balaton after 14.00 on Fridays, nor return in the evening on Sundays.

The water of the lake originates from 40 different, mostly minor water-courses. Only one river, the Zala, flows into the lake. It is mildly alkaline with traces of calcium, magnesium and hydrocarbonates. The water is lost through evaporation and through the canal at Siófok, which links the lake to the Danube. Due to the shallowness of the water the lake often freezes in winter and the ice can grow as thick as 20–25cm. Horse-drawn carts used to cross the frozen lake. Today it can be used for ice-skating and other winter sports.

About 2000 species of plants have been found in the Balaton region, while the number of aquatic or marsh plants is over 500. Different kinds of algae numbering 400 have been discovered. Among the 40 species of fish in the water the most valuable are the pike-perch, and the carp. Bream are also found in large numbers.

There are a great variety of birds living around the lake (over 250 species have been counted). The Tihany Peninsula is particularly rich in bird life. The black-headed gulls are the only kind of gulls that breed in colonies in Hungary. Other kinds mostly migrate over the country or settle on the lake for winter. The northern side of the lake is rich in woodland and is more hilly than the south. The hills, which in some places are near the lake, provide ample opportunites for walking and relaxation. The woods, especially in the Keszthely Hills to the W of the lake, are rich in game.

History. The human history of the region goes back to the Ice Age. Archaeological excavations have found traces of prehistoric people who were here even before the lake came into being as a result of movements in the earth's crust about 20–22,000 years ago. In the first half of the first millennium BC, during the Iron Age, large earthworks were built on the shore. In the second half of that century the Celts settled in the region and tilled the land with iron implements.

The Romans arrived around the beginning of the 1C AD. They called the province Pannonia after the Pannon tribes they found with the Celts. They built roads and over 60 settlements, and utilised a number of springs which they found. It was the Romans who introduced viticulture to the region. Remains of one of the Roman fortifications built in the 3C and 4C can be seen near Fenékpuszta at the SW corner of the lake.

Between the departure of the Romans and the arrival of the Magyars the region was settled by a variety of peoples including the Huns, Lombards, Avars, Franks and Slavs. The name Balaton itself is of Slav origin. The Hungarians brought the techniques of fishing, agriculture and livestock-breeding, and the area became densely populated. Royal estates were developed and the first Hungarian kings gave large tracts of land to the Church. Many churches were built at this time. King Andrew I's foundation deed (1055) of the Benedictine Abbey at Tihany is the earliest surviving written record in the Hungarian language. It is preserved at Pannonhalma Abbey near Győr.

As elsewhere in the country, the Mongol invasion of 1241–42 brought great destruction. Surviving elements of ecclesiatical architecture, however, can be seen at Egregy, Felsőörs and in the crypt of the Abbey church at Tihany. In the following 300 years castles were built or strengthened and towns were redeveloped. By the 16C there were over 100 populated settlements around the lake.

The Turks occupied the whole of the southern shore following the fall of Szigetvár in 1566, while the northern shore became a borderland subject to continual attacks by the Turkish forces. Eventually most of the castles on the northern side were taken by the Turks though some changed hands several times between the Turks and the Habsburgs who were occupying the NW part of the country. Meanwhile the population decreased and many settlements disappeared completely. After the Turks had been finally driven out of Hungary toward the end of the 17C the Habsburg ruler, Leopold I, ordered that the Hungarian castles be blown up. Only Nagyvázsony and Sümeg, near Balaton, escaped this fate and their remains can still be seen today.

In the 18C the population started to increase. Landowners brought in peasants to work on their estates. Hence Germans, Slovaks and Croats settled in the area. Agriculture, wine and fruit growing, and livestock-breeding were the chief occupations. The century was one of Baroque building and decoration. The outstanding remains of this are the church at Tihany, the Festetics mansion

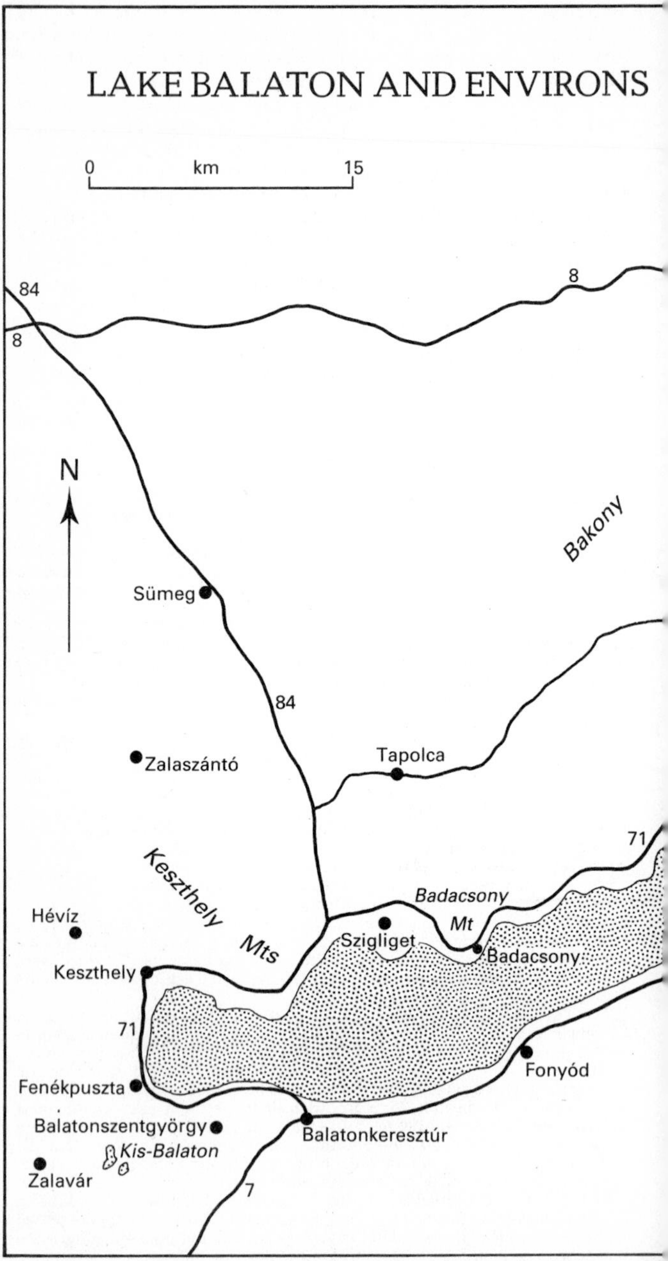
LAKE BALATON AND ENVIRONS
0
km
15
84
8
8
N
Bakony
Sümeg
84
Tapolca
Zalaszántó
71
Keszthely Mts
Badacsony
Mt
Hévíz
Szigliget
Badacsony
Keszthely
71
Fonyód
Fenékpuszta
Balatonszentgyörgy
Balatonkeresztúr
Kis-Balaton
Zalavár
7

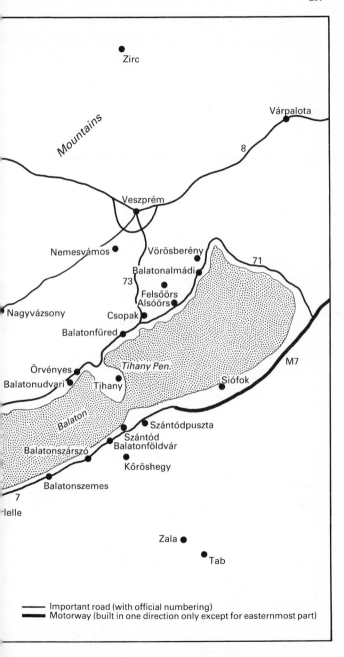

Important road (with official numbering)
Motorway (built in one direction only except for easternmost part)

at Keszthely and the frescoes of the parish church at Sümeg. By 1828, there were 34,000 people living on the shores of the lake.

Although use was made of the medicinal springs around the lake in the 18C it was not until the 19C that the area started to take off in terms of bathing and spa facilities. In 1785 Balatonfüred was officially declared a 'spa' and an official physician was appointed. A pharmacy was established and the spring water was scientifically analysed. Around the same time the progressive aristocrat and landowner, Count György Festetics, had a road built to the warm-water lake fed by the spring at Héviz at the western end of Lake Balaton, where he set up the first bathing establishment. For a long time Balatonfüred and Héviz were the only established centres of bathing in the area.

During the Reform Period of the second quarter of the 19C Balatonfüred became a popular resort for progressive and nationalistic-minded writers, artists and politicians. A theatre was built here in 1831 with the intention of developing dramatic writing and acting in Hungarian, as opposed to more widespread German. Bathing in the open-air became fashionable and in 1836 Baron Miklós Wesselényi, one of the leading reformers of the time, was the first to swim from Tihany to Balatonfüred. The political leader Lajos Kossuth suggested introducing steamboats on the lake and his contemporary István Széchenyi put the idea into effect by helping to found the Balaton Steamship Company. The first Balaton steamer, the 'Kisfaludy', was launched in 1846. It was built in Óbuda but the engine was supplied by the London firm of Penn. Landing-stages were built all around the Lake and the steamship service greatly increased the possibilites for travelling to different parts of the region. Further development was facilitated by the coming of the railways at the end of the century. The construction of the line, which still runs around the Lake near to the water's edge, necessitated the regulation of the shore and the enlargement of the Sió Canal.

In the 19C Lake Balaton had been primarily a playground for the wealthy. During the period of the Republic of Councils in 1919 some attempt was made to open up the resorts to the poorer members of society, but these came to a full stop with the arrival of the Horthy regime. The custom of spending the weekend in the country began in the inter-war period and it was then that catering establishments, boarding houses and hotels were built on a large scale. The road around the lake was also completed and motor traffic began.

Towards the end of World War II, in the course of fighting in the Balaton region, many hotels, summer houses and other buildings were damaged or destroyed. Reconstruction after the war was undertaken with a view to turning Lake Balaton into an area for mass-recreation. Cheap holidays were organised by the trade unions which still run many holiday hotels and camps around the lake. Private tourism in recent decades has led to a growth of privately-run services and facilities. Although not often frequented by English-speaking visitors, Lake Balaton is today a popular attraction for Austrian and German tourists and in an ironic twist, German has become, in some areas around the lake, the first language of communication.

The M7 motorway leads all the way from Budapest to the E of Lake Balaton, a distance of some 100km. It is a good, fast road with two lanes on each carriageway, but due to crowded traffic conditions it is best avoided at the beginning and the end of the weekend in the summer months. Trains from the Southern Railway Station (Déli pályaudvar), above the Buda terminus of metro Line No. 2, run to all major places along both shores of the lake.

A.   The Northern Shore

Road 71. Total distance c 100km. (**Budapest**—M7 turning for Road 71 c100km)—21km *Balatonalmádi* and turning for (2km) **Vörösberény**—6km *Alsóörs* and turning for (3km) **Felsőörs**—2.5km turning for Road 73 and **Csopak**—3.5km **Balatonfüred**—4km **Tihany Peninsula**—2km **Örvényes**—2km **Balatonudvari**—29km **Badacsony**—c 7km **Szigliget**—5km turning for Road 84 and (22km) **Sümeg**—15km **Keszthely**.

The route describes the main sights and places of interest along and near the shore.

Road 71 follows the line of the northern shore. It leaves the M7 motorway at the E end of the Lake in the direction of Balatonfüred. It winds through the villages of Balatonkenese and Balatonfűzfő at the most northerly tip of the lake and then sweeps round towards the SW.

Vörösberény is a small village connected to and 2km from the centre of Balatonalmádi, the next place on Road 70. (Follow the road signposted Veszprém opposite the railway station in the town centre.) The Baroque *Catholic Church* here was built in 1776–79. The interior is decorated with frescoes by Ferenc Bucher. On the left are portraits of the benefactors of the church dressed in costumes of the period and looking out of windows. Another fresco shows the founding of a nunnery in the Veszprém valley. On the ceiling are characteristic Baroque allegories of war and peace and, in the centre, St. Ignatius of Loyola can be seen writing his 'Spiritual Exercises'. Ignatius of Loyola (1491–1556) was the founder of the Jesuit order, which had a religious house in the two-storey, Baroque building next to the church.

Some way up the hill is a good example of a so-called *fortress church* surrounded by a wall. It was originally built around the 13C but has been rebuilt several times, though the Gothic doorway remains. Today it is a Lutheran church.

Felsőörs is 3km N of Alsóörs, which lies on Road 71 between Balatonalmádi and Balatonfüred. The 13C **Provostal church** here, built of pinkish sandstone, is an outstanding relic of Romanesque architecture in Hungary. A notable feature is the squat, square tower on the W façade, with its elaborate 14C door. On the façade there are three windows with semicircular arches divided by columns decorated with double knots. Above the windows the tower becomes octagonal and is crowned with a spire. Restoration took place in the 1960s, which was when the medieval details of the twin windows and some triforia were brought to light. The wooden furnishings inside, including the pulpit which is in peasant Baroque style, date from the 18C. In the porch there is a Romanesque sepulchre gravestone. (The porch is open daily 7.00–19.00. There is a text in English here giving greater details about the church. The interior can be visited on weekdays 10.00–13.00 and 15.00–18.00, and on Sundays 11.00–12.00 and 17.00–18.00. The keys can be obtained at the presbytery nearby.)

The *Local History Collection* is across the road from the church in the Baroque former provost's mansion. It covers the history of the village and local wine-making. (Open 10.00–12.00, 14.00–18.00 except Monday.)

Csopak is 2.5km W of Alsóörs by Road 73 which runs N to **Veszprém** (see Rte 9). At No. 28 Kisfaludy u. here, in an old water mill, there is a *Mill Museum*.

BALATONFÜRED, the major resort on the northern shore of Lake Balaton, is approximately 33km from the M7 and 125km from Budapest.

It is the oldest resort and watering place on the lake with many holiday homes, hospitals and other health and recreation establishments. It is a busy port and has an important shipyard. The curative properties of the local waters have been the subject of several poems. As early as the 18C the Benedictines of Tihany were familiar with and utilised the spring waters and created a bathing house. The town became a spa in the 19C which was when open-air bathing also became popular. Progressive intellectuals during the Reform Period used to congregate in Balatonfüred which was considered a fashionable place by the nobility in general. In the 20C it was recognised that the local spring water was especially useful in the treatment of heart diseases and the Heart Hospital of Balatonfüred became frequented not only by specialists but also by patients from all over the world, as is testified by the row of trees planted by distinguished visitors near the lakeside.

An easy way to see the main sights of the resort is to start at the W end of Blaha Lujza u., by the *Round Church* (Kerek templom). The neo-classical church was designed by Antal Fruman and built between 1841–46. The *Mór Jókai Memorial Museum* is across the junction to the W of the church on the corner of Jókai Mór u. and Honvéd u. Built in early-Eclectic style in 1870 it served as a regular summer house for Mór Jókai (1825–1904), a writer of popular romantic novels who is sometimes described as the Hungarian Dickens. The museum exhibits items relating to the novelist and Lake Balaton. (Open May–Sept 9.00–18.00; Oct 10.00–17.00; closed Tuesdays.) The neo-classical house at *No. 4* Blaha Lujza u. was the summer home of Lujza Blaha (1850–1926) a popular actress and singer known as 'the nation's nightingale'. The local *Tourist Information Office*, Balatontourist Nord, is situated opposite at No. 5 (tel. 42-822).

The centre of the old spa, GYÓGY TÉR, lies at the eastern end of Blaha Lujza u. and has preserved its 19C atmosphere. In the centre is the neo-classical *Kossuth Well*, which was built in 1800. Medicinal spring water can be sampled here. On the E side is the *Heart Hospital*, and to the N the *Trade Union Sanatorium*, which was built in 1802 and which has been the site of many so-called 'Anna Balls' held in July. The first Anna Ball was organised in 1825 by the Szentgyörgyi-Horváth family for their daughter Anna. The family owned the *Horváth House* still standing on the W side of the square (at the end of Blaha Lujza u.). Built in 1798 in Louis XVI style it is today a miners' holiday home. It was in the square that the first permanent Hungarian-language theatre in Transdanubia stood from 1831–73. It was erected in the Reform Period with a view to promoting the use of Hungarian language on stage.

From the S side of the square a park stretches down to the lake. By the lakeside there is a statue of *István Széchenyi* (János Andrássy Kurta, 1941). The quotation on the back reads: 'If a man tired of work sees the water of Lake Balaton, then he feels new blood in his veins.' The promenade of plane trees by the waterside stretches for almost a kilometre. To the W there is a series of statues of people who have had connections with Balatonfüred and a memorial grove of trees planted by various visitors. The tradition started when the Nobel Prize-winning Indian poet Rabindranath Tagore visited Balatonfüred for treatment in 1926. He planted a lime tree and wrote a poem here in memory of his stay. A small statue of the poet and an inscription of the poem can be found at the western end of the promenade which carries his name (Rabindranath Tagore sétány).

On the edge of the water, to the left of the short pier, there are sculptures representing two of Balatonfüred's traditional occupations—'The Fisherman' and 'The Ferryman' (János Pásztor, 1941). From the pier ferry boats run to Tihany and to Siófok on the S shore.

From Balatonfüred excursions can be made to the southern reaches of the Bakonyi Hills. The largest town in the vicinity is Veszprém, some 20km to the NE via Road 73. (For details see Rte 9.)

The **TIHANY PENINSULA** lies a few kilometres to the W of Balatonfüred via Road 71. The 12 sq km of the peninsula reach for more than
5km into the lake, making the shortest passage between the northern
and southern shores.

In 1952 the peninsula was declared a national park and a natural conservation
area was established. Building is now strictly limited. In the NE part of the
nature reserve the rocky walls of the *Óvár* (Old Castle), with rows of cells
carved by Russian Orthodox monks brought here by King Andrew I in the
mid-11C, can be seen. The area is a relic of volcanic activity and some hot
springs still gush up. The *Inner Lake* is in the centre of the peninsula. 700m by
400m, it has been created by precipitation and is 25m higher than Lake Balaton.
The *Outer Lake*, a short distance to the NE, is of a similar size. At one time it
dried up and was used for pasture. Now it has been filled with water and
restored to its original state. Today it is noted for its bird population. There used
to be more than 100 active geysers on the peninsula, which caused the
formation of a series of cones made up of different minerals. The scenic view
from the heights of the peninsula is most spectacular.

The twin-spired **Abbey Church** in Tihany village on the top of the
peninsula is one of Hungary's most significant Baroque art monuments. It was built between 1740 and 1754 and the interior decorative wood-carving is outstanding. The altar, the pulpit, the organ
loft and the sacristy furnishings were all carved by the lay brother
Sebestyén Stuhlhoff who worked for the monastery until his death in
1799. The frescoes, however, were added in the 19C when the
church was being restored and are by Bertalan Székely, Károly Lotz
and Lajos Deák-Ébner. (Open 10.00–18.00 during mass
times.)

The present church stands on the site of a Romanesque church belonging to a
Benedictine abbey founded by King Andrew I in 1055. The foundation deed,
preserved at Pannonhalma Abbey near Győr, although largely in Latin, contains 100 words in Hungarian and is the oldest surviving written source of the
Hungarian language. The *crypt* of the present church is formed from the
remains of the original Romanesque building. Here is the white marble-covered
grave of King Andrew who died in 1060 at Zirc to the N of Veszprém. This is the
only Hungarian royal tomb still in its original location.

The **Tihany Museum** is located next to the church in a former
Benedictine priory. The originally medieval building has been
rebuilt several times and the present Baroque structure dates from
the first half of the 18C. The exhibitions cover the general cultural
history of the region including exhibits of the various craft guilds of
Veszprém county. There is a memorial room to the university teacher
and physicist Loránd Eötvös (1849–1919) who in the 1890s spent a
considerable time in a tent on the ice of Lake Balaton in order to test
his invention, the torsion pendulum, used in geophysical research.
The library, with its Baroque furnishings, is a listed monument. The
lapidarium in the basement contains relics from the Roman and
medieval periods. (Open 10.00–18.00 except Monday.)

A few metres in front of the main façade of the church is Imre
Varga's basalt and aluminium statue of *King Andrew I* entitled 'The
Founder' (1972). A short way to the N, along the pathway which
gives a panoramic view towards Balatonfüred, is the entrance to the
small *Open-Air Ethnographical Museum*. The two main exhibits are
a small-holder's cottage with cart-shed and stable, and the former
Tihany fishermen's guild-house, the only surviving guild-house in
the region of Lake Balaton. Various items of furniture, utensils and
implements are on display in both houses. (Open 10.00–19.00 except
Tuesday; shorter hours in the winter months.)

The *Folk Art House* (Népművészeti ház) nearby is built in local architectural style with an arched porch. Handicraft products can be purchased here. The small, round look-out area at the end of the path is known as *Echo Hill* (Visszhang domb) since in previous times clear sounds could be heard echoed back from the church wall.

The local *Tourist Information Office* is situated on the main road below the church at No. 20 Kossuth Lajos u. This road leads southwards down to the tip of the Peninsula where there is a 'Club Tihany' holiday village run by a Hungarian-Austrian-Danish joint venture. A regular car-ferry service crosses the lake from the tip of the peninsula to Szántód and passenger ferries also ply from here to Balatonfüred nearby on the N side and Balatonföldvár on the S.

This has always been Lake Balaton's busiest crossing point as it is here that the distance between the two shores is narrowest. The present journey takes about 10–15 minutes. Before the days of steamboats oars were generally used, sometimes supplemented by sails if there was a wind. Not all the crossings were calm. In 1818 François Sulpice Beudant, Professor of Mineralogy at the University of Paris, crossed the Lake here in stormy weather and later recorded that 'it took more than two hours to reach the opposite shore. The lake was rough and looked like a real little sea. The boat rolled, we staggered this way and that, and the pale faces, silence and rigidity of most of the women passengers showed that they felt sick. It reminded one of the effects of a sea voyage.'

Road 71 continues westwards around the lake from the peninsula. **Örvényes** is a small village by the roadside a few kilometres to the W. The 18C *Water-mill* here is a valuable monument of peasant architecture and still in good condition and working order. (Turn right just before the village sign.) In the miller's room there is an ethnographical collection of folk art pieces, wood-carvings, pottery, pipes and furniture. (Open 8.00–17.00; Oct–April 8.00–16.00.) On the little hill above the water-mill there stand the ruins of a small Romanesque *chapel* of which the chancel has survived. The protective roof was built in the course of restoration in the late 1950s.

Balantonudvari is the next village, 2km to the W. In the cemetery on the right at the edge of the village there are about 50 unusual white limestone *heart-shaped tombstones* dating from the turn of the 18C–19C which are now listed as art monuments.

The heart motif, which is also popular in folk art, appeared in Hungarian cemeteries at the beginning of the 18C at the same time as it did in Austria and Germany. At first popular among the more well-to-do classes, they later were also used by ordinary people. The tombstones here are irregularly placed with each stone standing at the western end of its grave with the inscription facing W.

A number of roads from this stretch of the lakeside highway (for example from Aszófő, Balatonakali and Zánka) lead N to **Nagyvázsony**, about 15km from the lake. Here, among other things, there is a 15C castle and keep which has survived in relatively good condition. (For details see p 285.)

Road 71 continues along the northern shore passing through several resorts and small villages. Approximately 37km to the W of Balatonfüred it reaches the resort of **Badacsony**, which lies about two thirds of the way towards the end of the lake. The *József Egry Memorial Museum* is on the left just over the railway level-crossing to N of the main road. Egry (1883–1951) was born locally into a poor family, worked as a locksmith and roofer and eventually obtained a scholarship in Paris. Ill at ease, he returned and was admitted to the Academy of Fine Arts but left after two years. He is considered one of the main painters of the Balaton region and his former home and studio here now houses a selection of his paintings. (Open May–Sept 10.00–18.00 except Monday.) A bust of the artist stands in front of the museum (Miklós Borsos, 1976).

The area surrounding Badacsony has traditionally been wine-producing. Small country mansions and even press houses in the vineyards were built in Baroque style. A good example of the latter is the late-18C **Róza Szegedy House** on the hillside above the town. The two-storey building with its colonnaded portico and projecting balcony is a protected art monument and for many years housed a literary museum devoted to the poet Sándor Kisfaludy (1772–1844) who was married to Róza Szegedy. The restaurant just above, nearby, is also a former wine-press. It belonged to the Kisfaludy family. (The buildings are situated some 3km from the town centre and can be reached by following the signs for the Kisfaludy Ház restaurant.) At the time of writing the Róza Szegedy House was closed for renovations and the future plans for the building were not decided. It is advisable, therefore, before making the climb to the house, to enquire at the tourist office in the village at the foot of the hill. At the last turning before the final climb up to the Róza Szegedy House a stone-paved road leads to a *Wine Museum* (Bormúzeum). (Open 20 May–10 October 10.00–15.45 except Monday.)

The volcanic basalt **Badacsony Mountain** is a rare relic of geohistory. Here and there the mountain side consists of huge, tower-like basalt pillars rather like a series of organ pipes. Formerly much damage was done because the basalt was quarried on a large scale. Since the 1960s, however, conservation measures and afforestation have all but covered the scars left by quarrying. The purplish-blue and the strange shapes of the basalt mountain side can be clearly seen from Road 71 to the W of Badacsony.

Szigliget is approximately 7km W along the road from Badacsony. The area used to be an island and its name is a compound of Hungarian for island (sziget) and grove (liget). The surrounding landscape is beautiful and the village is picturesque. The *castle ruins* on top of the hill date from the 13C. The steep hillside and swampy surroundings kept it well protected and the Turks were never able to capture it. During the Turkish wars the Hungarian Balaton fleet was moored at Szigliget. After the Turks, however, the castle lost its significance and in the early 18C the Habsburgs had it demolished along with a whole series of fortifications throughout Hungary for fear that they could be used as bases in an anti-imperial revolt.

The village of Szigliget stretches from the SW side of Castle Hill. The *Esterházy Summer Mansion* in Fő tér was built in the 18C and rebuilt in neo-classical style in the 19C. Today it is a holiday home for writers. Its 10-hectare park is a nature conservation area with a botanical collection of over 500 kinds of ornamental trees and shrubs. (Permission to visit can be obtained from the home.) In the square in front of the mansion stands László Marton's statue *Reading Woman* (1925).

Kossuth Lajos u., which runs S from the square, contains most of the former outbuildings of the estate. The buildings, with their thatched roofs and porches, have been well preserved and constitute an attractive architectural ensemble.

Tapolca, 10km to the N, lies in the centre of a basin surrounded by a wreath of volcanic hills. The road via Hegymagas and Raposka passes by one of the most outstanding of these, *Mount St. George* (Szent-györgy-hegy). Fields, vineyards and orchards cover the slopes and then, above the woods, rises a row of basalt towers. The last eruption created a separate cone on the 414m high summit. Tapolca (pop. 18,000) is the centre of bauxite mining in the Bakony region. Hungary is generally not rich in mineral resources but it is one of the main sources in Europe for bauxite, the raw material for aluminium. The chief domestic source of the ore is the Bakony hills. There is an *Aluminium Industry Exhibition* at No. 2 Batsányi tér, which deals with the history of bauxite mining in the region and has a collection of minerals. (Open weekdays 9.00–15.00.)

One of the main attractions of Tapolca used to be its *Lake Cave*, but mining has caused the water to disappear. However the cave can still be visited and is open all year round except on Sundays (entrance in Batthyány tér).

At Balatonederics, 5km to the W of Szigliget, Road 71 is joined by Road 84 from Sopron. **SÜMEG** lies 22km to the N along this fast, flat road. In the 18C the bishops of Veszprém lived here and enriched the town. Today, although it is only a small town (pop. 7000) which has lost its former cultural and economic significance, it has some unique attractions.

The **Castle** standing on top of a 270m limestone hill dominates the surrounding landscape and is an imposing sight on the approaches to the town, rising like a small volcano in a plain. The fortress dates from the 13C and was later strengthened during the Ottoman wars. The Turks were unable to capture the castle but a fire in 1714 caused serious damage and the structure later fell into decline. Reconstruction was undertaken in the early 1960s. There is an exhibition about the history of the castle inside the walls.

The Baroque mid-18C building of the former bishop's stables, by the car park below the steps leading up to the castle, has been restored and contains a *Saddlery Museum*. (Open 8.00–11.30, 14.00–17.00.)

The **Parish Church** in Deák Ferenc tér was built in 1756–57. Unremarkable as a building it is a significant monument because of the *interior frescoes* which cover every inch of the walls and ceiling and which were painted by the Austrian artist, Franz Anton Maulbertsch (1757–58), somewhat dilapidated now, they are still counted among the loveliest series of Baroque frescoes in Hungary and were painted over the two years following the construction of the church.

Maulbertsch's skill in composition is well displayed here. The complex scheme of iconography in the paintings on the vaulted ceiling ranges from the Annunciation to the advent of the Holy Spirit. The Ascension of Christ is depicted on the main altar, whilst the patriarchs and symbolic representations of the Victorious and Suffering Church can be seen on both sides. The recessed side chapels have frescoed walls adorned with paintings following the iconographical theme of the ceiling.

F.A. Maulbertsch (1724–96) lived and worked in Hungary for almost four decades. He decorated dozens of churches and mansions and painted over 20 large altarpieces, but the Sümeg frescoes are considered among his finest.

The mid-18C single-storey Baroque building at No. 10 Deák Ferenc u. to the rear of the church was the birthplace of Vince Ramassetter (1806–78) a local man of commerce who donated much of his wealth to the town. The parallel street to the S is named after him and at the top of it, on Kossuth Lajos u., there is a statue of him by János Istók.

One of Franz Anton Maulbertsch's frescoes in the parish church at Sümeg.

Deák Ferenc u. leads up and across Kossuth Lajos u. to SZENT ISTVÁN TÉR at the foot of Castle Hill. The *Kisfaludy Memorial Museum* is at the NE corner of the square. It occupies the birthplace of the poet Sándor Kisfaludy (1772–1844) whose bust stands in the square at the lower end of the park area. The museum includes items relating to the poet and his younger brother, Károly, a dramatist and poet (1788–1830). (Open May–Sept 10.00–18.00; Sept–April 10.00–14.00; closed Mondays.)

At the top end of the square is the former *Episcopal Palace*, built in Baroque style between 1748 and 1753. Today it is a students' hostel. The former *Franciscan Church* nearby was originally built in 1649 and extended in 1720 by Ferenc Witner. A notable feature is the

carved Baroque altar, the work of Ferenc Richter, a Carmelite monk
from Győr (1743). The wooden *pietà* (1653) in the centre has been an
object of adoration over the centuries. The primitive paintings at the
rear of the church tesify to the various miracles attributed to the
'Sümegi Szűz Mária' (Blessed Virgin of Sümeg).

Türje (16km to the W of Sümeg) has a church dating from the first
half of the 13C. The façade has preserved its original form though the
church was remodelled in the 18C. The interior has a Gothic
tabernacle and some Baroque elements. The altarpiece and the
frescoes of the chapel are the work of István Dorfmeister (c 1760).

KESZTHELY (pop. 23,000) is situated at the western end of Lake
Balaton just under 70km from Balatonfüred on Road 71. (From
Sümeg an alternative route to Road 84 is via Zalaszántó which has a
13C restored Gothic church.)

The present main street of Keszthely, Kossuth Lajos u., runs along the line of a
former road built by the Romans who constructed a fortification (*Valcum*) a few
kilometres to the S near the present-day village of Fenékpuszta. In the 16C the
Ottoman armies were unable to capture the fortified church and monastery of
Keszthely but they did sack the town. In 1739 the Festetics family acquired
Keszthely and they retained extensive property and estates here until 1945.
One of the family, György Festetics (1755–1819), was an enlightened aristocrat
who did much for the town. In 1797 he founded here the first agricultural
academy in Europe, the Georgikon. He established a large, originally public,
library, had ships built, and began the development of nearby Hévíz into a spa.

The **Festetics Mansion**, a short distance to the N of the town centre at
the end of Kossuth Lajos u., is one of the largest and certainly one of
the most impressive mansions in Hungary. The Baroque palace was
constructed in stages in the second half of the 18C, though alterations in the 1880s gave it its present form. Today it houses a music
school and functions as a conference centre and venue for orchestral
and chamber concerts. The grounds, however, and the southern
wing are open to the public. Apart from the items of furniture,
materials relating to the activities of the Festetics family and a
collection of hunting trophies exhibited in the various rooms, the
principal sight is the *Helikon Library* which was established by
György Festetics in the 1790s. The carved oak furniture is the work of
a local cabinet maker, János Kerbl. Local craftsmen were also used to
bind the original collection of mainly legal, economic and agricultural books in leather. At first the library was open to the public,
but later entry was restricted and then it was closed, although the
work of cataloguing proceeded. In 1948 it was nationalised and today
its 80,000 volumes belong to the National Széchenyi Library. It was
declared a public monument library in 1974. (Open 10.00–18.00; July
and Aug 9.00–19.00; Oct–March 9.00–16.30; closed Mondays.)

The statue of *György Festetics* in front of the mansion is the work of Lajos
Lukácsy. On the right-hand wall in the gateway of the S wing there is a tablet to
the memory of the English doctor, scientist and traveller, *Richard Bright* (1789–
1859) who stayed here as a guest in 1815 and was the first to make an accurate
description of Lake Balaton in English. The façade facing the grounds at the
rear is decorated with horses, in the centre, and, above the S wing, with statues
of Ceres and Neptune, symbolising the horse breeding, agricultural and ship-
building activities of the owners.

Europe's first agricultural institute, the Georgikon, was established
in 1797 by György Festetics and functioned until 1848. The three-
year course in agricultural science included both theoretical and
practical studies. Most of the buildings of the institute's model farm

have survived and in 1972 they were opened as the *Georgikon Farm Museum* (entrance at No. 67 Bercsényi u.) The exhibitions of the museum include the history of the Georgikon and the later University of Agriculture, wine-making in the 19C, farm implements and farming practices from the 18C to the present century. (Open April–Oct 10.00–17.00, Sun 10.00–18.00, closed Mondays.)

The Gothic **Parish Church** on Fő tér in the centre of the town was originally built in the 1380s for Franciscan monks by the Palatine István Lackffy. The aisleless church was fortified in 1550 in the face of the Turkish advance and later rebuilt in Baroque style in 1747. It belonged to the Premonstratensians in the 19C and in 1878 further neo-Gothic alterations were made and the present tower erected. The stained-glass windows are the work of Miksa Róth (1896). Despite these many additions and alterations the church remains an impressive monument of medieval Hungary particularly in view of the discovery in 1974 of fine 14C and 15C *frescoes* on the chancel walls. Excavations have revealed the foundations walls of an earlier romanesque church. They can be seen adjoining the S side of the present church.

Kossuth Lajos u. runs southwards from Fő tér. Approximately 1km along here stands the neo-Baroque building of the **Balaton Museum**. It was designed by Dénes György and built in 1928 for the museum which was founded at the turn of the century. The exhibitions cover the general geological and ethnographic history and way of life of the Balaton region. There is also a collection of Roman and medieval stonework, and a display of paintings of the area. (Open 10.00–18.00 except Monday.)

Fenékpuszta (7.5km to the S on Road 71) used to be the Roman settlement of *Valcum*. In the 4C a large fortress was built to protect the busy town. Some of the remains have been unearthed and the surroundings have been laid out as a park.

Zalavár is 20km to the SW of Keszthely via Sármellék. The first Hungarian King, Stephen I, founded a Benedictine abbey here in the 11C. It was built in honour of St. Hadrian, to whom an earlier church had been dedicated. The area had previously been the 9C seat of the Slav prince, Pribina. The foundations of the nave, two aisles and apse of the basilica have been excavated.

Hévíz, 8km to the NW of Keszthely, is one of the oldest spas in Hungary. It has the largest lake in Europe with natural thermal curative water (50,000 sq m). The temperature, even in winter, rarely falls below 30°C, thus bathing is possible all the year round. Bathing, medicinal and recreational establishments have been erected on and around the lakeside. To the E at *Egregy*, which is today part of Hévíz, there is a small 13C Romanesque church with a square chancel and stone spire. The thatched white building of the *Gyöngyösi Csárda* some way to the N on the road towards Zalaszántó was built in 1728 and is one of the few genuine 'highwaymen's inns' remaining in Hungary.

B. The Southern Shore

Road 7. Total distance 70km. (**Budapest**—M7 106km **Siófok**)—Road
7—12km **Szántódpuszta**—c 5km turning for (3km) **Kőröshegy**, and
(14km) road to **Tab** and **Zala**—7km **Balatonszárszó**—5km
Balatonszemes—32km **Balatonkeresztúr**—2.5km turning for Road
76 and (4km) **Balatonszentgyörgy**.

The Southern Shore of Lake Balaton stretches for approximately
70km and consists almost entirely of a string of holiday resorts. Road
7 runs from Siófok to Balatonkeresztúr. The railway line was originally constructed in the 1860s and still runs close to the lakeside
linking all the towns and villages along the shore. The sandy beaches
and shallow, warm water of the lake have led to the development of
the resorts making the southern shore primarily an area of recreation.
However, there are a number of monuments, museums and other
places of interest in the vicinity of the lakeside.

Siófok (pop. 24,000) lies near the eastern end of the lake at the end
of the M7 motorway 106km from Budapest. It is the largest resort on
Lake Balaton and in the summer its hotels, guest-houses and
entertainment facilities cater for visitors numbering many times more
than its permanent population.

The *József Beszédes Water Management Museum* (Beszédes
József Vízgazdálkodási Múzeum) is situated at No. 2 Sió u. near the
Sió Bridge. József Beszédes (1787–1852) was a water-engineer who
planned much of the drainage and regulation of the waters of the
lake. The exhibitions cover the history of Hungarian hydro-
engineering, the Danube and the control of Lake Balaton. (Open
May–Oct 9.00–13.00 and 14.00–18.00, closed Mondays.)

Imre Kálmán (1882–1953) was born in Siófok, the son of a wealthy
corn dealer, and later studied at the Academy of Music in Budapest.
The première of his first operetta, 'The Mongol Invasion', took place
at the Gaiety Theatre in Budapest in 1908. In the inter-war period he
was the leading composer of Hungarian operettas, which were an
extremely popular form of entertainment at the time. 'The Csárdás
Queen' is his most popular operetta and it has been peformed
throughout Europe. There is an *Imre Kálmán Memorial House* at No.
5 Kálmán Imre sétány, which is devoted to his life and works. In the
same street, at No. 10, there is an *Exhibition of Minerals of the
Carparthian Basin* (Kárpát Medence Ásványai Kiállítás). It is a
private collection but can be viewed by the public. (Open 9.00–19.00
except Monday.)

Szántódpuszta is situated on Road 7 approximately 12km to the W
of Siófok. The collection of farm buildings here is the largest
ensemble of vernacular architecture preserved as a museum where
the buildings are on their original site. It comprises farm labourers'
dwellings, stables, animal houses, workshops, a large wine cellar and
a small church. The 30 buildings were constructed in the 18C and
19C, the earliest dating from the time when the estate used to belong
to the Benedictines of Tihany. Today it is a tourist and cultural centre
where activities of various kinds are organised.

The former servants' quarters by the car park is today a tourist information
office. The mansion to the left (1716) houses temporary exhibitions. Permanent
exhibitions inside the grounds include folk handicrafts of South Transdanubia,
the history of the Szántód ferry, local lace-making from Balatonendréd, the
agricultural history of the farmstead, regional fauna and flora, and the work of
the poet Ádám Pálóczi Horváth (1760–1820) who lived on the estate for a time.

There is an aquarium, wine-cellar, blacksmiths, bakery and other workshops. The Baroque St. Christopher (Kristóf) Chapel which stands on a small hill overlooking the settlement, dates from 1735. Cart, horse and pony rides are available and the visitors' facilities include two 'csárda' (inns), a café, wine bar and folk shop. (Open 16 April–30 May, 9.00–17.00; June–Aug 9.00–19.00; 1 Sept–14 Oct, 9.00–17.00; 15 October–15 April, 8.00–16.30, Sun 8.00–12.00; closed Mondays.)

Kőröshegy is 3km S of Road 7 along the road signposted Kaposvár at the W end of Szántód. The Gothic Roman Catholic Church here dates from the 15C and has survived almost undamaged. The aisleless church was originally built for the Franciscans. There are peasant carvings on the walls of the long chancel. The altarpiece depicting the Crucifixion is believed to be the work of the Viennese artist Hofbauer. A noteworthy feature is the small carved rose window above the Gothic doorway.

The road through Kőröshegy leads S to Kereki and Pusztaszemes. Pusztaszemes is a pretty village, characteristic in that it stretches for some distance along the length of the road with the houses built individually at right-angles to it. 14km S of Kőröshegy there is a junction for **Tab**, c 4km to the E. In the village, on a small hill rising to the left of the main road, there is a Baroque Church, dating from 1762, which has frescoes painted on its dome by István Dorfmeister. The small memorial tablet on the right-hand wall inside was placed there by Poles who fled from their country to Hungary in 1939.

Just before Tab there is a junction for the village of **Zala**, 3km to the N. Here the painter Mihály Zichy (1827–1906) used to have a country house which is today a Zichy Memorial Museum. The artist spent most of his life in Russia as the Tsar's court painter. He is known throughout Europe for his historical paintings and book-illustrations. The museum exhibits some of his works, documents referring to his life and work, his library and a selection of his collection of Asiatic objects (furniture, carpets, vases, weapons et al.) (Open 10.00–18.00; Nov–March 10.00–16.00; closed Mondays.)

Balatonszárszó is on Road 7 by the lake, approximately half-way along the southern shore. It was here that the working-class poet Attila József committed suicide under wheels of a train on 3 December 1937 at the age of 32. He had spent the last few weeks of his life in the village trying to recuperate from a bout of depression. The former Magda Pension, where he was staying, has been turned into the Attila József Memorial Museum (No. 7 József Attila u., to the right just before the railway crossing.) The exhibition covers the poet's literary career and his last days in the village. A guide to the exhibition in English giving biographical notes and translations of his poems is available. (Open 10.00–18.00; Nov–March 10.00–14.00; closed Mondays.)

The Postal Museum (Postamúzeum) at **Balatonszemes** is situated on the S side of Road 7, 5km to the W of Balatonszárszó. The Baroque building used to serve as a mail-coach station in the 19C. Today it exhibits old postal equipment, uniforms and stamps. Old mail coaches are in the courtyard. (Open June–Sept 10.00–18.00 except Monday.)

Fő u. runs northwards from the main road a few metres to the W of the museum. The Roman Catholic Church, which is 200m down this road, was originally built in the 15C in Gothic style and some details from this period remain. An interesting feature is the decorated tabernacle in the chancel wall which dates from 1517.

The village of **Balatonkeresztúr** lies at the SW end of Lake Balaton approximately 60km from Siófok on Road 7. The *Baroque Church* which stands on raised ground at the main cross-roads was designed by Kristóf Hofstädter, the architect of the Festetics estates, and built between 1753 and 1758. The rich interior frescoes illustrating Biblical scenes which decorate the church from top to bottom were painted in the 1760s. The artist is unknown, but the style clearly follows that of the Austrian painter, Franz Anton Maulbertsch, who produced the remarkable series of frescoes in the parish church at Sümeg (see above). Portraits of members of the Festetics family are included among the frescoes. Krisfóf Festetics is pictured to the left of the altar and at the rear of the church, also on the left, is his wife Judit Szegedi. The church is a listed art monument and was beautifully restored in 1985.

Balatonszentgyörgy is a small village a few kilometres to the W on Road 76, which joins Road 7 a short distance beyond Balatonkeresztúr. Csillagvár u., which leads off the main road at rightangles, has some interesting features. At the junction there is an unusual *stone crucifix*, with Christ shown on both sides of the cross. The *Holy Trinity Statue* in the churchyard on the left dates from 1616. In front of No. 52 there is a stone cross with a relief of St. George dating from 1800 and further on the right by the calvary there is a statue of St. Wendelin from 1900.

The *Peasant House* at No. 68 on the left dates from 1836 and is characteristic of the folk architecture of the region. Today it functions as a small folk museum. (Open 15 April–31 May, 9.00–17.00; June– Aug 9.00–19.00; 1 September–11 October, 9.00–17.00; closed Mondays.)

At a fork in the road some distance beyond the museum there stands a *cross* erected in 1907 to mark the departure of 22 members of the village who emigrated to the United States. Their names are inscribed on a tablet. The main road to the right of the cross and then left at the first signposted junction leads to the so-called *Csillagvár* (Star Castle) a former hunting lodge built in the early 1820s in early-Romantic style for the Festetics family. The name derives from the star-shaped ground plan and the fact that for a long time it was thought to have originally been some kind of border-fortress. Today it is open in the summer months as a museum devoted to the lifestyle of the warriors of the border fortresses which were situated on the boundaries of Turkish-occupied Hungary in the 16C and 17C.

Little Balaton (Kis-Balaton) is the name given to the 3500 hectares of marshland at the SW tip of Lake Balaton which used to be the large western bay of the lake. Gradually sand and clay brought by the river Zala filled up the gulf and the area is now mostly covered with reeds. In 1949 approximately half of the area was declared a nature conservation zone, with a view to protecting its fauna and flora and in particular its rare species of waterfowl and other birds. Ornithologists have found more than 80 breeds here including the white egret, cormorants, grey spoonbills, black-headed gulls and various breeds of geese. The conservation area can only be visited with special permission from the National Office for Nature Conservation and Environmental Protection (Országos Környezet-és Természetvédelmi Hivatal) at No. 25 Arany János u., Budapest, V (1327-371).

Little Balaton can be approached from **Vörs**, 5km SW of Balatonszentgyörgy. The 19C peasant house at No. 17 Dózsa György u. here has been transformed into a *museum* covering local folk art and the neighbouring conservation area. (Open April–Oct 10.00–18.00.) The village also has a small *Museum of Fire-Fighting services* at No. 1 Flórián tér. (Open April–Oct 10.00–12.00 and 14.00–18.00 except Monday.)

8 Székesfehérvár

Although **Székesfehérvár** (pop. 113,000) is often by-passed by foreign visitors, the M7 motorway cutting the town off the Budapest–Balaton route, there are quite a number of historical monuments worth visiting. This pleasant, large provincial town is only 60km from Budapest and can easily be reached either via the M7 motorway or by train from the Southern Railway Station.

Tourist Information: Albatours, 6 Szabadság tér (22/12-494).

Rail Station: Béke tér. 1 hour by Express from the Southern Railway Station, Budapest.

Bus Station: Piac tér. 1 1/2 hours from Engels tér, Budapest.

Post Office: 16 Kossuth u. on the corner with Petőfi u.

Police: 12 Dózsa György tér.

History. Székesfehérvár was the second most important town after Esztergom during the early years of the Hungarian state. Its foundations were laid by Prince Géza when he built a palace and a church dedicated to St. Peter here. Géza was buried in this Byzantine-style cathedral in 997. His son, King Stephen I, also made Székesfehérvár one of his royal seats. In fact because of its more central position Fehérvár (in Latin known as *Alba Regia*) became more important than Esztergom. Its name (White Castle) derived from the glittering white limestone church built by Géza which stood on a hill top and was visible for miles around. The town was situated at the meeting point of three large areas of marshland which were crossed with great difficulty. This provided a defensive ring for centuries which even the Mongols were not able to penetrate.

Stephen had a palace built for himself at Székesfehérvár and also a splendid cathedral, where in 1031 he buried his son, Imre, who had died young in a hunting accident. Stephen himself was also buried here in 1038. According to contemporary accounts, the cathedral, which was built by Italian architects, was a masterpiece. Its walls and pillars were of limestone, its patterned floor of marble, and its altars decorated with gold, silver and precious stones. The crown jewels and the national archives were kept here for centuries. Hungarian kings were crowned, married and buried here until the 16C. The Turks captured the town in 1543 and during their occupation the royal tombs were sacked and the coronation church blown up. Only the foundation walls remain today.

When the Turks were driven out of Hungary in 1688 Székesfehérvár was a deserted heap of ruins. Rebuilding was slow but took off in the 18C after the town became the seat of an episcopal see. Further expansion occurred in the 19C after the marshes had been drained and the Sávíz river had been diverted.

Serious damage occurred during battles towards the end of World War II, but post-war reconstuction has turned Székesfehérvár and its region into a major industrial area. Among the many local industrial enterprises is the Videoton computer, radio and televison company which has its own football team of European fame.

The route begins in SZABADSÁG TÉR in the centre of the town and then explores the areas to the N and S of the centre.

The **Town Hall** stands on the S side of the square at No. 6 and is in two parts. The two-storey right side dates from 1690, though it was restored in Louis XVI style towards the end of the following century. The main entrance is on the left of the building above which is a balcony with a stone balustrade with statues of Justice and Prudence.

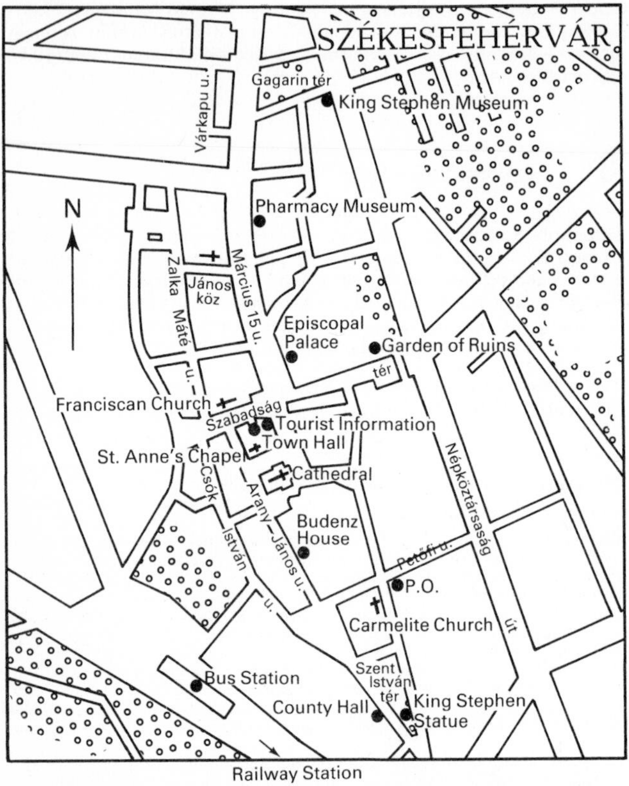

Railway Station

Above the richly decorated balcony door the orb, crown and imperial eagle can be seen. The three-storey wing, to the left, is the former Zichy Mansion and was built at the end of the 18C. The local *Tourist Information Office*, Albatours, is on the ground floor of this building.

Moving round the square in a clockwise direction, the equestrian statue by the right-hand end of the Town Hall is a *monument to the Tenth Hussars* (1939), a local regiment, and is the work of the sculptor Pál Pátzay. The monument at the W end of the square is a memorial to those killed in 1944–45. The corner house with a decorated oriel window, to the right of this monument at No. 1 Jókai u., is the so-called *Hiemer House* which formerly belonged to Mihály Hiemer, the town magistrate. The building was reconstructed in the late 18C. In the niche on the façade there is a statue of St. Sebastian. The main façade of the former *Franciscan church* overlooks Zalka Máté u. which joins Szabadság tér opposite the Hussars' memorial. The church was constructed in provincial Baroque style between 1720 and 1742, though the tower was built to its present height in the 1860s. The Esterházy coat of arms can be seen above the main entrance and there is also a niche on the façade with a statue of St. Francis. On the side of the church overlooking Szabadság tér there is an aluminium copy of Jánus Fadrusz's 1892 'Christ on the Cross'. The building adjoining the back of the church (No. 9 Szabadság tér) is the *former Franciscan House* and was built in 1741–43. Above the wall-well on the corner there is a *relief* by Ferenc Medgyessy depicting battle scenes. It was placed here in 1938 to commemorate the 250th anniversary of the liberation of Székesfehérvár from the Turks.

In the centre of the square is the round *National Orb* (1938), the work of the sculptor Béla Ohmann. The inscription around it refers to the freedom of the city being granted by King Stephen.

The **Episcopal Palace** stands in the northern section of the square at No. 10. The two-storey building in Louis XVI style and overlooking three streets was built in 1800–01. In the middle of the tympanum there is the Baroque coat of arms of the bishop. The *Medieval Garden of Ruins* (Romkert) lies behind the Bishop's Palace (access to the right of the palace from the eastern section of Szabadság tér). Here are the remains of the medieval cathedral and other buildings. Once the most important church in Hungary, 37 kings were crowned and 17 buried here. The Turks used it as a gunpowder store and during a siege in 1601 it was blown up and reduced to ruins. The stones were used during the building of the Bishop's Palace at the beginning of the 19C and very little of the original church remains, though the original ground plan has been established. Excavations in 1848 revealed the tombs of Béla III and his wife, which were taken to Budapest and can still be seen in the Matthias Church on Castle Hill. There are plans to establish a national memorial site here by 1996, the 1100th anniversary of the Hungarian Conquest.

The *Stonework Museum* in the garden contains the richly orna-mented Roman sarcophagus that was found in 1803 and is believed to contain the remains of King Stephen. The lapidarium exhibits remains of Romanesque, Gothic and Renaissance carvings found during excavations of the cathedral. (Open April–Oct 9.00–17.00 except Monday.)

Stephen I died in Székesfehérvár on 15 August 1038. He was canonised 45 years later, and for centuries he has been revered as the founder of the Hungarian state. In fact he carried on the work begun by his father Prince Géza, the great-grandson of Árpád, who began the process of Christianising the Hungarians and consolidating Hungarian rule in the Carpathian Basin.

After Géza's death in 997, Stephen was helped by Bavarian knights to crush a pagan insurrection. He later received an apostolic cross and crown from Pope Sylvester II and was crowned King of Hungary on Christmas Day in the year 1000 at Esztergom, his birthplace on the Danube. The importance of the coronation was that it signified the entry of Hungary into the family of European nations as an independent entity, and one not tied to the Holy Roman Empire.

Stephen carried through the conversion of the nation. He established dioceses, archdioceses and abbeys, which he reinforced with lavishly endowed monastic foundations. He promoted agriculture and safeguarded private prop-erty and continued with his father's foreign policy of non-interference and independence. Good relations with the West were helped by the fact that in 996 he had married a Bavarian princess, Gizella. His brother-in-law, Henry II, was a German King and also, from 1013, Holy Roman Emperor.

The cult of Stephen was based on his Christianity, his unification of the nation, and his alleged wisdom. In his 'Admonitions', written as recommen-dations to his son Imre, he says: 'Kings that have tolerance, rule; but the intolerant ones are tyrants in governing ... Have moderation, so you will never punish or blame any person beyond measure'. He also had some ideas about the multinational state which would be progressive in many countries even today: 'Immigrants are of great benefit ... They bring with them different tongues and customs, different skills and weapons, and all that is an ornament to the country ... A nation with but one tongue and one custom is feeble and frail'.

Some of Stephen's activities, however, are a little difficult to describe as Christian. When Imre, his only son, died early after a hunting accident, it left open the question of succession. Vászoly, the last male descendant of the House of Árpád, was a pagan and a supporter of the old order. To prevent him from asserting his rights, Vászoly was blinded and molten lead poured into his ears. Stephen then named his son-in-law, Peter Orseolo, as his heir.

Over the centuries 20 August, the date of Stephen's canonisation, was celebrated every year with a national holiday and processions. The last great fling of the Stephen cult before the Second World War occurred in 1938 on the occasion of the 900th anniversary of his death. Commemorative events were organised on a grand scale throughout the country. After the war the religious cult was officially discouraged as part of the anti-Church policies of the time, which were given support by the fact that ultra-conservative and right-wing forces had often used the Stephen cult for political purposes. 20 August, although still a national holiday, was now celebrated as Constitution Day, recalling the date when Hungary's new constitution was adopted in 1949. In recent years, however, a change has been taking place following the reconciliation between Church and State, and in 1988 the 950th anniversary of Stephen's death was commemorated with great pomp and many public celebrations (see p 179).

The route now continues along MÁRCIUS 15 UTCA which runs northwards from Szabadság tér. The Baroque **Church of St. John of Nepomuk**, on the left, is the most prominent building in the street. It was originally built in 1745–51 for the Jesuits and their coat of arms can be seen above the gate. The church was subsequently used by the Pauline order, the Germans of the inner city and eventually by the Cistercians. Significant features are the finely carved pulpit and the frescoes by C.F. Sambach of the Viennese Academy of Art. The former Jesuit and later Cistercian House is to the right of the church at *No. 6.* The Baroque building was designed by P. Hatzinger and built between 1744 and 1763. It today belongs to the local County Museum Directorate but there is no exhibition here.

Behind the church at No. 1 Bartók Béla tér there is the *István Csók Gallery* where temporary exhibitions of paintings are held. (Open 10.00–18.00; closed first Monday in the month.) The gallery is named after the painter István Csók (1865–1961) who was born in the local Fejér county. (To reach the square take János köz at the side of the church, then turn right along Zalka Máté u.)

The *Black Eagle* (Fekete Sas) *Pharmacy Museum* is at No. 9 Március 15 u. on the other side of the street from the church. The exhibition here presents the history of the former Jesuit pharmacy which moved into this building in 1745. Note the Baroque fittings and Empire counter. The name was given to the pharmacy by a certain Ferenc Valter who bought it from the Jesuits after the suppression of the order in 1773. It functioned as a pharmacy until 1971. (Open 10.00–18.00 except Monday.)

Gagarin tér, with its floral clock, is further along Március 15 u. on the right-hand side. Just before the square, at the beginning of Várkapu u. which leads off the street to the left, there is a statue of *György Varkocs* by Dezső Erdey. Varkocs was a captain of the castle who died in 1543 while defending Székesfehérvár from the armies of Sultan Süleyman II.

The *King Stephen Museum* (István Király Múzeum) can be found at No. 3 Gagarin tér at the SW corner of the square. There are permanent exhibitions dealing with Fejér county from prehistoric to Roman times and the 1000 years of Székesfehérvár. The modern building was constructed for the museum in 1929. (Open 10.00–18.00 except Monday.)

The early classical building with the ornamented oriel window and richly decorated reliefs at *No. 13* Március 15 u., on the corner of Gagarin tér, received its present form c 1810 though there is mention of the building in documents as early as 1727. The *Vörösmarty*

Theatre, on the left of Március 15 u. just beyond Gagarin tér was originally built in Eclectic style in 1872–74. However, serious fire damage in 1945 necessitated reconstruction and although the façade has retained its Eclectic form the interior was completely refashioned. The early classical building of the *Velence Hotel*, beyond the theatre, is believed to have been designed by Mihály Pollack. The first owner of the building was Tamás Schmidegg whose name appears on maps of 1828. In the mid-19C it became the property of Jenő Zichy a noted traveller and researcher of the Caucasus, and then, from the end of the century to 1945, it functioned as the Hungarian King Hotel. The female figure holding a palm branch, which can be seen at the end of Március 15 u. in the southern part of Dózsa György tér, is the *Liberation Monument* and was made by Sándor Mikus.

The route now returns to Szabadság tér and proceeds S along ARANY JÁNOS UTCA which runs from the right-hand side of the Town Hall.

A short distance along here, set back a little from the street, is the only remaining medieval building in Székesfehérvár, **St. Anne's Chapel**. This little Gothic chapel was built c 1470 though there have been later additions. The tower, for example, was added in the 18C and on the façade, although the gate is Gothic, the rose window above it is actually 19C. During the Turkish occupation the chapel was used as a prayer house and the remains of some Turkish paintings can be seen inside. The Baroque altar is early 18C. In front of the chapel stands a statue by Béla Ohmann of *Domonkos Kál-máncsehi* (died 1501), a humanist bishop who originated from a peasant family and rose to be a Chief Justice. From 1474–95 he was Provost of Székesfehérvár. In his left hand is the founding document of the St. Anne Chapel and his right hand is resting on a model of the chapel. Kálmáncsehi is depicted looking up at **St. Stephen's Cathedral**.

The church was originally built in the 13C, but later rebuildings have left it in a basically Baroque style. King Béla IV was crowned here in 1235 and in the Middle Ages the church was known as the Peter-Paul Church. It was used as a mosque in Turkish times, after which it was in the hands of the Jesuits. In 1702 Viennese architects restored the building, then at the end of the 1750s it was rebuilt in Baroque style. The towers were heightened in 1848–66 and further restoration work has taken place in the 20C.

The statues on the Baroque façade are of SS. Stephen, Ladislas and Imre. Above the gate the coat of arms of Székesfehérvár can be seen. The ceiling frescoes inside were painted in 1768 by Johann Ignác Cymbal, an Austrian artist who worked a great deal in Transdanubia. The chancel and the main altar were designed by his compatriot, F.A. Hillebrandt, the court architect of Maria Theresa who played a major role in the reconstruction of the Royal Palace at Buda in the 18C. The white statues on either side are of SS. Elizabeth and Theresa. The main altarpiece was painted in 1775 by Fischer Vinzenz of the Vienna Academy of Art. It depicts Stephen in Hungarian dress offering the crown to the Virgin after the death of his son Imre. Mary is shown as she used to be depicted on old Hungarian coins. In the paving in front of the cathedral there is an outline of the foundations of an even earlier church which stood on this site and which was possibly built in the 10C.

No. 10 Arany János u. was built in its present Louis XVI style in 1790 as a dwelling house. Today it belongs to the National Inspectorate of Historical Monuments and its showroom has occasional exhibitions on related themes. (Open May–Oct 10.00–16.00 except Monday.) No. 12 next door is the so-called *Budenz House*, named after József Budenz (1836–92) a Hungarian linguist of German origins who lived here in the late 1850s and taught at the Cistercian 'gimnázium' in Székesfehérvár. The present Copf-style building dates from 1781 as indicated by the year on the keystone of the gate, though it was built on the site of a medieval dwelling house. A 13C well was found in the cellar here in the 1960s. Today it houses the collection of 19C and 20C fine and applied art which belonged to the art historian Ervin Ybl (1890–1965) and which he left to the town.

The simple *Maulbertsch Well* stands at the end of Arany János u. It was placed here in the 1930s during a period of redevelopment. Petőfi u. runs to the E from here. *No. 6* on the right is a former seminary built for the Carmelite order in 1732. The Baroque **Carmelite church** next door dates from the mid 18C but an earthquake in 1802 necessitated much reconstruction work. The interior of the church is particularly fine, including the Rococo furnishings. Of especial note are the *frescoes* by the Austrian painter Franz Anton Maulbertsch depicting various scenes from the life of the Virgin Mary. He painted the ceiling of the nave and the chancel, and the pictures on the side altar. They are among the best examples of his work in Hungary. The well at the beginning of the street was erected in his memory. The statue on the wall of the church facing Kossuth Lajos u. is of Louis the Great, King of Hungary from 1342–82, and is the work of Ödön Moiret.

The *Town Gallery* (Városi Képtár) is situated a short distance to the N at No. 15 Kossuth Lajos u. in the former Pelikan Inn dating from 1756. The exhibition is devoted to 20C Hungarian art. (Open 10.00–18.00 except Monday.)

In the opposite direction, Kossuth u. leads S to ISTVÁN TÉR, which contains a number of historic buildings. In the middle of the square is an equestrian statue of *King Stephen* by Ferenc Sidló. It was erected in 1938 on the 900th anniversary of Stephen's death. The **County Hall** stands on the W side of the triangular square. It was built between 1807 and 1812.

The neo-classical façade was designed by Mihály Pollack and played a part in the development of 19C Hungarian architecture and politics. The original plans for the building were drawn up in Vienna but the local county authorities were dissatisfied with the proposed Baroque design and commissioned alternatives. Pollack's design became a model for other county halls and marked a historical turning point as local authorities asserted themselves against the Habsburg centre.

On the opposite side is a row of houses all of which are listed buildings. *No. 1*, was built around 1820 in neo-classical style. *No. 2* was originally Baroque but has neo-classical additions. *No. 3*, also renovated in neo-classical style, was originally late-18C Baroque. *Nos 4 and 5* are examples of late 18C building in Louis XVI style.

Other places of interest. Two additional specialist museums can be found in Székesfehérvár. The *Aluminium Industry Museum* is situated some way to the NE of the centre at No. 12 Zombori u. (Open 14.00–17.00; Sun and Holidays 10.00–17.00; closed Mondays.) There is also a specialist collection of documents and materials relating to *animal breeding* at the office of the local county inspectorate, situated at No. 39 Vörös Hadsereg u., to the E of the centre.

The mid-18C **Serbian Orthodox Church** is situated on Rác u. to the W of the centre. A semicircular choir with a domed roof connects with the Baroque vaulted nave. The paintings depicting scenes from the life of Christ and John the Baptist date from 1775–76. Restoration of the church and the mural paintings, which are particularly beautiful, was completed in the early 1980s, but at the time of writing the church was not open to the public. The row of vernacular houses across from the church was restored in the late 1980s. they now constitute a local folk-history museum containing original furniture, tools, etc. (Open 10.00–18.00 except Monday.)

Excursions from Székesfehérvár

Szabadbattyán is 10km to the SW of Székesfehérvár on Road 70. The Gothic *Kula Tower* here was built in the Middle Ages to defend a road that ran through the marshy region around Székesfehérvár. Today it is a museum which exhibits weapons and other items from the Turkish period. (Open 15 March–31 October 10.00–18.00 except Monday.)

Tác is a small village 5km to the S of Szabadbattyán. Nearby are one of the largest Roman finds in Hungary, the ruins of *Gorsium*. (Tác/Gorsium is also signposted at the nearest exit on the M7 motorway.) The area was conquered by the Romans in the 1C AD and a camp set up here for 500 troops. At the beginning of the 2C, after the province of Pannonia was divided into two, Aquincum, near present-day Óbuda, became the chief town of Pannonia Inferior and Gorsium became the religious centre. Towards the end of the 2C the town was destroyed during an attack but was rebuilt at the beginning of the following century. It was laid waste again around 260 and rebuilt once more later when it was renamed Herculiana. The town remained inhabited even after the Romans left in the 5C. Full-scale excavations began in the 20C and are still continuing. Today Gorsium is an open-air museum where one can see the remains of the centre of the town which covered an area of 2 sq km. The remains include that of a palace, an ancient Christian basilica, a five-room temple for the cult of the emperor, a cemetery, dwelling houses, and the Forum which was surrounded by shops, a court and civic buildings. The lapidarium contains items that have been found during excavations. Other pieces of pottery, glassware, buckles and bronze-work are exhibited at the King Stephen Museum in Székesfehérvár. The open-air museum at Gorsium is open May–Oct 10.00–17.00; Nov–April 8.00–16.00; closed Mondays.

Lake Velence (Velencei tó) is about 10km to the SE of Székesfehérvár and covers an area of about 26 sq km much of which is covered by reeds. Although the lake is being developed for tourism, the SW part is a nature conservation area and many varieties of birds nest here. There are beaches around the lake, and sailing and angling are popular sports here. The resort areas lie mainly on the southern shore of the lake in the villages strung along Road 70.

At *Agárd*, on the southern shore, the birthplace of the writer Géza Gárdonyi (1863–1922) has been turned into a *Gárdonyi Memorial House*. Gárdonyi was the author of the popular 'Stars of Eger' children's novel, which recounted the heroic defence of Eger against the Turks in 1552. Inside the house there is an exhibition about fishing and reed-cutting on Lake Velence. The latter is an important local activity and provides material for thatched roofs. The kitchen is in peasant style. (Open 10.00–18.00 except Monday.)

Kápolnásnyék is by the NE corner of the lake. The poet and playwright Mihály Vörösmarty (1800–55) died in the village and his former wine-press on Vörösmarty u., which was built in Baroque style in the second half of the 18C, has been turned into a *Vörösmarty Memorial Museum.* (Open 10.00–18.00 except Monday.)

Sukoró is on the northern side of the lake on a minor road which runs parallel to the motorway. The peasant house at No. 7 Szilvás sor has been turned into a *Folk Museum* to show the style and interior of local peasant dwelling houses. (Open 10.00–18.00 except Monday.)

Pákozd is on the same road 6km to the W. On Mészeg Hill, on the outskirts of the village, a stone obelisk recalls the first victorious battle of the Hungarian War of Independence fought here on 29 September 1848 when a mobilised peasantry forced the Lieutenant-General Jelačić to flee. The *Pákozd Battle Memorial Exhibition* here displays items and documents relating to the battle and the 1848–49 War. (Open 15 March–7 November 10.00–18.00 except Monday.) There is a good view of the surrounding area from the obelisk.

Várpalota (pop. 28,000) is 20km to the W of Székesfehérvár on Road 8. Today it is an industrial town, noted for its aluminium, chemical and oil-refining plants, though the settlement is ancient and is mentioned in documents of the 13C. The castle here was erected in the middle of the 15C and was an important border fortress in the Turkish period. Under the leadership of György Thúry (?–1571) it was able to resist the Turkish attacks for a long time. Today the castle, which had architectural additions in the 18C and 19C, houses the *Hungarian Chemical Museum* which has exhibitions about the history of chemistry and the chemical industry in Hungary over the centuries. (Open April–Oct 11.00–17.00 except Monday.) The castle also has a local *Mining History Collection* which deals with the history of coal mining in the Várpalota region over the last 100 years. (Open April–Oct 11.00–17.00 except Monday.) The former Zichy Mansion, built in Baroque style in 1825 and redesigned in Romantic style by Miklós Ybl in 1863, is today a specialist *Artillery Museum* which traces the use of artillery in Hungarian military history. (Open 10.00–16.00 except Monday.)

Martonvásár lies mid-way between Székesfehérvár and Budapest on Road 70, c 33km from the capital. There is a signposted exit from the M7 motorway which passes 3km to the N of the village. The **Brunswick Mansion** here was built for Count Antal Brunswick in 1773–75 in Baroque style. In 1875 it was rebuilt in English neo-Gothic style and as such is one of the finest Hungarian Romantic mansions. At the end of the century the estate came into the possession of Archduke Joseph and later still into that of the Dreher brewing family. Since 1949 it has belonged to the Agricultural Research Institute of the Hungarian Academy of Sciences. The *park* was declared a nature conservation area in 1953 and is one of the best kept historical gardens.

The garden was laid out in English style in the 19C when there was a fashion in Hungary for English gardens. Hundreds were laid out at mansions and country houses throughout the land. The garden architect, Petri Bernhard (1768–1855) spent four years in England and on his return was responsible for designing many gardens in Hungary. Henry Nebbien, who won the competition for the design of the City Park in Budapest in 1817, was also influenced by the English garden.

The Brunswick family were noted for their progressive attitudes and espousal of social progress during the Reform Period. Theresa Brunswick (1775–1861) was a pioneer of nursery education in Hungary. She was influenced by the Swiss educational reformer Pestalozzi, whom she met in Switzerland in 1808, and by the English social reformer Robert Owen. She established the first Hungarian kindergarten in Buda in 1828. It was known as the 'Garden of Angels'. By 1836 the Society for Promoting Nursery Schools in Hungary had established 14 throughout the country and in 1837 the first kindergarten teachers' training college was opened in Tolna.

Beethoven stayed at the mansion several times as a friend of the family. Part of the mansion has been turned into a *Beethoven Memorial Exhibition* (open weekends 10.00–18.00) and Beethoven concerts take place in the park during the summer months.

9 Veszprém

The entire castle area of **Veszprém**, with its ensemble of mainly Baroque buildings, is a designated protected area and a walk along its single street, Vár utca, gives a real feeling of walking back in time almost unparalleled elsewhere in Hungary. Although the present form of Veszprém dates from post-Turkish times, the town has a very ancient history. Its proximity to Lake Balaton makes it a perfect place for an excursion from the lake.

Tourist Information: Balatontourist, 3 Münnich Ferenc tér (80/26-277).

Rail Station: 2km to the N of the centre. 90 minutes by express from Budapest.

Bus Station: Felszabadulás tér, behind Piac tér. 2 hours from Engels tér, Budapest.

Post Office: 19 Kossuth Lajos u.

Police: 34 Bajcsy-Zsilinszky út.

History. During the time of Prince Géza, King Stephen I's father, one of the earliest dioceses was established here. A cathedral and a royal palace were built in the walled-in castle area on the town's highest hill and Veszprém became one of the centres of the Queen's household. The queen's palace was on the site of today's Baroque bishop's palace. Some 13C frescoes from its chapel at the side can still be seen.

Like several Hungarian towns, ruin and decline commenced in Veszprém even before the Turks arrived. In the years following the battle of Mohács in 1526, there were two rival claimants to the throne, Ferdinand of Habsburg and János Szapolyai. The town was destroyed as a result of the strife between the followers of the two rivals. First one, then the other, overran it. The palaces were burnt and the stones used to fortify the fortress walls. By 1538 Bishop Márton Kecsethy was writing: 'Apart from the ruined chapter buildings, there are only about 38 houses, if hovels made of mud and roofed with straw can be called houses at all.'

The Turkish wars added further destruction, particularly as Veszprém was in one of the areas of disputed territory between Turkish-held and Habsburg-dominated Hungary. The castle was finally demolished on the orders of Vienna in 1702, though further fighting in the 1703–11 War of Independence brought more destruction. It was only after this that reconstruction was able to take place.

Today Veszprém (pop. 66,000) has become a centre of industry and education. It has a university specialising in chemistry and several chemical institutes. Its protected castle area, cultural attractions and proximity to Lake Balaton make it a lively tourist centre.

The route begins in VÖRÖS HADSEREG TÉR, explores the neighbouring Castle Hill and then continues from the square in the direction of some interesting buildings lying to the S of the town centre.

The so-called *Pósa House* stands at No. 3 Vörös Hadsereg tér on its S side. The name is taken from that of a printer and bookseller who

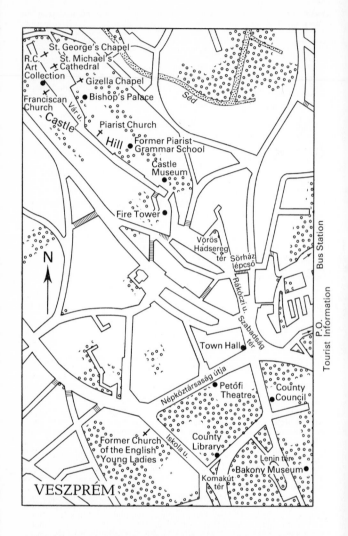

once owned the building. The Copf, two-storey building with an iron balcony was originally built for the Cistercian order in 1793. On the ledge are vases and two coats of arms. The symbol of the Cistercians is on the left. On the right a crane, symbolising vigilance. Nos 4, 5 and 6 to the right are all 18C dwelling houses. Opposite stand the *Memorial to Soviet Heroes* and, towards the NW corner of the square, a bronze statue entitled *Girl With Jug* (Korsós Lány) by local female sculptor Lenke R. Kiss (1962).

Veszprém's **Fire Tower** (Tűztorony) rises behind Nos 7 and 8 on the W side of the square. It was built on medieval foundations but an earthquake in 1810 damaged it and necessitated reconstruction in the following years.

John Paget, an Englishman who travelled extensively throughout the country in the 1830s and later settled in Hungary, visited Veszprém and recorded the following amusing observation about the tower. 'One slender minaret, erected by the Turks above an old Gothic tower, still retains its elegant proportions. It now serves as a watch-tower against fire. Where the Muezzim daily called the faithful Muslim to his spiritual duties, a watchman now warns his Christian brethren of danger to their wordly goods.'

At the end of the square the street starts to rise towards CASTLE HILL. The statue in the niche on the left, with the Latin inscription, is of *St. John of Nepomuk* and dates from 1785. VÁR UTCA, the main street of the Castle area, actually begins on the incline before the route passes through the gate. (The name means 'Castle street'. Until the late 1980s it was called Tolbuhin u., after one of the Soviet military commanders in Hungary during World War II.)

No. 1 Vár u., on the left, is a former fire station built at public expense in Copf style between 1811 and 1814. Fire-fighting vehicles used to emerge through the two gates on either side. In the niche is a statue of *St. Florian*, the patron saint of fire-fighters, which dates from 1788. The first floor used to be occupied by council offices until 1885 when it became the headquarters of an industrial and trades association. The old Veszprém coat of arms above the main ledge shows a mounted knight with sword. It was put here in 1933. Above it are symbols of various trades. 15 iron cannon balls on the façade of the building are a reminder of past battles in Veszprém.

The neo-Romanesque *Heroes' Gate* (Hősök Kapuja), through which Vár u. enters the castle area proper, was designed by István Pázmándy and erected in 1936 on the site of a former medieval castle gate as a First World War memorial. In the niches above the arch there are angels with bay leaf wreaths and a sword with bay leaves. The date 1914–18 can also be seen. The *Castle Museum* in the tower to the right has an exhibition about the military history of Veszprém castle. (Open May–Sept 10.00–18.00 except Monday.)

No. 17 Vár u. is on the left just beyond the gate. The Baroque house was built in 1798 for a lawyer. In 1887–98 Canon Gustav Jánosi lived here. He translated many foreign works into Hungarian, including Milton's 'Paradise Lost'. The large *iron tablet* on the side of the building was made in 1926 and gives a history of the town in Hungarian and German.

No. 6, on the right, dates from 1775. *No. 8* next door was built in Eclectic style in 1897 to the design of Frigyes Kovács. Originally an ecclesiastical building it today belongs to the town authorities. The long building on the other side at *No. 19* is the County Court. It was built in 1905. The building to the left of No. 8 was constructed as a wing of the *former Piarist Grammar School*, which stands behind the wall at No. 10 Vár u. The Piarist 'gimnázium' was built in 1740, though the upper floors were added in the 19C. The *ornamented gate* is the work of a local mason. The Latin inscription on the gate reads: 'To the youth of the country, to patriotism and science—erected in the time of Maria Theresa.' The wing on the right was added in 1905. On its façade overlooking the street there is a *memorial plaque* recording that the poet János Batsányi was a pupil at the school. Batsányi (1763–1845) worked with Ferenc Kazinczy in establishing the first Hungarian-language literary journal, 'Hungarian Museum'. He participated in the anti-Habsburg

'Jacobin' plot at the end of the 18C and was imprisoned and exiled to Linz. The U-shaped building opposite the school at *No. 21* was designed by Jakab Fellner and originally built in 1778 as a hostel for students at the Piarist school. It was taken over by the Veszprém diocese and turned into a home for elderly priests. The rear of the building by the side of the valley has three storeys.

The *former Piarist Monastery* stands at No. 12, to the left of the school. On the façade overlooking the street there are *two niches* with Baroque frescoes in them. The lower one depicts the founder of the order, St. Joseph Calasanctius, with the rule book of the order in his hand. The two female figures in the upper niche under the Baroque shell-like ornamentation were added at a later date during a restoration of the building. The neo-classical *Piarist Church* next door was built between 1828 and 1836. The paintings inside were finished in 1840. The Greek letters for MMT on the façade represent the Piarists' motto, Mary, Mother, God (Maria, Mater, Teo). The church is today used for temporary exhibitions. (Open May–Oct 9.00–17.00.) Up to the middle of the 18C there used to be an inner wall and gate across the street just beyond the church.

The so-called *Dubniczay House* is at No. 29 on the left beyond the protruding corner. It was built for Canon István Dubniczay in 1751. The year of construction can be seen above the gate. Above the first floor window there is Dubniczay's Latin motto and coat of arms. On top of the tympanum two angels hold a representation of the Mother

Thirteenth-century frescoes in the Gizella Chapel, Veszprém.

of God. Inside the gateway there is a copy of Imre Varga's statue of King Stephen which stands in the Hungarian Chapel in St. Peter's in Rome. The building today is occupied by a registry office and the Castle Gallery.

The E-shaped building of the Baroque **Bishop's Palace** stands opposite, at No. 16. Above the protruding balcony there is the coat of arms of Ignác Koller, the bishop who had it built in 1767. The architect was Jakab Fellner who also designed the building to the right at No. 14 for the employees of the bishop's household. The **Gizella Chapel**, tucked away on the left of the Bishop's Palace, came to light when the palace was being built in the 18C. The name, that of King Stephen's wife, was given at that time but a queen's palace and chapel used to stand here up to 1313. Reconstruction took place in the 18C but in 1937 restoration work removed the Baroque elements. The chapel was Byzantine in style and original carvings can be seen on the keystones of the vaults. The main significance of the chapel lies in the 13C *frescoes* of six apostles discovered on the N wall. The first pair from the left were repainted in the 18C. The others, although in a worse condition, are as original. (Open May–Oct 10.00–17.00 except Monday.)

The *Provost's House* at No. 18 to the left got its present form during this century following a fire in 1909. Restoration work also took place in the late 1980s. Albert Vetési was the Bishop of Veszprém from 1458 to 1486. The round structure of the *Castle Well* in front of the Gizella Chapel was erected in 1936 on the 450th anniversary of his death, although a well functioned here up to the late 16C. The Latin inscription says that Veszprém is the town where the sources of Hungarian culture were plentiful. Another bishop, Márton Bíró, commissioned the nearby *Holy Trinity Statue* in 1750. The designer, Tamás Walch, represented the Father, Son and Holy Spirit surrounded by statues and reliefs of various saints. Ferenc Schmidt was the sculptor.

The former *Franciscan Church and Monastery* are on the left side of the street. The Franciscans arrived in Veszprém in 1681 and their church, dedicated to St. Stephen, was consecrated c 1730. The monastery, to the right of the church at No. 33, was built in 1776. The fire of 1909 caused serious damage to the church and a neo-Romanesque style was adopted for the restoration work. The stone-framed door of the monastery has the latin motto of the order.

St. Michael's Cathedral stands to the N of the Trinity statue. An 11C cathedral stood here but fires and rebuilding occurred on several occasions. In 1400 it was reconsecrated with four side chapels and a total of 26 altars. The Turks burnt this church down and only the crypt survives. It was rebuilt in 1723 in Baroque style, but the present neo-Romanesque appearance dates from the last major restoration which took place in 1907–10. On the N side of the cathedral, below ground level, there are the excavated remains of *St. George's Chapel* which was originally built in 1016–18 and housed a relic of St. George brought by King Stephen. Originally separate from the cathedral it was connected to the larger church in the second third of the 13C and rebuilt as a Gothic vaulted chapel. For many years it was a place of pilgrimage until the tribulations of the 16C left it in ruins. Excavations were only undertaken in the 1950s. The bronze statue of *St. Imre* (Emeric) in front is by Dezső Erdei (1940). Legend has it that Imre, Stephen's son, took an oath of virginity in the chapel here.

No. 35, opposite the cathedral's main façade, is a former Canon's House and was built around 1772. Today there are two museums inside the building. The Veszprém *Roman Catholic Ecclesiastical Collection* of Christian art is on the ground floor. (Open May–Oct 9.00–17.00.) In the basement there is a *Museum of Brick Manufacture.* (Open May–Oct 9.00–17.00.) The neighbouring building at *No. 37* was built in 1769–70 and was probably designed by Jakab Fellner. Above the gate there is the coat of arms of Canon Dravecz. Today it is the local seat of the Academy of Sciences. The end building on the left, *No. 39*, is the so-called Körmendy House. The name is that of a canon whose mansion this was. It was built in the early 18C, though rebuilt in 1823 which was when the ornamented main gate was added. The U-shaped Baroque building opposite was built as the *Large Seminary* (Nagyszeminárium) between 1773 and 1782. The top floor was added in the 1930s and towards the end of the same decade the wall in front of the building was also added.

The statues of *King Stephen and Gizella* on the ledge at the end of the street were erected on the 900th anniversary of Stephen's death (József Ispánky, 1938). The crowned Stephen is holding a sword and an orb. His wife is depicted with a model of Veszprém's original cathedral. From the parapet there is a good view of the NW part of Veszprém. To the left there is the *Valley Bridge* which was built in 1936. To the right, the white rocks and cross of St. Benedict Hill can be seen.

The route now returns to Vörös Hadsereg tér and continues along Rákóczi u. which leads off from the SE corner of the square. Note the alleyway with steps just before the beginning of the street at the side of No. 26 Vörös Hadsereg tér. This is known as *Sörház lépcső* (Beerhouse steps) and dates from the 18C. Half-way along Rákóczi u., at the junction of Vörös Csillag u. on the left, there is a statue of the poet *Attila József* (1905–37) by István Tar.

The street leads into Szabadság tér where, at No. 1 on the right, there stands the *Town Hall.* The building was constructed for the Kapuváry family in 1793, and their coat of arms can still be seen above the central balcony. The town bought it in 1885. The S wing, facing Népköztársaság út, was added in 1907, which was when a new attic with the Veszprém coat of arms was added.

Lenin tér is due S of Szabadság tér. The Eclectic building of the *County Council* stands here at No. 5 on the left (István Kiss, 1886–87). In the 18C a salt house stood on this site. A short way across the square to the W the rear of the Art Nouveau **Petőfi Theatre** can be seen. (It actually faces Népköztársaság útja at No. 2.) Designed by István Medgyasszay and built in 1908, it was the first large building in Hungary to be constructed entirely from reinforced concrete. A notable feature is the circular *stained glass window* at the front. It is the work of Sándor Nagy, one of the leading members of the Gödöllő, Pre-Raphaelite workshop.

The design of the window, entitled 'The Magic of Folk Art', is a good example in practice of one of the central ideas of Hungarian Secessionism—the notion that fine art and folk art can be combined. The window contains several sections of a narrative character and depicts figures representing various components of Hungarian society as well as symbolic animals such as rams and deer. In the background a ploughman can be seen, symbolising peasant culture and the artist's affinity with rural life. Nagy was responsible also for the decoration at the rear of the theatre depicting 'The Hunting of the Magic Deer', a classic tale of Hungarian mythology.

The **Bakony Museum** is on the E side of Lenin Liget, which is the small park area to the S of Lenin tér. The museum belongs to the county and was founded in 1903. The present building was designed for the museum by István Medgyasszay and built between 1914 and 1922. The exhibitions cover the general history of the region including a display of folk art. (Open March–Sept 10.00–18.00; Nov–Feb 10.00–14.00; closed Mondays.) A few metres to the right of the museum there is the so-called *Bakony House* (Bakonyi Ház). It was built in 1935 in the style of a house in Öcs, a village to the W of Veszprém in the middle of the Bakony Hills. Inside are items relating to the local peasant way of life. (Open March–Sept 10.00–18.00; Nov–Feb 10.00–14.00; closed Mondays.)

Two buildings of architectural interest are nearby to the W of Lenin tér. The *County Library*, facing Komakút tér, is a Romantic-style building designed by Henrik Schmahl and originally constructed in 1900–02 for the management of the bishop's estates. Around the corner in Iskola u., which runs along the W side of the square, stands the former *Angolkisasszonyok temploma* (the Church of the English Young Ladies—the Hungarian name for the Mary Ward Nuns). The church and its group of buildings to the right were designed by József Szentirmai in 1860. The Romantic style of the buildings, perhaps appropriately, is English Gothic revival.

Veszprém's *Zoo and Botanical Gardens* are not on the route but are situated a short distance to the W of the centre on Kittenbeger Kálmán u. which runs from Jókai Mór u. below the western side of Castle Hill.

Excursions from Veszprém

One of Hungary's famous (and in this case genuine) highwaymen's inns, the **Vámosi csárda**, can be found 5km SW of Veszprém beside the main road to Nagyvázsony. The two-storey Baroque building stands in a courtyard surrounded by a wall. With its veranda and outbuildings it is a typical example of an 18C building in the Bakony region. In the last century it was the haunt of the notorious highwayman, Jóska Savanyú, who was immortalised in many folk-songs. Today it operates as a *csárda* (inn) catering in the summer mainly for tourist groups, but it is also open to individuals. Shows of folk music and dancing occasionally take place in the courtyard and an atmosphere of rustic revelry is maintained.

The earliest and largest known Roman ruins discovered in the Balaton region are at **Balácapuszta**, near the village of Nemesvámos which lies to the S of the main road via the junction near the *csárda*. The remains of several farm buildings and those of a villa with reconstructed frescoes and mosaics can be seen. (Open May–Sept 10.00–18.00 except Monday.)

Nagyvázsony is c 23km SW of Veszprém. Its main attraction is the restored *Kinizsi Castle*.

A castle and keep were built here in the 15C. In 1472 King Matthias Corvinus presented the castle to one of his favourite generals, Pál Kinizsi, who had it reconstructed. Kinizsi, who took part in campaigns against the Turks, was surrounded by many myths and legends. He was believed to have been a miller's assistant who attracted the King's attention through his great strength and courage. Folk myth also has it that after the battle of Kenyérmező, in 1479, he danced a triumphal dance holding three Turks, one of them between his teeth by his clothes. He died in 1494 and was buried in the Pauline monastery which he had founded at Nagyvázsony.

During the Turkish period Kinizsi's castle was one of the border fortresses lying between Turkish and Habsburg-ruled Hungary. It was also used by the insurgents during the War of Independence at the beginning of the 18C. In contrast to most of the other castles in the Balaton area it was not later deliberately destroyed by the Habsburgs. Over the years, however, the greater part of the castle fell into decline with only parts of the defensive works and the keep surviving. Excavations began in the 1950s and today it is an attractive memorial of castle life in old Hungary.

The castle is now a museum. The 30m-high *keep*, which covers a ground space of 10m by 12m, has four floors and a terrace. On display are items of furniture and weapons from the time when the keep was inhabited. In the 18C it was used for a while as a prison, and shackles and other material relating to this period are also on display. In the restored *chapel*, across from the keep, there is the cover of Pál Kinizsi's carved red marble sarcophagus, which was brought here from his original burial place, and documents illustrating his career. Below the chapel there is a small *lapidarium* with carved stones from various periods found during the excavations. (Open 8.00–17.00; June–Aug 8.00–19.00.)

The building on raised ground by the car park near the entrance to the castle contains a *Postal Museum*. (Open 10.00–18.00; Nov–Feb 10.00–14.00; closed Mondays.) The peasant house at No. 21 Bercsényi u. nearby, which was built in 1825, is today a small *Ethnographical Museum* which has a weaving shed and copper workshop. (Open 10.00–18.00 except Monday.)

Herend 12km NW of Veszprém just off Road 8, is known throughout the world because of the porcelain made here. The porcelain factory was opened in 1839 and achieved fame at the Great Exhibition in London where Queen Victoria ordered a complete set. A few years later, at the New York Exhibition, President Pierce purchased virtually the entire stock of Herend porcelain on display. The *Porcelain Museum* at the factory on Kossuth u. has an exhibition of Herend porcelain and a display about the technologies which have been utilised over the years. (Open April–Oct 8.30–16.30 except Monday; Nov–March 8.00–16.00 except Sunday.)

Zirc is 21km to the N of Veszprém on Road 82 in the middle of the Bakony Hills. The fomer Cistercian *Abbey Church* here was built between 1739 and 1753. A particular feature are the altarpieces by the Austrian painter Franz Anton Maulbertsch. The neo-classical façade of the adjoining abbey buildings date from 1854. Inside there are the exhibitions of the *Bakony Natural History Museum* (Bakony Természettudományi Múzeum, open 9.00–17.00; Nov–April 9.00–13; closed Mondays) and a library with Empire-style furnishings from the 1820s. It is named after Antal Reguly (1819–58) who was born in Zirc and who became an ethnographer and pioneer of Finno-Ugric linguistic research.

The *local history and folk art collection* can be found in the cultural centre at No. 1 Rákóczi tér. (Open April–Oct 9.00–17.00; Sat 9.00–16.00; closed Mondays.) Here is also the entrance to the local *Arboretum*. (Open Jan–Nov every day except Monday.)

10 Budapest to Pécs

Roads 70 and 6. Total distance 198km. **Budapest**—Road 70 21km
Érd—Road 6 46km **Dunaújváros**—20km **Dunaföldvár**—20km
Páks—27km turning for Road 56 and (3km) **Szekszárd**—20km
Bonyhád—10km **Mecseknádasd**—11km **Pécsvárad**—23km **Pécs**.

Pécs lies 198km SW of Budapest on Road 6 which forks from Road 70
21km SW of the capital at Érd. At **Érd** there is a 15C Catholic Church
which was later rebuilt in Baroque style, and the remains of a
mid-16C Turkish mosque. On the main road, at No. 4 Budai út, there
is a specialist *Geographical Museum* (Magyar Földrajzi Gyűtemény).
(Open Tues–Fri 14.00–18.00, weekends 10.00–18.00.)

67km S of Budapest the road by-passes the town of **Dunaújváros**,
which was founded as Sztálinváros (Stalin Town) in 1950 to serve as
a model new town of 'iron and steel' in line with the political
emphasis on heavy industry at the time. The Danube Ironworks is the
largest plant in the town but many other important industrial enterprises are also based here. The new town was created just to the S of
the ancient settlement of *Dunapentele* where previously the Romans
had erected a fortification known as Intercisa. The *Intercisa Museum*
at No. 10 Lenin tér has exhibitions covering the local history of the
area from prehistoric times to the present day. (Open 10.00–18.00
except Monday.) On Vörös Hadsereg útja, in the former village of
Dunapentele, there is a Baroque *Serbian church* dating from 1748.

Dunaföldvár is 20km S of Dunaújváros. It is the site of an old
Danube crossing. A castle was built here in the 16C to protect the
crossing. The tower is still standing and a *Castle Museum* (Vármúzeum) has been established inside. (Open 10.00–18.00, Sat and
Sun 10.00–20.00; Nov–March 10.00–18.00; closed Mondays.) The
bridge nearby connects Transdanubia with the road to Kecskemét
and the Great Plain.

In the 4C the area belonged to the Roman province of Pannonia and the Romans
built a fortress here. Situated by the bank of the river it was completely covered
when the level of the Danube rose. In the late 1980s carved Roman stones were
found below the level of the water. Underwater excavations revealed the walls
of a fortress 70m sq dating from the first half of the 4C. Some of the stones which
have been raised are on display in front of the Ádám Béri Balogh Museum in
Szekszárd.

20km further along Road 6 is the town of **Páks**, which is today noted
as the site of Hungary's first and only nuclear power plant. It was
constructed by the Danube on the S side of the town in the 1980s.
The old Paks railway station, built in 1896, is today a *Railway
Museum* (Vasúti Múzeum) where old trains and items of railway
equipment are displayed. (Open 10.00–18.00 except Monday.) There
is a *Halászcsárda* (fish restaurant) by the side of Road 6 in Páks
famous for its Halászlé (fish soup). There is a similar Halászcsárda at
Dunakömlőd a few kilometres to the N of the town on the main road.

The junction for **Szekszárd** (Road 56) lies 27km to the S of Paks
along Road 6. The *Old County Hall* here is a fine example of
Hungarian neo-classical architecture. It was built in 1828–33 to the
design of Mihály Pollack. A neo-classical palace stands on *Castle Hill*
in Béla tér. Remains of an abbey church from the age of Árpád and
the foundation wall of an early Christian sepulchral chapel have
been found in the courtyard of the palace. The *Ádám Béri Balogh
Museum* is situated in an 1895 neo-Renaissance building at No. 26
Mártírok tere. Balogh (c 1665–1711) was a *Kuruc* fighter who was

captured by imperial forces near the town and taken to Buda where he was executed. The county museum has exhibitions on the local history of the region as well as Renaissance, Baroque and 19C paintings. (Open 10.00–18.00 except Monday.)

The *Gemenc Nature Reserve* lies to the SE of Szekszárd towards the Danube.

The regulation of the Danube in this Sárköz stretch of the river was undertaken later than in other places and was completed only in the early years of this century. The river was shortened by 60km and hundreds of meandering curves were cut off. The old forest backwaters and branches dried out and the area was freed from annual flood water. However, streams, pools and marshland remained, offering refuge to game and birds. Human intervention has further created a game park. As well as the boar, wild cats, otters and deer, the area has a rich variety of birds including falcons, hawks, bald eagles and black storks.

20km SW of the Szekszárd junction Road 6 passes **Bonyhád**. A Baroque *Catholic Church* dating from the 1770s stands on the main square. There is also a Louis XVI-style *synagogue* and a Baroque *mansion* which both date from 1780. *Grábóc* is a few kilometres to the E of Bonyhád via Börzsöny. The *Serbian Orthodox Church* here has a particularly beautiful iconostasis.

The German-speaking village of **Mecseknádasd** is 10km to the S of Bonyhád on Road 6. The Baroque *Parish Church*, which was built by Bishop György Klimó of Pécs in 1771 has a relic of St. Margaret of Scotland set into the interior wall on the right. Above it hangs a painting of her by the Scottish artist Gregory Smith, donated to Mecseknádasd in 1975. The church has the additional peculiarity of one of the earliest specimens of Hungarian neo-Gothic work in the pointed arches of the choir (1785).

It is believed that St. Margaret of Scotland (1046–93) was born in this area. Margaret was the granddaughter of King Stephen of Hungary. Her mother, Ágota, had married Edward, the elder son of the English king Edmund Ironside. Stephen had granted Edward some land in the region of Mecseknádasd. Margaret herself married the Scottish king Malcolm III in 1069. She died in 1093 and was canonised in 1251. Acknowledged for her religious activity in Scotland (she founded several monasteries) she was named patron of that country in 1673.

Just to the S of the village, on a bend in the main road as it begins to climb the hill, is a small cemetery chapel, the former *Church of St. Stephen*, which dates from the 14C. The monument was restored in the 1970s and the original frescoes of the interior are visible even if the church is closed.

Road 6 now begins to climb and wind through the SE range of the *Mecsek Hills*. The Mecsek is an isolated range of karstic mountains. An interesting feaure of the flora of this immense limestone block is that many elements of Mediterranean life can be found here. The southern slopes have indigenous sweet chestnuts as well as fig and almond trees. On the western range of the mountains there is uranium ore, which accumulated in the red sandstone layers 200 million years ago. Uranium is one of Hungary's most important raw materials. Here, too, good anthracite coal is mined. The mineral resources of the mountains have helped developed Pécs, the largest town of Transdanubia.

Pécsvárad is 11km to the S of Mecseknádasd just off Road 6. The castle-like building of a *former Benedictine abbey* stands at the far end of the village. It was founded in the early 11C though the upper floors are additions from the 14C and 15C. Here there is now a permanent exhibition of the history of the building and of sculptures of Sándor Kígyós. (Open daily 10.00–18.00.) The *cemetery chapel*, a short way up the hill on the right, was originally 12C and was enlarged in the 15C.

The outskirts of **Pécs** (see below) begin approximately 25km after Pécsvárad.

11 Pécs

PÉCS is a town for art lovers. Outside Budapest and Szentendre there are probably more galleries here than anywhere else in Hungary. Pécs also has some of the most significant early Christian remains in the country as well as some outstanding Turkish relics. For those who simply want to relax Pécs is also attractive. Its climate is generally warmer than elsewhere and it has two large squares right in the centre. In addition the hills on the northern edge of the town provide good opportunities for excursions.

Tourist Information: Mecsek Tourist, 1 Széchenyi tér (72/14-866).

Rail Station: Lenin tér. 3 hours by express from the Southern Railway Station, Budapest.

Bus Station: Szalay András út (between Bajcsy-Zsilinszky u. and Rózsa Ferenc u.) 4½ hours from Engels tér, Budapest.

Post Office: 10 Jókai u.

Police: 3 Killián György u.

History. Because of its Roman connections Pécs is often referred to as the '2000-year-old town'. In fact, finds have been made here from the neolithic, Bronze and Copper Ages. The first peoples mentioned by written sources were the Illyrians and the Pannons, followed in the 5C–4C BC by the Celts. At the height of the Roman period in the first four centuries AD the town was known as *Sopianae*. At the end of the 3C Sopianae became the centre of civil administration of the newly-organised province of Pannonia Valeria and much construction work was undertaken. It was at this time, too, that Christianity started to spread in the area.

The Magyars arrived around the end of the 9C following waves of various settlers including the Huns, Eastern Goths and Avars. Building on the long-established traditions of Christianity in the area, King Stephen gave Pécs a central place in his organisation of church activity by announcing the foundation of the Pécs diocese in a charter dated August 1009. Pécs in the Middle Ages was an important ecclesiastical centre with a series of eminent bishops which included Janus Pannonius (Bishop 1459–72) whose poetry was known throughout Europe. The high level of cultural activity in Pécs at the time was manifested by the foundation of Hungary's first university here in 1367. Traces of this, however, along with other elements of medieval life, all but disappeared following the occupation of Pécs by the Turks in 1543.

During the 143 years of Ottoman rule the town acquired an oriental character. The indigenous population was forced outside the walls and the centre was occupied by Turks, Greeks, Bosnians and Serbs. Churches were pulled down or transformed into mosques. The leather industry, viticulture and the fruit trade grew, despite the constant state of war. Turkish rule ended with the occupation of Pécs by Louis of Baden's army in 1686 by which time the town had almost been levelled to the ground. Looting followed the battle and the Hungarian population was virtually left to starve to death.

Revival of the town was inevitably slow and further devastation occurred during the Rákóczi War of Independence and a plague of 1710. Economic recovery was helped by the long-standing traditions of viticulture and by the discovery of coal in the mid-18C. In 1780 Pécs was granted the privileges of a royal free town. Cultural life developed at this time under Bishop György Klimó (1710–77).

Pécs played only a minor role in the events of 1848–49. In the second half of the 19C the town began to develop into an industrial centre with a strong labour

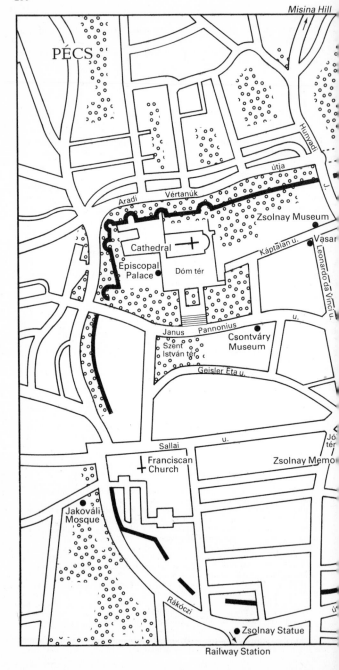

Misina Hill

PÉCS

Hunyadi

útja

Aradi

Vértanúk

Zsolnay Museum

Vásár

Cathedral

Káptalan u.

Leonardo da Vinci u.

Episcopal
Palace

Dóm tér

u.

Janus Pannonius

Szent
István tér

Csontváry
Museum

Geisler Eta u.

Sallai

u.

Jó
tér

Zsolnay Memo

Franciscan
Church

Jakováli
Mosque

Rákóczi

Zsolnay Statue

Railway Station

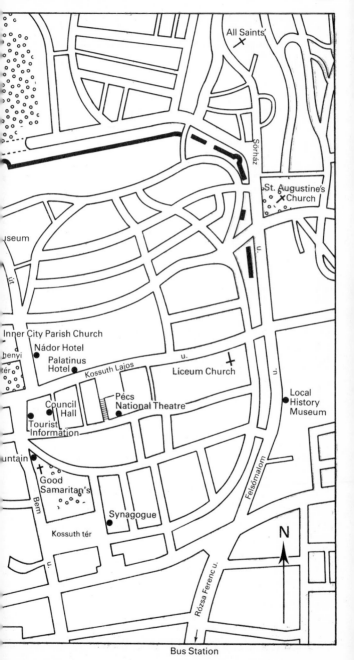

All Saints' ✗

Sörház

St. Augustine's ✗ Church

useum

u.

Inner City Parish Church

Nádor Hotel ●

Palatinus
Hotel ●

benyi
tér

Kossuth Lajos

u.

Líceum Church ✝

u.

Local
History
Museum ●

Council ● Hall
Tourist
Information

Pécs
National Theatre

Felsőmalom

untain ●

✝ Good
Samaritan's

Bem

Synagogue ●

Kossuth tér

N

u.

Rózsa Ferenc u.

Bus Station

movement. The town was occupied by Serbian forces in October 1918 and kept under occupation until August 1921. Pécs was fortunate in the Second World War in that neither air raids nor ground battles caused much damage and consequently post-war development began more speedily than elsewhere. Today Pécs is both an industrial and a cultural centre with several universities and research institutes, and many museums and art galleries. The climate is generally warmer than elsewhere being almost Mediterranean in character.

The route begins at SZÉCHENYI TÉR in the centre of the town. In the northern half of the square stands the largest relic of Turkish architecture of Hungary, the **former djami of Pasha Gazi Kassim** which is today the Roman Catholic Inner City Parish Church (Belvárosi plébániatemplom). In the Middle Ages the large Gothic Church of St. Bertalan stood here. Its stones were used by the Turks to build the mosque in the late 16C. After the expulsion of the Turks the mosque was turned into a church by the Jesuits who undertook numerous transformations, adding a chapel and sacristy and removing the Turkish entrance. The minaret was pulled down in 1753. Archaeological excavation of the mosque was carried out between 1939 and 1942 and was followed by restorations involving the removal of many later additions. The original cupola was restored in the 1950s. Elements of the original mosque can be seen inside in the form of two prayer niches facing Mecca and some Turkish windows.

A tablet in memory of the *former Pécs Battalion* stands on the terrace in front of the building (Ferenc Sidló, 1937) while in the lower part of the square there is the *Holy Trinity Statue* (Szentháromság-szobor). In 1713 the town council decided to erect a Trinity statue on the main square which was then known as Trinity Square. The present statue is the third one to stand here. It dates from 1908 and is the work of György Kiss. A bronze equestrian statue of *János Hunyadi* (c 1407–56) stands at the SE corner of the central area of the square. It was erected in August 1956 to commemorate the 500th anniversary of Hunyadi's important victory over the Turks at Nándorfehérvár (Belgrade). The sculptor who won the commission, following a competition, was Pál Pátzay.

The row of buildings on the E side of Széchenyi tér begins at the N end with the early-Eclectic *Baranya County Court* at No. 14. The building dates from 1891 and was designed by the Pécs architect Imre Schlauch. There used to be a medieval bath here which was rebuilt by the Turks and which was later used as a county prison in the 1720s. The *Nádor Hotel* is next door at No. 15. A Romantic-style hotel with the same name was opened here in 1846. Together with its coffee house it was a popular Pécs meeting place in the second half of the 19C. It was pulled down in 1902 and replaced with a larger, more luxurious hotel designed by Imre Schlauch. The present coffee house on the ground floor still maintains its old atmosphere. The Romantic apartment house at *No. 17* was built for the Zsolnay family in 1845 at the same time as Nos 16 and 18. The building houses the editorial offices of 'Jelenkor' (Present Age) the local literary periodical.

The four-storey Eclectic *Council Hall*, the former Town Hall, with a clock tower over its N façade, stands at the end of Kossuth Lajos u. which joins the E side of Széchenyi tér. The building houses Pécs' first department store, the *Centrum Áruház* and the local office of Mecsek Tourist, the county *Tourist Information Office* (entrance on the eastern side of the building at No. 1 Széchenyi tér).

KOSSUTH LAJOS UTCA has always been one of the main streets of Pécs and the route now proceeds some way along it before returning to Széchenyi tér. The *Palatinus Hotel*, at No. 5 Kossuth Lajos u. on the left, is the former Pannonnia Hotel which was built in 1913–15 in Art Nouveau style to the design of Andor Pilch. Its large hall was the most elite ballroom in Pécs and occasionally concert performances were also given here.

The hotel was closed in the 1970s and for many years stood empty. Plans to connect its rear with the back of the Nádor Hotel in Széchenyi tér to form one large hotel were shelved due to financial considerations. Meanwhile the hotel's old name was taken over by a new hotel constructed on Rákóczi út, not far away. The hotel and its Art Nouveau hall were eventually entirely reconstructed and reopened under the new name in 1988.

The two-storey Romantic house at *No. 8* on the right has ceramic ornamentation made at the local Zsolnay factory. This was a popular way of ornamenting buildings in Pécs. The house was owned by the Nendtvich family among whose members numbered a mayor of Pécs and Tamás Nendtvich (1782–1858), a chemist and natural scientist after whom a rare plant of the Mecsek region is named (Doronicum Nendtvich). The *Baranya County Archives* occupy No. 11 on the left in a three-storey building constructed in 1872 utilising some walls of a former Salt Depot which stood here. It is Hungary's largest provincial archive and is a centre for local historical research.

Set back a little from Kossuth Lajos u., the *Pécs National Theatre* (Pécsi Nemzeti Színház) stands in Színház tér. The neo-Renaissance theatre was designed by Antal Lang and Antal Steinhardt and built in 1893–95. A *Genius statue* made of gilded tin stands on the main cupola (György Kiss). The allegorical relief on the tympanum and the female trio above it, together with the reliefs of Mihály Vörösmarty, Ferenc Erkel, Gergely Csiky, Ede Szigligeti and Károly Kisfaludy were all made of pyrogranite in the Zsolnay factory.

No. 13 was built in 1895 (Ágoston Kirstein and Imre Schlauch) and is the former National Casino. It was modernised in the 1970s but the original Eclectic façade remains. Since the war it has been used primarily as an armed forces club. The two-storey building next door at *No. 15* dates from the early 19C. It was turned into a guest house and became a venue of balls and concerts.

The *Vasváry House* stands at No. 19 Kossuth Lajos u. It is in early Eclectic style. The exact date of construction is unknown but probably is the result of the transformation of an earlier building from the 1870s or 1880s. It was owned by the Treiber family who changed their name to Vasváry in 1883. The family ran a hardware shop on the ground floor. The inscription 'Vasváry ház' can be seen on the façade and above it an allegoric female figure with the Vasváry coat of arms. There is rich relief decoration between the far end windows. The allegoric figures and stucco decoration were made of pyrogranite in the Zsolnay factory and put on the façade in 1897.

The *'Lyceum' Church and Széchenyi Grammar School* are further along Kossuth Lajos u. on the right at No. 44.

Construction of the church, which originally belonged to the Pauline Order, began in 1741 and was completed in 1756. Four years later a new monastery for the order was opened beside the church. The spires of the church were added in 1779. Both the church and the monastery were built in Baroque style and were designed by Máté Vépi, a Pauline monk originally from Nagyszombat. Joseph II dissolved the order in 1786 following which both the church and the monastery were used for a variety of purposes including a storehouse, theatre and military hospital. Bishop Szepesy bought the buildings in 1832. The church was reconsecrated and a high school set up in the former monastery. It has operated as a school since then, with occasional interruptions to serve as a teachers' training college and a law academy. The church was renovated in the 1920s and again after World War II.

The route now returns along Kossuth Lajos u. to Széchenyi tér.

The corner building to the S of the Council Hall at the junction of Perczel u. and Munkácsy M. u. (No. 2 Széchenyi tér) is the so-called *Lóránt Palace*, built in 1883 and named after its original owner, Dr Lipót Lóránt. It was the first building in Pécs to have a lift. The Central Coffee House which used to occupy the ground floor was a popular meeting place at the turn of the 20C century. In 1913 the Workers' Casino was opened in the building by József Pécs, a labour movement sympathiser.

The *Church of the Good Samaritans* (Irgalmas rendiek temploma) stands at the S end of Széchenyi tér to the left of Bem u. It originally belonged to the Capuchins and was consecrated in 1727. The western chapel was added by the monks in 1734. In 1891 the N façade was rebuilt in neo-Renaissance style to the designs of Ágoston Kirstein. In 1908 a local painter, Ede Graits, decorated the vault of the church interior with copies of Tiepolo paintings. In the niche on the façade above the entrance there is a statue of the Virgin Mary by György Kiss, and on the exterior wall facing Bem u., to the right, there is a relief of St. John (Ede Mayer, 1905). Since 1930 the *Vilmos Zsolnay memorial fountain* has stood in front of the church. Designed by Andor Pilch it was made from glazed pyrogranite at the Zsolnay factory in Pécs in 1912. The Art Nouveau ox-headed gargoyles of the fountain and the ornaments are decorated with eosin glaze, which was invented by the factory's founder Vilmos Zsolnay and by the chemist Vince Wartha. The design is taken from gold vessels dating from the time of the Magyar conquest, which were found at Nagyszentmiklós in Transylvania and which are today in the Kunsthistorisches Museum in Vienna.

No. 9–10 Széchenyi tér (on the W side level with the steps in front of the Trinity statue) is the *former Savings Bank*. The four-storey,

Detail of the Vilmos Zsolnay memorial fountain (Andor Pilch, 1912), Pécs.

ornamented, Eclectic building was constructed in 1898. From 1950 to 1979 it was the headquarters of the County Council. The building next door, at *No. 11* Széchenyi tér was originally built as a Jesuit monastery in the early 18C. Since then it has been a law academy, a military hospital, a barracks and a grammar school. Today, after several reconstructions, it functions as a secondary school students' hostel. There is a 33m *open-air swimming pool* in the courtyard which is open to the public in the summer. The white marble bust of *Leonardo da Vinci* in front of the hostel is the work of György Baksa Soós (1958).

The two-storey Baroque building with neo-classical elements standing at the N end of the square behind the former mosque (No. 12) houses the *Janus Pannonius Museum's Archaeological Section.* The exhibition inside covers the history of Baranya county from prehistoric times to the Árpád dynasty. (Open 10.00–16.00 except Monday.)

The route now continues up LEONARDO DA VINCI U. from the NW corner of the square. The three-storey corner building on the left at *No. 1* is a school and was built in Eclectic style in the 1880s. The *University Library* is half-way up the street at No. 3 on the left. The neo-classical building with four Tuscan columns was designed by József Piatsek and built in 1830. Bishop Ignác Szepesy intended the building to be a college and it was opened as such in 1831. Soon after, however, the college moved to the former Pauline monastery in what is now Kossuth Lajos u. and the 'Klimó collection', the library founded by Bishop György Klimó in 1774, was moved here. At that time there were already about 33,000 volumes in the collection. Klimó's dictum for the library he founded was: 'You don't have to pay anything. Depart enriched. Return more frequently.' At present it is the central library of the Janus Pannonius University of Arts.

The **Zsolnay Ceramics Exhibition** (Zsolnay Kerámia Kiállítása) of the Janus Pannonius Museum is on the first floor of the building facing the top of Leonardo da Vinci u., at No. 2 Káptalan u. Inside the same building there is the *Amerigo Tot Museum* which exhibits works by the Hungarian-born sculptor Amerigo Tot (born Imre Tóth) (1909–84). (Both open 10.00–18.00 except Monday.)

Records about the building itself go back to 1324. In the Middle Ages it belonged to the local provost. In 1476, Provost Zsigmond Hampó established one of Hungary's first public libraries here. In 1520 it was rebuilt in Renaissance style. During Turkish times Gazi Kassim, the high priest of the *djami*, lived here. Reconstructions and renovations continued in the 18C and 19C. The 20C renovations have revealed the Baroque and medieval parts of the building.

The neo-classical corner building on the other side of the street at No. 3 Káptalan u. was designed by József Piatsek in 1838. Since 1976 the **Vasarely Museum** has been based here. The artist Victor Vasarely was born as Győző Vásárhelyi here in 1908. (Open 10.00–18.00 except Monday.) The building also contains an *underground mining museum.* (Open 10.00–17.00 except Monday.)

The route continues westwards along KÁPTALAN UTCA. The *former prebendal house*, at No. 4, is set back from the road on the right. Originally medieval, it was rebuilt after the Turkish period, though 20C restoration has uncovered several medieval remains. Today the building houses the *Uitz Museum* which contains works of the painter Béla Uitz (1887–1972) who lived in the Soviet Union for 50 years after 1919. There is also a selection of modern Hungarian painting from the first half of the 20C. (Open 10.00–18.00 except Monday.) Another modern art exhibition, the *Endre Nemes Museum* opened in 1984 at No. 5 Káptalan u. On display are paintings by Endre Nemes (1909–85) who was born at Pécsvárad near Pécs and spent much of his life in Sweden. (Open 10.00–18.00 except Monday.)

The *modern prebendal house* at No. 6 on the right was built with neo-classical elements in 1841 and designed by a local architect, Ferenc Windisch. In the early 1890s it was redesigned by Ágoston Kirstein in Eclectic style. The double-pillared portico preserves traces of the earlier classicism. In the niches are statues of St. Peter and St. Paul. The building is the former home of Ferenc Martyn (1899–1986) an early representative of non-figurative painting in Hungary. The *Ferenc Martyn Collection* is on the ground floor. (Open 10.00–18.00 except Monday.)

Káptalan u. swings to the left down a short incline but a roadway continues in front of No. 6 and then through an archway into DÓM TÉR, the historic ecclesiastical centre of Pécs. The **Cathedral** which dominates the sloping square on its N side has become a symbol of Pécs.

It is believed that the site of the crypt was an early Christian basilica which developed as a church with the present ground plan by the 9C. The earliest relics originate from the 11C. It was during this and the following century that the towers were built. The entrances to the crypt date from the 12C, though what remains of the crypt itself is entirely 11C. The Cathedral burnt down on several occasions. It was completely changed in each rebuilding. The Turks used the church as a mosque—one of the towers became the minaret. After the Turkish period remodelling of the church continued, which eventually resulted in rebuilding in Baroque style.

In the early 19C the architect Mihály Pollack was commissioned to transform the exterior of the Baroque cathedral into a neo-classical style, although the interior remained Gothic and the furnishings Baroque. At the end of the last century reconstruction started again. Bishop Nándor Dulánszky wanted to restore the 'original' cathedral from the Árpád period. A 'new' design was prepared by the Austrian architect Friedrich von Schmidt and the building, under the direction of Ágoston Kirstein, was completed in 1891. Eminent artists of the time, including Karl Andreä, Károly Lotz and Bertalan Székely, were entrusted with the interior paintings. György Zala produced replicas of the original medieval reliefs on the entrance to the crypt and György Kiss made statues of the apostles for the exterior, though these were replaced by new examples by Károly Antal in 1963.

The 70m by 22m neo-Romanesque Cathedral has three aisles. Its sanctuary is on a raised level and has a large canopied main altar. The *Corpus Christi Chapel*, inside by the SW tower, has paintings by Károly Lotz. The 16C red marble tabernacle of Bishop Szatmáry here is considered to be one of the finest works of the Hungarian Renaissance. The chapel next to the tower at the SE corner of the cathedral is named after the Pécs bishop, *St. Mór*. It has richly carved pews and contains the skeleton of St. Faustinus which was brought from Rome in 1781. Bertalan Székely painted the murals which includes his noted 'Crowning of Andrew I'. Székely also painted the *Mary Chapel* on the NW side. The alabaster engraving here was made in Rome in the 16C. The paintings in the *Heart of Jesus Chapel* by the NE corner are by Károly Lotz, the statue on the altar by György Zala.

The **Episcopal Palace** stands on the W side of Dóm tér. The present neo-Renaissance form dates from 1832 to 1852 and was designed by Ferenc Windisch for Bishop János Scytovszky, although a bishop's palace has stood on this site since the 12C. There is a life-size statue of *Ferenc Liszt* on the balcony at the S end of the façade overlooking the square (Imre Varga, 1983).

On the opposite side of the square stands the *Chapter Archives and Parish Rectory*. The two-storey building was designed by an Italian architect named Sartory and built in the 1780s. The protruding section to the S, which because of the slope of the square has three levels, was designed by Matthias Fölsinger of Pécs in 1794.

The stone balustrades ending in *sandstone obelisks* on either side of the square were built at the end of the 19C. Bishop Dulánszky's coat of arms can be seen on the side of the obelisks. A bronze statue of a former Bishop of Pécs, *Ignác Szepesy*, stands in the southern part of the square (György Kiss, 1893). On the base two bronze reliefs depict events from the history of the town. The **Csontváry Museum** is to the E of the statue at No. 11–13 Janus Pannonius u., in the former Catholic Young Men's club built in Eclectic style in 1895 to the design of Ágoston Kirstein. Paintings and drawings by the former village assistant pharmacist and self-taught painter Tivadar Csontváry Kosztka (1853–1919) are exhibited inside.

Csontváry's colourful post-Impressionist canvases were virtually unknown in Hungary during the artist's lifetime. It is only in recent decades that his work has become appreciated both at home and abroad. On seeing his paintings at an exhibition in Paris in the 1940s Pablo Picasso commented: 'I did not know that there was another great painter in our century besides me.'

To the W of the Szepesy statue stretches the so-called Barbican garden, at the far end of which is Miklós Borsos' 1972 bronze statue of *Janus Pannonius* (1434–72). In the hand of the one-time Bishop of Pécs is a book, symbolising this humanist poet's love of learning. Janus Pannonius' Latin poems where known throughout Europe. He wrote elegies lamenting Hungary's backwardness, satirical epigrams and lyrical poems. Nearby is the only surviving round stone bastion of the former city walls of Pécs, known as the **Barbican**. It was built in the 15C allegedly on the instructions of the military commander Pál Kinizsi (died 1494) and hence is sometimes known locally as the 'Kinizsi Bastion'.

Evidence suggests that walls were originally built around Pécs in the 13C following the Mongol invasion of 1241–42, but because of the high ground to the N of the town they were not of a sufficiently defensive character. In the period of decline after King Matthias, with the increased threat from the Turks, strengthening work was carried out on the walls. The Turkish victory at Mohács in 1526 led to panic throughout the country and in 1528 Ferdinand I gave the town temporary exemption from taxation in return for the increased fortification of the defence network. In 1543, however, the Turks occupied Pécs with little difficulty. In the Turkish period the walls were left to decay although some repair work was carried out in the 17C. By the 18C the walls had lost all defensive significance. Excavation started in the 1970s and reconstruction of sections of the wall was helped by a precise plan made by Josef Haüy in 1687. There are particularly good views of the walls to the W and N of the Barbican from Landler Jenő u. and Aradi Vértanúk útja.

To the S of the Barbican garden in the park section of Szent István tér stands a statue of *Zoltán Kodály*. The work of Imre Varga, it was unveiled in 1976. In the middle of Szent István tér, down the steps directly below the Szepesy statue, is the entrance to the **Early Christian Mausoleum** (Ókeresztény mauzóleum). The mausoleum was discovered by accident in 1975 and is Hungary's most significant early Christian find. The chapel which stood here was probably built around AD 350–360 for a wealthy inhabitant, hence the designation of mausoleum. Excavation has revealed frescoes of, among others, The Fall of Adam and Eve and Daniel in the Lion's Den. Part of a large white marble sarcophagus is one of the other items carefully preserved. (Open 10.00–18.00 except Monday.)

A huge cemetery was established between the area of today's Sallai u. and the cathedral during the period in which Sopianae flourished in the 3C–4C AD. Most of the graves found so far have been in Dóm tér and Geisler Eta u. After the Roman period, when Pécs, like the rest of Hungary, experienced a wave of migrations of different peoples, the tombs and underground burial chambers were used as a refuge and considerably altered. By the time the Cathedral was built they were already covered with a layer of earth between 5m and 6m deep.

At the lower end of the square is a three-storey college building which occupies the site of the *former Convent of the Order of Our Lady*. It was built in 1847–54 in neo-classical style. The Romantic *Nunnery Church* on its right was added over the following three years.

The route now follows Geisler Eta u. westwards as it swings to the left downhill. To the right, on the curve of the road, is Pál Pátzay's statue *Sisters* (1942). At the bottom of the hill at the junction with Sallai u. is a bronze statue of *St. Francis of Assisi* by György Bársony (1939). Two pigeons sit on the ledge of a basin by the pedestal. The saint also holds a pigeon in his hand. Hence it is often known locally as the 'Galambos-kút' (Pigeon fountain).

The **Franciscan Church** stands on the other side of Sallai u. The present structure dates from the first half of the 18C though alterations were made during the 19C. The simple exterior belies the rich interior of the church. The fine Baroque work, for example the *series of chapels* on the northern wall, is probably the work of Franciscan brothers. Noteworthy too is the inlaid Baroque *line of cabinets* in the choir, the work of Brother Lukács Jani dating from 1745.

The Hotel Minaret next to the church is the *former Franciscan monastery* which was constructed in the 1720s and 1730s though it has been altered several times since. Records show that the Franciscans had a monastery here as early as the 14C. A few metres to the E of the church, just before Váradi Antal u., is the small *Garden of Ruins* standing on the site of the bath of Pasha Memi which was pulled down in 1880. Excavation was begun in 1976.

The route now climbs uphill along Sallai u. back towards Széchenyi tér. *No. 24* on the left dates from the 1770s. It consists of two buildings which were erected at right-angles to the street, a characteristic form of Pécs architecture. One of the finest examples of Romantic architecture in Pécs is the building at *No. 14* further up the hill.

JÓKAI TÉR is at the top of Sallai u. The *Zsolnay Centenary Fountain* stands in the middle of the square. The glazed pyrogranite fountain was designed by Antal Gazder and erected in 1968 on the 100th anniversary of the foundation of the Zsolnay factory. Behind it is the so-called *Elephant Block*, the name given to the group of five buildings standing between Jókai tér and Széchenyi tér. This complex of Eclectic, Baroque, neo-classical and Romantic buildings has been renovated and functions as a mini arts centre. The neo-classical *Elephant House* overlooking Jókai tér, from which the block derives its name, was a bakery in the early 18C and later became a restaurant. For a while in the 1870s it was a grocers. The building was renovated in 1984 and today again houses a restaurant.

The oldest pharmacy in Pécs, the *Saracen Pharmacy* (Szerecsen Patika), is nearby at No. 1 Geisler Eta u. (round the corner to the left from the N of Jókai tér). A pharmacy was founded here in 1697 by János Sietz. The neo-Rococo oak fittings date from 1897 which was when the present building was erected. Above the shelving is a white cornice decorated by flowered ceramic tiles from the Zsolnay factory. The tiled basin is early 20C. A yellow-aproned Saracen is depicted above, which was also made in the Zsolnay factory.

Széchenyi tér, the start of the route, lies a few metres to the E.

Other places of interest. Rákóczi út and Felsőmalom u., which run around the town centre from SW to SE, have a number of places of interest not included on the main route.

The **Mosque of Pasha Yakovali Hassan** with its ribbed dome and minaret stands at No. 2 Rákóczi út opposite the new Pannonia Hotel on the SW side of the centre. It dates from the second half of the 16C but after the Turks were driven out Bishop Nesselrode turned the mosque into a chapel dedicated to St. John of Nepomuk. Later the building was reconstructed in Baroque style and it became the chapel of the University hospital built next door. Restoration began in the 1950s and the mosque was reconstructed in line with its original purpose. Albeit a result of restoration it is one of the finest Turkish relics in Hungary. Excerpts from the Koran and floral ornamentation have been uncovered on the plaster of the dome. There is a permanent exhibition of Turkish finds in Hungary inside the entrance hall. (Open 10.00–13.00, 14.00–18.00 except Wednesday.)

The Janus Pannonius Museum has a *Folk Art Exhibition* (Néprajzi Kiállítás) at No. 15 Rákóczi út just beyond the southern end of Váradi Antal u. Folk art and folk costumes of Baranya county are on display as well as the interior of a house from the local Ormánság region. (Open 10.00–16.00 except Monday.)

A statue of *Vilmos Zsolnay*, the founder of the famous Pécs ceramics factory, stands nearby at the junction of Rákóczi út and Szabadság u. (János Horvay, 1907).

A selection of Hungarian painting from 1950 to the present day is on display at the *Modern Hungarian Gallery* situated at No. 2 Szabadság u. Opened in 1957 the collection belongs to the Janus Pannonius Museum. (Open 12.00–18.00 except Monday.)

Hal tér lies on Rákóczi út some way to the E beyond Bem u. From here Kossuth tér is a short distance to the N. On the E side of the square stands the *Synagogue* built in Romantic style to the designs of Frigyes Feszl, Károly Gerster and Lipót Kauser in 1865–69. The first synagogue of Pécs was built in Citrom u. nearby in 1843 and was demolished when the present building was opened. The synagogue has a valuable organ made in the Angster factory in Pécs. At the other end of Kossuth tér there is a statue of *Lajos Kossuth* by local sculptor János Horvay (1908).

The *Geographical Exhibition* of the Janus Pannonius Museum is situated at No. 64 Rákóczi út. On display are pictures of the fauna and flora of the Mecsek region. (Closed Mondays.)

Rákóczi út swings N into Felsőmalom u. at the junction where Road No. 6 reaches the inner city of Pécs as Zsolnay Vilmos u. The *Local History Museum* (Várostörténeti és Munkásmozgalmi Múzeum) is situated at No. 9 Felsőmalom u. on the E side of the road. Opened in 1985 in a former tannery which occupied the late-Baroque 1786 building, the exhibitions cover the history of Pécs and its labour movement from 1686 to 1948, and the history of leatherwork in Pécs. There is also a special collection of old Hungarian playing cards. In the courtyard there are some 18C–19C statues from Pécs. (Open 10.00–18.00 except Monday.)

Sörház u. continues from the N end of Felsőmalom u. Ágoston tér lies 200m along this. Here stands the *Church of St. Augustine* (Szent Ágoston-templom). A church stood here in the Middle Ages which the Turks used as a mosque. It was completely destroyed by fire in 1750 and had to be rebuilt. Remains of Turkish windows can still be seen, however, on the southern wall.

All Saints Church (Mindszentek temploma) stands to the NE of the town centre at the end of Sörház u. by Tettye u. It was built in the 13C but reconstructed in late-Gothic style two centuries later when a new sanctuary was erected with buttresses. During Turkish times this was the only Christian church in Pécs. Further reconstruction took place in the 18C when it was transformed into a three-aisled church and the tower with its onion dome was built.

Excursions from Pécs

Misina Hill is one of the peaks of the Mecsek Hills rising 534m just to the N of the city. The 176m-high TV tower which stands here has a coffee bar and a terrace from where a splendid view of the surroundings can be had. From here there are well-marked walking routes to various beauty spots in the surrounding hills. Below the peak, on Beloiannisz u. which leads up to the tower, there is a small zoo. Bus No. 35 goes to the TV tower from the railway station in Lenin tér, which is to the S of the centre.

Abaliget is situated 18km NW of Pécs. Here, 220m above sea level, is a cave of stalagmites, with a main passage 466m long. The cave has a healing atmosphere due to its constant temperature, high humidity and the salt content of the dripping water. There is a tourist hotel, camping site and restaurant nearby.

Mánfa, 11km N of Pécs on Road 66, has a late 12C Romanesque church which was altered in the following century and then again in the 14C in Gothic style. Nevertheless, it is one of the earliest surviving churches in Hungary. Two original medieval stone fonts still remain inside.

Cserkút, 8km W of Pécs via Road 6, has an originally 13C Romanesque Catholic church in which some frescoes have survived. The church at *Kővágószőlős* 1km beyond Cserkút was originally 12C but was rebuilt in Gothic style in the 15C.

Szigetvár lies 33km to the W of Pécs on Road 6. (Regular rail connection from the Lenin tér station.) In 1566 the Turkish sultan Süleyman the Magnificent besieged the castle here at the head of an army of 100,000. The 2400 defenders, under the command of Miklós Zrínyi (c 1508–66), held out for 33 days. When finally Zrínyi and his Hungarian and Croatian soldiers broke out of the burning castle they engaged in bloody hand-to-hand combat until they had virtually all been killed. The Habsburg king, Maximilian I, had meanwhile been waiting with a mercenary force at Győr but refused to heed Zrínyi's calls for assistance. Although it was rebuilt by the Turks, the castle underwent centuries of neglect until it was finally completely restored in the 1960s. The *Zrínyi Miklós Castle Museum* is situated within the castle walls in a 16C building which was used as a mosque by the Turks. (Open 8.00–18.00; Nov–March 10.00–15.00; closed Mondays.) At No. 3 Bástya u., outside the walls, there is a 16C Turkish dwelling house which has been turned into a museum. (Open May–Sept 10.00–12.00, 14.00–16.00, closed Mondays.)

Siklós is approximately 30km to the S of Pécs via Road 58. (There is a regular bus service from the long-distance bus station in Pécs near the junction of Szalay András u. and Rózsa Ferenc u.) The *Castle* here was built at the turn of the 15C and enlarged at the beginning of the 16C. Its present appearance dates from the beginning of the 18C. The medieval fortress section has remained almost completely intact—a rarity in Hungary. The chapel, with its arched windows, fragments of frescoes and Renaissance stone carvings is a particularly noteworthy piece of Gothic architecture which dates from the first half of the 15C. The Castle Museum is situated inside the walls. Inside is a special glove collection. (Open 9.00–18.00 except Monday.)

Harkány, 6km to the W of Siklós, is a thermal spa resort at the foot of the Villány mountains. Hot waters containing sulphur and fluoride were discovered in the early 19C and have been used in health treatments ever since.

Villány, 13km E of Siklós, has been a wine-producing centre for almost 2000 years. The *Wine Museum* (Bormúzeum) at No. 8 Bem u. has an exhibition of 19C wine production, barrel-making and other aspects of the history of the local viticulure. (Open 9.00–17.00 except Monday.)

12 Budapest to Szeged via Kecskemét

Road 5. Total distance 171km. **Budapest**—Road 5 (30km **Ócsa**) 40km **Dabas**—27km **Lajosmizse**—18km **Kecskemét**—28km **Kiskunfélegyháza** (15km **Bugac**)—30km Kistelek and turning for (10km) **Ópusztaszer**—20km **Fehér-tó**—8km **Szeged**.

Szeged lies 171km to the SE of Budapest near the Yugoslav and Romanian borders. Road 5 from Boráros tér at the Pest end of Petőfi Bridge runs all the way to Szeged through the flat lands of the western part of the Great Plain. The road passes through Kecskemét roughly half-way between Budapest and Szeged. Motorway M5 runs for 75km in the direction of Kecskemét and then joins Road 5 (though only the first 38km has two lanes in each direction). The motorway leaves Nagykőrösi út in the Kispest district of Budapest to the SE of the city centre (take Üllői út from Kálvin tér and follow the signs for the M5).

The village of **Ócsa** is 30km from the centre of Budapest mid-way between the M5 Motorway and Road 5 (there is an exit from the motorway). The *Calvinist Church* here was built c 1250, originally for the Premonstratensians. It has belonged to the Reformed church since 1562. Fire caused some damage in the late 1880s and the towers date from the 1920s, but some rare 13C frescoes remain on the interior walls. The church was closed for restoration in the late 1980s and at the time of writing it was not yet clear when it would be reopened.

The *Ócsa Conservation Area* lies to the S of the village. Its 3575 hectares of bogs and forests were turned into a protected area in 1975 in view of the rich fauna and flora and many insects, butterflies and birds found here. The life and traditions of the region are the subject of the displays at the *local museum* situated in a peasant house at No. 4 Bercsényi u., Ócsa. (Open at weekends 10.00–15.00; Nov–March Sunday only.)

Dabas, 10km beyond Ócsa by Road 5, is noted for its early 19C neo-classical mansions on Biksa Miklós u. The residence of the Kossuth family used to be situated here.

The geographical centre of Hungary (17°11′N; 19°30′E) is marked by a 10m-high *symbolic tower* at *Pusztavacs* a few kilometres to the

W of the M5 (exit after the 52km mark). The tower was designed by
József Kerény and erected in 1978. The sundial is by Gábor Gáta.

Road 5 passes through **Lajosmizse**, which is about 18km before
Kecskemét. This is the beginning of a traditional area of individual
farms set in isolation. The *Farm Museum* (Tanyamúzeum) by the
roadside a few kilometres beyond the village preserves two farms
characteristic of the region between the Danube and the Tisza rivers
at the turn of the century. One is concerned with animal husbandry,
the other with horticulture. (Open 1 February–15 March and 16
October–15 December, 10.00–15.00; 16 March–15 October, 10.00–
18.00; closed Mondays.) Imre Varga's 1956 statue of *The Sower*
(Magvető) stands in front of the farm museum.

85km from Budapest Road 5 passes through the outskirts of
KECSKEMÉT (pop. 105,000), a traditional market town of the Great
Plain.

Hungary's largest fruit orchards are in the region, and from the
chief fruit, apricots, the famous Kecskemét apricot brandy is made.
There are vast vineyards around the town and these produce approximately 30 per cent of the country's wine.

The area was inhabited as early as the 1C AD. The conquering
Magyars established a settlement here and by the Middle Ages
Kecskemét had become a flourishing market town. The Mongol and
Turkish invasions both led to destruction but as Kecskemét was
governed directly by the Sultan it enjoyed some security during
Turkish times. Economic prosperity started to grow in the middle of
the 19C with the beginning of large-scale wine and fruit production.

Kecskemét still has a small town atmosphere but a number of
interesting and, in some cases, very colourful Hungarian Art
Nouveau buildings give an urban, turn-of-the-century feel to parts of
the centre. The restoration of these and other buildings and the
process of adapting modern ones to fit in naturally with the older
environment, under the direction of the architect József Kerény, has
won much praise for Kecskemét.

Tourist Information: Pusztatourist, 2 Szabadság tér (76/29-499).

Rail Station: Köztársaság tér. 1½ hours by express from the Western Railway
Station, Budapest.

Bus Station: Felszabadulás park. 1¾ hours from the Népstadion Bus Station,
Budapest.

Post Office: 10 Kálvin tér.

Police: 17–19 Rákóczi út.

The route in Kecskemét begins on KOSSUTH TÉR in the centre of the
town and describes a rough circle in an anti-clockwise direction
around this and the neighbouring SZABADSÁG TÉR.

The Baroque Catholic church on the square is known as the **Old
Church** (Öregtemplom) and sometimes as the **Big Church**
(Nagytemplom). It was designed by a Piarist father, Oswald Gáspár,
and built between 1774 and 1806. The reliefs on the façade are
memorials to (left) the 'Seventh Wilhelm Hussars' and (right) those
'Kecskemét citizens killed in 1848–49' during the War of Independence. Above the main door is a group of statues depicting Christ
giving the keys of Heaven to St. Peter, and on the façade there are
further statues of St. Stephen, St. Ladislas, St. Peter and St. Paul. The
main altarpiece inside depicts the Ascension of Christ. The artist was
Ferenc Falconer who also made the paintings on the two side altars.
The ceiling frescoes are the work of Ignác Roskovics and date from

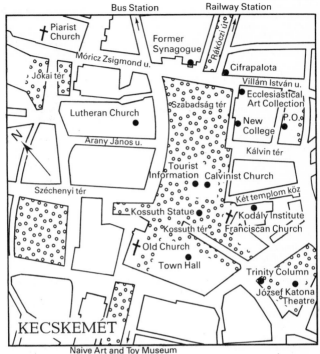

Bus Station · Railway Station

KECSKEMÉT

Naive Art and Toy Museum

1902. The church has been restored several times, most recently in the 1970s. The modern *Aranyhomok Szálló* (Golden Sands Hotel) on the N side of the square was designed by István Janáky and built in 1962.

The **Town Hall** to the S of the church was built in 1893–96 and designed by Ödön Lechner and Gyula Pártos. It was the first building where Lechner attempted to create a Hungarian national style by adding coloured folk ornamentation, and it pre-figures his later buildings in Budapest such as the Museum of Applied Arts and the Postal Savings Bank. The ceremonial hall inside has frescoes by Bertalan Székely. The bells on the façade play snippets of Kodály, Erkel, Handel, Beethoven and Mozart at regular intervals.

Lechner once wrote that 'the Town Hall of Kecskemét was made under the influence of a short visit to England' where he thought that British architecture 'had preserved a great deal of its original rural simplicity'. Whether the judgement was correct or not Lechner's followers, who started to develop a National Romantic *style* of architecture as opposed to what they considered to be his surface ornamentation, were certainly also influenced by English tendencies, particularly the Arts and Crafts movement. Nevertheless, the Kecskemét Town Hall can be seen as the beginning of a specifically Hungarian architectural development.

Just in front of the Town Hall is a stone block split in two, the *József Katona Memorial*. The inscription reads: 'One of Kecskemét's greatest sons broke his heart here', for it was on this spot that the dramatist József Katona (1791–1830) died of a heart attack.

József Katona was born in Kecskemét, the son of a local weaver. He attended
school here and studied law in Budapest. Later he worked as a public prosecutor
in Kecskemét. He was writing plays at the age of 20 but his early dramas were
never staged. His 'Bánk bán', which has become one of the seminal plays of
Hungarian national drama, was written in 1814 for a competition held for the
opening of the National Theatre in Kolozsvár in Transylvania (today Cluj). It
failed even to get a mention by the jury. It was revised a few years later but
performances were banned by the censor. Finally published in 1820 it received
little attention and was never performed in the author's lifetime.

'Bánk bán' has a historical theme based around the rebellion of the potentate
Bánk and the murder of Queen Gertrude while King Andrew II was away at
war. It is based on real events. The historical tragedy in five acts, although
having a medieval setting, was seen as having very relevant contemporary
national themes and this accounted for its later success. It was first performed in
Kassa (Košice, Czechoslovakia) in 1833 and then in 1839 at the National
Theatre in Pest. It was regularly on the bill here during the 1848–49 War of
Independence, but afterwards it was banned for a decade. Since then, however,
it has never lost its popularity. Composer Ferenc Erkel wrote an opera from it
which was first performed in 1861 and it has been a regular feature of
Hungarian repertoires ever since.

Facing the Town Hall is Ede Telcs' statue (1906) of *Lajos Kossuth*
(1802–94) the political leader of the struggle for Hungarian independence in the mid-19C. Behind the statue, at No. 2 Kossuth tér, is the
county *Tourist Information Office*, Pusztatourist. (Open Mon–Thurs
8.00–17.00; Fri 8.00–16.30; closed Saturdays and Sundays.) Just to
the left of the Town Hall, in the small park area, is a bust of Péter
Lestár (1819–96) a former mayor and leading participant from Kecskemét in the 1848–49 War of Independence.

The Baroque *Holy Trinity Column* (Szentháromság-oszlop) stands
a short way to the S in Katona József tér. It was designed by Lipót
Antal Conti and erected in 1742 following the plague of 1739–40 in
which nearly 6000 people died out of a population of 18,000. The
statues around the octagonal balustrade were restored in 1972–74.

The *József Katona Theatre* here was built in 1895–96 and designed
by the Viennese architects Helmer and Fellner. It is a smaller version
of the Vígszínház (Gaiety Theatre) on Budapest's Szent István körút
which they also designed. On the left of the theatre is a statue of
József Katona by Tamás Vígh and to the right is a *memorial* to the
38th Infantry Regiment (Zsigmond Kisfaludi Strobl, 1942).

Opposite the SE corner of the Town Hall in Kossuth Lajos tér
stands the **Franciscan Church**. It is the oldest church in the town and
dates from the Middle Ages. In the 16C it was jointly used by
Catholics and Calvinists but in 1678 it passed into the hands of the
Franciscans. In the same year the wooden tower burnt down. The
Baroque stone tower was built 100 years later. An earthquake in 1911
caused serious damage which resulted in reconstruction. A notable
feature is the wrought-iron gate by the small courtyard. It is the work
of Ferenc Tiringer, a local master, and was made in 1930.

The **Zoltán Kodály Institute of Music Education** (Kodály Zoltán
Zenepedagógiai Inézet) is behind the church in Kéttemplom köz. It
occupies the former Franciscan monastery which was built in
Baroque style in 1702–36. The building was redesigned by József
Kerényi in the early 1970s for the Institute.

Zoltán Kodály (1882–1967) was born in Kecskemét and became, along with
Béla Bartók, one of the founders of modern Hungarian music. He was a
composer, a musicologist and a pioneer of music education. The so-called
'Kodály method', which places great emphasis on choral singing and the
enjoyment of song as the basis of musical education, has been taken up and
applied worldwide. Surprisingly perhaps for a man who is deemed to have
created a specifically Hungarian approach to music, Kodály acknowledged that

he learnt much from his visits to England. 'The high level of English choral singing', he once wrote, 'was for us a stimulating example.' He drew on English music practice and in music teaching applied John Curwen's Tonic Sol-Fa method. He visited and conducted in Britain several times and had a close relationship with the English musicologist, Edward J. Dent. The Kodály seminars at the Institute regularly attract music teachers from all over the world.

On the ground floor of the building there is a small exhibition about Kodály and his work. (Open Mon–Fri 12.00–13.00 and 16.00–18.00; Sat and Sun 10.00–18.00.)

The *Calvinist Church* is just across from the N end of Kéttemplom köz and faces E into the park area of Szabadság tér. The present church dates from 1790–92. It was built on the walls of a 15C Catholic church. The tower, with its Renaissance twin windows, is the work of local builder Boldizsár Fischer.

No. 7 on the S side of the square, the **New College** (Új-kollégium), was built in 1911–13 to the designs of Valér Mende and Lajos Dombi.

The building is a good example of Hungarian National Romantic architecture and shows clearly the development that had taken place in this style since the period of Lechner's use of folk ornamentation, as seen on Kecskemét's Town Hall. Although Zsolnay ceramics were used on this building, the emphasis was on architectural designs the form of which was authentically Hungarian and not just the decoration. The 'rural' character of the building stems from the attempt to incorporate traditional Hungarian peasant styles into the new buildings of the time.

The rear end facing Búzác u. was rebuilt in 1927 by Jenő Szappanos for the Calvinist grammar school and law academy. Today the building houses a music school and the offices and library of the local Reformed Church. Around the corner on the W side of the building facing Villám u. is the entrance to the *Ecclesiastical Art Collection* of the Reformed Episcopacy of the Danube region. (Open 10.00–18.00 except Monday.)

Across the road, on the corner of Villám u. and the wide Rákóczi út, stands one of the most colourful and unusual buildings in Hungary, the **Cifrapalota** (Ornamental Palace). The building, adorned with coloured ceramics, was designed by Géza Márkus and built in 1902. It is one of the most lively examples of Hungarian Art Nouveau (known in Hungary as Secessionist style). Today it is a county trade union headquarters and also houses the *Kecskemét Gallery* (Kecskeméti Képtár) which exhibits Hungarian paintings and graphics from the present and last century, work of the artist Menyhért Tóth (1904–80) and an exhibition of enamel work. (Open 10.00–18.00 except Monday.)

The large *statue* at the end of Rákóczi út is a monument to those killed during the suppression of the 1919 Hungarian Republic of Councils (Klára Merezeg and József Körner, 1959). The impressive Romantic, Moorish-style building to the left of the monument is the former **Synagogue**, built between 1862 and 1871 to the plans of János Zitterbarth. The present Persian-style dome was erected after an earthquake of 1911 which toppled the previous onion-shaped one. The synagogue was devastated by the Germans in 1944 at the time of the deportation of the Jews. It was restored by József Kerényi in 1973 and was further renovated at the end of the 1980s.

Across from the former synagogue, at *No. 3* Szabadság tér, there is another example of National Romanticism (Valér Mende, 1911). Note how the modern corner building next to it, which extends round into Móricz Zsigmond u., has been designed to blend with it.

The 'Cifrapalota'. A striking example of Hungarian Art Nouveau in Kecskemét.

This is characteristic of modern Hungarian architecture which has to comply with regulations stipulating that new buildings do not spoil the existing environment. Some architects go beyond this and incorporate traditional elements into their work. József Kerény, the architect who played a leading role in the modern town planning of Kecskemét, once wrote: 'In order that our communities should not be the realised failures of a utopia of a sterile order, we have to keep alive the memory of our past; we have to defend and use the materials and intellectual heritage of our predecessors.'

Móricz Zsigmond u. leads northwards and runs into Jókai u. at Komszomol tér. On the right stands the Baroque **Piarist Church**, designed by András Mayerhoffer and built in 1724–30. The tower was added in 1765 by József Peithmüller. On the façade are statues of St. Stephen and St. Ladislas, two 11C Hungarian kings (István and László) who are often portrayed together in statues. Above the door in the niche is a statue of St. Joseph of Calasanctius who founded the Piarist order. The buildings to the left and right of the church were built for the order in 1720–25 and 1825–32 respectively. The large building across from the church on the N side of Komszomol tér is today occupied by a Piarist secondary school, a state primary school and a workers' technical college.

A short distance to the SW of Komszomol tér at No. 1 Arany János u. stands the *Lutheran Church* built in the form of a Greek cross in 1863 and designed by Miklós Ybl. Originally there were four corner towers, but these were destroyed during the earthquake of 19ll. A notable feature of the interior is the wrought-iron work. A short way to the N, at No. 1 Lugosi u., is the international *Ceramics Studio*, the first of its kind in the country. The building was restored by József Kerényi in 1977.

Other places of interest. Kecskemét has a number of interesting museums outside the central area of the town, but all are within walking distance of the centre. Four are situated to the SW of the centre.

The *Medical Collection* (Orvosés Gyógyszerészettörténeti Gyűjtemény) at No. 3 Kölcsey u. exhibits items connected with the history of medicine in the county (Bács-Kiskun) over the past 200 years. (Open 10.00–18.00 except Monday.)

The *Museum of Naïve Art* (Naiv Művészek Múzeuma) at No. 11 Gáspár András u. was opened in 1976 in a provincial Baroque dwelling house dating from 1730. It has a collection of 20C Hungarian naïve paintings ranging from pre-World War I work to the 1980s. (Open 10.00–18.00 except Monday.)

In 1981 the *Toy Museum* (Szórakaténusz Játékműhely és Múzeum) opened in a specially designed building (József Kerényi) at the corner of Gáspár András u. and Hosszú u. The exhibitions cover the history of toy design and manufacture, toys from festive occasions and international toys. Children can play with some of the toys at weekends. (Open 10.00–18.00 except Monday.)

The *Museum of Hungarian Folk Craft* (Magyar Népi Iparművészeti Múzeum) was opened in 1983 in a late-18C Baroque house at No. 19/a Külső Szabadság u. across Szalvai körút. The exhibition includes samples of the last 35 years of folk art (embroidery, pottery, weaving, etc.) and has a memorial room dedicated to the memory of the folk art specialist and historian, Gyula Ortutay (1910–78). (Open 9.00–17.00 except Monday and Tuesday.)

Bánk bán u. is SE of the centre not far from the József Katona Theatre. Here, at No. 9, is the *Modern History Museum* (Újkori Történeti Múzeum). Opened in 1986, it covers the history of Kecskemét in the 19C and 20C. (Open 10.00–18.00 except Monday.)

The *Bozsó Collection* (Bozsó Gyűjtemény) is in a Baroque house built in 1786 at No. 34 Klapka u. to the NE of the centre. As well as paintings by János Bozsó, a living local artist, there is a display of applied and folk art from his own collection and that of the town. (Open Fri, Sat and Sun 10.00–18.00.)

The *József Katona Museum* is the county museum and has a general collection about the history of the region. It is situated near the railway station at No. 1 Bethlen körút at the N end of the park to the NE of the centre. (Open 10.00–18.00 except Monday.)

Further to the NE, at No. 19 Liszt Ferenc u., in the building of the

Kiskunság National Park Directorate, there is a *National Park Exhibi-tion Room* with displays about the National Park's animal and plant life. (Open Sundays and holidays 10.00–12.00.)

Excursions from Kecskemét

Nagykőrös (pop. 27,000) lies 16km NE of Kecskemét on Road 441. Historically it was a market town and is today one of the county's main vegetable and fruit producing centres. The *Town Hall* on Szabadság tér dates from c 1710 though parts were added in the 19C. The statue in front of the building is of Lajos Kossuth who gave a speech from the balcony here in September 1848. Árpád Somogyi's *Liberation Monument* stands nearby. The Catholic *Church of St. Ladislas* in the square was built in Louis XVI style in the 1780s to the plans of the Kecskemét architect Boldizsár Fischer. The *Calvinist Church*, also in Szabadság tér, was originally 15C Gothic but has been altered several times. The celebrated epic poet, János Arany (1817–82) taught at the local grammar school here from 1851 to 1860. The *János Arany Museum* is situated at No. 19 Ceglédi út, just under 1km to the N from the main square. The exhibition inside covers the history of the region from the Magyar Conquest to the present time with particular reference to literary history. (Open 10.00–18.00 except Monday.)

The route to Szeged continues from Kecskemét on Road 5.

Kiskunfélegyháza, 28km SE of Kecskemét on Road 5, was settled by the Cumanians in the Middle Ages. Completely destroyed during the Turkish occupation it was later settled in the 1740s by the Jazygians, who like the Cumanians before them were a nomadic people from the east who migrated to Hungary in the 13C.

The *Little Cumania Museum* (Kiskun Múzeum) is at No. 9 Vöröshadsereg u. (on the left of Road 5 before the main crossroads of the town). The exhibitions cover the history of the region and include paintings by local artist László Holló (1887–1976). Part of the complex of buildings served as a prison from 1753 to 1919 and this today is maintained as a *prison museum* covering the history of prisons in Hungary from 1514 to 1919. In the yard at the back there is a characteristic local windmill dating from 1860. It was moved here from its original site at Mindszent on the banks of the Tisza, 30km to the SE. (Open April–Oct 13.00–17.00 except Monday.)

An impressive Hungarian Secessionist *Town Hall* with majolica decoration stands at the main crossroads in the centre of Kiskun-félegyháza. It was designed by Nándor Morbitzer and József Vass and built in 1912.

The birthplace of the writer, journalist and museologist, Ferenc Móra (1879–1934) is at No. 19 Móra Ferenc u., S from Bajcsy-Zsilinszki u. which runs eastwards from the Town Hall. His birth-place has been turned into a *Ferenc Móra Memorial House* devoted to his life and work. (Open Thurs, Fri and Sat 10.00–14.00.)

A significant proportion of the area between the Danube and the Tisza around Kiskunfélegyháza, the so-called **Kiskunság** (Little Cumania), is a sandy table-land sparsely covered with patches of grass which over the centuries afforded little possibility of farming apart from the breeding of sheep. Since the beginning of the 19C, the shifting sand has been gradually stabilised and the prairie turned into cultivated land with afforestation, the planting of grapes and other fruit. Kiskunság apricots, summer apples and table grapes have become valuable export items for the country. Despite the development of horticulture, however, certain sections of the area still preserve the natural landscape of the region. The *Kiskunság National Park*, the second national park in Hungary, was established on 30,000 hectares to protect the indigenous plant and animal life, reed-filled marshes and wild bird life. The *Bugac* is the most famous prairie of this protected territory. The *Kiskunság National Park Museum* is situated in the village of **Bugac** 15km to the W of Kiskunfélegyháza. It depicts the old shepherd's life of wandering from place to place in search of pastures and their buildings made from reeds and twigs. (Open May–Oct 10.00–17.00 except Monday.)

At Kistelek, 30km S of Kiskunfélegyháza on Road 5, there is a well-marked turning for **Ópusztaszer**, 10km to the E. Here, just outside the village, is the *National Historical Memorial Park* (Nemzeti Történeti Emlékpark). (Open April–Oct 9.00–17.00 except Monday.) According to Anonymus, the chronicler of Béla III, Árpád and the other chiefs of the conquering Magyars held their first 'parliamentary session' here. At any rate, this is the spot where Lajos Lovas' *memorial* was erected in 1896 as part of the massive millennial celebrations held throughout Hungary in that year. This was also the place symbolically chosen for the first distribution of land after World War II. It took place on 29 March 1945.

The remains of a 13C Romanesque church and monastery have been discovered on the site and these have been excavated and the foundations can now be seen. An open-air *ethnographical museum* has been established here and traditional peasant and other houses have been brought from different parts of SE Hungary. By the early 1990s it is expected that Árpád Feszty's monumental *Cyclorama* will be restored and ready to be placed in a special building being erected here to house it.

This huge canvas, depicting Árpád leading the Magyars into the valley of Munkács (today Mukachevo in the Soviet Union), was made for the Millennium celebrations in 1896 and exhibited in a special building on the site where the Budapest Museum of Fine Arts stands today. In 1899 it was exhibited in London. In 1908 it moved to another building in the City Park near the Széchenyi Baths. Damaged during the siege of 1944–45 it has been under the attention of restorers for several years.

The 14 sq km area known as **Fehér-Tó** (White Lake) is 20km to the S of Kistelek. This is the deepest point of the Great Plain and is designated a protected bird sanctuary by the International Bird Protection Council of UNESCO. Over 250 species have been observed. The look-out tower for bird-watchers is approached from the Szatymaz cemetery hill.

Kiskundorozsma is 3km to the W of Road 5 just before it reaches the outskirts of Szeged. Here a traditional *windmill* dating from 1821 has been restored and is preserved as a monument which can be visited. (Open 15 April–31 October, 13.00–17.00 except Monday.)

13   Szeged

The key date in the modern history of **SZEGED** (pop. 188,000) is
1879. In March of that year the Tisza river, on which Szeged stands,
overflowed its banks in a tremendous flood which destroyed the
town and left over 6000 homes in ruins. The town had to be almost
completely rebuilt. The style generally adopted was the then popular
Eclectic style which had just been employed on Budapest's specially
constructed Nagykörút and many other buildings in the capital.
Szeged, therefore, is a unique example of a Hungarian town almost
entirely constructed in this style of architecture. Its broad avenues
and sweeping curved boulevards were a model of late-19C town
planning, the atmosphere of which has still remained. In recognition
of the international assistance the town received for rebuilding after
the flood, stretches of Szeged's Great Boulevard (Nagykörút) encircling the town were named after the cities, which included London,
that provided help. The Moscow section, however, was only thus
named after 1945.

Tourist Information: Szeged Tourist, 1 Victor Hugo u. (62/11-711).

Rail Station: Indóház tér. 2¹/₂ hours by express from the Western Railway
Station, Budapest.

Bus Station: Marx tér. 3¹/₂ hours from the Népstadion Bus Station, Budapest.

Post Office: 1 Széchenyi tér.

Police: 42 Párizsi körút.

History. The area of Szeged has been inhabited for many centuries. Before the
Hungarians a succession of different peoples settled here: Illyrians, Celts,
Jazygians, Huns, Gepids and Avars. During the years following the foundation
of the Hungarian state Szeged became an important centre for salt distribution.
The Mongol invasion (1241–42) disrupted the town's development as did the
Turkish occupation which began in 1543. Because of its geographical position
Szeged was a Turkish stronghold, being in the heart of Turkish-occupied
Hungary. However, virtually no traces of the Turkish period have survived, not
even to the minimal extent that they have in Pécs which was in a similar
position, geographically speaking.
  Development only really took off in the period of reconstruction after the 1879
flood. Post-World War II planning added residential and industrial areas so that
today, apart from the capital, Szeged is the third largest city in terms of
population (after Debrecen and Miskolc). Paprika and fruit production are
important as is the food industry (salami, canned foods, paprika processing),
textiles and other branches of industry. The proximity of both the Yugoslav and
the Romanian border makes the city a major traffic junction for international road
transport. Szeged is a university city and has a major biological research institute.
Its open-air theatre festival, held every summer, was initiated in the 1930s and is
a significant cultural attraction for both Hungarian and foreign visitors.

The route begins in SZÉCHENYI TÉR, which is one of the most attractive
public squares in the country. It covers more than 50,000 sq m, and
with its trees, statues, fountains and harmonious surrounding buildings is virtually an inner-city park.
  The **Town Hall** stands on the W side of the square at No. 10. It was
built in 1883 and designed by Ödön Lechner and Gyula Pártos.

The neo-Baroque style is rather unusual for this pair of architects as it was they
who later went on the develop a particularly Hungarian architecture using folk
ornamentation (Kecskemét Town Hall, Budapest Museum of Applied Arts, etc.).
A rather pointed comment was made by Lechner who later wrote: 'Without
modesty I can say that from the point of view of Baroque style I can compete
with anybody. I showed that with the Szeged town hall ... but I don't regard it
as a task for an artist ... if we don't do what is ours but simply regurgitate a

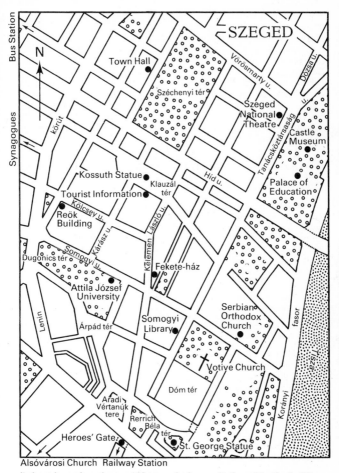

Alsóvárosi Church Railway Station

died-out form of another era.' Not everybody was displeased by the building, however. The poet Mihály Babits (1883–1941) who taught in Szeged in the early years of this century said that the town hall was 'like a lace-covered young woman dancing in the moonlight'.

The neighbouring building to the S at *No. 11* was built in 1870 to the plans of Gyula Wegman and József Adolf Scherrer as a residential block. After the flood of 1879 it was converted into offices. The 'bridge of sighs' between the two buildings was added in 1883.

The classical building on the other side of the Town Hall at *No. 9*, which today has a restaurant on the ground floor, was built in 1844 for a distillery. In 1848 it was used as a military hospital and barracks. In 1849, during the War of Independence, two sessions of the independent Parliament were held here at which the Nationalities Law was enacted.

The two fountains opposite the Town Hall in the park area of the square are entitled 'The blessing and the angry' (Az Áldáshozó és a

Romboló) and are allegories of the river Tisza (János Pásztor, 1930).
They were actually intended for Tihany at Lake Balaton as allegories
of the lake, but were placed here in 1934.

The building of the *Savings Bank* (Takarékpénztár) at No. 7 on the
N side of the square was designed in Secessionist style by Lipót
Baumhorn who made use of modern ferro-concrete techniques.

From the N to the S in the central, park area of the square is a series
of four statues. At the N end stands György Zala's 1914 statue of
Ferenc Deák (1803–76) who was the Hungarian politician most
responsible for the Austro-Hungarian Compromise of 1867 which
established the Dual Monarchy and gave Hungary a limited amount
of independence.

The inscription on the base is a quotation from Deák and reads: 'What force and
power may take away, that can be brought back by time and good fortune; but
what a nation itself fearing suffering has given up—regaining it is difficult and
always doubtful.'

The next statue is of *Lajos Tisza* (1832–98) the Minister of Labour and
Transport in the early 1870s and a man instrumental in the rebuilding of Szeged after the flood (János Fadrusz, 1904). To the S is a
bronze statue of *Pál Vásárhelyi* (1795–1846), the engineer who laid
the plans for the regulation of the river Tisza in the 1840s (Lajos
Matrai, 1905).

It was one of the world's largest flood control projects at the time and another of
the projects which Count István Széchenyi promoted. 120 large bends of the
river were cut through and straight channels dug, shortening the river by
450km. 4000km of dykes secured about 3 million hectares (7.4 million acres) of
land from flood devastation. The proposals generated much heated argument
and in the midst of intense debate Vásárhelyi died of a heart attack before the
project was begun.

The statue at the S end of the square is of *István Széchenyi* (1791–
1860), the leading economic and social reformer of the 1825–48
Reform Period (Alajos Stróbl, 1912). On the limestone base there is a
relief of the Chain Bridge in Budapest, the building of which
Széchenyi had initiated.

The route continues along the pedestrian precinct of Kárász u.
which leads off from the middle of the S end of Széchenyi tér.
KLAUZÁL TÉR is 100m to the S. A statue of *Lajos Kossuth* (1802–94)
the political leader of the movement for national independence in the
last century stands in the square, to the left (József Róna, 1902).

In 1905 the square was the scene of a bloody incident when a group of mutinous
soldiers laid a wreath at the statue. The police attacked wounding several
civilians in the crowd. When news of the event spread, demonstrators bearing
the national colours came from all over the country to protest.

The other statue in the square, to the right, is entitled *The Breadcut-
ter* and is the work of Pál Pátzay. The classical building at *No. 5*
nearby has some historical associations. The last speech of Lajos
Kossuth during the War of Independence was delivered here from
the balcony in 1849. 'If Debrecen is the place where we gained our
independence', he said, 'then Szeged will be the place where
freedom is announced to Europe.' (A reference to the overthrow of
the Habsburgs which had been declared by Kossuth in the Great
Calvinist Church at Debrecen.) The writer Ferenc Móra also spoke
from the same balcony announcing the formation of a republican
government in October 1918.

There is a *Tourist Information Office* (Szeged Tourist) at *No. 2*

Klauzál tér. (Open Mon–Fri 9.00–6.00, Sat 9.00–2.00; open every day and until later during the summer festival.)

Kölcsey u. is the first street to cross Kárász u. as it continues to the S of the square. 100m to the right on the corner is the so-called **Reök Building**, which is one of the most notable pieces of Art Nouveau in Szeged. Built in 1907, it was designed by Ede Magyar for Iván Reök, the nephew of the painter Mihály Munkácsy. A notable feature is the intricate wrought-iron bannister in the stairway (access via the side door round the corner). It is the work of a local craftsman, Pál Fekete.

DUGONICS TÉR lies a short distance to the S. In the park area on the W side of the square there is a statue of *András Dugonics* (1740–1818), a local writer, university teacher and member of the Piarist order (Miklós Izsó and Adolf Huszár, 1876). The central building of the *Attila József University* stands on the E side of the square. It was designed in early-Eclectic style by Antal Skalnitczky and built in 1873 originally for a science secondary school. The university is today named after its most famous pupil, the poet Attila József (1905–37). There is a statue of him by Imre Varga near the right-hand corner of the building (1964).

The proletarian poet was not always so revered. He was actually expelled from the university in 1924 after an uproar following the publication of his poem 'With a Pure Heart' which opened with the lines 'I have no father and no mother, I have no country and no god,' and later continues 'with a pure heart, I'll burn and loot, and if I have to, I'll even shoot.'

In front of the university is a musical fountain (it plays only in the summer months). Around it are some words from 'A Sonnet to Szeged', a poem by Gyula Juhász (1883–1937) a poet, journalist and member of the 'Nyugat' circle who was born and who died in Szeged.

The route now leaves Dugonics tér at the SE corner and via the street passing through Árpád tér by the modern shopping centre reaches ARADI VÉRTANÚK TERE. The name of the square (Arad Martyrs Square) recalls the 13 Hungarian generals who were executed by the Austrians in Arad, Transylvania, in October 1849 at the end of the War of Independence. A mounted statue of *Ferenc Rákóczi II*, leader of the 1703–11 anti-Habsburg struggle stands in the square (György Vastagh, 1911). Nearby is the *Memorial Column* to the Hungarians killed at the battle of Szőreg a few kilometres from Szeged on 5 August 1849. *Heroes' Gate*, which dominates the S side of the square and leads to the broad April 4th Avenue, was built in 1936 to the design of Móric Pogány. The statues of soldiers on the Aradi Vértanúk tere façade are the work of Éva Lőte.

The garden of Rerrich Béla tér is just to the E. Here is a copy of what many consider to be one of the finest medieval Hungarian sculptures, *St. George and the Dragon* by the Kolozsvári brothers, the original of which (1373) can be seen in Prague.

The small-bodied horse of the statue is a typically Hungarian breed. The saddle is the type used by the Magyars since the Conquest. The garments and equipment of the knight are also characteristically Hungarian. Thus, not only was it one of the earliest sculptures in Europe conceived in the round and designed to be independent of a building, but it is also thoroughly Hungarian in content, form and detail.

The building to the S of the statue was designed in early-Eclectic style by Viktor Bachó and built in 1886 originally as a Piarist secondary school. It became part of the university of Kolozsvár in

1921 and today it belongs to the institutes of higher education, along with the adjoining buildings here and in Dóm tér.

DÓM TÉR (Cathedral Square) to the N can be reached through archways from either Rerrich Béla tér or Aradi Vértanúk tere. The 12,000 sq m area was created in 1920 by demolishing the small streets which stood here previously. The architect, Béla Rerrich, created a three-sided, arcaded building which today, along with some later additions, is occupied by university buildings, halls of residence, a bishop's palace and theological academy. The reliefs of saints around the walls are the work of Béla Ohmann and the iron work that of Pál Virágh. On the S façade there is a *musical clock*. During the festival time moving figures representing university professors, artistic and scientific personalities appear when the music is played. The *National Pantheon* is a series of statues and reliefs that runs along the arcade around the square. It was begun in the late 1920s. Leading personalities of Hungarian history from all walks of life are represented here. Strangely, not one woman is represented among the more than 80 figures. The square is undoubtedly spoilt by the scaffolding and seating of the open-air theatre's 6000-seat auditorium which is left here permanently throughout the year. Summer performances began here in 1931 and continued until the Second World War. Revived in 1959 they are the central part of Szeged's summer festival which takes place annually in July and August.

Szeged's only relic of Romanesque architecture, the *St. Demetrius Tower* (Dömötör-torony) stands towards the NW corner of the square. The foundations are 11C, the lower, square part is 12C, and the upper octagonal part was added in the 13C. It was restored by Béla Rerrich in 1931 following a public debate as to whether it should be demolished. A 12C stone relief of the *Lamb of God*, one of Szeged's oldest relics, was placed inside. The Lamb used to be in Szeged's coat of arms until 1950.

The **Votive Church** on the N side of Dóm tér has become the symbol of Szeged. Following the great flood of 1879 the city fathers were determined to erect a vast church as a plea to God for protection against further floods. The neo-Romanesque cathedral with its 93m-high towers was begun in 1913 to the plans of Frigyes Schulek, the architect who had remodelled and restored the Matthias Church in Buda in the last decades of the 19C. After Schulek's death in 1919 the work was finished under the direction of Ernő Foerk and completed in 1930. The façade has a mosaic of the twelve apostles and above the main gate is a marble statue of the Virgin Mary. The interior is richly decorated. On the ceiling above the chancel is a large mosaic by Ferenc Marton showing the Virgin Mary in traditional folk costume from the Szeged region. Note also the huge organ which has a total of over 9000 pipes. The church is open on weekdays 9.00–18.00 (though on certain unspecified days it may be closed in the morning for cleaning), and on Sundays 9.30–10.00, 11.00–11.30 and 12.30 to 18.00.

The modern building on the W side of the church is the new building of the *Somogyi Library* (see p 315). It was constructed between 1978 and 1984 according to a prize-winning design of the Budapest City Planning Architects' Office under the direction of János Pomsár and Borbála Péterfia.

The **Serbian Orthodox Church** is behind the Votive Church at the side of Somogyi u. It was designed by János Dobi and built in 1773–78 for the Serbians who settled in Szeged after the Turkish period.

The iconostasis, which had belonged to a church which had previously stood here, is the work of Jovan Popovich (1761). It has a pear tree frame and 80 icons. There are also some 16C icons in the church. The ceiling fresco depicting the Creation is by János Hodina. (The church is open at irregular times, though a plaque indicates that the official opening times are: 9.30–11.30, 15.00–17.00 and on Sundays and holidays in the afternoon.)

The route now continues E along Somogyi u. to the river and then left to the N along the upper embankment, Korányi fasor.

The first steamer appeared on the Tisza in September 1833. To investigate the possibilities of steamship navigation István Széchenyi himself sailed down the Danube and up the Tisza from the junction of the two rivers. The arrival of his SS 'Duna' created a great impression. One Pest newspaper reported that 'the Serbs stood astounded while their wives made the sign of the cross; but the Hungarians noisily rejoiced and as the steamer cut through the waves they raced, following her on the bank, some on foot, some on horseback and some in carriages.' A regular service, began in the following decade, although it was not until later, when the river was properly regulated, that services were speeded up and fully established. In earlier times boats towed by horses on the bank were common. At the end of the 18C, when Joseph II abolished the death penalty, convicts were used to tow the boats.

The present *bridge* over the Tisza was built in 1948 to replace an earlier one built by the French Eiffel Company in 1883 which was destroyed by the Germans in 1944. Just before the bridge on the left is a statue of *Gyula Juhász* (1883–1937) the poet from Szeged who wrote many verses about the Tisza (György Segesdi, 1957).

The road from the W end of the bridge cuts across Roosevelt tér, on the N side of which stands the so-called **Palace of Education** (Közművelődési palota). It was built in 1896 by the Viennese architects Antal Steinhardt and Adolf Lang. Since 1899 it has been occupied by the local town museum which, since 1950, has been known as the *Ferenc Móra Museum*. The exhibition covers the general history of Csongrád county, including peasant furniture and costumes, and has a memorial room to Ferenc Móra (1879–1934) a writer, journalist and from 1917 until his death the director of the museum. (Open 10.00–18.00 except Monday.)

The building was originally intended for the Somogyi Library. In 1881 Károly Somogyi, the Esztergom Canon, donated the 43,000 volumes of his library to Szeged writing 'Culture has to be given to Szeged until it has its own university—that's why I offer it, and through it my country, what I have'. The library continued to be based here until it moved to a new building near the Votive Church in 1984.

By the columns beneath the tympanum there are statues of Socrates and Homer and in front of the building in the park there are statues of Ferenc Móra (to the E) and István Tömörkény, both former directors of the museum. They are the work of Antal Tápai from 1939 and 1943 respectively. There are other statues and busts in the park of the writer Kálmán Mikszáth (Lajos Ungvári, 1961), the politician Gábor Klauzál (György Vastagh Jr, 1906) and the pioneer of Hungarian shorthand, Iván Markovits (Géza Horváth, 1913).

The *Castle Museum* is situated in the grounds to the rear of the Palace of Education. Szeged castle was one of the series of castles built in the 13C following the Mongol invasion. It was used for a variety of purposes over the centuries including a prison under Joseph II. The ramparts extended westwards from the river almost to today's Széchenyi tér. The castle was pulled down after the flood in 1880–82 to make way for new buildings. The museum has a display of stonework from the castle as well as an exhibition of local history. (Open 10.00–18.00 except Monday.)

A few metres to the E of the museum, in Tanácsköztársaság útja, stands the Eclectic building of the *Szeged National Theatre* (Nemzeti Színház). It was constructed after the flood in 1883 to the plans of the Viennese architects Ferdinand Fellner and Herman Helmer who also designed the Gaiety Theatre in Budapest and the József Katona Theatre in Kecskemét. It was burnt out in 1885 but reopened the following year. The statues on the façade of the composer Ferenc Erkel and the playwright József Katona are by Antal Tápai (1956). A plaque on the wall commemorates the foundation here in December 1944 of the Hungarian National Independence Front, the predecessor of today's Patriotic People's Front. Across the road, facing Vörösmarty u., is the *Memorial to the 1919 Republic of Councils* (Tanácsköztársasági emlékmű) the work of György Segesdi and erected in 1959.

A short way to the N on the right hand side of Dózsa u. is Ede Margó's 1912 statue of *Pista Dankó* (1858–1903) a famous gipsy violinist whose compositions were popularised by the singer Lujza Blaha. Dankó came to Szeged when he was 15 to play in a gipsy band. Later he travelled all over the country with his own group. Unable to write music he had to rely on others to note down his compositions. He died of tuberculosis and was buried in Szeged. Behind the statue is the former *Kass Hotel*, designed by Antal Steinhardt and built in 1898. The building was restored and renovated at the end of the 1980s. The so-called *Deutsch Mansion* on the other side of the road at No. 2 Dózsa u. was designed in Secessionist style by Mihály Erdélyi, though the façade with its ceramic tiles is the work of Ödön Lechner. The building was restored in 1988–89.

Vörösmarty u., at the side of the National Theatre, leads back to Széchenyi tér and the start of the route.

Other places of interest. There are two synagogues to the W of the town centre just beyond Lenin körút. The *Old Synagogue*, at No. 12 Hajnóczi u., was designed by Henrik and József Lipovszky in classical style in 1843. The marble plaque on the Hajnóczy u. side shows the height of the water on 12 March during the flood of 1879.

There was already a Jewish population in Szeged before the Turks arrived. After their expulsion Jews were only allowed to settle if they agreed to be baptised. Towards the end of the 18C, however, an act of Joseph II allowed Jews to move into Szeged. In 1808 there were only just over 300 but by 1861 their numbers had grown and Szeged was the first town where Jews received a subsidy to maintain their schools. Lipót Löw, the Rabbi from 1850–75, was imprisoned for a while following the War of Independence.

The **New Synagogue** is nearby at No. 20 Gutenberg u., on the corner with Jósika u. It was built in Hungarian Secessionist style with Moorish elements in 1903 to the design of Lipót Baumhorn assisted by Immanuel Löw, a scholarly rabbi and son of the aforementioned Lipót. The huge 48m dome represents the world; the 24 columns—the hours of the day; the white flowers of the rosehip bush—faith; the blue stars—the infinity of the universe. At the top is a Star of David with rays of sunshine. The stained glass windows depicting scenes from Jewish life and history are the work of Miksa Róth. On the wall of the entrance hall there is a *marble tablet* with the names of 1874 Jews killed in the Second World War. The interior furnishings are worth viewing, for example the tabernacle made from acacia wood from the Nile region.

The former Franciscan church known as the **Alsóvárosi Church** (Lower Town Church) is the sole Gothic building in Szeged and one of Hungary's most important Gothic monuments. It is situated in Mátyás tér to the S of the centre at the end of Hunyadi János u. (Bus No. 74 from the Marx tér bus station.)

Construction began in the late 15C and was completed in 1503 though several additions have changed its appearance somewhat. The Baroque tower on the N side, for example, was built in 1771 and the porch on the main façade and the interior furnishings are also Baroque. However, Gothic elements such as the windows remain. Particularly noteworthy is the interior vaulted ceiling above the nave and chancel.

Through the entrance and to the left is a *Black Madonna* (András Morvai, 1740) and next to it a poem by Gyula Juhász about the church, Our Lady and Hungary. The *altarpiece* above the Baroque main altar depicts the Virgin Mary. Many miracles have been associated with it and it has been an object of adoration over the centuries. The *pulpit* dates from 1714 and is the work of a monk, Antal Gráff. Above it St. Michael is depicted defeating Satan; below is the Ark of the Covenant and the tablets with the Ten Commandments. At the front the Holy Spirit is represented by a dove accompanied by four cherubs holding the symbols of Faith (a cross), Hope (an anchor), Charity (a heart) and Justice (scales). The Good Shepherd and the four evangelists were added in 1781 and are by an unknown artist.

To the left of the main entrance stands the *former Franciscan monastery*. On the wall a Baroque sun dial can be seen. On the right-hand exterior wall of the church there is a copy of the so-called 'Bautzen Matthias relief', an authentic representation of King Matthias made in 1486 which can be found in the German city of Bautzen. The copy was placed here in 1931 in the erroneous belief that King Matthias had had the church built.

Mátyás tér itself somewhat resembles a village green and indeed the small streets and single-storey houses to the S of the square are rather like a village and give some idea of what old Szeged used to be like.

Szeged has some interesting museums which are not included on the main route. The *Kass Gallery* is situated at No. 7 Vár u. not far from the National Theatre. János Kass is a local graphic artist born in 1927. A selection of his work is exhibited here. (Open 10.00–18.00 except Monday.)

The *Fekete-ház* (Black House) at No. 13 Somogyi Béla u., on the corner of Kelemen László u., houses an exhibition of Csongrád county labour movement history 1867–1945. (Open 10.00–18.00 except Monday.) The building itself, which dates from 1857, managed to escape the flood and is a rare example in Szeged of the Romantic style. The name Black House comes from the dark mortar of the exterior. It was designed by Károly Gerster for Ferdinánd Mayer, a local businessman and owner of an iron works.

In the first half of the 1860s the Black House functioned as the Inner City Casino, a gentlemen's club. At the end of the First World War it was turned into a workers' centre. A memorial plaque recalls that in the library here on 22 October 1918 the republican Szeged National Council was formed. These political associations led the poet Gyula Juhász to call the building the 'Szeged Pilvax', a reference to the Pilvax café in the capital which was a well-known political meeting place in the mid-19C.

To the S of the centre at No. 11/a Bécsi körút there is a *Theatre History Exhibition Room* which opened in 1987 to exhibit the work of the stage-designer Mátyás Varga (1910–). (Open 10.00–18.00 except Monday.)

Szeged is one of the main paprika-growing areas in Hungary which in turn has given rise to salami production. The *Salami Factory Historical Collection* can be viewed at No. 10 Felső-Tiszapart which runs along the embankment curving NE from the centre. The display covers the production of the local 'Pick' salami. (Open Tues and Thurs 15.30–17.00.)

3km to the E of Szeged, **Tápé** is a fishing community on the banks of the Tisza. The inhabitants have preserved their local songs, dances, customs and handicrafts over the years. A private *Ethnographical Collection* can be viewed at No. 4 Vártó u. On display are examples of the local bullrush-weaving, folk paintings, costumes and items connected with the fishing traditions. (Open 15.00–18.00 except Monday.) The original 13C *Church* was reconstructed in the 14C and 18C. It has 14C wall-paintings in the Gothic sanctuary.

14 Budapest to Eger

Roads 30, 3 and 25. Total distance 128km. **Budapest**—Road 30 29km **Gödöllő**—14km **Aszód**—15km **Hatvan**—23km **Gyöngyös**—Road 3 25km Kápolna and turning for (7km) **Feldebrő**—8km Kerecsend and Road 25—14km **Eger**.

Eger is 128km NE of Budapest via motorway M3, which leaves the capital at Hungária körút on the western side of the City Park (Városliget) in the direction of Miskolc. At present the motorway finishes a few kilometres before Gyöngyös, which is 81km from Budapest. The route continues along Road 3 to Kerecsend where there is the junction with Road 25 for Eger to the N. An alternative to the motorway is to take Road 30 to Gyöngyös via Gödöllő, Aszód and Hatvan, though there is also access to these places from the motorway.

GÖDÖLLŐ (pop. 30,000) is 29km from Budapest and today is one of the centres of agricultural science in Hungary, being the home of the University of Agricultural Science, agricultural research institutes and experimental stations. Gödöllő used to be the Hungarian summer residence of the Habsburgs.

The **Grassalkovich Mansion** on the S side of the main junction (Szabadság tér) is one of the largest manorhouses in Hungary. It was built in the 1740s for Antal Grassalkovich (1694–1771), a royal official of noble birth who became a personal friend and supporter of Maria Theresa. He acquired huge estates in Hungary in the middle of the 18C and had a number of mansions built. This one was designed by András Mayerhoffer and virtually created a new style of Baroque mansion building in Hungary. The wings do not surround the reception court but instead the upper garden, which was originally French Baroque in form and later English landscape in style. The Rococo chapel in the right wing dates from 1749.

Members of the Habsburg family took refuge here during the Napoleonic Wars. In 1864 it was bought by a Belgian bank but three years later the Hungarian state bought it back for the royal and later the governor's summer residence. The building was then redesigned by Miklós Ybl which was when the domes were added. During the

Second World War the mansion was pillaged and looted and not much care was taken of it until the 1980s when serious restoration work began.

The *Mary Column* (Mária-oszlop) in Szabadság tér dates from 1749 and is similar to one standing in Hainburg in Austria. Both are the work of Martin Vogerl. Four reliefs decorate the lower part of the column. Of the statues surrounding the column two are noteworthy: the Baroque statue of St. John of Nepomuk, the patron of bridges and river crossings, dates from 1750, while the 1823 classical statue of St. Florian is represented by a Roman soldier with a flag extinguishing a fire. The small Baroque *Calvinist Church* on the northern edge of the square was built in 1747, though the towers were renewed in 1912. No. 5 Szabadság tér houses the *Local History Museum*. There are exhibitions on the regional fauna and flora and on the Gödöllő Colony 1901–20. There is also a small memorial room dedicated to Queen Elizabeth, the wife of Emperor Francis Joseph I. (Open 10.00– 18.00 except Monday.) The museum is due to move into the Grassalkovich Mansion when restoration work is finally completed.

In the first two decades of the 20C Gödöllő was the home of a colony of artists and craftspeople strongly influenced by the English Pre-Raphaelites and the Arts and Crafts movement of John Ruskin and William Morris. The artist Walter Crane, an associate of Morris, had an immensely influential exhibition at the Museum of Applied Arts in Budapest in 1900. He came to Hungary to lecture and travelled the country researching local crafts. The leaders of the Gödöllő school were Sándor Nagy and Aladár Körösfői Kriesch, who wrote a book in Hungarian about Morris, Ruskin and their circle in 1904. The colony, which was organised on the lines of rural simplicity very much akin to English experiments such as the Edward Carpenter circle near Sheffield in the 1880s, attracted painters, artists, tapestry makers, book-binders and architects. One of Hungary's most important 20C architects Károly Kós, for example, was for a while closely involved with the colony. In the 1910s the year books of the English journal 'Studio' gave regular accounts of the the Gödöllő colony in a series entitled 'Hungarian Architecture and Decoration'. There are plans to open the former home and workshop of Sándor Nagy as a museum in the early 1990s.

5km out of Gödöllő, on Road 30 on the left, stands a *former Capuchin Church and Monastery* built in the 1760s. Members of the Grassalkovich family are buried here in the crypt. The large decorated gate near the roadside at the beginning of the driveway to the church is 20C, but is made in the style of traditional Transylvanian wooden gates.

Aszód is approximately 9km further on Road 30. The former *Podmaniczky Mansion* looks on to Szabadság tér. The older part is 18C late Baroque though construction work continued well into the present century. The main hall has a ceiling fresco by Johann Lukas Kracker, the Austrian artist who painted several important frescoes in Eger.

The *Petőfi Museum* at No. 2 Szontágy lépcső is housed in a former Lutheran grammar school built in late-Baroque style in 1820. The poet and political activist Sándor Petőfi (1823–49) attended school here from 1835 to 1838 and it was here that he started writing verse. The exhibitions cover his life and work in Aszód and the local folk and literary history of the area. (Open 10.00–18.00; Nov–March 9.00– 17.00; closed Mondays.) The *Lutheran Church* on the hill dates from the 15C though fire later destroyed much of the church. It was rebuilt in Baroque style in the 1720s and the tower was added in 1729. The attractive Baroque carved wooden altar is early 18C. The Baroque *Roman Catholic Church* was built between 1748 and 1750. The painting of the Holy Trinity here is the work of J.L. Kracker.

The town of **Hatvan** (pop. 25,000) is on the banks of the river
Zagyva 15km to the E of Aszód on Road 30. It was famous for its
sugar-beet industry. Here there is another *Grassalkovich Mansion*.
The two-storey Baroque mansion was built in 1754–63 and was later
owned by the Hatvany-Deutsch family, the owners of the big sugar
factory. Today it is a hospital. The *Roman Catholic Church* was
commissioned for Antal Grassalkovich and built in Baroque style
between 1751 and 1757. The *Lajos Hatvany Museum* at No. 3
Kossuth tér covers the history of the region. (Open 14.00–18.00
except Monday.) Baron Lajos Hatvany (1880–1961) was a writer,
critic, literary historian and one of the creators of the influential
journal 'Nyugat'. His family's estates used to be in the area.

Road 30 is joined by traffic from the M3 motorway about 6km
outside **GYÖNGYÖS**. The road to Eger continues through the town
just S of the centre. The places of interest near the town centre can be
reached by turning left at the first set of traffic lights just before the
OTP tower block.

Gyöngyös, situated at the foot of the Mátra Hills, was a market town as early as
the first half of the 14C. Despite attacks from both the Turks and the Habsburgs
it managed to develop into a trading and cultural centre during the years of
Turkish rule. In the first decade of the 18C it was a focal point for the
independence struggle led by Ferenc Rákóczi II. Traditionally noted for its
handicraft and textile industries the town today has a number of large-scale
plants and an open coal mine nearby to the east. Gyöngyös is also the centre of
a local wine-growing area.

The originally Gothic *St. Bartholomew's Church* (Szent Bertalan-
templom) at the N end of Fő tér dates from the mid-14C, though it
was remodelled in the 18C with Baroque features. Gothic elements
are discernible, however, in the structure. (Open in the mornings.)
The building immediately behind the church was originally built in
the 15C as a school. From 1634 and for the next 140 years the school
was run by the Jesuits. After that, between 1776 and 1896, it
belonged to the Franciscans. The present Baroque form of the
building dates from 1783. Today it is occupied by a music school. The
tall, slender statue just across from the SW corner of the church is of
King Charles Robert, the Anjou king who ruled Hungary from 1307
to 1342 (Pál Kő, 1984).

The *Old County Hall* (Régi Megyeháza) stands on Vármegyeház
tér on the far side of the Nagy-patak stream to the W of Fő tér (via
Beloiannisz u.). It was built in Baroque style in 1765 and was
originally intended for a barracks. The classical *former Synagogue*
nearby to the N was built in 1818–20 by Károly Rábl. In Nemecz
József tér to the SE of Fő tér there is a former *Franciscan Church* built
for the order by the Bárthori family around 1400. The medieval parts
of the church, however, were destroyed in a fire of 1526. It was
rebuilt in the early 18C, though the Baroque tower dates from 1755.
The coat of arms of the Bárthori family can be seen on the keystone in
the chancel. The former Franciscan monastery to the side was built in
1727.

The local history museum, the *Mátra Museum*, occupies the former
Orczy mansion at No. 40 Kossuth Lajos u., some way to the E of Fő
tér. The originally Baroque mansion was redesigned in classical style
in 1824 by Lőrinc Zofahl. The collections inside cover the geography
of the Mátra region and the history of Gyöngyös. (Open 9.00–17.00
except Monday.)

The main road to Eger continues from Gyöngyös as Road 3 in the
direction of Miskolc. At Kerecsend, a small village 33km to the E of

Gyöngyös, Road 25 branches off to the left. Eger is 14km to the N along here.

8km before Kerecsend, Road 3 passes through the village of Kápolna. 7km to the N from here, along the road signposted Verpelét, lies the village of **Feldebrő**. The parish church here, which was restored in the 1980s, is one of the earliest relics in Hungary from the age of the House of Árpád, and dates from the mid-11C.

The missionaries who came to Hungary in the early years of the state built churches in the style of their own homeland. The upper church had five aisles in the Byzantine style, probably with a central dome. Only some of its rising walls and pillars have survived. The crypt, however, has survived. It is divided by primitive columns into two. The chancel and vaulting were adorned around the middle of the 12C with frescoes depicting Christ, the prophets and Biblical scenes. The master was probably a painter from Northern Italy who, in accordance with the custom of the age, worked in the Byzantine style. (Viewing times: Tues–Sat 10.00–12.00, 14.00–16.00; Sun and holidays 11.00–12.00, 15.00–16.00; keys from the presbytery (plébánia) behind the church.)

Eger can be reached from Feldebrő via Verpelét to the N and then Egerszalók to the NE. In *Verpelét* there is a reconstructed *smith's workshop* at No. 54 Kossuth Lajos u. (Open 9.00–13.00 except Monday.)

15 Eger

Every Hungarian school child knows about **EGER**. About how, in 1552, the women of Eger fought alongside the 2000 soldiers in the castle and in a heroic struggle under the leadership of Captain István Dobó managed to repel an attack by Turkish forces six times their strength. 'The Stars of Eger' (Egri Csillagok), a novel by Géza Gárdonyi published in 1901, tells the story of the defence of Eger and the heroic deeds of the defenders. It has been virtually compulsory reading in all schools since it was published. No wonder that Eger Castle is one of the most popular places for Hungarian visitors in the whole of the country.

Tourist Information: Eger Tourist, 9 Bajcsy-Zsilinszky u. (36/11-724)

Rail Station: Lumumba tér. 2 hours by express from the Eastern Railway Station, Budapest.

Bus Station: 194 Lenin út (Felszabadulás tér). 2 hours from the Népstadion Bus Station, Budapest.

Post Office: 20–22 Széchenyi tér.

Police: 1–3 Szabadság tér.

History. The Eger Valley lies between the wooded Bükk and Mátra Mountains. It was settled by the first generation of Magyars to arrive in the Carpathian Basin. Stephen I made it an episcopal see at the beginning of the 11C and the town has been an ecclesiastical centre ever since.

The Mongol forces who came from the East burned the town down in 1241 and slaughtered many of the inhabitants. This was followed by a wave of immigration from Western Europe, and by the end of the 15C Eger was one of Hungary's main Renaissance centres. The defeat of the Turks in 1552 delayed the spread of the Ottoman Empire, but it could not stop it altogether and 44 years later, in 1596, Sultan Mohammed III was able to capture the castle and the Turks ruled Eger until 1687. Mosques and baths were built but today only one minaret remains standing.

In 1690 there were only 3500 residents, which included about 600 Muslims who stayed after the Turks had left and who were converted to Christianity and assimilated into Hungarian life. In 1702 the Habsburg Emperor Leopold I ordered the Castle walls to be blown up so that the fortress could not be used by Hungarian forces struggling for independence. Nevertheless Eger became one of the centres of resistance during the ensuing Rákóczi War of Independence.

Development in the 18C took place under the direction of the episcopal see which owned huge tracts of land in the region. This is when the town started to develop its characteristic Baroque appearance. Some fine works from this period remain, particularly in the field of wrought-iron work.

Industrial development in Eger only really took off after the Second World War and the population remains small even today, standing at 67,000. Apart from scholastic achievements, agriculture has always been important, particularly viticulture. Eger's famous 'Bulls Blood' (Egri Bikavér) is one of the best-known Hungarian wines in the West.

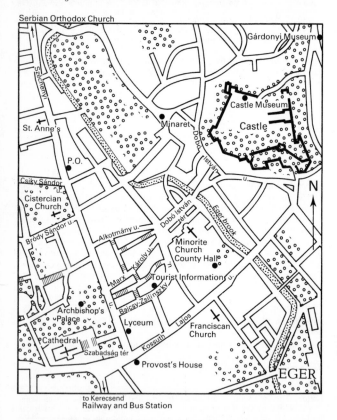

to Kerecsend
Railway and Bus Station

The **Cathedral** is a huge, dominating neo-classical structure in Szabadság tér at the N end of Lenin út along which the road from Budapest arrives. It stands on a hill and there has been a church on this site since the 11C when King Stephen I established the see of Eger. The present building, which the Pope designated as a Basilica in 1970, was designed by József Hild and constructed extremely quickly between 1831 and 1836 following the demolition of a

Baroque church which had previously stood here. The consecration of the new church, dedicated to St. Michael and St. John of Nepomuk, was performed in early May 1837.

The imposing effect of the main façade, with its 17m Corinthian columns, is heightened by the flight of steps from the square below. At the bottom of the steps are statues of 11C Hungarian kings: St. Stephen (1000–38) and, on the left, St. Ladislas (1077–95). Curiously they are dressed in 19C Hungarian robes. At the beginning of the second flight there are statues of the apostles St. Peter, with the key of Heaven and St. Paul. Paul's sword is made from iron from Szilvásvárad, 20km to the N of Eger, as the inscription on it testifies. The statues, like the allegorical figures of Faith, Hope and Charity on the central ledge above the tympanum, and the winged angels representing Divine Truth and Love on either side, are the work of the Italian-born sculptor, Marco Casagrande (1806–80) who was invited to Eger to work on the cathedral and stayed in Hungary for 30 years working mainly on ecclesiastical buildings in Budapest and Esztergom. The reliefs depicting scenes from Christ's life to the left and the right of the portico, and above the doors, are also the work of Casagrande, as are a further 24 reliefs inside.

A vast colonnade divides the nave from the aisles. Originally the nave and aisles were bare. Most of the painting and decoration here was added much later, not being completed, in fact, until the late 1940s.

The paintings on the side altars near the entrance depicting (on the right) 'St. Stephen offering the crown to the Virgin' and (on the left) 'St. Ladislas kneeling before the Madonna' are by Johann Lukas Kracker and were made in the 1770s for the previous Baroque church which stood here. (The Viennese J.L. Kracker (1717–79) painted many of the church frescoes in Prague in the early 1760s. In 1764 he was invited to Hungary and worked here until his death in Eger.) The small marble statues on the main altar of Jesus and Mary are the work of Miklós Köllő, while the angels and cherubs were sculpted by Casagrande in Carrara marble. The large painting on the main altar of 'The Martyrdom of St. John' (1834–35) is by the Viennese artist Joseph Danhauser. The white marble pulpit on the S side, placed here in 1910, has a relief decoration of St. John the Evangelist by József Damkó.

The **Lyceum** stands opposite the cathedral. The four-winged building with a courtyard was built in 1765–85 to the designs of József Gerl and Jakab Fellner. The W façade is considered to be one of the finest examples of Copf architecture in Hungary. The Lyceum was originally intended to be a university, but the plans were thwarted by a decree of Maria Theresa in 1777 which ruled that there could only be one university in Hungary—in Buda. It was a Catholic training college for most of its life until nationalisation after 1945. Today the building is occupied by the Ho Chi Minh Teachers' Training College.

The grand hall in the W wing has frescoes by the Viennese artist, Franz Sigrist. The chapel in the N wing has a fresco by Franz Anton Maulbertsch and above the altar, made from Hungarian marble, is a painting by Hesz Mihály from 1813. However, it is the fresco on the ceiling of the *library* on the first floor of the S wing which is the main attraction of the Lyceum and which is considered one of the masterpieces of Hungarian art.

The huge fresco depicting a session of the Council of Trent (1545–63) was painted by Johann Lukas Kracker and his son-in-law József Zach in 1778. Although the Gothic structure in the background is a product of the artist's imagination, many of the 132 figures represent real people. The central section

shows the Spanish Jesuit Salmeron in the pulpit. Below him, to the left, sits
Charles V and to his left on a raised platform are four cardinals. Among the
figures below them is the Pécs bishop, György Draskovich, the representative of
the king of Hungary, Ferdinand I. In the four corners are illustrations of various
decisions of the Council, for example the lightning and book representing the
Index of banned books.

The oak shelving of the library was carved by a local carpenter,
Tamás Lotter in 1778–80. When it was opened in 1793 there were
20,000 volumes which had been collected from all over the world.
Today there are over 76,000 volumes which include several medieval
codices and Hungarian manuscripts of great value. The library,
which still belongs to the Church, can be used by researchers. As
such it is the only public ecclesiastical library in Hungary. Visitors
can inspect the library and its fresco. (Open 9.30–12.30 except
Monday.)

At the top of the tower in the E wing there is an *Observatory* and a
small museum where by use of a *camera obscura* mirror the whole
town can be seen. The revolving dome is the work of Lénárd Fazela
(1779), and some of the original instruments, which included
English equipment, are on display. (Open 9.30–13.00; 20 May–10
July, 13.00–15.30; closed 20 December–31 January and every
Monday.)

The County *Tourist Information Office*, Eger Tourist, is situated
near the NE corner of the Lyceum at No. 9 Bajcsy-Zsilinszky u. The
Stephen Well (István-kút) nearby at the end of Fellner u. was erected
in 1986 by the local Town Preservation Association (Városszépítő
Egyesület).

The route proceeds along KOSSUTH LAJOS UTCA which runs
eastwards from the S side of the Lyceum. The *Provost's House*
(Kispréposti lak) stands at No. 4 across the road from the Lyceum.
This fine Rococo building, with its richly carved stone vases in niches
on either side of the entrance, was designed by Matthias Gerl and
built in 1758. The iron lattice of the balcony was made by Henrik
Fazola. The Baroque house with its rich gate and stone vases at *No. 6*
next door also dates from the 18C. Above the gate in a niche is a
statue of Justitia.

The former Leánygimnázium (Girls' school) is at *No. 8*. Above the
carved gate is the coat of arms of the Foglár family who once owned
the building, and above that in a niche is a statue of the Madonna.
The building has been used for a variety of purposes including a
medical school, a boys' school and a military hospital. For nearly a
century from 1852 to 1948 it was a school belonging to the English-
founded Mary Ward nuns and carried the name of the order as it was
known in Hungary—Angolkisasszonyok iskola (School of the English Young Ladies). In the first courtyard there is a bust of the poet
Attila József (1905–37). *No. 10* Kossuth Lajos u. dates from 1733 and
is the oldest house in the street. Canon András Püspöky commissioned G.B. Marloné to design this Baroque dwelling.

The *Franciscan Church* on the right, just past the end of Jókai u.,
was built in 1736–55 to the plans of János Nietschmann from remains
of a former mosque which stood here in Turkish times. The ornamented Copf-style gate dates from 1793. The Baroque interior was
excavated in the late 1980s. The large Baroque building at No. 9 on
the left is the **County Hall**, designed by the Viennese architect
Matthias Gerl between 1748 and 1756. On the façade there are three
coats of arms. In the middle is the Hungarian arms, to the left that of
Bishop Barkóczy who had the building erected, and to the right the

local Heves County arms. The county arms shows a stork with a snake in its beak, representing the marshy area to the S of Eger, and a wine grape in its claw, which represents local viticulture. The iron work above the main gate and the two *wrought-iron gates* to the left and the right at the far end of the gateway are the work of Henrik Fazola. The gates, completed in 1761, are two of the finest specimens of Baroque iron work in Hungary. They are decorated with coats of arms and motifs including figures representing Truth, Faith and Hope. Fazola (1730–99) was born in Würzburg and moved to Eger at the invitation of the local bishop. His splendid work decorates many of the buildings around the town. A former *prison* stands in the courtyard of the County Hall. There is a large, high relief of the Crucifixion on the wall by the entrance. Executions used to take place here.

Henrik Fazola's wrought-iron gate at the County Hall, Eger (1761).

No. 13 Kossuth Lajos u. is the former Lion restaurant and dates from the mid-18C, though it was restored after World War II. On 27 August 1827 a fire started in the stables here which swept through the whole of Eger. The *County Library* is at No. 16 in the former Provost's House. The Baroque building was begun in 1774 to the plans of Jakab Fellner and completed in 1780. *No. 18* was built in early Eclectic, neo-Renaissance style in 1867–68.

Kossuth Lajos u. continues across a small bridge over the river Eger and swings up leftwards to Dózsa György tér. *No. 1–3* here is the site of a former Turkish bath which was built at the beginning of the 17C for the Sultan Valide. It was a six-chamber bath and had a dome covered with red ceramics. It was excavated in the 1980s.

A road leads up from Dózsa György tér to the lower gate of the **Castle**. On the right is a *large bronze relief* by István Tar and Gyula Illés commemorating the victorious defence of the castle against the Turks in 1552. It was erected in 1952 to mark the 400th anniversary. The gate itself probably dates from the 1580s. The road leads up past the Gergely Bastion on the right and a medieval Gothic gate tower to its left, and then passes through a gateway in the Varkoch bastion to the inner castle area.

Although the history of the fort dates back to the foundation of Eger's episcopate and the construction of a cathedral in the 11C, its main development took place only in the 16C when Péter Perényi had it built up by the Italian architect, Alessandro da Vedano following the Turkish victory at Mohács in 1526. István Dobó became captain of the fortress in 1549 and collected taxes to help reinforce the castle. Italian and German masters were brought from Vienna to participate and local people from surrounding villages brought wood, lime, stones and clay. An inventory made in the year preceeding the Turkish attack noted that there was enough grain for half a year as well as smoked beef, lamb, bacon, salted fish and lots of soured cabbage stored in barrels. Herds of oxes, cows, goats, sheep and many chickens had also been gathered.

By the summer of 1552 Temesvár, Veszprém and other Hungarian forts had fallen into Turkish hands. The capture of Szolnok by the Turks on 4 September left the way open to Eger. The attack began on 14 September by a Turkish force of over 10,000 which vastly outnumbered the Hungarians under Dobó. The grim battle continued for a month until, on 18 October, the tired and greatly reduced Turkish army retreated leaving the fort's walls almost in ruins. Eger's victory soon became known all over Europe. However, despite reconstruction in the 1570s by the castle architect Ottavio Baldigara, Eger was unable to withstand the Turkish attack which came 40 years later, and from 1596 to 1687 the castle was in Turkish hands.

The Habsburg rulers of Hungary ordered the outer walls to be blown up in 1702 for fear the castle would become a stronghold in the struggle for Hungarian independence. Despite this Eger did become one of the most important *Kuruc* forts during the War of Independence in the first decade of the 18C. Eger's Bishop Telekessy (1699–1715) was the only Catholic prelate who declared himself in support of Prince Rákóczi. But the fort was forced to surrender to imperial forces in 1710. Following decades of neglect, restoration of the castle has been undertaken in stages throughout the 19C and 20C.

The path leads up through the inner courtyard to a two-storey, late-19C building which is the entrance to the **Castle Museum** (Dobó István Vármúzeum). (Open 9.00–17.00 except Monday.) In the gateway on the right is a bronze relief depicting the Battle of Eger Castle by György Zala which was originally in Heroes' Square in Budapest under a statue of King Ferdinand I.

The *Picture Gallery* (Egri Képtár) to the left, occupies a building erected for the army in the 1880s, as was the building to the right. The gallery exhibits 16C, 17C and 18C Italian and Dutch paintings as well as 18C and 19C Hungarian and Austrian works.

Directly ahead is the former **Bishop's Palace**. The arched Gothic arcade in the front of the building dates from around 1470. It is one of the few Gothic structures still intact in the eastern part of Hungary. In the late 15C, following the construction of the original palace, the bishop's seat of residence was furnished like a royal court and it became a centre of humanist culture with a rich library. The small *Hall of Heroes* is situated on the ground floor. It was restored in 1957–65. In the middle of the Hall is the red marble tomb of Captain Dobó. It was carved after his death in 1572 and brought here in 1832 from Dobóruszka where the family burial chapel stood. The figure is life-sized and the style of dress follows the fashion of the time—armour, chain mail and shoes of soft leather. In his left hand is a parchment with a quotation from the Bible, and in the right hand a flag. It is probably the only authentic representation of István Dobó.

Dobó (c 1500–72) was a landowning aristocrat of northern Hungary, in command of various border fortresses. He was based at Eger between 1549 and 1552 after which he was 'voivode' (commander) of Transylvania. He was counted among those aristocrats dissatisfied with the ineffectiveness of Habsburg military leadership and in 1569 was imprisoned on suspicion of conspiracy. He was released only shortly before his death.

On either side of the tomb there are statues representing defenders of the fortress (István Kiss, 1965), and in the stone cases next to the statues are bones of those who fell in 1552, which have been found in the course of excavations. The names of the defenders are on the back wall. In the 18C the hall was used as a prison chapel and under the slabs on the back wall there is a drawing made by the prisoners. Upstairs there is an exhibition of the history of the castle and the palace containing documents, old weapons, household items and other relics.

The foundation stones of the former *Cathedral of St. John the Evangelist* are to the E of the Castle Museum.

The first cathedral built on this site was erected in the 11C after Stephen I had established the diocese of Eger. The Romanesque church was covered with paintings and the floor was of marble mosaic. According to the chronicles King Imre was buried here in 1204. The church was destroyed during the Mongol invasion in 1241. Rebuilding in Gothic style was initiated by Bishop Lambert in 1248. Later two large towers were added at the western façade and later still two side chapels on the S side. In the 15C plans were made to increase its size and richness in accordance with the economic and political power of the local episcopacy which was then at its zenith. However, a great fire in 1506 destroyed the building, including the parts that had already been finished. The situation following the battle of Mohács in 1526 made it impossible for construction to continue and the building gradually started to deteriorate. In 1542 the Gothic stones were taken and used for fortification work and the sanctuary was transformed into a bastion. During the siege of 1552 the gunpowder stored in the sanctuary blew up and a great part of the building was destroyed. In Turkish times, too, it was used as an arsenal. Final demolition of the church came in the 18C and the remaining parts were covered over. Work to uncover the ruins began in 1860 and continued in the 1920s. A statue of *King Stephen I* by the Italian sculptor Marco Casagrande was placed in the middle of the ruins after 1830.

To the S of the ruins is the entrance to the *underground fortifications*, some of which can be visited in the company of a guide. There is a small exhibition on the castle's architectural history here. The underground passages form a network of tunnels and rooms connecting the bastions. They were fashioned by being first dug out and then covered over.

The *three wooden crosses* on the small hill nearby are the remains of a stations of the cross erected here in the last century by János Pyrker (1772–1847) who became Archbishop of Eger in 1827.

In the SE corner of the inner area of the Castle is the *tomb of Géza Gárdonyi* (1863–1922) the author of the renowned 'Stars of Eger'. The words 'Csak a teste' (Only his body lies here) are inscribed on the stone slab. In the writer's former home, at 28 Gárdonyi u, 250m from the NE corner of the Castle, there is a *Géza Gárdonyi Memorial Room.* (Open 9.00–17.00 except Monday.)

The route now continues from the main entrance to the Castle westwards along Dobó István u. which leads to a short street curving to the left in the direction of DOBÓ ISTVÁN TÉR. One of the finest examples of Hungarian Baroque ecclesiastical architecture, the former **Minorite Church**, stands on the S side of the square. It was built in 1758–73 to the plans of the Prague architect Kilián Ignaz

Dientzenhofer. The projecting central section, accentuated by two
pairs of columns, dominates the façade with its two 57m towers.
Above the entrance is the Latin inscription 'Pro Deo Nunquam Satis'
(Nothing is Enough for God). Above this there are two crossed arms,
the insignia of the Franciscans. (The church belonged to a branch of
this order, the *fraters minores*. They lived in the building on the left
which was constructed soon after the church.) The Roman numerals
above the insignia show the date of completion, 1771. Above the
protruding ledge there is a devotional inscription in Latin to the
patron of the church, St. Anthony of Padua. His statue at the top of
the façade is by a local sculptor, János Hössz.

The exterior of the church was restored in 1962–64. Unfortunately
the interior was not and this is now in a state of decay. Nevertheless
some idea of the former splendour remains. The altarpiece (1771) is
by Johann Lukas Kracker who painted the celebrated fresco in the
Lyceum Library. The ceiling frescoes are the work of the Pozsony
(Bratislava) painter Márton Raindl. The pulpit, pews and organ loft
are all finely carved.

The *István Dobó* statue at the E side of the square is the work of
Alajos Stróbl (1907). Alongside Dobó there is a knight and a woman,
representing the defenders of the castle. Another monument to the
defence of Eger in 1552 stands towards the W side of the square. This
Monument to the Gallant Border Warriors (Végvári harcosok emlék-
műve) was sculpted by Zsigmond Kisfaludi Strobl and erected in
1967. The building of the **Town Council** is behind the statue at No. 2
on the SW corner of Dobó István tér. This two-storey Eclectic
building was erected at the beginning of the 20C on the site of a
previous Baroque town hall. The Eger coat of arms, dating from 1695,
can be seen on the façade. *No. 1* at the W end of the square is the so-
called Forst House. This two-storey Baroque house was designed by
János Povolry and built in the second half of the 18C.

Marx Károly u. leads from the left of the Forst House westwards to
SZÉCHENYI UTCA. The large U-shaped Baroque building at No. 1–2
Széchenyi u. to the N of Szabadság tér is the **Archbishop's Palace**,
which was built in stages throughout the 18C. The oldest part is the
middle section which was begun by Bishop Gábor Erdődy in the
1720s and 1730s. Later bishops added the third floor and the wings
over the next 30 years. The wrought-iron gates at the entrance to the
garden are particularly beautiful. They are the work of Lénárd Fazela
and date from 1778. The building is partly occupied today by the
central offices of Egervin, the local wine company.

Moving northwards along the pleasant pedestrian precinct section
of Széchenyi u., the elegant *Dobos eszpresszó* is at No. 6 on the right.
The neo-classical building at *No. 8* dates from 1820 and the Baroque
building at *No. 10* from 1748. The Baroque building with two statues
in niches at *No. 13* on the left is the so-called Carlone House and was
designed around 1725 by the Italian Giovanni Battista Carlone who
had been commissioned to design the Baroque church which previously occupied the site of today's Cathedral.

The former *Cistercian Church* stands at the corner of Széchenyi u.
and Bródy Sándor u. on the left. The church, which originally
belonged to the Jesuits, was built in the first half of the 18C. The
Rococo decoration on the doorway was added in 1743 and the statues
on the façade in 1773. In the same year the Cistercians took over the
church. At the beginning of the 20C the front end of the church was
redesigned by Ignác Alpár, the architect of several huge Eclectic
buildings in Budapest, including the National Bank and the former

Stock Exchange. At No. 14 on the right there is the *Telekessy Pharmacy Museum* (Telekessy Patikamúzeum). The Baroque building with Copf elements was designed by József Francz and erected in 1763. The pharmacy itself was founded earlier elsewhere by the Eger bishop, István Telekessy (1633–1715) following a plague of 1710. For many years the Jesuits ran the pharmacy which moved to the present building in 1900. The Baroque interior fittings were restored in the mid-1980s. *No. 16* is a former gentlemen's club, the Eger Casino. There are four large iron columns on the second floor and two classical doors to the right and left on the ground floor. The Latin inscription about the role of fate which appears on the façade was added following a great fire in the 1820s. The Casino functioned here until 1945 when it became a trade union headquarters. Today it is a youth centre.

The building at *No. 19* Széchenyi u., on the corner of Csiky Sándor u., is the former Jesuit secondary school which is today the István Dobó Secondary School and Forestry Technical School. It was built in 1750–54 and belonged to the Jesuits until 1773, the year the order was disbanded. Later it was given to the Cistercians. It has been used for a variety of purposes including a barracks but has been a school since 1892. The building has been damaged by fire and reconstructed several times. The Baroque elements have only been preserved on the gable end facing S. Above the gate to the left are cherubs holding the coat of arms of the Jesuits, and above them there is a memorial plaque of the foundation of the building and, higher still in a niche, a statue of the Virgin Mary. At the sides are statues of St. Ignatius and St. Aloysius.

Other places of interest. *St. Anne's Church* (Szent Anna templom) stands some way further along Széchenyi u. next to the county hospital at No. 27–29. The Baroque church was built in 1729–33 from the stones of a former mosque which stood here. The interior, however, is neo-Gothic and dates from the mid-19C. There are statues of the Virgin Mary and St. Anne on the façade. The classical building of the hospital used to function as an almshouse.

The *Serbian Orthodox church*, on the hill overlooking the town, can be approached via the arcaded flight of steps behind the church presbytery (1760) at No. 55 Széchenyi u. just over 1km N of the town centre. It was built in Copf style to the design of János Povolny between 1784 and 1799, following a decision of Joseph II to allow the construction of an Orthodox church in Eger. Inside there is a beautifully carved iconostasis, and a Copf-style pulpit. The gravestones in the chuchyard are from the 18C and 19C. There is a good view of the town from the hilltop.

An early 17C 14-sided 40m-high **Minaret** stands on a little square in front of No. 1 Knézich Károly u. a short distance to the N of Dobó István tér. Stairs lead up to a round balcony at the top. The mosque which stood by the minaret was demolished in 1841.

Excursions from Eger

The **Bükk Mountains** lie to the NE of Eger. Among the mountains in the area the *Istállóskő* (959m) and the *Bálvány* (956m) are the highest. The central part of the range is a 20km long by 6km wide plateau, formed by ocean deposits and surrounded by steep rocky cliffs. The mountainous terrain is covered by a forest of mainly beech trees and is rich in springs and mountain streams. There are almost

500 caves, cavities and rare geological formations in the interior of
the mountain range and a number of plants and animals are found
only here. 38,000 hectares of the area were turned into a National
Park in 1976. Further information can be obtained from the office of
the Bükk National Park at No. 6 Sánc u., Eger (tel: 12-791).

Bélapátfalva is about 20km N of Eger (turn right after Szarvaskő on
Road 25). The *Romanesque abbey church*, 1km to the E of the village,
was founded in 1232 by a group of Cistercian monks who settled here
from France. It is the only surviving example of Cistercian Romanesque architecture in Hungary. The plan is a Latin cross. Noteworthy
are the semicircular arches of the main entrance and the ornamented
rose window above. The windows are Romanesque but the arches
inside are Gothic, the result of later rebuilding.

At *Mikófalva*, 2km W of Bélapátfalva, a 19C blacksmith's workshop has been reconstructed in the peasant house at No. 25 Kossuth
u. (Open 10.00–12.00, 14.00–16.00 except Monday.)

Szilvásvárad is 8km to the N of Bélapátfalva. The village is the
centre of Lippizaner horse breeding in Hungary. A covered manège
and large-capacity race course have been constructed here. At No. 8
Park u. there is a *Horsebreeding Exhibition* (Lótenyésztéstörténeti
Kiállítás) about the origin, breeding and use of the Lippizaner horses
together with a display of coaches. (Open 9.00–17.00 except Monday.) The neo-classical circular *Reformed Church* was built in 1837–
41. Notable features inside the church are the 16 Doric columns, the
cylindrical pulpit and the octagonal altar. The walks along the
Szalajka stream are a popular attraction in this part of the Bükk Hills.
There are a series of terraced waterfalls forming pools where trout
are raised. The fish is a speciality of local restaurants. The open-air
Forestry Museum (Szabadtéri Erdészeti Múzeum) is in the valley not
far from the stream. Items displayed cover the local iron, glass,
logging, charcoal-burning and other industries of the last two centuries. (Open April–Nov 9.00–16.00 except Monday.)

Noszvaj lies 13km to the NE of Eger. Here, set in a park, is the
Rococo *De la Motte Mansion* (open to visitors), designed by the Eger
architect János Povolny and built in 1774–78. It was later bought by
the Frenchman, Anton de la Motte, a colonel of the Emperor. The
smallholder's dwelling at No. 40 Lenin út has been turned into a
museum. (Open 14.00–18.00 except Monday.)

Szépasszony völgy (Valley of the Beautiful Lady) a few kilometres to
the W of Eger is a popular attraction due to the abundance of wine
cellars here and the opportunities they provide for wine-tasting
together with open-air festivities organised in the summer months.
Eger's vine-growing area, comprising more that 3700 hectares,
produces the well-known dark red Egri bikavér (Bull's Blood).
Among other wines exported are the dark red, strong, sweet dessert
wine, Medoc Noir and the honey-coloured Egri leányka. The *Wine
Cellar Museum* (Pincemúzeum) at Szépasszony völgy which
occupies former wine cellars has displays relating to grape production and wine-making. (Open April–Oct, Fri–Sat–Sun 10.00–18.00.)

Feldebrő, 20km to the SW of Eger via Verpelét, has a church with a
12C crypt which is one of Hungary's oldest surviving architectural
monuments. (For further details see page 321.)

16   Budapest to Debrecen

A.   Via Szolnok

Road 4. Total distance 226km. **Budapest**—Road 4 70km **Cegléd**—
17km **Abony**—13km **Szolnok**—46km **Kisújszállás**—17km **Karcag**—
40km **Hajdúszoboszló**—23km **Debrecen**.

Debrecen is 226km E from Budapest on Road 4 via Szolnok and the
Great Plain (Alföld). Road 4 begins in Budapest as Üllői út, which
starts from Kálvin tér and runs through the city passed the People's
Park (Népliget) and Ferihegy Airport. The road is flat and fast,
although there is no motorway or long dual-carriageway section and
so heavy traffic on this road, which is for the most part a main
through-route to Romania, can cause hold-ups. There are no major
towns of architectural significance on the route, but several places
are of historical or ethnographical interest.

70km from Budapest Road 4 passes by **Cegléd**, a small town (pop.
40,000) of some historical importance. Cegléd was the scene in 1514
of a speech given by György Dózsa, the leader of the peasant revolt
of that year, calling the whole nation to war. It was here, too, that
Lajos Kossuth, the political leader of the 1848–49 War of Independence, summoned the inhabitants of the Great Plain to arms against
the Habsburgs. In 1877, when Kossuth was in exile in Turin, over 100
citizens of Cegléd travelled to Italy to ask him to return to Hungary
and be their member of Parliament. When they came back the
delegation was greeted by rapturous crowds throughout the country.
Kossuth's son, Ferenc, was MP for Cegléd from 1894, as was Count
Mihály Károlyi during the First World War. In the late 19C the town
was also the centre of the agricultural labourers' movement. In 1897
the first National Agricultural Workers' Congress was held here.

The *Kossuth Museum* at No. 5 Marx u., on the corner of Rákóczi út in a
former industrial bank building, was founded in 1917 on the basis of
2000 items which had been bequeathed by Ferenc Kossuth. Apart from
local history, the exhibition includes items relating to Lajos Kossuth and
1848, a 'Turin room', various personal possessions of Kossuth and
material about his burial in 1894 when his body was returned from
Turin and when 2000 citizens of Cegléd walked to Pest for the funeral.
(Open 10.00–18.00; Nov–April 9.00–17.00; closed Mondays.)

One of the biggest Reformed churches of the Great Plain stands in
Szabadság tér. This neo-classical **Calvinist Church**, which seats over
2000 people, was planned by József Hild and begun in 1836,
although it was redecorated with Eclectic elements later in the
century. Miklós Borsos' memorial relief by the entrance has a portrait
of István Szegedi Kis (1505–72), a follower of Zwingli and one of the
leading figures of the Protestant Reformation in Hungary. He was a
minister in Cegléd in 1545–48. The *school* opposite the Calvinist
church was built in 1858 and also designed by Hild. It was originally
founded by István Szegedi Kis in 1545.

The Catholic Parish *Church of the Holy Cross* (Szent Kereszt-
templom) stands to the E of the Reformed church. It was designed in
neo-classical style by Ferenc Homályossi Tunkel and built in the
1820s. In front of the church stands an 18C *Holy Trinity Column*
which was placed here in 1896. It was on this spot that Lajos Kossuth

delivered his legendary speech of 24 September 1848 standing on an oak table which had been brought from the Town Hall nearby. The writer Mór Jókai was present and described how Kossuth's delivery 'magically impassioned the crowd and made it into a flood of volunteers'. At the back of the church, in Kossuth tér, there is József Somogyi's statue of *György Dózsa*, erected on the 500th anniversary of his birth (1970) in memory of the historic speech that he too, according to tradition, made in Cegléd.

György Dózsa (c 1470–1514) was a soldier of the border fortresses in southern Hungary who won a title of nobility with his military exploits as an officer of the garrison of Nándorfehérvár (Belgrade, Yugoslavia). In 1514 Archbishop Tamás Bakócz of Esztergom appointed him commander of a crusading army against the Turks. The grievances of the peasants who joined his army and the obstacles he encountered in preparing his anti-Turkish campaign induced him to turn his army against the landlords and to lead the peasant war which was flaring up throughout the country. After a victorious advance through the Great Plain his army was defeated at Temesvár (Timişoara, Romania). Dózsa was captured and, in one of those classic examples of the powerful taking revenge on one of their rebellious sons, he was tortured to death on a red-hot iron throne.

Abony (pop. 15,000) lies 17km beyond Cegléd on Road 4. The Baroque *St. Stephen's Church* in Kossuth tér dates from 1773–85. The main altar (1800) is by Mihály Sperer. The classical statue of *St. John of Nepomuk* in front of the church dates from 1826. The *Reformed church* in Lenin u. is in late Baroque style and dates from 1785. The wooden ceiling above the choir is from an earlier church.

At No. 16 Zalka Máté tér, in a former mid-18C Baroque granary, there is the *Lajos Abonyi Village Museum*, which exhibits items relating to the local peasant economy of vine-growing, rope-making, weaving and barrel-making. (Open 9.00–17.00 except Monday.) Lajos Abonyi (1833–98) was an Alföld writer who was originally called Ferenc Márton. He studied in Pest and Kecskemét and at the age of 15 joined the National Guard during the War of Independence. He ran a farm in Abony from 1853 until his death.

Road 4 reaches **SZOLNOK** on the river Tisza 13km after Abony.

It was the Tisza that brought Szolnok into existence as the town developed around the middle of the Tisza valley where the vast flood area narrowed and permitted an easy crossing. Thus Szolnok became one of the centres of communication of the Great Plain and the river's most important port. For centuries blocks of salt were brought here by boat from Transylvania to be crushed before being delivered to every part of the country. Timber from the Carpathians was also brought by river to be prepared in Szolnok for further transport. The aspect of the town as a trade depot was also enhanced by the fact that the north–south waterway intersected here with the east–west overland routes between the Balkans and the Middle East and Central and Western Europe.

Szolnok's fortress here played an important role in the Turkish wars until 1552 when it was finally taken and after which it became a Turkish administrative centre for 130 years. At the beginning of the 1703–11 War of Independence the fortress fell into the hands of Rákóczi's supporters though it was finally captured by Habsburg forces in 1706, after which the imperial commander, Rabutin, ordered the destruction of its bastions and fortifications. The remaining walls were finally demolished in the mid-18C and the stones used in the rebuilding of the town centre. The Budapest–Szolnok railway line, the second in the country, was opened in 1847 and thus the town was an important strategic centre during the events of 1848–49. The modern appearance of present-day Szolnok (pop. 81,000) is due to the fact that the town was almost completely destroyed during the Second World War.

Kossuth Lajos tér forms the centre of the town. The Szolnok county museum, the *János Damjanich Museum*, is at No. 4, in the late-classical, former Magyar Király (Hungarian King) Hotel (Lajos Obermayer, 1860). The exhibitions include the local history of the region and archaeological finds from prehistoric times to the Turkish period. (Open 10.00–18.00; Nov–March 9.00–17.00; closed Mondays.) János Damjanich (1804–49), after whom the museum is named, was a general during the War of Independence and the victorious commander at the Battle of Szolnok on 5 March 1849. He was one of the 13 Hungarian generals executed by the Austrians on 6 October 1849 at Arad. There is a Carrara marble memorial to him by Béla Radnai in Gutenberg tér to the E, across the river Zagyva.

The Szolnok artists' colony was established here between the Zagyva and the Tisza in an English-style park in 1902. Among the leading painters have been László Mednyánszky (1852–1919) and Adolf Fényes (1867–1945). The paintings of one of the members of the colony, Ferenc Chiovini (1899–1981), are displayed at No. 4 Gutenberg tér in the *Chiovini Exhibition*. (Open 10.00–18.00; Nov–March 9.00–17.00; closed Mondays.)

The *Szolnok Gallery* is situated to the S of the town centre (No. 2 Koltói Anna u.) in a former synagogue designed by Lipót Baumhorn in Romantic style and built in 1899. Temporary exhibitions are held here. (Open 10.00–18.00; Nov–March 9.00–17.00; closed Mondays.) The Baroque former Franciscan church and house nearby were both built in the first half of the 18C.

Szolnok's specialist museum is the *Open-air Water Management Museum* which covers the history of the regulation of the Tisza—a major project of the last century. Much of the pumping equipment was made in England and installed by the Clayton and Shuttleworth company in 1878. The museum is situated in the Millér district of Szolnok. (Open 10.00–16.00 except Monday.)

The region beyond the Tisza to the east (known as Tiszántúl) has a low rainfall and has frequently suffered from drought. It is a flat undistinguished area with settlements relatively far from each other. After the Second World War the government established small farming centres to provide economic and cultural opportunities. Agriculture has been encouraged by irrigation systems and industrial centres have also been set up.

Kisújszállás is 46km beyond Szolnok on Road 4 after Törökszentmiklós. There is a regional *Folk Art Exhibition* at No. 5 Petőfi u. (Open Wed and Sat 10.00–12.00.) Temporary exhibitions are held at the *Kisgaléria* (Small Gallery) in the Cultural Centre at No. 1 Szabadság tér.

Karcag is a further 17km. One of Central Europe's largest rice-hulling mills has been here since the 1950s. The Baroque *Calvinist church* standing in Kossuth tér in the centre of the town dates from 1745–55, though the tower was added in 1789. The area is noted for its folk crafts and in particular its pottery. At the *Pottery House* (Fazekasház) at No. 1 Erkel Ferenc u., a late 19C peasant house, there is an exhibition of the pottery of the local craftsman Sándor Kántor. (Open April–Oct 10.00–18.00 except Monday.) The regional museum at No. 4 Kálvin tér, is the *István Győrffy Museum*. Győrffy (1884–1939) a folk art specialist and university teacher was born in Karcag. The collection, housed in a neo-classical mansion built in 1830, covers regional folk art and Győrffy's work. (Open April–Oct 10.00–18.00 except Monday; Nov–March 9.00–17.00, Sat 10.00–15.00, closed Sundays and Mondays.) At No. 16 Jókai u. there is a *peasant dwelling house* built c 1850 and furnished in the traditional style of the region. (Open April–Oct 10.00–18.00 every day except Monday.)

Road 4 now begins to pass through the area known as the *Hajdúság*.

The term *hajdú* refers to a group of people brought together by social and political ties. Some were descendants of people involved in the medieval cattle trade, others were descended from Southern Slavs who arrived during the Turkish wars, yet others were peasants made homeless during the many years of fighting. The 'hajdú's were hardened fighters and fought together as footsoldiers and cavalry against the Habsburgs in the armies of István Bocskai (1557–1606), the Prince of Transylvania. They helped him gain a decisive victory in 1604. In return the prince provided them with land and they settled down in communities and attached the term 'hajdú' as a prefix to the names of the settlements. As a group they enjoyed certain privileges and the Hajdú district operated as an independent administrative unit even up to 1876.

Hajdúszoboszló, on Road 4, 40km after Karcag, is Hungary's largest spa. Hot water springs, at a temperature of 73°C, were first discovered here in 1925 during drilling operations for oil and natural gas. Today there are 16 pools and over 30 different therapeutic services which function all the year round.

The central museum is the *István Bocskai Museum* at No. 12 Bocskai u. The exhibition covers the history of the town and its people over nine centuries up to 1975. The museum also runs an *exhibition hall* at No. 21 in the same street. It has a display of folk art from the Hajdúság region. (Both open 9.00–13.00, 15.00–19.00; Oct–April 9.00–13.00, 14.00–18.00; closed Mondays.) There is a private collection of local folk art, ceramics and furnishings at No. 2 Ady Endre u. (Open Monday 8.00–16.00.)

Road 4 reaches **Debrecen** (see Rte 17) after a further 22km.

B.   Via the Hortobágy

Roads 30, 3 and 33. Total distance 232km. **Budapest**—M3 Roads 30 and 3 120km junction of Road 33 (near Füzesabony)—Road 33 5km **Dormánd**. Alternatively **Budapest**—Road 31 79km **Jászberény**—6km *Jászjákóhalma*—13km **Jászapáti**—15km *Heves*—16km **Dormánd** and Road 33. This second route adds only 4km to the total distance but is much slower. Then for both routes **Dormánd**—Road 33 32km Tiszafüred—35km **Hortobágy**—40km **Debrecen**.

The Hortobágy is an area of more that 2000 sq km to the west of Debrecen of which 630 sq km are taken up by the **Hortobágy National Park**. Founded in 1973, it was the first such national park in Hungary. From the point of view of its natural endowments and its historic and ethnographic traditions the area is unique in Hungary.

The Hortobágy can be reached en route to Debrecen by taking the M3 Motorway from Budapest, then Road 3 to the junction of Road 33 near Füzesabony, 5km after the village of Kerecsend. Road 33 runs from here to Debrecen via Tiszafüred and the Hortobágy National Park. This route to Debrecen is a few kilometres longer than that via Road 4 (232km) but due to the motorway section and traffic conditions it can be much quicker. (For the section up to Kerecsend see Rte 14.)

An alternative, slightly longer, way of reaching Road 33 is via Jászberény on Road 31 which originates in Budapest in the Kőbánya district. **Jászberény** (79km from Budapest) was the centre of the former province of Jászság. The Jazygians were a nomadic people who settled along the Zagyva River in the first half of the 13C during the reign of Béla IV. The *Jász Museum* is situated at No. 5 Táncsis u. in a former Jazygian military headquarters originally built in 1782. The exhibition covers the history of the ethnic group with archaeological material dating back to the Age of Migrations. Of particular significance is the so-called Lehel Horn, an 8C Byzantine work carved from ivory. Legend has it that Lehel, one of the Magyar leaders at the Battle of Augsburg in 955, struck the emperor with this horn. The name Lehel is more widely known today as the name of the local refrigerator manufacturer. The museum has a section dealing with the history of the factory. (Open April–Oct 9.00–17.00 except Monday; Nov–March 9.00–15.00, weekends 9.00–13.00, closed Mondays)

At *Jászjákóhalma*, 6km beyond Jászberény on Road 31, there is a *Village Museum* (Bajcsy-Zsilinszky út) covering the history of the village and containing items of folk art. (Open Sundays and holidays 14.00–17.00.) *Jászapáti*, a further 13km, has a *Local History Museum* at No. 21 Beloiannisz u. Inside there is a memorial room to the locally-born painter, Pál Vágó (1853–1928), a village kitchen and equipment of traditional hemp-making. (Open Tues 14.00–17.00, Thurs 9.00–12.00, Sun 9.00–12.00 and 14.00–17.00.) Local residents have also established a *Homestead Museum* in the village, with tools, furniture, clothing and implements from the beginning of the present century. (Open April–Oct, Sat and Sun 10.00–18.00.)

Road 31 passes through (15km) Heves and joins Road 33 at (16km) Dormánd, 5km S of its junction with Road 3.

Road 33 crosses the river Tisza, passes through Tiszafüred and then, for the 74km stretch to Debrecen, crosses the **Hortobágy**.

This area of the Great Plain was once covered with forests and marshland and was densely populated, but the Mongol and Turkish invasions destroyed over 50 settlements. The frequent floods of the river Tisza washed away the upper soil leaving, together with the effect of the winds, the present general look of the puszta (plain). After the regulation of the Tisza in the 19C the marshes remained in the low-lying areas and the sodic subsoil came to the surface. The only mounds on the puszta were former look-out hills and burial places dating from the Age of Migrations. Otherwise the land differs in height only by a few centimetres.

The climate of the Hortobágy is very dry, although the temperature fluctuates a great deal throughout the seasons. In the great heat of the summer a special natural phenomenom can sometimes be seen above the endless plain—the *délibáb*, a mirage caused by the diffusion of light resulting from the meeting of humid layers of air of differing temperatures. Painters, writers, travellers and modern-day photographers have all testified to the visual splendour of the Hortobágy.

The construction of the Eastern and Western main canals and the digging of drainage channels has led to an improvement of the harsh natural conditions. In the area between the two canals 5000 hectares of fish lakes have been created.

Traditionally the Hortobágy has been a centre of one of the oldest occupations in Hungary—cattle-breeding. Hungarian grey cattle can still occasionally be seen. Black and white, twisted horn Racka sheep are also characteristic of the extensive, but meagre grazing areas. They are watched over by Hungarian pumi and puli dogs.

The bird life of the puszta is unique. Such rarities as the little ringed plover and stone curlew can be found here. Nests of godwits, redshanks, terns, white storks, great bustards, spoonbill cranes and occasionally great white egrets can also be found. The white-tailed eagle, imperial eagle, the buzzard and the osprey are also regular inhabitants of the Hortobágy. Twice a year, in autumn and spring, the Hortobágy becomes one of the main resting places in Europe for millions of migratory birds. More than 236 species have been counted, that is more than half of the bird species of Europe.

The Hortobágy National Park (HNP) *Patkos Inn* is on Road 33, 8km after Tiszafüred by the junction for Tiszacsege. Designed by Nándor Paár and István Nagy, it was built in 1975. There is an information office here and temporary exhibitions are also sometimes organised here. (Open mid-May to Sept 9.00–18.00 except Monday.) After a further 8km there is a turning for *Nagyiván*, 7km to the S. Nagyiván is a small village, characteristic of the Hortobágy. The *Megyes Csárda Museum* is a few kilometres further along Road 33. The ensemble of buildings here was constructed in the 1760s. (Open mid-May to Sept 9.00–18.00 except Monday.) The *Fish Lake* (Halastó) *Exhibition* is situated on the right, a further 7km along Road 33. On display are items relating to the water world of the Hortobágy—the fish ponds, geese, bogs, snails, crabs, reptiles etc. (Open mid-May to Sep 9.00–18.00 except Monday.)

The village of **Hortobágy** is a further 5km. This is the centre of the National Park. Road 33 arrives at the village across the so-called *Nine-holed Bridge*. It has nine arches and is one of the longest stone bridges in Hungary. It was built in 1827–33 to replace an earlier wooden structure and was designed by Ferenc Povolny on commission from the Debrecen town authorities. The bridge has been painted and mentioned in literature many times and has become one of the symbols of the Hortobágy. Every August the Hortobágy Bridge Fair takes place as a reminder of the traditional life-style of the puszta. The *Hortobágy Csárda* is immediately across the bridge on the left. It was built in 1781 in peasant Baroque style, though the eastern classical wing was added in the early 19C. The *Hortobágy Gallery* is along the road by the side of the csárda on the left. Paintings of the Hortobágy and the Alföld are exhibited here. (Open 9.00–17.00; Oct–March 10.00–12.00, 12.30–16.00; closed Mondays.) Across the road from the csárda, in a former cart shed and stables built in 1785, there is the *Pastoral Museum*, which contains an exhibition about the historic traditions of the Hortobágy, in particular animal raising, and the life of the shepherds at the turn of the century. (Open 9.00–17.00 except Monday; shorter hours in the

A traditional peasant house of the Great Plain. This one is at Kismarja near the Romanian border. The traditional wall decoration is not paper but is put on with a roller.

winter months.) The circular barn building of the *National Park Exhibition* nearby has a display about the fauna and flora of the Hortobágy. (Open May to mid-Oct 9.00–18.00 except Monday.)

Horse-breeding was one of the traditional activities of the puszta. At *Máta*, a short distance along the road leading northwards from the W side of the bridge, there is a stud farm and stables. The Hortobágy International Horse Show is held each year in June.

Road 33 leads from Hortobágy directly to **Debrecen** (see Rte 17), a distance of some 39km. Several kilometres after the village, on the left, there is the *Szálkahalom Museum* which has a display about the geological formation of the region.

17 Debrecen

DEBRECEN is the major town of the Great Plain and the centre of Protestant Hungary. Its population has crept up in recent years to 217,000 making it the second most populous place in Hungary after Budapest. Though the fact that its population is just over 10 per cent of the capital's indicates the degree of difference between the size of Budapest and that of everywhere else in the country.

Tourist Information: Hajdú Tourist, 2/a Kálvin tér (52/15-588).

Rail Station: Petőfi tér. 2½ hours by express from the Western Railway Station, Budapest.

Post Office: 5–9 Hatvan u.

Police: 5–7 Becskereki u.

History. Debrecen is one of the oldest of Hungarian towns. It was originally formed by the fusion of villages in the 13C and later acquired municipal status under Louis the Great (1342–82). The town developed as a market town such that by the end of the 15C there were eight annual fairs held in Debrecen attended by traders from all over Europe.

The town became known as the 'Calvinist Rome' as the Protestant Reformation gained a strong foothold in Debrecen even before the Turkish times. In 1552 it was enacted that only Calvinists would be allowed to settle in the city, and its Calvinist College became a cultural and educational centre with a significant influence in the surrounding region. Debrecen has remained the centre of the Reformed Church in Hungary even to this day. The Great Calvinist Church and the College behind it have become symbols of the town.

During the Turkish period Debrecen was near the border of all three parts of Hungary—the Turkish-occupied territory, the Hungarian Principality of Transylvania and the Habsburg-ruled Hungarian kingdom. Despite being surrounded by a theatre of war, the town managed to survive relatively independently and even prospered. Debrecen cattle-dealers drove their Hortobágy-bred grey Hungarian cattle with forked horns as far as Vienna, Prague and even parts of Germany.

The town suffered serious damage during the War of Independence in the early 18C and was plundered and burned more than once by the Imperial forces. Distance from Austria and strong Calvinist roots meant that the Counter-Reformation had little long-term success in Debrecen. Baroque influences were therefore minimal in the town.

Debrecen has played an important part in the political history of Hungary. During the 1848–49 War of Independence the Kossuth government had its headquarters transferred to Debrecen and it was here that the overthrow of the House of Habsburg was proclaimed in April 1849. Towards the end of the Second World War, after the city was finally liberated in October 1944, the Provisional National Government was set up in Debrecen and introduced some important laws including that of land reform.

Since the war Debrecen has become a centre of the pharmaceutical, medical

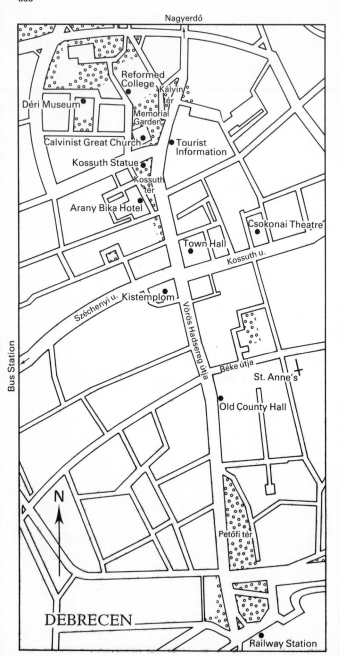

Nagyerdő

Reformed College

Kálvin tér

Déri Museum

Memorial Garden

Calvinist Great Church

Tourist Information

Kossuth Statue

Kossuth tér

Arany Bika Hotel

Csokonai Theatre

Town Hall

Kossuth u.

Széchenyi u.   Kistemplom

Vörös Hadsereg útja

Béke útja

St. Anne's

Bus Station

Old County Hall

N

Petőfi tér

DEBRECEN

Railway Station

instrument, food-processing and light engineering industries, but it has also retained its role as a cultural centre and has three universities.

VÖRÖS HADSEREG ÚTJA runs in a S–N direction from the railway station in Petőfi tér to the Great Church. (Tram No. 1 runs the length of the street.) The *Railway Station* (Nagyállomás) was originally built in 1857 for the opening of the line from Szolnok. A 15-minute bombing raid in June 1944 destroyed the old station and killed 1000 people in the vicinity. The new station building was designed by László Kelemen and built in 1961. The decoration inside shows scenes of the famous old markets of Debrecen. PETŐFI TÉR in front of the station has two memorials. In the southern corner stands the *Soviet war memorial* and at the N end there is a statue of the poet and political activist, *Sándor Petőfi* (1823–49). The statue is by Ferenc Medgyessy and was erected in 1948.

The **Old County Hall** (Régi megyeháza) is at No. 54 on the right of Vörös Hadsereg útja some distance to the N of Petőfi tér. The Secessionist building was constructed in 1912 and designed by Zoltán Bálint and Lajos Jámbor. The pyrogranite ornamentation on the façade depicting armed 'Hajdús' was made at the Zsolnay factory in Pécs. The elaborate stained-glass windows of the main hall (see above the entrance) are the work of Károly Kernstok and depict the seven chiefs of the ancient Magyars. The County Council still meets in the building.

In the gateway are two memorial plaques to the right and left. The one on the right records that the first Hungarian language theatre performance was held here in the summer of 1798 in the courtyard of a hotel which stood here. The other is a memorial to the Debrecen and Hajdu County 16th Hussar Regiment of the last century. The relief of the battle scene is by Manno Miltiades.

St. Anne's Church is in Béke útja which runs off Vörös Hadsereg útja to the E just beyond the Old County Hall. The church was built between 1721 and 1746 and financed by Cardinal Imre Csáky. (The towers were added in the 1830s.) The cardinal's coat of arms can be seen above the portal. The church, which was designed by Giovanni Battista Carlone, was originally built as a monastic church for the Piarists, who ran the parish from 1719 to 1807. To the right was the Piarist monastery and to the left their grammar school. (In the present school there is a *school museum* which has an exhibition of documents and teaching apparatus. Open 1 September–15 June 8.00–14.00 except weekends and holidays.)

The façade of the church is also adorned with the coat of arms of the Piarists, the Virgin Mary with the child Jesus, and statues of St. Stephen and St. Imre. The main altarpiece (date unknown) showing St. Anne and Mary is by the Viennese artist Karl Rahl. The four large sculptures here are of the Popes St. Augustus, St. Gregory, St. Leo and St. Ambrose.

The so-called *Csanak House* is at No. 51 Vörös Hadsereg útja, on the left as the route proceeds northwards. This corner house was designed by Antal Szkalnitzky and built in 1874 for the merchant József Csanak, a local self-made man and patron of the arts. The church on the left, at the corner of Vörös Hadsereg útja and Széchenyi u., is known as the **Kistemplom** (Small Church). A wooden ecclesiastical building stood here in the 17C which was rebuilt in brick in 1670 and called the Kistemplom. This was destroyed in a fire of 1719. Rebuilding started in 1720 but over the decades constant problems demanding repairs led to the complete reconstruction of the church in the 1870s under the direction of the architect Antal

Szkalnitzky. The Romantic style dates from that time. Szkalnitzky had an onion-shaped dome erected on top of the tower. This was blown off during a storm in 1909, after which the bastion-like top was added. The church is sometimes, therefore, called the 'csonka' (mutilated) templom. In 1860 the church was the scene of a meeting in protest against a law of 1859 which did away with the autonomy of the Protestant Churches. The meeting was banned and a confrontation with the police occurred. The corner building at *No. 22* opposite the church with the elaborate gilded Art Nouveau doorway was originally built for the First Savings Bank of Debrecen, which was founded in 1846. Today the building is the home of the Hungarian People's Army Club.

100m along Széchenyi u., at No. 6 on the left, is the *Old Post Office Restaurant* (Régi Posta étterem). It was built in the 1690s and with its arcaded loggia is a rare surviving example of rural architecture in central Debrecen. The interior has been reconstructed several times. At the beginning of the 18C the house was owned by Sámuel Diószegi, the postmaster and, for a while, chief justice of Debrecen. The plaque on the exterior wall recalls that Charles XII of Sweden stayed here on his return from exile in Turkey on 13 November 1714.

Kossuth Lajos u. runs eastward from Vörös Hadsereg útja, opposite Széchenyi u. The **Csokonai Theatre**, on the left at No. 10, was built in Romantic style with Moorish-Byzantine ornamentation in 1861–65 to the design of Antal Szkalnitzky. The façade is adorned with two allegorical female figures and six poets—Petőfi, Csokonai, Kazinczy, Vörösmarty, Kölcsey and Károly Kisfaludy. Mihály Csokonai Vitéz (1773–1805), a poet of the Hungarian Enlightenment, was born and died in Debrecen. The bust in front of the theatre, by Nándor Berky, is of Árpád Horváth, a noted director of the theatre. The so-called Financial Palace (Pénzügy Palota) stands next to the theatre, at *No. 12–14* Kossuth Lajos u. It was designed by János Bobula and built in 1911–12. The plaque on the wall records that in the winter of 1944–45 this was the headquarters of the Provisional Hungarian government for a while.

A short distance along Kossuth Lajos u., in Méliusz tér, stands the *Verestemplom*. 'Veres' is an old Hungarian word meaning 'red' and is used here to describe the red-brick church which was designed by Sámuel Pecz and built in 1887. The interior furnishings were carved by Endre Ték. The frescoes were painted in 1937 by Jenő Haranghy.

The neo-classical building at *No. 29* Vörös Hadsereg útja is known as the Podmaniczky House and dates from the 1820s. The Upper House met in the main hall here in 1849. The plaque on the wall of *No. 31* next door records that Lajos Kossuth gave a rousing speech here in January 1849. The neo-classical **Town Hall** (Városi Tanácsháza) on the other side of the road at No. 20 stands on the site of the meeting place of the local authority since the 16C. The present building was begun following a fire in 1802, although the façade was designed by Ferenc Povolny in 1837 and modified later by József Ságodi. The only ornamentation is the old coat of arms of Debrecen above the main entrance. It depicts a phoenix rising from the flames, possibly a reference to the many fires of the town, or to the frequent occasions when the town has been burned by invaders. During the first months of 1849 Lajos Kossuth lived in the left wing of the building and the National Defence Committee also met here. From 14 April 1849, Kossuth was Provisional Head of State and Governing President.

No. 18, to the N of the Town Hall, is the local headquarters of the Hungarian State Railways. A plaque on the wall indicates that in 1862 the first music research association was established here. The *Liberation Monument* nearby has the names of Soviet soldiers who died here inscribed on a tablet. The statue was designed by Pál Pátzay and was erected in 1967. The **Arany Bika** (Golden Bull) **Hotel** stands opposite at No. 11–15 Vörös Hadsereg útja. There was an inn here from the end of the 17C. The name comes from a former owner who was called János Bika. That hotel was pulled down in 1882 and another one, designed in neo-classical style by Imre Steindl, was erected. It had two storeys and, being considered too small, was demolished in 1913. The present building was constructed in the following years to the plans of Alfréd Hajos and Lajos Villányi and was opened in 1915. Much of the interior retains its characteristic Art Nouveau style. The modern wing was added in 1976.

Vörös Hadsereg útja ends in KOSSUTH TÉR, which may be regarded as the centre of Debrecen. Towards the NW corner of the square, in the park area, there is a statue of *Lajos Kossuth* (1802–94; statue by Ede Margo and Sigfrid Pongrácz, 1914) the leader of the 1848–49 struggle against the Habsburgs. The other people represented all took part in the events. They are Zsigmond Perényi, speaker of the Upper House, Imre Szacsvay, secretary of the House of Representatives, and Mihály Könyves Tóth, pastor of Debrecen. Perényi and Szacsvay were later executed. Tóth's death sentence was commuted to 20 years' imprisonment.

The **Calvinist Great Church** (Nagytemplom) at the N end of the square has become the symbol of Debrecen. (Open Mon–Fri 9.00–12.00 and 14.00–16.00; Sat 9.00–12.00; Sun 11.00–16.00.) It was built in the first decades of the 19C and finished in 1823. The neo-classical design of Mihály Péchy is somewhat unusual in that although other ecclesiastical buildings were constructed in classical style (such as the cathedral at Eger) neo-classicism was primarily used for secular building in Hungary. Nevertheless, the monumentality and early construction of the Great Church helped to establish neo-classicism as the architectural style of the first half of the 19C.

In contrast with the (Roman Catholic) cathedral at Eger, however, the church, in keeping with the puritanism of its denomination, is simple and unornamented both inside and out. The Empire pulpit was made in the Pest workshop of Sebestyén Vogel. The benches and the Lord's table were made locally by József Doháńyosi. The organ dates from 1838 and was made in the Vienna workshop of Jakab Deutschmann. The seating between the plain, whitewashed walls was made to hold 3000. Due to the number of people that could be accommodated, and to the acquiescence of the church authorities, it was here that on 14 April 1849 Lajos Kossuth read out the Declaration of Independence and announced the dethronement of the House of Habsburg. On the centenary, in 1949, a ceremonial meeting of Parliament took place here, after the church had been repaired following severe bomb damage in the Second World War. Excavations in the 1980s have revealed remains of St. Andrew's Church which stood here in the 17C. Some parts of its walls can be seen. The church fell victim to the fire of 1802.

The County *Tourist Information Office* (Hajdútourist) is situated to the right of the main façade of the Great Church, at No. 2/a Kálvin tér. The small park behind the church is called the *Memorial Garden* (Emlékkert). In the centre stands a statue of *István Bocskai* which was erected by the local council in 1906 to mark the 300th anniversary of the Vienna Peace Treaty. The statue is a copy of one in Budapest by Barnabás Holló.

Bocskai (1557–1606) was a big landowner of the Tisza region. At first he headed the Transylvanian Habsburg faction and was the military leader of several victories against the Turks. He later led the struggle of the Hungarian nobles against Habsburg absolutism and in 1604 he organised an insurrection with the support of the Turks. At the 1606 Peace of Vienna he won self-government for the Hungarian nobility and religious freedom for Protestants. He endowed the hajdu soldiers who had fought in his campaign with collective privileges and settled them on his estates. The hajdu figures depicted on the base of the statue are the work of András Tóth.

The *memorial column* standing nearby since 1895 is to the memory of 41 Protestant ministers sold as galley slaves after a trial of 1673. The inscription reads: 'For their beliefs they were taken as convicts to Naples.' Across the road, to the E, there is a statue of the Debrecen poet *Mihály Csokonai Vitéz* (1773–1805).

Debrecen's celebrated **Reformed College** (Református Kollégium) stands on the N side of the Memorial Garden.

In the Middle Ages a Dominican Latin language school stood here. In 1538 the Reformed Church took over the building and set up a school based on the Württemberg University education system. The school had a basic influence on the area to the east of the river Tisza and it became one of the most important educational establishments of Hungary. For centuries it was supported by the Transylvanian princes, local manufacturers and Reformed Church communities.

Strict discipline characterised the life of the students. Up to the end of the 18C they had to rise at 3.00 and go to bed by 9.00. Residential students had to provide their own food, heating and other requirements. A register of 1706 records that poor students had to go around the locality begging for support.

Protestantism took root in eastern Hungary partly because of the more radical traditions of independence in Transylvania and partly because of the Reformation's inherent appeal to the poorer sections of society. Another factor was that many Franciscans, members of the most popular order, supported the Reformation and converted their followers as well. The spirit of independence, coupled with the distance from Vienna, meant that the Counter-Reformation, spearheaded from Austria, was unable to wipe out the Protestant tradition in the years following the expulsion of the Turks.

Protestantism advocated not only liberty of conscience, but social justice as well. Protestant preachers, who mainly came from peasant backgrounds, denounced the tyranny of landlords. The Hungarian Calvinists were very much influenced by the English Revolution and denounced the entire serf system. The big Calvinist colleges, like the one in Debrecen, were hotbeds of new ideas. Thousands of Hungarian students visited the universities of the Netherlands, Germany and England and were influenced by political ideas and rational thinking. The Debrecen College was also at the forefront of language reform. From 1797 all sciences were taught in Hungarian. The use of Hungarian in science and learning, however, was nothing new for Reformed Church thinkers. In the previous century the Calvinist János Apáczai Csere had written the first Hungarian language encyclopaedia.

Naturally this spirit of independence sometimes provoked opposition. In 1769 Maria Theresa prohibited the town council from supporting the college. During her reign a request for aid was sent to Thomas Harring, Archbishop of Canterbury, who, with the support of the English bishops and the universities of Oxford and Cambridge, arranged an endowment for the Reformed College. However, a tradition of sympathetic feeling in England towards the Protestants in Hungary had already been established for over a century. Milton, as secretary to Cromwell, wrote several letters to the Prince of Transylvania, György Rákóczi II, and in his 'Areopagitica' praised the Transylvanian students. The names of Transylvanian princes were well known in England and at one time English anti-Royalists were dubbed 'Teckelites' after one of them, Imre Thököly. It was in Debrecen that the first English grammar was published in Hungary in 1664.

The present building of the Reformed College dates from the early

19C as Debrecen's large fire of June 1802 destroyed the old southern wing. The fire took place during the Whitsun break, but the few students who were there managed to save the library and archives. Mihály Péchy was commissioned to design a new building. The first part was completed in 1816 but due to lack of funds his plans had to be simplified. The wings were added in 1870–74 to the plans of Alajos Vasél. The façade is decorated with memorial tablets to the religious reformers Calvin and Zwingli and to the outstanding educators and students of the college. The writer Zsigmond Móricz, and the poets Mihály Csokonai Vitéz, János Arany, Ferenc Kölcsey and Mihály Fazekas are portrayed.

The building today contains a secondary school, a theological college, a hostel, library and two exhibitions (college history and ecclesiastical art). The parts of the building which contain the exhibitions, the library and the historic oratory can be visited by the public. (Entrance on the left of the main façade. Open Tues–Sat 9.00–17.00; Sun 9.00–13.00.) The *College History Exhibition* is on the ground floor and describes the life of the students at the time, their foreign connections, uniforms and extra-curricular activities—the fire service, choir, etc. Some former teaching aids are on display together with certain personal possessions of various famous Hungarians. Also on the ground floor is the *Exhibition of Ecclesiastical Art*. On display are various textiles, items of goldsmiths' work and furniture used by the Reformed Church. The *Library*, on the second floor, is the biggest of the Reformed Church and has more than half a million items, including 14C codices, printed books from the 15C, and 200 versions of the Bible in various languages and translations. The wooden columns and shelving of the library date from 1827 and are the work of local carpenter József Dohányosi.

The large frescoes, which begin on the walls of the staircase above the first floor, show scenes from the history of the college. They were painted by Kálmán Gáborjáni Szabó in 1938 to commemorate the 400th anniversary of the founding of the Reformed College. Also dating from the same year is the stained-glass window by Oszwald Thoroczkai in the niche on the second floor landing. It is in memory of István Hatvani (1718–86), a mathematician and scientist, a former student of the college and later head of the philosophy and mathematics department. He was one of the first to teach chemistry in Hungary. The *Oratory* is opposite the Library on the second floor. Like the library, the woodwork was made by József Dohányosi.

On the last day of 1848 the Parliament in Pest decided that the government and Defence Committee should move to Debrecen. Hence, from 9 January to 31 May 1849, the National Assembly's Chamber of Deputies met here. (It was the only large meeting hall with heating which could be found.) Brass plates with the names of various deputies can be seen on several benches. Kossuth's is at the front on the right. The government mint also worked in the college building, issuing the so-called 'Kossuth bank notes' which today have become collectors' items. The staff and students of the college welcomed the move. 130 students joined the Hungarian army as volunteers.

On 21 December 1944 the Provisional National Assembly also met here. (This was the temporary government established to take over while the Germans were being driven out of Hungary.) A photograph of this meeting can be seen at the back of the hall, and there is a memorial tablet recalling the event outside, by the door of the Oratory.

The **Déri Museum** is 100m to the W of the Reformed College, in Déri tér. (Open 10.00–18.00; Nov–March 10.00–16.00; closed Mondays.)

It is named after Frigyes Déri (1852–1924) who was born in Hungary but studied in Vienna and set up silk factories there. He had a mansion in the Austrian capital and it was there that he began his art collection. Within a decade he had built up a small but valuable collection. Déri had no ties with Debrecen, he simply wanted to donate his collection to a public museum in a university town.

The museum, in neo-Empire style, was designed by György Dénes and Aladár Münich. Work began on the site of the former botanical gardens in 1923. Financial problems led to delays and it was not until 25 May 1930 that the museum was finally opened. The four symbolic statues in front of the building, representing archaeology, science, art and ethnography, are by Ferenc Medgyessy and won a grand prix at the Paris World Exhibition of 1937.

One of Ferenc Medgyessy's 1937 Paris World Exhibition prize-winning statues outside the Déri Museum, Debrecen.

The Hungarian holdings of the museum are especially rich in the field of fine arts. Some of the best examples of 19C National Romanticism and Realism are on display in the specially-built, glass-roofed *Munkácsy Room*. In the decades following the defeat of the 1848–49 War of Independence the desire to strengthen patriotic feelings took on a new impetus. The works of Viktor Madarász and Bertalan Székely served this aim. The former's 'National Assembly at Ónod' (1879), on display here, is based on an episode of the Rákóczi War of Independence, while the latter's 'Zrínyi's Sortee' (1885) takes its theme from the period of the Turkish wars. Folk genre scenes are well illustrated here by the works of János Jankó and Károly Lotz as well as by Mihály Munkácsy's 'Woebegone Highwayman' (1865). The pride of the exhibition, however, is Munkácsy's huge canvas, 'Ecce Homo'.

Mihály Munkácsy was born in 1844 at Munkács (today Mukachevo in the Soviet Union). After a difficult childhood he studied art in Pest and later in Vienna. After Munich and Düsseldorf, he settled down in Paris in 1871, where he matured and became the most internationally well-known of 19C Hungarian painters. Distance from Hungarian life led to a certain over-romanticism which can be seen in some of the paintings here. 'Ecce Homo' is part of Munkácsy's Christ Trilogy. 'Christ Before Pilate' and 'Golgotha' were painted in 1881 and 1884 respectively. They were shown throughout Europe and the United States, where they were finally bought and hung in the chapel of the Wanamaker Department Store in Philadelphia.

'Ecce Homo' was finished in 1896 and exhibited first in Paris, then at the Millennial Exhibition in Budapest. A delegation took it around the world, hoping that from the proceeds they could buy it for the Hungarian state. In 1898 it was displayed in London and the following year at the Royal Academy in Dublin. In 1914–15 the painting was once more exhibited in Hungary and it was then that it was bought by Frigyes Déri.

Although the theme is taken from the New Testament, 'Ecce Homo' is not simply a religious painting. It is Munkácsy's view of good and evil, of truth and falsehood. Its dramatic quality and powerful portrayal of character was commented on by James Joyce, who viewed the painting in Dublin: 'It is a mistake to limit drama to the stage; a drama can be painted as well as sung or acted, and 'Ecce Homo' is a drama.'

Frigyes Déri's collection was not restricted to paintings. Apart from the works of art in the Munkácsy Room, the museum also has an Egyptian, Greek and Roman collection, an Oriental exhibition, a Japanese collection, a collection of medieval European coats of armour, a collection of coins and medals, a collection of 15C–17C drawings and engravings, and a collection of folk art, which was assembled by Györgyi Déri, the younger brother of the museum's founder.

Péterfia u. runs northwards from the E side of the Reformed College. The *Medgyessy Memorial Museum* is a short distance along here at No. 28 on the left. The exhibition covers the life work of the sculptor Ferenc Medgyessy (1881–1958), who was born in Debrecen. (Open 10.00–18.00; Nov–March 10.00–16.00; closed Mondays.)

The **Nagyerdő** (Great Wood) is situated 2.5km to the N along Péterfia u., through Bem tér and along Simonyi út (No. 1 tram runs there). The area used to be outside the city boundary, but today it has the character of an urban park and contains an open-air theatre, sports grounds, an amusement park and a small zoo. Behind the neoclassical *Vigadó Restaurant* (Ferenc Povolny, 1826) is the *Spa*. There are four thermal baths in the domed pool hall and facilities for a total of over 3000 bathers a day.

The main building of the **Lajos Kossuth University** stands on the W side of the park facing Egyetem tér. Erected in late-Eclectic/neo-Baroque style in 1927–32 it is Debrecen's largest building. The French garden in front of the university was laid out in the 1930s. The large fountain was placed here in 1965. The neo-classical former University Calvinist Church stands to the right of the building. It was designed by József Borsos and built in 1940. The *University Botanical Garden* nearby is open in the summer from 8.00 to 18.00 and in the winter from 8.00 to 16.00. A short distance to the NE, along Nagyerdei körút, are the buildings of the Medical University and Teaching Hospitals.

Other places of interest. *The Debrecen Literary Museum*, at No. 1

Borsos József tér, deals with the role of Debrecen in Hungarian literature. (Open 10.00–16.00 except Monday.) *The Postal Museum* is situated at No. 1 Bethlen u. (Open Wed, Sat and Sun 14.00–18.00.) *The László Holló Museum* on Margit u., has paintings by this artist who died in Debrecen in 1976.

Excursions from Debrecen

The Nyírség is the name given to the area to the N and NE of Debrecen. It is slightly higher than the rest of the Great Plain as over the centuries winds have brought sand from the Tisza area and deposited it here in thick layers. The sand eventually became covered with birch forests which grew alongside stagnant water arising from below the surface. Drainage projects in the last century turned the area into agricultural land and today the Nyírség is dotted with numerous large orchards.

Nyírbátor (pop. 14,000) lies c 50km to the NE of Debrecen on Road 471. It has a number of important art monuments. The single nave **Calvinist Church** here is one of Hungary's most important late-Gothic buildings. Although only a Reformed church since the late 16C, it was built by the Transylvanian Voivode István Báthori between 1484 and 1488. The spaces between the exterior buttresses are broken by huge Gothic windows and adorned by the Renaissance coats of arms of the founder. The long and conspicuously high interior is roofed with Gothic reticulated vaulting. The Renaissance sedilia inside indicate that the Báthori family probably had access to the royal building workshop and also show that Gothic and Renaissance lived side by side in 15C Hungary. The church was originally built as a family burial church and the Gothic tomb of the founder, dating from 1490, can still be seen. The *wooden belfry* beside the church was built around 1640 and is a good example of the several splendidly carved and solidly built belfries which can still be found in northern and eastern Hungary. The turreted spire reverts to Gothic style, while the arcade is more in the spirit of the Renaissance. (Up to the end of the 18C Protestant churches were not allowed to have towers built of more solid materials.)

Nyírbátor's former Franciscan, **Minorite Church** was also built for István Báthori around 1480. It was plundered by the Turks in 1587 and later, in 1717, was restored in Baroque style by Sándor Károlyi. The richly decorated altars and pulpit were made in the workshop of a sculptor at Eperjes (Prešov, Czechoslovakia) around 1730. Of particular note is the highly decorated *Krucsay Altar* on the left towards the chancel. The name comes from János Krucsay, who commissioned it in memory of his wife.

The *István Báthori Museum* is situated in the former Minorite monastery, which was built in the first half of the 18C on medieval foundations (No. 15 Károlyi u.). The exhibitions cover local history and that of the Báthori family. (Open 10.00–17.00 except Monday.)

Nyíregyháza is 50km N of Debrecen on Road 4. It is the central town of the Nyírség and although much larger than Nyírbátor (pop. 119,000) it is not so rich in monuments. The central museum, at No. 21 Benczúr tér, is the *András Jósa Museum*, named after the archaeologist, doctor, anthropologist and first director of the county museum. Jósa died in Nyíregyháza in 1918. The large collections include archaeological and ethnographical material from the region and items relating to the history of the town. There are also memorial rooms to the painter Gyula Benczúr (1844–1920) and the writer Gyula Krúdy (1878–1933), both of whom were born in Nyíregyháza. (Open Tues–Fri 9.30–17.30, Sat and Sun 9.00–17.00.)

At *Sóstófürdő*, 6km N of the centre via Kossuth Lajos u., there are thermal baths and an open-air *Ethnographical Museum* which describes the traditional vernacular architecture, way of life and economic activity of the region. (Open April–Oct 9.00–17.00 except Monday.)

18 North-East Hungary

Roads 3 and 37. Total distance c 135km. **Budapest**—M3 Roads 30 and 3 115km **Kerecsend**—Road 3 20km **Mezőkövesd**—45km **Miskolc** (5km **Diósgyőr**; 8km **Lillafüred**; 5km **Miskolctapolca**)— 35km **Szerencs** (9km *Monok*)—10km turning for Road 38 and (8km) **Tokaj**—25km **Sárospatak**.

Due to its geographical position and distance from Budapest, the North-East region of Hungary is one of the least visited by foreigners. There are, however, a number of places of interest in the area and this route gives a general idea of what can be found here.

Leave Budapest via Road 30 or the M3. (Rte 14 covers this route up to the village of Kerecsend.) **Mezőkövesd** is on Road 3, 20km beyond Kerecsend. Traditionally it is the centre of the Matyós, an ethnic group living on the southern slopes of the Bükk Mountains. The local costumes, embroidery and folk art have become famous and several places in the town (pop. 18,000) are devoted to preserving the traditions. The *Matyó Museum*, at No. 20 Béke tér, is a regional museum devoted to recording the life and traditions of the Matyó people. (Open 9.00–17.00 except Monday.) The *Bori Kis Jankó Memorial House*, occupies a peasant house built c 1850 at No. 22 in the street which bears her name. Kis Jankó (1876–1954) was a local embroidery specialist. Samples of her work are exhibited here. (Open 9.00–17.00; Nov–March 9.00–12.00; closed Mondays.) Peasant dwelling houses with traditional interior furnishings can be viewed at Nos 12 and 21 Kis Jankó Bori u., and at No. 4 Mogyoró köz. (All three are open 9.00–17.00 except Monday.) The *Town Gallery* is situated in the local cultural centre at No. 7 Béke tér. Matyó folk art is exhibited here. (Open 9.00–17.00 except Monday.)

MISKOLC (pop. 210,000) is 45km N of Mezőkövesd on Road 3. Since 1945 the town has been the second most important industrial centre in Hungary after Budapest. Miskolc was ravaged by the Turks and by the Austrian Imperial forces during the 1703–11 War of Independence. Industrial development started in the last century and came to dominate the area, although the country's first Hungarian language theatre was built in Miskolc in 1823, preceding that in Budapest by 14 years.

Avas Hill is near the centre of the town. It has hundreds of cellars in its side, hollowed out over the centuries for the storage of wine. Some cellars reach a depth of 50m and many are over 300 years old. The look-out platform on the radio and TV tower on the top of the hill offers a good view of the surroundings.

A Gothic **Calvinist Church**, with a chapel dating from the mid-13C, stands on the side of the hill by the town. The chapel was enlarged at the end of the 14C and 100 years later it was converted into a three-aisled Gothic church. Burnt by the Turks in 1544 it was rebuilt in the 1560s as a Calvinist church. The pews, made in Renaissance style, date from the 18C. On their backs there is flower decoration revealing a combination of folk art and Rococo. The *wooden belfry* with its Renaissance gallery next to the church dates from 1557. The cemetery has been in use since the 11C.

The **Orthodox Church** stands in the courtyard of the house at No. 7 Deák Ferenc tér. It was originally built in Louis XVI style between 1785 and 1806 by descendants of Greeks who had fled from the Turks. Of special note is the iconostasis with its 'Black Mary of Kazan' icon, which was given to the church by Tsarina Catherine II when she passed through Miskolc on her way to Vienna. The 'Mount Athos Cross', decorated with precious stones, was brought by the first Greek settlers and dates from 1590. The *Orthodox Ecclesiastical Museum* here was opened in 1986. The collection includes Orthodox religious works of art from the whole of Hungary. (Open 10.00–18.00; Nov–March 10.00–16.00; closed Mondays.) Nearby, on the N side of Hősök tere, stands the *former Minorite Church*. Both it and the adjoining former monastery were built in Baroque style between 1729 and 1740. Also nearby, at No. 13 Kossuth u., in the *Borsod-Miskolc Museum* there is a permanent exhibition of the paintings of Béla Kondor (1931–72) (Open 10.00–18.00; Nov–March 10.00–16.00; closed Mondays.)

Two other museums can be found to the S of the centre. The county museum, the *Ottó Herman Museum*, is at No. 28 Felszabadítók útja. Herman (1835–1914) was a natural historian and folk art researcher who finished his studies in Miskolc. The permanent exhibition is entitled 'Two centuries of Hungarian painting'. (Open 10.00–18.00; Nov–March 10.00–16.00; closed Mondays.) At the Heavy Industry Technical University, in the campus district of Miskolc, there is a specialist *University History Collection* dealing with the development of Hungarian mining and foundry work and its associated research and training. (Open 10.00–13.00 except weekends.)

The *Hairdressing Museum* (Fodrász Múzeum) at No. 8 Park u. has a specialist collection of instruments. (Open 10.00–16.00; Sat 10.00–12.00; closed Sunday.) One of the country's largest industrial plants, the Lenin Metallurgical Works, is situated on the western side of Miskolc. The *Central Museum of Metallurgy* (Központi Kohászati Múzeum) is nearby at No. 22 Palota u. The exhibition covers the history of iron and steel production in Hungary. (Open 9.00–17.00 except Monday.)

Diósgyőr, the oldest part of Miskolc, is further to the W, beyond the iron works district. The *Medieval Castle* here is one of Hungary's most important monuments from pre-Turkish times.

The second half of the 14C saw the introduction of the southern Italian type of castle. The central section was a palace with windows opening onto the outside. At each of the four corners there were usually four-sided towers. The royal castle at Diósgyőr was built for King Louis the Great between 1350 and 1375. Both Sigismund of Luxemburg and King Matthias had it extended and further adorned. It was the traditional dower house of the queen and hence was sometimes known as the 'Queen's Castle'. The castle served as a recreation centre for the royal family as it was situated in picturesque woodland and in the middle of good hunting grounds.

The castle frequently changed hands at the beginning of the 18C during the War of Independence, and later it gradually fell into ruin. Restoration of the castle took place in the 1960s. Prior archaeological excavations revealed that it had been built on the site of an earlier castle. The oval ground plan of this castle was discovered but the only traces were some remains of the foundation walls.

Three towers of the later, ruined castle were restored and the fourth preserved as it was found. The early 16C rondella at the NE corner was covered to provide a hall for the *Castle Museum* (Open April–Oct 9.00–18.00 except Monday.)

Also in the castle is the so-called *Déryné House*. Róza Széppataki (often known as Mrs Déry; 1793–1872) was a popular actress and one of the first opera singers in Hungary. She died in Miskolc. There is a memorial room here as well as a display of the history of photography in Miskolc. (Open April–Dec 9.00– 18.00 except Monday.)

The resort of **Lillafüred** is a few kilometres to the W of Diósgyőr. The neo-Eclectic former *Palace Hotel*, by Lake Hámori was built between 1927 and 1930 and is today a trade union recreation centre. A number of caves can be visited in the area, including the *Szeleta Caves*, where Ice Age remains were discovered at the beginning of the century. Near the *István Caves*, at No. 33 Erzsébet sétány, is the former villa of the archaeologist and ethnographer Ottó Herman (1835–1914). The *Herman Memorial House* has exhibitions about his life and work and about the fauna of the Bükk region. (Open 10.00– 18.00 except Monday.)

The *Újmassa Foundry* was developed from the first foundry in Hungary and is one of the oldest surviving foundries in Europe. (Take the road W from the Palace Hotel along the shore of the Lake.)

Henrik Fazola, the locksmith and wrought-iron specialist who worked at Eger, set up a blast-furnace for developing the iron-ore deposits in the northern Bükk Hills. The crude iron was processed at Hámor. His son, Frigyes, had this foundry constructed between 1810 and 1813 in order to expand the operations. It operated for 60 years. After the Second World War it was reconstructed and preserved as an industrial monument. The small museum on the site covers the history of foundry work in the area. (Open 9.00–17.00 except Monday.)

Miskolctapolca is another resort, lying 7km to the S of the centre of Miskolc via the university district (Egyetemváros). The natural spring thermal waters here have turned the area into a spa. The mildly radioactive waters were utilised as early as the Middle Ages, but the first stone buildings around the spa were not constructed until the 18C. Several pools and baths can be visited, including medicinal and therapeutic baths, a cave bath, formed inside a natural rock cave, and indoor and outdoor pools. The spa has a lake and a large park.

Szerencs is 35km to the E of Miskolc on Road 37. The *Castle* here was originally built in the middle of the 16C on the foundations of a Benedictine monastery founded in the second half of the 13C. In 1583 it came into the possession of the Rákóczi family, whose members led the struggles for independence against the Habsburgs. Here István Bocskai (1557–1606) was first elected Prince of Hungary. After the failure of the War of Independence in 1711, which had been led by Ferenc Rákóczi II, the castle lost its political and military importance. The castle and its estate were confiscated by the Vienna authorites and given to aristocrats who supported the Habsburgs. The castle was restored after World War II. The *Zemplén Museum* in the castle has exhibitions relating to local history and the Rákóczi period, and also has a large, unique collection of picture postcards of Hungary. (The museum is closed at the time of writing.) The *Calvinist Church* of Szerencs was built in the first half of the 14C and remodelled c 1480. The church is surrounded by a medieval fortress wall. Prince Zsigmond Rákóczi and his wife are buried here in a red marble sarcophagus.

Monok, 9km to the N of Szerencs, is the birthplace of Lajos Kossuth, the leading political figure of the struggle for independence in the 1848–49 period. The late-18C, Louis XVI style manor house where he was born (No. 18 Kossuth u.) is today a *Kossuth Memorial Museum* belonging to the Hungarian National Museum. As well as momentoes of Kossuth and the War of Independence there are items of local history and folk art. (Open 8.00–18.00 on request.)

18km from Szerencs, via Road 37 and then Road 38, lies the village of **Tokaj**. Although only small (pop. 5000) and far from Budapest, the name of Tokaj is known throughout the world because of the special local wines made here.

Actually Tokaj is only one of several communities which make up the vine-growing region. Vineyards have been cultivated here for many centuries. The environmental and climatic conditions are favourable. The soil of the local hills is made up of rocks and earth of volcanic origin. The Carpathians act as a shield against the northern winds and the autumn is usually long and dry with plenty of sunshine. The grapes are harvested later than normal here, usually from the end of October. A special paste made from the withered grapes is added in various proportions to the pressed-out grape juice. The fermentation process is slow and it can take up to eight years for Tokaj wine to mature, after which it can be stored for hundreds of years.

The popularity of the wine began in the Middle Ages, first in Poland and then it spread to Russia, Greece, Germany and Scandinavia. Numerous stories and historical anecdotes are attached to it. Pope Pius IV is said to have commented favourably on the wine at the Council of Trent. Louis XIV of France, who was sent the wine by Prince Rákóczi, is attributed with calling it 'the wine of kings—the king of wines'. Tsar Peter the Great even purchased several vineyards in the area. Voltaire wrote that 'Tokaj stimulates the brain cells and kindles words of genius', while Schubert immortalised it in song.

The *Tokaj Museum* at No. 7 Bethlen Gábor u. is a regional museum of local history containing items connected with the history of Tokaj and its grape and wine culture. There is also a small liturgical collection here. (Open 10.00–18.00 except Monday.) The *Cellar Museum* (Pincemúzeum) on Petőfi út is also devoted to the history of Tokaj wines. (Open 9.00–17.00 except Monday.) There are several wine shops and cellars located in different parts of the town, and traditional festivities take place annually at harvest time.

Sárospatak is near the NE Hungarian border, about 65km from Miskolc on Road 37. Although only a small town (pop. 15,000) it has played a significant role in history and has some important monuments.

The first mention of Sárospatak **Castle** dates from 1262. However, the keep which is the oldest surviving part of the castle was built at the end of the 15C. Between 1534 and 1563, the Perényi family who owned the castle rebuilt it in Renaissance style and added a palace surrounded by a rampart with Italian bastions. At the beginning of the 17C, the new owner, Prince George Rákóczi I, built a palace here and in 1645 the earlier Renaissance palace and the keep were connected by a late-Renaissance loggia.

In 1702 the castle was badly damaged by explosives on the orders of the Austrian War Council. (This happened in many places throughout the country and helps to explain why few ancient castles have survived in Hungary.) During the Rákóczi War of Independence (1703–11) one of the most important meetings of the Diet took place here in 1708. After the war the castle was confiscated and given to Habsburg supporters. The new owners added Baroque elements and further additions were made in the 19C. After World War II the castle was restored and converted into a museum. The ground floor of the keep was unearthed and many Renaissance details were restored to their original form. The 18C and 19C changes, however, were left untouched.

There are four collections inside the old castle area. The *Rákóczi Museum* exhibition covers the history of the castle, the Rákóczi family and the War of Independence. As well as weapons and a collection of Renaissance stonework, there are items of furniture and local applied arts. (During a campaign of 1645 Prince György Rákóczi moved some 50 Anabaptist craftsmen and their families here from the Moravian border area. They included cloth-makers, carpenters, wheelwrights, brewers, gardeners, knifemakers and potters.) The adjoining *Sárospatak Gallery* contains modern Hungarian paintings. (Both open 10.00–18.00 except Monday.) A short distance to the N is the *Roman Catholic Ecclesiastical Collection* in a former Jesuit monastery built in late-Renaissance and Baroque styles on medieval foundations, though with a present appearance owing much to 19C changes. The exhibition covers the history of the Sárospatak Castle chapel. (Open May–Oct 9.00–17.00, Sun 12.00–17.00, closed Monday.) Also nearby is the *Andrássy Kurta Collection*, where the sculptures of János Andrássy Kurta are on permanent display. (Open 10.00–18.00 except Monday.)

The **Parish Church** on Kádár Kata u. is one of Eastern Hungary's largest Gothic hall churches. It originally dates from the 14C, was rebuilt at the end of the following century and has been remodelled several times since. A notable feature is the huge Baroque *high altar*, which was brought here from the Carmelite church in Buda Castle when their order was banned in 1784. The two Rococo side altars came from the local church of the Trinitarians.

The **Calvinist College** at the N end of Rákóczi út was founded in 1531 and has played an important role in the educational and cultural life of the country.

The golden age of the college coincided with the arrival of the humanist educationalist John Amos Comenius in 1650. During his four years at the college he reorganised the school and the teaching system. A printing press was put at his disposal by György Rákóczi and one of his major works, 'Orbis Pictus', was written here. His textbooks were in use for many years and were repeatedly printed in new editions.

The Counter-Reformation in the second half of the 17C forced the college to close for a while. At first it moved to Gönc, on the far side of the Zemplén Hills to the NW, then it operated in Kassa (Košice, Czechoslovakia). It was able to return to Sárospatak only after 1703.

The college's reputation has been enhanced by the fact that over the years many eminent Hungarians have studied here, including the language reformer Ferenc Kazinczy, the statesman Lajos Kossuth and the writer Zsigmond Móricz. As with the Reformed College at Debrecen (see Rte 17) there have been strong English connections with this Calvinist college and English has been taught as a special subject for many years.

The present neo-classical main building of the college dates from the beginning of the last century. In the remains of the older parts there is a *Calvinist Museum* which has an exhibition of regional ecclesiastical applied arts and items relating to the history of the college, in particular the impact of Comenius.

19 Other Places of Interest in Hungary

A. Hollókő

To reach Hollókő by car (103km from Budapest) take the M3 motorway from
Budapest to Hatvan, then Road 21 towards Salgótarján and turn off before
Pásztó towards Szécsény. 3km after Felsőtold on this road an approach road
leads to Hollókő.
   A bus can be taken from the Népstadion Bus Station (departs 7.00) to Szécsény,
from where another bus (departing 9.50) takes 30 minutes to reach Hollókő.
Trains depart from the Eastern Railway station (7.40) to Pásztó (arriving 9.14).
From here there is a 45 minute rail connection to Hollókő. On weekdays there is a
2-hour wait for the connection at Pásztó. At weekends it is only 45 minutes.
(Times can be checked in advance at Tourinform or travel agencies.)

The village of **Hollókő** in Northern Hungary, one of a handful of
protected rural settlements in the country, is inhabited by Palóc
people who still speak an old dialect of Hungarian, and who have
preserved both their characteristic architecture and their folk costumes. Recognition of the cultural significance of the settlement was
given in 1988 when Hollókő was the first village in the world to be
added to UNESCO's World Heritage List.

   The village, which lies in a valley amid the wooded Cserhát Hills,
has burned down several times (the last time was in 1909) but each
time the inhabitants rebuilt their houses in almost exactly the same
shape and form. Of the 52 houses around the 14C wooden-towered
church a museum village has been made. Several of the buildings,
many of which have traditional carved wooden porticos, serve some
kind of public function such as post office, surgery, hostel, etc. There
is *an exhibition of local folk art* at No. 99 Kossuth u. (open 10.00–
14.00 except Monday and Wednesday) and a *village museum* at No.
82 (open Tues–Fri 10.00–14.00, Sat 10.00–16.00; Nov–March, Sat
10.00–12.00, Sun 10.00–14.00). On traditional holidays the villagers
wear their local folk costumes and throughout the year there are
various festivities and activities.

   A handicrafts cooperative functions in the village and weaving and
woodcarving are taught to foreign students. On the hill overlooking
the village there are the ruins of a 13C fortress. There are plans to
involve other local villages nearby in the burgeoning rural tourist
industry. Special excursions and accommodation in the village can
be booked at travel agencies in Budapest.

B. Ják

Ják is a remote village in western Hungary 10km to the S of
Szombathely near the Austrian border. Although Ják has never been
more than a small village, the former **Benedictine Abbey Church**
here is the most ornamental Romanesque architectural monument in
Hungary. The church was commissioned by Márton Nagy of the Ják
clan. Building began in 1220 but it was consecrated and dedicated to
St. George only in 1256.

Conversion to Christianity and the building of churches by converts in Hungary
began in the 11C, most of the early churches being built on royal estates.
Subsequently the establishing of monasteries, particularly in Transdanubia, the
area to the west of the Danube, became an expression of power and wealth by

Main portal of the church at Ják, the outstanding relic of Romanesque architecture in Hungary.

leading local families. The ground plan of the church is characteristic of those early churches founded by nobles (cf. Lébény, Türje and Zsámbék) as is the gallery, reserved for the noble and his family, constructed between the towers, and the placing of the towers over the first bay of the side aisles.

The Mongols probably never reached Ják, which helps to explain the survival of the building. Many other Romanesque constructions were destroyed during the invasion of 1241–42. However destruction did take place during the Turkish period and there were several later restorations.

The latest and most fundamental reconstruction of the church took place between 1896 and 1904 according to the plans of Frigyes Schulek, the architect who supervised the reconstruction of the Matthias Church in Budapest. The crumbling remains of the elaborate carvings on the main portal were replaced by others, and a new relief was set up in the tympanum above it. The original height of the towers was restored, but the Baroque spires, which had been added, were replaced by copies of the original stone spires of the church at Zsámbék. The exterior walls were repaired and the windows carved in the Baroque period were done away with. Although it was not the intention of Schulek, it is possible to distinguish the original stonework from the turn of the century additions.

The most significant decorative feature of the building is the *main portal* which is a Norman-style pillared doorway with rows of apostles above and a figure of Christ at the top. The ornamentation of the columns continues along the length of the arches above. (A copy of the portal can be seen at the Vajdahunyad Castle in the City Park in Budapest. See p 204.) The characteristics of the ornamental motifs, although originating in Northern France, can be found on the castles at Bamberg and Regensburg, and it may be from here that the Hungarian craftsmen derived their knowledge of this style. The church of the Scottish Benedictines in Regensburg was the point from which the style spread over Central Europe.

The figures of Christ and the apostles standing in gradually ascending niches are considered some of the most significant examples of Romanesque sculpture in Hungary, although, due to damage and replacements, the only original heads are those of Christ and the two apostles beside him.

The 13C *Chapel of St. James* in front of the Abbey Church was at one time the parish church.

A convenient way for motorists to visit Ják is by entering or leaving Hungary via the Rattersdorf/Kőszeg crossing or the Schachendorf/Bucsu crossing near Szombathely.

Kőszeg (pop. 14,000) has entered the annals of Hungarian history as the town where, in 1532, Captain Miklós Jurisich heroically headed a handful of troops and managed to resist an onslaught of Turkish forces far superior in numbers, thus halting the Ottoman drive towards Vienna. The castle here was rebuilt between 1958 and 1962 and today houses the Jurisich Museum which displays items illustrating the history of the town. The originally 15C *Church of St. James* in Jurisich tér is a valuable monument of Hungarian Gothic and still contains some 15C frescoes. The town's general appearance dates from the 18C though there are also some interesting Renaissance houses which have survived.

Szombathely (pop. 87,000) has some of the most important Roman remains in Hungary. Emperor Claudius founded the settlement of *Savaria* here in AD 43. The Garden of Ruins by Alkotmány u. contains the ruins of the *Basilica of St. Quirinus*, the largest Christian church of Pannonia. At No. 2 Rákóczi Ferenc u. there are the remains of the late 2C *Temple of Isis*, while further Roman stonework finds have been collected at the indoor Savaria Museum at No. 9 Kisfaludy Sándor u. The *Szombathely Picture Gallery* at No. 12 Rákóczi Ferenc u. is a specialist museum devoted to socialist art of the first half of the 20C. The exhibition includes works by two leading left-wing proletarian artists: the locally-born Gyula Derkovits (1894–1934) and István Dési Huber (1895–1944).

C. Zsámbék

Zsámbék can be reached by car from Budapest either via the M1 motorway for approximately 25km, then north, or via a country road through Páty beyond Budakeszi on the western side of the capital. A regular bus service runs to the village from Széna tér, which adjoins the NE corner of Moszkva tér (on No. 2 metro) in Buda.

The village of **Zsámbék** is 33km to the W of Budapest. Although in ruins, the 13C **Church** here is one of the important monuments of Romanesque architecture in Hungary. It was originally built for the

Premonstratensian order by the Ainard family, who were of French descent. Work began on the three-aisled, two-towered church in 1220 but was only completed in 1258. In 1475 it came into the possession of the Pauline order who renovated it and made Gothic additions. The church was destroyed in an earthquake of 1763 but the walls which remained standing have been preserved. (A replica of the church was built in Budapest in the 1930s and stands in Élmunkás tér, one stop northwards from the Western Railway Station on the No. 3 metro.)

In the village, at No. 18 Magyar u., there is a small *Lamp Museum* which exhibits items relating to the history of lighting. (Open Tues and Fri 14.00–18.00, Wed and Thurs 8.00–12.00, Sat and Sun 8.00–18.00.)

D. Ráckeve

Ráckeve is a pleasant little town 46km to the S of Budapest towards the southern end of Csepel Island. It has two important monuments—a Baroque mansion and an Orthodox church—and can easily be reached in an hour by taking the HÉV suburban railway from the junction of Soroksári út and Kvassay Jenő út (bus 54 or 23 from Boráros tér), or by car via Road 51 and then to the W after Kiskunlacháza.

According to documents, in 1440 King Ulászló I (1440–44) settled a Rác (Serbian) population here from Keve (to the south) which was threatened by the Turks. In the 16C the population increased with an influx mainly of Hungarians, and Ráckeve became an important centre of the Reformation. In the 18C German settlers arrived and the three nationalities, Serbian, Hungarian and German, with their three religions, Orthodox, Catholic and Protestant, lived together, even rotating the offices of judge and magistrates among themselves. Development slowed down in the 19C and therefore the old structure of the town has remained.

The terminus of the HÉV railway is at the northern end of Ráckeve. The splendid **Savoy Mansion** stands a short distance to the south. It was one of the first Hungarian manor houses to be built in Hungary after the expulsion of the Turks. Eugene of Savoy, the Imperial Commander of the united Christian armies, purchased the estate in 1698 and commissioned the Austrian architect Johann Lucas von Hildebrandt to build a manor-house. Work began in 1702 and was completed in 1722. The stables were added in 1750. The original single-storey building, with a courtyard and octagon-shaped, domed state-room, faces the Danube. The ground plan reflects the influence of French Baroque, the richly ornamented façade that of Italian Baroque.

After the death of Eugene of Savoy the estate came into the possession of the House of Habsburgs. In 1814 the dome burnt down and was rebuilt in neo-classical style. In the second half of the 19C another storey was added. Between the two wars it was used as a granary and after the last war served various temporary purposes and rapidly deteriorated. The mansion was fully restored in the late 1970s and today is an architects' recreation centre. It is also used for cultural and professional events and has a restaurant in the cellar.

The *statue of Árpád*, the military leader of the Hungarian conquest, standing near the mansion, was made by Gyula Szász for the

Millenary celebrations in 1896. The reliefs on the base depict celebrations at the birth of Árpád's son, Zsolt.

The **Serbian Orthodox Church** is on the W side of the town centre. It was built as a hall church with reticulated vaulting in late-Gothic style in 1487 for the Serbs who had fled here. In the 16C it was enlarged with two high-roofed, Gothic chapels on the southern side and a separate tower was also built. The present upper parts of the tower are in Copf style and date from 1758. The interior wooden structure divides the church into a sanctuary sealed off with an iconostasis, a nave and a vestibule. The frescoes, depicting scenes from the lives of Jesus, Mary and the saints, were painted by Tódor Gruntovich between 1765 and 1771. The fine carvings of the rich Baroque iconostasis, along with the other interior carvings, also date from the 18C.

At **Szigetbecse**, 4km to the S of Ráckeve, there is a *Kertész Museum* (No. 40 Makádi út) which has an exhibition of the work of the internationally renowned photographer André Kertész (1894–1985) who spent his childhood in this village. (Open 10.00–18.00; Oct–April 9.00–17.00; closed Mondays.)

INDEX

Topographical names are printed in **bold** type, names of persons in *italics*, and other entries (including sub-indexes of large towns) in Roman type.

Abaliget 300
Aba Novák, Vilmos 140
Abda 88
Abony 332
Abonyi, Lajos 332
Adami, Carlo 161
Ady, Endre 49, 163, 197, 198, 210, 211
Agárd 277
Agriculture 31
Alba Regia 271
Alessandro da Vedano 326
Alpár, Ignác 158, 172, 178, 180, 204
Althan, Károly, Bishop 250
Altomonte, Andreas 107
Altomonte, Bartolomeo 107
Altomonte, Martino 93
Ámos, Imre 140
Andrássy, Gyula 195
Andrássy Kurta, János 351
Andreä, Karl 296
Andrew I, King 261
Andrew II, King 15, 99
Andrew III, King 15, 115, 125
Anne of Châtillon 128
Anonymus, the notary 115, 239
Antal, Károly 129, 143, 181, 187
Apáczai Csere, János 342
Aquincum 115, 220
Arany, János 48, 161, 169, 308
Árkay, Aladár 149
Árpád 13, 115
Arrabona 91
Arrow Cross 26, 118, 150, 181
Aszód 319
Atzél, Béla 190
Auer, Leopold 53
Ausgleich 22

Babits, Mihály 49, 211, 247, 311
Baccio del Bianco 37, 98
Badacsony 262
Badacsony Mountain 263
Bajcsy-Zsilinszky, Endre 110, 172

Bajor, Gizi 225
Bakfark, Valentin 52
Bakócz, Tamás 37, 240, 243
Balácapuszta 285
Balantonudvari 262
Balassi, Bálint 44, 199, 245
Balatonederics 264
Balatonfüred 259
Balatonkeresztúr 270
Balatonszárszó 269
Balatonszemes 269
Balatonszentgyörgy 270
Balf 110
Bálint, Endre 141
Bálint, Zoltán 339
Balogh, Ádám Béri 287
Barabás, Miklós 139, 148
Barcsay, Jenő 140, 141, 231
Bársony, György 298
Bartók, Béla 53, 130, 211, 225
Bashkiria 13
Báthori, Miklós, Bishop 249
Batsányi, János 281
Batthyány, Lajos, Count 22, 162, 181, 194
Baumhorn, Lipót 316, 333
Beatrice of Aragon 52, 116
Bebó, Károly 150, 218
Bechert, Joseph 250
Beethoven, Ludwig von 279
Béla III, King 15, 35, 128, 273
Béla IV, King 15, 35, 115, 247, 275
Bélapátfalva 35, 330
Bem, Joseph 152, 177
Benczúr, Gyula 40, 139, 179, 347
Beregszászy, Dezső 150
Berény, Róbert 140
Berlioz, Hector 166
Bernardt, Győző 212
Bernáth, Aurél 177
Bernhard, Petri 278
Berzsenyi, Dániel 109, 169
Bessenyei György 46
Bethlen, Gábor 19

Blaas, Karl 111, 249
Blaha, Lujza 192, 260
Bocskai, István 19, 334, 341, 349
Bodor, Ádám 50
Bogdanich, Imre Dániel 144
Böhm, Henrik 161
Bonani, Pietro 240, 241
Bone, Edith 251
Bonfini, Antonio 116
Bonyhád 288
Bornemisza, Péter 44
Borsos, József 139
Borsos, Miklós 96, 149, 297
Börzsöny Mountains 252
Bottyán, János 247
Bottyán, Vak 199, 250
Bozsó, János 307
Brein, Ferenc 197
Brennbergbánya 110
Bright, Richard 266
Brocky, Károly 139
Brunswick, Antal, Count 278
Brunswick, Theresa 278
Buda 15, 35, 36, 115, 116, 121
Buda, capture of 19
Budakalász 248
BUDAPEST 114
  Academy of Fine Arts 198
  Academy of Music 211
  Academy of Sciences 176
  Akadémia u. 177
  Állatkerti körút 203
  Alpári Gyula u. 178, 179
  Árpád Bridge 217
  Astoria Hotel 190
  Atrium-Hyatt Hotel 175
  Attila út 147
  Bakáts tér 206
  Baross tér 194
  Baross u. 207
  Batthányi tér 150
  Bécsi kapu tér 131
  Béke Hotel 212
  Bem József tér 152
  Biermann István tér 172
  Blaha Lujza tér 192, 209
  Bolgár Elek tér 151

BUDAPEST (contd)
British Embassy 156
Boráros tér 205
Brcdy Sándor u. 169
Castle District 119
Castle Theatre 122
Central Bus Station
178
Central Market 165
Central Police HQ
172
Central Synagogue
170
Chain Bridge 148
Circus 203
Churhes
  Basilica 178
  Calvinist 166
  Christina Town
  147
  Elizabeth Town
  194
  Élmunkás tér 213
  English Young
  Ladies' 188
  Franciscan 189
  Francis Town 206
  Greek Orthodox
  188
  Inner City 185
  Joseph Town 207
  Lutheran 171
  Matthias 125
  Óbuda 217
  St. Anne's 150
  St. Ladislas' 223
  St. Roch Chapel
  192
  Serbian Orthodox
  163
  Servite 160
  Tabán 146
  Theresa Town 197
  University 163
  Újlak 223
Church services 68
Citadel 144
City Park 204
Clark Ádám tér 148
Cog-wheel Railway
221
Corso, The 173
Corvin tér 149
Csepel 225
Császár Baths 153
Deák tér 171
Dimitrov tér 165
Dísz tér 122
Döbrenti tér 145
Dózsa György út 202
Duna
  Intercontinental
  Hotel 175
Eastern Railway
  Station 194
Economics
  University 165
Egyetem tér 162
Elizabeth Bridge 145

BUDAPEST (contd)
EMKE Hotel 193
Engels tér 178
Erkel Theatre 193
Exhibition Hall, The
200
Felszabadulás tér
189
Ferenc körút 206
Fishermen's Bastion
129
Flórián tér 219
Fortuna u. 131
Forum Hotel 175
Fő tér 218
Fő u. 149
Fun Fair 203
Funicular 149
Gaity Theatre 213
Gellért Hill 143
Gellért Hotel and
  Baths 143
Gellért Monument
144
Gellért tér 143
Gerbaud's 159
Gresham Palace 177
Gutenberg tér 208
Heroes' Square 200
Hess András tér 129
Hilton Hotel 129
Honvéd u. 214
Horváth Mihály tér
207
Hungarian
  Television 180
Hűvösvölgy 222
International Fair
224
János-hegy 222
Jászai Mari tér 214
József Attila u. 178
József körút 207
József Nádor tér 177
Jubilee Park 144
Kálvin tér 166
Kapistrán tér 132
Károlyi Mihály u.
162
Kerepesi Cemetery
194
Kispest 225
Király Baths 151
Klotild Palaces 189
Kőbánya 223
Kodály Körönd 199
Kórház u. 219
Korvin Ottó tér 218
Korvin Ottó u. 220
Kossuth Lajos tér 182
Kossuth Lajos u. 189
Köztársaság tér 193
Lehel market 213
Lenin körút 210
Libegő (Chair Lift)
222
Liberation
  Monument 143
Liberty Bridge 164

BUDAPEST (contd)
Liszt Ferenc tér 198,
  211
Lost property 68
Lukács Baths 153
Madách Imre tér 171
Madách Theatre 210
March 15th Square
185
Margaret Bridge 215
Margaret Island 215
Markets 72
Martinelli tér 160
Marx tér 213
Millenary Monument
200
Museum Garden 169
Museums
  Acquincum 220
  Agriculture 205
  Ambulance Service
  226
  Applied Arts 206
  Architecture 130
  Attila József 226
  Bakery 226
  Béla Bartók 225
  Bible 166
  Budapest History
  141
  Commerce and
  Catering 132
  Communist Party
  213
  Csepel Labour
  Movement 225
  Csepel Local
  History 225
  Eastern Asiatic Art
  199
  Ecclesiastical Art
  128
  Electricity Industry
  226
  Endre Ady 163
  Ferenc Liszt 198
  Foundry 152
  Ethnographical 185
  Fine Arts 202
  Fire Service 224
  Folk Art 219
  Geological
  Institute 226
  Hercules Villa 220
  Imre Varga 219
  Jewish Prayer
  House 131
  Kiscell 225
  Kőbánya Local
  History 223
  Labour History 136
  Lajos Kassák 219
  Law 85
  Lift 226
  Literary 162
  Meat Processing
  226
  Medical History
  147

BUDAPEST (contd)
  Military History 133
  Milling Industry 226
  Music History 130
  Museum Ship 175
  Nagytétény 226
  'Nyugat' 226
  Natural History 168
  National Gallery 136
  National Jewish 171
  National Lutheran 172
  National Museum 167
  PE and Sport 226
  Pharmacy 124
  Philatelic 211
  Post Office 195
  Roman Baths 220
  Roman Camp 220
  Sewage Disposal 226
  Textile 226
  Theatre 225
  Transport 205
  Underground 171
  Veterinary Science 226
  Victor Vasarely 218
  Wax Works 134
  Múzeum körút 167
  Múzeum u. 167
  Nagy-Mező u. 197
  Nagyrét 222
  National Széchényi Library 142
  National Bank 180
  Nemzeti Hotel 209
  Néphadsereg tér 214
  Népköztársaság útja 195
  New York Palace 210
  Normafa 222
  November 7 tér 198
  Óbuda Island 217
  Opera House 196
  Orientation 71
  Országház u. 132
  Palace Hotel 193
  Palatinus Baths 216
  Pálvölgy Cave 223
  Párisi udvar 189
  Parliament Building 182
  Pataki István tér 223
  Petőfi tér 188
  Pilvax Coffee House 161
  Pioneers' Railway 222
  Planetarium 227
  Public transport 63

BUDAPEST (contd)
  Puppet Theatre(s) 198
  Rác Baths 145
  Rajk László u. 214
  Rákóczi tér 208
  Rákóczi út 191
  Roosevelt tér 175
  Rosenberg házaspár u. 181
  Royal Hotel 211
  Royal Palace 135
  Rudas Baths 144
  Ságvári-liget 222
  Skating Rink 204
  Southern Railway Station 147
  Szabadság-hegy 221
  Szabadság tér 180
  Szabad Sajtó u. 189
  Szabó Ervin tér 166
  Szarvas tér 147
  Széchenyi Baths 203
  Széchenyi-hegy 222
  Szemlőhegy Cave 223
  Szentháromság tér 124
  Szentháromság u. 124, 125
  Szent István körút 213
  Szent István tér 178
  Szilágyi Dezső tér 150
  Tabán, The 146
  Tanács körút 170
  Táncsis Mihály u. 130
  Tárnok u. 124
  Taxis 64
  Tolbuhin körút 165
  Tomb of Gül Baba 153
  Tóth Árpád sétány 133
  Tourinform 172
  Tunnel, The 149
  Új Köztemető Cemetery 224
  Üllői út 206
  Úri u. 134
  US Embassy 181
  Váci u. 153, 188
  Vajdahunyad Castle 204
  Városház u. 161
  Vas u. 192
  Veres Pálné u. 163, 165
  Vérmező 147
  Vigadó tér 173
  Visegrád u. 213
  Vörösmarty tér 159
  Western Railway Station 212
  Ybl Miklós tér 146
  Zalka Máté tér 223
  Zoo 203

Bugac 309
Bükk Mountains 329
Bükk National Park 330
Bukovics, Gyula 184

Canevale, Isidore 37, 38, 250, 251, 252
Carlone, Carlo Martino 37
Carlone, Giovanni Battista 37, 328, 339
Casagrande, Marco 323, 327
Cegléd 331
Çelebi, Evliya 116
Charlemagne 13
Charles IV, King 126
Charles Robert, King 15, 35, 115, 237
Children 32
Chiovini, Ferenc 333
Chrismar, F.S. 157
Churches, access to 67
Clark, Adam 146, 148, 149
Clark, William Tierney 148
Climate 68
Comenius, John Amos 351
Compromise of 1867 22, 117
Conti, Lipót Antal 304
Crnojevič, Arsen, Patriarch 230
Cserhalmy, József 91
Cserhát Hills 352
Cserkút 300
Csók, István 274
Csokonai Vitéz, Mihály 340, 342
Csontváry Kosztka, Tivadar 42, 140, 297
Csopak 259
Csorna 113
Cumanians, the 308
Cymbal, Johann Ignác 275
Czigány, Dezső 42, 140
Czigler, Győző 190, 195
Czóbel, Béla 140, 233

Dabas 301
Damjanich, János 333
Damkó, József 133, 187
Dankó, Márton 133
Dankó, Pista 316
Danninger, Franz Anton 241
Deák, Ferenc 22, 173, 176, 194, 312
Deák-Ébner, Lajos 201, 261
DEBRECEN 337
  Calvinist Great Church 341

DEBRECEN (contd)
Csokonai Theatre
340
Déri Museum 344
Kossuth tér 341
Nagyerdő 345
Reformed College
342
St. Anne's Church
339
Vörös Hadsereg útja
339
Déri, Frigyes 344
Déri, Tibor 162
Derkovits, Gyula 140,
354
Dési Huber, István 354
Dientzenhofer, Kilián
Ignaz 328
Diescher, Antal 165
Dimitrov, Georgi 165
Diósgyőr 36, 348
Dobi, János 314
Dobó, István 19, 326,
327, 328
Dobogókő 248
Dombi, Lajos 41, 305
Dömös 238
Donát, János 139
Donáth, Gyula 90, 135
Donner, Georg
Raphael 38
Doppler, Ferenc 191
Doppler, Károly 191
Dorfmeister, István 38,
103, 107, 112, 266,
269
Dormánd 335
Dorog 248
Dózsa, György 17, 332
Dubniczay, Canon
István 282
Dugonics, András 46,
313
Dunabogdány 236
Dunaföldvár 287
Dunaisky, László 132,
158
Dunaisky, Lőrinc 207
Dunakeszi 248
Dunapentele 287
Dunaújváros 287

Éder, József 90
Education 32
EGER 321
Archbishop's Palace
328
Castle 326
Cathedral 322
County Hall 324
Dobó István tér 327
Kossuth Lajos u. 324
Lyceum 323
Minaret 329
Minorite Church 327
Széchenyi u. 328
Egregy 267
Egry, József 262

1848 Revolution 21,
117, 161, 167, 190
Elizabeth, Empress 145
Elizabeth, Queen 87
Emergencies 68
Endre, Béla 140
Enese 113
Engel, József 176
Entzenhoffer, Johann
225
Eötvös, József, Baron
47, 175
Eötvös, Loránd 156,
163, 261
Eravisci 115
Érd 287
Erkel, Ferenc 53, 196
Ernst, Lajos 197
Esterházy, Miklós,
Prince 112
Esterházy, Péter 43, 50
ESZTERGOM 238
Bajcsy-Zsilinsky út
245
Bakócz Chapel 240
Bottyán János u. 247
Castle Museum 243
Cathedral 240
Cathedral Treasury
243
Christian Museum
245
Hydrology Museum
247
St. Thomas Hill 244
Széchenyi tér 246
Watertown 245
Eusebius, Canon 163

Fadrusz, János 136, 185
Faludi, Ferenc 45, 151
Faragó, Ödön 158
Fátay, Tamás 91
Fáy, András 249
Fazola, Henrik 38, 325,
349
Fehér-Tó 309
Feketeházi, János 194
Feldebrő 35, 321, 330
Fellner, Ferdinánd 316
Fellner, Jakab 38, 89,
90, 282, 283, 284,
323, 325
Fellner, Sándor 125
Felsőörs 259
Fenékpuszta 266, 267
Fényes, Adolf 42, 140,
333
Ferenc I, King 89
Ferenczy, Béni 156,
187, 233
Ferenczy, István 39,
139, 149, 187, 242
Ferenczy, Károly 140,
233, 234
Ferenczy, Noémi 233
Ferenczy, Valér 233
Ferrucci, Andrea 240
Fertőd 37, 112

Fertőrákos 110
Fessl, József 189
Fessler, Leó 179
Festetics, György,
Count 258, 266
Feszl, Frigyes 39, 170,
173
Feszty, Adolf 195
Feszty, Árpád 236, 309
Finta, József 157, 175
Fischer, Joseph
Emanuel 96
Fitzjames, James 116
Fledderus, Jan 166
Fodor, József 208
Fodor, Oszkár 210
Förster, Lajos 104, 170
Fót 248
Francis Joseph,
Emperor 126, 175
Frankel, Leó 153
Freund, Miklós 195
Frigyes, Karinthy 211
Fruman, Antal 260
Further Reading 69

Gádor, István 141
Gál, Bertalan 157
Ganz, Ábrahám 152
Gárdonyi, Géza 277,
321, 327
Gazder, Antal 298
Gazi Kassim, Pasha
292
Gellért, Bishop 143,
144
Gemenc Nature
Reserve 288
Gergely, Sándor 141
Gerl, József 323
Gerl, Matthias 324
Géza I, King 168, 250
Géza, Prince 13, 99,
115, 238, 271
Giergl, Kálmán 160,
189, 210, 211
Ginesser, Mátyás 234
Giuliano da Sangallo
240
Glatz, Oszkár 140
Göd 249
Gödöllő 318
Gödöllő Colony 42,
252, 319
Goldmann, György 141
Gömbös, Gyula 145
Gorka, Géza 252
Gorsium 277
Gouin, Ernest 215
Gráboc 288
Grassalkovich, Antal
318
Great Flood of 1838
117, 188, 189, 206
Gresham Circle 141,
177
Grigoletti,
Michelangelo 241,
242

Group of Eight 140
Grundemann, Johann
Basilius 112
Grünwald, Béla Iványi
140
Güll Baba 153
Gulyás, Zoltán 160
Gundel, János 203
Gundel, Károly 203
Gyöngyös 320
Gyöngyösi, István 45
GYŐR 91
Carmelite Church 92
Cathedral 94
Church of St.
Ignatius 98
Gutenberg tér 96
János Xantus
Museum 97
Köztársaság tér 92
Liszt Frenc u. 98
Martinovics tér 95
Szabadság tér 91
Széchenyi tér 96
Győrffy, István 333

Hadik, András 134
Hajdú, the 334
Hajdúság 334
Hajdúszoboszló 334
Hajós, Alfréd 341
Halbig, Johann 178
Hamon, Kristóf 150,
223
Handler, Ferdinand
105, 107
Handler, József 108
Hanság, the 88
Haranghy, Jenő 212
Harkány 301
Hartmann, Antal 246,
247
Hatvan 320
Hatvany, Lajos, Baron
131, 320
Hatzinger, P. 274
Hauszmann, Alajos
135, 157, 185, 210,
212
Haydn, Joseph 52, 113
Haynau, Julius 162
Health and Medicine
70
Health Service 31
Hebenstreit, József 163
Hegedüs, Ármin 143,
161
Hegyeshalom 87
Helmer, Herman 316
Herend 286
Herend Porcelain
Factory 39
Herman, Ottó 169, 348,
349
Herzog, Fülöp 201, 202
Herzog, György 247
Hess, András 129
Heves 335
Hevesy, György 177

Hévíz 267
Hidegség 112
Hikisch, Rezső 101
Hild, Ferdinand 108
Hild, János 178, 187
Hild, József 39, 158,
162, 163, 166, 171,
173, 177, 178, 191,
206, 207, 214, 240,
245, 246, 322, 331
Hildebrandt, Johann
Lucas 37, 355
Hillebrandt, Franz
Anton 132, 275
Hincz, Gyula 251
Hoepfner, Guido 133
Hofrichter, József 166
Hofstädter, Kristóf 270
Holló, Barnabás 139,
149
Holló, László 346
Hollókő 352
Hollósy, Simon 42, 140
Hopp, Ferenc 199
Horthy, Miklós 25
Hortobágy 336
Hortobágy National
Park 334
Horváth, Árpád 340
Housing 31
Hubay, Jenő 191
Hüber, Jenő 91
Huns 13
Hunyadi, János 16,
116, 129, 292
Hunyadi, Mátyás 17
Hussars 122
Huszár, Adolf 176
Hűvösvölgy 222

Ignjatovic, Jakov 231,
232
Imre, King 327
Imre, Prince 14, 43, 271
Innocent XI, Pope 116
Intercisa 287
Ipoly valley 253
Ipolydamásd 253
Ipolyi, Arnold, Bishop
137
Ipolytölgyes 253
Ippolito d'Este 37, 240
Irányi, Dániel 162
Ispánky, József 284
Istók, János 152
István Caves 349
Izsó, Miklós 40, 139,
188

Jadot, Jean Nicolas
135
Jäger, János Henrik
219
Ják 35, 352
Jakab, Dezső 193
Jámbor, Lajos 339
Jankovich, Miklós 188
Jankovits, Gyula 144,
176

János-hegy 222
Jánszky, Béla 252
Jászai, Mari 214
Jászapáti 335
Jászberény 334
Jászjákóhalma 335
Jazygians, the 308
Jelačić, Josip 21, 278
Joachim, Joseph 53
Jókai, Mór 48, 162,
198, 211, 221, 260
Joseph, Archduke 117,
177
Joseph II 19, 117
József, Attila 50, 158,
162, 183, 193, 226,
269, 313
Juhász, Gyula 313, 315
Julianus and Gellért
129
Jung, József 188, 192
Jungfer, Gyula 135,
158, 167, 194, 199, 212
Jurisich, Miklós,
Captain 354

Kádár, János 28, 194,
195
Kallina, Mór 149, 159
Kalló, Viktor 193
Kallós, Ede 151
Kálmán, Imre 268
Kálmán, King 15
Kálmáncsehi,
Domonkos, Bishop
275
Kalocsa 35
Kántor, Sándor 333
Kápolna 321
Kápolnásnyék 278
Kapuvár 113
Karadzic, Vuk 147
Karcag 333
Kardetter, Tamás 192
Károlyi, Gáspár 44
Károlyi, István 249
Károlyi, Mihály, Count
23, 159, 162, 185
Kass, János 317
Kassák, Lajos 42, 140,
141, 158, 213, 219
Kasselik, Ferenc 144,
165
Kasselik, Fidél 197
Katona, József 303
Kauser, József 179
Kazinczy, Ferenc 21,
46, 131, 147, 169, 351
KECSKEMÉT 302
Cifrapalota 305
Franciscan Church
304
Kodály Institute 304
Naive Art Museum
307
Piarist Church 306
Synagogue 305
Town Hall 303
Toy Museum 307

Keleti, Hermann 210
Kemény, Zsigmond 48
Kempelen, Farkas 123
Kerecsend 320
Kereki 269
Kerény, József 305, 306
Kerényi, Jenő 210, 235
Kernstok, Károly 42, 140
Kertész, André 356
Kessler, Adolf 176
KESZTHELY 266
Kiegyezés 22
Kinizsi, Pál 285
Kirstein, Ágoston 296
Kis Jankó, Bori 347
Kisfaludi Strobl, Zsigmond 101,141, 143, 183, 202, 304, 328
Kisfaludy, Károly 139, 157, 265
Kisfaludy, Sándor 169, 265
Kiskundorozsma 309
Kiskunfélegyháza 308
Kiskunság 308
Kisoroszi 236
Kiss, Bálint 139
Kiss, György 178, 208, 240, 242, 246, 292, 293, 294, 296, 297
Kiss, István 147, 202, 216, 284, 327
Kiss Kovács, Gyula 166, 199, 210
Kiss Nagy, András 198
Kistelek 309
Kisújszállás 333
Klapka, György 177
Klimó, György, Bishop 295
Kmetty, János 140, 232
Kocsis, András 147
Kodály, Zoltán 53, 199, 211, 304
Kölcsey, Ferenc 46, 151
Kollár, Ján 193
Kollina, Mór 131
Kolozsvári, György 36
Kolozsvári, Márton 36
Kolozsvári, Tamás 246
Komor, Marcell 193
Kondor, Béla 348
Korb, Flóris 160, 189, 210, 211
Körner, József 195
Korniss, Dezső 140
Körösfői Kriesch, Aladár 42, 140, 211, 252, 319
Kőröshegy 269
Kós, Károly 42, 203, 218, 225, 252, 319
Kossuth, Lajos 21, 22, 181, 183, 194, 304, 308, 312, 331, 340, 341, 349, 351

Kőszeg 354
Koszta, József 140
Kosztolányi, Dezső 49
Kovács, Frigyes 281
Kovács, Margit 96, 157, 233
Kovács, Mihály 139
Kővágószőlős 300
Kővári, György 148
Kracker, Johann Lucas 38, 319, 323, 328
Kratzmann, Ede 128
Kraus, János 171
Kresz, Géza 226
Krúdy, Gyula 197, 208, 210, 219, 347
Kühneland, Pál 240
Kun, Béla 148, 213
Kuny, Domokos 89
Kupelwieser, Leopold 207
Kuttner, József 90

Lajosmizse 302
Lajta, Béla 41, 161, 191, 192
LAKE BALATON 254
Lake Velence 277
Landherer, András 218
Lantai, Lajos 126
Lantos, Sebestyén Tinódi 52
Lascaris, Mária 247
László (Ladislas) I, King 15, 36, 43, 94, 99
László II, King 90
Lázár, Tzar 235
Leányfalu 236
Lébénymiklós 35, 88, 113
Lechner, Ödön 40, 158, 181, 191, 197, 204, 206, 207, 223, 226, 303, 310, 316
Lékai, Cardinal 30
Lendvay, Márton 132
Leo XI, Pope 19
Ligeti, Miklós 136, 141, 205
Lillafüred 349
Lippert, József 245
Liszt, Ferenc 53, 158, 196, 198, 211, 240
Little Balaton 270
Little Plain 88
Lost Property 68
Lotz, Károly 40, 126, 128, 139, 168, 169, 182, 185, 191, 194, 195, 196, 197, 198, 206, 210, 261, 296
Louis II, King 17
Louis the Great, King 15, 92, 115
Lovas, Lajos 309
Lövér Hills 110
Löw, Immanuel 316
Löw, Lipót, Rabbi 316

Lukács, George 42, 164, 172
Luther, Martin 172

Madách, Imre 48, 216
Madarász, Viktor 40, 139
Magyar, Ede 313
Magyars, the 13
Máltás, Hugó 149, 178
Mánfa 300
Mann, Thomas 131
Mányoki, Ádám 38, 137
Márffy, Ödön 140
Margaret Capet, (Queen) 244
Margó, Ede 316
Maria Theresa, Empress 19, 113, 117, 251
Markó, Iván 98
Markó, Károly the Elder 139
Márkus, Géza 305
Marosits, István 245
Maróthi, György 52
Maróty, Géza 158
Marschalkó, János 148
Martinelli, Anton Erhard 37, 161
Martinovics, Ignác 21, 95, 117, 134, 147
Marton, László 183, 199
Martonvásár 278
Martyn, Ferenc 296
Master MS 137, 246
Máta 337
Mátra Hills 320
Matrai, Lajos 312
Matthias Corvinus, King 17, 36, 52, 116, 119, 141, 237
Maulbertsch, Franz Anton 38, 94, 139, 246, 250, 264, 276, 286, 323
Mayer, Ede 146, 176, 191, 294
Mayerhoffer, András 37, 162, 163, 187, 233, 247, 306, 318
Mechwart, András 152
Mecsek Hills 288
Mecseknádasd 288
Medgyasszay, István 284, 285
Medgyessy, Ferenc 94, 132, 273, 339, 344, 345
Mednyánszky, László 333
Medveczky, Jenő 140
Meissl, Joseph 250
Meixner, Johann 240, 242, 243
Mende, Valér 41, 305
Mészáros, László 141

Mészöly, Géza 139
Mező, Imre 194
Mezőkövesd 347
*Migazzi, Kristóf,
Bishop* 250, 251, 252
Mikes, Kelemen 45
Mikófalva 330
Mikszáth, Kálmán 48
Mikus, Sándor 91
Milldorfer, Josef Ignaz
112
Millenary celebrations,
1896 23, 90, 118, 204
Milton, John 342
Mindszenty, Cardinal
181
Misina Hill 300
MISKOLC 347
Miskolctapolca 349
Modok, Mária 233
Mohács, battle of 17,
116
Mohammed III, Sultan
321
Moholy-Nagy, László
42
Molnár, Ferenc 207
Molnár, Pál C. 140,
187
Monok 349
*Monti, Alessandro,
Baron* 169
Móra, Ferenc 212, 308,
312, 315
Moralt, Ludwig 241,
242
Morbitzer, Nándor 308
Móricz, Zsigmond 49,
162, 165, 211, 236,
351
Mosonmagyaróvár 87
Mount St. George 264
Munkácsy, Mihály 40,
139, 345
Münnich, Ferenc 214
Murad, Sultan 235
Museums 70

Nádas, Péter 50
Nagy, Imre 27, 33,
151, 199, 202, 224
Nagy, Jenő 197
Nagy, Sándor 140, 284,
319
Nagybánya colony 42
Nagybörzsöny 253
Nagycenk 111
Nagyiván 336
Nagykőrös 308
Nagymaros 252
Nagyvázsony 262, 285
Nándorfehérvár 17, 116
Napoleon 91, 94
National Romanticism
41, 252, 305
Nebojsza, Mitric 147
Nemes, Endre 296
*Nemes Lampérth,
József* 140

Nemesvámos 285
Németh, Kálmán 249
Nendtvich, Tamás 293
Nepauer, Mátyás 150,
152
*Neuschloss-Knüsli,
Kornél* 203
New Economic
Mechanism 28, 29
Niccolò di Tommaso
244
Nikisch, Arthur 53
1956 Uprising 27, 88,
152, 170, 188, 193,
202, 206
Normafa 222
Noszvaj 330
Nyírbátor 346
Nyíregyháza 346
Nyírség, The 346
'Nyugat' 49, 50, 210,
211, 226

Óbuda 115
Ob-Ugors 13
Ócsa 301
Ohmann, Béla 131, 273
Olhauer, József 235
Ópusztaszer 309
Oracsek, Ignác 250
Orbán, Dezső 140
Orseolo, Peter 274
Orth, Ambrus 109
Örvényes 262
Ostoič, Vasilije 234
Osvát, Ernő 210
Öttevény 88

Paál, László 139
Packh, János 240, 247
Paget, John 281
Pákozd 278
Paks 287
Palóc people 352
Pálóczi Horváth, Ádám
268
Pannonhalma 35, 99
Pannonia 13, 115, 255
*Pannonius, Janus,
Bishop* 44, 289, 297
Pártos, Gyula 40, 158,
197, 206, 303, 310
Pásztor, János 141, 312
Pátzay, Pál 91, 113,
124, 141, 153, 199,
202, 214, 272, 292,
298, 312, 341
Paur, János György
187, 217
Pázmándy, István 281
Pázmány, Péter 45,
163, 208, 242
Péchy, Mihály 38, 341,
343
PÉCS 289
Barbican 297
Cathedral 296
Csontváry Museum
297

PÉCS (contd)
Early Christian
Mausoleum 297
Felsőmalom u. 299
Former mosques 292,
299
Franciscan Church
298
Jókai tér 298
Káptalan u. 295
Kossuth Lajos u. 292
Leonardo da Vinci u.
295
National Theatre 293
Rákóczi út 299
Sallai u. 298
Synagogue 299
Széchenyi tér 292
Vasarely Museum
295
Zsolnay Ceramics
Exhibition 295
Pécsvárad 288
Pecz, Sámuel 150, 165
Pekáry, Imre 197
Pest 115, 117
Pető Institute 32, 221
Petőfi, Sándor 21, 47,
152, 161, 162, 167,
172, 188, 319
Petrich, Soma Orlai
139
Petzval, József 252
Pietro della Vedova
242
Pilch, Andor 293, 294
Pilgram, Franz Anton
250
Pilinszky, János 50
Pilis Hills 248
Pilismarót 238, 253
Pilisszentkereszt 248
Pilisszentlászló 235
Politics 33
Pollack, Mihály 39,
167, 171, 192, 275,
276, 287, 296
Pomáz 248
Popovich, Jovan 315
Pór, Bertalan 140
Post Office Services 71
Povolny, Ferenc 336,
340
Povolny, János 329,
330
Pozsony 117
Public Holidays 72
*Puskás, Tivadar and
Ferenc* 208
Pusztaszemes 269
Pusztavacs 301
*Pyrker, László,
Archbishop* 136

Quittner, Zsigmond
177, 195, 196

Ráckeve 355
Ráday, Mihály 125

Ráday, Pál 166
Radnóti, Miklós 88,
158, 162
Rahl, Karl 339
Rajk, László 27, 195,
214
Rákóczi II, Ferenc,
Prince 19, 117, 182
Rákóczi, Zsigmond
349
Rákosi, Mátyás 27,
119, 224
Ráskai, Lea 216
Reform Period 21, 38,
53, 111, 117
Reményi, Attila 91
Reményi, Ede 53, 188
Republic of Councils,
1919 25, 42, 118, 258
Rerrich, Béla 314
Révai, Miklós 106
Richter, Franz 93
Richter, Hans 53
Riegl, Anton 162
Ringer, József 112
Rippl-Rónai, József 42,
140, 197
Rochlitz, Gyula 194
Romans, the 13, 220,
255, 277
Róna, Erzsébet 150
Róna, József 136, 199,
312
Róth, Miksa 159, 267,
316
Rothermere, Lord 167,
180

Ságvári, Endre 184
St. Elizabeth of the
House of Árpád 194
St. John Capistranus
17, 133
St. John of Nepomuk
43, 218
St. Margaret of
Hungary 215, 216
St. Margaret of
Scotland 288
Salamon, Ferenc 176
Sambach, C.F. 274
Sárospatak 350
Savanyú, Jóska 285
Savaria 354
Sávoly, Pál 145
Scarbantia 100
Schickedanz, Albert
200, 201, 202
Schmahl, Henrik 189,
191, 192, 285
Schmidt, Friedrich von
296
Schönbrunn Peace
Treaty 89
Schulek, Frigyes 126,
128, 129, 222, 314,
353
Sebestyén, Artúr 143
Sebestyén, Loránd 150

Second economy 30
Semmelweis, Ignác
147, 192
Senyei, Károly 135,
139, 185, 210
Serres, August de
212
Shopping 72
Sidló, Ferenc 172
Sigismund, King 16,
36, 89, 116
Sigl, Márton 124
Siklós 300
Simor, János,
Archbishop 242, 245
Siófok 268
Skalnitczky, Antal 313
Sokoli Mustapha,
Pasha 144
Somló, Emil 109
Sommer, August 165
Somogyi, Árpád 185
Somogyi, József 210,
332
Somogyi, Károly 315
Sopianae 289
SOPRON 100
Fegyvertár u. 104
Fire Tower 101
Fő tér 102
Goat Church 103
Hátsókapu 106
Ikva Híd 107
Lenin körút 106
Medieval Synagogue
105
Orsolya tér 105
Petőfi tér 108
St. George's Church
106
St. Michael's Church
107
Sopron Museum 109
Széchenyi tér 108
Szent György u. 105
Színház u. 108
Templom u. 104
Új u. 105
Sopronbánfalva 110
Sopronkőhida 110
Sóstófürdő 347
Stéger, Ferenc 232
Steindl, Imre 182, 194,
341
Stephen (István) I,
King 13, 35, 43, 115,
168, 179, 238, 271,
273
Sterk, Izidor 143
Storno, Ferenc 102, 107
Strauss, Johann, the
Younger 106
Stróbl, Alajos 111, 129,
136, 139, 141, 152,
179, 192, 196, 198,
206, 222, 242, 312,
328
Stuhlhoff, Sebestyén
261

Stüler, Friedrich
August 176
Sukoró 278
Süleyman the
Magnificent 17, 300
Sümeg 264
Sylvester II, Pope 13,
115, 168
Szabadbattyán 277
Szabó, Ervin 166
Szalajka stream 330
Számord, Ignác 247
Szántódpuszta 268
Szarvas, Gábor 176
Széchényi, Ferenc,
Count 111, 142, 167,
169
Széchenyi, István,
Count 21, 111, 112,
148, 176, 212, 217,
258, 312, 315
Széchenyi, Ödön 149
Széchenyi-hegy 222
Szécsi, Antal 194
SZEGED 310
Alsóvárosi Church
317
Aradi Vértanuk tere
313
Castle Museum 315
Dóm tér 314
Dugonics tér 313
Klauzál tér 312
National Theatre 316
New Synagogue 316
Palace of Education
315
Reök Building 313
Széchenyi tér 310
Szerbian Orthodox
Church 314
Town Hall 310
Votive Church 314
Szegedi Kis, István 331
Szegedy, Róza 263
Székely, Aladár 207
Székely, Bertalan 40,
126, 128, 139, 196,
261, 296, 303, 236
SZÉKESFEHÉRVÁR
15, 271
Arany János u. 275
Carmelite Church
276
Cathedral 275
Garden of Ruins 273
István tér 276
King Stephen
Museum 274
Március 15 u. 274
Pharmacy Museum
274
St. Anne's Chapel
275
Serbian Orthodox
Church 274
Szabadság tér 271
Szekszárd 287
Szeleta Caves 349

SZENTENDRE 230
Artists' Colony 235
Belgrade Church 233
Blagoveštenska
Church 233
Bogdányi u. 234
Czóbel Museum 233
Dumtsa Jenő u. 231
Fő tér 232
Kossuth Lajos u. 230
Margit Kovács
Collection 233
Open-air Museum
235
Orthodox Art
Museum 234
Parish Church 233
Peter-Paul Church
232
Požaravačka Church
231
Preobraženska
Church 235
Szentendre Island 236
Szent-györgy-hegy 264
Szentgyörgyi, István
141
Szentirmai, József 285
Szépasszony-völgy
330
Széppataki, Róza 349
Szerencs 349
Szigetbecse 356
Szigetvár 300
Szigliget 263
Szilágyi, Erzsébet 204
Szilvásvárad 330
Szinyei Merse, Pál 40,
139
Szkalnitzky, Antal 340
Szob 252
Sződliget 249
Sződy, Szilárd 153
Szolnok 332
Szolnok colony 333
Szombathely 354
Szondi, György 199,
212
Szőnyi, István 140,
252

Tab 269
Tác 277
Tahitófalu 236
Táncsics, Mihály 130
Tándor, Ottó 223
Tápé 318
Tapolca 264
Tar, István 284
Tartsay, Vilmos 197
Tata 89
Tatabánya 90
Telcs, Ede 159
Telekessy, István 96
Teleki, József, Count
176
Thallher, József 207
Than, Mór 139, 168,
194, 196, 206

Theatre and Concert
Tickets 74
Thék, Endre 167
Thorma, János 140
Thury, György 278
Tihany 35, 261
Tihanyi, Lajos 42, 140
Time 74
Tipping 74
Tisza, Lajos 312
Tisza river 310, 312,
315, 332, 333, 335
Tiszafüred 335
Tiszántúl 333
Tokaj 350
Toldi, Miklós 216
Tornyai, János 140
Tot, Amerigo 184, 295
Tóth, Árpad 131
Tourist Information
65
Transylvania 17, 19,
152, 204
Trianon Peace Treaty,
1920 25, 34, 102, 200
Troger, Paul 38, 98
Türje 266
Türr, István 158

Uhrl, Ferenc 189
Uitz, Béla 295
Ulcisia Castra 230

VÁC 249
Vácrátot 249
Vágó, Jószef 177, 191
Vágó, László 177, 191
Vágó, Pál 335
Vajda, Lajos 234
Valcum 266, 267
Vámosi csárda 285
Varga, Imre 148, 171,
185, 206, 214, 219,
261, 283, 296, 297,
302, 313
Varga, Mátyás 318
Várpalota 278
Vas, Zoltán 119
Vasarely, Victor 98,
148, 218, 295
Vásárhelyi, Pál 312
Vass, József 308
Vászoly, Prince 273
Veres, Pálné, née
Hermin Beniczky 165,
178
Verőcemaros 252
Verpelét 321
Vértes, László 90
Vértesszőlős 90
VESZPRÉM 35, 38, 279
Bakony Museum 284
Bishop's Palace 283
Fire Tower 280
Gizella Chapel 283
Lenin tér 284
Petőfi Theatre 284
St. Michael's
Cathedral 283

VESZPRÉM (contd)
Vár u. 281
Vörös Hadsereg tér
279
Vidor, Emil 157, 215
Villány 301
Villány mountains 301
Villányi, Lajos 341
Vilt, Tibor 141
Vinzenz, Fischer 275
Virág, Benedek 146
Visegrád 36, 237
Vitéz, János 239, 243
Vitnyédi, István 105
Vogerl, Martin 319
Vogl, Gergely 150
Vörösberény 259
Vörösmarty, Mihály 46,
47, 157, 159, 249, 278
Vörs 270

Wächtler, Lajos 108
Wagner, Otto 171
Wágner, Sándor 139
Walch, Tamás 283
Wallenberg, Raoul 214
War of Independence,
1703–11 19, 113, 350
War of Independence,
1848–49 22, 39, 122,
278, 331, 337
Ward, Mary 188
Weichinger, Károly
143
Wesselényi, Miklós,
Baron 189, 258
Wheelchair Access 74
Wieser, Ferenc 179
Wittwer, Martin 92, 97
Wladislas II, King 17
Women, situation of 31
Woronieczky,
Mieczslaw, Duke 184

Xantus, János 203

Ybl, Ervin 276
Ybl, Miklós 39, 111,
135, 145, 146, 165,
170, 178, 188, 196,
206, 221, 223, 249,
278, 307, 318

Zach, József 323
Zagyva River 335
Zala 269
Zala, György 124, 139,
140, 145, 185, 200,
296, 312, 326
Zalaszántó 266
Zalavár 267
Zebegény 252
Zichy, Mihály 40, 128,
139, 269
Zirc 286
Zitterbarth, János
305
Zitterbarth Jr, Mátyás
177

Zitterbarth, Mátyás
144
Živkovič, Mihailo 233

Zrínyi, Miklós 19, 45,
199, 213, 300
Zrumeczky, Dezső 218

Zsámbék 35,
354
Zsolnay, Vilmos 294

CHANGED NAMES OF STREETS

The following street names have changed, or are in the process of changing. Street name plates and maps, however, may show the old name for some time. The old names are given throughout the *Blue Guide*.

Old Name   *New Name*

Budapest
(district in brackets)

Old Name	New Name
Dimitrov tér (V, IX)	Fővám tér
Engels tér (V)	Erzsébet tér
Guszev u. (V)	Sas u.
Károlyi Mihály u. (at the beginning) (V)	Ferenciek tere
Korvin Ottó tér (III)	Szentlélek tér
Korvin Ottó u. (III)	Pacsirtamező u.
Lenin körút (VI)	Teréz körút
Lenin körút (VII)	Erzsébet körút
Majakovskij u. (VI, VII)	Király u.
Néphadsereg tér (V)	Honvéd tér
Néphöztársaság útja (VI)	Andrássy út
November 7 tér (VI)	Oktogon
Rajk László u. (XIII)	Pannónia u.
Rosenberg házaspár u. (V)	Hold u.
Ságvári tér (V)	Vértanuk tere
Tolbuhin körút (V, IX)	Vámház körút

Debrecen

Old Name	New Name
Vörös Hadsereg útja	Piac u.

Eger

Old Name	New Name
Lumumba tér	Állomás tér
Szabadság tér	Eszterházy tér
Lenin tér	Hösök tere
Lenin út (first part)	Deák Ferenc u.
Felszabadulás tér	Pyrker tér
Marx Károly u.	Érsek u.

Esztergom

Old Name	New Name
Makarenkó út	Majer István u.
Bajcsy-Zsilinszky út (western part)	Pázmány Péter u.

Győr

Old Name	New Name
Tanácsköztársaság útja	Szent István út

Sopron

Old Name	New Name
Lenin körút	Várkerület
Május I tér	Deák tér

Szeged

Old Name	New Name
Lenin körút	Tisza Lajos körút

Székesfehérvár

Old Name	New Name
Népköztársaság út	Vár körút

Veszprém

Old Name	New Name
Vörös Hadsereg tér	Óváros tér
Lenin tér	Megyeház tér